ABC's of NATURE

Reader's Digest

ABC's of NATURE

A Family Answer Book

THE READER'S DIGEST ASSOCIATION, INC. · PLEASANTVILLE, NEW YORK · MONTREAL

ABC's of NATURE

Editor: Richard L. Scheffel
Art Editor: Gilbert L. Nielsen
Associate Editors: Susan Brackett
                     W. Clotilde Lanig
Art Production Editor: Dorothy R. Schmidt
Art Associate: Janet G. Tenenzaph
Picture Editor: Robert J. Woodward
Special Typesetting: Grace Del Bagno
Editorial Assistant: Annette Koshut
Contributing Editor: Katharine R. O'Hare

With special contributions by
Senior Staff Editor Susan J. Wernert

Consultants

Durward L. Allen, *Professor of Wildlife Ecology*
Purdue University
Rhodes W. Fairbridge, *Professor of Geological*
Sciences, Columbia University
William C. Steere, *Professor Emeritus and Senior*
Scientist, The New York Botanical Garden

Contributors

Copy Editor: Patricia M. Godfrey
Contributing Writers: Vic Cox, George S. Fichter,
Ruth Kirk, Peter R. Limburg, Edward R. Ricciuti

Library of Congress Cataloging in Publication Data

Main entry under title:

ABC's of nature.

   At head of title: Reader's digest.
   Summary: Answers questions about the physical world,
its plants and animals, and the adaptations and interactions
of plants and animals in various environments such as
deserts, mountains, and seashores.

   1. Natural history—Miscellanea. [1. Natural history—
Miscellanea. 2. Questions and answers] I. Reader's Digest
Association. II. Reader's Digest. III. Title: A B C's of nature.
QH45.5.A23 1984   508   83-60796
ISBN 0-89577-169-1

Printed in the United States of America
Fifth Printing, July 1988

About this book...

ABC's OF NATURE is designed to inform and entertain readers both young and old with explanations of the mysteries and marvels of the world all around us, from our planet's position in space to its many forms of life. The book's question-and-answer format was chosen to provide clear, concise information on the subjects readers are most likely to ask about, and to put it in perspective with what they may already know. In addition, the text frequently expands on related topics to give a more complete picture of the subject's place and function in the natural world. The book does not attempt to describe every natural phenomenon or every kind of living thing; instead, it highlights the most familiar and important ones—the ones that you as a reader are most likely to wonder about.

Because it covers such a broad range of subject matter, ABC's OF NATURE is divided into four sections. Part 1, The World Itself, deals with the physical world, from the earth and its atmosphere to geological processes and landforms. Part 2, The World of Plants, is about the earth's infinitely varied mantle of vegetation. Part 3, The Animal World, covers the characteristics and life-styles of the many kinds of creatures that share our planet. Part 4, Many Worlds of Life, explores the adaptations and interactions of plants and animals in various environments such as deserts, mountains, and seashores.

The four sections are distinguished by color-coded tabs printed at the upper right-hand edges of the pages. A different color is used for each of the four parts, and the tabs are visible even when the book is closed so that you can easily find the part that interests you. In addition, each part begins with its own detailed table of contents that will lead you to specific subjects. A comprehensive index pinpoints other references to particular subjects throughout the book. But we hope you will often find that the most rewarding way of using ABC's OF NATURE is to open the book at random, browse, and linger over the questions—and answers—that arouse your curiosity and satisfy your desire to understand and appreciate the ever fascinating world of nature.

—The Editors

THE WORLD ITSELF

PART ONE
8

Spinning in space, the earth is a small but remarkable part of the universe. Storms, tides, earthquakes, glaciers—these are some of the physical forces that shape its landforms and keep its restless surface in a subtle but persistent state of flux.

THE WORLD OF PLANTS

PART TWO
72

Whether on land or in water, plants seem to thrive everywhere on earth. Infinitely varied in form and life-style, many of them have become adapted for surviving even such extremes as drought and flood, scorching heat and freezing cold.

THE ANIMAL WORLD

Penguins and polar bears, streamlined sharks and fragile seashells, leaping frogs and fluttering butterflies—such is the diversity of the creatures that make up the animal kingdom. Beautiful or bizarre, each one is ideally equipped for its own way of life.

MANY WORLDS OF LIFE

From wetlands with their wading birds to forests filled with trees, the earth contains all sorts of living spaces. Each one supports its own distinctive community of plants and animals; each is a fascinating world in and of itself.

The Earth, veiled by clouds, looms before the Apollo 12 spacecraft; arching across the foreground are Mexico and Central America.

THE WORLD ITSELF

The Earth in Space

What is the solar system?

The sun is just one of billions of stars in the universe. As it travels through space, it is circled by an array of other celestial bodies that, together with the sun, make up the solar system.

The largest objects held in orbit by the sun's gravitational field are the nine known planets, some of them circled in turn by their own satellites, or moons. Thousands of smaller planet-like asteroids also travel around the sun. Smaller still are the countless meteoroids—chunks of rock and metal that sometimes brighten the night sky with the streaks of light known as shooting stars. Finally, in addition to interplanetary dust and gas, the sun's entourage includes the comets. Sweeping in from far out in space, these mysterious trails of light may be visible for days to months, then disappear for years or even centuries on their far-flung orbits.

Where is the earth located in our solar system?

The nine planets circle the hub of the solar system with the precision of clockwork. Mercury is closest to the sun, followed by Venus, Earth's "twin" in size and our nearest planetary neighbor. Earth is the third planet from the sun, at a distance of about 93 million miles. Beyond lies Mars, followed by a band of orbiting mini-planets, the asteroids. The fifth planet, Jupiter, is the giant of them all, with a diameter more than 11 times that of Earth. Saturn, the sixth planet, is the second largest and is best known for its encircling rings. Next come Uranus and Neptune. Then, finally, there is Pluto, the ninth and outermost planet. Although Mercury was long thought to be the smallest planet, recent discoveries have shown that Pluto is even smaller, with a diameter less than our own moon's.

Where is the solar system in space?

Just as the earth revolves around the sun, so the sun too is moving—around the center of our galaxy, the Milky Way. This collection of some 200 billion stars includes every one that is visible to the naked eye at night. The glowing trail of stars across the sky that is commonly called the Milky Way is actually only a small part of the galaxy.

If we could see the entire Milky Way, it would resemble a gigantic disk. From the top it would look like a pinwheel, with long star- and gas-filled arms spiraling around the center. The solar system is in one of these arms, about three-fifths of the way out from the heart of the galaxy.

As the entire Milky Way rotates around its mysterious center, stars closer to the hub move faster than those on its outer edge. Hurtling through space, at 150 miles per sec-

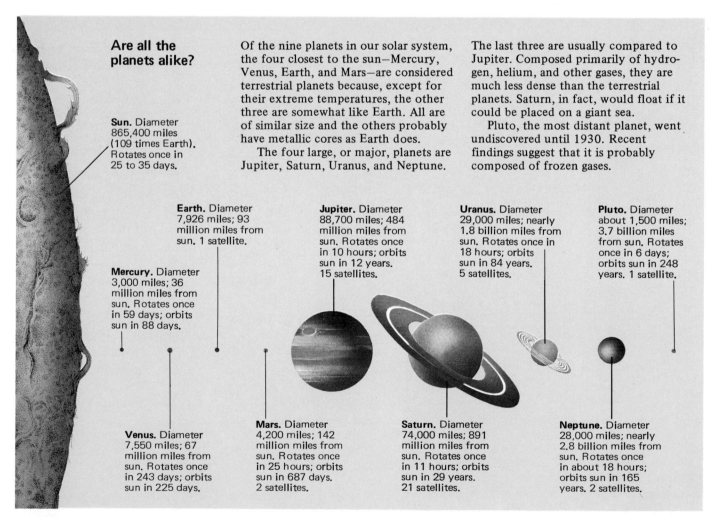

Are all the planets alike?

Of the nine planets in our solar system, the four closest to the sun—Mercury, Venus, Earth, and Mars—are considered terrestrial planets because, except for their extreme temperatures, the other three are somewhat like Earth. All are of similar size and the others probably have metallic cores as Earth does.

The four large, or major, planets are Jupiter, Saturn, Uranus, and Neptune.

The last three are usually compared to Jupiter. Composed primarily of hydrogen, helium, and other gases, they are much less dense than the terrestrial planets. Saturn, in fact, would float if it could be placed on a giant sea.

Pluto, the most distant planet, went undiscovered until 1930. Recent findings suggest that it is probably composed of frozen gases.

Sun. Diameter 865,400 miles (109 times Earth). Rotates once in 25 to 35 days.

Earth. Diameter 7,926 miles; 93 million miles from sun. 1 satellite.

Mercury. Diameter 3,000 miles; 36 million miles from sun. Rotates once in 59 days; orbits sun in 88 days.

Jupiter. Diameter 88,700 miles; 484 million miles from sun. Rotates once in 10 hours; orbits sun in 12 years. 15 satellites.

Uranus. Diameter 29,000 miles; nearly 1.8 billion miles from sun. Rotates once in 18 hours; orbits sun in 84 years. 5 satellites.

Pluto. Diameter about 1,500 miles; 3.7 billion miles from sun. Rotates once in 6 days; orbits sun in 248 years. 1 satellite.

Venus. Diameter 7,550 miles; 67 million miles from sun. Rotates once in 243 days; orbits sun in 225 days.

Mars. Diameter 4,200 miles; 142 million miles from sun. Rotates once in 25 hours; orbits sun in 687 days. 2 satellites.

Saturn. Diameter 74,000 miles; 891 million miles from sun. Rotates once in 11 hours; orbits sun in 29 years. 21 satellites.

Neptune. Diameter 28,000 miles; nearly 2.8 billion miles from sun. Rotates once in about 18 hours; orbits sun in 165 years. 2 satellites.

ond, our own sun and neighboring stars complete one circuit of the galaxy every 225 million years.

How big is the Milky Way?

The immensity of space defies the imagination. The distances involved are so vast that astronomers measure them not in miles or kilometers, but in terms of the speed of light, which passes through a vacuum at a rate of 186,282 miles per second. Light from the sun, for example, travels the 93 million miles to Earth in approximately 8 minutes.

But even that distance is just a short hop in astronomical terms. In reckoning the dimensions of space, astronomers use the light-year; this is the distance light travels in one year, or about 6 million million miles. Thus the stars nearest our sun in the Milky Way are 4.3 light-years away. The entire galaxy in turn is about 100,000 light-years in diameter. And far beyond our own Milky Way, in the void of space, uncountable other galaxies are speeding through the immensity of the universe.

Why does the sun shine?

The sun, source of the constant stream of heat and light essential to life on Earth, is a gaseous ball some 865,000 miles in diameter. Its inner temperature is measured in millions of degrees, and disturbances on its surface send streams of glowing gas tens of thousands of miles into space. Even today, when scientists are beginning to comprehend the sun's inner workings, the extent of its power remains difficult to grasp.

The source of all the sun's energy lies far below its visible surface, in its thermonuclear core. Temperatures in the core reach nearly 30,000,000° F, and pressures are so enormous that the gases there—mainly hydrogen and helium—are compressed to a density 14 times that of lead.

Under so much heat and pressure, the hydrogen is transformed into helium in thermonuclear reactions that release massive amounts of energy. The energy then passes through a thick zone of hot gases that blankets the inner core, and it eventually reaches the sun's surface, where it is radiated into space as heat and light.

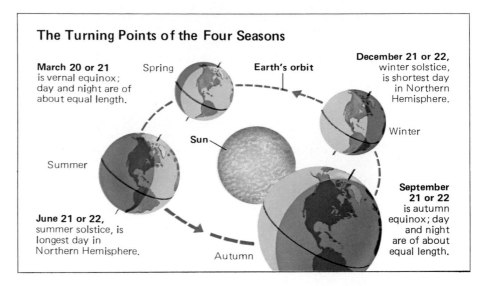

Why do the seasons change?

The earth's unending spin on its axis—the line connecting the North and the South Pole—is the cause of day and night. The seasons, in turn, result from the fact that the axis is tilted in relation to the earth's orbit around the sun.

In the course of the earth's annual orbit, the tilted axis causes the North Pole to lean toward the sun during part of the year. The Northern Hemisphere then has its summer: days are long and hot, and for part of the time the region around the pole is never in shadow. This is the time of year when far northern lands bask in the light of the midnight sun.

In winter, when the earth is on the opposite side of the sun, the North Pole leans away from the sun, and the Northern Hemisphere cools down. For a time the Far North is shrouded in 24-hour darkness. At the same time, the South Pole is tilted toward the sun, and the Southern Hemisphere enjoys the long days of summer.

The so-called summer solstice occurs on June 21 or 22 in the Northern Hemisphere; it is the longest day of the year there and marks the beginning of summer. The winter solstice, about December 21, is the shortest day and is considered to be the first day of that season.

The turning points for spring and fall are the equinoxes (from the Latin for "equal night"). The vernal, or spring, equinox occurs about March 21, and the autumnal equinox falls on September 21 or 22. On these dates, the dividing line between light and darkness on the globe cuts across both the North and the South Pole, and throughout the world day and night are of nearly equal length.

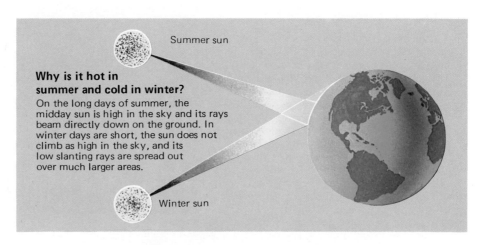

Why is it hot in summer and cold in winter?

On the long days of summer, the midday sun is high in the sky and its rays beam directly down on the ground. In winter days are short, the sun does not climb as high in the sky, and its low slanting rays are spread out over much larger areas.

The Sky Above

How many stars are there?

The star-strewn night sky has long been a source of fascination. Seemingly countless specks of light stretch from horizon to horizon, especially on the dark nights of a new moon. (None are visible by day because then our own star, the sun, outshines all others.) Yet the visible stars are only a fraction of the 200 billion or so that make up our galaxy. In any one place, the naked eye can distinguish at most 2,000 or so individual stars.

Our brightest star is Sirius, the Dog Star, in the constellation Canis Major. The most important "landmark" star in the Northern Hemisphere is Polaris, the North Star. Located almost exactly above the North Pole, it remains in the same position throughout the night while, as the earth turns, all other stars appear to revolve around it. As a result, Polaris has traditionally been a reference point for navigators, and it remains a major "signpost" for modern stargazers.

How big is the moon?

Aglow with reflected sunlight, the moon seems by far the largest object in the night sky. In reality it is tiny in comparison with the sun. But the earth's only natural satellite is also its nearest neighbor in space: on the average the moon is only about 240,000 miles from the earth. And so, because it is so near, it seems very large.

The moon's actual diameter is 2,160 miles, about one-fourth the earth's diameter. Several moons in the solar system are larger than our own: Jupiter's Ganymede is bigger than the planet Mercury. Even so, the earth and the moon are closer in size than any other planet-satellite pair.

Why does the moon change in size?

Everyone has been startled from time to time by the gigantic size of a full moon rising above the horizon. Then as it climbs higher in the sky, it seems to shrink to its normal size. Yet photographs have proved that the moon's face remains nearly the same size. The seeming change is apparently a trick played by our own perceptions. At the horizon, we compare the moon to known landmarks and it seems enormous. High in the sky, it is by itself and we perceive it as smaller.

Over the course of the month, however, the moon really does change in apparent size. This happens because its orbit is not a perfect circle. The nearest point on its orbit is 25,000 miles closer to the earth than its farthest point. And when the moon is closer, it looks noticeably larger.

What causes an eclipse?

Among the most awesome celestial events is a total solar eclipse. The daytime sky darkens, and people look up in wonder as the sun is temporarily blotted out. Such an event is visible somewhere on the earth at least twice a year. It comes about during times of the new moon, when the sun, moon, and earth become aligned so that the moon casts its shadow on the earth.

Within the umbra (the dark part of the shadow) the eclipse is total: for a time the moon completely covers the sun. Observers in the penumbra (the larger, lighter part of the shadow) see a partial eclipse: the moon's disk passes across the face of the sun but never covers it completely.

What are the phases of the moon?

Over the course of the 29½-day lunar month, the moon appears to wax, or grow in size, to a full moon, then wane, or shrink, to nothing. This happens because, during most of the month, only part of the sunlit half of the moon is visible from the earth. The photographs at the right show the phases of the moon during a lunar month. The numbers correspond to the positions of the moon on its monthly orbit, shown in the diagram below.

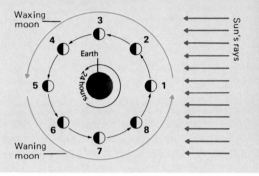

1. New moon

5. Full moon

2. Waxing crescent

6. Waning gibbous

3. First quarter

7. Last quarter

4. Waxing gibbous

8. Waning crescent

What are constellations?

Although stars may be trillions of miles apart, some of them seem to form distinct groups in the sky. These clusters, called constellations, have been recognized since ancient times, and early astronomers named many of them for animals, mythological figures, and other objects that the stars seemed to outline. The resemblances in some cases are obvious. The Big Dipper looks unmistakably like a dipper. It is more difficult to see the mythological queen of Ethiopia in the five bright stars of Cassiopeia, although some claim to see at least the outline of her chair.

Cassiopeia

Polaris

Big Dipper

Eclipses of the moon are less dramatic but equally intriguing. They occur when the earth is in line between a full moon and the sun, so that the moon passes through the earth's

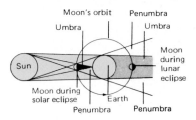

shadow. Even during a total eclipse, however, the moon usually does not disappear completely. Some of the sun's rays are refracted, or bent, as they pass through the earth's atmosphere and enter the shadow, illuminating the moon with a more or less coppery glow.

Where do comets come from?

Of all the objects that brighten the night sky, comets are the rarest and most elusive. Yet these glowing spheres with long streaming tails of light produce some of the most thrilling celestial spectacles.

The orbits of the visible comets are long ellipses. Some of them swing out beyond the realm of Pluto, then travel back toward the sun, coming even closer to it than Mercury. Some comets return again and again on a predictable schedule; others are seen once or twice, then vanish forever.

The actual origin of comets is uncertain. One theory suggests that they are leftovers from the formation of the solar system, and that billions are circling at the outer reaches of the system. Occasionally one is diverted from this orbit and moves in toward the sun. The comet itself is thought to be a mass of dust and frozen gases. As it approaches the sun only the bright head is visible at first. But as it gets nearer, the comet develops a tail (sometimes millions of miles long) composed of dust and gas.

Comets are usually named for their discoverers. Our most famous comet is named for Edmund Halley, the British astronomer who correctly calculated its 76-year timetable in the 17th century. Halley's comet was last seen— right on schedule—in 1910 and is expected to visit our skies again in 1986.

What are shooting stars?

Although comets may remain visible for weeks or even months at a time, so-called shooting stars streak across the sky and vanish within moments. Most are the legacy of comets, caused by bits of debris that remain in space after the comet has passed by. When the fragments enter the atmosphere, friction causes them to vaporize and produce the streaks of light known as meteors, or shooting stars. Others are caused by larger chunks of interplanetary debris that burn as they enter the atmosphere.

The most predictable displays of shooting stars are called meteor showers. Recurring year after year on about the same date, they happen when the earth passes through the orbit of a bygone comet. At the height of a shower, dozens of meteors may fall every hour, all seeming to radiate from a particular constellation. During the Leonid meteor shower, about November 16, great shows of shooting stars have been seen in the vicinity of the constellation Leo, and the Perseid meteor showers, in early August, center on the constellation Perseus.

Do meteors ever reach the earth?

Difficult as it may be to believe, rocks can and do fall from the sky. Hundreds of them fall to earth each year, but most land in the oceans, and the majority are very small.

These rocks from outer space, called meteors as they speed through the atmosphere, are known as meteorites if they reach the earth. They range in size from a few ounces to several tons. The largest known meteorite was found in Namibia (South-West Africa) and weighed about 60 tons. Another, much larger, once crashed into the Arizona desert and exploded on impact. All that remains is Meteor Crater, a hole some 4,000 feet in diameter and nearly 600 feet deep.

A comet (lower left) sweeps across the solar system in the vicinity of Saturn. Its orbit will take it on a hairpin turn around the sun before it sweeps back into outer space.

Our Ocean of Air

What is air made of?

Invisible and unnoticed except when it moves as wind, the air we breathe is basically a mixture of gases. About 78 percent of completely dry air consists of nitrogen, and another 21 percent is the oxygen on which our lives depend. The remaining 1 percent is a mixture of carbon dioxide and other gases.

Air, of course, is seldom completely dry. It includes one other gas—water vapor—in amounts that vary from place to place and from time to time. Without this, there would be no clouds, no rain, and no life on earth.

Also adrift in the ocean of air are a host of microscopic particles. Even "pure" air over the middle of the sea contains thousands of bits of dust per cubic inch. Over an industrial city the number may rise to the millions. Soot, sand, salt from sea spray, plant spores, and pollen grains all float through the air, and a single volcanic eruption can spew tons of fine ash into the atmosphere. Even meteors add to the impurities in air. Remains from their fiery descent into the atmosphere rain slowly but continuously down to the surface of the earth.

How thick is the atmosphere?

In comparison with the size of the earth, the ocean of air enveloping our planet is only a thin film. Although the atmosphere has no clearly defined upper boundary, scientists generally consider it to be about 300 miles thick. Beyond that altitude, the thin gases of the atmosphere merge imperceptibly with the near vacuum of outer space.

Far from being uniform, the atmosphere is divided into four distinct layers. The lowest, the troposphere, averages about 10 miles in depth. It is there that most of our storms are born and the great wind systems keep the parade of clouds in motion.

The next layer, the stratosphere, lies between 10 and 30 miles above the earth. Unlike the turbulent troposphere, the stratosphere is calm; jet pilots fly their planes there to escape the stormy air below.

The third layer, the chilly mesosphere, extends from 30 to 50 miles out in space. It is there that the visible trails of meteors are formed. Beyond lies the extremely thin, electrically charged air of the thermosphere, the site of shimmering displays of northern and southern lights.

What is the ozone layer?

Compared to the rest of the atmosphere, the stratosphere contains a relatively higher concentration of ozone, a form of oxygen. It is constantly being produced there and then broken down again into oxygen by the absorption of ultraviolet radiation from the sun.

Although the amount of ozone is minute even in the ozone layer, it is crucial to life on earth. Because so much solar energy is absorbed in the production and breakdown of ozone, the stratosphere is warmer and more stable than the troposphere below; it acts as a roof, trapping weather systems in the lower atmosphere. More important, it prevents most of the life-destroying ultraviolet radiation from reaching earth. Only enough gets through to give sunbathers a good tan or, if they are careless, a sunburn.

How much does air weigh?

Just as water in the sea has weight, so does the ocean of air above us. About one ton of air presses down on the shoulders of the average person, but we do not feel it because we are held up by an equal amount of air pressure on all sides.

The usual weight of air at sea level is 14.7 pounds per square inch. Atmospheric pressure decreases rapidly with increasing altitude, however. At 10,000 feet it amounts to about 10 pounds per square inch. At 29,000 feet, the height of Mount Everest, the pressure is only 4.5 pounds per square inch. (The air is so thin at these heights that climbers must carry an extra supply of oxygen.)

The weight of our entire ocean of air is almost inconceivable. The mere 14.7 pounds per square inch at sea level adds up to an estimated total of 5,000 million *million* tons of air.

Why is the sky blue?

Molecules of gases in the air itself account for the color of the sky. The intense white light of the sun is actually a mixture of all the colors of the rainbow, and each color has its own wavelength. Red and yellow waves are the longest, blue and violet the shortest. The sky looks blue because the gas

Silhouetting moss-draped baldcypresses, a Florida sunset bathes the sky in color.

molecules deflect, or "scatter," the short wavelengths more thoroughly than the longer ones. The short blue wavelengths are scattered at random, changing direction again and again as they pass through the atmosphere. While the long wavelengths reach our eyes in almost a direct line from the

Wind Systems of the World

The globe is girdled by several zones of prevailing surface winds. Hot air at the equator expands and rises, and the dependable trade winds blow in to take its place. The air subsides again at the horse latitudes (belts of high pressure at about 30° N and 30° S), where it fuels both the trade winds and the westerlies. Closer to the poles, the air rises again at another low pressure zone, where the warm westerlies meet the cold polar air masses. This pattern of prevailing winds generally holds true; however, it is not unchanging. Uneven heating of the earth's surface and seasonal variations sometimes alter it substantially.

We see the rainbow because myriads of individual raindrops are acting as tiny prisms and mirrors. As a ray of sunlight enters each drop, it is bent, or refracted, and split into all the colors of the spectrum. The light is then reflected off the back of the raindrop and travels back to our eyes. Since the light of each color is bent at a slightly different angle, we see neat bands of colors from violet through green to yellow and red. The light reaches us at just the right angles from countless raindrops across the sky, and so we see the continuous arc of the rainbow.

Why does the wind blow?
Whether as gentle breezes or gale-force winds, the air of the lower atmosphere is constantly on the move. The propelling force for all this activity is energy from the sun. As air is warmed, it expands and rises, forming low pressure areas. And as it rises, nearby masses of denser, cooler air move in as wind to take its place.

Many other factors also come into play, such as the presence of mountains and deserts and the differential heating of large expanses of land and sea. Thus, in addition to the global system of prevailing winds, persistent local wind patterns affect many areas of the world.

The eastern Rocky Mountains, for example, are famous for the chinook, a hot, dry winter wind that periodically sweeps down the mountain slopes and out across the plains. Sometimes raising temperatures by 50° F in less than an hour, the chinook often lives up to its other name, the snow-eater. A similar hot, dry wind, common in parts of the Alps, is known as the foehn.

France's mistral, in contrast, is cold and dry. Low pressure areas over the Mediterranean cause blasts of frigid mountain air to funnel seaward down the Rhone Valley. Dreaded since Roman times, the mistral reaches speeds of 85 miles per hour and sometimes persists for days.

Deserts are also powerful wind generators. The hot siroccos, blowing north from the Sahara and the Arabian Desert, are well known. Another Saharan wind, the harmattan, blows westward toward the Atlantic. Hot, dry, and dusty, it often impairs visibility far out at sea.

sun, the blue waves reach us from all parts of the sky, and it appears blue.

In contrast to gas molecules, larger particles in the air scatter longer wavelengths as well as the blue. When enough of these larger particles are present, the scattering of the longer wavelengths diminishes the intensity of the blue we see, and the sky appears light blue or even milky white.

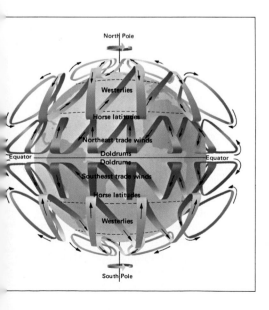

Why is the sky so colorful at sunset?
In the evening, as the sun begins to set, its beams travel a much longer distance through the atmosphere than when it is shining directly overhead. Large particles in the lower atmosphere scatter the light so intensely that only the longer red and yellow wavelengths reach our eyes directly. The sun itself may appear as a crimson sphere. Its rays, moreover, beaming from a low angle, tint the undersides of the clouds with dazzling colors.

The brilliance of a sunset (or a sunrise) depends on the amount and size of particles in the air. It is for this reason that dust storms and eruptions of volcanic ash often produce memorable sunsets far from their source.

How are rainbows formed?
On a sunny day anyone can see a rainbow in the spray from a garden hose. The trick is to stand so that the sun is behind you, shining into the spray. The same thing happens when a natural rainbow forms in the sky. But instead of shining into nearby spray, the sun is shining into a distant rain shower, and the banded arc of colors forms on a much larger scale.

15

The Cycle of Precipitation

Why don't we run out of water?
The world's water supply is enormous: it totals some 325 million cubic miles. At any one time, however, about 97 percent of all that water lies in the salty seas, and another 2 percent is trapped in glaciers and ice caps. Less than 1 percent is available as fresh, usable water in lakes and ponds, rivers and streams, and in the underground supplies we tap with wells.

If this meager supply of fresh water were not continually replenished, rivers and lakes would go dry, fields and forests would wither, and all life would come to an end. Fortunately, water is constantly on the move, circulating between ocean, air, and land in a complex, unending cycle.

The sun is the powerhouse that keeps the water cycle in operation. It warms the surface of the sea, changing water into vapor. Water also evaporates from lakes, streams, the leaves of plants, and even glaciers. In the air this invisible vapor condenses and forms the billions of minute droplets and ice crystals that make up the clouds. Eventually the moisture in the clouds returns to earth as rain, snow, and other forms of precipitation. And there it evaporates once again, continuing its never-ending cycle.

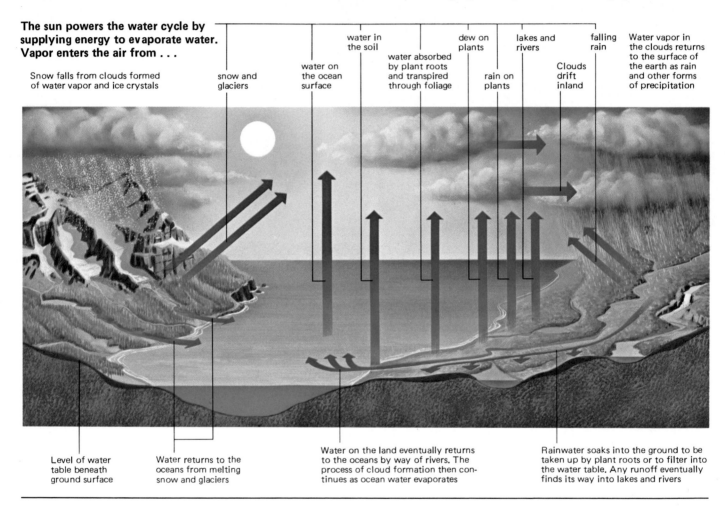

The sun powers the water cycle by supplying energy to evaporate water. Vapor enters the air from . . .

Snow falls from clouds formed of water vapor and ice crystals

snow and glaciers

water on the ocean surface

water in the soil

water absorbed by plant roots and transpired through foliage

dew on plants

rain on plants

lakes and rivers

Clouds drift inland

falling rain

Water vapor in the clouds returns to the surface of the earth as rain and other forms of precipitation

Level of water table beneath ground surface

Water returns to the oceans from melting snow and glaciers

Water on the land eventually returns to the oceans by way of rivers. The process of cloud formation then continues as ocean water evaporates

Rainwater soaks into the ground to be taken up by plant roots or to filter into the water table. Any runoff eventually finds its way into lakes and rivers

How do raindrops form?
The clouds that drift majestically across the sky are composed of billions upon billions of tiny water droplets and ice crystals. Yet though a single cloud may contain several tons of moisture, many of them pass by without producing so much as a shower. Only when conditions are right does some of that moisture fall to earth as liquid rain.

The myriads of water droplets in clouds form because, as warm, moist air rises, it eventually becomes so cold that the water vapor condenses. Collecting around bits of dust and other microscopic particles known as condensation nuclei, the droplets at first are so minute that they literally float on air. But as they ride the air currents, the droplets collide and coalesce, gradually forming larger and larger droplets. In time they may become big and heavy enough to fall as rain.

Other raindrops have a more complicated history. They begin as snow or ice crystals in the frigid upper reaches of a cloud, then melt as they pass through warmer air below and land on earth as rain. At least half of all rain probably begins as snow.

The smallest raindrops, classed as drizzle, drift so lazily to earth that they seem to float. The largest, nearly $\frac{1}{4}$ inch in diameter, pelt down at 25 feet per second. But whatever their size, none are teardrop-shaped. Although the largest drops are flattened on the bottom, most are round.

What causes snow?

When temperatures in a cloud are low enough, its moisture content may be released, not as rain, but as feather-light snowflakes. This happens because the water in clouds behaves in strange ways. At very low temperatures cloud droplets become supercooled, which means that they remain liquid even though their temperature is below freezing. Under certain conditions the supercooled droplets evaporate and the vapor then freezes directly into minute ice crystals. As more vapor freezes on the first tiny crystals, they grow into snowflakes.

Developing flakes take on different shapes, depending on the temperature and the amount of moisture in the air. Because of their crystalline structure, most snowflakes are about 90 percent air, a fact that makes them excellent insulators and mufflers of sound. But it also means that the water in 10 inches of snowfall equals only 1 inch of rain. Even so, snow is an important source of fresh water in many regions. Arid areas in the American West depend heavily on the spring runoff from snow in the Rocky Mountains.

Ephemeral icy feathers of frost on a windowpane are products of water's remarkable ability to freeze directly from its gaseous state into solid crystals of ice.

Some Snow Is Star-shaped

Although all snow crystals are constructed on a six-sided pattern, they are noted for the infinite variety of their forms. The most beautiful are the delicately symmetrical starlike flakes, like those shown above. Others may take the form of flat, hexagonal plates, needles, columns, cups, spools, or even irregular masses.

Are sleet and hail similar?

Freezing temperatures and turbulent winds can play many tricks on a raindrop. The falling drops may pass through a layer of very cold air and freeze into solid pellets, or sleet, that actually bounce when they hit the ground. Or the drops may become so cold that they freeze on impact and coat everything they touch with a glassy armor of ice.

Hailstones, in contrast, are born high up in turbulent thunderclouds. Caught alternately in updrafts and downdrafts, pellets of ice enlarge as they are coated with additional layers of ice. Their final size depends on how long they are buffeted about in the cloud. Most are the size of grapes when they finally fall to earth, but many grow as big as walnuts and a few are as large as tennis balls. One of the biggest on record was $5\frac{1}{2}$ inches in diameter and weighed $1\frac{1}{2}$ pounds.

The damage from hailstones can be catastrophic. They sometimes dent the roofs of cars and batter buildings, but their worst damage is to agriculture. Since they usually fall in summer, when thunderstorms are most common, they sometimes ruin entire fields of wheat and other crops.

Is frost frozen dew?

Seeing the tiny beads of dew that cling to spiderwebs at dawn or the tracery of frost on windowpanes is among the rewards of rising early. For as soon as the sun's rays strike, dew and frost begin to disappear.

Both are products of cold night air. As the air begins to cool after dark, it gradually approaches the dew point (the temperature at which it becomes saturated with water vapor). When the saturated air comes in contact with the slightly cooler surfaces of leaves and grass, the water vapor condenses and coats them with dew—just as it coats a glass of iced water on a hot and humid summer day.

Frost forms only when temperatures are below freezing. Then, when the saturated air comes in contact with a freezing cold surface, the water vapor does not condense into liquid but instead freezes directly from its gaseous state into minute crystals of ice. The crystals grow as more and more vapor freezes, sometimes forming delicate featherlike patterns.

How is fog formed?

Like frost and dew, fog is the product of saturated air. As the air reaches its dew point, water vapor in it condenses into tiny droplets that, like the droplets in a cloud, are too small and light to fall. Fog, in fact, is essentially a cloud formed at ground level.

Many different circumstances result in the formation of fog. It may form when the ground cools at night and chills the damp air above it. Or it can occur when warm moist air moves over a cold ocean current or cool land area. Fog can also be formed by the meeting of warm and cold air masses or by the cooling of moist air as it moves up a mountain slope.

Weather and Climate

What is the difference between weather and climate?

When we speak of a rainy day or a sunny day, a warm day or a cool one, we are referring to the weather. When we speak of a region's year-round balmy temperatures, however, we are talking about climate.

Both terms take into account all of the atmospheric conditions in an area, including temperature, humidity, precipitation, windiness, cloudiness, and so on. But weather is short-term and local; it may change daily or even within an hour. Climate, in contrast, applies to a larger area and covers a longer period of time; it is a composite of the various day-to-day weather conditions that are likely to prevail in a region. Thus, a rainy day is an unexpected bit of weather in the Sahara, but showers are almost daily occurrences in the warm, wet climate of Puerto Rico or Samoa.

Why do climates vary from place to place?

Climate depends first and foremost on latitude. Areas near the equator tend to be warm and wet, while the poles are cold and relatively dry, with drastic seasonal extremes. The mid-latitudes, in turn, have more moderate climates, neither as hot as the equator nor as cold as the poles.

A host of other factors, however, alter this general pattern. The British Isles, for example, are at the same latitude as Labrador, yet the two have entirely different climates. The warm Gulf Stream, sweeping northward from the tropics, keeps the British Isles relatively mild and moist.

Parts of Siberia at this same latitude, in turn, have violent seasonal extremes, with frigid winters and mild summers. The interiors of all the continents, in fact, have harsher climates than coastal zones, for the oceans are great moderators. Since water absorbs heat more slowly than land in summer and loses it more slowly in winter, the oceans tend to temper the climates of nearby seacoasts.

Elevation also plays a role. Africa's highest peak, Kilimanjaro, for instance, stands just south of the equator, yet its summit is perpetually covered with snow. By the same token, highlands everywhere have cooler, often wetter climates than surrounding lowlands.

Mountain barriers can create dramatic contrasts. In the Pacific Northwest, the western slopes of the Cascade Range receive abundant rain and snowfall, while the plains to their east are semiarid. Moist winds blowing in from the Pacific Ocean are, in effect, squeezed dry as they rise over the mountain barrier, leaving little moisture for the parched land to its east.

What are some climatic extremes?

Record temperatures and rainfalls are figures that fascinate. The world's all-time high—a scorching 136° F in the shade—was recorded at Al Aziziyah, in western Libya. Death Valley, California, is a close runner-up, with a high of 134° F. This lowest spot in North America also endured the record heat wave: temperatures once topped 120° F for 43 days in a row.

Antarctica has registered the lowest temperature. Vostok, a Soviet research station, has been chilled to − 127° F. The coldest permanently inhabited place, with a low of −96° F, is Oymyakon, a village high on a plateau in south-central Siberia.

The wettest spot is Mount Waialeale, in Hawaii. It gets rain up to 350 days each year, and its average annual rainfall exceeds 450 inches. The driest place is Chile's Atacama Desert; in some parts of this wasteland, no rain has ever fallen.

Why is weather so changeable?

Air in the lower atmosphere is constantly on the move. Masses of air that are cold or warm, wet or dry, move across land and sea, bringing weather changes as one air mass replaces another. The greatest changes occur along fronts, the boundaries between air masses. When warm air replaces cold air, the boundary is called a warm front. A cold front is the leading edge of a cold air mass. Cloudiness and precipitation usually mark the passage of a front.

Atmospheric pressure also varies. An atmospheric high resembles a mountain of cool, heavy air. As the air sinks and spirals out from the center of a high, it becomes warmer. Clouds evaporate and fair weather follows as a high drifts through.

Lows, in contrast, produce cloudy, sometimes stormy weather. Warm air spirals inward toward the center of a low. Rising at the center, the air ex-

---

When Warm and Cold Air Meet

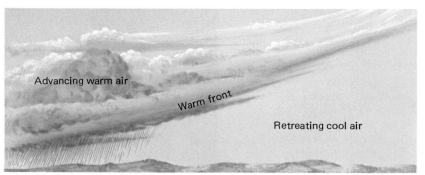

Advancing warm air

Warm front

Retreating cool air

Moving air masses are notable weather makers, especially along fronts, the boundaries between air masses with different temperatures. A warm front, like the one shown above, is the boundary between a warm air mass and a cooler one that it is replacing. When this happens, the warm air rides up over the cooler air, and its moisture begins to condense. High wispy clouds are the first signs of an advancing warm front. Gradually the clouds lower and thicken, and a long steady rainfall usually follows.

A cold front, in contrast, may arrive more suddenly as a mass of cold air wedges beneath warmer air. Showers and thunderstorms, followed by shifting winds, falling temperatures, and a clearing sky, mark a cold front's passage.

High clouds (above 20,000 ft.)

The high-flying, cirrus-type clouds, composed mainly of ice crystals, often form thin, transparent veils across the sky.

Cirrus
(wispy)

Cirrocumulus
(wispy, puffed up)

Cirrostratus
(wispy, layered)

Middle clouds (7,000 to 20,000 ft.)

Although cumulonimbus clouds have their bases low in the sky, the billowing thunderheads usually tower tens of thousands of feet into the air.

Altostratus
(high, layered)

Altocumulus
(high, puffed up)

Low clouds (below 7,000 ft.)

The mobile clouds are not always restricted to particular altitudes. Nimbostratus clouds, for example, are often seen at middle levels of the sky.

Cumulonimbus
(puffed up, rain cloud)

Cumulus
(puffed up)

Stratocumulus
(layered, puffed up)

Nimbostratus
(rain cloud, layered)

Stratus
(layered)

Fog

Do clouds have names?

No two clouds are alike. Even a single cloud continually changes as it drifts across the sky. Yet many are obviously of the same general type. Everyone recognizes the wispy mare's tails that form streaks high in the sky, and the towering thunderheads that produce summer cloudbursts.

Every type of cloud, in fact, has its own descriptive name. The system began in 1803 when Luke Howard, a London pharmacist, named the three basic groups. The wispy mare's tails he named cirrus, from the Latin for "lock of hair." He called the puffed-up cottony clouds cumulus, which means "heap" or "mass." His third name, stratus, for clouds in sheets or layers, is derived from the Latin word for "spread out."

The modern classification of clouds is based on Luke Howard's names, along with two additional terms. *Alto,* meaning "high," refers to clouds in the middle regions of the sky, and *nimbus,* the Latin for "dark rain cloud," is added to the names of clouds that portend bad weather.

Various combinations of these basic terms give us the names of the ten types of clouds that pass across the sky. Cirrostratus clouds, for example, form a thin, wispy layer high in the sky. They sometimes mean bad weather is on the way. Altocumulus clouds are patches of small puffed-up clouds in the middle sky. Nimbostratus clouds, in turn, are dark, gloomy rain clouds that spread out in a solid layer. They usually produce a steady, lasting downpour.

pands and cools; moisture condenses; and precipitation often follows.

Many other factors affect the circulation of the air, causing weather to change. Clouds may gather and spoil a picnic, or they may evaporate and transform a gloomy day into a pleasant one. Whatever the causes, changing weather inevitably affects our plans from day to day.

How do forecasters predict weather?

People have always searched the skies for clues to the weather. Farmers and seafarers down through the ages have learned to read the clouds and winds for signs of fair weather or foul. Today we rely on the predictions of professional meteorologists.

Their forecasts are the product of an international effort. Thousands of weather stations are located around the world, both on land and at sea. At each station, the weather is monitored at least four times daily: measurements are taken of such things as air pressure and temperature, wind speed, cloud cover, and precipitation. Elsewhere, upper-level observations are made by weather balloons, and satellites send a continuous flow of photographs back to earth.

All this information is relayed to national weather bureaus, where it is plotted on charts and analyzed by meteorologists. The information is then transmitted to newspapers and radio and television stations, where forecasts are issued to the public. Speed is essential in communicating weather data. Forecasters must be able to warn of hurricanes and tornadoes, floods and freezes. But obviously they most enjoy predicting fair weather for the weekend.

The Ways of Storms

How do thunderstorms develop?
The rapid growth of towering storm clouds and the damp, cool winds that herald an approaching thunderstorm are familiar in most temperate and tropical regions of the world. At any one time, in fact, an estimated 1,800 such storms are in progress somewhere around the globe.

The clouds begin to form when a strong updraft of warm, moist air develops in an unstable area of the atmosphere. Moisture condenses as the billowing cloud grows to heights of 40,000 feet or more. By this time, rain, snow, and even hail are falling within the cloud—so much so, in fact, that they create powerful downdrafts of cold air from high altitudes.

Before long, streaks of lightning flash across the sky, thunder echoes from the hills, and the countryside is drenched by a driving downpour as updrafts and downdrafts battle it out within the cloud. The downdrafts eventually win out, stifling the warm, moist updrafts. The rainfall slows down, the winds abate, and the storm ends almost as suddenly as it began.

Where does lightning come from?
Powerful electrical charges build up in the churning interior of a thundercloud. How this happens is not entirely understood, but it is known that a positive charge builds up near the top of the cloud and a negative charge is concentrated near its base.

This negative charge in turn is attracted to positively charged ground beneath the cloud. But the air is a good insulator, and for a time it prevents the flow of electricity that would equalize the charges.

When enough voltage finally does build up, a two-part stroke of lightning occurs. First a series of faint "leader" strokes zigzag down from the cloud. Electrically charged "streamers" flare up from the ground, and when the two meet, an electrical pathway is forged between earth and sky.

A powerful current of electricity then travels up this pathway into the cloud. This second "return stroke" produces the flash we see as lightning.

Does lightning ever strike twice?
Despite the old saying to the contrary, nearly every bolt of lightning strikes in

Two successive bolts of lightning, caught in a time exposure, light up the sky with a dazzling display of natural fireworks during a thunderstorm.

the same place not just once, but several times. Each flash of lightning that we see is actually a succession of leader and return strokes traveling along the same pathway through the sky. But the whole sequence of strokes is completed so quickly that we perceive them as a single flash.

The old saying does not even hold true over the long term. The electrical charge in the ground beneath a storm becomes concentrated in the highest objects, and this causes them to attract the leader strokes. Thus, tall trees and high buildings are indeed often struck more than once by lightning. The Empire State Building in New York City has been struck many times in the course of a single storm.

What causes thunder?
The temperature of a streak of lightning reaches 27,000° F or more—hotter than the surface of the sun. This blast of heat can explode trees by vaporizing their sap, and it sometimes melts sand into shards of glass.

Such temperatures also heat up the air along a stroke of lightning. The heated air expands so violently that it generates the shock waves we hear as thunder. A nearby stroke of lightning produces an explosive thunderclap. A more distant stroke produces a drawn-out rumbling, because the sound waves are refracted by the atmosphere and bounced off hills and other landforms.

Since light travels faster than sound,

So much snow is blown about in a blizzard that visibility is often reduced to zero. And in the storm's aftermath, the countryside is often paralyzed beneath enormous snowdrifts. A similar deadly storm in Siberia is known as a *purga* or a *buran*. But the worst blizzards are the ones that hit Antarctica, where they strike with winds of hurricane force.

What is an ice storm?

If ground temperatures are below freezing, even a light drizzle from a passing warm air mass can produce one of the most disruptive of winter storms. The falling rain freezes immediately upon impact and soon sheaths the entire landscape beneath a shimmering layer of ice.

An ice storm's handiwork can be incredibly beautiful: woodlands and parks are frequently transformed into fantasylands of fragile crystal. But the results can be deadly as well. Streets and sidewalks become sheets of ice. Branches bend until they finally snap, especially if strong winds are blowing. The deadliest damage comes when utility wires sag and then break beneath their burden of ice, leaving the storm's victims without heat or light.

Are desert storms dangerous?

Even in the driest of deserts, some rain usually falls from time to time. It can produce startling results. Following the brief annual rainy season, the deserts of the American West are transformed almost overnight into colorful tapestries of short-lived wildflowers.

Occasionally, however, desert areas are plagued by brief, torrential downpours that produce devastating flash floods. Runoff water drains into dry stream channels that are called arroyos in the Southwest and wadis in Arabic-speaking lands. Without warning, a wall of water hurtles downstream, washing out entire bridges, overturning cars, and destroying everything in its path.

Desert travelers can also be marooned by storms without rain. Fierce winds blowing across these parched lands sometimes whip up sand and dust storms that last for days at a time. Choking clouds of dust blot out the light of the sun, and sand piles up in drifts that make roads impassable.

Windshields are sandblasted into sheets of frosted glass, and paint is eaten away entirely.

Even nondesert areas can suffer from dust storms. During the drought years of the 1930's, a large area of the western United States was transformed into the notorious Dust Bowl. In recurring annual dust storms, untold quantities of precious topsoil were blown away and lost forever.

Why do monsoons bring so much rain?

Among the most predictable of all storm systems is the monsoon, a shifting seasonal wind pattern that brings months of unending rain followed by months of clear, dry weather. The world's best-known monsoon blows across the Indian Ocean, where for centuries seafarers have relied on the dependable seasonal winds.

Monsoon winds begin to blow inland with the onset of summer, when the land heats up more rapidly than the oceans. As heated air above the land expands and rises, a low pressure area forms and warm, moist ocean air moves in to take its place. Rising over

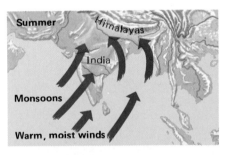

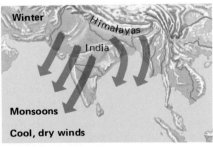

highlands and plateaus, the ocean winds then drop their moisture as torrential summer rains.

In autumn the situation is reversed as the land cools down more rapidly than the sea. Low pressure areas develop over the ocean, and for months on end, cool, dry winds blow steadily from land out to sea.

it is possible to determine just how far away lightning has struck. Counting the seconds between the visible flash and the audible blast, then dividing by five, yields the approximate distance in miles from the lightning stroke.

When does a snowstorm become a blizzard?

The howling winds and blinding snows of a blizzard can bring life to a standstill over hundreds of square miles—sometimes for days at a time. Although the term is used loosely for any severe storm, a blizzard is officially defined as a snowstorm with winds in excess of 35 miles per hour and temperatures below 20° F. If wind speeds reach 45 miles per hour and the temperature drops to 10° F, the blizzard is classed as severe.

Hurricanes and Tornadoes

What is a hurricane?

Dreaded wherever they are likely to occur, hurricanes are massive, rotating tropical storms characterized by powerful winds and torrential rains. The entire storm system is often some 500 miles in diameter and consists of high winds and lines of clouds that spiral in toward a common center known as the eye. The air is calm and cloudless in the eye itself, which is about 15 miles in diameter. But the eye is surrounded by a towering wall of dense clouds that produce the hurricane's greatest downpours. Here too are found the highest wind speeds. Although winds must blow at least 74 miles per hour for a storm to be classed as a hurricane, speeds around the eye often exceed 150 miles per hour.

Hurricanes characteristically sweep westward across the Atlantic Ocean and batter the islands of the Caribbean and the coasts of North America. Identical storms in the Pacific and Indian oceans are known as typhoons and tropical cyclones. But whatever the name, the result is usually the same—a gruesome toll in death and destruction.

What kinds of damage do hurricanes cause?

When hurricanes hit land, they pack a triple punch—wind, rain, and surging seas. The high winds around the eye can easily uproot trees, lift the roofs off buildings, and overturn cars. The storms typically drop as much as six inches of rain, usually in torrential downpours that cause widespread flooding. Even worse is the so-called storm surge. The winds whip up the sea into tremendous waves that sometimes wash far inland as solid walls of water, swamping everything that lies in their path.

Damage is especially severe along low-lying coasts. Some of the worst disasters have occurred along the densely populated shores of the Bay of Bengal. A storm that hit Calcutta, India, in 1737 took 300,000 lives. Estimates of the death toll from another storm, in 1970, this one in Bangladesh, were as high as 500,000.

Where do hurricanes form?

Born of the warm seas and moist winds of the tropics, all hurricanes originate in either of two relatively narrow belts to the north and south of the equator. The ones that strike North America typically begin over the Atlantic Ocean. Gathering strength over the course of several days, they drift westward toward the Caribbean, then generally veer northward before dying out.

Hurricanes formed off the west coast of Mexico are less dangerous, since they usually head out across the Pacific Ocean and do not strike land. Western Pacific storms, in contrast, frequently cause great damage as they batter the densely populated coasts of the Philippines, Japan, and the Asian mainland. The other great spawning area for these devastating tropical storms is over the Indian Ocean, where some veer north toward Asia and others turn south toward Madagascar and East Africa.

How do hurricanes develop?

No one knows precisely why some tropical storms grow to hurricane intensity and others do not, but heat and abundant moisture are essential ingredients. The storms are most common in late summer, when the surface of the sea has warmed to 80° F or more and humidity is high.

Hurricanes begin as small areas of low pressure over tropical seas. Warm, moist air rises rapidly in these centers, and as tons of water vapor condense, great quantities of heat are released to further fuel the upward rush of air. Soon moist winds are spiraling in from all directions and swirling up around the eye of the storm.

As the winds intensify, a full-scale hurricane takes shape. Its fury continues until it moves over land or a cold area of the sea, where its supply of heat and moisture is finally cut off.

How High Winds Circulate in a Hurricane

The illustration below, although much compressed, shows the general pattern of wind circulation in a hurricane. (The entire storm system is usually hundreds of miles in diameter.) Surface winds spiral in toward the center of the hurricane from all directions, rise rapidly around the eye, and finally escape the storm at high altitudes.

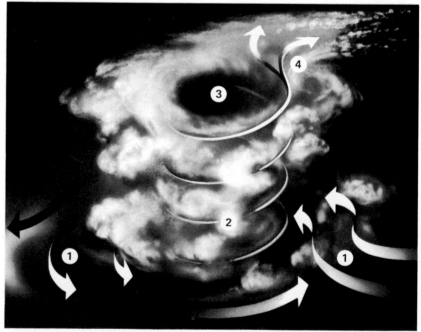

1. Moist surface winds spiral in toward the center of the storm.

2. Gales circle the eye at speeds of up to 200 miles per hour.

3. The calm central eye is usually about 15 miles wide.

4. The rising winds exit from the storm at high altitudes.

The partial vacuum and strong updrafts at the core of a tornado have played strange tricks. Entire railroad cars have been lifted from their tracks and dumped nearby. Yet, in another storm, a jar of pickles is said to have been blown 25 miles through the air and to have landed intact.

Where are twisters likely to form?

Hurricanes are born at sea, but tornadoes normally form over land. They can occur from time to time almost anywhere in the world, but are commonest over the Central Plains of the United States, especially in the spring and early summer months. Some 600 to 700 twisters develop in the United States each year. The worst-hit area, sometimes known as "Tornado Alley," is a broad swath extending northward from Texas and continuing across Oklahoma and Kansas.

What triggers tornadoes?

Although scientists do not know exactly what sets off these deadly whirlwinds, the storms are almost invariably associated with thunderclouds. Conditions are ideal when a mass of warm, moist air pushing north from the Gulf of Mexico becomes trapped beneath colder, heavier air from the north. Clouds form and storms develop in this turbulent zone, sometimes culminating in the violent, swirling uprush of warm air that is known as a tornado.

At first nothing more than a rounded lobe hangs from the base of the cloud. The lobe gradually elongates and finally touches ground, linking earth and cloud with a column of violently whirling winds. White at first from condensing moisture, the twister darkens and turns black as it sucks up dust and debris.

How long does a tornado last?

Once a tornado touches ground, it usually peters out within an hour or less, although some have lasted for several hours. Advancing across the countryside, the average tornado carves a path of destruction about 1,000 feet wide and up to 16 miles long. But some giants leave mile-wide tracks in their wake. And one tornado in 1917 carved a continuous swath 293 miles long.

Sheathed in swirling dust and debris, a tornado advances across a plain in Oklahoma. These most violent of all windstorms take a heavy toll in death and destruction.

Why are tornadoes so terrifying?

When the tip of a tornado touches ground, it traces a path of total destruction across the countryside. Advancing with a roar that has been likened to a squadron of jet planes, the typically funnel-shaped whirlwind can easily uproot trees and shatter entire buildings.

A tornado is essentially a vortex of wind whirling around a core that contains a partial vacuum. And it is the deadly combination of high winds and low atmospheric pressure that makes tornadoes, or twisters, so destructive. Wind speeds average about 200 miles per hour, but are thought to sometimes reach 500 miles per hour. Pieces of straw picked up by such winds have been known to pierce boards and tree trunks. One tornado even sent a plank through a $\frac{5}{8}$-inch sheet of iron.

The low pressure causes buildings to actually explode. When a twister passes, the sudden drop in atmospheric pressure causes air trapped in a building to expand so violently that it literally blows the walls down.

Earth's Restless Crust

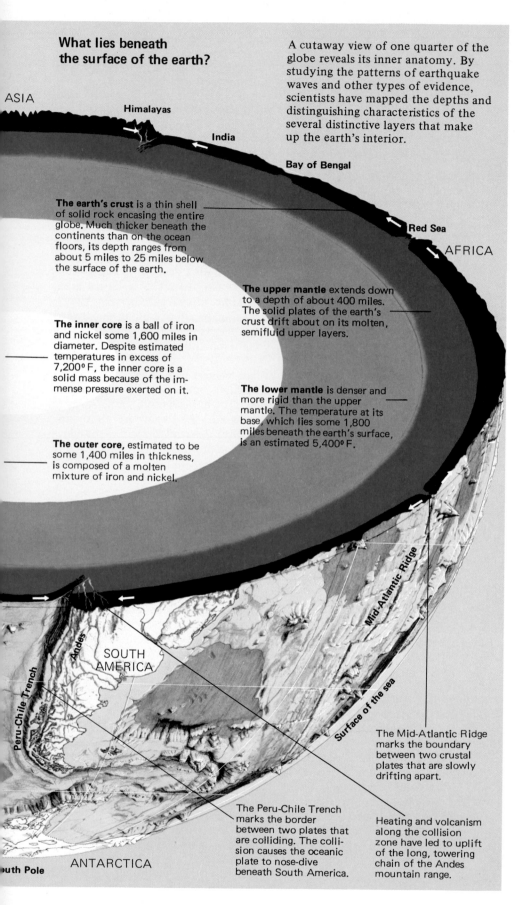

What lies beneath the surface of the earth?

A cutaway view of one quarter of the globe reveals its inner anatomy. By studying the patterns of earthquake waves and other types of evidence, scientists have mapped the depths and distinguishing characteristics of the several distinctive layers that make up the earth's interior.

ASIA

Himalayas

India

Bay of Bengal

The earth's crust is a thin shell of solid rock encasing the entire globe. Much thicker beneath the continents than on the ocean floors, its depth ranges from about 5 miles to 25 miles below the surface of the earth.

Red Sea

AFRICA

The upper mantle extends down to a depth of about 400 miles. The solid plates of the earth's crust drift about on its molten, semifluid upper layers.

The inner core is a ball of iron and nickel some 1,600 miles in diameter. Despite estimated temperatures in excess of 7,200° F, the inner core is a solid mass because of the immense pressure exerted on it.

The lower mantle is denser and more rigid than the upper mantle. The temperature at its base, which lies some 1,800 miles beneath the earth's surface, is an estimated 5,400° F.

The outer core, estimated to be some 1,400 miles in thickness, is composed of a molten mixture of iron and nickel.

Mid-Atlantic Ridge

Andes

SOUTH AMERICA

Peru-Chile Trench

Surface of the sea

The Mid-Atlantic Ridge marks the boundary between two crustal plates that are slowly drifting apart.

The Peru-Chile Trench marks the border between two plates that are colliding. The collision causes the oceanic plate to nose-dive beneath South America.

Heating and volcanism along the collision zone have led to uplift of the long, towering chain of the Andes mountain range.

ANTARCTICA

South Pole

Can the earth's crust move?

The solid ground beneath our feet—the rock that forms the earth's crust—is not as stable as it generally seems. The occasional jolts of earthquakes are cruel reminders of its restless, pent-up energy. But most of the movements are so subtle and take place over such long periods of time that we can only guess at their existence.

Yet by piecing together many bits of evidence, geologists have arrived at a convincing description of our planet's ever-changing face. Fossil seashells entombed on inland mountains, for example, demonstrate that the oceans at times have invaded now-dry land. Earth's mobile crust seems to have repeatedly sagged in some places, warped upward elsewhere, buckled, folded into gigantic rumples, and fractured and then slipped up, down, and sideways along the breaks.

Thus at one time there were no mountains at all where the Himalayas—the world's highest—now rise in southern Asia. By the same token, the Appalachians of eastern North America are the mere eroded roots of a range that may once have been as lofty as the Alps. Indeed, most geologists now believe that the continents themselves are constantly—though ever so slowly—on the move.

Where did the idea of drifting continents originate?

Earth's outer crust, ranging from 5 to 25 miles or so in thickness, is just a thin shell compared to the size of the globe. And most scientists now believe that the shell is broken. Instead of being a continuous skin, they theorize, it is composed of a mosaic of crustal plates. The plates, moreover, are moving in relation to one another and are carrying the continents with them.

As long ago as 1620 the British philosopher Francis Bacon commented on the similarity between the facing coasts of South America and Africa, which look as if they could fit together like the pieces of a puzzle. The theory of continental drift suggests that in fact the two continents once were connected and are slowly moving apart.

The theory was first proposed in the early 1900's by a German scientist, Alfred Wegener. But it was not until the 1950's and 1960's that evidence (mainly from studies of the ocean floor) began to accumulate to explain how such movements might occur.

How can continents move apart?

Much of the evidence supporting the concept of continental drift came from studies of the Mid-Atlantic Ridge. Curving south from Iceland like a giant seam, this submarine mountain range marks the boundary between adjoining crustal plates, as do similar ridges beneath the other oceans.

Such oceanic ridges are volcanic hot spots. Molten material from the earth's interior is constantly welling up along these ridges, where it solidifies and becomes part of the ocean floor. As bands of new rock are added to the edges of the crustal plates on each side of the ridge, the seafloor spreads slowly outward from the ridge. The younger rocks, in effect, push the older rocks aside.

The movement is generally only a couple of inches a year. But it was just this sort of conveyor-belt action that, over tens of millions of years, widened the Atlantic Ocean and separated South America from Africa.

What happens when crustal plates collide?

The crustal plates cannot continue to grow indefinitely, and where their outer margins collide the results are truly earthshaking. When the plate carrying the Indian subcontinent drifted north against the Eurasian Plate, the collision produced the long line of the Himalayas.

Elsewhere, the collision zones are marked by deep ocean trenches. They were formed as the leading edge of one crustal plate nose-dived beneath another and then was melted as it angled back down into the earth's hot interior. When an oceanic plate meets a continental plate, as along the west coast of South America, the collision is accompanied by earthquakes, volcanoes, and violently upthrust mountains such as the Andes. Where two oceanic plates collide beneath the sea, curved chains of volcanic islands rise from the ocean floor, as is the case in Indonesia, Japan, and the Philippines.

How long have the continents been adrift?

At one time, geologists theorize, all the present-day continents drifted together to form a single gigantic landmass. Its name, Pangaea, is from the Greek for "all lands." For reasons that are still unclear, this supercontinent then began to break up again nearly 200 million years ago.

First the northern half (containing the future North America, Europe, and most of Asia) broke away from the southern half (including South America, Africa, Australia, India, and Antarctica). Then, as time passed, further rifts developed, and these two landmasses fragmented into the continents we know today. Carried about on crustal plates that grew along the margins of the rifts, the continents gradually drifted into their present positions.

And the movement continues. Steadily, though imperceptibly, Europe and North America are drifting farther apart as the Atlantic Ocean continues to widen. The Red Sea, in turn, marks a comparatively recent rift in the earth's crust. As new material is added to its floor, the Red Sea may one day become an ocean even wider than the Atlantic.

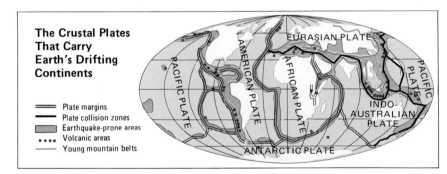

The Crustal Plates That Carry Earth's Drifting Continents

- Plate margins
- Plate collision zones
- Earthquake-prone areas
- Volcanic areas
- Young mountain belts

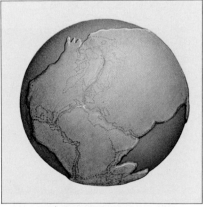

Scientists believe that some 200 million years ago all the continents were united in one supercontinent known as Pangaea.

Pangaea eventually broke up into many pieces—the present-day continents—that slowly began to drift apart.

The continents, shown in their present positions, are probably still moving, though much too slowly to be observed.

Rocks and Minerals

What are minerals?

The building blocks of rocks—minerals—are all around us. They include such common, everyday substances as salt, the graphite in pencil lead, and the talc used to make talcum powder. But they also include rarities such as silver, gold, and diamonds. Despite their variety, all these substances have several common traits: each is a solid with a uniform chemical composition; they all occur naturally on earth; each has a unique crystal structure; and most have never been part of a living thing. In all, scientists have identified more than 2,000 minerals. Yet only about 20 of them make up more than 95 percent of the earth's solid crust.

How are minerals identified?

The two basic properties of a mineral, its chemical composition and its crystal structure, can often be determined only in a laboratory. But many other characteristics are useful in distinguishing one mineral from another.

Shape and color are sometimes helpful, although crystals often crowd together and become distorted as they grow, and they are frequently discolored by impurities. When minerals are scratched against a rough white surface however, many of them leave a distinctive streak of color. Hematite, the commonest iron ore, for example, varies from brownish red to black. But it always produces a red streak.

A mineral's luster is the way it reflects light. It may be glassy, metallic, pearly, waxy, and so on. Hardness is determined by a specimen's ability to scratch certain other minerals whose hardnesses are rated on a scale of 1 to 10. Talc, among the softest of minerals, has a hardness of 1; 10 is reserved for diamonds, the hardest materials in nature.

Cleavage, the way some minerals break along certain planes, is another clue. Mica, one of the most distinctive, cleaves into thin parallel sheets. Specific gravity—weight compared to size—can be estimated by the heft of the mineral in the hand; lead, for example, feels noticeably heavier than an equal volume of sulfur.

Are all rocks made of minerals?

Just as a cake is a mixture of several ingredients, most rocks are composed of one or more minerals combined in various ways. Granite, for example, is formed mainly of the minerals quartz and feldspar. A few types of rocks, however, are made up of the remains of living things. Coal is a solid mass of fossilized plant material. Several types of limestone are formed from the shells and skeletons of various kinds of marine animals, from corals to clams. And some of the oldest limestones were produced by microscopic algae.

How are rocks formed?

All rocks on earth are divided into three large groups—igneous, sedimentary, and metamorphic—depending on the way they were produced. Igneous rocks, named from the Latin word that means "fiery," begin as magma, the molten material of the earth's interior. When magma hardens underground, it cools slowly to form granite and other coarse-grained rocks. Magma that erupts onto the surface cools rapidly into basalt and other kinds of volcanic rocks.

Sedimentary rocks result when layers of water- or wind-borne materials are consolidated into stone. Some, such as sandstone and shale, are made up of eroded debris from older rocks. Others, including certain types of limestone, are composed of plant and animal remains. And still others, including gypsum, rock salt, and many limestones, are made up of minerals that were once dissolved in water. Layers of sedimentary rock, called strata, can be just a few inches or many hundreds of feet thick.

When existing rocks are subjected to intense heat and pressure, new crystals grow within the masses, transforming them into metamorphic rocks. Granite, for example, can become a rock called gneiss, shale becomes slate, limestone metamor-

---

The Many Uses of Minerals

Minerals, with their varied shapes and colors, have fascinated humanity since the earliest of times. Neanderthal man sprinkled hematite, a blood-red mineral, on the dead, possibly in an attempt to restore a ruddy complexion, and bits of gold have been found in the graves of Neolithic man. In later ages, amethysts were said to prevent drunkenness, and opals were believed to bring bad luck. Today gemstones are still treasured for their beauty and rarity. But a host of other, more mundane minerals are of even greater value, for they serve as the basic raw materials of industry.

Malachite is prized for its color, and is often cut and polished for ornaments. It is also mined as a copper ore.

Diamonds, so hard they can only be polished by other diamonds, are valued as both gems and industrial abrasives.

Sulfur, the brimstone of former times, is a basic raw material that is used in countless industrial processes.

phoses into marble, and sandstones usually turn into quartzite. Metamorphic rocks in time can be further transformed into other kinds of metamorphic rocks.

Are all gems minerals?

A few of the world's treasured ornamental stones—pearls, coral, amber, and jet—are plant and animal products. But the vast majority of the precious and semiprecious stones called gems are minerals. Diamonds, emeralds, sapphires, and rubies, in particular, are the royalty of the mineral world. Their flawless transparency, dazzling color, hardness, and rarity have made them the most valuable gemstones of all.

Precious stones of various kinds are found all around the world, but southern Africa remains the major source of diamonds. One mine there, the Kimberley, produced about three tons of diamonds in 42 years of operation. Another mine nearby, the Premier, in 1905 yielded the famed Cullinan diamond. At 3,025 carats, or 1.3 pounds, it was the largest diamond ever found.

The finest emeralds, in turn, are mined in Colombia, South America. The best rubies come from Burma, and quality sapphires are found chiefly in southern Asia.

What causes the colors of gems?

Some minerals are invariably the same hue. Malachite is always green, azurite is blue, and realgar, used in making fireworks, is red. But many occur in a variety of colors, resulting from mixing with other minerals, chemical impurities, and other causes.

Quartz is typically as clear as glass. Traces of titanium, however, transform it into rose quartz, while small amounts of iron result in the purple variety known as amethyst. Brownish smoky quartz, in contrast, is believed to be the result of natural radiation.

Impurities have transformed another colorless mineral, corundum, into precious gems. Sapphires are crystals of corundum tinted with titanium; rubies also are corundum crystals, colored with traces of chromium. Emeralds and aquamarines, in turn, are simply differently colored forms of the mineral beryl, made precious by the presence of impurities.

How are star sapphires formed?

The slender six-pointed star pattern radiating from the center of a star sapphire is a quirk of its creation. During its formation, needlelike impurities of another mineral, usually rutile, were lined up inside it in a crisscross pattern. Light reflected from these impurities produces the beautiful six-pointed star that makes the stone so valuable. Star rubies also exhibit this property, called asterism, and are formed in the same way.

A somewhat similar effect, called chatoyancy, is well displayed by the variety of chrysoberyl known as cat's-eye. In this case the presence of parallel needles of impurities produces a lustrous band of light that moves as the stone is turned.

Where do metals come from?

Gems are the glamorous minerals, but the hardworking metallic minerals have played a far more important role in human history. Ever since early man learned to fashion tools and weapons from bits of copper and iron, the search for valuable metals has been underway.

Certain metals, notably copper, silver, gold, and platinum, sometimes occur in pure, solid masses. But more often metals are found in association with other minerals in commercially valuable deposits called ores. The mineral galena, for example, is the richest source of lead. The bright red mineral cinnabar yields mercury, and cassiterite is the principal tin-bearing ore. Iron, the most important metal of all, is obtained chiefly from widespread deposits of hematite. Extracted from their ores by various processes, these and other metals, from aluminum to zinc, form the backbone of our industrialized world.

Fluorite, which comes in a rainbow of colors, is used in the manufacture of steel and a host of other products.

Halite, better known as common salt, is a necessity for life and has been an object of trade and commerce since ancient times. Its crystals are perfect cubes.

Turquoise occurs in seams and masses, and gets its color from traces of copper. It is found in America's Southwest, but the finest specimens come from Iran.

Fossils: Clues to the Past

What is a fossil?

The remains of ancient seashells encased in rock are fossils, as are the bones and teeth of bygone mammals. So are the delicate forms of insects entombed in amber, and massive, multicolored chunks of petrified wood. Even the footprints of dinosaurs that lumbered across now vanished mud flats are considered fossils. A fossil, in fact, is any trace or remains of a plant or animal that lived in the prehistoric past.

The oldest known fossils are traces of microscopic algae and bacteria that lived more than 3 billion years ago. Among the youngest are the frozen carcasses of mammoths that roamed the Arctic tundra within the past few thousand years. All that we know of the amazing variety of plants and animals that flourished on earth in the intervening millennia has been learned from fossils. To paleontologists—scientists who study prehistoric forms of life—the fossils embedded in successive layers of rocks are like printing on the pages of a book. They tell the story of the ever-changing parade of life on earth.

When this fish died many millions of years ago, its body was covered by a layer of silt that eventually turned to stone. Minerals then replaced the bones, exactly preserving its form.

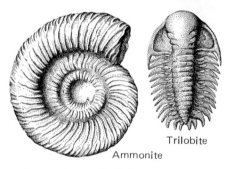

Ammonite
Trilobite

Ammonites and trilobites are common, widespread fossils of long-vanished creatures that lived in ancient seas.

Petrified wood was formed when minerals seeped into buried logs and, cell by cell, replaced the original wood.

stone, and sandstone—where the organisms were buried as sediments accumulated. They are extremely rare in metamorphic rocks, since any fossils in the original rock layers were usually destroyed during the process of transformation.

Some sedimentary rocks are almost solid deposits of fossils. The White Cliffs of Dover on the English Channel, for example, are made up of thick deposits of chalk. And chalk, a type of limestone, is composed almost entirely of fragments of minute seashells and the calcium carbonate remains of tiny marine animals.

On very rare occasions, molds are found of plants and animals that were engulfed by lava flows. An extraordinary find in Oregon proved to be a mold of the entire body of a type of rhinoceros that had been trapped by a volcanic eruption that took place some 20 million years ago.

Is amber a fossil?

The discovery of a piece of amber containing the intact form of a tiny insect is a double fossil find, for amber itself is a fossil. The yellowish glassy material, prized since ancient times, is a fossilized mass of resin. Most of it is found along the coast of the Baltic Sea, where it was formed from the resin of now extinct coniferous trees.

Insects, leaves, and other bits of plant material were sometimes trapped in the sticky resin before it hardened into amber. Preserved in minute detail—even wing veins are clearly visible—the insects look as if they are still in the amber. In fact, all that remains is a hollow mold, lined with a film of residue from the vanished creatures.

Where are dinosaur fossils found?

For many people, the most exciting of all fossil finds are those of the remains of dinosaurs, the great reptiles that became extinct some 65 million years ago. Many species, both large and small, were often trapped in lowland swamps and quicksands. (Some, discovered in the Gobi desert, were apparently buried in sandstorms.) Great quantities of their bones, including entire skeletons, have been excavated on every continent except Antarctica.

But we know the dinosaurs by more

How are fossils formed?

Quick burial in sediments—usually under water—is the commonest route to fossilization. Although the fleshy parts of the buried creatures quickly rot away, the hard parts such as bones or shells remain. In some cases these hard structures survive virtually intact. But more often, their pores and open spaces are partially or entirely impregnated with mineral deposits from seeping groundwater, and the structures are turned to stone. In the case of petrified wood the original material may be replaced, molecule by molecule, by minerals, mainly silica. When this happens, features such as annual growth rings and even cellular structure are perfectly preserved.

In another type of fossilization, the original structure completely dissolves away, leaving an opening or natural mold in the rock. The mold retains the exact shape of the original. Sometimes other materials infiltrate the mold, producing a cast of the original.

Molds of leaves and other very thin structures are known as imprints. Leaves and soft-bodied animals can also be preserved as films of carbon that form silhouettes of the originals. Intricately detailed fossil fern leaves that were produced in this way are especially beautiful.

What kinds of rocks contain fossils?

The vast majority of fossils are found in sedimentary rocks—shale, lime-

than just their bones, for they left footprints behind as well. Tracks of all shapes and sizes have been found in the Connecticut River valley in New England, for example. It is seldom possible to determine just which species made each track. Even so, the prints tell us a great deal about the way their makers wandered around on mud flats, walking, running, and sometimes slipping in the soft mud.

Much rarer than dinosaur tracks are the eggs. The most sensational discovery was made in 1922, when fossil eggs and dinosaur skeletons were found together in a large deposit in Mongolia. Many more eggs have since been unearthed, but, as with the tracks, it is usually difficult to say which species they belong to.

Are whole animals ever fossilized?
No matter how quick the burial, the fleshy parts of an animal normally decay long before its bones begin to fossilize. But remarkable exceptions to this rule have been found in the deep-freeze climates of Arctic Alaska and Siberia. Complete specimens of mammoths and woolly rhinoceroses have been unearthed from time to time. Frozen for thousands of years, some of them were preserved with fur, skin, flesh, and even internal organs completely intact. Intrepid paleontologists who have sampled the meat have found it to be perfectly edible.

What are the La Brea tar pits?
Near the end of the last ice age, mammoths, mastodons, and a host of other now extinct animals roamed the grasslands around what is now Los Angeles, California. And many suffered a common fate; they were mired in a series of tar pits at Rancho La Brea, located within the present-day city limits. These pools of viscous asphalt, formed by seepage from petroleum deposits, were natural death traps. Animals came to drink from pools of water that collected atop the asphalt, and many became hopelessly bogged down in the tar. The list of victims includes familiar creatures such as coyotes and weasels, and more exotic ones as well, including ground sloths, saber-toothed cats, camels, dire wolves, and now extinct species of condors and storks. One of the richest fossil sites ever discovered, the tar pits have yielded more than a million fossil remains of an incredible array of vanished wildlife.

What have we learned from fossils?
Carefully excavated from the rocks that protected them through the ages, fossils have supplied many clues to the earth's past. From the oldest to the youngest rocks around the world, the fossil record reveals the ever-changing development of life on earth. Fossils also tell us much about the earth itself. Petrified seashells high in the Andes, for example, are mute testimony to past convulsions of the earth's crust. Remains of palm trees in Greenland tell of a time when the climate there was far different from that of today.

Fossils, in fact, are the major evidence on which the geologic time chart—a sort of calendar of the earth's history—is based. Eras, the longest time spans, are divided into periods, and the more recent periods are divided into epochs. From bottom to top, the chart summarizes the milestones in earth's history from the earliest known events to the most recent.

GEOLOGIC TIME CHART

ERA	PERIOD	EPOCH	MAJOR EVENTS
CENOZOIC	QUATERNARY	**Holocene** From 10,000 years ago	Ice sheets melt, sea level rises. Towns and cities are built.
		Pleistocene 1.8 million years ago	Ice Age. Mastodons die out. Modern man emerges.
		Pliocene 5 million years ago	Large carnivores are the dominant land animals.
	TERTIARY	**Miocene** 26 million years ago	Renewed uplift of Rockies. Apelike hominids appear.
		Oligocene 37 million years ago	Alps and Himalayas begin to rise. Mastodons and apes appear.
		Eocene 53 million years ago	Grasses develop and spread. Earliest horses appear.
		Paleocene 65 million years ago	Rocky Mountains take shape. Mammals diversify rapidly.
MESOZOIC	**CRETACEOUS PERIOD** 143 million years ago		Dinosaurs die out. Flowering plants develop.
	JURASSIC PERIOD 212 million years ago		Dinosaurs abundant. Birds appear. Conifers, cycads abound.
	TRIASSIC PERIOD 246 million years ago		Reptiles expand dramatically. First mammals appear.
UPPER PALEOZOIC	**PERMIAN PERIOD** 289 million years ago		Insects appear. Amphibians increase. Trilobites die out.
	CARBONIFEROUS PERIOD 367 million years ago		Appalachians rise. Coal-forming forests flourish. Reptiles appear.
	DEVONIAN PERIOD 416 million years ago		Sharks and other large fish are widespread. Vegetation increases.
LOWER PALEOZOIC	**SILURIAN PERIOD** 446 million years ago		Plants begin to invade dry land. Shelled cephalopods abound.
	ORDOVICIAN PERIOD 508 million years ago		Primitive fish and corals appear. Marine invertebrates diversify.
	CAMBRIAN PERIOD 575 million years ago		Seas cover most of North America. Trilobites are common.
ARCHEOZOIC / PROTEROZOIC	**PRECAMBRIAN PERIOD** 4 to 6 billion years ago		Earth's crust forms. Primitive plants and animals appear.

Erosion: The Master Sculptor

What is erosion?

Great canyons and coastal cliffs, rocky crags and awesome caverns—all are products of various kinds of erosion. The term, from the Latin for "gnaw away," refers to the wearing down of the earth's surface by natural forces. The agents responsible for this endless sculpting of earth's outer crust are as varied as wind, water, ice, and even living plants and repeated fluctuations in temperature.

The changes wrought by erosion can take place within minutes, as when the whole side of a mountain gives way in a thundering landslide. Or they can be as slow and subtle as the wearing away of the inscription on an ancient tombstone. But whatever the rates or methods of erosion, the result is constant alteration of the lay of the land.

How does water shape the land?

The Grand Canyon of the Colorado River is a classic example of the erosive power of moving water. On a less dramatic scale, running water everywhere is continuously reshaping the land by carrying soil and debris steadily downslope. As it moves along, this eroded material itself becomes an important erosive force. Bouncing along the bottoms of streams and rivers, the fragments can scour away solid bedrock and eventually carve deep chasms.

Along seacoasts, the movements of waves and tides continually alter the shoreline by gnawing away at the beaches, building sandbars, and undermining cliffs. Storm-driven waves sometimes batter the coasts with the violence of pile drivers and cause dramatic changes in their contours within a matter of hours.

Glaciers, in turn, are water in another guise. These slow-moving rivers of ice can carve mountain peaks into jagged spires, pluck great chunks of bedrock from the slopes, and deepen valleys into dramatic fjords.

Can the wind cause erosion?

The slow but steady migration of sand dunes along seashores is ample testimony to the wind's power to transport solids. Wherever the land has no protective cover of plants, in fact, the wind easily picks up particles of soil, sand, and dust and carries them away. In arid regions and in times of drought, tons of fertile topsoil are lost through wind erosion.

The windblown grains of sand are themselves powerful cutting tools. But since the wind can lift sand only a few feet above the ground, the sandblasting effect of desert winds is concentrated around the bases of rocks and cliffs. The results are sometimes fantastic forms, such as mushroom-shaped rocks with large caps resting atop graceful, sandblasted stalks.

Why do rocks sometimes fall apart?

In time all rocks decay and break up into ever smaller fragments by a process known as weathering. Water, which picks up acid-forming substances from the air and soil, plays an important role. Seeping into cracks and pores, this slightly acidic water slowly attacks the rock, corroding it and wearing it away. In some cases, such as with limestone, the rock is completely dissolved. (Most caves are formed in this way.) By decomposing the minerals in other types of rock, water causes them to gradually disintegrate. This so-called chemical weathering can eventually reduce seemingly indestructible granite to a mass of sand and clay.

Mechanical weathering, in turn, is the breakdown of rock by physical forces. Water, for example, expands when it turns into ice. Thus, if it seeps into cracks and then freezes, it acts as a wedge, prying the rock apart with forces of up to 2,000 pounds per square inch. Ice in surface cracks chips off small flakes of rock; in deeper crevices it can loosen huge chunks and send them tumbling downslope.

The roots of plants are equally powerful wedges. Sections of sidewalks that have been lifted by the roots of trees are familiar examples of the effectiveness of plants as rock breakers and movers.

Temperature changes also play a part in weathering. Just as a pitcher

Australia's Wave Rock, looming some 50 feet above its surroundings like a petrified wall of surf, is the eroded edge of an outcrop of solid granite.

may crack when filled with boiling liquid, so rocks can be fractured by alternately expanding and contracting when they are heated and cooled. This sort of weathering is especially important in deserts, where hot days alternate with chilly nights.

What sets off landslides?
Though relatively rare, large-scale landslides can be terrifying events. In the Peruvian Andes in 1962, an avalanche of rocks and debris hurtled nine miles downslope in a matter of minutes. By the time it ended, eight villages had been destroyed and 3,500 lives lost.

Such massive earth movements usually occur on slopes that are so steep that the friction between soil particles or rock layers is barely enough to withstand the downward pull of gravity. Landslides are often triggered by earthquakes that disturb the precarious balance or by heavy rains that saturate the soil, making it heavier and more fluid. The bedrock itself may slide if enough water seeps in and lubricates the boundaries between rock layers.

Sometimes the movements are less dramatic. Lobes of saturated soil simply slump down a hillside, just as they do along recently excavated road cuts. Though relatively slow, this kind of slumpage can cause great damage in populated areas by carrying entire buildings down the slopes.

Can soil creep downhill?
The covering of soil and rocks on every hillside is constantly slipping downward in a slow-motion version of a landslide. Known as soil creep, this mostly imperceptible movement is caused by many things. In cold climates, frost heaving plays a role. When the ground freezes, soil and rocks are lifted up at right angles to the slope; when it thaws, they are dropped slightly downslope. Swelling of the soil when it is wet and shrinkage when it dries also rearrange soil particles and pebbles. So do the growth and decay of plant roots and the burrowing and trampling of animals.

Soil creep takes place so slowly that we can detect it only by its indirect effects. It is, in fact, the force that causes fence posts and utility poles on slopes

to gradually assume a downhill slant. But while soil creep is subtle and unseen, over the course of a year it probably moves more material downhill than all the world's visible landslides combined.

What causes badlands?
The famed Badlands of South Dakota are a colorful wilderness of deep gullies, steep ridges, and jagged pinnacles of fantastic form. They got their name from early French trappers and explorers who called them *mauvaises*

terres—"bad lands"—because they were so difficult to cross.

The Dakota Badlands and similar landscapes in other parts of the world occur where deep beds of clay and soft, weak rocks are found in arid regions. The rainfall in such areas is not enough to support a protective cover of vegetation. But when the rain does come, it usually falls in violent cloudbursts. The heavy rainfall easily washes gullies in the soft, unprotected ground, creating bizarre, often beautiful formations.

Delicate Arch, one of many in Arches National Park in Utah, is the fanciful creation of uplift and erosion.

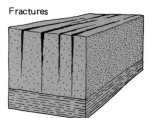
1. Crustal movements created deep fractures in the rock.

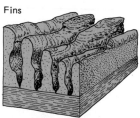
2. Weathering and water carved narrow upright fins.

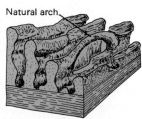
3. Further weathering pierced a fin to produce an arch.

How are natural arches formed?
The graceful spans of natural arches are largely the creation of long, slow weathering. For those in the southwestern United States, the stage was set when movements of the earth's crust produced deep fractures in thick sandstone formations. Running water and weathering enlarged the fractures, leaving widely spaced, upright fins of rock. Further weathering then ate through the bases of the fins, in

some cases producing monumental natural arches.

Natural bridges, in contrast, are usually produced where a meandering river loops around a projecting fin of rock. Eventually the river erodes a hole through the fin and flows straight through the opening, which enlarges and leaves a natural bridge. In limestone regions bridges may also be formed by the collapse of all but one narrow span of a cave ceiling.

When the Earth Quakes

Are earthquakes common?
Although the ground beneath our feet seems solid and unmoving, earth's restless crust trembles with surprising frequency. Scientists estimate that a million or more tremors occur somewhere in the earth's crust every year. Most are so slight that they can be detected only with sensitive instruments, but others are powerful. On the average, 15 to 25 major quakes occur annually, sometimes with devastating effect. In densely populated areas, these most awesome of all natural disasters may kill thousands of people, cause billions of dollars in damage, and visibly alter the lay of the land.

What causes earthquakes?
Earth's outer crust is not one solid piece like the shell of an egg. It consists of a dozen or so enormous plates that float on the more plastic mantle below. As they slowly but continually jostle each other, great stress builds up along their edges. Eventually the pressure becomes so intense that the plates give way with a jolt. This slippage relieves the stress, at least temporarily, but it also causes the earth to shake—sometimes over distances of hundreds of miles.

Most earthquakes result from these movements of the crustal plates, particularly around the margins of the Pacific Ocean and in a belt that stretches across southern Europe into Asia. But there are other causes. Some parts of the globe are still recovering from the effects of the Ice Age, which ended only about 10,000 years ago. Relieved of its tremendous burden of ice, the crust shudders with occasional quakes as it slowly rebounds.

Small localized earthquakes can also be set off by volcanic eruptions and landslides. Earth tremors have been triggered, too, by underground nuclear blasts and even by the filling of reservoirs. But these are insignificant compared to the great quakes that take place along the crustal margins and release waves of energy equivalent to dozens of atomic bombs.

How long does an earthquake last?
The devastating jolt of an earthquake's main shock rarely lasts as long as a minute. But in many cases it is preceded by minor tremors, or foreshocks, often occurring hours, weeks, or even months before the most violent shock. Then a series of aftershocks takes place as the earth stabilizes once again. Although the aftershocks are not nearly as strong as the main shock, they often cause considerable damage to structures that have already been weakened by the earthquake.

On March 27, 1964, the Anchorage, Alaska, area was hit by one of the strongest earthquakes ever recorded. In the convulsion, this city street was ripped apart and sections of it slumped some 10 feet below their prequake level.

Can quakes occur under the sea?
Blocks of the earth's crust can slip along submarine faults just as they do on dry land. The resultant earthquakes have little effect in the immediate area; a passing ship may be jolted but is unlikely to be damaged.

Yet submarine earthquakes or those occurring very near a seacoast are the principal cause of one of the most terrifying of all natural disasters. The tremors sometimes set in motion the giant walls of water popularly called tidal waves but better described by their Japanese name, tsunamis. The waves, traveling up to 500 miles an hour, appear as only moderate swells over the deep water of the open sea. But as they approach the shallows near shore, the waves slow down dramatically and walls of water pile up to heights of as much as 200 feet. Crashing on land with tremendous force, the waves leave unimaginable death and destruction in their wake.

Tsunamis, moreover, take their toll far from the site of the earthquake that triggered them. The 1964 quake in Alaska created a tsunami that caused extensive damage on the California coast. Another one, generated by the great 1960 earthquake in Chile, struck Japan more than a day later, after a journey of some 12,000 miles.

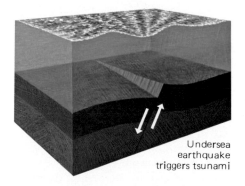

Undersea earthquake triggers tsunami

How does a seismograph work?
Seismologists, the scientists who specialize in the study of earthquakes, use a variety of sophisticated instruments in their research. But their basic tool is the seismograph, a highly sensitive device that can detect the slightest vibrations in the earth. The movements are recorded by a stylus that traces a line on paper wrapped around a revolving cylinder. (On some, the line is made by a thin beam of light directed onto photosensitive paper.) When there are no vibrations, the line is straight. Minor tremors cause slight wavers in the line; major jolts produce broad up and down strokes.

Seismograph stations are located all around the world. When seismic waves of significant size are registered, comparisons of the intensity of the waves and of the times it took them to reach several stations enable scientists to pinpoint the location and intensity of the earthquake.

What is the Richter scale?
In 1935 an American seismologist, Charles F. Richter, devised a numerical scale for rating the strength of earthquakes. Each successive number in the scale represents a tenfold increase in the amount of energy released by a quake. An earthquake rated 2 releases 10 times as much energy as a quake rated 1, for example, and a 3 is 10 times stronger than a 2.

Seismographs record hundreds of minor tremors each day, but magnitudes of less than 2 are not noticeable by humans. Structural damage is unlikely unless an earthquake rates a 5 or more. Severe earthquakes are in the 7-and-up category. The truly great earthquakes are the few with magnitudes of more than 8. Only two have ever reached a magnitude of 8.9—one in Colombia and Ecuador in 1906, the other in Japan in 1933.

Why is the San Andreas Fault so famous?
Size and continuing earthquake activity have earned worldwide notoriety for California's San Andreas Fault. Unlike most faults, which are simply fractures in rock formations, this gigantic rift marks the boundary between two of the earth's great shifting crustal plates. Nearly 700 miles long, it extends northwestward from the Gulf of California and continues out to sea north of San Francisco.

All along the fault, the land is subject to frequent tremors and occasional severe earthquakes. This happens because the two crustal plates are grinding against each other with a sideswiping motion. While the American Plate east of the fault is fairly steady, the Pacific Plate to the west is moving toward the north.

This slippage has been going on for millions of years and continues at a rate of about two inches a year. The movement occurs in fits and starts as pressure builds up along the fault and is suddenly released. More than 100 tremors are registered each year, and occasionally there is a major earth-

quake. During the San Francisco quake of 1906, which measured about 8.3 on the Richter scale, the earth in places shifted more than 15 feet.

How dangerous are earthquakes?
Millions of people around the world have lost their lives in earthquakes. China has perhaps suffered the most: an earthquake in 1556 is said to have killed some 830,000 people and another in 1976 claimed 242,000 victims. Japan's 1923 earthquake killed more than 140,000 people and destroyed countless buildings. India has also been hard hit: its 1737 earthquake took a toll of some 300,000 lives. The statistics are equally grim for Italy, Iran, and other countries that are prone to earthquakes.

North American quakes to date have killed far fewer people. The 1906 San Francisco earthquake leveled the city, but only about 700 lost their lives, many in the fires that followed. Alaska's 1964 earthquake measured about 8.5 on the Richter scale and permanently altered some 77,000 square miles of land. But only 131 people died in that calamitous quake.

Volcanoes

What is a volcano?

Among the most powerful forces in nature, volcanoes have always inspired awe and terror. When a volcano erupts, walls of lava may ooze down a mountainside, destroying everything in their path. Or the mountain may blow its top with a thunderous explosion, sending clouds of gases and debris into the sky. Whatever the form of the eruption, these natural fireworks alter their surroundings for all time.

Strictly speaking, a volcano is an opening in the earth's crust through which magma, or molten rock, escapes from the earth's interior. The term is also applied to the mountain of debris that piles up around the vent. Built up over the course of thousands of years, a volcano may grow to enormous size. Kilimanjaro, the highest mountain in Africa, for example, is a volcano that towers some 16,000 feet above the surrounding plains.

Do all volcanoes erupt lava?

When magma erupts on the surface, it is known as lava and is the usual form of erupted material. Emerging at temperatures of 2000° F or more, some lavas are very fluid; they can flow many miles before cooling enough to solidify. Other lavas, with a different mineral composition and temperature, are much less runny and solidify more rapidly. In fact, they sometimes harden in the volcano's vent and form a plug that ends the eruption.

Eventually, however, gases in the magma build up enough pressure to blast away the plug with an explosion that hurls many solid fragments into the sky. Blocks of rock may be torn from the crater walls and thrown down the slopes. Blobs of lava hurtling through the air can harden and fall as rounded or spindle-shaped volcanic bombs. Rocks, cinders, and pebbly fragments known as lapilli (Italian for "little stones") may also rain down on the surroundings. And tremendous quantities of fine-grained volcanic ash and dust may darken the cloud of steam and other gases that escape during an explosion.

Are all eruptions alike?

Just as lavas differ in temperature and composition, eruptions vary enormously in their severity. The least violent are Hawaiian-type eruptions, in which very fluid lava flows quietly from the vent and builds up a broad dome. In Strombolian eruptions, clots of somewhat thicker lava are expelled in more or less continuous but relatively mild explosions. Vulcanian eruptions are much more severe. Lava forms a plug that blocks the volcano's vent between eruptions. The quiet period ends with a violent explosion as extreme pressure "uncorks" the vent. Most violent of all are Pelean eruptions, typified by Mont Pelée on the Caribbean island of Martinique. In this case the explosion sets off an avalanche of incandescent gas and ash that sweeps down the slopes, annihilating everything in its path. In the

How are volcanoes formed?

Most volcanoes are either broad, dome-shaped shield volcanoes or steep-sided, conical stratovolcanoes. Shield volcanoes are built up, layer upon layer, by successive flows of very fluid lava that travels long distances before solidifying. The result is a low, domelike profile resembling an inverted saucer. Though the slopes are not steep, shield volcanoes may grow to enormous size. Hawaii's Mauna Kea, a classic example of a shield volcano, rises from the ocean floor to a height of more than 30,000 feet. Mauna Kea is, in fact, the highest mountain in the world, dwarfing even Mount Everest in the Himalayas.

Stratovolcanoes result from a more complex cycle of eruption. Flows of molten lava from the summit crater alternate with explosions of ash and other solid materials. Thus the steep slopes are built up of alternating layers of lava and other debris. Sometimes the lava breaks through auxiliary vents and forms so-called parasitic cones on the slopes. But in some cases no irregularities mar the slopes, and many stratovolcanoes, such as Japan's Fujiyama, are noted for their near-perfect symmetry.

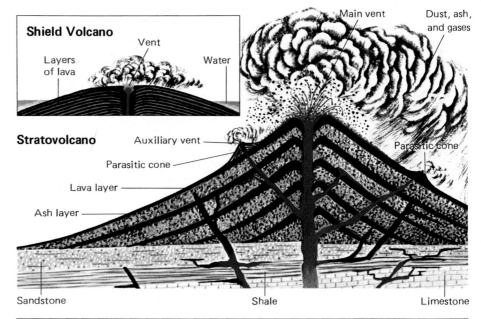

Shield Volcano — Layers of lava — Vent — Water

Stratovolcano — Auxiliary vent — Parasitic cone — Lava layer — Ash layer — Sandstone — Shale — Limestone

Main vent — Dust, ash, and gases — Parasitic cone

1902 eruption of Mont Pelée, a fiery cloud of this sort destroyed the entire city of St.-Pierre at its base.

What was the worst eruption?

Perhaps the most famous of all eruptions took place in A.D. 79, when Italy's Vesuvius blew its top and, within hours, entombed the entire city of Pompeii. But the most powerful explosion in modern times was the one that destroyed the Indonesian island of Krakatoa on August 27, 1883. The blast was heard some 2,200 miles away in Australia. The explosion triggered 100-foot-high tidal waves that drowned some 36,000 people. And the cloud of ash that was blown sky-high made Krakatoa famous everywhere:

34

The fiery eruption of a Guatemalan volcano releases some of the tremendous heat and pressure seething beneath the earth's crust.

encircling the globe, the wind-borne layer of ash caused spectacular sunsets all around the world for over a year.

Where are most volcanoes found?
Volcanoes tend to be located along unstable areas of the earth's crust—on midocean ridges and in rift valleys where crustal plates are moving apart, and along continental margins where they are colliding. In such areas the land shudders frequently with earthquakes, and volcanoes now and then burst to life. The greatest concentration of all is in the so-called Ring of Fire, the belt of volcanoes that nearly encircles the Pacific Ocean and encompasses more than half of the world's active volcanoes.

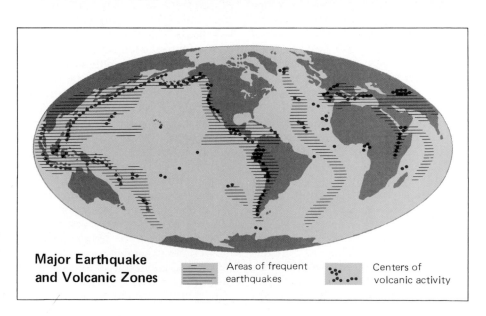

Major Earthquake and Volcanic Zones

— Areas of frequent earthquakes

Centers of volcanic activity

Volcanic Landforms

How are crater lakes formed?
Perched high in the Cascade Range in western Oregon is a glistening deep blue expanse of water known as Crater Lake. Nearly circular, it is some 6 miles in diameter, 1,932 feet deep, and rimmed by cliffs up to 2,000 feet high. Although it sits atop a volcanic mountain, its basin is not actually a crater.

Like many other so-called crater lakes, it occupies a broad saucerlike depression known as a caldera.

Sometimes, such a gigantic cousin of a crater has been formed when a volcano exploded so violently that much of the mountaintop was blasted away, leaving a gaping hole. More often, as in the case of Crater Lake,

calderas are formed when, after a series of eruptions, the top of the mountain collapses into the magma chamber below. Some of these basins fill with water and become lakes. Others remain dry. Africa's huge Ngorongoro caldera encompasses both land and a lake. Ngorongoro supports such a variety of wildlife, it is called "a zoo in a volcano."

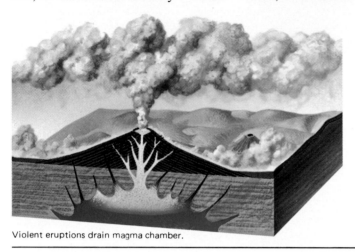

Violent eruptions drain magma chamber.

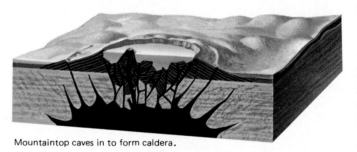

Although some mountaintop lakes are water-filled volcanic craters, the larger ones—often several miles across—usually occupy calderas. Most were formed after eruptions emptied the volcano's magma chamber. The massive cone then collapsed, and a broad, saucerlike depression known as a caldera was left.

Mountaintop caves in to form caldera.

Are all volcanic lakes found on mountaintops?
Parts of western Europe, such as the Eifel plateau in West Germany, are pockmarked with circular depressions that look much like giant bomb craters. Although there are no high mountains in the area, the depressions, known as maars, are products of volcanism. Violent explosions of ash and cinder scooped out the flat-bottomed depressions, many of which are now filled with water and form lovely, placid lakes. In other parts of the world, lakes have been formed where lava flows created natural dams across river valleys.

What are volcanic necks?
Ship Rock Peak, a well-known landmark in northwestern New Mexico, is a craggy spire of rock that rises some 1,400 feet above the surrounding desert. A spectacular remnant of a long-extinct volcano, it is composed of lava that hardened in the vent of the volcano. Over the years since the volcano died down, the mountain itself has been worn away, leaving only this erosion-resistant plug of rock known as a volcanic neck.

Steep-sloped and difficult to ap-

proach, volcanic necks once were favored sites for building castles and cathedrals. Among the most famous of all volcanic necks is the one in Scotland known as Castle Rock. Crowning its rocky cliffs are the ramparts of Edinburgh Castle.

Do volcanic eruptions always build mountains?
The lava, ash, and cinders expelled by volcanoes usually accumulate around the vent and form impressive mountain peaks. But in some cases the lava escapes through long cracks or fissures in the earth's crust and flows across the countryside in broad sheets. In Iceland in the late 1700's, lava began to flow from a fissure some 20 miles long. By the time the eruption had ended, the lava flow had covered about 800 square miles and killed one-fifth of the island's population.

Similar fissure eruptions have occurred in many areas of the world. Craters of the Moon, in southern Idaho, is a celebated showcase of volcanic landforms. An eerie moonscape of lava flows, cinder cones, and craters, it was created by a long series of eruptions from a fissure some 50 miles long. Southern Idaho, in fact, is part of

a much larger area known as the Columbia Plateau, which covers much of Washington and Oregon and parts of adjacent states. Built up by repeated fissure eruptions over millions of years, the plateau encompasses an area of some 200,000 square miles and is underlain by layers of lava up to 6,000 feet thick.

Does magma ever harden underground?
In earth's restless interior, pockets of magma have often welled upward into overlying layers of rocks, then cooled and hardened without ever breaking through the surface. Later exposed by the erosion of the surrounding rocks, the once molten masses sometimes form entire mountains; an impressive example is the striking dome of Stone Mountain in Georgia.

Devils Tower in Wyoming was formed by a similar, though smaller-scale, intrusion of molten magma into deep layers of sedimentary rock. As it cooled, the magma cracked into slender fluted columns of hard volcanic rock that remained intact while the softer surrounding rocks were worn away. Today the tower looms like a giant stump some 865 feet high.

Vertical sheetlike intrusions of molten magma are known as dikes. The tops of several dikes radiate like walls from the base of Ship Rock Peak in New Mexico.

A sill, in contrast, is a horizontal intrusion of a mass of volcanic rock between older layers of sedimentary rock. The striking cliffs known as the Palisades along the Hudson River in New Jersey and New York originated in this way. They are the exposed edge of a once molten sheet of magma that long ago forced its way between older rock layers.

What are lava tubes?

Long tunnellike caves penetrate some of the lava flows in Craters of the Moon and other volcanic areas. One in Africa, now broken into sections by earth tremors, originally was a continuous tunnel more than five miles long. Known as lava tubes, these openings were formed when the surface of the lava flow began to cool and harden. Beneath this solid crust, streams of still-molten lava sometimes drained away, leaving long tunnellike openings in the flows. Some lava tubes are even decorated with lava stalactites formed from hot lava that dripped from their ceilings.

Can volcanoes erupt under the sea?

Just after dawn on November 14, 1963, a fisherman off the coast of Iceland noticed strange clouds of smoke rising from the sea. Before long, billows of steam, smoke, and debris were rising 12,000 feet into the air. Investigation the next day revealed a small island where there had been none before. A submarine volcano had broken through the surface of the sea.

Eruptions continued in the months that followed. By the time they ended, the island covered an area of one square mile and rose more than 500 feet above the sea. Local people named the island Surtsey, after Surtr, the god of fire in Norse mythology.

Thousands of other sea islands have been formed much as Surtsey was. All of the Hawaiian Islands are the exposed tips of submarine volcanoes, as are the Galápagos, the Azores, the Canary Islands, and many more. But Surtsey remains unique, for it was the first volcanic island whose actual birth was witnessed by humans and recorded on film.

Are volcanoes ever beneficial?

Volcanic eruptions are rightly feared. They have taken an uncounted toll in human lives and suffering, obliterated entire towns, and transformed vast tracts into wastelands. Yet their aftermath is often beneficial. In time the mineral-rich volcanic debris weathers into fertile soil. Natural vegetation makes a comeback, and people reinhabit volcanic areas to till the soil that produces such bountiful crops.

Lava and other volcanic rocks are useful building materials for roads and houses, and some old volcanoes are important sources of sulfur and other valuable minerals. Some scientists have even suggested that most of the water now on earth is the product of steam and other gases that escaped from volcanoes billions of years ago.

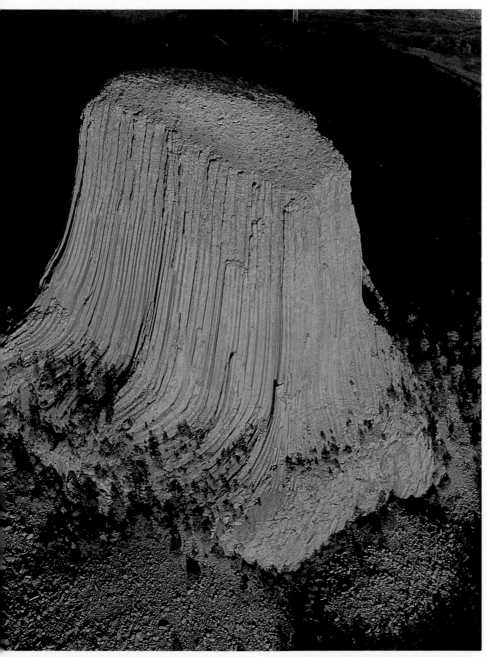

Devils Tower, a massive monolith rising above the plains of Wyoming, was formed from a plug of molten magma that long ago welled up from the earth's interior.

Many Kinds of Mountains

How are mountains formed?

Mountains are monuments of great upheavals in the earth's crust. They vary in size and shape from place to place, and also vary in their origins. Some of the most beautiful mountains are volcanoes—isolated symmetrical cones such as Fujiyama in Japan, Mount Mayon in the Philippines, or Mount Shasta in northern California.

Volcanoes build up on top of the earth's crust, but other mountains are formed by movements of the crust itself. Sometimes great cracks or faults develop in the crust and huge blocks of rock slip up or drop down along these fractures. The Teton Range, in Wyoming, is a good example of such fault-block mountains. Rising like a wall from the floor of Jackson Hole, the eastern front of the range is the edge of a crustal block that tilted up along a fault while the valley floor dropped down on its opposite side.

Elsewhere stresses have caused the crust to rumple into giant wavelike folds, producing long parallel lines of ridges and valleys. The Appalachians are eroded remnants of folded mountains. Large sections of the Alps are also severely folded mountains.

Most dome mountains are caused by intrusions of magma that forced overlying rock layers to arch up in a bulge. In time, these covering rocks usually wear away, exposing the intruded mass of igneous rock.

The Drakensberg (the name means "Mountain of the Dragon") in southern Africa is the eroded edge of a thick lava plateau. In places sheer escarpments rise thousands of feet above the grasslands at its base. Many flat-topped massifs in northern South America, in contrast, are isolated remnants of a plateau that once covered the entire region. Mountains in other areas had still other origins. But whatever their causes, they are testimony to the awesome power of the forces that have shaped the earth's crust.

Three Kinds of Mountains

Fault-block mountains   Folded mountains   Dome mountains

Where are the world's highest mountains?

If mountains were measured from base to summit, the highest in the world would be the Hawaiian Islands' Mauna Kea. An enormous volcano, it rises more than 30,000 feet from the ocean floor. But less than half of the mountain projects above the sea.

Measured from sea level to summit, the world's loftiest peaks are clustered in the Himalayas. This great mountain wall, which sweeps some 1,500 miles across southern Asia, includes more than 30 peaks that exceed 24,000 feet. The giant of them all, Mount Everest, towers to a dizzying height of 29,108 feet above sea level.

The high point of South America is Argentina's Aconcagua, at 22,835 feet. Mount McKinley in Alaska takes top honors for North America, with an elevation of 20,320 feet. With its summit at 19,340 feet above sea level, Tanzania's Kilimanjaro is the highest peak in Africa, while Europe's is Mount Elbrus in the U.S.S.R., at 18,481 feet. Even Antarctica has some impressive elevations; its highest mountain is the Vinson Massif, which rises to 16,860 feet. Relief is far more modest in Australia, where the loftiest summit is Mount Kosciusko, at 7,310 feet.

What are mountain systems?

Volcanoes sometimes stand in splendid isolation. No neighboring peaks detract from the grandeur of Kilimanjaro in Tanzania or Italy's Mount Etna. But most mountains occur in groups or ranges—lines of peaks with more or less similar origins. Ranges in turn are often intertwined into long, complex mountain systems, such as the Rockies and the Himalayas. Systems generally result from a variety of mountain-building forces.

Although the Himalayas are the highest mountains in the world, the Andes are the longest mountain system. From the shores of the Caribbean to the mountainous islands near Cape Horn, they form a continuous line of peaks extending 5,500 miles down the west coast of South America.

The individual ranges of the Andes are known as cordilleras, from a Spanish word for "rope." Some were formed by the folding and faulting of sedimentary rocks. Others were heaved up by masses of intruded magma known as batholiths. And all along their length, the Andes are crowned with towering volcanoes.

Why are the Rockies so much higher than the Appalachians?

The Rocky Mountains of western North America are rugged and imposing, with lofty peaks and precipitous slopes. The Appalachians, paralleling the east coast, are low and smoothly rounded, composed of long rows of undulating ridges. The highest summit in the Rockies, Mount Elbert in

Colorado, is 14,431 feet high. North Carolina's Mount Mitchell, the highest of the Appalachians, reaches only 6,684 feet.

The contrast between the two mountain chains is mainly a matter of age, for the Appalachians are ancient, the Rockies relatively young. Subjected to erosion for more than 300 million years, the Appalachians are mere remnants of mountains that may once have rivaled the Alps. The Rockies, in contrast, began to take form only about 65 million years ago and still retain the rugged contours of youthful mountains everywhere.

How were the Alps created?

Like the Himalayas and other great mountain systems of the world, the Alps are believed to be the result of a collision of two of the drifting plates that make up the earth's crust. Over the course of tens of millions of years, the crustal plate underlying Africa nudged relentlessly against the so-

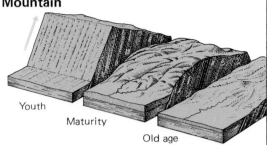

Life Cycle of a Fault-Block Mountain

Contours are often clues to a mountain's age. Young fault-block ranges have steep, rugged faces. In maturity, erosion levels the summits, and in old age the mountains are worn down to plains. Even then, renewed uplift may form new mountains and start the cycle again.

Youth

Maturity

Old age

called Eurasian Plate. Under the intense pressure of the collision, rock layers were rumpled up into great folds and broken up by faults. Volcanic activity took place, and deeply buried rocks were metamorphosed into other, harder types of crystalline rocks. In the course of the paroxysm, once horizontal rock layers were upended and now stand vertically; other layers were overturned completely.

The end result was an arc of moun-

tains extending some 750 miles across southern Europe like a rugged spine. Honed to their present form by repeated glaciation, the Alps are studded with famous peaks: Mont Blanc (at 15,772 feet, the highest summit), the spirelike Matterhorn, the imposing trio of the Jungfrau, Mönch, and Eiger, and many others. Renowned around the world for their beauty, the Alps in fact are many people's idea of what mountains should look like.

Crowning a snowy ridge of the Great Himalayas is the jagged crest of Kanchenjunga, the third tallest mountain in the world.

Glaciers: Rivers of Ice

What are glaciers?
An alpine glacier is an impressive sight. From its source on a mountainside to its lower end, or snout, it may be miles long, and it may be hundreds of feet thick. Filling a valley from wall to wall with ice, it resembles an immense frozen river. And, like a river, a valley glacier of this sort may be swollen along its descent by tributary glaciers flowing into the main ice stream. Valley glaciers are typical of the Alps and other high mountains around the world.

A second type, the piedmont glacier, forms when a valley glacier descends all the way to the lowlands at the foot of a mountain. With no valley walls to confine it, the ice spreads out to form a broad lobe, sometimes of gigantic size.

Ice sheets, in turn, are immense domes of ice that can cover entire mountain ranges, islands, or even continents. Ice sheets once covered much of North America and northern Europe, and still cover most of Greenland and Antarctica.

Why do glaciers form?
Whenever more snow falls in winter than is lost by melting or evaporation, conditions are right for the birth of a glacier. Year after year more snow and ice build up in the accumulation zone

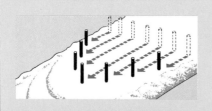

Measuring Glacial Speed
Glacial movement was first studied in the 1840's by the naturalist Louis Agassiz, who drove a line of iron stakes across a glacier and noted gradual changes in their positions. He found not only that the ice moves, but that it moves at different speeds: faster in the center and slower along the sides, where friction slows it down. Scientists later discovered that friction also causes the bottom of a glacier to flow more slowly than its upper surface.

at the head of the valley. Eventually the weight and pressure become so great that the ice begins to ooze slowly downslope, or, in the case of an ice sheet, to spread outward on all sides.

Where does the ice come from?
The snow that falls on a glacier's accumulation zone is just like snow everywhere else. But over the course of time natural processes convert it into ice. Repeated thawing and refreezing first transform the snowflakes into a mass of small ice granules called firn or névé. As more snow piles on top of it, the firn becomes more and more tightly packed. Finally, when the accumulation is about 150 feet deep, weight and pressure cause the lowest layers to recrystallize into ice.

How does a glacier move?
Despite their seeming stability, glaciers can and do move—sometimes with surprising speed. Generally the movement is barely perceptible, with the ice advancing less than a foot a day, but some glaciers maintain a steady daily pace of 50 feet or more. And occasionally, for complex reasons, a glacier may undergo a "surge," sliding forward for several miles at a rate of 300 feet or more a day.

A glacier does not begin to move until the ice is about 200 feet deep. Then, under tremendous pressure, the normally brittle ice begins to flow somewhat like a mass of frigid molasses. Some of the movement is due to the pull of gravity. Some is due to the slippage of ice crystals over one another. Melting along the bottom of the glacier also plays a role by "oiling" the track. This happens because ice melts if it is under enough pressure, and the pressure at the bottom of a glacier may be as much as 28 tons per square foot. (In much the same way, the weight of an ice skater causes a film of water to form beneath his blades, easing their glide across the ice.)

The upper layers of the ice remain brittle, however, since they are under much less pressure. Thus, they crack quite easily under stress. When the glacier passes over an obstruction or begins an abrupt descent, for example, its surface may break open into gigantic fissures, known as crevasses, sometimes more than 150 feet deep.

Can a glacier grow indefinitely?
As a glacier descends a mountainside, it eventually reaches elevations where the ice at its lower end begins to melt and evaporate. When the annual loss of ice at the snout equals the amount accumulated at its head, the glacier stops advancing. If the rate of loss ex-

Anatomy of a Valley Glacier

1. Head of valley

2. Accumulation zone, where snow turns to ice

3. Crevasses form where glacier passes over surface irregularities

4. Tributary glacier feeds into main glacier

5. Rock debris, carried beneath the glacier, abrades the bedrock

6. Subglacial pocket of meltwater

7. Ridge of resistant rock impedes glacier's movement and causes crevasses to form

8. Subglacial cavity

9. Glacier's snout, or lower end

10. Block of ice broken from main ice mass

11. Recessional moraine, a ridge of debris left by retreating snout

12. Meltwater stream flows from tunnel beneath glacier's snout

13. Lake of glacial meltwater

14. Terminal moraine marks farthest extent of glacier's advance

ceeds the glacier's rate of flow, its snout begins to retreat upslope.

Moraines—accumulations of rubble —build up around a glacier's melting snout. A terminal moraine marks the site of a glacier's maximum advance; recessional moraines are deposited along the path of a retreating glacier.

How Glaciers Shape the Land

Can glaciers carve solid rock?

A slowly moving glacier has tremendous cutting power. In a process called plucking, the ice actually loosens huge chunks of bedrock and carries them along as it creeps downslope.

Embedded in the glacier, the rocks and boulders—sometimes as big as houses—rasp away like the teeth of a file. Grinding against the bedrock, they smooth down projections and carve deep grooves and hollows. In time, many of the embedded rocks are themselves worn down to bits of sand that further polish the bedrock.

Eventually the debris reaches the snout of the glacier, where it is dropped in long ridgelike moraines by the melting ice. Streams flowing from glaciers are so heavily laden with rock flour—finely ground particles of once solid rock—that glacier-fed lakes have a characteristic milky look.

What are cirques?

Mountain climbers frequently encounter deep, bowllike hollows high on the slopes. Known as cirques, they mark the birthplaces of bygone glaciers. Cirques begin as sheltered hollows where snow accumulates at the heads of mountain valleys. As the glacier grows and moves downslope, it plucks blocks of rock from the walls and floor of the hollow. Gradually the hollow is enlarged to a steep-walled basin known as a cirque.

Where two side-by-side cirques grow toward each other, they erode the mountainside into a jagged, razor-edged ridge called an arête. When cirques on opposite sides of a mountain ridge meet, they often eat through the ridge to form a notch, or col. Such notches have served as strategic passes for centuries. If a mountaintop is ringed by several cirques, they can carve it into a spirelike peak, or horn, like the one on Switzerland's famous Matterhorn.

Are glacial valleys distinctive?

While stream-carved mountain valleys have a more or less V-shaped cross section, glacier-carved valleys have an unmistakable U-shape. Sheer walls often rise abruptly from the valley floor. In California's glacier-carved Yosemite Valley, the walls in places are more than 3,000 feet high.

Far above the main valley, moreover, "hanging valleys" may open abruptly on the cliffsides. These were formed by tributary glaciers that flowed into the main glacier, which carved a deeper trench. Waterfalls often spill from hanging valleys, adding to the beauty of the scene.

What forces shaped fjords?

Long, narrow inlets known as fjords notch many seacoasts. The best known are in Norway, but there are spectacular fjords in Alaska, Canada, Greenland, Chile, and New Zealand, and elsewhere. All are the handiwork of glaciers that excavated deep valleys opening on the sea.

Fjords are found on mountainous coasts where tongues of ice from great inland ice sheets moved seaward down river valleys and gouged out their floors to a depth far below sea level. During the Ice Age, sea levels were lower than today because so much water was locked up in the ice sheets. When the ice melted, the seas rose and flooded the valleys.

The results are often truly breathtaking. Norway's famous Sogne Fjord, for example, extends about 125 miles inland. In places its walls soar more than 3,000 feet above the water. But the visible walls reveal only part of the power of the glacier that carved the fjord; below the waterline the walls of

Signs of Vanished Ice Sheets

Time and again during the last 2½ million years, large areas of North America, Europe, and other parts of the globe have been buried beneath vast continental ice sheets. Advancing and retreating with the changing climate, they have left many signs of their passage across the landscape. Moraines and outwash plains cover large areas with eroded debris. Other characteristic glacial landforms are as varied as kames and kettle holes, eskers and erratics, and the streamlined hills called drumlins.

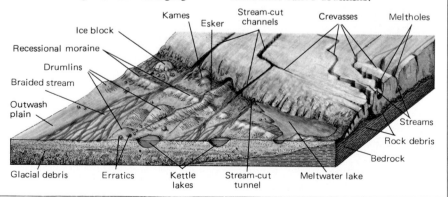

A sweeping U-shaped cross section is evidence of the glacial origin of the Klön Valley in Switzerland's Glarus Alps.

the mighty trench plunge to a maximum depth of almost 4,300 feet.

Where did ice sheets dump debris?
Like valley glaciers, the continental ice sheets deposited huge moraines along their melting fronts. In Finland, for instance, two parallel moraines sweep across the countryside and mark two stages in the retreat of an ice sheet. Known as the Salpausselka, they form a barrier 300 miles long and in places rise to heights of 260 feet.

Streams flowing from the melting ice fronts also deposited broad aprons of debris, called outwash plains. Long Island and other islands off the southern coast of New England, for example, are composed of glacial moraines and outwash plains.

Boulders scattered across the coun-tryside are another glacial relic. Known as erratics, they were picked up by the advancing ice and then deposited far from their original locations.

What are kames and kettles?
Irregular hills in many glaciated areas are known as kames. They formed where glacial meltwater poured into crevasses or along the edge of an ice sheet, dumping mounds of debris that remained as hills. Kames are often quarried for sand and gravel.

Somewhat similar are the narrow, winding ridges of debris called eskers. They are thought to have been formed by streams that flowed in subglacial tunnels and dropped sediments in their beds as the glaciers retreated.

Kettles, in contrast, are rounded basins, often occupied by ponds. As the ice sheets retreated, chunks of ice sometimes broke off and were buried in sand and gravel. When the ice melted, the covering debris caved in, forming the distinctive basins.

How were drumlins formed?
Many glaciated areas are dotted with long, streamlined, domelike hills called drumlins. Shaped like half of a hard-boiled egg that has been sliced lengthwise, they often were formed when an advancing ice sheet plastered debris around some obstruction such as a resistant knob of bedrock.

Drumlins are common in parts of the United States. (Bunker Hill in Boston is a drumlin.) Many are also found in Scandinavia and the British Isles. Their name, in fact, comes from a Gaelic word meaning "ridge."

Earth's Mantle of Soil

What is soil?

Whether it is black or brown or red or yellow, whether it forms a thick deposit or a thin veneer over the rock below, soil is a complex substance. Weathered and eroded rock fragments—clay, silt, and sand—are its basic constituents. But these building blocks are transformed into soil only by the addition of organic material, the dead and decaying remains of plants and animals. The film of water clinging to these countless individual fragments and the air filling the pore spaces between them are also essential ingredients of soil.

Far from being sterile, soil teems with life, especially in its upper layers. Some of the life is visible. Plant roots penetrate the soil in all directions, and earthworms, insects, moles, and other creatures burrow through it. But the vast majority of soil inhabitants live their lives unseen. Miles of fungal threads, millions of bacteria, and a host of other microorganisms thrive in every acre of life-giving soil.

Where does soil come from?

Life on land with its unending cycle of growth and decay would not be possible without the earth's rich mantle of soil. For soil is the laboratory where minerals become food for growing plants, and dying plants and animals in turn are reduced to their components—nutrients upon which new plants can survive and prosper.

Yet soil has not always covered the globe. For millions of years the earth's dry land was barren rock. Gradually the rocks were worn down and pulverized into the fragments that form the skeleton of soil. Expansion and contraction caused by freezing and thawing splintered rocks apart. Chemical weathering disintegrated them. Wind and water eroded the rocks and moved their remains from place to place. Slow-moving glaciers also pushed, scraped, and crushed the rocks into fine particles.

Eventually land plants appeared and gained a foothold, some on the bare rocks themselves, others on the accumulated blanket of debris. Generation after generation, the plants lived and died, and their remains were incorporated into the lifeless masses of mineral particles, transforming them into the miraculous, life-supporting substance we call soil.

Is soil still being formed?

Soil continually comes and goes. Transported by wind and water, much of it is ultimately washed into the sea, where, after millions of years, it is consolidated into rock. But new mountains rise and are attacked by weathering and erosion. As the rocks crumble, their fragments supply the grist for the formation of new soil.

Though the process is a slow one, it is possible to observe soil being formed on a small scale. On barren rocky outcrops, the first and sometimes only plants to take hold are tenacious, crusty patches of lichens. Able to live without soil, these strange and primitive plants produce acids that actually help disintegrate the surface of the rock.

A bit downslope, the weathered rock fragments and the dead remains of lichens may collect in pockets. Soon mosses gain a foothold, and their remains in turn are incorporated into the patch of soil-in-the-making. Where enough debris has accumulated, a few weeds and perhaps even a shrub or two take root. In time a sizable layer of soil forms where once there was only bare rock.

Are all soils alike?

Soil differs dramatically from place to place. The type of rock from which it was formed affects the nature of a soil. The plants that grow on it leave their own special imprint. Climate also plays a role. Temperature and humidity, for example, determine how fast organic matter decomposes, releasing nutrients that increase the fertility of the soil.

Scientists recognize about a dozen major soil types, with hundreds of variations on these general patterns. (Four types are shown below.) The types are classified according to characteristic layers that generally develop in soils. Sometimes the layers, or horizons, are made obvious by distinct color changes. But more often one layer blends imperceptibly into the next.

The topsoil, or A horizon, usually contains the most decomposing organic matter. The subsoil, or B horizon, collects nutrients that seep down from above. The C horizon consists of loose weathered rock fragments lying atop the solid bedrock.

Prairie soil, found in moderately moist regions, has no clearly defined layers. It is the fertile soil of North America's corn belt.

Chernozem (from the Russian for "black earth") is topped by a dark humus layer. Extremely fertile, it produces bumper crops of grain.

Podzol (from the Russian for "ashes") is the acid, infertile soil of the cool, moist northern coniferous forests.

Gray-brown podzolic soil forms under temperate broadleaf forests. With proper treatment, it can support a wide variety of crops.

Flat, fertile, well-watered lowlands in the Netherlands are covered by a mosaic of varied crops. In a land where much of the soil has been reclaimed from the sea, this precious natural resource is treated with meticulous care.

Why do plants need soil?

Simple plants such as lichens need little more than air and moisture to survive. Air plants—plants, such as Spanish moss, that live perched on the branches of trees—also manage to get along without soil, as do floating aquatic plants.

But for rooted land plants, soil is a necessity for life. Most important is its function as the reservoir their probing roots tap for the water and essential nutrients they use (along with air) to manufacture food. Soil also protects the roots from rapid fluctuations in temperature. Just below the surface, the temperature scarcely changes from day to night. And, of course, soil supplies the firm anchorage that plants need for support as they reach for the sun.

What is loam?

Soils vary in texture, depending on the size of the rock fragments they contain. The smallest particles are microscopic bits of clay; the largest, sand grains of various sizes. The intermediate particles are classed as silt. (Many soils also contain variable amounts of larger stones and pebbles.)

Loam is a soil that is composed of particles of all three sizes—clay, silt, and sand. Depending on the amount of humus (decayed organic matter) it contains, loam is usually the most productive type of soil. Light, sandy soils, for instance, are so porous that they retain very little water. Heavy, clayey soils can hold more water, but the particles are so tightly packed together that they leave little room for the air that plant roots need for survival.

Loams have the best qualities of both: they retain water well but also have ample pore space for air.

Why does jungle soil seem so fertile?

The great tropical rain forests of equatorial Africa and South America are perhaps the most luxuriant in the world. Huge trees, vines, and a profusion of other plants flourish in the warm, moist climate.

Yet the soil that supports them is surprisingly infertile. Because of the heavy rainfall, essential nutrients are eventually washed away. Fertility is maintained only because the high heat and humidity promote rapid growth and, in turn, the rapid decay of fallen plant remains, which returns nutrients to the soil. If the trees are cut, the land can be farmed for only a few years before it becomes sterile and nearly useless for agriculture.

Can soil be destroyed?

Soil protected by a cover of vegetation can remain productive indefinitely. Leaves and branches lessen the impact of pounding raindrops, and tangles of plant roots hold the particles of soil in place.

Once the plant cover is removed, however, the soil becomes vulnerable to the ravages of erosion. Heavy rains quickly carve deep gullies in unprotected slopes. Even light rains wash away thin films of particles that, over the course of months, can amount to tons of valuable topsoil. Winds, too, can carry away huge quantities of soil, particularly in times of drought. And once gone, the soil is lost forever.

Fortunately, many measures can be taken to protect croplands from erosion. Shelterbelts of trees—windbreaks—slow down the wind and protect the land on their lee side. Cover crops of fast-growing plants bind the soil in place on idle land. Plowing across rather than up and down slopes slows the runoff of rain. So does terracing and planting alternating strips of different crops across the slopes. In a system called minimum tillage, crops such as soybeans are planted without first plowing and so disturbing the soil surface. With these and other methods, farmers around the world are working to keep their precious soil from washing away.

Our Encircling Sea

How many oceans are there?
The great sea of saltwater that encircles the globe is usually divided into four units: the Pacific Ocean, the Atlantic Ocean, the Indian Ocean, and the Arctic Ocean. The Antarctic Ocean, surrounding Antarctica, is also considered a distinct ocean by some.

In fact all the oceans are interconnected into one great, continuous body of water. Encircling all the continents, the worldwide ocean covers about 71 percent of the earth's surface and contains an estimated 315 million cubic miles of water.

Which is the largest ocean?
With an area of approximately 64 million square miles, the Pacific Ocean is larger than the Atlantic and Indian oceans combined. (The Atlantic Ocean covers 32 million square miles, the Indian Ocean, about 28 million.) More than a third of the earth's surface, in fact, is covered by the waters of the Pacific. At its widest point, just north of the equator, it stretches 11,000 miles from the Isthmus of Panama to the Malay Peninsula in Asia—almost halfway around the world.

What causes ocean currents?
All the water in the sea is in constant circulation, moving about in an orderly, well-defined pattern of currents. The best known of these ocean rivers, the Gulf Stream, is nowhere less than 50 miles wide and travels at speeds of

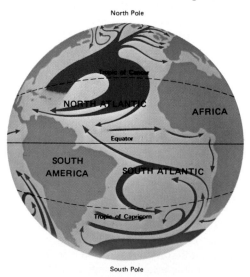

Red arrows indicate the warm currents, and blue arrows the cold currents that circulate in the Atlantic Ocean.

up to 4 miles per hour. It sweeps up the coast of North America and flows across the North Atlantic, where it moderates the climate of northern Europe. A similar stream of warm water flowing up from the tropics—the North Pacific Current—warms the western coast of North America.

Prevailing winds are the main force that keeps the currents in motion. Differences in density also play a role. Cold water is denser than warm water, and so it sinks, while less dense water rises. Thus cold water near the poles sinks and flows beneath the ocean surface toward the equator. There it rises to replace warm water that the surface currents are constantly carrying toward the poles.

Islands and continental coasts also influence the currents, deflecting them or splitting them into separate branches. But in general, the major currents tend to flow in great swirls around the various ocean basins. Deflected by the earth's rotation on its axis, the swirls flow clockwise in the Northern Hemisphere, counterclockwise in the Southern Hemisphere.

What is the Sargasso Sea?
In the middle reaches of the North Atlantic, between Florida and the Azores, there is a broad expanse of calm water awash with a type of seaweed called sargassum. For centuries it was feared by mariners as a place where ships were doomed to drift forever, tangled in the floating plants.

In fact ships can sail through quite easily. The sea is simply the calm center of the great swirl of currents that circle the North Atlantic. Similar calms exist within the swirls of currents in other oceans. But none is as conspicuous as the Sargasso Sea, with all its floating seaweed. And scientists have found that, far from being fearsome, it is a fascinating place inhabited by many unusual creatures.

Why is the sea salty?
The water in the sea is a salty brew. The amount differs from place to place, but on the average about 3.5 percent of seawater is dissolved mineral salts. The commonest by far is sodium chloride, ordinary table salt.

Some of the salts were contributed by submarine volcanoes, but most originated in the rocks of the earth's crust. As the rocks were disintegrated by weathering, the salts were released, and rivers carried them to the sea. As the seawater evaporated in the never-ending water cycle, the salts were left behind and gradually accumulated to their present concentrations. In all, the oceans contain enough salt to form a layer some 500 feet thick over all the dry land on earth.

Why do the tides rise and fall?
Twice a day, with predictable regularity, the sea level alternately rises and falls along most shorelines. For slightly more than six hours the tide flows in, or floods. Then for an equal length of time it falls back, or ebbs.

The ebb and flow of the tides are produced mainly by the gravitational pull on the earth of the moon and, to a lesser degree, of the more distant sun. This pull causes the ocean's water to pile up in a bulge; centrifugal force resulting from the earth's spin on its axis causes a corresponding bulge to form on the opposite side of the globe. As the bulge moves in toward shore, sea level goes up as the rising tide, then just as predictably falls again.

At any one place, the tidal range

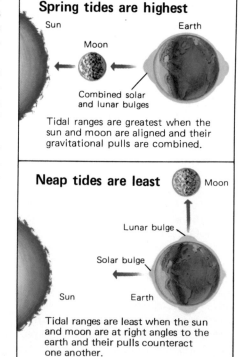

Spring tides are highest
Sun — Moon — Earth
Combined solar and lunar bulges
Tidal ranges are greatest when the sun and moon are aligned and their gravitational pulls are combined.

Neap tides are least
Moon
Lunar bulge
Solar bulge
Sun — Earth
Tidal ranges are least when the sun and moon are at right angles to the earth and their pulls counteract one another.

How Waves Stir the Water

Although water seems to move forward with the waves, it is actually stirred up and down in a circular motion. In the diagram below, the black dot shows the path of an individual water particle. As a wave advances, it moves up the front of the wave, then slides down the back of the crest, moving in a complete circle from trough to trough. In the same way, ducks are not carried forward by advancing waves but simply bob up and down.

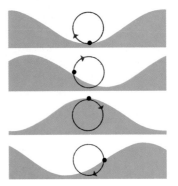

Whitecaps—waves with windblown crests broken into foam—undulate across the open sea.

varies over the course of each month. The highest and lowest tides, called spring tides, occur twice a month, at the times of the new and full moons; since the sun and the moon are then in a straight line with the earth, their gravitational pulls are combined. The lowest tidal ranges, or neap tides, occur when the sun and moon are at right angles to the earth and their pulls counteract each other.

Where are the highest tides?

Depending on the shapes of ocean basins and coastal contours, and on other factors, the difference between high and low tide can vary widely. In some areas it is only a foot or two; elsewhere it is much greater. Tides of 35 to 40 feet are common along the coasts of England and Alaska. Similar high tides in the Rance Estuary in France have been harnessed to generate electricity. But the highest tides of all occur in Canada's Bay of Fundy, a funnel-shaped indentation between New Brunswick and Nova Scotia. In parts of the bay the water rises more than 50 feet with each incoming tide.

What are tidal bores?

In places where exceptionally high tides are forced into narrow or shallow channels, the water sometimes advances upstream in a solid wall known as a tidal bore. With each rising tide a great crest of water surges far inland along the Amazon River. Other well-known tidal bores occur in Alaska's Cook Inlet, the Severn River in Great Britain, and China's Hangchow Bay.

The Bay of Fundy's tidal bore advances at about 8½ miles an hour. When it reaches the mouth of the St. John River, it produces the strange spectacle of the river's famed Reversing Falls. With each incoming tide, the wall of water surges *up* a substantial stretch of rapids. When the tide recedes, the river resumes its normal downstream flow.

How are waves formed?

Waves roll continually across the sea. Sometimes they are smooth and gentle; sometimes they are high and powerful, pounding and tearing at the shore. Except for those generated by earthquakes or volcanic explosions, most are caused by winds blowing over the sea. Waves stirred up by distant storms can travel hundreds of miles before reaching shore.

Most waves are less than 10 feet high, measured from their top, or crest, to the bottom of the trough between waves. But in stormy seas they can be much higher. The biggest wave on record, observed in the Pacific in 1933, was 112 feet high.

Are maelstroms dangerous?

Writers from Homer to Edgar Allan Poe have told terrifying tales of giant whirlpools, or maelstroms, that supposedly could suck entire ships into the ocean depths. Generally caused by strong tidal currents surging through constricted channels, maelstroms can indeed be dangerous to smaller boats. They can easily smash such vessels against nearby reefs and rocks.

Maelstroms are named for a famous whirlpool off the coast of Norway. Other well-known maelstroms regularly stir the waters of the Strait of Messina off the coast of Sicily and the Naruto Strait of Japan's Inland Sea.

The Ocean Floor

Is the ocean floor flat?
Once it was believed that the land underneath the sea sloped gently downward from all shores to vast, featureless plains on the floors of the oceans. The lack of knowledge of the earth's dark, deep "inner space" was understandable. Until recent times the only way to probe the depths was by dropping weighted lines until they touched bottom. The method was laborious at best, and the measurements were often inaccurate.

Today depths are measured by echo soundings. Ultrasonic pulses transmitted from ships travel swiftly to the floor of the sea, then bounce back. Exact depths are quickly calculated by measuring the time it takes the echo to reach the ship. Television cameras can also be lowered into the depths to get accurate pictures of the ocean floor.

From the information gathered by these and other methods, it is now known that large expanses of the ocean floors are indeed flat—the so-called abyssal plains—and are covered with thick deposits of sediments that have slowly rained down from the waters above. But elsewhere the ocean floor is as varied as the surface of the continents—dotted with great volcanoes, crossed by mountain ranges, and scarred by canyonlike trenches.

What is the continental shelf?
The edges of a few landmasses such as volcanic islands drop off abruptly into the depths of the sea. But the continents for the most part are surrounded by relatively shallow water covering shelflike extensions of the landmasses. These continental shelves usually slope gradually to a depth of about 650 feet below sea level, then plunge steeply to the ocean floor. (The steep edge of the shelf is called the continental slope.) Off most shores the shelf is about 50 miles wide, but in some places it is much narrower. Off the northern coast of Siberia, in contrast, it extends 800 miles into the Arctic Ocean. Most commercial fish harvests are taken from the rich waters over continental shelves, and countries also claim ownership of the oil, minerals, and other resources on this seaward extension of their land areas.

Can rivers carve submarine canyons?
The edges of the continental shelves in many places are scarred by canyons larger than even the Grand Canyon. Some, aligned with the outlets of great rivers, may have been carved, at least in part, by the rivers at times when sea level was lower than today. The Hudson Canyon, off the east coast of North America, extends far out to sea, and another canyon forms a long undersea extension of the Congo River. The deep waters over the Ganges Canyon, a notable fishing area, have earned the colorful name Swatch of No Ground.

But other submarine canyons are nowhere near any river mouths. They seem to have been carved by turbidity currents—massive underwater mudflows. Sweeping down the continental slope, these sand- and mud-laden streams of water have gradually gnawed the great hidden chasms of the deep.

Two maps of portions of the world's ocean floor reveal the great complexity of its topography. The map on the left shows parts of the Indian and Pacific oceans; on the right is the Atlantic Ocean, bisected by the long line of the Mid-Atlantic Ridge.

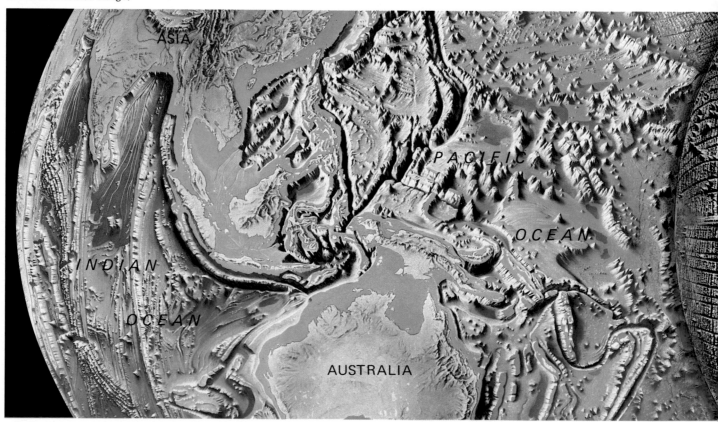

How deep are the oceans?
The smallest of the oceans—the Arctic Ocean—is also the shallowest, with an average depth of about 5,000 feet. But like the others, it is crossed by mountain ranges separating deep basins, one of which is 17,880 feet deep.

The next larger, the Indian Ocean, averages about 13,000 feet but at its deepest, in the Java Trench, reaches down 25,344 feet. The Atlantic is only slightly deeper, averaging 14,000 feet; it has a maximum depth of 28,374 feet in the Puerto Rico Trench, a great chasm just north of the West Indies.

The largest ocean, the Pacific, like the Atlantic has an average depth of 14,000 feet. But its vast expanse conceals the deepest known scar in the earth's crust. The Mariana Trench, a deep gash near Guam, at one point plunges to a depth of 36,198 feet. Its bottom is nearly seven miles beneath the surface of the sea—more than a mile deeper than Mount Everest's height above sea level.

Where are undersea mountains found?
The best-known undersea mountain range is the Mid-Atlantic Ridge, angling in a broad S-curve south from Iceland. Yet it is only part of a vast interconnected mountain system that extends more than 40,000 miles through the Atlantic, Pacific, and Indian oceans. All these mid-ocean ridges are volcanic mountain ranges formed where new material is being added to the seafloors along the margins of adjoining crustal plates.

Smaller ranges subdivide various ocean basins. Also scattered across the ocean floor, especially in the Pacific, are volcanoes known as seamounts. Many of them are thousands of feet high. Submarine mountains of another type, called guyots, have flat, tablelike tops. Apparently their peaks were sheared off by the waves at a time when the mountaintops were near the surface of the sea. Later sagging of the ocean floor lowered them far below sea level.

Is there anything valuable on the ocean floor?
Over the centuries, countless ships have gone to watery graves beneath the sea, some of them laden with precious cargoes of silver, gold, and gems. Great treasures have been retrieved from lost Spanish galleons, homeward bound with booty from the Americas. And in 1981 a team of divers recovered 11,206 pounds of gold ingots from the hold of a British ship that had been sunk during World War II.

The sea contains many natural treasures as well. A large part of the world's supply of petroleum and natural gas now comes from offshore wells on the continental shelves in the Gulf of Mexico and the Persian Gulf and elsewhere. A great deal of magnesium and various mineral salts are also extracted from seawater.

But much of the sea's mineral bounty remains untapped. Although every cubic mile of seawater contains tons of gold and other valuable metals, minerals, and salts, economical methods of recovering them have yet to be developed. Huge areas of the ocean floor are littered with large nodules composed of manganese, iron, and other metals. But again, attempts to mine them have not yet proven profitable. The riches of the sea, it seems, are vast, virtually untouched, and still being discovered.

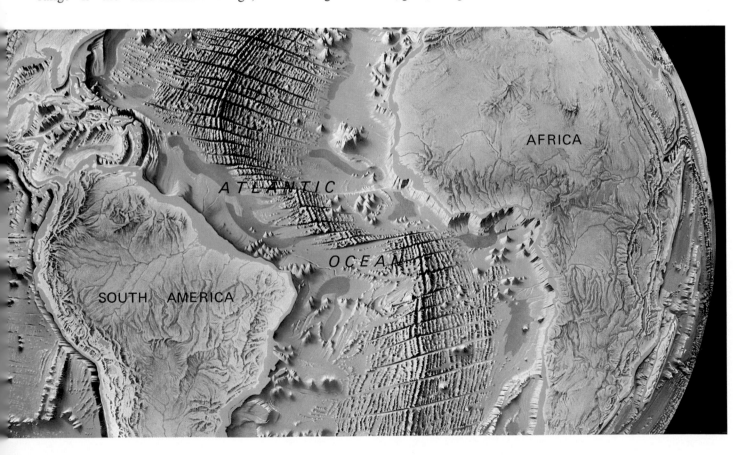

Sandy Seashores

What are the forces that shape sandy beaches?

Although sandy shores may seem to change little from day to day, they are in a constant state of flux. Waves lapping at the beach, coastal currents, and breezes blowing in from the sea all play a role in keeping the sand in constant motion.

The water in the zone where the waves break is loaded with sand that has been churned up by its turbulence. As each breaking wave rushes up on the beach, some of this sand is carried along and left behind when the water flows back down.

Individual sand grains also move sideways along the beach. Longshore currents, flowing parallel to the coast, carry some of the stirred-up sand along with them. In addition, waves usually come in at an angle to the shore. As a result the water follows a curved path as it rushes up the beach and flows back down to sea, and it carries sand grains on this same curved pathway. (The steady movement of sand along the beach in this way is called longshore drift.)

Sand deposited on the beach is further rearranged by the wind. When the sand dries out, even gentle breezes can pick up individual sand grains and bounce them along the surface. Blown inland, the sand grains lodge behind obstructions and eventually pile up into dunes. In time the wind causes the dunes themselves to migrate slowly inland from the beach.

Even a gentle surf, lapping endlessly at a sandy shore, keeps it in a constant state of change as the waves shift the sand from place to place.

Cross Section of a Sandy Shore

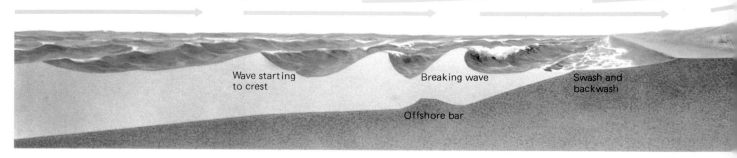

Winds generate waves and pile sand into dunes.

Wave starting to crest

Breaking wave

Swash and backwash

Offshore bar

Where does all the sand come from?

The blanket of sand that lines long stretches of seacoast around the world comes from many sources. Some was washed down from inland glacial deposits. Some was created locally, when waves undermined seaside cliffs and ground down the fallen boulders. Sand sometimes contains pulverized seashells and, in tropical areas, sand is often formed of coral from offshore reefs that have been battered relentlessly by the waves.

But most of the sand is brought down to the sea by rivers that carry weathered and eroded rock debris from inland areas. Fine particles of silt and clay tend to remain in suspension and are carried far out to sea. But the larger, heavier sand grains settle out near shore, where ocean waves and currents distribute them along the margin of the land.

What colors are sand grains?

Look closely at a handful of sand and chances are that you will see grains of several colors. Their varied hues depend on the materials from which the sand is derived. Grains of quartz, for example, are a translucent white, tan, or yellow; feldspar is gray or pink. Fragments of seashells are usually white and opaque. On some beaches the sand contains red garnet and black magnetite; on others flecks of mica give the sand a golden tinge.

Most beaches in temperate regions are light in color because the sand is composed mainly of quartz. In the tropics the sand may be white fragments of coral. And on Tahiti and other volcanic islands there are beaches of black sand, derived from the lava that formed the islands.

Why do waves break?

Watching lines of waves breaking into foaming surf is one of the pleasures of visiting sandy seashores. The ceaseless drama takes place because the motion of the waves changes as they advance into shallow water.

As the waves move into water about half as deep as the distance between crests, they slow down, grow higher and steeper, and begin to peak. Then at a critical point—when the height of the crest is about three-fourths the depth of water beneath it—the wave

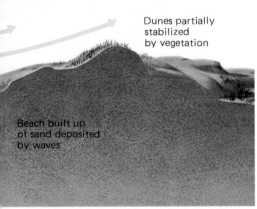

Dunes partially stabilized by vegetation

Beach built up of sand deposited by waves

can no longer maintain its form. The crest topples forward as a breaker, and its foaming remains rush up the beach as an apron of "swash."

Some of the water soaks into the porous sand; the rest glides back to sea as "backwash." Then the drama immediately repeats itself as the next wave collapses into a wall of surf.

Is undertow really dangerous?
Scientists have yet to prove the existence of the supposedly fatal underwater current that sucks unwary bathers seaward beneath the waves. The backwash from a breaking wave can be strong enough to knock a person down and wash him into the surf. But it can carry him no farther than the next incoming wave.

Rip currents, on the other hand, can be a real hazard. These narrow channels of water flowing swiftly away from shore sometimes occur at intervals along sandy beaches. They form when breaking waves and longshore currents cause water to surge up along the shore faster than it can flow seaward against the incoming waves. Finally so much water piles up that it seeks an escape route. Eroding a channel across an offshore bar, a powerful current rushes out to sea at more or less a right angle to the shore.

Few swimmers can fight against the force of a rip current. If caught in one, the best way to escape is to swim parallel to the shore. Since rip currents are usually quite narrow, the swimmer soon finds his way into calmer water.

What causes spits and bars?
Individual grains of sand are constantly moving along the length of a beach. Waves striking the coast at an angle keep them moving in a zigzag pattern along the shore. The longshore current that generally flows parallel to the coast also picks up sand and carries it along.

A spit may form if, at the end of the beach, the coastline makes a sharp turn. Instead of being carried around the bend, the sand continues to move in a straight line out into open water. Eventually enough sand accumulates to form an underwater bar and, if the same conditions continue to prevail, the bar rises above sea level to become a long narrow spit of land projecting into the water.

Under certain circumstances, waves and currents cause the tip of the spit to curve back on itself like a fishhook. Spits forming at the mouth of a bay sometimes grow long enough to seal off the bay completely, transforming it into a closed lagoon.

How do sand dunes form?
On the dry upper beach, even a light wind can dislodge sand grains and send them bouncing along the surface. When the wind meets an obstruction such as a clump of grass, however, it slows down and drops the sand on the leeward side of the windbreak. In time enough sand may accumulate to form a sizable dune.

Most coastal dunes are less than 50

feet high, but they sometimes grow much higher. Dunes on the Oregon coast and along the coast of North Carolina near Cape Hatteras are more than 100 feet high, and some in the Gironde region of France top out at more than 300 feet.

Dunes never stop changing as they grow. Some even "march" slowly inland. Strong, steady winds pick up sand on the windward side of the dune and drop it on the lee side, causing the dune to advance. Marching dunes can bury buildings and even entire forests that lie in their paths.

Dunes can be stabilized if grass and other plants gain a foothold. The plants shield the sand from the wind and anchor it with their roots. But dunes are fragile despite their bulk. A break in the plant cover—from fire, footpaths, or other causes—gives the wind a chance to resume its attack. It rapidly enlarges the eroded area, and before long the entire dune may once again be on the move.

Magnification reveals the infinite variety of sizes, shapes, and colors of sand grains, the basic building blocks of sandy beaches. This sample is from a Hawaiian seashore.

Rocky Coastlines

Why is every rocky coast different?

Few places can equal a rocky shore for sheer beauty and drama. The scenery is in continual motion, the result of the endless interplay of seemingly unyielding land and surging sea.

The rocky foundations of this drama vary around the world. Layers of chalk, a type of limestone, form dazzling white cliffs on both sides of the English Channel. The rugged coast of northern New England is mostly granite. Halfway round the world, on the Hawaiian island of Kauai, volcanic basalt has been carved into stupendous 2,000-foot escarpments.

The contours of these coasts, moreover, are as varied as the rocks that form them. Some are fronted by long lines of vertical cliffs. Elsewhere looming headlands alternate with sheltered coves. Frequently the rocks have been sculpted into tunnels, caves, and arches. But all are alike in one respect. All are dominated by the thunder of pounding surf, the chief architect of their scenic splendor.

How do waves carve solid rock?

The "pounding surf" is no idle expression. Waves, especially during storms, slam against the rocks with the power of battering rams. One estimate of the force of winter waves in the Pacific Northwest compared their impact to that of a car crashing into a stone wall at 90 miles per hour.

The breaking waves, moreover, usually are loaded with pebbles, stones, and even boulders. Hurtled against the coast like shrapnel, these chunks of debris rasp away at the rocks and grind them into pieces.

The waves attack in a less obvious way as well. Crashing against the rocks, they trap air in cracks and crevices and cause explosive bursts of high air-pressure. Repeated again and again, these miniature explosions can loosen enormous chunks of rock and send them toppling into the sea.

Many other forces contribute to the sculpting of coastal cliffs. Chemical weathering weakens the rocks. Pieces are pried loose when fresh water freezes and expands in cracks. Even

Red sandstone cliffs on Canada's Magdalen Islands have been intricately sculpted by the sea.

plants and animals play a role. Certain algae secrete acids that help dissolve the rocks. And animals such as snails, sea urchins, and worms can bore holes into rocks, increasing their susceptibility to the surf.

What causes cliffs and coves?

Sea cliffs usually begin as steep slopes plunging down to the water's edge. In the first stage of their development, the pounding surf carves a shallow notch along the base of the slope. As the notch deepens, the overlying rocks collapse, and a cliff begins to form. The waves continue their attack, cutting the cliff back into the rising slope and so increasing its height.

If the rocks are uniform in their composition, a long straight line of cliffs will form. But more often the rocks vary in their resistance to erosion. The weaker portions of the rocks are quickly worn away, and the coast becomes indented with countless caves and coves. The more resistant rock formations remain intact, projecting out to sea as lofty headlands and peninsulas.

Can an arch become a sea stack?

Graceful wave-cut arches and surf-beaten offshore pillars, or sea stacks, are picturesque features of many rocky coasts. Arches form where waves and crosscurrents attack the sides of headlands or fins of rock projecting from a cliff. Gnawing away at weak areas in the rock, they eventually bore an opening all the way through. In time the top of the arch may collapse, and the seaward end remains standing as a stack.

An imposing example of a sea stack

What makes a blowhole blow?

On many rocky coasts, water erupts like geysers from natural blowholes in the rocks. The essential ingredients of these spectacular jets are strong surf and a seaside cave with a hole in its roof. At times of low tide, the water may barely enter the cave (below, left). Even at high tide, calm seas may simply lap at the back of the cave (below, center). But when storm-driven surf crashes into the opening, the cavity fills with water, and successive waves send fountains of spray spurting through the blow-hole (below, right).

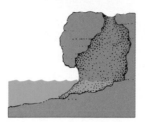

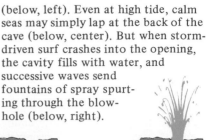

is the Old Man of Hoy, a slender 450-foot sandstone pinnacle off the coast of Scotland's Orkney Islands. A notable array of stacks and arches lines the 20-mile-long stretch of Port Campbell Cliffs in southeastern Australia. An impressive double arch there is known as the London Bridge and a striking group of stacks is called the Twelve Apostles. Even more unusual is the Great Blowhole: waves surge through a long tunnel in a massive seaside cliff and then erupt like geysers through a hole in its roof.

Where do sea caves form?

The caves that penetrate many rocky cliffs have small beginnings. They start to form when the surf gnaws at a zone of weakness in the rock, perhaps a tiny crack or fissure. As the opening grows larger, the heaving waters wrench great chunks of rocks from the walls and hurl them about in the cavity. And so the opening continues to grow larger and larger.

The resultant sea caves are often places of special beauty. One of the most famous is the Blue Grotto on Italy's isle of Capri. Its name refers to the ethereal effect of light in its interior, reflected from the blue waters of the Mediterranean. Another celebrated grotto is Fingal's Cave in the Scottish Hebrides. The rhythmic surge of the surf in its dim interior inspired Felix Mendelssohn's well-known "Hebrides Overture."

What is a "drowned" coast?

When the last ice age ended some 10,000 years ago, the melting of continental ice sheets caused a dramatic rise in sea level all around the world. In many areas, former river valleys were invaded by the sea, becoming picturesque embayments. In places such as the coast of Maine, where the surface of the land had been depressed by the weight of the ice, mountain ridges now form long peninsulas jutting out to sea. The myriad offshore islands are the exposed tops of drowned mountains.

In other places, uplift of the land has created an entirely different sort of topography. Along such emergent coasts, alternating cliffs and wave-cut terraces often rise inland like a giant staircase. Each "riser" on the staircase was once a seaside cliff that has now been uplifted above sea level.

Three Stages in the Sculpting of a Rocky Coast

The erosion of a rocky shore leaves a headland of resistant rock projecting out to sea (bottom). Waves and currents may then bore a hole through the headland, creating an arch (center). When the roof of the arch caves in, the end of the headland remains standing as an isolated sea stack (top).

Rivers and Streams

Do rivers change along their length?
From source to sea, most rivers pass through three stages of development: youth, maturity, and old age. In its rambunctious youth in upland areas, a river rushes down the slopes, spilling over rapids and waterfalls and carving deep, steep-sided ravines. As it passes into the foothills, the river enters maturity. Its pace slows down, its valley widens, and it begins to flow in gentle curves. In old age, the river meanders lazily in looping curves across a nearly flat plain, then finally merges with the sea. In time continued erosion may cause the mature section of a river to acquire the characteristics of old age. Or renewed uplift of the landscape may transform a mature river into a youthful river once again.

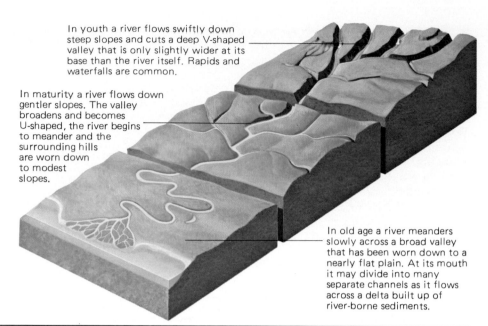

In youth a river flows swiftly down steep slopes and cuts a deep V-shaped valley that is only slightly wider at its base than the river itself. Rapids and waterfalls are common.

In maturity a river flows down gentler slopes. The valley broadens and becomes U-shaped, the river begins to meander and the surrounding hills are worn down to modest slopes.

In old age a river meanders slowly across a broad valley that has been worn down to a nearly flat plain. At its mouth it may divide into many separate channels as it flows across a delta built up of river-borne sediments.

Can rivers build levees?

Rivers flowing across flat plains are often hemmed in on both banks by mounds of sediment— natural levees built up by the rivers themselves. In times of flood, when muddy water spills over the banks, coarse sediments are dropped along the river's edge as the water spreads across the plain. In time the levees may become so high, as in the case of the lower Mississippi, that the water level in the river is well above the surrounding plain.

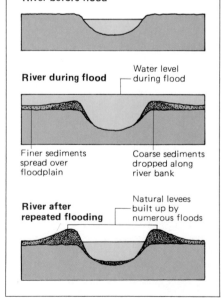

River before flood

River during flood

Water level during flood

Finer sediments spread over floodplain

Coarse sediments dropped along river bank

River after repeated flooding

Natural levees built up by numerous floods

Which are the longest rivers?
The Nile, among the most historic of all rivers, is also the longest in the world. From its source in central Africa it flows northward 4,132 miles to its outlet on the Mediterranean Sea. The second longest, the Amazon, extends almost all the way across South America. Rising high on the eastern slopes of the Andes, it travels some 4,000 miles before emptying into the Atlantic Ocean. The lower Mississippi River and its major tributary, the Missouri, together make up the world's third longest river, with a total length of 3,740 miles.

In terms of volume, however, the Amazon is by far the giant among the world's rivers. It drains an area nearly as large as the contiguous United States, much of it steaming tropical rain forest where rain falls some 200 days a year. Gathering the flow of countless tributaries, it spills an average of 28 billion gallons of water a minute into the sea.

What is a river system?
Follow any rivulet far enough downstream and chances are that it will eventually empty into a larger stream. The larger stream in turn will be joined by still more tributaries, or side streams, and finally it will merge with an even larger stream or perhaps a river that empties into the sea.

The river that flows into the sea, and all of the lesser streams that flow into the river, make up a river system. The area drained by a river system is known as a river basin. The basin of a major river can be immense. The basin of the Mississippi-Missouri River, for example, stretches from the Appalachian Mountains to the Rockies and covers 1,244,000 square miles.

The ridges of high ground separating drainage basins are called divides. A continental divide, in turn, separates the areas that drain into different oceans on opposite sides of a continent. In North America, the continental divide is a line along the jagged crests of the Rocky Mountains. Rivers on one side of the divide flow ultimately into the Atlantic and Arctic oceans. Rivers on the other side drain into the Pacific. In South America the continental divide runs along the high peaks of the Andes.

Do all rivers empty into the sea?
In most areas, every river system has its ultimate outlet in the ocean. But there are exceptions. The mighty Volga in the U.S.S.R. ends in the Caspian Sea, which, cupped at the heart of a vast landlocked basin, is not connected to any ocean at all. Its surface, in fact, lies nearly 100 feet below sea level. Great Salt Lake, in the western United States, and Lake Chad, in Africa, lie at the centers of similar enclosed drainage basins. Rivers flow

What are meandering streams?
Few streams or rivers follow straight courses for long distances. On floodplains, in particular, they tend to flow in looping curves known as meanders. The word is derived from the name of a river in Asia Minor that was famed for its convoluted course.

The pattern of the loops on such a river is continually changing. Slow-moving water on the inside of a bend drops its load of sediments and builds a bar; swifter currents on the outside of the bend undercut the bank and gradually extend the loop. Meanders along the Mississippi have been

known to move 60 feet or more in a single year.

In time, the river may cut a new channel across the base of a loop, isolating the bend as a crescent-shaped oxbow lake. Floods may then fill the lake with sediment, transforming it into a marsh and then into dry land.

An intricate pattern of meandering loops and oxbow lakes that have been cut off from the main stream is characteristic of floodplains like this one in central Alaska.

How Meanders Become Oxbow Lakes

Direction of flow

Sediment is deposited on inside of bends, where the water moves relatively slowly.

Fast-moving water undercuts the outer bank as it flows around each bend.

Continued erosion tightens the bends until only a thin neck of land separates adjacent meanders.

River eventually cuts across the neck. Silt accumulates at the ends of old meander and seals it off.

Former river channel

Former meander remains as an oxbow lake

Direction of flow

into the lakes, but none flow out; water escapes only by evaporation.

In many desert regions, rivers simply come to a dead end. Many rivers flowing southward from the mountains of northern Africa, for example, slow to a trickle as they approach the Sahara and finally disappear in the parched desert sands.

Why do rivers flood?
Occasional flooding is a natural occurrence in the life of any river. Exceptionally heavy rain or rapidly melting snow may result in more water than the channels can hold. And so the water spills over the banks and spreads across the river's floodplain.

In many places, human activity has increased the severity of floods. Cutting down forests in headwater areas has reduced the land's ability to soak up rainfall and release it gradually into the river system. People, moreover, have traditionally lived along rivers because they are convenient

sources of water and avenues for transportation. But by building on floodplains, humans have put themselves directly in the paths of floods.

Around the world, countless dams have been built to contain floodwaters. River channels have been deepened and straightened to speed the runoff of excess water. Great levees have been built along many rivers to increase their capacity. All these and other measures have been effective in controlling floods or at least reducing their damage. But perhaps the best solutions to the problem of flooding are to maintain healthy forests and other plant covers in catchment areas and to avoid building on floodplains.

How do deltas form?
Many great rivers of the world end their journeys to the sea by fanning out across seaward extensions of land, called deltas. The term was coined in the fifth century B.C. by the Greek historian Herodotus, who noted the simi-

larity of the Nile's outlet to the triangle-shaped Greek letter delta.

A delta is simply an accumulation of waterborne sediment that builds up at a river's mouth. As the river empties into a lake or ocean, it slows down and drops its load of debris, which forms low-lying marshlands that gradually extend farther out from shore. As sediment blocks the main channel, water spills over the banks and carves new channels that flow into the sea. Clogged in turn with more debris, these secondary channels give way to new ones, and so the delta gradually changes in shape.

Wondrous mixtures of shifting river courses, marshes, ponds, and dry land, many deltas are havens for waterfowl and other wildlife. Among the most famous are the Danube delta on the Black Sea, Las Marismas at the mouth of the Guadalquivir in Spain, and France's Camargue at the outlet of the Rhone, famed for its flamingoes and herds of half-wild white horses.

Canyons: Rivers' Masterworks

**What is the difference between
a canyon and a valley?**
Canyons are long, deep, relatively narrow river valleys bordered by steep slopes or even vertical cliffs. Some are simple trenches carved by a single river; others have branches, where side canyons join the main stream. Similar, smaller-scale trenches are usually called gorges. The term "valley," in contrast, customarily refers to a river-carved depression that is bordered by much gentler slopes.

The differing contours of canyons and valleys usually result from differences in climate. Most of the great canyons of the world are found in arid and semiarid regions. Since there is little rainfall on the surrounding terrain, rushing rivers can deepen their channels much faster than weathering and erosion wear away the rocks on either side. And so the canyon walls remain steep. In wetter areas the entire land surface is gradually worn away, so that the river valley is bordered by gently rounded hills.

How are canyons formed?
A swiftly flowing river is a first requirement for the formation of a canyon, for the faster a river flows, the greater the load of rocks and other debris it can carry. And the more debris rolls and bounces along the river bottom, the faster the bedrock is eaten away. Canyon-carving rivers, in fact, have been compared to endless belts of sandpaper that slowly but relentlessly rasp away the streambed.

Gradual uplift or tilting of the land surface is often involved as well. As the surface tilts, a river that once meandered across a plain is transformed into a torrent that rapidly deepens its channel. The current may undercut projecting fins of rock, producing natural arches and leaving the old channel high and dry. Side streams flowing into the main canyon may isolate buttes that rise from the canyon floor. Layers of erosion-resistant rocks often project as ledges from the walls. Bit by bit the varied scenery of each canyon takes shape.

**Are all gorges created
in the same way?**
No two gorges have identical origins. Switzerland's Aar Gorge, for example,
is a mere slot through a massive limestone formation; only 3 feet wide in places, it is bounded by cliffs up to 165 feet high. The gorge was carved by torrential runoff from a melting glacier at the end of the Ice Age.

Many gorges in arid regions of northern Africa, in turn, contain mere trickles or are even bone-dry much of the time. But when rain falls in the mountains upstream, it falls in drenching downpours. Walls of water then surge through the normally dry river channels and continue their intermittent deepening of the gorges.

Other gorges originated when a block of the earth's crust shifted along a fault, causing a fault-block mountain to rise across a river's path. But downward erosion by the river kept pace with the rate of uplift of the mountain, and so the barrier was traversed in time by a canyon.

How fast can a river carve a canyon?
Some canyons are very young, and were formed in just a few thousand years. Others have been millions of
years in the making. The rate at which a river carves a canyon depends on many things. Its speed, its volume, and the quantity of debris it carries all play a role in determining its rate of erosion. So does the hardness of the bedrock: a river flowing over shale will deepen its channel much faster than one flowing over granite.

Even so, it is difficult to grasp the slow but steady pace at which most canyons form. Imagine, for instance, a river that was grinding away its channel at a rate of just one one-hundredth of an inch each year—less than the thickness of a sheet of paper. In a century it would wear away 1 inch of rock, and in 1,000 years, 10 inches. But in a million years—a mere moment in geological time—it could carve a chasm more than 800 feet deep.

How big is the Grand Canyon?
Unsurpassed by any other natural wonder, the Grand Canyon of the Colorado River is the largest in the world. Angling some 277 miles across northwestern Arizona, this awesome gash is 18 miles wide in places and about 1 mile deep. It is, most visitors agree, all but unbelievable.

The chasm began to take shape less than 10 million years ago, when gradual uplift of the region forced the Colorado River to increase its speed. Scouring its channel ever deeper into the bedrock, the rushing river probably carved only a narrow gorge at first. Weathering of the exposed rocks, periodic landslides, and other tools of erosion gradually widened the cleft and carved the canyon's intricately sculpted rock formations.

In recent years, a dam upstream from the canyon has reduced the river's flow and, as a result, its power to erode. Even so, the canyon is still growing and changing. Waterborne debris continues to rasp away at the riverbed, and from time to time boulders topple from the canyon's rim, slowly but surely altering its contours for all time.

What kinds of rocks form the Grand Canyon's walls?
Part of the spectacle of the Grand Canyon is the varied colors of its many rock formations. The most ancient, at the bottom of the gorge, are schists

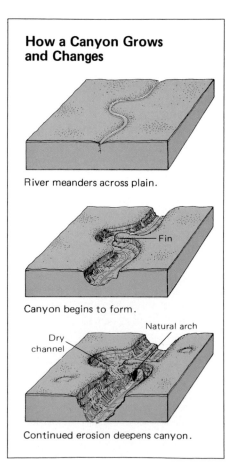

**How a Canyon Grows
and Changes**

River meanders across plain.

Fin

Canyon begins to form.

Natural arch

Dry
channel

Continued erosion deepens canyon.

and granites that were formed 2 billion years ago. Piled on top of them are layers of sedimentary rocks—sandstones, shales, and limestones—that range in color from shades of russet and tan to subtle pinks and white. They were formed between 600 million and 200 million years ago.

Descent into the canyon is thus, in a sense, a journey back through time. Along the way you pass older and older rock formations, each containing fossils of progressively more primitive forms of life. Finally at the bottom you stand on the ancient schists and granites. Completely devoid of fossils, they are among the oldest rocks exposed anywhere on earth.

Where are some other great canyons?
Although the Grand Canyon is the largest in the world, it is not the deepest. In North America, its 1-mile depth is exceeded by Hell's Canyon on the Idaho-Oregon border. Carved by the Snake River, this giant cleft has a maximum depth of 7,900 feet.

Another impressive gorge is Mexico's Barranca del Cobre ("Copper Canyon"). Although it is only 30 miles long, it has nearly vertical walls that rise to heights of 4,600 feet above the canyon floor.

Among the most famous in Europe is the Verdon Gorge in southern France. Slashed through a limestone plateau by the Verdon River, it is bordered by precipitous cliffs up to 2,300 feet high. It is thought that the Verdon may once have been an underground river, and that the gorge was formed in part by collapse of the overlying rocks.

Also notable are China's Ichang Gorges, a series of narrow clefts carved by the Yangtze River. Only about 500 feet wide as it passes through the gorges, the river is hemmed in by sheer walls as much as 2,000 feet high. Within the narrow confines of the gorges, the river reaches depths of 600 feet, making this sector of the Yangtze the deepest river in the world.

The Colorado River, glinting in the dim depths of the Grand Canyon, seems a relatively placid stream. But in fact it was the master sculptor of the awesome, multicolored chasm.

Wondrous Waterfalls

What causes waterfalls to form?

Whether slender ribbons or seething walls of foam, all waterfalls owe their existence to an abrupt change in the level of a river's channel. Many of the world's greatest falls—in South America, Africa, and India, for example—spill off the margins of broad, elevated plateaus. Heavy rainfall assures an ample supply of water for rivers that course across the plateaus and have nowhere to go but down when they reach the edge.

Or the cliffs may have been formed by crustal movements. After the earth's surface moved up or down on opposite sides of a fault, rivers that once flowed across flat land were forced to leap down escarpments.

Steep mountain slopes, too, are laced with numerous waterfalls and rapids. Some of the most spectacular are found in mountains that have been carved by glaciers. Where small tributary glaciers joined a main valley glacier, the main valley was often deepened into a steep-walled trench. The tributary glaciers carved much shallower depressions that were left perched at the tops of cliffs as "hanging valleys." Rivers now pouring from the mouths of such valleys form some of the loveliest falls in the Alps. The fjords of Norway, too, are adorned with plumelike waterfalls that spill from hanging valleys.

Are waterfalls permanent?

Every waterfall is doomed to disappear. The process is a gradual one with many variations, but the life cycle of a waterfall generally follows either of two basic patterns. One involves the slow cutting down of a resistant ridge of rock as a river seeks to smooth irregularities in its channel. Where this happens, a single waterfall may evolve into a series of smaller cascades. Further erosion then hones down the cascades into a stretch of turbulent white water, or rapids, that eventually blends in with the smooth flow of the rest of the river.

In other cases, the top layer of rock may be harder than those beneath it, forming an erosion-resistant "cap." Then most of the erosion takes place at the base of the falls, where falling water carves out a deep plunge pool, or basin, in the riverbed. At the same

time, churning debris wears away the weaker rocks in the lower part of the cliff. In time the cap rock is undermined and breaks off, sometimes in massive chunks, and leaves a new crest slightly upstream. As the process is repeated, the falls slowly migrate upstream, often leaving a series of plunge pools in the riverbed that mark the former locations of the falls.

Where are the highest waterfalls?

In 1935, an American aviator, Jimmy Angel, was prospecting for gold in southeastern Venezuela when he discovered treasure of a different sort. Flying his small plane up a narrow canyon, he came upon a plume of water plummeting off a sheer cliff. Its source proved to be a river that spills off a high plateau. Subsequently named Angel Falls, the cascade is the highest in the world. It drops a total of 3,212 feet.

Steep escarpments have produced other notable waterfalls, including Angel's closest rival; Tugela Falls in South Africa also plunges off a plateau, with a total drop of 3,110 feet.

The third highest in the world, Yosemite Falls in California, tumbles from the mouth of a hanging valley for a total distance of 2,425 feet.

Which falls are most powerful?

High waterfalls may be spectacular, but in terms of volume of flow, the most powerful are generally wide and relatively low. Among the titans is Khone Falls, on the Mekong River in Laos. It drops only 72 feet, yet has an average discharge of 400,000 cubic feet of water per second.

But perhaps the greatest of all "falls makers" is the Río Paraná in South America. One of its tributaries is the site of Iguassú Falls, pouring over a cliff more than 2 miles wide. Although its average discharge is only about 60,000 cubic feet per second, the figure increases to more than 400,000 in times of flood. Downstream on the Paraná itself Guaíra Falls—with 7½ times the average discharge of Iguassú—was the mightiest cataract on earth until it was flooded out of existence by the construction of the Itaipu dam, completed in 1982.

Some 275 separate cascades contribute to the overwhelming grandeur of Iguassú Falls on the Brazil-Argentina border.

How was Niagara Falls formed?

Although far from the highest, Niagara Falls is among the most famous in the world. Located near the midpoint of the Niagara River, which flows from Lake Erie into Lake Ontario, the falls are twin cascades with a total drop of about 180 feet. On one side of an island in the river is the long, straight line of American Falls; on the other, the graceful crescent of Horseshoe Falls.

The falls came into being about 10,000 years ago, at the end of the Ice Age. Originally they fell over an escarpment capped by an extremely hard layer of dolomite. As plunging water wore away softer underlying layers of shale and sandstone, large sections of the cap rock collapsed. Over the years, continued undercutting of the dolomite has caused the falls to migrate about seven miles upstream to their present site. In time—but not for at least 25,000 years—the falls may retreat all the way to Lake Erie and disappear entirely.

The Evolution of a Natural Wonder: Niagara Falls Then and Now

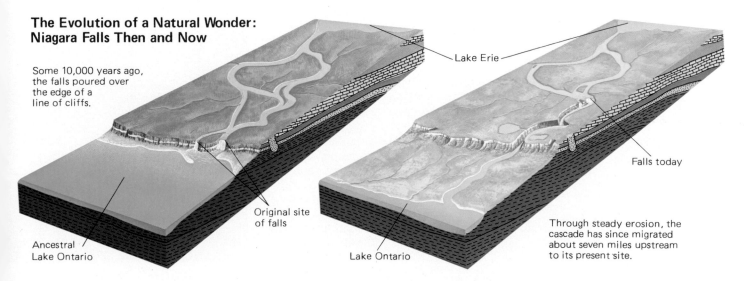

Some 10,000 years ago, the falls poured over the edge of a line of cliffs.

Ancestral Lake Ontario

Original site of falls

Lake Erie

Falls today

Lake Ontario

Through steady erosion, the cascade has since migrated about seven miles upstream to its present site.

Lakes and Ponds

How were most lakes formed?
Ponds and lakes come in all shapes and sizes, as a result of differences in the forces that created them. The vast majority have one thing in common, however: most lakes and ponds are products of some form of glaciation.

During the Ice Age, continental ice sheets gouged countless hollows in the bedrock, carving the myriads of lake basins that dot heavily glaciated regions such as central Canada and much of Finland. The ice sheets also played a major role in excavating the Great Lakes of North America.

High on mountain slopes, valley glaciers scooped out the basins of little lakes called tarns. Moraines—deposits of debris left by melting glaciers— form natural dams holding back the waters of Italy's Lake Maggiore and many other lakes in the Alps. Kettle holes are another type of glacial lake.

The Varied Origins of Lakes

Some lakes occupy grabens, steep-sided basins that formed when a block of the earth's crust dropped downward between parallel faults, or fractures.

Gentle warping of the earth's crust sometimes produces broad, shallow basins that are later filled with water.

Crater lakes are water-filled volcanic craters. Some so-called crater lakes actually occupy calderas, much larger basins caused by the collapse of a volcano's entire summit.

Tarns are one of many types of lakes carved by glaciers. They fill shallow basins near the heads of glacial valleys high on mountain slopes.

The basins, caused by the melting of blocks of ice that were buried in rubble, later filled with water to form typically circular ponds.

Can other forces create lakes?
Some major lakes in the world are the result of massive movements of the earth's crust. Lake Tanganyika and its neighbors in Africa's Great Rift Valley occupy grabens—elongated basins formed by the slumping of segments of the crust between faults. Nearby Lake Victoria, in contrast, came into being when a gentle warping of the earth's crust produced a shallow basin.

Volcanoes also can create lakes. Their craters and calderas sometimes become filled with water and so form lakes. A special type of volcanic lake, called a maar, is caused by a violent explosion that blasts out a nearly circular depression in the earth. And lakes can be impounded behind dams formed by lava flows. Africa's Lake Kivu is a notable example. (Landslides also create natural barriers that transform river valleys into lakes.)

In limestone regions many lakes and ponds occupy basins that were hollowed out when the rock itself was dissolved. Oxbow lakes are born when rivers change courses and cut off loops along their channels. Shifting spits and dunes along seacoasts sometimes block off river mouths, creating freshwater ponds. Even meteors occasionally play a role; Crater Lake in northern Quebec is cupped at the bottom of a basin that was scooped out when a giant meteorite crashed to earth. And of course beavers are industrious dam builders and have created countless woodland lakes and ponds in many parts of North America.

What's the difference between a lake and a pond?
According to some definitions, a pond is a body of standing water that is shallow enough to allow sunlight to reach its bottom—usually no more than about 15 feet. Rooted plants can thus grow on its bottom from shore to shore. Since lakes are larger and deeper, rooted plants grow only along their margins and in shallow coves.

But in common usage, many enclosed bodies of water do not fit these definitions. Some so-called ponds are

very deep; other extensive "lakes" are so shallow that their surfaces are almost entirely covered by plants. For most people, in fact, size is the main distinguishing feature between lakes and ponds. Ponds are small, while lakes are large.

How big are man-made lakes?
In addition to all the natural lakes and ponds that dot the earth, many more have been created by humans. Countless ponds have been dug or dammed to provide water for farm animals or for recreation, and to slow surface runoff. But the most impressive man-made lakes are the reservoirs held

Islands and islets of every shape and size dot the many glistening glacier-carved lakes in Finland's idyllic Lake Region.

back by gigantic dams. The reservoirs provide water for domestic use, irrigation, and recreation. They help control and even prevent disastrous floods. And their water is used to spin turbines that generate electricity.

The size of some of these man-made lakes is truly impressive. The largest in North America, Canada's Manicouagan Reservoir, has a capacity of 115 million acre-feet of water. (An acre-foot is the amount of water needed to cover an acre to a depth of one foot.) The largest man-made lake of all is the Bratsk Reservoir on the Angara River in the U.S.S.R. It holds 137 million acre-feet of water.

Where are the world's largest lakes?
The Great Lakes of North America deserve their name. The five lakes— Superior, Michigan, Huron, Erie, and Ontario—form a chain along the U.S.-Canadian border. Their combined surface area of 94,460 square miles is the world's largest expanse of fresh water. Lake Superior alone covers 31,700 square miles, and is thus the world's largest freshwater lake in terms of area.

In terms of volume, however, the largest is Lake Baikal in the U.S.S.R. Nearly 400 miles long and 30 miles wide, it contains some 5,500 cubic miles of water—about as much as all five Great Lakes combined. If all the rivers in the world emptied into Baikal's basin, it would take them nearly a year to fill the narrow trench. And a trench it is: with a maximum depth of 5,315 feet, Baikal is also the deepest lake in the world.

Why is Great Salt Lake so salty?
Great Salt Lake in the western United States, the largest salt lake in the Western Hemisphere, is but a remnant of its former self. At the close of the Ice Age the entire region was submerged beneath a lake of meltwater, shown in light blue on the map above. Overflow from the lake escaped to the Pacific Ocean through the Snake and Columbia rivers.

Then the climate changed, and the region became warm and dry. Evaporation exceeded the inflow of fresh water and the lake began to shrink, leaving its former outlet high and dry. Continued evaporation reduced the lake to one-twentieth of its former size. And as the water evaporated, the traces of dissolved salts that are present in all fresh water were gradually concentrated in the shrinking puddle. Today some parts of the lake are nearly eight times saltier than the sea.

Similar salt lakes lie within enclosed drainage basins in many parts of the world. The largest is the Caspian Sea in Eurasia; the briniest—ten times saltier than the sea—is Lake Assal in East Africa.

Waterlogged Wetlands

What are wetlands?
Swamps, bogs, marshes—all of these soggy, low places on earth, where the land is perpetually saturated or even partly submerged, are included in the convenient, one-word term "wetlands." In some such places the water is fresh, in others salty; but almost all of them are teeming with life.

For those who do not know them at first hand, mention of swamps and marshes often conjures up images of gloomy wastelands. Yet as breeding grounds for birds, fish, and other wildlife, wetlands have few rivals in the natural world. For some species, such as America's endangered whooping cranes, these watery wonderlands are the last strongholds on earth.

How does a marsh differ from a swamp?
Although the two terms are sometimes used interchangeably, marshes and swamps are as different as fields and forests. Like fields, marshes are open, airy places covered mainly by water-tolerant grasses and similar plants such as sedges and cattails. Swamps, on the other hand, are wet forests; they are dominated by trees and shrubs. Baldcypresses, tupelos, and other trees that can survive with their roots underwater are found in fresh-water swamps. Coastal swamps in the tropics are tangles of mangrove.

The distinction between swamps and marshes, however, is not always clear-cut. Some swamps are dotted with marshy areas, and many marshes include patches of swamp. And both swamps and marshes are often interrupted by tracts of open water, spangled here and there perhaps with the floating pads and bright blossoms of water lilies.

Where do wetlands develop?
Swamps and marshes are common in lowlands and areas with poor drainage. The floodplains and muddy deltas of rivers are often covered with soggy wetlands. Or wetlands may be the final stages in the filling in of a pond or lake. Over the course of time, lake basins gradually fill up with the remains of plants and with sediments washed in from the surrounding land. The lake first becomes a marsh as grasses and sedges move in from the shore and spread across what was once open water. Eventually trees may take over and the marsh becomes a swamp.

Salt marshes are a special case. They are found along seacoasts, frequently near shallow lagoons partially enclosed behind sandbars or barrier islands. Twice a day the tide surges in and out and floods most of the marsh. Constantly drenched in this way with fresh supplies of nutrients, salt marshes rank among the most productive habitats in the world.

How do bogs come into being?
In northern regions, a lake or pond with extremely poor drainage sometimes develops into a special type of wetland called a bog. Typically a floating mat of sphagnum moss and sedges forms along the shoreline and gradually extends inward toward the center of the pond. The mat thickens as individual moss plants grow up at their tips while the lower parts die off. From time to time chunks of dead moss drop from the floating mat and accumulate on the bottom of the basin.

When the mat becomes solid enough, shrubs and then trees take root on its spongy surface. Bogs, in fact, can often be recognized by the surface pattern of vegetation: an "eye" of open water is surrounded by a floating mat of sphagnum and sedges, which is circled in turn by a shrubby zone and then by a ring of water-tolerant trees such as larches. In time the eye of the bog may be sealed completely by the encroaching moss, and the whole basin may then be covered by swampy forest.

The material that eventually fills a bog is peat, the partially decomposed remains of sphagnum and other bog plants. It forms because few living things—not even the microorganisms that cause decay—can thrive in the extremely acid, oxygen-poor water of a bog. Decay proceeds so slowly, in fact, that some bogs have yielded mummified human corpses hundreds of years old. One astounding find was a remarkably well preserved specimen from a Danish bog, buried more than 2,000 years ago.

Is quicksand really as dangerous as people say it is?
To be sucked from sight in a trap of quicksand is a real fear of many who wander in wild places. Although most tales of such events are greatly exaggerated, quicksand can indeed be dangerous. During World War II an entire U.S. Army truck was engulfed by quicksand in Germany.

Quicksand is a pocket of ordinary sand that has been saturated by water moving in from an underground source. This forces the sand grains apart, forming a souplike mixture in which heavy objects sink.

If caught in quicksand, don't panic. Discard any extra weight such as a backpack. Then lie on your back with legs and arms spread out, and try to squirm to the safety of solid ground.

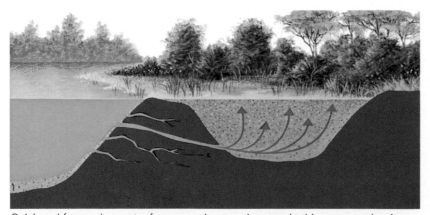

Quicksand forms when water from an underground source, in this case a nearby river, seeps upward through the sand and makes a soupy mixture as it forces the grains apart.

Bog with large area of open water   **Bog nearly filled with peat**

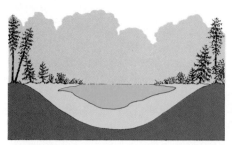 

As the floating mat of sphagnum in a bog extends outward from all shores, the "eye" of open water gradually shrinks, and the basin fills with peat (above). In time, all the open water disappears, as in the bog below.

What are mangrove swamps?

Throughout the tropics and subtropics, long stretches of muddy seacoast are bordered by mangrove swamps. Fringing bays, filling lagoons, and extending far inland along tidal rivers, thickets of these salt-tolerant trees form nearly impenetrable barriers.

In some areas mangrove swamps help to extend the coast seaward over the years. Red mangroves, among the most picturesque of the several kinds, produce aerial roots that grow down like stilts from the branches. Other roots, called prop roots, arch from the sides of the trunks, giving the trees the odd appearance of walking, spider-fashion, out to sea.

These dense tangles of roots, penetrating the water like so many fingers, act as sediment traps. Mud and debris washed in with the tides, and dead leaves falling from the trees, are caught among the roots and gradually accumulate to build dry land. The labyrinths of roots also make it difficult for marauding animals to travel through mangrove swamps. Thus in many areas they are favored as nesting sites by large colonies of herons, pelicans, and other water birds.

Are the Everglades a swamp?

Sprawled across the southern tip of the Florida peninsula is one of the most unusual wetlands in the world—the famed Everglades. They are not the dark junglelike swampland, rank with undergrowth, that many imagine. Instead, much of the Everglades is a wide-open, sun-drenched, water-logged prairie—a sea of waving saw grass. And the saw grass is not a grass at all; it is a sedge with sharp saw-toothed leaves. Here and there "islands" of trees, called hammocks, rise above the marshy flatness. But only along the southern coast is there an extensive wilderness of trees, a wide belt of mangrove swamp.

Nowhere more than 10 feet above sea level, the Everglades occupy a broad shallow trough extending southward toward the sea from Lake Okeechobee. Spillover from the lake is funneled south across the Everglades. In this "river of grass" the slope is so gentle—only a few inches per mile—that the water flows over the surface in a barely perceptible way.

Underground Water

How does water get underground?
An unseen ocean of water lies beneath the surface of the land. Some is "fossil water" that was trapped in deep layers of porous rock when they were being formed, and some seeped in as melt-water from Ice Age glaciers. But most underground water comes from recent rain and melting snow.

This moisture percolates through pores and cracks in soil and even solid rock, seeping down until it reaches an impermeable layer. Then it begins to fill the available spaces in the porous material, saturating it with water.

A permeable formation that holds water is called an aquifer, from the Latin for "water-bearer." Some aquifers are composed of sand or gravel, some of rock. Most rocks are capable of holding some water, but porous types such as limestone and sandstone have the greatest capacity.

The contents of such a subterranean reservoir are called groundwater; the water in lakes and streams is called surface water. Tapped by wells and springs, groundwater is, in many areas, the purest source of water for drinking and may also be used for irrigation and other purposes.

What is the water table?
Aquifers are seldom saturated all the way to the surface of the earth. The top of the saturated zone is called the water table. Above it, no more than a thin film of water clings to soil particles, and the pore spaces are filled with air.

How deep the water table lies beneath the surface varies with the amount of rainfall and with other factors such as the removal of water by humans. You can see the water table if you look into a shallow well; the surface of the water glinting in its depths is at the level of the water table.

Where does spring water come from?
It's no coincidence that so many places are named for springs, since springs are among man's oldest water sources. There is a Springston, New Zealand, for example, an Alice Springs, Australia, and more than a dozen Springfields in the United States.

These natural outflows of underground water are found in many places: on hillsides, in valleys, in the midst of bone-dry deserts, at the feet or even on the faces of cliffs. Springs sometimes flow directly into the beds of lakes and streams, and there are even springs on the ocean floor.

Some springs are mere seeps that barely dampen the surface of the ground, while the water literally gushes from others. A few, such as Silver Springs in Florida and the Fontaine de Vaucluse in France, spill out millions of gallons per minute.

Most of the very large springs are the outlets of underground rivers flowing through channels that have been dissolved in limestone. Or water in an aquifer that is capped by a layer of impervious rock may escape to the surface through fractures in the impervious layer. But springs most commonly occur where an aquifer comes in contact with a sloping land surface, and the water is able to move out through weak spots or crevices.

How do artesian wells work?
As early as the 12th century, monks in the French region of Artois noted that the wells there were different from most others. When they were dug, water rose to the surface under pressure and even gushed into the air. Similar wells found elsewhere, called artesian wells, are named for Artois.

The Natural Plumbing System of an Artesian Spring

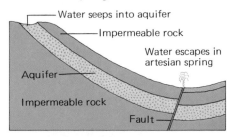

Artesian wells exist only under certain conditions. First, the aquifer tapped by the well must be tilted, sloping down to a considerable depth. And it must be sandwiched between two impervious layers.

Surface water seeps into the upper end of the aquifer and moves slowly through it. Trapped between the impermeable layers, water toward the bottom of the aquifer is under tremendous pressure because of the weight on top. When a well pierces the imper-meable layer above the aquifer, the pressure is released and water gushes up. If the pressure is great enough, water may spurt into the air in a spectacular fountain.

Artesian springs operate in the same way. But instead of escaping through man-made wells, the water rises to the surface through natural breaks that occur in the cap of impermeable rock.

Are all oases alike?
For the weary desert traveler, no sight is more welcome than an oasis, an island of vegetation in an otherwise barren land. In the Sahara and the Middle East, many oases have been occupied for centuries by humans who have used their scant water supplies to irrigate date palms and other crops.

Oases exist because groundwater underlies even the driest of deserts. Where the water table lies close enough to the surface, wells are often dug to create or expand oases. Wind-blown hollows sometimes become deep enough to expose the water table. And here and there deserts are dotted with natural seeps and springs—often artesian—that bring water to the surface. In most cases, the life-sustaining water of these springs originates as rain and snow on distant mountains; it may travel hundreds of miles through a porous aquifer before surfacing at an oasis.

Rivers flowing from highlands into the desert also support oases in the form of ribbons of greenery along their banks. The swaths of lush, cultivated land on both sides of the lower Nile are sometimes considered the largest oasis of this type in the world.

What causes hot springs?
Ever since ancient times, people have sought relief from various ailments at natural hot springs. These are found in many places, called thermal areas, where pockets of magma lie fairly close to the surface and heat the overlying rocks. Groundwater is heated as it circulates through fissures in the rock, and emerges in the pools of hot springs. Besides being warm, the water is usually laden with dissolved minerals that are sometimes deposited around the spring in fantastic, often colorful formations.

Thermal areas often have fumaroles and mud pots as well. In fumaroles, plumes of steam and other gases escape through vents or cracks in the rock. Mud pots form when the emerging steam contains acids that decompose the rocks around the vent into pools of mud. The surface of a mud pot, like a pot of simmering oatmeal, is in constant turmoil, sputtering and bubbling as the steam escapes.

Why do geysers erupt?

By far the most spectacular features of thermal areas are geysers, periodically erupting with explosive bursts of steam and hot water. As water collects in a geyser's long contorted tube, it becomes superheated to temperatures far beyond the normal boiling point. (An increase in pressure, caused in this case by the weight of all the water in the tube, raises the boiling point of water.) But eventually the boiling point is reached, forcing some of the water up and out. With this sudden reduction in pressure, superheated water in the tube flashes into steam, and a jet of steam and scalding water spurts high into the air. When the geyser dies down, more water begins to seep into the tube, setting the stage for the next eruption.

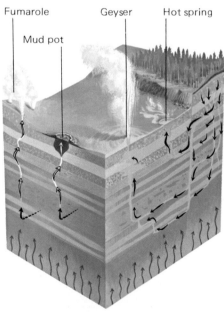

In thermal areas, heat from a pocket of magma warms the overlying rocks. Groundwater is heated as it circulates through fissures, then emerges from hot springs and other outlets.

Beehive Geyser, one of about 300 geysers in Yellowstone National Park in the western United States, regularly erupts with powerful jets of steam and scalding water.

65

Caves and Cave Systems

How are caves formed?

Slowly seeping water is the master sculptor of most of the world's great caves. Typically found in massive beds of limestone, many caves are complex systems of passageways that are dozens of miles long and penetrate hundreds of feet beneath the surface. These hidden underground spaces owe their existence to the ability of water, under certain circumstances, to dissolve solid rock.

Rainwater leaching through the soil takes on enough carbon dioxide to form a mild solution of carbonic acid. Penetrating the networks of natural cracks and fissures that crisscross any limestone formation, the acidic water eats away at the rock, dissolves its minerals, and carries them off in solution. In time, tiny crevices grow to the size of man-made tunnels or even larger. The weakened rock may also cave in. The collapse of ceilings sometimes results in the formation of huge vaulted chambers.

When the water level in the limestone eventually drops, vast air-filled caverns and passageways remain. But mineral-laden water continues to seep downward. Streams cut deeper into cavern floors, and water dripping from the ceilings begins to form fantastic displays of stalactites and other cave formations.

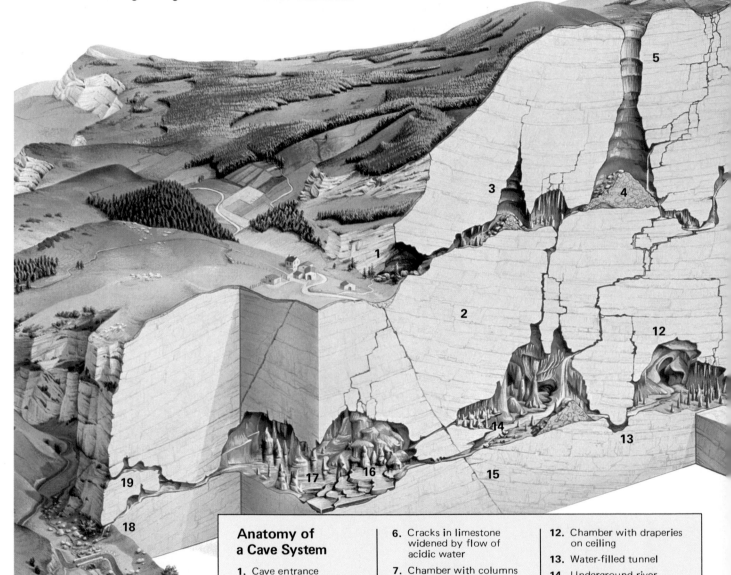

Anatomy of a Cave System

1. Cave entrance
2. Limestone riddled with network of cracks
3. Chamber formed by collapse of ceiling.
4. Mound of rubble
5. Chimneylike shaft to surface sinkhole
6. Cracks in limestone widened by flow of acidic water
7. Chamber with columns and stalagmites
8. Eroded surface rocks
9. Chamber with lake
10. Active underground stream channel
11. Waterfall to large lake-filled chamber
12. Chamber with draperies on ceiling
13. Water-filled tunnel
14. Underground river
15. Fault
16. Rimstone dams and stepped pools of water
17. Underground lake
18. Active spring
19. Inactive spring

Where are the largest caverns?

Mammoth Cave in Kentucky has always been noted for its great size. But no one realized its full extent until 1972, when a link was discovered between it and another cave system. With nearly 200 miles of passageways explored to date, Mammoth is the world's longest cave system.

Honors for the deepest cave go to Pierre-St.-Martin Cavern in France. From its uppermost opening to its lowermost known passageway, it is 4,364 feet deep. The largest cave chamber, in turn, is in Spain's Carlista Cavern; it includes one room with a floor covering more than 20 acres and a ceiling arching 400 feet overhead.

Yet even these records may be temporary. As long as exploration goes on, even longer, bigger, deeper caverns may be discovered.

Can signs of caves be seen above ground?

The surest sign of cave country is the prevalence of disappearing streams. Surface streams may flow into holes on hillsides or funnel into saucer-shaped sinkholes. Miles downstream, the water may reappear at springs, flow only short distances, then plunge once again underground.

The land surface also tends to be very rugged, marred by valleys and circular depressions caused by the collapse of cave ceilings. Even surface outcrops are at the mercy of the water's power to dissolve; large expanses of rock are often scarred with dramatic grooves and ridges.

What are cave formations?

In addition to familiar stalactites and stalagmites, a seemingly endless variety of formations adorn many caves. All are formed of dissolved minerals that have been redeposited on surfaces. Films of water flowing down the walls leave undulating cascades of flowstone. Translucent draperies hang from ceilings. Sunbursts and crystalline "flowers" may spangle the walls, and helictites zigzag in all directions. Where a stream flows down a slope, tiers of crescent-shaped dams may form, each encircling a pool of water. Often breathtakingly beautiful, these monuments of stone all lend an air of fantasy to the world of caves.

How are floor-to-ceiling columns formed in caves?

Water dripping into a cave is saturated with dissolved minerals. When it enters the damp cave air, some of the minerals are forced out of solution and deposited, crystal by crystal, on walls and other surfaces. Slender stalactites slowly lengthen and thicken, like icicles hanging from the ceiling. Water splashing on the ground below builds up the irregular domes of stalagmites. In time the two often merge to form stout floor-to-ceiling columns.

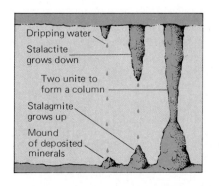

Dripping water
Stalactite grows down
Two unite to form a column
Stalagmite grows up
Mound of deposited minerals

Deserts Around the World

Why are deserts so dry?
Scanty rainfall, the common characteristic of deserts everywhere, results from a variety of circumstances. Some of the world's great deserts, including the Sahara and the Australian deserts, are located in zones of permanent high atmospheric pressure. Continuously descending dry air masses in the highs have practically no moisture to drop as they drift endlessly across these arid lands.

Other deserts lie in the "rain shadows" of major mountain ranges. In western North America moisture-laden winds from the Pacific are forced up by coastal mountains. The air is chilled as it rises and drops nearly all its moisture as rain and snow on the western slopes. Essentially "wrung dry" when it climbs the mountains, the air descends the eastern slopes as dry winds that blow across the deserts of the Great Basin.

Cold ocean currents account for the Atacama Desert of Chile and Peru and the Namib Desert in southern Africa. In these cases, moist onshore winds lose their moisture, mainly in the form of fog, as they pass over the cold water. Practically none is left to fall as rain on the long, narrow strips of coastal desert. Still other deserts, such as the Gobi in central Asia, are simply so far from any ocean that little moisture ever reaches them.

How Mountains Create Rain Shadows

Forced up by mountain barriers, moist onshore winds drop abundant rain and snow on windward slopes.

Little moisture is left as the winds descend leeward slopes, and precipitation is scanty in the mountain's inland rain shadow.

How much rain falls on deserts?
According to one definition of deserts, they are areas that receive, on the average, no more than 10 inches of rain a year. In fact, many deserts receive far less than that. Rainfall in parts of central Australia averages five inches a year, and the figure for Death Valley in the western United States is less than two inches annually. Driest of all are parts of the Atacama Desert in Chile, where no rain has ever been known to fall.

Averages, however, tell only part of the story. A few deserts have a more or less regular annual rainy season, but generally rainfall is totally unpredictable. An area may receive no rain for years on end, then a sudden cloudburst may deluge it with rain.

Sometimes, too, in these parched lands, passing clouds offer the promise of relief. But only a "ghost rain" falls: water showering from the clouds evaporates in the hot, dry air long before reaching ground.

Are deserts always hot?
On September 13, 1922, in a Saharan outpost in western Libya, the air temperature soared to 136° F in the shade—the highest ever recorded anywhere on earth. Soil temperatures in deserts get even higher: in Death Valley they have been known to reach an intense 190° F.

Not all deserts reach such extremes, of course, but they do become hotter than humid regions at the same latitudes. This happens because in humid areas less than half of the sun's radiation reaches the earth. The rest is screened out by clouds and water vapor in the air or is reflected back into space by leaves and water surfaces. In the dry, sparsely vegetated desert environment, with its clear cloudless skies, nearly all the sun's radiation comes through to heat the bare ground and the air above it.

At night, however, desert temperatures usually drop dramatically as heat is radiated back into space. At one spot in the Sahara, the temperature once dropped 100 degrees within 24 hours, from a scorching 126° F to a bone-chilling 26°.

Are there lakes in the desert?
Some deserts are dotted here and there with permanent lakes. While their water may look inviting, it is generally unfit to drink, for most are salt lakes. Like Great Salt Lake in the western United States, they usually are cupped in enclosed drainage basins with no outlet. Seasonal rains on surrounding uplands keep them supplied with water. But intense evaporation over the years has resulted in a great concentration of the dissolved mineral salts that are continually being washed into the lakes.

Most desert lakes, however, are strictly temporary. Occasional rains fill them, perhaps to a depth of several feet, but within a matter of weeks or months all the water evaporates. Nothing remains but the dry lake beds, called playas. Some are simply broad, flat expanses of sun-baked mud; others are covered with a glittering crust of salts.

One of the strangest of all desert lakes is Lake Eyre in south central Australia. About 3,600 square miles in area, it is bone-dry most of the time. Only twice since its discovery in 1840 has it been completely filled with water. But each time the lake vanished once again within a few years, its water completely evaporated by the hot, dry desert air.

What is desert varnish?

In many deserts, cliffs are stained with streaks of color ranging from tan to dark red to black. Even rocks on the desert floor are covered by a thin, lacquerlike film. The coating, called desert varnish, was long a mystery to desert travelers.

The varnish is actually a thin layer of metallic oxides that have been deposited on the rock surfaces and then burnished by windblown sand. It is believed that dew dissolves the metallic elements from the rocks and they remain as a surface coating when the dew evaporates. Studies suggest that microorganisms may also play a role in the creation of desert varnish.

Are all deserts sandy?

Contrary to the popular conception of deserts as vast, unending tracts of undulating dunes, only about one-fifth of the world's desert area is covered with sand. Even so, many of the "seas of sand" are impressive; some in the Sahara, where they are called ergs, cover tens of thousands of square miles. (The Sahara itself, with an area of some 3.5 million square miles, is the largest desert in the world.) The sand is washed in from adjoining uplands or derived from the weathering of desert rocks. Constantly moved about by the wind, the sand eventually accumulates in low spots or basins on the desert floor.

Beyond the dune fields, most deserts present a variety of other landscapes. Many include large areas of bare, windswept bedrock, known as hammadas in northern Africa. Usually there are extensive plains, called regs, that are littered with loose stones and gravel. Sometimes, as sand and dust between the stones on a plain are blown or washed away, the stones settle together to form a solid armor of fragments known as desert pavement. Mountains, steep-sided plateaus dissected by deep gorges, buttes, natural arches, glistening salt flats, and many other landforms contribute to the infinite variety of desert scenery.

What causes desert dunes?

Two things are needed for the formation of dunes: a plentiful supply of sand and persistent wind. Depending on such things as the nature of the

Patterns of light and shadow accentuate the dramatic forms of the dunes on a Saharan erg, as such areas of shifting sand are called. Modeled by incessant wind, the dunes are constantly being changed in shape and size.

Some Common Desert Dune Formations

Transverse dunes are long ridges of sand that form at right angles to the path of the prevailing wind.

Barchan dunes are shaped like horseshoes, with their tapered tips facing away from the oncoming wind.

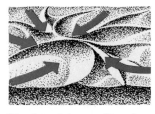

Star-shaped dunes, often of enormous size, are produced by shifting winds that blow from various directions.

sand, the lay of the land, and the strength of the wind, the dunes take on a variety of shapes.

One common type—called transverse dunes—forms long ridges across the path of the prevailing wind, like waves at sea. (The dunes along most seashores are transverse dunes.) Seif dunes (from the Arabic word for "sword"), in contrast, lie parallel to the prevailing wind direction. Sculpted by very powerful winds, they are often many miles long and up to 300 feet high. The bare, windswept troughs between rows of seif dunes have traditionally been used as highways by nomadic desert peoples.

Barchans are shaped like crescents, with their tips pointing downwind. Found where sand is relatively scarce, they travel across gravelly surfaces or even bare bedrock. Barchans are among the most active dunes, migrating up to 100 feet per year.

Some dunes are mountainous, star-shaped formations up to 1,000 feet high. Created by winds that blow alternately from various directions, these dunes tend to remain where they were formed.

The Polar Regions

Where is the Arctic?

If three geographers were asked to define the exact boundaries of the Arctic, they might well give three different answers. Some say the Arctic is simply the region enclosed by the Arctic Circle, the imaginary line on the earth's surface north of which the sun does not set on the longest day of the year nor rise above the horizon on the shortest day. Others place the boundary at the line along which average summer temperatures do not exceed 50° F—a line reaching well south of the Arctic Circle in some places. Still others say the Arctic begins at the northern limit of tree growth.

But if its borders are debatable, the Arctic itself is unquestionably unique. It includes an ice-covered, nearly landlocked sea, the northern fringes of Eurasia and North America, plus Greenland and other islands.

The outstanding feature of the region is its climate, dominated by the long darkness of winter and summer's midnight sun. Actually the brief Arctic summer can be surprisingly mild in some land areas, where the snow cover melts away and July temperatures may rise well above 50° F. But winter is long and very cold indeed. January

Calved from an Antarctic ice shelf, an iceberg glistens in the warm light of the southern midnight sun. Small by Antarctic standards, this one is about half a mile long and 100 feet high.

temperatures average about −30° F over most of the region.

What is Antarctica like?

The polar regions are alike in being cold and isolated, but in many ways they are strikingly different. While the Arctic is primarily a landlocked sea, Antarctica is a continent covering more than 5 million square miles. It is, moreover, the earth's highest continent, with an average land height of 6,000 feet. And virtually all that land is topped by a vast ice cap thousands of feet thick.

The average year-round temperature in parts of the interior is −70° F. (One time the temperature plunged to a world record of −127° F.) Although coastal areas are not nearly as cold, they are sometimes assaulted by violent blizzards with gales of up to 200 miles per hour.

Only about 2 percent of Antarctica's land area is free of the immense ice cap, which in many places extends far offshore in the form of partially floating ice shelves. All in all, this frozen land is the least hospitable to life of all the earth's continents.

Where do icebergs come from?

Icebergs—floating mountains of ice adrift in polar seas—are found in both the Arctic and the Antarctic. The best known are the Arctic bergs, which sometimes drift down into the heavily

traveled shipping lanes of the North Atlantic. Most originate on the west coast of Greenland. Huge glaciers from the edges of the ice cap push out to sea until finally great masses of ice break off with a thunderous roar, a process called calving.

Arctic bergs may weigh more than a million tons and tower 400 feet above the sea, though most of their bulk remains submerged. Yet even the biggest are dwarfed by the flat-topped icebergs of the Antarctic. Calved from the margins of ice shelves that fringe the continent, these floating islands of ice are measured not in feet, but in miles. The largest on record was 60 miles wide and 208 miles long.

Are the polar seas frozen solid?

Much of the Arctic Ocean is covered by a slowly drifting mass of ice, called pack ice, that grows in area in winter, then shrinks again in summer. A zone of pack ice also rings Antarctica and varies in extent with the seasons.

Winds, tides, and currents keep the pack ice in constant motion and break it up into pieces, large and small, called ice floes. Like floating islands, floes may drift apart and become separated by channels of open water that then freeze over. When floes collide, the ice buckles up in jagged pressure ridges, perhaps 20 feet high. Or one floe may ride up over another, creating a jumble of huge ice blocks.

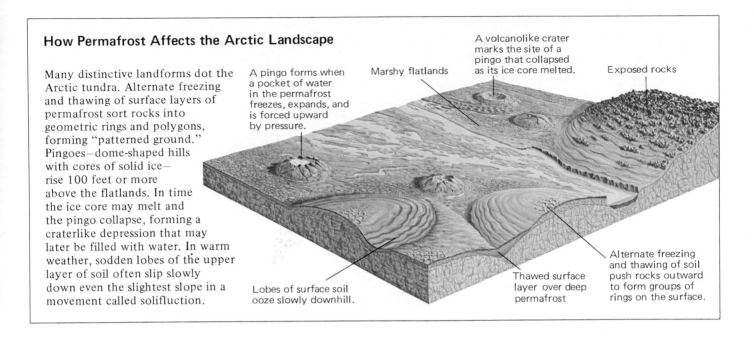

How Permafrost Affects the Arctic Landscape

Many distinctive landforms dot the Arctic tundra. Alternate freezing and thawing of surface layers of permafrost sort rocks into geometric rings and polygons, forming "patterned ground." Pingoes—dome-shaped hills with cores of solid ice— rise 100 feet or more above the flatlands. In time the ice core may melt and the pingo collapse, forming a craterlike depression that may later be filled with water. In warm weather, sodden lobes of the upper layer of soil often slip slowly down even the slightest slope in a movement called solifluction.

A pingo forms when a pocket of water in the permafrost freezes, expands, and is forced upward by pressure.

Marshy flatlands

A volcanolike crater marks the site of a pingo that collapsed as its ice core melted.

Exposed rocks

Lobes of surface soil ooze slowly downhill.

Thawed surface layer over deep permafrost

Alternate freezing and thawing of soil push rocks outward to form groups of rings on the surface.

Yet even these scenes of desolation are not lifeless. In the Antarctic seals and penguins ride on the drifting floes, while in the Far North polar bears wander now and then across the shifting pack ice.

What is permafrost?

One of the most important effects of extreme cold in Arctic lands is the presence of permafrost, a deep layer of permanently frozen ground. In the North American Arctic, the permafrost averages about 1,000 feet in thickness; in parts of Siberia it extends to depths of more than 2,000 feet.

Only the top few inches or feet of surface soil thaw in summer. The tundra—the characteristic treeless plains of the Arctic—is then transformed into a soggy landscape. Because of poor drainage, large areas are dotted with countless marshes, ponds, and shallow lakes. When winter returns, the land and water are once again covered by an armor of ice and snow.

Permafrost poses many problems for would-be builders in the Arctic.

Stripping away the insulating cover of vegetation—to build a road, for example—causes the permafrost to melt. So does the warmth from improperly built houses. And when the permafrost melts, the land shifts and settles, and structures built on it tilt or crack. Special techniques are used to prevent such damage. Houses are built on deep-seated pilings or on insulating pads of gravel. Roads are routed over bedrock where possible; elsewhere, thick layers of gravel are used to protect the fragile permafrost.

California poppies, native to the western United States, are treasured as garden flowers in many parts of the world.

THE WORLD OF PLANTS

Many Kinds of Plants

Are all plants green and leafy?
Stroll through any park or garden and you may find yourself surrounded by the green and leafy living things people think of as typical plants. The trees overhead and the shrubs in dense hedges are clearly plants. So are the roses, zinnias, and marigolds growing in neatly tended beds, and the lawns' carpet of grass. Perhaps a few patches of moss or clumps of ferns grow in shady nooks. They also are plants.

But what about the mushrooms, ghostly white and leafless, poking up through the grass? They are fungi, another type of plant. Boulders may be blotched with colorful crusty patches, like smears of paint. These are lichens, clinging to the rocks; they have no leaves, no stems, no roots, but they too are plants. The greenish tint on tree trunks is yet another type of plant—microscopic one-celled algae. A closer look at a woodlot, a marsh, or almost any other habitat would reveal similar diversity in the colors, forms, and sizes of the living things we call plants.

What is the difference between plants and animals?
Plants and animals are as different as dandelions and deer. But while some of the distinctions between them are obvious, others are not so clear-cut. Most animals, for instance, can move about actively. Most plants cannot, although certain one-celled algae have whiplike structures called flagella that enable them to swim.

Most plants contain the green pigment chlorophyll, which permits them to manufacture their own food through the process of photosynthesis. Animals must rely on the food manufactured by green plants. But again, there are exceptions. The fungi and even certain flowering plants contain no chlorophyll and so cannot manufacture their own food.

Unlike animals, plants have no nervous system and so do not normally react quickly to stimuli. Yet the leaves of the sensitive plant quickly fold up when touched. And the growing tip of a morning glory manages to "feel" a potential support and soon begins to twine around it.

Even the cellular structure of plants and animals is different. Most plants have rigid cell walls containing cellulose, a substance not found in any animals. These two types of living things also grow differently. Animals grow only until they reach maturity; plants never stop growing until they die.

How many kinds of plants are there?
Plants of some sort live nearly everywhere on earth—on the land, in the sea, from deserts to rain forests, and even on and inside the bodies of animals. They include some of the smallest living things—one-celled bacteria and algae so minute that they can be seen only with the aid of microscopes—and the largest of all living things—the giant sequoia trees of western North America. In all, scientists estimate that the vast and varied plant kingdom includes more than 350,000 species. In terms of sheer numbers of individuals, there are far more plants than animals in the world. And in terms of combined mass, the plants account for nearly all the living matter that exists on earth.

Are all plants related?
Biologists believe that plants, like all other forms of life, originated in primeval seas. Fossils of the earliest forms are rare; the oldest known are traces of algae that lived more than 3 billion years ago. Over the ensuing eons, all the more complex plants developed gradually from these primitive beginnings.

A long time elapsed before any plants managed to invade the land, however. The first of these pioneers began colonizing muddy shores more than 400 million years ago. Some types of early land plants flourished for a time, and then died out; others

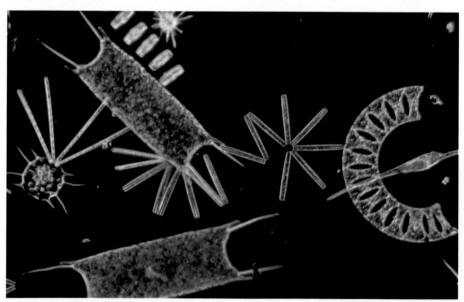

Diatoms, microscopic single-celled algae, are among the most abundant plants in oceans around the world.

Ferns and other plants flourish in rain-drenched forests on the slopes of Mount Waialeale in the Hawaiian Islands.

were the ancestors of plants that exist today, such as the mosses and their relatives the liverworts.

The next great advance occurred about 345 million years ago. It was then that the forebears of the so-called higher plants first left their traces in the fossil record—plants with specialized water-conducting cells and true roots, stems, and leaves. Among the survivors of this line of development are such plants as the present-day club mosses, horsetails, and ferns.

The first true seed-bearing plants entered the picture about 225 million years ago and gave rise to the modern conifers and a few rather obscure plant groups. But the most revolutionary development took place a mere 135 million years before the present. Flowering plants appeared for the first time and since then have inherited the earth. Now the largest plant group in the world, the flowering plants include an amazing assortment of trees, shrubs, vines, grasses, crop plants, wildflowers, weeds, and nearly all the other familiar plants we encounter in our everyday lives.

Could we live without plants?

Without earth's green mantle of vegetation, animal life as we know it could not exist. For plants, from the loftiest trees to the tiniest algae adrift in the sea, are the ultimate source of the very food we eat and the oxygen in the air we breathe.

In the process of photosynthesis, green plants form simple sugars in the presence of sunlight. As part of the reaction, they release oxygen into the atmosphere—the oxygen that all animals need to survive. In a never-ending cycle, the animals in turn exhale the carbon dioxide that plants require for photosynthesis.

Since plants alone can manufacture food, all animals must rely on them for nourishment. Some animals eat the leaves, fruits, and other parts of the plants themselves. Others feed on animals that in turn fed on plants.

Humans use plants in countless other ways as well. Plants supply us with fibers for textiles and ropes; wood products for buildings and furniture; paper for a multitude of purposes; and even many lifesaving medicines.

Giant proteas of southern Africa have showy flower heads that are as much as 10 inches in diameter.

Giant sequoias, conifers native to the mountains of California, are the most massive of all living things.

Algae Are Simple Plants

What are algae?

Rockweed, kelp, sea lettuce, dulse, and all the other well-known seaweeds are algae. So is the bubbly green scum that forms in stagnating ponds, and the greenish film that develops on the walls of aquariums.

In all, more than 25,000 species of plants are classed as algae. Despite a tremendous diversity in shape and size, all share several traits. Like the majority of plants, most algae contain chlorophyll, the green substance that enables them to manufacture their own food. But unlike the more familiar plants of fields and forests, algae do not bear flowers or produce seeds. They do not even have true leaves, stems, or roots, although the larger kinds are often intricately branched. And many are microscopic in size, self-contained in a single cell.

Algae multiply in a variety of ways. The single-celled species can simply divide to form two new individuals.

A Gallery of Algae

The 25,000 or more species of plants classed as algae range from microscopic forms to large and complexly branched seaweeds. Single-celled *Euglena* is propelled by a hairlike flagellum. *Spirogyra* lives in threadlike colonies of cells joined end to end. *Polysiphonia* is a fragile seaweed formed of many branching filaments, and sea lettuce fronds resemble large, thin leaves of lettuce.

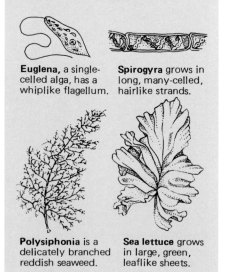

Euglena, a single-celled alga, has a whiplike flagellum.

Spirogyra grows in long, many-celled, hairlike strands.

Polysiphonia is a delicately branched reddish seaweed.

Sea lettuce grows in large, green, leaflike sheets.

Some produce spores that grow into new plants. In a process called fragmentation, pieces may be broken off and, if conditions are favorable, continue to grow on their own. Some algae can reproduce sexually by the fusion of male and female germ cells.

How big are algae?

The tiniest algae are single-celled forms, so minute that millions can exist unseen in a gallon of seawater. When viewed through a microscope, however, many reveal a surprising beauty and symmetry of form. At the other extreme are the giant kelps. Some of these are more than 200 feet long; one type can grow to its full length of 150 feet in just one year.

Yet even the microscopic species are sometimes visible because of their sheer abundance. The thin green film that forms on moist stones, flowerpots, and the shady side of trees is actually millions of individual single-celled algae. Other kinds can transform stagnant pools into a thick greenish soup.

The Red Sea, in turn, is noted for the reddish algae that sometimes tint its water. Similarly, "red tides" in the ocean are caused by population explosions of algae. These strange outbreaks can have devastating effects, for the algae sometimes produce poisons that kill millions of fish.

Eeriest of all are certain of the dinoflagellates—minute, one-celled algae that swim about by whipping long, oarlike hairs. Some of these tiny plants are phosphorescent and produce the pinpricks of light that are often seen flashing in tropical seas.

Where do algae live?

Water, both salt and fresh, is the natural habitat of most algae. But these incredibly adaptable plants thrive in many other places as well. Some live in the upper layers of the soil, on rocks, tree trunks, and even on the walls and roofs of buildings. Many kinds survive in the frigid climates of both the Arctic and Antarctica; others are equally at home in hot springs with temperatures as high as 185° F.

Algae also live in and on the bodies of other plants and animals. Microscopic single-celled animals called paramecia often have numbers of even tinier algae living within their

bodies. A type of European flatworm gets its dark green color from the many algae that live and multiply beneath its skin. Turtles are often camouflaged by colonies of larger algae that live attached to their shells. And sloths, large mammals that inhabit the treetops of tropical rain forests, frequently have a greenish tinge from the many algae that live on their fur.

Are all algae green?

Although all algae contain the green coloring matter chlorophyll, not all of them are green. Other pigments frequently mask the chlorophyll, tinting different kinds with a rainbow of hues. Many of the large, familiar seaweeds, for example, are various shades of brown. But dulse, a widespread species, is purplish red, and Irish moss is sometimes purplish, sometimes yellow. Others range from delicate pink to deep violet.

The microscopic varieties are equally colorful. The kinds that live in hot springs tinge the walls with splashes of brilliant yellow, orange, and red. Myriads of algae cause the strange phenomenon of red snow: living on the surface of snowfields and glaciers, they sometimes stain them with a reddish bloom. Algae are also responsible for an alternative name for the gigantic blue whale: colonies of minute yellowish diatoms on its underside have earned it the name sulfurbottomed whale.

Are algae edible?

People who live near the ocean have always collected seaweed. They fertilize their crops with it, they feed it to farm animals, and they eat it themselves. Laver, dulse, various kinds of kelp, and other sorts of seaweed are still used in a wide variety of preparations. Dried, shredded, ground, and in many other guises, they are eaten as vegetables, bread, confections, beverages, and other foods. In Japan, especially, seaweeds are cultivated for human consumption.

Animals, too, take advantage of algae. Sheep have been known to patrol beaches at low tide in search of laver. Horses, cattle, and pigs are fed seaweed in coastal areas. Elsewhere large amounts are ground up for use as livestock food supplements.

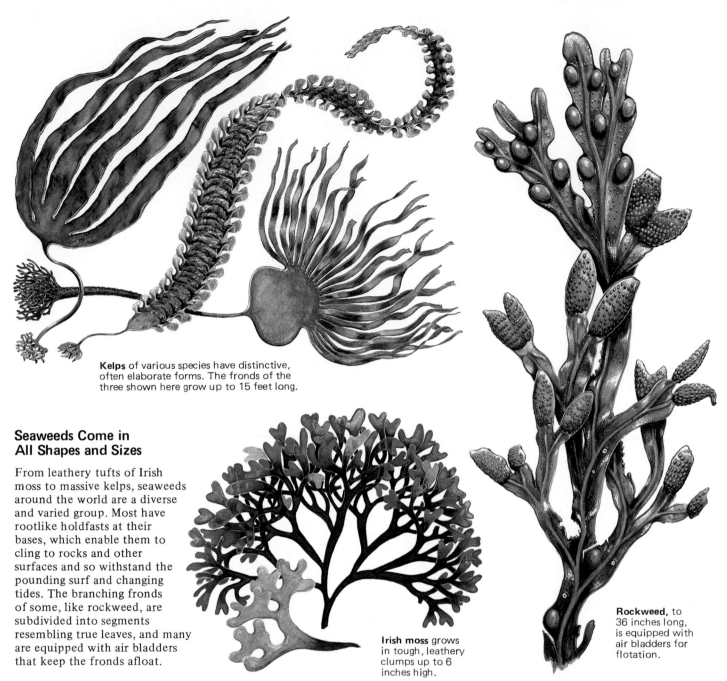

Kelps of various species have distinctive, often elaborate forms. The fronds of the three shown here grow up to 15 feet long.

Seaweeds Come in All Shapes and Sizes

From leathery tufts of Irish moss to massive kelps, seaweeds around the world are a diverse and varied group. Most have rootlike holdfasts at their bases, which enable them to cling to rocks and other surfaces and so withstand the pounding surf and changing tides. The branching fronds of some, like rockweed, are subdivided into segments resembling true leaves, and many are equipped with air bladders that keep the fronds afloat.

Irish moss grows in tough, leathery clumps up to 6 inches high.

Rockweed, to 36 inches long, is equipped with air bladders for flotation.

But algae are most important as an indirect food source. The microscopic floating algae, so abundant that they have been called the grass of the sea, are the basis of all marine food chains. The primary producers of food in the ocean and other bodies of water, they are fed upon by microscopic animals that are eaten in turn by larger animals. Without the hosts of unseen algae adrift in the sea, there would be no shrimp, no clams, no oysters, nor any other seafood delicacies.

What else are algae used for?

Probing the secrets of seaweeds, scientists have come up with a surprising number of uses for these versatile plants. Antibiotics have been developed from several species. Agar, a jellylike substance derived from certain seaweeds, is used as a culture medium in biological research, as well as in the manufacture of products ranging from adhesives, soaps, and shaving creams to foods and pharmaceuticals. Alginic acid, extracted from kelp, acts as a sta-

bilizer in ice cream, salad dressings, and other foods. It is also used in the preparation of surgical thread, films, plastics, papers, and other products.

Among the many other important algal products is diatomaceous earth, deposited over the ages by diatoms—tiny one-celled algae with silica in their cell walls. This gritty material is used as a mild abrasive in toothpastes and metal polishes. It also serves as a filter in sugar refining and an absorbent in the manufacture of dynamite.

Of Molds and Mushrooms

What are fungi?

Like algae, fungi are simple non-flowering plants that lack true leaves, stems, and roots. But unlike algae, they contain no chlorophyll and so are unable to manufacture their own food.

Mushrooms are the best known of the more than 75,000 species of plants classed as fungi. The one-celled yeasts that cause bread to rise and juices to ferment are also fungi, as is the mildew that may form on a pair of shoes in a damp closet. Still other types of fungi cause the various rust and smut diseases that afflict plants, and the ringworm and athlete's foot infections of human skin.

The mold that appears on decaying fruit and the fuzzy mold that sometimes forms on bread are fungi, too. Blue cheeses, Roquefort, and Camembert owe their distinctive flavors to molds, and another mold is the source of healing penicillin.

How do mushrooms and other fungi reproduce?

If you squeeze a ripe puffball, a cloud of dark "dust" spurts out. And if you tap a mushroom cap over a piece of white paper, the paper is peppered with similar specks. These are spores, the reproductive units of fungi. Occurring in a variety of shapes and colors, they all have the ability to develop into new plants.

Fungi generally produce huge numbers of spores. A single mushroom may release billions of them. Some spores are shot from the parent plant. Others are scattered by falling raindrops. But most are spread by the wind. Tiny and lightweight, they can ride through the air for thousands of miles. So many eventually land and germinate that fungi are among the most widespread of all living things.

Can mushrooms grow up overnight?

A mushroom is only the fruiting, or reproductive, structure of a much larger fungus body that grows out of sight in rotting logs, rich humus, and similar dark, damp places. The hidden part of the plant consists of a multitude of minute, threadlike filaments, called hyphae, that form a tangled mass known as the mycelium.

In many of the familiar mushrooms, the fruiting bodies are fleshy and umbrella-shaped. Warm, damp weather triggers their sudden appearance. First to show up is a small round "button" composed of densely packed hyphae. Soon the outer covering ruptures, the stem elongates, and the cap enlarges to its full size. The entire process can indeed happen overnight.

How Mushrooms Grow and Multiply

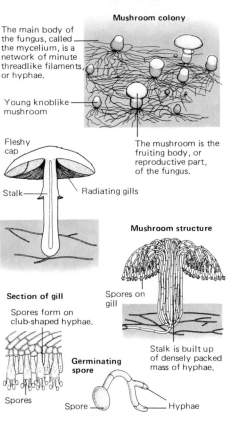

Mushroom colony

The main body of the fungus, called the mycelium, is a network of minute threadlike filaments, or hyphae.

Young knoblike mushroom

The mushroom is the fruiting body, or reproductive part, of the fungus.

Fleshy cap

Stalk

Radiating gills

Mushroom structure

Section of gill

Spores form on club-shaped hyphae.

Spores on gill

Germinating spore

Stalk is built up of densely packed mass of hyphae.

Spores

Spore

Hyphae

Most mushrooms shed their spores and wither away within a few days. But the mycelium persists, sometimes living for decades. Whenever favorable conditions return, it forms new fruiting bodies that pop up on the surface and produce more spores.

What do fungi feed on?

Unable to produce their own food, all fungi take their nourishment from the bodies of other plants and animals, both living and dead. Thousands of plant diseases are caused by parasitic fungi that attack living plants. One kind of fungus is even predatory. It snares microscopic nematode worms in nooselike growths on its hyphae, then absorbs their substance.

Other kinds of fungi live in close association with the roots of pines, orchids, and other types of plants. The hyphae grow around the root tips of the larger plants and sometimes even penetrate them. This combination of plant root and fungal mycelium is called a mycorrhiza, a word meaning "fungus root." In this case the relationship is mutually beneficial, not parasitic; the fungi supply the roots with water and nutrients and in return receive essential food.

But the majority of fungi live on the remains of plants and animals. Their hyphae permeate the dead tissue, hastening its breakdown and decay. Fungi, in fact, are invaluable for their role in decomposing organic matter.

Are all big fungi shaped like mushrooms?

The fruiting bodies of fungi come in a seemingly endless array of forms and colors. Many are variations on the familiar stalk-and-cap pattern of the mushrooms sold in stores, although some, instead of gills, have minute spore-bearing pores on the undersides of the caps. But many other fungi do not resemble mushrooms at all. Puffballs are solid, fleshy spheres. Bird's nest fungi form little cups containing "eggs" packed with spores. One kind of fungus looks like a head of cauliflower, and others resemble upright branching clumps of coral. Still others protrude like shelves from tree trunks, and other kinds look like glistening blobs of jelly.

Earthstars have an outer layer that splits open to reveal the spore sac.

Common morels have patterns of pits and ridges on their caps.

Are toadstools a type of mushroom?

In common usage, mushroomlike fungi that are poisonous or inedible are often called toadstools. The word originated in times gone by, when toads were considered vile, poisonous creatures, and the fungi found with them in damp, dark places were presumed to be poisonous too. But while the word is certainly picturesque, it is not used by scientists who study fungi. They consider it a useless catchall term lumping many species that are not even closely related.

How can you tell if a mushroom is poisonous?

Many kinds of mushrooms have been enjoyed as food since ancient times. But many others have long been known to be poisonous. Some of the toxic kinds cause only mild discomfort; others are lethal. Some kinds may be poisonous to one person and not to others, or they may have ill effects only if eaten in large quantities. And some are hallucinogens, causing severe distortions of perception.

Unfortunately, there is no easy way to tell if a mushroom is poisonous. Some of the edible kinds are quite easily recognized, but others have lethal look-alikes that can only be distinguished by experts with many years of experience. For the average person, the safest way to enjoy mushrooms is to eat only the commercially grown kinds that are sold in markets.

What causes fairy rings to form?

Long ago it was believed that the circles of mushrooms that sometimes form in meadows marked the places where fairies danced at night. The rings actually mark the edges of the underground network of hyphae that grow outward from the center. Mushrooms pop up from the margin, thus forming the circle.

Fairy ring mushrooms, to three inches tall, are the usual producers of these enchanting circles.

Where do truffles come from?

Perhaps the most prized of all edible fungi are the gourmet's delights called truffles. Found mainly in western Europe, they grow in open woodlands near the roots of trees. The fruiting bodies, ranging from white to grayish brown to nearly black, are fragrant, fleshy structures, usually about the size of golf balls.

Truffles are difficult to find because, unlike typical mushrooms, they develop underground. Truffle hunters use specially trained dogs and pigs to find the flavorful morsels. Both animals have a keen sense of smell and are attracted by the strong, nutlike aroma of the truffles. Pigs, in fact, can scent a truffle from 20 feet away. They rush to the spot and quickly root out the precious prize.

What are slime molds?

Among the most peculiar of all living things are the 500 or so species of fungi known as slime molds; for much of their lives they act more like animals than plants. In their active phase, slime molds are jellylike blobs, sometimes brightly colored and often several inches in diameter, that flourish among decaying vegetation. Creeping along like giant amoebas, they ingest microorganisms and bits of rotting plant debris.

Eventually, however, the slime molds make their way to higher, drier places, and the masses of protoplasm are gradually transformed into fruiting bodies. These stalked, often ornately formed structures then release myriads of spores that germinate and start the cycle anew.

Giant puffballs are big globes that can grow to the size of volleyballs.

Fly agarics are large, colorful, and extremely poisonous mushrooms.

Sulfur polypores grow like brackets from trees, stumps, and logs.

Lichens: Two Plants in One

What are lichens?

To the casual observer, lichens, despite their sometimes strange forms, seem like fairly ordinary plants. But microscopic examination reveals them to be far from simple. For, whatever their shapes and sizes, each and every type of lichen is actually composed of two separate plants—a fungus and an alga—living in close association. The bulk of the lichen is made up of a meshwork of minute, threadlike fungal filaments; embedded within this network are multitudes of microscopic one-celled algae.

Both members benefit from this partnership. The fungus absorbs the moisture that the algae need, and may supply them with essential minerals. It supplies the algae with a living place; anchored to the surface by rootlike structures, the fungus also furnishes stability. The algae are the food-producing members of the partnership, and supply the fungus with carbohydrates. Lichens, in fact, are notable examples of mutualism—a case of two different organisms living together to the advantage of both.

Bare rocks on a windswept mountaintop have been colonized by crustose lichens.

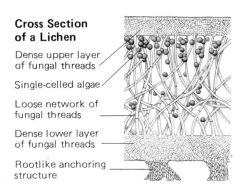

Cross Section of a Lichen

Dense upper layer of fungal threads

Single-celled algae

Loose network of fungal threads

Dense lower layer of fungal threads

Rootlike anchoring structure

How do lichens spread?

Reproduction would seem to be a tricky problem for a compound organism like a lichen, which is formed of two totally unrelated plants. Yet lichens can and do multiply and spread.

The chanciest method is by producing spores. The fungi in lichens form reproductive organs, often brilliantly colored, that release countless microscopic spores. If the spores alight in the right sort of habitat, they develop into tiny fungus plants. And if, as they grow, they happen to come into contact with exactly the right species of alga, the two develop into a lichen. But

oftener than not, the fungus fails to find the right partner and dies.

Other methods leave less to chance. Lichens become brittle when they dry out, and fragments tend to break off and blow away. If the pieces land in moist places, they revive, take hold, and continue to grow. Lichens also produce little clumps of fungal threads and algal cells on their upper surfaces. Broken off and carried away by wind or water, these tiny structures develop into mature lichens.

Where do lichens live?

Lichens flourish in all sorts of habitats, from dripping rain forests to searing deserts. Some have been found high above the timberline in the Himalayas, others within 250 miles of the South Pole. Lichens grow on rocks, trees, and bare soil as well as on gravestones, buildings, and even sun-bleached bones and the backs of certain weevils.

Lichens, in fact, frequently thrive where no other plants can survive.

They are, in a sense, the pioneers of the plant world. By colonizing such inhospitable habitats as bare rock, they play a part in preparing the way for other plants. They help break down the rock and so create pockets of soil, which furnish a suitable environment where spores and seeds of other plants can gain a foothold.

How do lichens survive?

The lichens that live in Antarctica regularly endure temperatures that fall far below 0° F. Desert species live on rocks that sometimes become literally too hot to touch. In one experiment, some lichens were baked for seven hours at a temperature of 434° F—more than twice the temperature of boiling water. And they survived.

One secret of lichens' success, however, is that they normally avoid such extremes by drying out and becoming dormant. When favorable conditions return, they soak up moisture and begin to grow actively again.

Yet even the hardy lichens cannot

survive everywhere. Despite their adaptability, most species are extremely sensitive to air pollution. As a result, large cities and industrial areas are among the few places where lichens are generally not found. But there are exceptions even to this rule; in Great Britain one kind of lichen is actually increasing in abundance in areas of severe air pollution.

Are all lichens alike?
Scientists recognize some 15,000 species of lichens, each consisting of one particular kind of fungus combined with a specific algal partner. This bewildering array is usually divided into three groups, each determined by the way the plants grow.

One group, the crustose lichens, includes all the species that grow as thin, flat crusts on rocks and other surfaces. Usually no more than a few inches in diameter, many of them are dull green while others are brilliant yellows, oranges, and reds.

The foliose lichens look more or less like leaves that have been carelessly pasted down and are loose at the edges. Rock tripe, a typical example, resembles leathery brownish leaves with ruffled edges.

The third group is called fruticose lichens, from the Latin word for "shrub." Some of these, such as reindeer moss, grow on the ground in upright branching tufts. Others, such as the beard lichens, hang like tassels from the limbs of trees. Some of the hanging types are nine feet long.

How long do lichens live?
The longevity of lichens varies, depending on the species and many other factors. In temperate regions, a full-grown lichen is likely to be as much as 50 years old. But specimens of some rock-encrusting types in the Arctic may be up to 4,500 years old.

Long life spans and slow growth rates often go together, and this is certainly true of the lichens. The fastest-growing types expand by less than half an inch per year, and the crustlike types grow even slower. Some of the Arctic species need hundreds of years to grow a single inch. These incredibly slow growth rates are no doubt linked to the harsh environments in which the lichens live.

Are any lichens useful?
Lichens, like every living thing, have a role in the general scheme of nature. They not only help form soil from solid rock but also serve as food for animals from reindeer to snails and tiny insects.

Man, too, has found many special uses for lichens. People from the ancient Greeks to 19th-century European peasants relied on lichen extracts to treat a wide variety of ailments. Although most of these remedies were in fact worthless, modern researchers have found a useful antibiotic in certain kinds of lichens.

Another traditional lichen product is dyes, including scarlets, purples, blues, browns, and yellows. Scottish craftsmen still use lichen dyes to color their famous Harris tweeds. Lichens are also the source of litmus, the dye used in chemical tests for acidity.

Although most lichens are inedible, the leaflike species called Iceland moss yields a starchy food that poor people used to eat. Reindeer moss and rock tripe have also served as emergency rations. And some scholars believe the manna that sustained the ancient Israelites in the wilderness was a type of lichen still eaten by desert tribes.

The Many Life-styles of Lichens

From tundra to tropics, the pioneering lichens live in all sorts of places. Reindeer moss lives mainly in soil; beard lichen hangs from the branches of coniferous trees. Lung lichen and cracked shield lichen both cling to tree trunks. Dog lichen prefers moist sandy soil, while the three species shown at the bottom are most at home in dry sunny places such as sandy soil or on old pieces of wood.

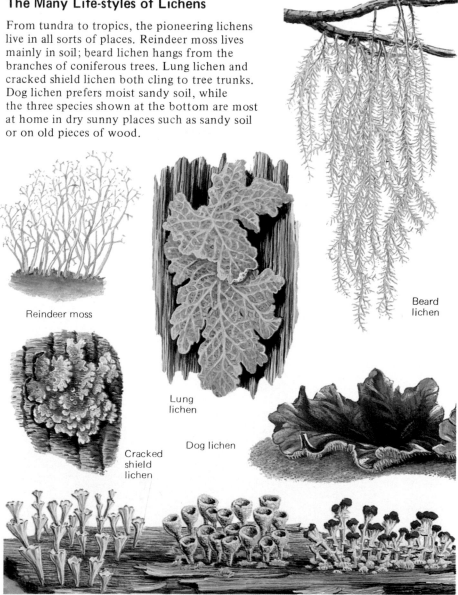

Reindeer moss

Beard lichen

Lung lichen

Cracked shield lichen

Dog lichen

Ladder lichen

Pyxie cups

British soldiers

The Diminutive Mosses

What are mosses?

Among the most primitive of all land-dwelling plants, mosses made their first appearance on earth more than 350 million years ago—long before the days of the dinosaurs. They are members of a group of plants called bryophytes, which also includes the less familiar liverworts and hornworts.

Mosses generally are small, standing no more than a few inches high or creeping flat across the ground and other surfaces. Unlike the more advanced land plants, most mosses lack any specialized tissue for transporting food or water from one part of the plant to another. Because they have no such "plumbing" system, they are not considered to have true roots, stems, or leaves. The "roots" of a moss, for example, serve only to hold it in place, not to bring water and nutrients up from the ground; the whole surface of the plant absorbs these vital substances. And the "leaves," except at their midribs, are usually only a single cell thick.

Nor do mosses produce any flowers or seeds. Instead they are generally topped by grainlike little spore capsules on long slender stalks. The spores germinate into plants that produce eggs and sperm. The fertilized eggs, in turn, give rise to a new generation of spore-producing plants. And so the cycle continues.

Where do mosses grow?

Although they may seem delicate and fragile, mosses are actually quite tough and hardy. Various kinds can be found from the shores of the Arctic Ocean through the tropics to parts of Antarctica. Some manage to survive in deserts and on sunbaked rocks, while others live in bogs and streams. But most mosses prefer damp, shaded locations in temperate climates. In forests they frequently form thick cushiony mats that completely cover rotting logs and the woodland floor.

Some of the mosses require specialized living conditions. Certain species grow only on acid soil, others only on alkaline. Still others, the so-called copper mosses, live only in the vicinity of copper and furnish valuable clues to the presence of ore deposits.

Another specialized type, luminous moss, is restricted to caves, recesses under the roots of trees, and similar dimly lit places. Equipped with cells shaped like tiny lenses, it focuses what little light there is on its food-making chlorophyll granules. In the near-darkness of the places where it grows, luminous moss seems to glow with a golden-green light. It really shines by reflected light, not its own.

Is it true that moss grows only on the north side of trees?

Folklore tells of many a person, lost in the woods, who found his way to safety by using moss as a kind of natural compass indicating north. And in fact, moss does tend to grow more luxuriantly on the north side of tree trunks, for that is usually the shadier, moister side. But other factors, such as the presence or absence of nearby trees, also influence the growth of moss, and it can be found on any and all sides of trees. So while the moss on tree trunks frequently gives a clue to general direction, it is a far from foolproof "compass."

Can mosses endure drought?

Although mosses are moisture-loving plants, most kinds can survive long severe dry spells. For one thing, they can store large quantities of water in their cells and draw on this reserve during the first few days or weeks of drought. Then, when this water is almost gone, they simply go dormant.

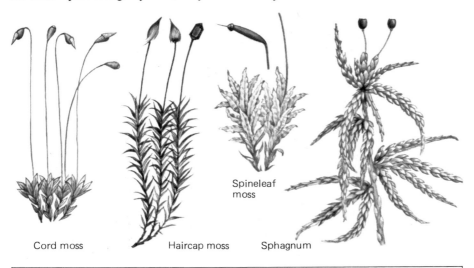

Cord moss   Haircap moss   Spineleaf moss   Sphagnum

How do mosses reproduce?

The two-stage life cycle of a moss plant begins with a spore that spills from the spore capsule of a parent plant. The spore germinates into a branching green thread, and buds along its length sprout into new moss plants. In many species some of these grow into male, sperm-producing plants, others into female, egg-producing plants. When they are mature, a sperm cell from a male plant swims through a film of dew or other moisture to a nearby female plant and fertilizes an egg cell. The fertilized egg then grows into a spore-producing plant—a slender stalk topped by a spore capsule—that remains attached to the parent plant. When spores are released from the capsule, the two-stage cycle begins again.

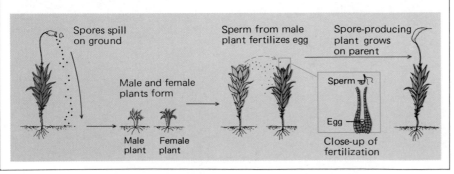

Spores spill on ground

Male and female plants form

Male plant   Female plant

Sperm from male plant fertilizes egg

Spore-producing plant grows on parent

Sperm

Egg

Close-up of fertilization

Their leaves curl up, so that no remaining moisture evaporates. The whole plant shrivels, turns brown, and looks completely dead. But the spark of life remains. As soon as the rains return, the plants become green and fresh again, almost overnight, and resume their vital processes.

When is a moss not a moss?
Down through the ages, many a plant has come to be called a moss even though it is not related to mosses at all. Irish moss, for example, is an edible alga that grows in leathery tufts along northern seacoasts, and so-called sea moss is another seaweed. Iceland moss is a kind of lichen that was once made into a type of bread. Reindeer moss, another lichen, is a mainstay in the diets of reindeer and caribou in far northern lands. And club mosses, a whole group of plants that often look mossy indeed, are actually only very

distantly related to mosses. But the least mosslike of all in the family tree of plants is Spanish moss, which hangs in grayish festoons from trees in the southeastern United States. Though its blossoms are minute and seldom noticed, it is in fact a flowering plant of the pineapple family.

Are mosses useful to man?
Mosses play an important role in forming soil in which other plants can take root. These low-growing plants protect bare soil from erosion, and when they decay they too turn into components of soil.

But for the most part, mosses have seldom been of great importance to people. Some kinds have traditionally been used for stuffing mattresses. Just as many birds line their nests with moss, so in Lapland, mothers use it to line their infants' cradles. In North America, pioneers employed moss to

chink the cracks in their log cabins. And in Japan, gardens are sometimes planted with nothing but mosses.

Today, however, the only mosses with widespread commercial value are the many kinds of sphagnum, or peat moss. Most gardeners are well acquainted with sphagnum. Because it retains moisture so well (sphagnum can absorb 20 times its own weight in water), mail-order nurseries frequently pack it around the roots of plants before shipment. The shredded plants are also dug into garden soil to improve its texture.

Among the mosses that thrive in water, sphagnum can fill in entire ponds and transform them into bogs. In time the sphagnum in bogs is compressed into peat. When cut into slabs and dried, peat makes a good fuel that burns with some smoke. It was once widely used in northern Europe and is still a valued energy source in Ireland.

Sphagnum, the characteristic moss of northern bogs, can soak up as much as 20 times its own dry weight in water.

Club Mosses and Horsetails

How do club mosses differ from true mosses?

The creeping evergreen woodland plants commonly known as ground pine and running cedar are familiar examples of club mosses. Although they are neither conifers nor mosses, some do indeed resemble miniature pines and cedars, and others are decidedly mosslike in appearance.

But unlike true mosses, club mosses and their relatives—spike mosses, quillworts, and horsetails—all have true leaves, stems, and roots. The leaves often are narrow, scalelike, and densely packed around the stems, giving many species their mossy look.

And unlike the true mosses and other simpler plants, club mosses and their kin are equipped with special water-conducting tissues—a vascular, or circulatory, system. Well-developed bundles of tubelike cells transport water and nutrients from the roots to the leaves; similar sets of cells distribute food throughout the plants.

Do all club mosses creep across the ground?

In temperate climates club mosses are primarily low-growing plants of moist, shaded woodlands. Typically, branching stems spread across the ground, sending up leafy stalks all along their length. Colonies of the plants sometimes cover sizable areas.

But the majority of club mosses live in the tropics and subtropics, where many of them have adopted a different life-style. Instead of sprawling on the ground, they cling to the trunks and limbs of trees, their roots anchored in debris that has collected in crevices and crannies.

The closely related spike mosses, also mainly tropical, are more varied. Some look mossy, others resemble miniature ferns; some creep, some stand erect, and others form filmy mats. One species grown as an ornamental is called resurrection plant. When dry, its stems curl up into a tight ball; when moistened, they unfurl as if by magic.

What are the clubs on club mosses?

The upright stems of many club mosses are topped with slender little clublike structures that account for the plants' common name. On some

The ground pines are not pines but club mosses that spread by means of horizontal stems creeping across the ground. The upright branches are 4 to 10 inches high.

Ground pine

species they are branched like delicate little candelabra. The clubs, known as strobili, are actually spore-bearing structures. They are made up of small overlapping scales, each concealing a tiny spore case. (In species without strobili, the spore cases are scattered along the stems.)

When the spores are ripe, they are released and blown about by the wind. But the spores of some species of ground pine sometimes do not escape to fulfill their natural role in reproduction. The highly flammable golden "dust," known as vegetable sulfur, is collected for medical purposes and also for use in manufacturing fireworks.

Do the spores sprout into new plants?

The club mosses we see on the forest floor do not grow directly from spores. When the spores germinate, each one develops into a diminutive plant, called a prothallus, that looks nothing like the parent plant. In most tropical species, the prothalli are so small that

they are rarely noticed—just little green specks that grow on the ground.

The prothalli of cool-climate species are larger, sometimes as big as grapes. But they too go unnoticed, for they usually develop underground. Some are shaped like gnarled little carrots; others are disklike or irregularly lobed. They get their nourishment from fungi that live embedded within the prothallus.

At maturity, sex organs develop on the prothallus, some producing male reproductive cells, others female cells. Fertilization takes place when a male cell, or sperm, swims through a film of water and unites with a female cell, or egg. The fertilized egg then develops into a green spore-producing plant.

In most tropical species, all this happens within a matter of months. Temperate-region kinds develop more slowly. Frequently two or three years pass before the spores even germinate. Then 10 years or more may elapse while the prothallus matures, leading its hidden life underfoot.

What are horsetails?

Some two dozen or so species of the strange and simple plants called horsetails thrive in waste places around much of the globe. Most are less than 3 feet tall, although one vinelike horsetail of the American tropics occasionally reaches heights of 30 feet.

In some species, whorls of slender green side branches grow from the joints, or nodes, along the delicately fluted main stem, producing a fancied resemblance to a horse's tail. In most, the stems are hollow except at the joints, where they are ringed by tiny, scalelike leaves. (Photosynthesis takes place in the plants' green stems.)

Many of the horsetails have conelike spore-producing structures at the tips of the stems. Others send up special spore-producing shoots that die back after the spores are shed. The spores, like those of the club mosses, germinate into inconspicuous prothalli, which then produce the familiar spore-bearing plants.

Why are some horsetails called scouring rushes?

The stems of many horsetails have a gritty feel, the result of silica deposits in some of their cells. (Silica is the hard, glassy mineral of which quartz and sand grains are composed.) In one species, an unbranched type that grows in moist places, so much silica is present that the plant has earned the name scouring rush. In the days before chemical cleansers were invented, these plants were used for scouring pots and pans and scrubbing wooden floors. A few craftsmen still rely on horsetails when a gentle fine sanding is required, as in the making of wooden musical instruments. And the "rushes" continue to serve as an ingredient in a few abrasive powders. Except for these incidental uses, however, horsetails have few practical applications today.

Are fossil forms valuable?

During the Carboniferous period, more than 300 million years ago, forests flourished on this planet. The climate was warm and moist, and vast wetlands were covered with trees—the forebears of present-day horsetails, ferns, and club mosses.

Some of the long-extinct horsetails

were some 50 feet tall. The ancestors of today's lowly club mosses were even bigger, with trunks up to 100 feet tall and 3 feet in diameter. Their spore-bearing cones were up to a foot long, and some had leaves more than three feet long.

The Carboniferous forests were odd places indeed. There were no flowers, no birds, no mammals. Fish splashed occasionally in the shallow water, giant salamanderlike amphibians sprawled along the shores, and huge insects lurked in the damp debris. But for the most part, the forests were eerily silent, monotonously green.

Yet without them, life on earth would be far different from what it is today. The remains of those lush, long-gone forests accumulated in thick layers of organic matter. Subsequently buried beneath younger sedimentary rocks, they were compressed into tremendous deposits of coal.

Some of the fossil ancestors of modern horsetails grew like trees up to 50 feet high. Field horsetail (below) rarely exceeds 2½ feet in height. Its spore cases are borne on separate shoots that wither after the spores are shed.

Field horsetail

Fabulous Ferns

Are ferns very common?

To many people, ferns are familiar only as house and garden plants, and as the sprays of greenery that florists include with bunches of cut flowers. Or they may be acquainted with one or two lacy-leaved types that grow in damp, dark woodlands.

In fact, ferns are a widespread group of plants including some 10,000 species. They are most abundant in warm, moist tropical regions, but some range northward into the tundra, others grow in dry rocky places, and a few even live in water. They range in size from kinds so small that they resemble carpets of moss to others that are as tall as trees.

How do ferns grow?

Although ferns are among the many plants that lack flowers, they do possess true leaves, stems, and roots. The stems usually go unnoticed, however, since they generally trail underground. The visible part of the plant consists only of leaves, or fronds, rising at intervals from the underground stem. When the leaves first appear, their tips are tightly coiled like watch springs. Then they gradually unfurl as the leaves elongate. The tender young shoots are called fiddleheads, and those of certain species are sometimes eaten as vegetables.

In cool climates the leaves of most ferns die back in autumn and are replaced by new growth the following spring. In warmer regions, many species grow as epiphytes attached to the trunks and branches of trees and remain green all the year round.

What are the dots on fern fronds?

Many a plant lover has been alarmed at the discovery of small dark spots on the undersides of the leaves of a favorite fern. Far from being the result of some disease or insect pest, however, the spots are actually clusters of spore sacs. In some species, the spots, called sori, are bare; in others, each is covered by a little flap of tissue. Depending on the type of fern, the sori may be round, curved, long and slender, or take a variety of other shapes.

Although the dotlike clusters of spore sacs are typical, in many species the spore sacs are arranged differently. In some cases, spores are produced only on special fertile fronds that look nothing like normal leaves. Or spore sacs may be restricted to just a few leaflets on each frond. On interrupted ferns, for example, the green leaflets on certain fronds are "interrupted" partway down the central stalk by a cluster of twisted, brownish spore-producing leaflets.

How do ferns reproduce?

Whatever the arrangement of a fern's spore sacs, their ultimate fate is the same: when the spores are mature, the sacs burst open and scatter the dust-like granules to the wind. Those that land in favorable places germinate into small, flat, usually heart-shaped plants called prothalli. Most are less than half an inch long.

Like those of club mosses and horsetails, fern prothalli produce male and female sex cells—sperms and eggs. When they are mature, the sperms unite with the eggs. And from each fertilized egg a new spore-producing fern plant grows.

Ferns also multiply by other means. New clusters of leaves may rise from the spreading underground stems, and in this way large colonies may be produced. Some ferns produce tiny bulb-like growths on the undersides of their leaflets. At maturity, the bulblets fall off and grow into new plants. And the walking fern gets its name from its habit of producing new plantlets at the tips of its lance-shaped leaves; the leaves arch down and touch the soil, permitting the plantlets to take root and so "walk" away.

Can any ferns float?

Among the least fernlike of ferns are the several kinds that live in water. Some—the water clovers, with their shamrock-shaped fronds—grow rooted in the mud in shallow ponds. Others have dispensed with roots entirely and simply float on the surface of lakes, ponds, and sluggish streams.

One of the floaters, water spangles, has rows of nearly circular leaves, and carpets the water with masses of greenery. Others, the mosquito ferns, have even tinier leaves. But they form such dense mats that they have sometimes been used for mosquito control. The leaves grow so profusely that mosquito larvae are unable to break

In the common polypody, the undersides of the leathery, evergreen leaves, or fronds, are dotted with dark, conspicuous clusters of spore sacs.

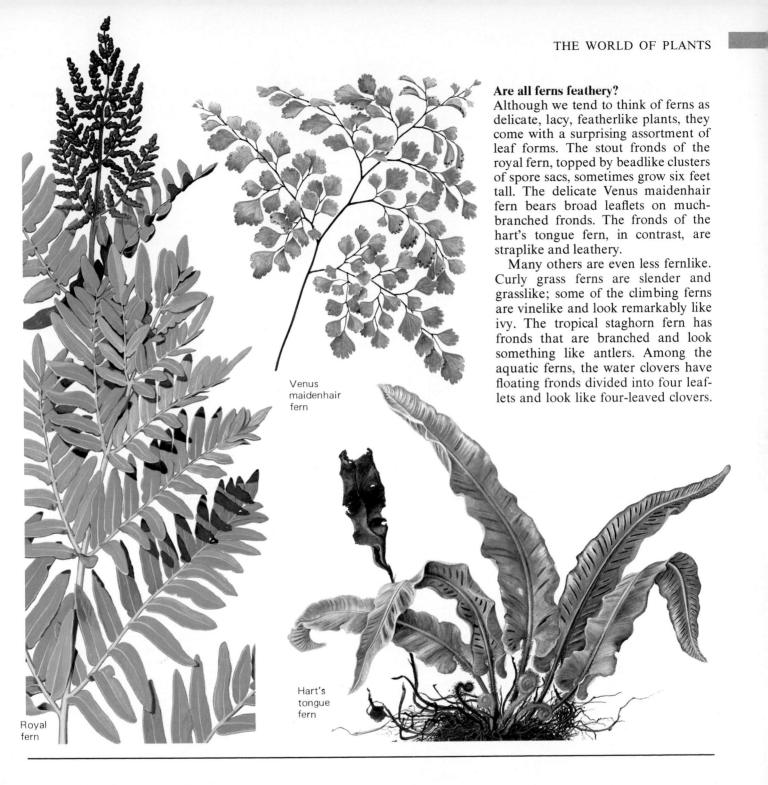

Venus
maidenhair
fern

Hart's
tongue
fern

Royal
fern

Are all ferns feathery?

Although we tend to think of ferns as delicate, lacy, featherlike plants, they come with a surprising assortment of leaf forms. The stout fronds of the royal fern, topped by beadlike clusters of spore sacs, sometimes grow six feet tall. The delicate Venus maidenhair fern bears broad leaflets on much-branched fronds. The fronds of the hart's tongue fern, in contrast, are straplike and leathery.

Many others are even less fernlike. Curly grass ferns are slender and grasslike; some of the climbing ferns are vinelike and look remarkably like ivy. The tropical staghorn fern has fronds that are branched and look something like antlers. Among the aquatic ferns, the water clovers have floating fronds divided into four leaflets and look like four-leaved clovers.

through to the surface to breathe. The plants are even considered pests in some areas; the choking growths of the midget ferns are sometimes so dense that they interfere with boating, fishing, and other uses of waterways.

What are tree ferns?

Ferns as big as trees were common in the swampy forests that flourished in the Carboniferous period, more than 300 million years ago. Some had trunks several feet in diameter and as much as 100 feet tall. Topped by crowns of lacy fronds up to 15 feet long, they looked much like present-day palms. Their dead remains, along with those of the giant club mosses and horsetails that lived in the same forests, were compacted into the coal deposits we mine today.

Similar-looking tree ferns still survive in many parts of the world, especially in warm, moist tropical rain forests. Some of them reach heights of 70 feet or more, and are the largest of all living ferns. In places like the Hawaiian Islands, these giants sometimes grow in solid stands. Damp and dim, and dappled by light filtering down through the canopy of feathery fronds, these groves of tree ferns are magical places; they have the power to transport visitors back through time, recalling those long-gone forests that we know only through their fossils.

Some Plants Have Seeds

What is the difference between spores and seeds?

The development of seeds was a great leap forward in the history of plant life. Like spores, their sole function is to produce new generations of plants and so ensure the survival of the species. But seeds accomplish this task much more efficiently.

Spores leave a great deal to chance. Each one consists of a single cell that contains little or no food reserve—just a genetic "blueprint" for a new plant. And it can germinate and survive only if it happens to land in a place where conditions are just right for growth. As a result, mosses, ferns, and similar plants must produce spores by the millions to overcome the great odds against their survival.

Seeds, on the other hand, give the next generation a head start in the struggle to mature into new plants. Each one consists of many cells within a protective covering. The cells, moreover, are usually organized into an entire embryonic plant, one that is complete with rudimentary root, stem, and leaves. And in almost all cases, the seeds contain a food supply that supports the emerging plantlet until the seedling can exist on its own. Seeds are so much more efficient than spores, in fact, that the plants that bear them have become the dominant vegetation on earth.

Two Kinds of Seed Plants

Firs, pines, and other conifers, as well as a few other obscure plant groups, produce seeds in cones and other specialized structures. The commonest seed-producers, however, are the enormously varied flowering plants.

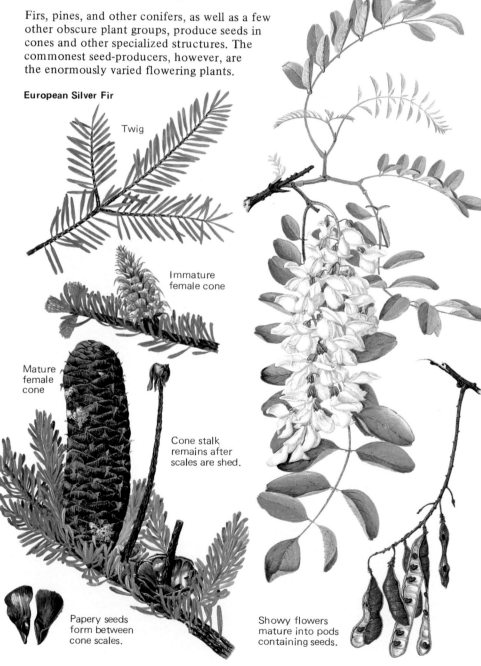

Black Locust

European Silver Fir

Twig

Immature female cone

Mature female cone

Cone stalk remains after scales are shed.

Papery seeds form between cone scales.

Showy flowers mature into pods containing seeds.

Which sorts of plants produce seeds?

The flowering plants are the commonest, most widespread seed-producers on earth today. Everyone is familiar with apple trees that blossom in the spring and then, in the fall, yield plump fruits containing "packets" of seeds—the pips—in their cores.

On some flowering plants, the flowers, unlike the showy ones of apple blossoms, orchids, and the like, have been greatly modified or reduced in size, so that they do not look like flowers at all. But the basic parts are there in one form or another. Corn, for instance, is a flowering plant. The tassels are clusters of pollen-producing male flowers. The ears are formed from spikes of female flowers, and each kernel of corn is, of course, a seed.

Certain nonflowering plants also produce seeds. The best-known examples are the conifers, such as pines, spruces, and firs. Instead of developing from flowers, their seeds are formed between the scales of their woody cones. One kind, the pinyon pine of the American Southwest, produces the large edible seeds commonly known as pinyon nuts. The *pignoli* nuts of southern Europe are the large, tasty seeds of another kind of pine.

How many kinds of seed plants are there?

In all, more than 235,000 species of plants produce seeds. The vast majority are the flowering plants. The nonflowering seed-producers—conifers and a few other types of plants—number only about 800 species.

Botanists have special names for these two types of plants. The nonflowering seed plants are called gymnosperms, from the Greek for "naked seeds." This does not mean that the seeds lack protective coverings. The term refers to the fact that the ovules, which develop into seeds, are borne unprotected on the bare surfaces of the cone scales or similar structures.

The flowering plants are called angiosperms, meaning "enclosed seeds." Their ovules develop into seeds within the protective enclosure of a structure called the ovary, usually located at the center of the flower. The ovary—sometimes along with other parts of the flower as well—matures into a fruit encasing the seeds. Following pollination, the ovary of the edible plum, for example, develops into a

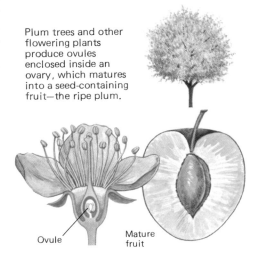

Plum trees and other flowering plants produce ovules enclosed inside an ovary, which matures into a seed-containing fruit—the ripe plum.

Ovule   Mature fruit

fleshy fruit with a seed inside the stony pit at its center. Other flowering plants bear their seeds in fruits as varied as acorns and apples, blueberries and beans, chestnuts and cranberries.

What are some differences between flowering plants and conifers?

The flowering plants are a varied lot indeed. In addition to producing flowers and fruits, they differ from the conifers in many ways. All the conifers, for instance, are woody plants that grow as trees or shrubs; some flowering plants are trees, but the majority are low-growing plants with soft, juicy stems. (The tree types have a much more complex and efficient circulatory system than any of the conifers.) Instead of evergreen needles or scalelike leaves, the flowering plants bear broad leaves in a multitude of shapes and sizes. While the conifers all live for many years, vast numbers of flowering plants can complete their life cycles in a single growing season. All the coni-

fers, moreover, are pollinated by the wind. The flowering plants have a more sophisticated system; most rely on insects or other animals to transfer pollen to the female flower parts.

The flowering plants, in short, have become supremely adaptable. From lawn grasses and garden flowers to trees more than 100 feet tall, they include far more species than any other plant group on earth today.

How are ginkgo trees related to conifers?

Pines, hemlocks, and other conifers are the most successful and widespread of the plants that produce seeds without flowers. They are found from the equator to the frigid Far North, from windswept mountaintops to humid lowlands and semideserts. All are woody plants that have needlelike or scalelike leaves, and in all but a few cases they are evergreen. True to their name, almost all the conifers produce their seeds in woody cones.

The gymnosperms that are not conifers are an odd assortment of plants with little in common except for their mode of reproduction. The best known is the ginkgo, which is widely planted as an ornamental tree. Growing to 70 feet, it is covered with fan-shaped leaves that are shed in autumn.

The cycads, another type of gymnosperm, are a primitive group of plants that grow mainly in tropical areas. Most resemble palm trees, with large, leathery, fernlike leaves. Some species produce enormous seed cones. On one kind the cones grow more than 3 feet long and weigh almost 90 pounds.

Finally there are the Gnetales, another mainly tropical group of plants, which is so small and obscure that it does not even have a common name. The strangest member of this strange group is the welwitschia, found only in a few desert areas of southern Africa.

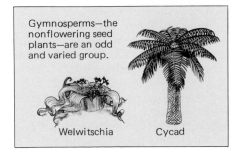

Gymnosperms—the nonflowering seed plants—are an odd and varied group.

Welwitschia   Cycad

From the top of its huge stumplike stem sprout two long, straplike permanent leaves—the only leaves it produces in its entire lifetime of a century or more. Because the leaves fray from the tips into a ring of twisted segments, the welwitschia has sometimes been described as the "desert octopus."

Why is the ginkgo sometimes called a living fossil?

The stately ginkgo, or maidenhair tree, has an ancient lineage. As much as 150 million years ago, its ancestors flourished in forests throughout the Northern Hemisphere. And the fossil remains of some are almost identical to the living trees.

Ginkgo

The ginkgo has fan-shaped leaves and fleshy, foul-smelling fruits.

In fact it is only by chance that the ginkgo itself has survived to this day. It nearly perished during the Ice Age, but was narrowly saved from extinction when Chinese monks began to plant it in their temple gardens about the 10th century A.D.

As a result, the hardy, pollution-resistant trees are now a familiar sight on big-city streets in many parts of the world. Only male trees are used for street plantings, however; the cherry-sized fruits produced by the female trees have fleshy coverings that make a foul-smelling mess when they fall.

Conifers: Trees for All Seasons

Do all conifers have cones?

Everyone is familiar with pinecones of one sort or another—often shaped like miniature copies of the trees themselves. Spruces, firs, and most other conifers, as their name implies, also produce cones. In fact, they have two types of cones: the less familiar male cones, producing pollen; and the female cones, bearing seeds between their typically woody scales.

Mature female cones come in many shapes and sizes. Those of some of the hemlocks are only half an inch long, but the sugar pine of the western United States has cones up to two feet

Common juniper, a widespread shrubby species, produces cones that resemble small, fleshy berries.

long. And some do not even look like cones. On junipers the scales remain fleshy, and the cones resemble berries. (The "berries" of the common juniper are used for flavoring gin.)

A few kinds of conifers do not produce any cones at all. The nutlike seeds of yews are nearly enclosed by succulent, bright red "cups." The California nutmeg (a very different species from the spice-producing tree, which is not a conifer) and the plum yews of the Far East also bear nutlike seeds with fleshy, fruitlike coverings.

Northern white cedar

The leaves are tiny overlapping scales.

Are needles all alike?

Just as the cones of conifers differ from species to species, so their foliage is also distinctive and often supplies a clue to identification. The slender leaves of the pines are the most needlelike. (On the North American longleaf pine they are up to 18 inches long.) The short, stiff leaves of most spruces are also needlelike. But pine needles almost always grow in clusters of two to five; the leaves of spruces and most other conifers grow singly.

Slightly less needlelike are the broader leaves of firs, hemlocks, yews, and others. Some have sharp tips, others are blunt, but all are flattened from side to side. The leaves of the cedars, of most junipers, and of several other conifers are entirely different. They are tiny, overlapping scales that completely cover the twigs.

Are all conifers evergreen?

Like maples, oaks, and other broad-leaved trees, all the conifers shed their foliage periodically. But most conifers do not shed all their needles at the same time, and so they remain green all year round.

Conifers are not the only evergreens. Some broad-leaved trees and shrubs, such as hollies and rhododendrons, also retain green leaves throughout the year. Nor are all conifers evergreen. The larches turn a golden color in autumn, and all the needles soon fall off. The twigs remain bare through the winter, and new needles appear in spring.

The baldcypress, another kind of conifer, sheds not only its needles but also the slender branches on which the needles grow. Another leaf-dropping conifer is the dawn redwood. Once known only from fossils, the tree was believed extinct until living specimens were discovered in a remote area of China in the 1940's. The tree is now widely planted as an ornamental.

How long do conifers live?

All the conifers are woody trees and shrubs that survive for many years. Life spans of a century or even several centuries are not uncommon. But the reigning monarchs of the clan, found in western North America, have been on earth for thousands of years. Some of the redwoods are more than 2,000 years old, and many giant sequoias are well over 3,000.

The most ancient of all living trees, however, are bristlecone pines, found in scattered stands on the White Mountains in California. Growing near the timberline, some of these gnarled and twisted trees are more than 4,600 years old—approximately the same age as the Great Pyramid of Cheops in Egypt.

Which are the largest conifers?

The most massive of all living things are the giant sequoias of the western United States. The current record holder, the General Sherman tree, is located in Sequoia National Park in California. This giant is 275 feet tall; its trunk, some 32 feet in diameter, weighs an estimated 1,385 tons. Its seeds, in contrast, are so small that 8,000 of them may weigh no more than an ounce.

The world's tallest trees, the red-

Three Giant Conifers

Redwood

Giant sequoia

Douglas fir

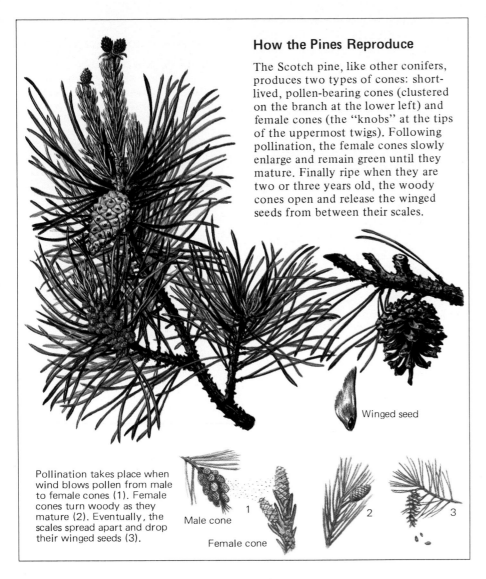

How the Pines Reproduce

The Scotch pine, like other conifers, produces two types of cones: short-lived, pollen-bearing cones (clustered on the branch at the lower left) and female cones (the "knobs" at the tips of the uppermost twigs). Following pollination, the female cones slowly enlarge and remain green until they mature. Finally ripe when they are two or three years old, the woody cones open and release the winged seeds from between their scales.

Winged seed

Pollination takes place when wind blows pollen from male to female cones (1). Female cones turn woody as they mature (2). Eventually, the scales spread apart and drop their winged seeds (3).

Male cone

Female cone

1

2

3

What are conifers used for?

No other trees can match the conifers in contributing to our way of life. They furnish some 75 percent of all the timber that is cut, and their uses range from building construction to furniture, fence posts, pencils, plywood, and veneers. The pulp for most paper comes from conifers, as does much of the cellulose used in the manufacture of such things as cellophane and rayon. Turpentine, resin, and various tars are among the many other products derived from conifers.

Because of their great commercial value, the trees are grown in scientifically managed forests and large-scale plantations in many parts of the world. The most widely planted pine in Australia, New Zealand, and other lands of the Southern Hemisphere is the Monterey pine, a native of coastal California. Transplanted to these distant lands, it flourishes as the world's fastest-growing timber tree.

Shortleaf pine, of the southeastern United States, is a valuable timber tree. It yields lumber for a variety of uses, it furnishes pulpwood for paper, and it is an important source of turpentine.

Western hemlock, of northwestern North America, supplies wood for flooring and pulp for paper, plastics, and rayon. Its bark is a source of the tannic acid used for tanning leather.

woods, are also native to California. Slimmer than the giant sequoias, these graceful conifers commonly grow to heights of 275 feet or more. The tallest on record towers more than 360 feet above the surface.

Another giant among the conifers is the Douglas fir of the western United States. Under ideal conditions, it sometimes reaches heights of 250 feet.

Where do conifers live?

Cool-climate regions are the favored haunts of most conifers. They thrive in the broad band of evergreen forest that spans northern Eurasia and North America. Farther south they find similar living conditions on mountain slopes, where they also form extensive forests.

Tolerant of poor sandy or rocky soils, some of the conifers do well in much warmer climates. There are large forests of pines in the southeastern United States, for example. Conifers are a familiar sight around the Mediterranean as well. The famed cedar of Lebanon, one of the Mediterranean species, has long since been heavily cut on its original range. But many of the same rocky hillsides have been reforested with North American pinyon pines.

The Southern Hemisphere also has its share of conifers. Some, such as the Norfolk Island pine and the closely related monkey puzzle tree, are grown elsewhere as ornamentals. The yew-like podocarps include the smallest of all conifers—New Zealand's pygmy pine, which produces cones when it is only three inches tall.

Our lives are also enriched by the sheer beauty of the conifers. The pines of Rome inspired Ottorino Respighi to write one of his best-loved symphonic works. Countless horticultural varieties of conifers have been developed for the enhancement of our landscapes. And the conifers account for the special qualities of some of the most famous forests in the world, from the dark beauty of the Black Forest in West Germany to the awesome grandeur of California's redwood groves.

The Flowering Plants

Why do plants have flowers?

Whether large or small, colorful or inconspicuous, all flowers have the same basic function: to produce seeds and so perpetuate the species. They perform this role so well that the flowering plants, or angiosperms, have become the most abundant and varied group of plants on earth today.

All the parts of a flower contribute to its success as a reproductive structure. Although there are many variations on the general theme, the "typical" flower consists of concentric rings of sepals, petals, and stamens, with one or more pistils at the center.

The sepals, generally green, enclose the bud and protect its contents until the flower opens. (All the sepals together form the calyx.) The petals (collectively called the corolla) are usually bright and colorful, serving as signals to attract insects and other pollinators. The stamens consist of threadlike stalks—the filaments—supporting saclike anthers, which produce the pollen.

The central pistil normally has three parts—stigma, style, and ovary. The stigma, often sticky or fuzzy, traps pollen grains that touch it. A tube from the pollen then grows down through the necklike style and fertilizes the egg cells, which are encased within the ovary. After fertilization, the ovary matures into a fruit that helps protect the seeds.

Do all flowers have the same parts?

From the simplicity of buttercups to the extravagant complexity of orchids, the forms of flowers are incredibly diverse. Depending on the species, there may be many or few of each of the basic parts, or some of them may have been lost entirely.

On some flowers, the sepals are colored and look exactly like petals. Sometimes the petals are ruffled or fringed, or they may be fused together to form tubes, bells, or other fanciful shapes. And many species have two different kinds of flowers—male, or staminate, flowers that have stamens but no pistils, and female, or pistillate, flowers that have pistils but no stamens. In some species both kinds of flowers are borne on the same plant; other species produce them on separate male and female plants.

This seemingly endless variety in form is one of the things that make flowers such a delight to study. But botanists have found that the variations are by no means random. The classification of plant families, in fact, is based mainly on differences in the arrangement of the floral parts.

Are flowering plants important?

The flowering plants are everywhere around us. Growing as trees, shrubs, vines, and soft-stemmed herbs, they have come to dominate most of the world's dry land. Many thrive in fresh water, and some even live in salt water near the margins of the sea.

These abundant, adaptable plants affect our lives in many ways. Growing wild, they are vital links in the web of life. They protect the soil from erosion and supply valuable timber. We cultivate many species as ornamentals or as windbreaks, and for shade. Flowering plants are the source of almost all the food that we eat—either directly, as grains, fruits, and vegetables, or indirectly as milk, meat, and eggs. They also yield medicines, spices, oils, and countless other useful products.

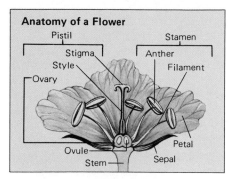

Anatomy of a Flower

Pistil — Stigma, Style, Ovary

Stamen — Anther, Filament

Ovule, Stem, Sepal, Petal

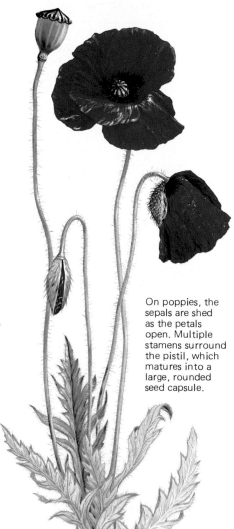

On poppies, the sepals are shed as the petals open. Multiple stamens surround the pistil, which matures into a large, rounded seed capsule.

When is a flower many flowers?

Some flowers grow singly, one to a stem; others, such as lilacs and lupines, grow in characteristic clusters called inflorescences. In some cases the clusters are so compact that people think of the whole mass as a single bloom. The "petals" of a poinsettia, for instance, are colorful bracts (modified leaves) surrounding a group of tiny flowers. The composite family has a different arrangement: on daisies each "petal" is a separate flower, and the eye at the center is dozens of individual florets. Arums such as jack-in-the-pulpit and calla lilies are even more deceptive; the "petal" is a spathe (a specialized bract) enclosing a rodlike, flower-studded spadix.

Dandelions are members of the composite family; each of the "petals" is actually an individual floret.

Red clover, of the pea family, has blooms that are in fact masses of florets resembling miniature sweet peas.

bages, are biennials. But we usually harvest them in their first year of growth, never giving them a chance to blossom and produce seeds.

The longest-lived are the perennials, which continue to flower and set seed year after year. Flowering trees and shrubs are woody perennials. Many soft-stemmed herbs are also perennials. Except in the tropics, every autumn their leaves and stems die back. But their roots and other storage structures remain dormant in the soil, ready to send up shoots at the onset of the next growing season.

How big can flowers be?
The largest of all blossoms are produced by *Rafflesia,* a parasitic plant that lives in Southeast Asia. Each of its

giant blooms is up to 3 feet in diameter and commonly weighs more than 10 pounds. Another giant of the plant world is *Puya raimondii,* a South American relative of the pineapple. Although its individual flowers are small, as many as 8,000 of them may be clustered in huge upright spikes some 35 feet high and 8 feet across.

At the opposite end of the scale is *Wolffia* (also known as watermeal or duckweed), the smallest of all flowering plants. Tiny specks of green that float on fresh water, the individual plants are a mere fiftieth of an inch across. Yet from time to time they bloom, producing male flowers, each consisting of a single minute stamen, and female flowers, each of which is nothing more than a tiny pistil.

Lords-and-ladies, a European arum, has a leaflike spathe surrounding a fleshy spadix that produces groups of tiny male and female flowers.

Spathe

Male flowers

Spadix

Female flowers

How long do flowering plants live?
The life expectancies of the flowering plants differ dramatically from species to species. A sunflower lives for less than a year, for example, but an oak may continue to grow for centuries.

The many plants that, like the sunflower, have their entire life cycle compressed into a single growing season are called annuals. They germinate, flower, set seed, and then die within a matter of days, weeks, or months.

Biennials are plants that live for two years. They grow and store food in their first season, remain dormant over the winter, and then flower and die in their second year. Many garden vegetables, such as carrots and cab-

Do all trees have flowers?
Except for the conifers and other gymnosperms, all the trees in the world are flowering plants. On some, such as magnolias, cherries, and horse chestnuts, the blossoms are large and

showy. On others, the flowers are inconspicuous and easily overlooked—so much so, in fact, that people are often more likely to notice the fruits than the flowers that produced them. The acorns on oaks, the winged seeds of maples, and the berries on hollies are all the products of flowering trees.

Some of the simplest flowers are borne on species pollinated by the wind. The European black poplar, like all poplars, for example, bears its blossoms in tassellike clusters called catkins. The male catkins are reddish; each "flower" is little more than a cluster of stamens. The female catkins, growing on separate trees, are greenish. The pistil of each female flower matures into a capsule that bursts open and releases cottony seeds.

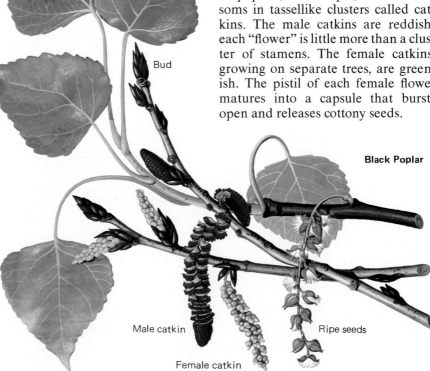

Bud

Black Poplar

Male catkin

Female catkin

Ripe seeds

The Miracle of Pollination

What is pollination?

In all of the plant kingdom, only the seed-bearing plants produce pollen. Pollination is the process of transferring these minute male reproductive units from the parts that produce them to the plants' female structures. The transfer is accomplished in several ways. Conifers and many flowering plants rely on the wind to carry their pollen to its destination. A few flowering plants are pollinated by splashing raindrops. But the majority depend on insects and other animals.

If seeds are to be produced, pollination must be followed by fertilization of the egg cells. The pollen of conifers adheres directly to the ovules, which contain the egg cells and are exposed on young female cones. In the flowering plants, the ovules are enclosed within the pistil. When a pollen grain lands on a receptive stigma, a pollen tube grows down through the style until it reaches an ovule. There it releases a sperm cell that fertilizes an egg cell, and the ovule eventually matures into a seed.

How does wind pollination work?

Plants that rely on the wind for pollination have no need for special lures to attract insects. Their flowers and cones are small and inconspicuous, and male and female organs are often on separate plants. On flowering species, long stamens hold the pollen-producing anthers out to every passing breeze; on many, such as oaks and birches, the male flowers are clustered in dangling catkins. The pistils of female flowers frequently have feathery stigmas, the better to entrap any passing pollen grains. The pollen itself is lightweight, buoyant, and able to travel long distances on the wind.

Despite these adaptations, wind pollination remains a hit-or-miss process. Plants that rely on it must produce enormous quantities of pollen to ensure that some hits the target. A single birch catkin, for example, releases about 5.5 million grains of pollen, and there may be hundreds of catkins on a single tree. During peak pollination periods, sidewalks and ponds are often covered with a visible film of pollen. These, too, are the times when hay fever sufferers endure the greatest discomfort from their allergic reactions to the windblown pollen of ragweed and several kinds of wind-pollinated trees.

How do plants attract pollinators?

Food is the reward that insects and other creatures receive in exchange for their services as pollinators. Some animals eat the pollen itself; others feed on the nectar secreted by special glands that are hidden deep within the blossom. Typically the insect or other visitor receives a dusting of pollen as it probes for food, then unwittingly transfers some of this pollen to the stigma of the next flower it visits.

Most flowers do a superb job of advertising their wares. Showy petals signal the presence of food and furnish convenient landing platforms. Patterns of lines and spots, called honey guides, lead insect visitors to the stores of nectar or pollen. Tiny flowers are often massed in clusters that make them more conspicuous and supply better footing. Scent is another powerful attractant, especially on night-blooming species that otherwise might be difficult to find.

Can plants play tricks on insects?

The flowering plants have developed many ways of ensuring pollination. Some devices are purely mechanical; the mere weight of an insect on a petal

One Way to Dust a Bee With Pollen

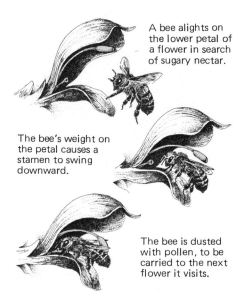

A bee alights on the lower petal of a flower in search of sugary nectar.

The bee's weight on the petal causes a stamen to swing downward.

The bee is dusted with pollen, to be carried to the next flower it visits.

may cause the stamens to tap it on the back and sprinkle it with pollen. Mountain laurel and Scotch broom have triggering mechanisms that cause the stamens to snap against visiting insects and dust them with pollen. On milkweeds, pollen is borne in paired sacs that resemble miniature saddlebags; hooked over the feet of a visiting butterfly, the sacs are carried to the stigma of the next floret.

Other plants have gone to even greater extremes of trickery. Some orchids lure male flies and wasps with scents that match the mating odors of their females. Other orchids look so much like the female insects that the males actually attempt to mate with them, pollinating the flowers in the process. Traps are another common device. On the arum lords-and-ladies, for one, insects are lured into a vaselike chamber and remain imprisoned there by downward-pointing hairs until pollination occurs.

What does pollen look like?

Generally yellow or orange, all pollen appears pretty much the same to the unaided eye. But viewed through a microscope, the minute, dustlike granules reveal an extraordinary diversity of forms, each unique to a particular species of flowering plant.

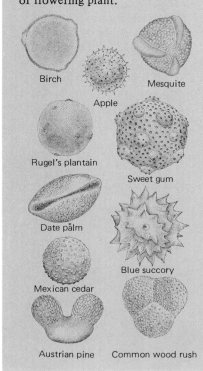

Birch

Mesquite

Apple

Rugel's plantain

Sweet gum

Date palm

Mexican cedar

Blue succory

Austrian pine

Common wood rush

Which are the major pollinators?

Insects, even more numerous than the flowering plants, are the pollinators par excellence. The best known and most important are honeybees, on which most of our fruit and vegetable crops depend. But a host of other insects also contribute their services. Beetles, bumblebees, wasps, flies, and butterflies are just a few of the many kinds of pollinating insects.

Birds play an important role, too, especially in the tropics. Picking up pollen as they probe for nectar, New World hummingbirds, Old World sunbirds, and many others contribute to the survival of the plants they visit.

Among the mammal pollinators are Australia's mouselike honey possums. Clambering up banksias and other trees to feed on nectar, they transfer pollen with their fur. Some of the tropical bats also specialize in diets of nectar and pollen. Bat-pollinated flowers tend to be large and sturdy, offering firm surfaces that the bats can cling to as they feed.

Are plants particular about their pollinators?

Many plants attract a variety of insect visitors, but others are more specific in their requirements for pollination. Honeysuckles, for example, are pollinated primarily by night-flying moths, the common red clover mainly by bumblebees. When red clover was introduced into Australia, where there are no native bumblebees, the plants failed to set seed until bumblebees too were imported.

Some plants have even more specialized insect partnerships. One orchid in Madagascar is pollinated by a single kind of hawkmoth, the only creature in the vicinity with mouthparts long enough to reach its deeply hidden supply of nectar. Figs rely on one type of tiny gall wasp, while the North American yuccas are completely dependent on insects called yucca moths for pollination. The female moth collects a ball of pollen from one blossom and then, after depositing a few eggs in the ovaries of another flower, presses the ball of pollen onto its stigma. The moth larvae feed on the developing yucca seeds, but they leave more than enough for the plant to reproduce.

Hovering in midair, a diminutive hummingbird receives a light dusting of pollen as it sips nectar from the dangling blossom of a fuchsia.

From Flower to Fruit

What's the difference between a fruit and a vegetable?

In everyday usage, apples, oranges, and the like are called fruits; vegetables include such edibles as carrots, asparagus, tomatoes, and corn. Botanists, however, are more precise in their terminology. They say that a fruit is the mature, seed-bearing ovary of a flowering plant, sometimes with other parts of the plant attached. Thus all the seed-containing vegetables—eggplants and tomatoes, for example—are actually fruits. So too are such unfruitlike fruits as milkweed pods and the winged keys of maples.

Many other vegetables are not true fruits but simply edible plant parts. Radishes and carrots are roots, lettuce and spinach are leaves, and broccoli and cauliflower are tightly clustered flower buds. Rhubarb, on the other hand, is commonly called a fruit but is not really a fruit in botanical terms; the rosy-red stalks are the edible stems of oversized leaves.

How does a flower become a fruit?

Only the flowering plants produce fruits. The process begins when pollen fertilizes an egg inside an ovule. While the ovule is developing into a seed, the ovary (the flower part that holds the ovule) goes through changes of its own. In some cases the ovary wall develops into three distinct layers—an outer exocarp, a middle mesocarp, and an inner layer called the endo-carp. All three layers together make up the pericarp.

The layers are most obvious in cherries, peaches, plums, and the other stone fruits, which are known as drupes. In a peach, for example, the thin fuzzy skin is the exocarp, the juicy flesh is the mesocarp, and the stony pit that encloses the seed is the endocarp.

Apples develop differently. In their case, the pericarp forms only the seed-containing core at the center of the fruit. The edible flesh is formed by the enlargement of the floral tube that originally surrounded the ovary. Apples, pears, quinces, and all the other core fruits are called pomes.

Are all fruits fleshy?

Only berries, pomes, drupes, and a few other kinds of fruits are moist and fleshy. Many more are dry, with woody or papery pericarps. The pods of peas and beans, for example, are called legumes. They are usually harvested and eaten while still green and moist, but if allowed to mature on the plants, they eventually dry out and split open to release their seeds. The long, slender pods of mustard plants are dry fruits of another type, known as siliques, while the winged fruits of maples and elms are samaras.

In the case of true nuts such as hazelnuts, the oily meat that we eat is the seed and the hard shell is the pericarp. The sunflower seeds that we feed to birds are yet another example of dry fruits, of a kind technically known as achenes. Birds crack open the tough outer covering—the pericarp—to get at the true seed inside.

Is the blueberry a true berry?

Berries, in botanical terms, include such seemingly diverse fruits as grapes and tomatoes, avocados and eggplants. All are alike in being simple fruits with entirely fleshy pericarps that enclose one or many seeds. The citrus fruits such as oranges are also a type of berry, distinguished by the possession of a leathery outer rind.

Blueberries, on the other hand, are classed as false berries. Although

berrylike at first glance, the mature fruits are formed from other floral parts in addition to the ovary wall. Look closely and you can see remnants of the sepals still attached to the tips of each fruit. Watermelons, cucumbers, and squashes are false berries of another type, called pepos. Like blueberries, they have at least part of the outer skin derived from the floral tube that encased the ovary.

Blackberries and raspberries, in contrast, are not berries at all. Each segment of a ripe raspberry is actually a separate fruit that developed from one of many individual ovaries in a single flower. All grew together as they matured to form what botanists call an aggregate fruit. The individual segments are drupelets, comparable in structure to miniature cherries.

Why do fruits change color as they ripen?

The fleshy fruits undergo many complex changes as they approach maturity. Color is the most obvious. Tomatoes turn from green to red, plums become red or blue, and so on. Flesh that was hard and sour, bitter, or otherwise unpalatable frequently be-

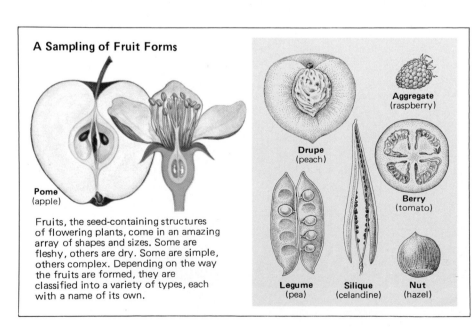

A Sampling of Fruit Forms

Pome (apple)

Fruits, the seed-containing structures of flowering plants, come in an amazing array of shapes and sizes. Some are fleshy, others are dry. Some are simple, others complex. Depending on the way the fruits are formed, they are classified into a variety of types, each with a name of its own.

Drupe (peach)

Aggregate (raspberry)

Berry (tomato)

Legume (pea)

Silique (celandine)

Nut (hazel)

comes soft, juicy, sweet, and fragrant.

All these changes are related to the fruit's role in reproduction. The green color of immature fruit helps keep it hidden among the plant's foliage. Unpleasant flavors also deter animals from eating it before the seeds are fully matured.

Ripe fruit, colorful and succulent, on the other hand, offers an irresistible invitation to hungry birds and other creatures. When they eat the fruits, small seeds pass unharmed through their digestive tracts and later are deposited far from the parent plant, along with a dose of natural fertilizer. If the seeds are too big to swallow, animals are likely to drag the fruit off and eat it elsewhere, leaving the seeds to sprout when conditions are favorable.

Are nuts a special kind of fruit?

Acorns are the most familiar examples of the kinds of fruits that are classed as nuts. Each consists of a single seed enclosed in a hard, seamless shell. In most cases the nut is partly covered by modified leaves called bracts. The cups of acorns are made up of many scalelike bracts. On hazelnuts, another true nut, the bracts are thin and leaflike.

Many of the things commonly called nuts are really the edible parts of various other kinds of fruits. Peanuts are the seeds of pealike plants; they grow underground in legumelike pods. Coconuts are the inner parts of large dry drupes; their thick, fibrous husks, removed

before shipment, are comparable to the flesh of a peach. Almonds are the seeds of another stone fruit. Brazil nuts, cashews, and pistachios are other familiar examples of "nuts" that are not true nuts.

Acorns

Hazelnuts

How do strawberries develop?

Succulent strawberries, studded with tiny seeds, are among the most deceptive of fruits. Like blackberries and raspberries, they are aggregate fruits, each one formed from a single flower that contained many separate ovaries. But in the case of strawberries, each ovary matures into a dry, one-seeded achene. Thus the "seeds" are actually individual dry fruits. The juicy red edible part of the strawberry is the much enlarged, fleshy receptacle, the tip of the flower stem to which the ovaries were attached.

Pineapples are even stranger, for they form, not from one, but from a whole cluster of flowers that fuse into a single fleshy mass. The bulk of the pineapple's flesh is formed from the matured sepals and ovaries of the many individual flowers; the tough inner core develops from the upright stalk on which the flowers grew.

How big can fruits become?

The ovary that gives rise to a fruit often enlarges enormously as it matures. A full-grown tomato, for instance, may be as much as 100,000 times the size of the ovary from which it developed, and an avocado 300,000 times its original size.

Not surprisingly, some of the largest fruits are produced by cultivated plants, which are of course selectively bred. Some varieties of watermelon yield fruits that weigh 50 pounds, and 100-pound pumpkins are a common sight at country fairs. But the record may well be held by a squash raised by an Indiana family in 1977; it weighed 513 pounds.

It is difficult to say which fruit is the smallest, since many plants produce tiny dry fruits that we ordinarily think of as seeds. Each "seed" of a daisy, dandelion, or buttercup, for example, is a complete fruit in and of itself.

All Sorts of Seeds

Are all seeds the same inside?

When corn sprouts, only a single leaf lifts out of the kernel. For corn belongs to the group of plants called monocots; *mono* means "one," and *cot* refers to the cotyledon, or seed leaf, that forms inside the seed. Beans are dicots: in contrast to corn, a sprouting bean seed unfolds two seed leaves.

This division into monocots and dicots is the major one among flowering plants, and it shows up not only in the seeds and seedlings but in the plants themselves. Monocots have narrow leaves with smooth edges and parallel veins. Their flower parts are in threes (or multiples of three), and the conducting, or vascular, tissues—visible if you look at the cut end of a stem—are scattered throughout the stem. The most important group of monocots is the grass family, which includes corn, wheat, rice, oats, and other cereal grains as well as lawn and pasture grasses. Orchids, lilies, palms, and bananas are also monocots.

A flowering plant that is not a monocot is a dicot. There are many more dicots than monocots, and their leaves are much more varied, ranging from simple flat blades to compound leaves divided into many leaflets. The edges of the leaves may be smooth, toothed, deeply lobed, or otherwise divided. The flower parts of dicots are generally in fours or fives, and the vascular tissues are in rings that encircle the center of the stem.

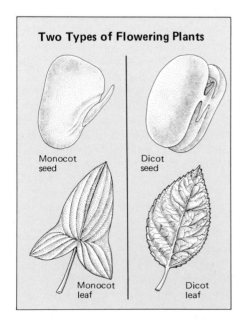

Two Types of Flowering Plants

Monocot seed

Dicot seed

Monocot leaf

Dicot leaf

Which seeds are giants and which are dwarfs?

You can't tell how big a plant will grow by looking at its seeds. Nor is the actual height of a plant much of a clue to the size of its seeds. A pea, for example, is the seed of a rather humble plant—yet it is far larger than that of the redwood, the world's tallest tree.

The largest seed of all is the coco-de-mer, the impressive product of a palm that grows on the Seychelles Islands, in the Indian Ocean. Weighing 40 pounds or more, the huge double-lobed coco-de-mer can measure 18 inches long and more than 8 inches

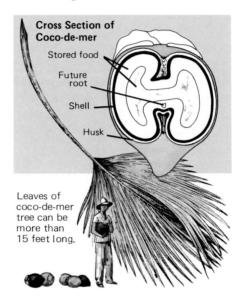

Cross Section of Coco-de-mer

Stored food

Future root

Shell

Husk

Leaves of coco-de-mer tree can be more than 15 feet long.

thick. The smallest are the seeds of a witchweed plant native to Asia, which measure less than a thousandth of an inch long. Orchids, too, have very small seeds, some so lightweight that there are 30 million to the ounce.

Why do plants produce seeds?

Seeds are more than a way for plants to perpetuate themselves, more than a way for plants to "sit out" such hostile conditions as cold and drought. Seeds are also the means by which plants travel—mostly for short distances but sometimes for hundreds or even thousands of miles. Seeds that sprout near their parent plants have to compete with them for light, water, and nutrients. By moving away, they improve their chances for growth.

The force that most frequently propels seeds from place to place is the wind. Specially equipped for wind-

powered flight, the seeds of dandelions and thistles have hairlike tufts or plumes that catch the wind; maple and elm seeds have wings serving as propellers or sails. Picked up by the slightest breeze, the tiniest seeds—orchid seeds, for example—travel as dust in the air. Tumbleweeds are perhaps the most spectacular wind travelers. Once their seeds have developed,

Wind-borne Seeds

Maple   Clematis   Dandelion

Seeds Spread by Animals

Avens   Blackberry   Mistletoe

Seeds Spread in Other Ways

Wild geranium   Water lily   Poppy

the round plant balls break off at ground level and roll across the landscape, scattering the seeds as they tumble along.

Water also helps fruits and seeds to travel about. Heavy rains wash them short distances; floods carry them for many miles. Some seeds transported by water have special "equipment" that helps them travel—the spongy tissues of the coconut and the water lily fruit, for example.

Do animals spread seeds?

Though plants cannot move from one place to another, their seeds may hitchhike on animals that can. Some fruits and seeds, such as those of sticktights and avens, are equipped with hooks or barbs that cling to feathers and fur; they may ride along for miles before they fall off. Wading birds pick up quantities of seeds in the muddy shallows of lakes, ponds, and streams, carrying them on their feet to new locations. Squirrels, woodpeckers, jays, and other animals hide fruits and seeds, sometimes in places ideal for the plants to sprout. Seeds swallowed by animals may pass through

How do seeds sprout?

Before sprouting, seeds must absorb water. The amount they need differs from species to species, some doing best when soaked and others needing only a slight film. Water softens the seed coat, enabling the plant embryo inside to push out and activating enzymes so that the growth process resumes. Oxygen is necessary too, for the rate of respiration increases greatly at the time of germination. Some seeds require light for germination; others will not sprout once they have been exposed to light. If a castor bean is exposed to the right conditions, it transforms into a seedling as shown in the drawings at right.

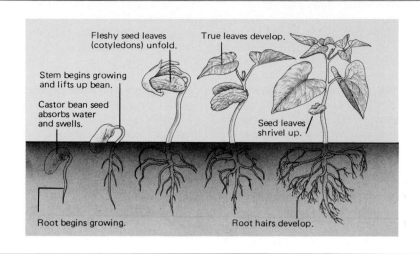

Fleshy seed leaves (cotyledons) unfold.

True leaves develop.

Stem begins growing and lifts up bean.

Castor bean seed absorbs water and swells.

Seed leaves shrivel up.

Root begins growing.

Root hairs develop.

the digestive system intact, then sprout where they are deposited. Mistletoe seeds, for example, stick onto the branches where they drop, germinating high above the ground. Today, of course, people are the greatest seed distributors. We transport the seeds of edible and ornamental plants deliberately, and many a weed seed has been relocated unintentionally.

Explosive Seeds

When witch hazel seeds are mature, the seed case contracts, propelling them outward with great force.

Aren't some seeds "shot" away from the parent plant?

As fruits ripen, physical tension may build up inside them, and eventually the seeds inside are forcibly expelled. If you touch the seedpod of a touch-me-not (also called *Impatiens* and jewelweed), it rips apart and throws its seeds a distance of six feet or more. Some violet pods also "explode" to release their seeds; squirting cucumbers send out their seeds in a fluid jet.

Do seeds ever sprout on the plant itself?

A squash called the chayote, native to the American tropics and subtropics, looks somewhat like a bleached green pepper. If left on the vine to develop (human hands may pick it first), it sprouts a new vine from its tip. And so, when the squash falls to the ground, it

is already a growing plant, having only to put out roots to establish itself in the soil.

This growth of the seed while still attached to its parent is called viviparity—the same term (it means "live birth") used for animals whose young develop inside the mother's body. Viviparity occurs in a number of other plants. Perhaps the best-known example is the red mangrove, a saltwater tree that forms dense thickets in warm coastal regions around the world. The roots and stem (but not the leaves) develop from the seed while it is still attached to the tree.

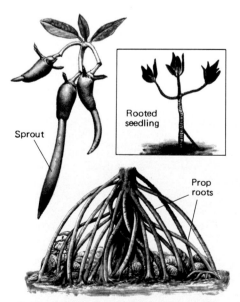

Sprout

Rooted seedling

Prop roots

Seeds of the red mangrove germinate while still attached to the plant. Once the seedling is anchored in the muddy bottom, an extensive system of prop roots develops.

How long does a seed stay alive?

Some seeds remain alive, or viable, for only a few days after they mature; unless they germinate right away, they will not germinate at all. Others, particularly those growing in cool climates, need a period of dormancy before they can sprout—a fact that enables them to survive during the cold winter months.

But if kept cool and dry, most seeds remain viable for more than from one season to the next, delaying their germination until conditions become suitable. The longevity record belongs to an Arctic lupine. Seeds stored in a northern lemming burrow some 10,000 years ago and then frozen were washed out recently in a mining operation. Most amazingly, some of them sprouted and actually grew into healthy plants.

What do people use seeds for?

Seeds are the most important food on earth. All of the grains (wheat, corn, rice, rye, among others) plus beans, peas, peanuts, soybeans, and other legumes are seeds eaten directly by man. Seed-eating poultry and livestock convert plant material into animal protein, which eventually becomes human food. Seeds supply vegetable oils used in cooking and in soaps, paints, lubricants, and other products. Some seeds add spice to our lives—among them, mustard, pepper, and caraway. We also consume seeds when we drink coffee, cocoa, and certain alcoholic beverages.

New Plants From Old

Can plants reproduce without seeds?

The ability to reproduce is essential to each and every form of life. Surprisingly, although flowering plants reproduce by seeds, many of them also propagate themselves in an entirely different way: through the process known as vegetative reproduction. The process has many variations, but generally it involves the growth of small roots and shoots on existing plants. Over time, these little growths develop into independent new plants. In similar fashion, many plants that reproduce by spores instead of seeds (ferns, for example) can reproduce vegetatively too.

Which parts of a plant produce new plants from old?

Those of us with green thumbs delight in the ease with which one house plant can be turned into two. Cut off a leafy section of a coleus or a grape ivy plant, put it in water until roots appear; then plant it and watch it grow.

But if one used just a leaf, rather than leaf *plus* stem, in following this process, nothing would happen. For only specific parts of a plant can be used to produce new plants from old, and which parts they are differ from one type of plant to another. This holds true not just for cultivated plants but for wild ones as well.

In some cases, it is the stem of a wild plant that will root itself, much as cuttings are rooted from houseplants. When the creeping stems of wild strawberry touch the soil, for example, roots and buds often develop at the point of contact and eventually grow into a new plant. In many species, it is the plant's underground parts that perform the task. Bracken fern multiplies—often far too efficiently, from a gardener's point of view—by sending out a rhizome, or underground stem, that creeps along and sends up new ferns en route.

Sometimes just a single leaf can give rise to a new plant. An African violet

Various kinds of cacti, such as these bristling opuntias, have "ears" that break off easily and develop into new plants. Cacti also reproduce by means of flowers and fruits.

can be made to do this (by planting one of its leaves); and kalanchoe (the fleshy air plant) develops little plantlets along the edges of its leaves. The walking fern sends out slender fronds (the fern equivalent of a leaf) that produce new plants where they touch the soil. In time, the connecting frond withers and the new fern becomes independent of its parent.

Why can't animals do the same?

Unlike most animals, plants can grow throughout their lives, and just a small portion of one of them can develop into an entirely new individual. Plants can do this because they have some tissue that is perpetually young.

Called meristem (from the Greek word for "to divide") and capable of infinitely dividing into new cells, this tissue generally occurs at the tips of roots and shoots and at the junction of leaf and stem. (It may occur elsewhere as well.) When you cut off the leafy tip of a grape ivy plant, both the cutting

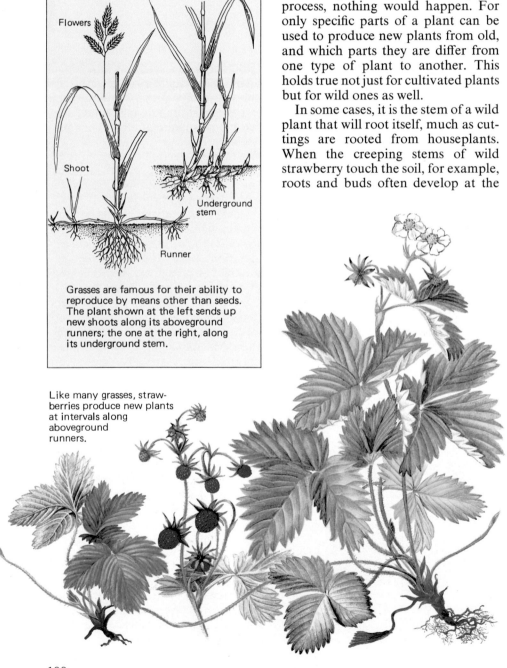

How Grasses Reproduce

Flowers

Shoot

Underground stem

Runner

Grasses are famous for their ability to reproduce by means other than seeds. The plant shown at the left sends up new shoots along its aboveground runners; the one at the right, along its underground stem.

Like many grasses, strawberries produce new plants at intervals along aboveground runners.

and the plant from which the cutting was made still contain meristematic tissue; and so both have the capacity for growth.

Even more remarkable is that cells from one part of a plant—say, a leaf—can turn into cells of a different part, such as roots. Though a leaf by itself has no perpetually young tissue, its cells are able to change their functions and take on new roles. This is why just a single leaf from an African violet can, under the right conditions, develop into a new beauty blossoming on its own.

How do bulbs make new plants?

Lilies are among the plants that grow from underground bulbs. On their own, these bulbs will produce smaller ones, which can be removed from the mother bulb and rooted. You can also break off some of the scales on the bulb and plant them separately; eventually new small bulbs will develop at

Tiger lilies have dark little bulbils at the bases of their leaves. The bulbils can be removed and planted like seeds.

the base of each scale. Certain lilies also produce little bulbs above ground, at the bases of the leaves.

Why is vegetative reproduction so important?

One major difference between reproducing by seeds and vegetative reproduction is the rate at which new plants are brought into being. Many lilies, for instance, do not flower until some seven seasons after the seeds have germinated; the same varieties propagated from offshoots of their bulbs may flower in just one or two.

Not surprisingly, this rapid growth rate is one reason why plant growers—commercial and amateur alike —use vegetative reproduction techniques. But even more important is the uniform quality of fruits and vegetables propagated vegetatively, in contrast to the unpredictable variations that arise among offspring produced by seed. Growers propagate roses, carnations, tulips, and numerous other flowers and ornamental plants vegetatively, and most of the apples, oranges, and other common fruits cultivated in temperate regions are handled the seedless way. In fact, several popular varieties cannot be propagated any other way—among them, cultivated bananas, navel oranges, and seedless grapes.

What is a clone?

In recent years a great deal of public attention has been focused on the subject of clones—exact duplicates of a living organism, generated under laboratory conditions from a sample of its tissue. The keenest interest, of course, has centered on the possibility of cloning various types of animals— and, conceivably, even human beings.

To those familiar with plants, there is really nothing new about this idea. In the language of horticulture, a clone consists of all the individual plants descended by vegetative reproduction from a single ancestor. When you grow a leaf cutting from an African violet or a "spider" from a spider plant, you are in effect cloning it. The genetic heritage of the new plant is the same as that of the old.

Under the right circumstances, a clone can grow to include millions of individual plants and perpetuate itself

over a very long period of time. Clones that have been in existence for a century or more are not uncommon, and certain varieties of grapes cultivated in Europe have actually been produced this way for more than 2,000 years. And every time you eat an apple of a particular variety—McIntosh, for example—you are eating part of one single clone.

Potatoes are actually swollen underground stems, and their eyes have buds that can produce new shoots. Potatoes sold in stores are often chemically treated to inhibit bud growth.

Why does a potato have eyes?

One common way in which plants reproduce without seeds is by sending out stems that grow underground. At first glance, these underground stems, called rhizomes, might look more like roots, but they are indeed stems, complete with buds and even leaves. Growing longer each year, the rhizomes produce roots that reach downward at certain points, and shoots that push up and grow into new plants.

In some plants, the tip of the rhizome develops into a tuber, an enlarged part used by the plant to store food. The best-known example of a tuber, the ordinary white potato, bears a number of small whitish indentations on its surface, which are often referred to as eyes. Each eye is actually a miniature leaf with several little buds. If you cut up the potato so that every piece has an eye, each will normally grow roots and stems.

Sweet potatoes are not technically tubers but true fleshy roots. (Though the distinction may seem trivial, it is not; the internal structure is very different.) Sweet potatoes have no eyes, but they too can produce shoots and roots under the right conditions.

Broad-leaved Trees

Do broad-leaved trees have anything in common besides broad leaves?
Trees are divided into two great groups: the broad-leaved species and the conifers. The palms form a third group, but because they are more like grasses than trees, they are not considered broad-leaved even though they have the broadest leaves of all.

As the name implies, broadleaf trees generally have leaves that are wide and flat; conifers have slender, needlelike leaves or tiny scalelike ones. Another difference is that the broadleaf trees have true flowers, while the conifers have cones. And most conifers produce resin, while few of the broadleaf trees do.

What is the difference between a broad-leaved and a deciduous tree?
"Deciduous" comes from the Latin for "falling down." Because such broad-leaved trees as maples and elms shed their leaves in autumn (as do most other broad-leaved trees in temperate regions), "deciduous" has become a synonym for "broadleaf." The conifers have been dubbed the evergreens because they stay green all year.

But this distinction, like so many in the botanical world, is imperfect. Many broad-leaved trees and shrubs, such as rhododendrons and live oaks, retain their foliage throughout the year. And larches, baldcypresses, and dawn redwoods—conifers all—shed their needles with the onset of cold.

Another distinction often made is between hardwoods (the broad-leaved trees) and softwoods (the conifers). In fact, there are many broadleaf trees, such as willows, with very soft wood, and some conifers, such as slash pine, whose wood is very hard.

Why do trees lose their leaves?
As the days grow short and cold weather approaches in autumn, deciduous trees shed their leaves en masse—a phenomenon so striking and regular that it gives its name to the entire fall season.

The principal reason for this annual shedding of foliage is not to stay warm but to conserve moisture. Broad leaves, with their large surface areas, give off huge quantities of moisture through evaporation. In winter, the freezing of the soil cuts off the supply of moisture to the roots, and water conservation becomes very important; for if broad-leaved trees retained their leaves, they might become fatally dried out.

Conifers, with their needlelike leaves, have a much smaller surface area and can survive without dropping their leaves. Keeping their leaves actually helps them survive: they can use them in photosynthesis on mild winter days.

What tells trees when to shed their leaves?
The seasonal shedding of leaves is governed by a combination of shortening hours of daylight and cooling temperatures. When the balance of daylight, darkness, and cold reaches a critical point, the typical broad-leaved tree responds by creating a barrier of special corky cells where the leaf stem joins the twig. Sealed off from the tree's circulatory system, the leaf slowly dies. Its attachment weakens, and it drops from the tree. (Dead leaves tend to stay longer on beeches and some oaks—a habit that often annoys homeowners because it means

How do leaves change color?

In autumn the leaves of a maple become sealed off from the rest of the tree. Deprived of nutrients and moisture, the leaves cannot form new chlorophyll. The old chlorophyll breaks down, and the green color disappears.

As the chlorophyll fades, the yellow and orange pigments—present all along but masked by the chlorophyll—begin to dominate. Reds and purples may also appear, produced during a series of chemical reactions involving sugars that build up in the leaf as nights grow cold.

The green pigment chlorophyll dominates the summer leaf.

In fall, chlorophyll production ceases, and other pigments appear.

The leaf's attachment to the twig weakens, and the leaf falls.

an extra leaf-raking chore in spring.) Another layer of specialized cells seals the tiny wound left when the leaf drops, protecting the tree against loss of moisture and the entry of fungi.

In parts of the world where there are strongly marked wet and dry seasons instead of freezing winters, trees drop their leaves at the beginning of the dry season. In this case it is the reduction in soil moisture that triggers the shedding of the leaves, and the trees leaf out again when the rains come.

What do buds do?

Long before its leaves fall, a tree is creating buds for the following year's growth. Buds usually form in the angles between the twigs and the leaf-stalks, and also at the ends of the twigs. Where they are and what they look like—sometimes an important clue in identifying a tree—can be seen especially clearly after the leaves fall.

Buds are usually covered with scales to protect them from drying out. Packed inside the scales are the cells that will develop into the next season's growth. Most buds produce leaves and shoots; some become flowers. All tend to be diminutive in fall and winter. In spring, responding to the lengthening days, flowing sap, and rising temperatures, they swell and burst.

Hormones produced by the tree control bud growth. A tree branch tends to grow in the direction toward which the bud points. If you are trying to shape a fruit or ornamental tree by pruning, you should prune just beyond a bud that points in the direction in which you want the branch to grow. Keep in mind, however, that shoots grow toward the light, and that the shade created by other branches may change the direction of growth.

Which tree flowers don't look like flowers?

Each spring, masses of catkins dangle from the spreading branches of oak trees, looking much like yellowish caterpillars. They are in fact composed of dozens of male flowers without petals or sepals, all crammed together for economy of space. Their job is to produce clouds of pollen, which the wind will carry to the inconspicuous female flowers that nestle in the joints of the leaf stems.

How to Tell One Tree From Another

Regardless of season, broad-leaved trees offer a variety of clues to what they are. The paintings here show the importance of overall shape, leaves, and fruits in identifying species. Other clues useful in identification are furnished by the tree's buds, twigs, and bark.

Black locust

Horse chestnut

Crab apple

European beech

European white birch

Many common trees in the Northern Hemisphere are wind-pollinated—among them, poplars, birches, walnuts, and elms. Petals would interfere with the wind's work of picking up and depositing pollen; nor are petals needed to attract insect pollinators.

Maples are in a halfway state. They have separate male and female flowers (which are sometimes on separate trees), and the pollen-producing male flowers typically grow in loose, catkin-like clusters, like those of many wind-pollinated trees. Their flowers are very small—another wind-pollinated trait. But some species of maples have tiny petals on their flowers, and still others produce fragrance and nectar to attract insect pollinators.

Are certain trees male and others female?

For pollination to occur, any plant, from the tiniest wildflower to the tallest tree, must have pollen-producing stamens and egg-containing pistils. Certain species have stamens and pistils in separate flowers (that is, some flowers are male and others female), and sometimes the separate flowers are on completely different plants. Persimmon trees are either male or female; so are the hollies, which is why at least two of them have to be planted for the attractive berries to be produced. Unlike animals, male and female plants look the same overall, and only their flowers and fruits can tell you which sex they are.

Leaves Are Food Factories

What is photosynthesis?

The basic raw materials utilized by plants in manufacturing food are amazingly simple—only water and carbon dioxide. The water is taken in by the roots, and carbon dioxide by pores in the leaves. From these ingredients the plant makes a simple sugar that is converted (by the plant itself or by plant-eating animals) into more complex sugars, starches, proteins, and fats. All life depends on this "putting together by light," which is what the word *photosynthesis* means. The light—solar energy—is captured by the plant and transformed into chemical energy contained in the sugar.

The whole process takes a fraction of a second. When light strikes the leaf, some of its energy is absorbed by the green pigment chlorophyll. Chlorophyll plays the key role in photosynthesis, acting as a catalyst to bring about the chemical reactions. In photosynthesis, water is split apart into hydrogen and oxygen. The oxygen is given off as a by-product, and the hydrogen is combined chemically with the carbon dioxide to produce the simple sugar, which dissolves easily in water and is transported throughout the plant.

Which parts of a plant can manufacture food?

Leaves are the most specialized and efficient food factories in plants. But many plants, most notably the cacti, have leaves greatly reduced in size or none at all. These plants manufacture food in their stems. Seedlings, green twigs, leafstalks, green stems—wherever there is chlorophyll, photosynthesis can occur. Although green is the reliable indication that chlorophyll is present, leaves that are not green may contain ample amounts too; in these leaves other pigments may be masking the chlorophyll.

Do all leaves on a particular plant get the same amount of light?

When trees, shrubs, and other tall plants are viewed from the side, the arrangement of their branches and leaves may appear rather random. But if viewed directly from above, these plants—even the tallest trees—form a surface of nearly solid green, with almost every leaf getting the same amount of exposure to the sun. Without light, of course, leaves cannot function, and those that develop in positions where they are completely deprived of light are eventually shed. This self-pruning is a constant process in trees and may include sizable branches as well as leaves.

In some plants changes take place constantly inside the leaves: the chloroplasts—the structures containing the chlorophyll—move about in the cells. To get more light, they turn so their flat sides are toward the source; if the light is too intense, they may turn edgewise or move deeper into the cell.

Can photosynthesis occur without plants?

The green chlorophyll in plants is not all the same. Rather, there are at least 10 types, each playing a distinct role in the food-manufacturing process. Once scientists understand precisely how each type functions, it should be possible to develop artificial photosynthetic membranes that would be even more efficient than those in plants. These membranes would use solar energy, carbon dioxide, and water to produce synthetic food.

Do plants give off a dangerous gas at night?

Years ago, when the chemistry of plants was just beginning to be understood, people genuinely worried that plants were the Jekyll-and-Hyde of nature. Though people recognized that healthy, growing plants give off oxygen during the day, they were concerned about the carbon dioxide given off at night—so concerned, in fact, that plants were kept out of bedrooms, especially if a person was ill.

Like every living thing, plants breathe, taking in oxygen and giving off carbon dioxide. Plant respiration is continuous night and day, but during the day the carbon dioxide produced is used in photosynthesis. When the food manufacturing stops at night, the carbon dioxide is released into the air—but definitely not in dangerous (or even harmful) amounts.

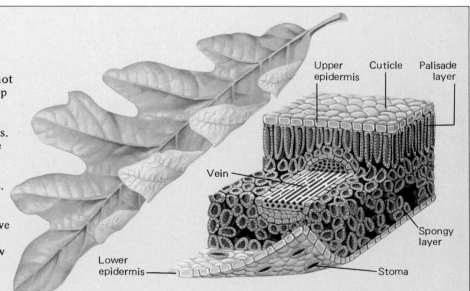

Leaves on a Broad-leaved Tree

When a section of leaf is examined under a microscope, it becomes apparent that the leaf's structure is not the same throughout. On the very top is a thin waterproof coat, known as the cuticle, overlying a layer of transparent cells, called the epidermis. Beneath the epidermis is the palisade layer, with tall, tightly packed cells that contain numerous chlorophyll-containing bodies called chloroplasts. Beneath the palisade layer are the loosely arranged cells of the spongy layer, where water and gases can move freely. Numerous openings, called stomata, in the lower epidermis allow gases and water to move in and out.

Upper epidermis

Cuticle

Palisade layer

Vein

Spongy layer

Lower epidermis

Stoma

What controls the amount of gases going into and out of the leaf?

Gases move into and out of the leaf through the special pores known as stomata. Although the pores are generally on the underside, some species also have pores on the upper surface; in water lilies and other plants with floating leaves, all the pores are topside, facing into the air.

The pore has a bean-shaped guard cell on each side. Because the guard cells contain chlorophyll, they can manufacture sugar in the presence of light. During the daytime, the sugar they make causes water to be drawn into the cells. As water is drawn in, the thinner-walled sides—those away from the opening—bow out, much like balloons filling with air. This pulls on the stiffer walls and opens the pore. The oxygen released as a by-product of photosynthesis escapes, and carbon dioxide moves in. When photosynthesis comes to a halt at night, the sugar level decreases in the guard cells, water moves out, and the pores close.

Are all leaves basically the same?

From the slender lance of a willow to the wide, deeply scalloped foliage of maples and oaks, leaves come in an incredible variety of sizes and shapes. But regardless of what they look like, leaves have the same basic function: to manufacture food.

The veins on a leaf are its distribution system, carrying water and nutrients throughout the leaf and taking away food. On a broad-leaved tree the veins form a branching network and keep the leaf spread out. In some species, such as elms, the veins angle away from a central main vein. In others, including the maples, several main veins spring from a junction at the base of the leaf.

Another difference among leaves is in the way they are attached to the twig. Leaves may grow opposite one another (as on a maple) or in an alternate pattern. In addition, some broad-leaved trees have compound leaves—that is, a number of smaller leaflets are attached to a central stem, which is itself attached to the twig. The leaflets may extend off the sides like seats off the aisle of a bus (ash is one example), or they may spread out fanwise, as in the horse chestnut.

Different Plants, Different Leaves

Within each species leaves grow in a characteristic pattern. The basic "choices" are shown below. Leaves can also be classified into one of two general groups—simple or compound—and then by shape and structure.

Leaf Arrangements

Alternate

Whorled

Opposite

Basal rosette

Simple Leaves

Parallel veins (lilies, grasses)

Fingerlike veins (maples, sycamores)

Featherlike veins (beeches, chestnuts)

Lobed leaves (oaks, tulip trees)

Toothed leaves (mulberries, elms)

Compound Leaves

Featherlike pattern

Fanlike pattern

Needles on a Conifer

Though the needles on a conifer function in the same way as the leaves on a broadleaf tree, their structure is quite different. For example, there is far less difference from top to bottom, and the outside is harder and waxier, cutting down on water loss. Evergreens retain their leaves all year, and photosynthesis can continue throughout.

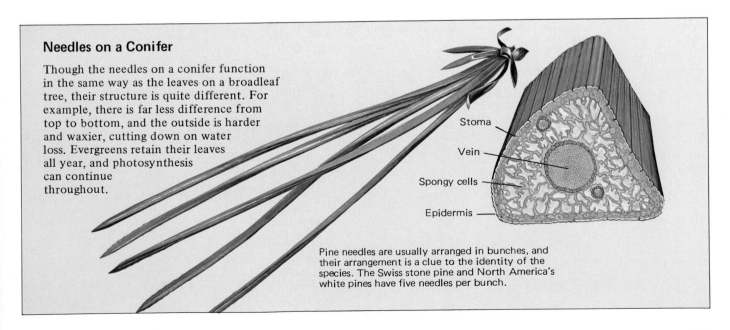

Stoma

Vein

Spongy cells

Epidermis

Pine needles are usually arranged in bunches, and their arrangement is a clue to the identity of the species. The Swiss stone pine and North America's white pines have five needles per bunch.

How Trees Grow

If you drive a nail into a sapling, how quickly will it rise?

A tree increases in height by building upward, with new cells forming atop the old. A branch that grows out of a trunk at four or five feet above the ground will remain at that height; it will not change its position with relation to the ground. Similarly, a nail driven into a trunk or a fence fastened to a tree will remain at precisely the same height. As the tree increases in circumference, it can grow around such objects, however, and over a period of years, they may become completely embedded in the trunk.

How can a hollow tree continue to grow?

It's not uncommon to find an actively growing tree with hollow, burned-out, or diseased insides. No matter what its age, a tree's growth occurs in a single layer of green cells that form the cambium, located under the bark and phloem. (The cambium layer can be seen most easily in a young woody twig, by gently scraping away the tender bark

with a knife or with your thumbnail.) Regardless of what has happened to the interior, a tree can live and grow as long as this cambium remains intact. Eventually it may topple, of course, for it requires the layers of wood inside as a support.

What does bark do for a tree?

When a ground fire creeps through a stand of giant sequoia trees, their thick, insulating bark protects them from injury. Indeed, the thick bark of many species gives some protection against fire. But this is only one of the ways bark protects trees.

The bark of many conifers exudes resin when it is wounded, sealing out fungi and other organisms of disease. Tough, hard bark may help to bar parasitic plants from gaining a toehold. And bark protects the tender living layer of the tree from sun and wind.

One of the most remarkable barks of all belongs to the eucalyptus family of trees and shrubs. Eucalypt bark oozes a protective gum when wounded, and is highly fire-resistant. If fire destroys

the leaves, the tree often can produce a new set of leaves from dormant buds hidden beneath the bark.

How does a tree heal itself?

Ice, windstorms, fires, axes—trees get wounds from many sources. At first the wound bleeds, leaking sap from the opening. In most cases, a callus soon begins to form at the edges of the wound, stopping the fluids from oozing. Cells from the cambium (the growth tissue) around the edges then begin to multiply, growing inward.

If the break is small, this inward growth may continue until the cells meet in the center. If the edges are jagged, as when a big limb breaks in a windstorm, the opening may never become completely closed. Large wounds form permanent scars on the surface, and all damage is recorded in the annual growth rings.

Why does water rise in a tree?

Hundreds of feet may separate a tree's roots from the leaves in its crown. Though the tree has no heart or com-

A Tree Trunk and Its Many Layers

A tree trunk is intricately designed to serve as a system of pipelines and as a support. The thinnest layer, the cambium, is perhaps the most important, for it produces all the others. When cambium cells divide, the ones toward the outside become phloem, which carries sugar throughout the tree. Old phloem becomes bark. The cells toward the interior become the water pipeline, called xylem. Young xylem cells form the sapwood and older ones, the heartwood.

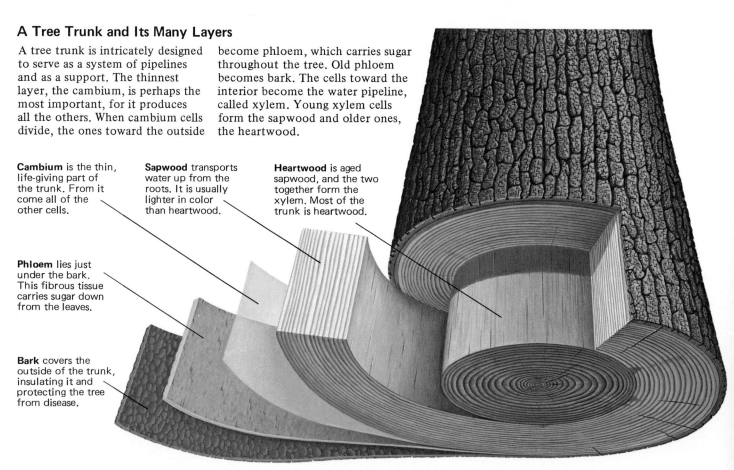

Cambium is the thin, life-giving part of the trunk. From it come all of the other cells.

Sapwood transports water up from the roots. It is usually lighter in color than heartwood.

Heartwood is aged sapwood, and the two together form the xylem. Most of the trunk is heartwood.

Phloem lies just under the bark. This fibrous tissue carries sugar down from the leaves.

Bark covers the outside of the trunk, insulating it and protecting the tree from disease.

parable pump, great volumes of water make this trip—in some trees, at the phenomenal speed of more than 100 feet per hour.

The journey begins at the roots, where water moves into the root hairs by osmosis. Cells in the root hairs contain dissolved sugars and salts, and the water moves into them from the surrounding soil to equalize the pressure. This increased water pressure in the

A Tree's Two Pipelines

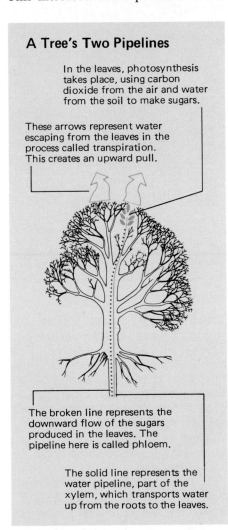

In the leaves, photosynthesis takes place, using carbon dioxide from the air and water from the soil to make sugars.

These arrows represent water escaping from the leaves in the process called transpiration. This creates an upward pull.

The broken line represents the downward flow of the sugars produced in the leaves. The pipeline here is called phloem.

The solid line represents the water pipeline, part of the xylem, which transports water up from the roots to the leaves.

root hairs forces water upward, cell by cell, through the roots and trunk toward the top of the tree.

This draw is made much stronger by still another force. During a growing season, a tree may pass literally tons of water into the atmosphere from its leaves. Some of the water taken in—only about 1 percent—is needed for photosynthesis; the remainder is lost by transpiration. In essence, this creates a partial vacuum that is

The Story in the Rings

Trees in temperate climates grow most rapidly in spring, when the thin-walled cells that form the water-conducting system (xylem) expand rapidly. In a cut trunk, these cells make up the light-colored rings known as spring wood. In late summer, growth slows, and the cells become smaller and thicker-walled. Called summer wood, these cells show as darker rings in the trunk. So each ring, a light and a dark, thus represents half of a growing season, and a tree's age can be determined by counting these rings. Each pair equals one year.

Unusual circumstances interrupt the regularity of the rings. Severe drought, late freezes, serious outbreaks of insect pests, and other disasters may cause a tree to lose all of its leaves after the start of the growing season, and the growth may not be resumed that year. Tree rings are not always symmetrical, for growth on one side may have been inhibited by some sort of obstacle. So from the width of the rings, scars, and other features, scientists can reconstruct many of the happenings in a tree's history.

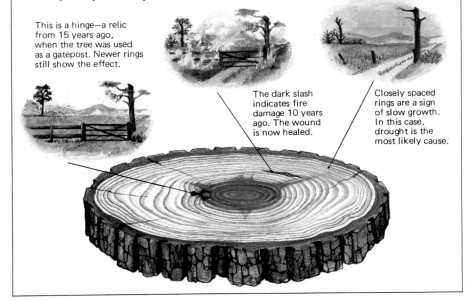

This is a hinge—a relic from 15 years ago, when the tree was used as a gatepost. Newer rings still show the effect.

The dark slash indicates fire damage 10 years ago. The wound is now healed.

Closely spaced rings are a sign of slow growth. In this case, drought is the most likely cause.

quickly filled by the water being pushed up from the roots. Water molecules stick together, and as water is lost through the leaves, this cohesion causes a chain reaction that is transmitted all the way down.

How can a tree's age be determined without cutting it down?

Signs on some trees in parks and forests give their ages, yet the trees are still standing. Foresters use a special instrument called an increment borer, which operates much like a brace and bit for boring holes in wood. The bit, or borer, is hollow. A hole is drilled straight to the center of the trunk, and then the bit is backed out. Inside the bit is a core of wood with a complete set of rings to be counted.

Reasonably accurate estimates of a mature tree's age can also be made by

measuring its circumference four or five feet off the ground. On the average, a tree increases in girth about one inch every year. (If the tree is in a crowded forest, the increase averages about half that.) So a tree with a trunk 48 inches in circumference that is growing under favorable conditions is roughly half a century old.

Do twigs reveal their age?

A tree grows upward from the tips of its stems. In deciduous trees, a new bud is formed at the end of a stem before the terminal leaf is shed. These buds swell in spring (or during the rainy season), producing the new stems and leaves. The point where a twig begins its growth each season is clearly evident by a scar that circles the stem, and counting the number of scars will tell you the age of the twig.

Curious Trees

What are the oddest trees?

By definition a tree has a single, slender trunk and leafy, spreading branches. Many trees, however, don't fit this pattern. Among the oddest are the baobabs of Africa and the related bottle trees of Australia. Both have enormously swollen, bulbous trunks topped with short scraggly limbs. A Bushman legend recounts that the hyena, a spirit of evil, spitefully planted the first baobab upside-down —for that is how a baobab looks.

A mature baobab is a reservoir of water. Inside its wrinkled bark the spongy wood is saturated with moisture. Thirsty elephants attack the great trunks with their tusks, leaving them dying wrecks. Old baobabs are often hollow. They are sometimes used as houses, and one famous tree served as a bus stop, accommodating as many as 30 travelers.

Another water-storing oddity is the boojum tree of Baja California. This extraordinary desert plant looks like an inverted carrot 10 to 30 feet tall. The green trunk bristles with short, wispy branches, leafless except after one of the infrequent rains. Boojum trees store water in their trunks, using it in times of extreme drought.

Very different from the baobab and the boojum tree, the remarkable banyan of India starts out as an epiphyte, or air plant. From its perch on another tree, it sends out aerial roots that descend to the ground. These roots thicken into scores of trunks, which hold up the banyan's heavy branches. An old specimen may be 100 feet tall and spread over several acres—a miniature forest composed of a single tree.

What makes palms different from other trees?

Not all of the 1,500 species of palms are trees, but the date, coconut, royal, and many others certainly qualify. Palms, however, are not woody plants; they do not have bark or annual rings. The interior of the trunk is fibrous, and the palm takes in water and nutrients all over.

Palms have only one growing point, a single bud at the center of the crown. At ground level, the bud appears as a tightly folded, cabbagelike bunch of leaves. As the plant develops, the bud

is carried upward on the developing trunk. As long as it remains intact, the palm continues to grow, unfolding a succession of fan-shaped leaves or feathery fronds. But if the bud is removed—perhaps for the delicacy known as hearts of palm—the tree will not survive.

Palm leaves are shed regularly; as they fall off, rows of scars remain, visible on most species. The rough trunks of date palms retain the leaf bases, and one Cuban species, the petticoat palm, holds its fan-shaped dead leaves around the trunk like a sagging undergarment. In contrast, the stately royal palm, lining many avenues in tropical and subtropical places, sheds its leaves cleanly, with no visible marks on its smooth polished trunk.

Do bananas grow on trees?

Though we may speak of banana trees, bananas actually grow on large flowering plants that have neither woody trunk nor branches. The thick stem, which is 10 to 25 feet tall, consists entirely of long leafstalks and blades wrapped tightly together. A growing banana plant produces a succession of broad, 10-foot leaves; with each new leaf the stem grows taller. After 12 to 15 months, the plant sends out a huge colorful bud, which dangles from a long stalk. When the bud opens, it reveals rows of flowers, some of which will become green bananas. After bearing one bunch of fruit, the whole plant dies.

Bananas originated in tropical Asia; they are cultivated extensively in South America and the Caribbean area, but most of the fruit in our markets comes from Central America. Popular in the tropics, the plantain is a close relative of the edible banana.

A rare relative of the banana plant is the traveler's-tree of Madagascar. The stalks of the large leaves are arranged in a fan shape on a short trunk, and hollows at the bases of the stalks form cups that may collect a quart of rainwater. A thirsty traveler in this arid island could cut through the base to reach the lifesaving liquid. The name is also explained by the belief

By shape alone these three trees are leading contenders for the title of the world's oddest tree. The African baobabs (far left) are natural water tanks, capable of storing more than 25,000 gallons. The Galápagos prickly pear (left) is a tree-sized cactus, and the Australian grass tree (below) is a 15-foot-high lily relative.

that the tree is oriented north to south—a sort of natural compass.

What is puzzling about the monkey puzzle tree?

An odd-looking tree from South America, the monkey puzzle (also called the Chile pine) is so closely covered with overlapping spiny scales on the trunk and branches that it is unclimbable—even by a monkey. That, at any rate, is the usual explanation of the curious name.

The monkey puzzle is a conifer with hard, dark green scales instead of nee-

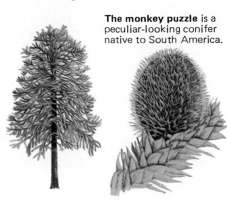

The monkey puzzle is a peculiar-looking conifer native to South America.

dles. Contained in large cones, its almond-size nuts were once a staple in the diet of the region's Araucanian Indians. In the damp, chilly forests of southern Chile and Argentina, monkey puzzles are frequented, not by monkeys, but by flocks of parrots, which extract the nuts with their powerful hooked bills.

Monkey puzzles were first planted in England in the 1790's, when seeds were introduced following Capt. George Vancouver's survey of the Chilean coast. The trees have an attractive pyramidal shape and are often planted in gardens and parks.

Which trees are pollinated by bats?

Most plants depend on insects or, more rarely, on birds to pollinate their flowers. The sausage tree, a native of tropical Africa and Madagascar, is different. With "sausages" dangling in appetizing array, this tree looks like an open-air delicatessen. (Unfortunately, the sausages are edible neither by man nor by beast.) The sausages develop from clusters of dark red flowers that

appear during the dry season, when the tree is leafless. The bats, in their search for nectar, find the big blossoms conveniently suspended before their very noses.

How did the Joshua tree get its name?

The Joshua tree grows in just one place in the world, in and around the Mojave Desert. A giant yucca, it belongs to the lily family, which also includes many handsome desert plants with tall, candelabra-shaped flower stalks and succulent leaves.

From time to time a Joshua tree puts out clusters of creamy white, bell-shaped flowers at the ends of its branches. After flowering, the tree produces additional arms at right angles to the original branches. As the tree grows, other arms are added until the tree assumes the strangely contorted silhouette of a gesticulating giant. The story is that Mormon pioneers, seeing the upraised arms of this unusual desert tree, named it after the biblical prophet who gave the signal for the capture of the city of Ai.

Roots: The Underground Connection

Why do plants need roots?

Water-dwelling plants often get along perfectly well without roots (although seaweeds and some others have rootlike organs called holdfasts to keep them anchored in place). But most familiar land plants could not exist without roots to support them and absorb water from the soil. Without roots, land plants would be limited to such small, humble forms as mosses and mushrooms.

Water is absorbed by roots through the fine hairs that grow near the root tips. It then passes into the central, woody portion of the root, which carries it to the stem and leaves. Roots keep growing until the plant dies, and often more of a plant's mass is below ground than above ground. The sheer volume of roots is amazing. A dogged researcher once found that a single rye plant had 13,815,762 roots, with a combined length of 387 miles! The total surface area of these slender roots was 2,554 square feet—more than half the size of a basketball court. The total daily growth of this plant's roots was estimated at 3.1 miles. The roots were equipped with more than 14 *billion* root hairs, whose combined length was calculated at about 6,600 feet.

How do roots grow?

The first part to emerge from a germinating seed is usually the root—a pallid, threadlike organ enveloped in a cloudlike puff of root hairs. The embryonic root grows rapidly, lengthening and thickening at a prodigious rate. The rootlet soon begins to branch out, seeking additional sources of water and of the nutrients dissolved in it. In time, roots may become very thick and develop growth rings similar to those on the trunk of a tree.

A root system is in some ways like a system of underground branches, although roots, unlike branches, lack joints and leaves. And like branches, roots grow from their tips. At the very tip of each root is a sheath of tough, hard cells called the root cap. The root cap's cells are continually being worn away by friction with the soil, but replacement cells are constantly being formed. The actual lengthwise growth takes place in a short zone just behind the root cap, where rapidly multiplying and expanding cells force the root cap forward.

What are root hairs?

Just behind a root tip's growth zone are the root hairs, often so fine and

The Mighty Root System of a Mighty Tree

Root systems develop in two different ways. Some species of plants have spreading, fibrous root systems in which there are many main roots, all about the same size. Others, such as the tree shown below, have a single main root, called the taproot, which has smaller side branches. The taproot is more or less straight and reaches fairly deep in relation to the size of the plant. At the ends of the side branches are the root tips, where water is absorbed and root growth occurs. The illustrations at right show the root tips with their spiky hairs and a hairless portion where growth takes place.

Root tips (upper illustration) and close-up of a root tip with microscopic root hairs (lower illustration)

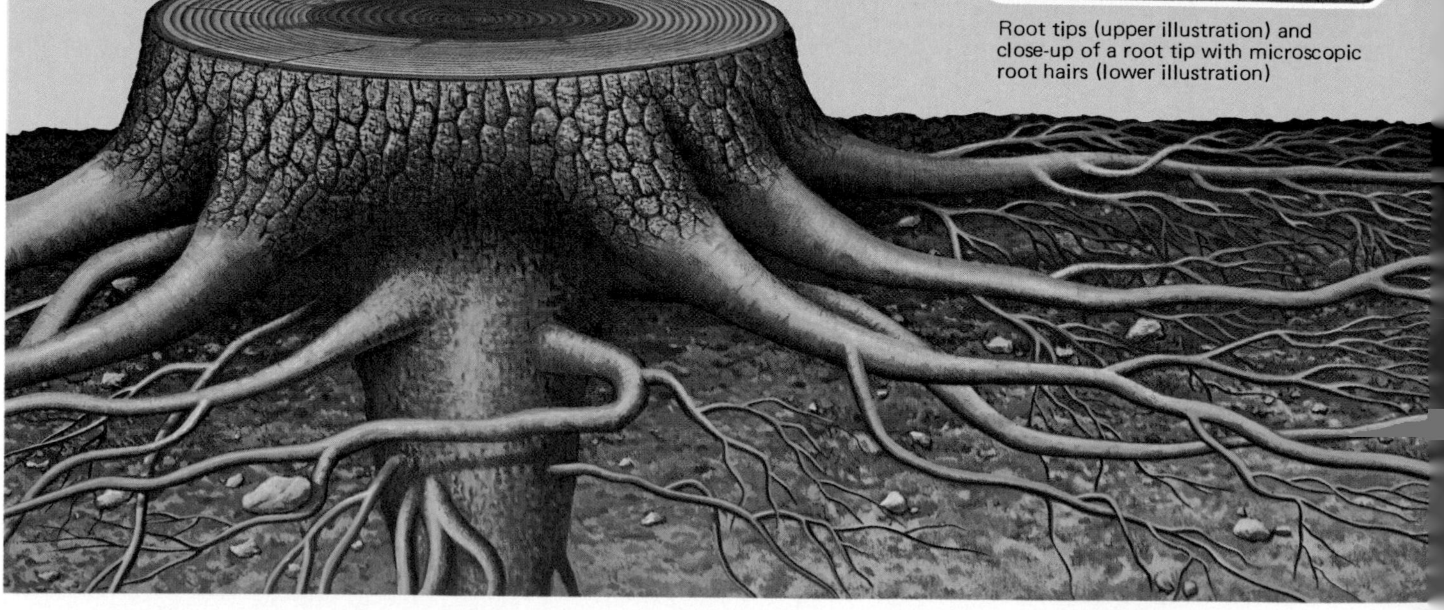

Taproot

Branching side roots

short that they cannot be seen with the naked eye. Even the mightiest oak trees depend on these little patches of fragile, short-lived hairs. The root hairs do almost all the actual work of absorbing the water and dissolved nutrients. They also anchor the root as the growing tip snakes forward between soil particles. However, they grow in only a very limited zone of the root tip, and an individual root hair lives for only a few days to a few weeks at most.

How deep do roots go?

The roots of some plants reach astoundingly deep. The taproot of a large old hickory or oak may extend as far down as 100 feet. The mesquite, a tree native to the arid American Southwest, may send its roots 50 feet or more beneath the ground. Alfalfa roots commonly grow 10 to 15 feet beneath the surface and may reach more than 30 feet down.

Many plants, including some sizable trees, have shallow, wide-spreading root systems. Hemlocks and most of the maples have their roots in the topmost two feet of the soil. These trees are more easily toppled by wind, and they cannot withstand drought as well as the deeper-rooted trees. Shallow roots, however, have the advantage of being able to soak up the water in the topmost soil layers—an especially important feature in dry places, where the infrequent rains seldom penetrate more than a few inches into the soil.

Do all roots grow underground?

Roots can appear in the strangest places—even in the air. Baldcypress trees, which grow in swamps in the southeastern United States, send up hollow, kneelike roots through which the tree obtains oxygen. English ivy sends out roots from its stem to grip the surfaces on which it climbs.

The huge banyan tree, native to southern Asia, starts life as an air plant. The roots grow downward until they reach the ground and anchor in the soil, turning into trunks. One banyan in India has 454 trunks, all of which began as aerial roots.

Banyans are not the only plants with aboveground supports. Corn plants sprout prop roots from their

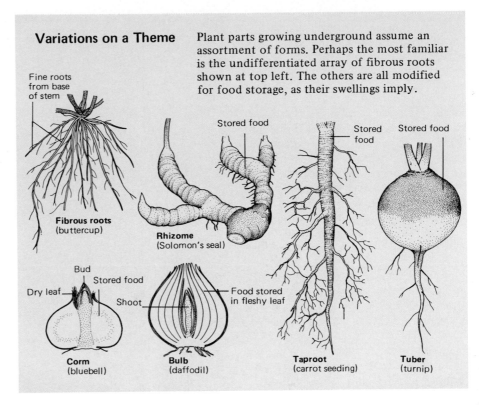

Variations on a Theme Plant parts growing underground assume an assortment of forms. Perhaps the most familiar is the undifferentiated array of fibrous roots shown at top left. The others are all modified for food storage, as their swellings imply.

Fine roots from base of stem

Fibrous roots (buttercup)

Stored food

Rhizome (Solomon's seal)

Stored food

Stored food

Bud
Dry leaf
Stored food
Shoot

Food stored in fleshy leaf

Corm (bluebell)

Bulb (daffodil)

Taproot (carrot seeding)

Tuber (turnip)

lower stem joints. The tropical pandanus tree, or screw pine, of the South Pacific has similar roots, so sturdy that they will support the tree even when its original base dies and decays. Red mangroves have high-arching stilt roots that keep the main trunks above high tide.

Is every underground plant part a root?

A black locust tree has a habit of sending up sprouts from underground. These sprouts come, not from its roots, but from specialized rootlike underground stems called rhizomes. Although rhizomes look like roots, biologically they are stems, since they have joints and buds and can send up leaves and sprouts.

Some plants have rhizomes with swollen tips in which food is stored. Such specialized tips are called tubers, and the potato is the best-known example. A daffodil bulb represents another kind of subterranean food-storage organ. A bulb is really an over-sized bud, made up of fleshy, scalelike leaves. An onion is a bulb, too. A crocus "bulb" is not really a bulb but a corm—a chunk of stem with some small food-storage leaves.

In what ways do people use roots?

Roots can be troublesome at times, as when they buckle sidewalks or invade drainpipes. However, they are far more useful than they are vexatious. Roots and such rootlike organs as tubers and bulbs are among man's chief sources of food.

Turnips, carrots, beets, radishes, potatoes, and onions are mainstays of the human diet. In tropical regions other root crops such as manioc and taro are staples. Yams and sweet potatoes supply calories and vitamin A over much of the world. Sugar beets yield sweet harvests in regions too cold for sugar cane. Even the humble dandelion root can be eaten if prepared in a way that removes its bitterness. Garlic and horseradish—the first a bulb and the second a fleshy root—add flavor to the menu.

Roots also yield dyes and drugs. American Indians used bloodroot for a red dye, and madder roots were a standard source of red in the Old World until the development of synthetic dyes. Elecampane root is made into cough medicine for man and horses. The bulbs of squill, a member of the lily family, are used in heart stimulants and diuretics.

The Surprising Mobility of Plants

Why do plants turn toward the light?
A plant set on a windowsill soon turns toward the outside and has to be rotated to maintain its shape. This inexorable orientation toward light is an automatic adjustment made by the plant as it grows. For the plant is not bending over as we humans do when we touch our toes; instead, it bends by growing in a particular direction. Though a plant's growth movements are very different from an animal's movements, they accomplish the same result—changing the position of the individual concerned.

A plant's growth movements are controlled by internal chemical substances. When one side of a plant is shaded, a growth hormone—called an auxin, from the Greek for "to grow"—moves to the darker side of the plant and causes that side to grow much faster. As a result, the stem becomes bent toward the light.

The reaction of some plants to light changes as they mature. The flower stalk of the peanut plant, for example, at first reacts positively to light (that is, it grows toward the sun). But after the flower is pollinated, the reaction reverses. The flower stalk then grows several inches into the soil, and the peanut develops underground.

Like sunbathers at the shore, sunflowers turn their heads to follow the sun.

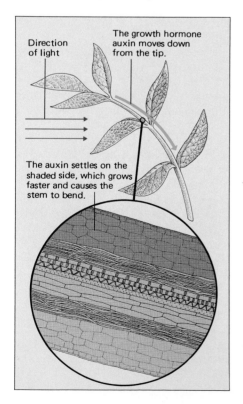

Direction of light

The growth hormone auxin moves down from the tip.

The auxin settles on the shaded side, which grows faster and causes the stem to bend.

What controls the growth movements of plants?
Like animals, plants produce chemical hormones that affect growth when present in even minute amounts. The best known of these chemical regulators are the auxins. Auxins occur in all of a plant's growth tissues, their production controlled by light and other factors. They move throughout the plant in the phloem, or sap, just as animal hormones do in the blood.

Growers use hormones to nurture their crops. A synthetic auxin, 2,4-D, is an important weed killer. Other auxin sprays are used to prevent fruit from dropping prematurely, to produce seedless fruits, and to delay the sprouting of potatoes and onions in storage. Among the other plant hormones are the gibberellins, present in large quantities in unripened seeds. Gibberellins are used by growers to cause stems to root and seeds to germinate. The dormins, another group, inhibit plant growth.

Why do roots grow away from light?
Searching for water, roots grow into the darkness of the soil—a movement that is both a negative reaction to light and a positive reaction to gravity. In growing downward, roots are reacting to the same plant hormone that causes stems to bend toward the light. The hormone collects on the underside of the root tip, but there it inhibits growth. The upper side grows faster, and the root tip bends down.

Do flowers move too?
Some plants are attracted to the sun so strongly that they begin their day facing east and then follow the sun as the earth turns. Among the most spectacular of these sun worshipers are common sunflowers. Although the movement of a single sunflower in a garden generally goes unnoticed, in a vast field the change in orientation is far too dramatic to go unnoticed. Literally thousands of blossoms slowly pivot as they keep the sun shining on their upturned heads.

Flowers move in another fashion, too. Brightly colored ones open during daylight hours, the unfolding of their petals triggered by light and heat. They close again at nightfall. (Such white ones as the night-blooming cereus—a cactus—and the jasmine from which oil is extracted for perfume open only at night, depending on fragrance to attract insect pollinators.) The time that some species open is so predictable that botanical gardens sometimes feature floral clocks that tell the time of day. Like the movement of sunflowers toward the sun, the opening and closing of flowers is caused by growth. When the inside of a petal grows faster than the outside (as happens to a day-blooming flower during the day), the petal opens; the reverse happens at night.

What makes a tendril coil?

Grapes are among the climbing plants with slim, almost threadlike tendrils that wrap tightly around a support.

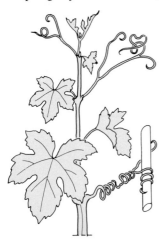

The effect of tendrils is to move the plant toward an object to which it can cling. So tendrils, too, are for plants a way of changing position.

A tendril begins to coil as soon as it makes contact with a firm support, and it can secure its hold with amazing speed. Tendrils of a closely watched cyclanthera (cyclantheras are cucumberlike vines) began their first turn within 20 seconds of making contact and had completed it in less than 4 minutes. The mechanism of coiling is similar to that of a plant's bending toward the light. Growth on the side of the tendril touching the support virtually stops; but on the opposite side, growth may be some 200 times as fast as normal.

How sensitive is a sensitive plant?

The speediest of all plant movements are the reactions that some species

have to touch. Leaflets of the mimosa, popularly called the sensitive plant, fold within seconds of being touched (they are also sensitive to raindrops, and to the blowing of the wind). When a leaflet folds, a rippling chain reaction is set off as a chemical activator moves throughout the plant. Leaflet after leaflet folds, and then entire leaves, until the entire plant droops.

Plants, of course, have no muscle tissue to help them move. Instead, in many cases, they use water to do the work. At the base of each mimosa leaflet is a saclike structure called the pulvinus. (The base of each whole mimosa leaf also has a pulvinus.) When water fills the pulvinus, it bulges, and the leaflet becomes erect. When the pulvinus suddenly drains, as it does when a leaflet is touched, the leaflet droops.

Why do prayer plants "pray" at night?

The popular houseplant known as the prayer plant is one of several species that fold their leaves at night. Clovers are another well-known example. Although a plant's sleep movements may prevent heat loss during the cool of the night, there is no completely satisfactory explanation of how the plant benefits. Certain species droop their leaves during the daytime, which seems easier to understand: when heat and light from the sun become too intense, the plants reduce their water loss by cutting down on the area exposed to the sun.

Why do Mexican jumping beans jump about?

Mexican jumping beans are, by themselves, as sedentary as any other bean. Their wiggling, snapping motions, which make them so popular as novelty items, come from the antics of a caterpillar inside. A certain kind of moth lays its eggs in the bean plant's flower or in a young pod. Caterpillars hatch from the eggs and burrow inside the developing bean. Generally it is the flexing of the caterpillar's body that makes the bean jump about. When the caterpillar is mature, it lines the inside of the bean with silk and transforms into a pupa. After several weeks a fully developed moth emerges from the hollowed-out bean, to start the cycle once again.

Wood sorrel leaves fold down at night.

The nightly opening of the evening primrose is another type of movement.

In Self-defense

Why do some plants have thorns?

Plants have developed an impressive range of defensive weapons to prevent their being eaten. Thorns come in many sizes and shapes, ranging from the short, stout, back-curving claws of the multiflora rose (a popular hedge plant) to the 3½-inch spikes of the camel thorn. All are effective deterrents. Very few animals, no matter how hungry, would care to lacerate their tongues and mouths.

Not all the prickling and scratching organs on plants are thorns, according to botanists. True thorns, such as the ones on hawthorns, are modified branches. Cacti are among the plants with spines, which are modified leaves. The thorn of a rose is actually a prickle, growing from the outer skin of the stem; prickles may also grow on leaves, which comes as no surprise to people who have met up with thistles. True thorns and spines are hard to break off because they are part of the woody structure of the plants, but prickles, attached only to the surface, break off easily.

Three-pronged and ferocious-looking, the spines on this honey locust keep plant-eating animals at a distance.

Can animals circumvent a thorny defense?

Despite their unpleasantness, thorns are not 100 percent effective in preventing the onslaughts of hungry herbivores. Thorns are "designed" to repel mammals, and they are ineffective against the many thousands of species of plant-eating insects. Moreover, some of the browsing and grazing animals have developed the ability to eat thorny or spiky-leaved plants.

Donkeys munch contentedly on thistles; camels browse on the shoulder-high camel thorn shrub; giraffes pluck leaves from thorny acacia twigs with their long, prehensile tongues. But these are exceptions. Most animals—and human beings too—stay away from thorns.

One thorny tree has a second line of defense. An acacia tree of Central and South America is known as the bullhorn acacia because of the size and shape of its paired thorns. The thorns are hollow, and biting ants nest in them. At the slightest disturbance the ants rush out and attack the intruder, repelling not only browsing mammals but also most insect pests. The tree supplies the ants with food as well as a nest site. Special glands on branches ooze a sweet nectar, and the leaflets bear small egglike globules rich in proteins, fats, and carbohydrates.

Why does a nettle sting?

Many plants are armed with irritating hairs, which break off when touched even lightly and work their way into unprotected areas of an attacker's flesh. This is an effective deterrent to browsing animals, with their tender nostrils and mouths. But nettles go one step further.

A nettle hair is stiff and hollow, like a hypodermic needle. Inside is a fluid that contains both histamine (one of the main factors in human allergies) and a substance similar to the venom produced by wasps. At the tip of the hair is a tiny bead that breaks off when an animal brushes against it. Even the slight force of the contact is enough to drive the hair's stiff shaft into the intruder's skin. Simultaneously, the soft base of the hair acts like a squeeze bulb and squirts the poisonous fluid into the wound.

Weapons at a Plant's Disposal

Browsing animals rely on plants for food, and over time plants have fashioned a counterattack. Thorns and stinging hairs are among the weapons deterring would-be diners.

Tansy has bitter-tasting foliage.

Gooseberries often have stout spines.

Holly leaves may be armed with spiny teeth.

How do plants poison their enemies?
Tansy, milkweed, and dogbane all taste bitter. Jimsonweed has a foul odor when crushed or bitten.

It is no coincidence that these particular plants—like so many other species that are unpleasant (to plant eaters, at least)—are poisonous. Poisons are often a plant's main line of defense, and the bad taste acts as a warning to would-be eaters. Grazing animals leave these plants alone. The plants avoid being eaten; the animals avoid being poisoned.

Not all plant poisons are the same. Dieffenbachia (dumb cane) and skunk cabbage contain needle-sharp crystals of calcium oxalate—crystals that penetrate the lining of the mouth and throat of any mammal that chews or swallows them, causing intense pain and inflammation. Members of the spurge family have an irritating, burning sap. Some plants operate in a subtler fashion: many members of the pea family, for example, contain poisonous amino acids that link up with an animal's normal proteins and disrupt its life processes.

Which insects can cope with poisonous plants?
Milkweeds contain heart poisons that can kill numerous types of insects, yet the caterpillars of monarch butterflies and milkweed tussock moths thrive on a diet of milkweed leaves. Certain insects have developed the ability to break down or neutralize particular plant poisons. The monarch butterfly has even gone a step farther: the caterpillar actually stores the milkweed poisons in its tissues, making it distasteful to insect-eating birds.

Insects that have evolved the ability to feed on a particular type of poisonous plant tend to feed mainly or exclusively on that plant. For the insects, a big advantage is that they have few competitors for their food. The advantage to the plants is not clear, although some scientists think that the insects and larvae give off an odor that repels plant-eating mammals.

Which plants produce natural insect repellents?
Poisons are not the only chemical defenses in the plant kingdom. Plants also secrete hormones that interfere ingeniously with the life cycle of insects. One is the juvenile hormone, which keeps larvae from maturing.

The existence of juvenile hormones in plants was discovered accidentally, when a researcher found that specimens of a European insect that he was working with would not mature. The cause was traced to a chemical in the paper towels he used to line the bottoms of the cages. Further research showed that newsprint and many other kinds of paper had the same result, and that the substance responsible came from the balsam fir tree.

Juvenile hormones give promise of becoming ecologically safe and effective insecticides. However, every insect species has its own juvenile hormone, and more work is necessary to tailor the synthetic hormones to match those of particular pests.

The popular garden flower ageratum counterattacks from another angle. Instead of keeping its insect pests in a permanent larval state, it produces a hormone that prematurely turns them into adults. The adult insects are dwarfed and sterile.

How do plants protect themselves against disease?
Plant diseases are caused by fungi, bacteria, and viruses. If these manage to gain an entry into the plant (through a wound, for example), the plant may still be able to fight them off. Many species, such as bouncing Bet and shepherd's purse, contain soaplike compounds called saponins. When their cells are invaded by fungi, the saponins attack the membranes of the fungus cells and kill them. (This does not work against all fungi, but it stops a good many.) Other chemicals may function as antibiotics.

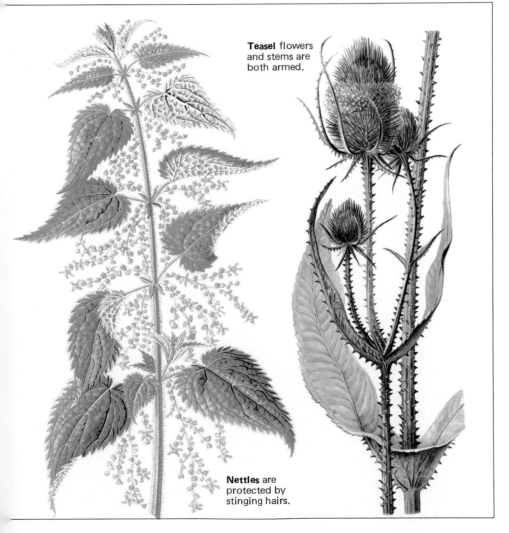

Teasel flowers and stems are both armed.

Nettles are protected by stinging hairs.

Plant Predators

Why are some plants carnivorous?

Some 500 species of plants around the world are carnivorous; that is, they get part of their nutrients from animals (generally insects) caught or trapped in one of several ingenious ways. Carnivorous plants are most abundant in soggy soils in or near bogs and swamps, where the animals they catch help alleviate the shortage of nitrogen. One exception is the European flycatcher, which grows in dry, rocky soil and is especially common in Portugal. Its sticky, grasslike leaves have been used locally as a natural flypaper.

Carnivorous plants do contain chlorophyll, and so they manufacture food like other green plants. They can, in fact, survive without eating animals, but they grow more vigorously and are healthier when they have this dietary supplement. All carnivorous plants produce flowers, some of them quite beautiful. Only incidentally, however, do the flowers help attract victims—but the plants have other ways.

What attracts victims to these death traps?

Carnivorous plants trap insects in their leaves. Often the leaves are colorful, luring insects and other animals accustomed to associating bright colors with sources of nectar. Many leaves also secrete a sweet-smelling fluid in their trapping devices. The bad odor of decaying victims may attract such insects as flies, which, of course, often find their food by zeroing in on a malodorous source.

How do sundews trap prey?

The leaves of sundews are covered with red or bright orange hairs, each tipped with a shiny drop of fluid that looks deceptively like honey. But a fly, an ant, or another hungry insect touching the droplet discovers instantly that the fluid is a powerful glue. The hapless creature's struggle to break free only stimulates the surrounding hairs to bend over the catch, which soon becomes coated with glue-like slime. The insect suffocates. The sundew then secretes an enzyme that digests the catch, leaving only the wings, the outer skeleton, and other hard parts. If a leaf catches two insects at once, the hairs divide their work and secure both.

Sundews attract prey with the glistening bright hairs on their leaves. The hairs are tipped, not with nectar, but with glue.

Butterworts catch insects in the sticky coating on their leaves. The leaves often actually curl over the trapped prey.

Butterworts operate much like the sundews, trapping insects in a sticky secretion on the long tapered leaves arranged in a rosette at the base of the plant. The edges of the leaves in most species may roll inward, enclosing the catch in a troughlike tube. Other leaf cells then secrete digestive enzymes. When the "meal" is absorbed, the leaf unrolls and is ready to act again. Most leaves make only two or three catches before they are shed and replaced.

Which carnivorous plants grow in water?

Nearly half of all the species of carnivorous plants belong to the bladderwort family, and most of them are aquatic plants with submerged feathery leaves and no roots. Their flowers are generally small and bright yellow.

Bladderworts have bladderlike catching devices where their leaves join the stems. The tiny bladders, rarely measuring more than a tenth of an inch across, are filled with air and have a single opening surrounded by bristles. The "door" remains closed until something pushes against it or touches the bristles. Either triggers it to pop open. Then the water literally rushes in, sucking in such small items as tiny crustaceans and larvae. The door closes again and cannot be opened from the inside. Eventually the water moves out of the bladder, but left behind is the "meal" to be digested and absorbed.

Not all bladderworts are aquatic. One tropical species thrives among damp mosses and other plants growing on trees. Another, with beautiful orchidlike flowers, grows in the water that collects in the center of bromeliads. (Bromeliads are pineapplelike plants that often grow on trees.) It reproduces by sending out tendrillike growths that produce new plants if they find another bromeliad.

Why do pitcher plants have pitchers?
Pitcher plants catch insects passively but effectively. Their tubular leaves form an urnlike basin in which rainwater collects. In some, the leaf has a funnel-shaped top that directs water inside; in others, the tip of the leaf is spread over the opening like a hood, limiting the amount of water that can enter and preventing an overflow in heavy rains.

Typically the lip of the pitcher (the

The Venus's-flytrap is unique among plants. When an insect touches the hairs on its hinged leaves, the trap springs shut, and the teeth lock over the victim.

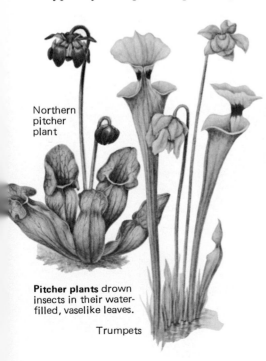

Northern pitcher plant

Pitcher plants drown insects in their water-filled, vaselike leaves.

Trumpets

outward-bending portion of the leaf) is scarlet, maroon, or purple, often striped with cream or bright yellow. Along the winglike ridge inside are cells exuding a sweet nectar. Below these is a band of stiff hairs that point downward—a bristly barricade that prevents a creature from crawling up and out of the pitcher. Wax secreted by cells on the smooth sides of most pitchers is a double preventive, making the surface so slippery that no hooks, claws, or suction pads can get a purchase. Once started into the pitcher, an insect or other creature is doomed, sliding down into the water where it drowns. Eventually it sinks to the bottom and decays, its soft parts absorbed by the plant.

Is the fluid in a pitcher plant dangerous?
Pitcher plants are sometimes called hunter's cups, for the liquid they contain is drinkable: the fluid at the top of the pitcher is clear, uncontaminated water. At the bottom, of course, are the remains—the indigestible hard parts—of the plant's "meals." But with care these can be avoided, and nearly every pitcher offers at least a swallow or two of water—and some much more.

How does the Venus's-flytrap capture flies?
Most carnivorous plants don't depend on speed to make their catch: they drown their victims in pools of water or catch them on sticky hairs or leaves. The Venus's-flytrap, an endangered species growing in the Carolina lowlands of North America, comes closest to being aggressive.

The tip of each leaf on the flytrap is hinged down the middle like a clamshell. Around its edges are stout toothlike spines, and in the rose-to-pink center of the leaf are three trigger hairs. An insect or other creature attracted to the leaf cannot avoid touching a trigger. Touching only one causes no reaction, but if two are touched—or one hair is jiggled twice—the two halves of the leaf snap shut. With its teeth interlocked and the two halves pushed tightly together, the leaf cannot be forced apart. Small soft-bodied creatures are trapped inside. If a leaf misses its catch or is triggered closed by nonliving material, it opens again within half an hour. Otherwise the leaf stays shut until it digests its victim, which may take several weeks. Most leaves make only two or three catches before they die and are replaced by new ones.

117

Parasites: The Dependent Ones

What do we mean by a parasitic plant?

Most green plants are quite self-sufficient, drawing water and minerals from the soil and creating their own food by means of photosynthesis. A sizable number, however, depend on other plants in one way or another for their survival. Not every dependent plant is a parasite—only those that draw sustenance from others and supply no benefit in return. Spanish moss and certain other plants, for example, attach themselves to others only to gain better exposure to sunlight. They take nothing from their host.

Plants that *do* come under the heading of parasites display different degrees of dependence and have different methods of survival. Some species have neither roots for obtaining water nor chlorophyll for converting sunlight into food. Prominent among this group are the dodders, toothworts, and broomrapes, as well as the exotic tropical plant *Rafflesia*. All are true parasites, totally dependent on other living plants for their survival. Various plants—among them the bird's-nest and coralroot orchids—can live either as parasites or as scavengers, according to the circumstances. Others are only partially parasitic. Mistletoe, for example, has chlorophyll and can synthesize its own food, but it depends on the host plant for water.

How do parasites feed on their hosts?

Just as a hungry mosquito penetrates the skin of its victim and draws blood for nourishment, so a parasitic plant must somehow tap the nutrient- and water-carrying tissues of its host. Unlike the mosquito, of course, a parasitic plant must establish a reliable, long-lasting connection. Most attach themselves to the root systems of their hosts, although some of the best known—including mistletoe and dodder—usually concentrate on the branches or stems.

Whatever its point of attack, a parasite uses as its primary weapon a specialized rootlike structure, called a haustorium (from the Latin for "to drink"). The haustorium penetrates the host's outer layer and then absorbs the nutrients circulating through the central tissues. Penetrating the normally tough outer layer is a strenuous task, and some parasites gain the necessary leverage by twining around the host and sending haustoria in from different directions. Others produce a second kind of structure that clamps firmly onto the host's surface, giving the would-be invader the solid grip it needs to drive its probes inward.

Are parasites always visible?

The best-known parasitic plants, such as mistletoe and dodder, are familiar largely because they are conspicuous. There are others, though, that manage to live for years while yielding scarcely a hint of their existence.

Many parasites attach themselves to the roots of trees and shrubs and do much of their growing underground. One such plant, the European tooth-

The Unusual Nature of Mistletoe

One of our most familiar Christmas decorations, mistletoe has served generations of well-wishers as a cue to give or receive a kiss. In times past it was thought to possess such special powers as repelling witches, enhancing fertility, and curing toothache. Early observers could scarcely have avoided the conclusion that this plant must be endowed with supernatural powers. Not only does it remain green all winter; it seldom if ever comes in contact with the earth.

Mistletoe is a perching plant, living on the branches of trees and shrubs. Its seeds reach their lofty position through the courtesy of birds, which eat the berries and then deposit the sticky seeds. The plant is able to make its own food (it has chlorophyll), but it must tap into the tree's pipeline for its water supply. (It develops rootlike processes that penetrate the tree.) Generally mistletoe does its host little or no harm.

wort, may live and thrive underground for as long as 10 years, disclosing its own presence only in the form of a few small, reddish flowers that break through the soil surface.

Probably the most striking example of unseen parasitism is that of the tropical plant *Rafflesia,* found in certain areas of the Far East. Rather than

Common European dodder twining around a stem

Enlarged view of dodder flowers

encircle the roots or stem of a host plant, *Rafflesia* lives entirely inside it, spreading thin filaments through the internal tissues so thoroughly that even experts have difficulty telling the parasite from the host. Further, when *Rafflesia* does reveal itself, it does so dramatically, producing the largest flower in the world—a foul-smelling brown and purple blossom measuring as much as three feet across.

Why is dodder called the "devil's sewing thread"?

One of the commonest of plant parasites, dodder begins its life in a most uncommon manner. The seed germinates in the soil and sends up a slender shoot, just like countless other plants. But here the similarity ends, for this young stem promptly begins to reach outward with a circular motion until it makes contact with a neighboring plant. If the newly discovered plant is of a suitable variety, the dodder's stem twines around it and begins to sink rootlike organs into its tissues. Once this connection is made, the dodder's original stem withers and breaks, so that its direct link with the ground is severed and it is left completely dependent on the host.

Fortified by an ample source of nourishment, the parasite continues to grow, and the defenseless host becomes entangled in an ever-larger network of thin stems. Their resemblance to sewing thread is easy to see, but what makes these threadlike stems so

The reddish glow on this hillside is dodder, which climbs over other plants and nourishes itself on their tissues. Dodders around the world have different colors.

devilish is the effect they have on the host plant. A single dodder may produce hundreds of feet of stem, along with numerous new rootlike probes through which it draws water and nutrients. When this happens, a parasitized shrub—and in some cases even a full-sized tree—can become completely enveloped, losing precious exposure to sunlight and generally being drained dry by the dodder's relentless growth.

Do parasites have parasites?

The survival of a parasite as a species depends on its success in bringing its seeds or seedlings into contact with suitable hosts. In some cases the seeds are dispersed in a manner specifically designed to make a parasitic connection, but more often they are dispersed by the same methods as the seeds of nonparasitic plants—that is, they are carried about by animals, and by wind and other forces.

Parasites vary greatly in their degrees of choosiness about what plants will make satisfactory hosts. Some are specialized indeed: a certain species might grow only on pines, for instance, and another only on junipers. Not surprisingly, though, this kind of selectiveness can only prevail in areas where a particular host plant grows abundantly. Most parasites are not so discriminating: one kind of dodder, for example, can parasitize more than a hundred hosts.

Ironically (and perhaps fittingly), many parasitic plants do not hesitate to take advantage of other parasites. It is not uncommon to find a mistletoe feeding on a tree and being parasitized in turn by another mistletoe.

What harm do parasites do?

Of the thousands of species of parasitic plants, most do not cause serious harm to the plants on which they depend: the typical parasite is so much smaller than its host plant that the amount of nourishment it extracts is inconsequential. But even though only a small percentage of parasites pose a serious threat to their hosts, the damage they do can be significant indeed—particularly when major food crops are involved. Certain types of dodder, for instance, can dramatically reduce the yields of alfalfa and clover.

119

Competition: The Endless Struggle

What are plants competing for?

Plants battle most strongly for whichever of their requirements is in shortest supply, be it water, sunlight, carbon dioxide, or mineral elements in the soil. In tropical rain forests, for example, water is plentiful, and the intense competition is not for water but for light. To succeed, a rain-forest species requiring a great deal of sunlight must shoot up quickly and break through the already existing leaf canopy that blocks out the light. The climbing habit—typified by vines—and the perching habit—by epiphytes, or "air plants"—are two other rainforest adaptations that help plants get their required measure of sun.

Creating shade is a slow but effective weapon for eliminating competitors, for it can reduce the rate of photosynthesis in sun-loving plants to a fraction of the full-sun rate. Trees and other tall plants shade out competition by virtue of their size. Large leaves are a way of accomplishing the same thing—and are, of course, important in helping the large-leaved plant to increase its own exposure to light.

Who competes with whom?

Any two plants growing near one another are at some time likely to be in competition, the growth of one impeding that of the other. But competition is usually fiercest among members of the same species, for only they share exactly the same requirements for growth. Over time many species of plants (and animals too) have developed their own niches—that is, lives for which they are suited especially well. One species of fern, for example, may thrive on sandstone rock; a closely related species, only on limestone. Because the needs of the two species are not the same, competition is reduced.

Do plants ever help one another rather than compete?

Plants don't exactly help one another—surely not in the sense of doing one another a good turn. But if you explore a forest or other wild place, you are certain to discover some plants that are making life better for others. Mosses soak up water, creating the moist conditions required by certain wildflowers and ferns. Towering trees furnish the shade that allows hemlock seedlings (and those of certain other species) to thrive. Such vines as bittersweet and greenbrier use thicker-stemmed plants for support.

What kinds of plants use chemical warfare?

Sharp-eyed observers noticed long ago that certain plants do not thrive in each other's company. Apple trees, for example, do poorly near black walnut trees, and tomatoes will not grow near them at all. The cause is a poison that is given off by the roots of the black walnut; its function is to inhibit some of the competing plants.

The effect is even more striking in a eucalyptus grove, where not a blade of grass or a single weed grows beneath the trees. In this case, the poison is produced in the leaves, and when the leaves drop off, rain washes the poison into the ground. Beech leaves, too, release a chemical—in this case, one that prevents the sprouting of its own (and other beeches') seeds.

In the deserts of the American

The Struggle for Water

Creosote bush

Night-blooming cereus

Water-storing bulb

Mesquite

Regular spacing caused by root poisons

Survival in the desert means soaking up as much water as possible and preventing others from doing the same. Creosote bushes poison rivals nearby; night-blooming cereus stores water from infrequent rains; mesquite digs deep.

Deep roots

The serenity of the redwood forest is deceptive. Though there is an abundance of greenery, the plants are all competing for water, sunlight, and nutrients.

Southwest are bushes that practice the same sort of chemical warfare. Sagebrush forms thickets in which no other plants can grow. Within the thickets not even seedlings grow. (Apparently the mature plants poison the seedlings, thus keeping competition for moisture to a minimum.) In a wide ring around the thicket grow sagebrush seedlings but nothing else. The drier the region, the fiercer this chemical warfare between plant and plant seems to become.

How does competition affect a plant's appearance?

Because of their size, it is trees that show the effect of competition most dramatically. A tree growing in the open (in a park, for example) may develop a huge trunk and a broad crown; a forest tree belonging to the same species will often be slender, with a long length of uninterrupted trunk before any branches shoot out.

Though growth may be stunted, most plants can survive for some time even if they are not growing in optimum conditions. But it is to provide the optimum that foresters thin stands of trees just as gardeners do their vegetables and ornamental plants. This reduces competition, and allows those that remain to grow more rapidly and productively.

Do animals ever influence competition between plants?

Rabbits were once abundant in the grasslands on England's chalky soil. Their constant foraging kept the grasses cropped short, and so many other kinds of flowering plants grew there. Then, in the late 1950's, a virus disease eliminated most of the rabbits. No longer controlled, the grass became thicker and spread. It choked out most of the other plants, which were unable to compete with the vigorous grass.

In reverse, the same effect can be seen on grasslands where livestock overgraze. When grasses are cropped too close or are eliminated, weedy plants move in quickly. In parts of the American Southwest, for example, the spread of prickly pear cactus and also of such woody-stemmed plants as mesquite can be traced to overgrazing by range animals.

Succession: The Ever-Changing Scene

Why do lakes and ponds disappear?
Nothing in nature is more constant than change. The seasons progress; young animals grow up; populations rise and fall. Outdoor scenes remembered from childhood may no longer be the same—and not only because of the hand of man. The natural condition is one of change.

In time, for example, the fish-filled open waters of most of today's lakes and ponds will become grasslands and forests. Small ponds may be converted to dry land in just a few years. For large lakes the transition may take many centuries, its progress barely measurable in human terms.

When a pond or lake forms (as when beavers dam a stream), it is generally just a water-filled basin with some small forms of life—floating algae, aquatic insects, and the like. Winds, bird visitors, and runoff waters filling the basin bring in new types of plants. The plants grow and die, and their remains add organic matter to the bottom of the basin. Large leafy plants begin to grow along the shore, building up the soil. Some are rooted in deeper water but have floating leaves. Eventually (the time involved depends on the size of the body of water, the climate, and the rate at which sediments are washed in), the basin becomes filled in.

What does the word "succession" mean?
As plants grow, they change the habitat where they are growing by creating more shade, for example, or by influencing the fertility of the soil. Eventually the area becomes less suitable for the plants currently growing there and more suitable for species with different requirements. Young plants of other species begin to thrive (seeds and spores are always waiting in the wings), and the mixture of species changes. Eventually a whole new group of plants dominates, victors in the battle for sunlight, water, and nutrients. As each changeover progresses, the animal population also undergoes alteration; for as the plants change, the types of food and shelter offered also change.

Succession in nature is an orderly (that is, predictable) series of changes in the plant life inhabiting a particular

To some an untended clearing is a landscape in disarray. To others it is a scene of beauty, a sign of nature's restorative power and an indication of forest to come.

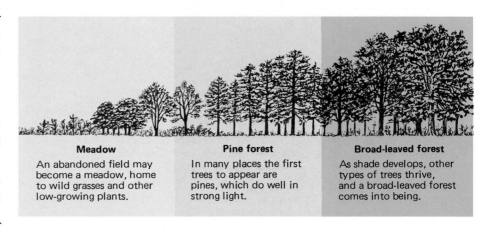

Meadow
An abandoned field may become a meadow, home to wild grasses and other low-growing plants.

Pine forest
In many places the first trees to appear are pines, which do well in strong light.

Broad-leaved forest
As shade develops, other types of trees thrive, and a broad-leaved forest comes into being.

area. Such changes continue until at some point the plant community becomes stable, and what ecologists call the climax community is achieved. Which plants belong to the climax community depends on a number of factors, especially climate and soil conditions. Grasses constitute the climax community on the Eurasian steppe and in the heartland of North America; spruces, firs, and other northern evergreens dominate a great region south of the Arctic Circle.

Where can you see succession in action?
Measured on our day-to-day time scale, most changes in the plant world come about slowly, and often the changes are unnoticed unless documented by camera or pen. The changes of succession, however, can be observed in another fashion—over space rather than time. There are sites where a panorama hundreds of years in the making is laid out within a few hundred feet.

Sand dunes are one such place. Built along shorelines by wind and waves, dunes are at first lifeless mounds, their sterile sand hostile to nearly all plant life (and to animals too, except for transients). But beach grasses soon appear, holding the particles of sand together with their sprawling stems and network of roots. Beach grasses stabilize the dunes, and when they die and decay, they enhance the fertility of the sand. As other kinds of plants begin to grow on the dunes, the grasses creep toward the shore, where wind and waves are building new dunes. Shrubs grow in the troughs between the dunes and up their slopes. Pines and then, in many places, broad-leaved trees take over. Along the coast or the shore of a lake, all these stages can be seen in a walk from the beach area inland over the dunes—from sterile sand to sparse vegetation, then shrubby growths, and finally a forest.

How does nature reclaim vacant lots?
One place where you can see succession happening over time is in a backyard or vacant lot. If the lawn is not mowed regularly (or if the vacant lot is left alone), weeds quickly appear. If the weeds with their deeper root systems are not controlled, they will compete successfully with the grass for water and nutrients. Left untended, the site will in time be invaded by shrubs, and then trees.

What forces interrupt a succession?
Fires, volcanic eruptions, dust storms, hurricanes, glaciers, floods—any disturbance that destroys vegetation will interrupt a succession, clearing the land partially or fully and setting it back to an earlier stage. (Usually some soil and plant life remain.)

The violent eruption of Krakatoa off the island of Java in 1883 killed all life nearby, burying it under ashes and cinders. Within the first year, grasses and other pioneer plants began to appear in the ashes; within 50 years, the islands were completely vegetated, their plant cover almost indistinguishable from that of other islands in the region. More recently, the recovery of the Mount St. Helens region in the Pacific Northwest began while the volcano still grumbled.

Jack pine is a sun-loving plant, and one that does remarkably well after fire. It generally takes a fire to open the cones and release the seeds.

Tightly closed cones

Part of the natural process that shapes the land, fires started by lightning have burned off many forests. Grasses soon sprout through the black-charred surface; so do certain pines (the jack pine, for example), whose cones are ordinarily opened only by the heat of fire. Under controlled conditions foresters use fire as a tool to give the forest a new start and increase the chances that the species they consider desirable will take over.

What role do people play in succession?
From coast to coast in North America, the original climax forests fell to the saw and the ax as land was cleared for farms and cities. Changes of this sort are not restricted to any particular continent; hundreds of years earlier they began in Europe, Asia, and much of Africa, and they are now also a fact of life in the remainder of the tropics. In some places, however (for example, in parks once disturbed by human activity), a secondary succession is taking place. Where natural events are allowed to proceed, vegetation resembling that of the primitive conditions (often coniferous or hardwood forest) is reclaiming the land.

Who are the pioneers?
Plant pioneers are species that do well in the earliest stage of a succession—for example, when lava from an eruption has hardened into rock. A Hawaiian plant called the sword fern grows in cracks soon after the lava has cooled; in other lands the deep pink blossoms of fireweed, or willow herb, blanket the earth after forest fires have denuded the soil.

Like human pioneers, the green ones must withstand the harshest of conditions—among them, intense sunlight and scarce or infertile soil. The growing conditions are not suitable for most other species, and pioneer plants have the field essentially to themselves. Few competitors will challenge their existence until the pioneers have done the homesteading, until the pioneers have changed the site enough for others to survive.

Mature seed capsule

From the ashes of newly scorched earth spring the beautiful blossoms of fireweed, or willow herb.

Adaptable Aquatics

Where do aquatic plants grow?

Aquatic plants grow in the water, of course, but not all water is the same. Generally, flowering species (most other water plants are algae) grow in fresh water, but a few flourish in the salty water of the sea. While most aquatic plants grow in quiet water or slow streams, water crowfoot and some others thrive in turbulent rivers.

In any type of aquatic habitat, different water plants tend to occupy different zones. Cattails and bulrushes grow in wet margins, their sturdy stems rising well above the water level. Pickerelweed prefers the shallows near the shore. Water lilies grow in water from 2 to 6 feet deep or more (the giant Amazon water lily must survive seasonal flood depths greater than 30 feet). Duckweed and water hyacinth float freely on the surface, while such aquatics as water milfoil and some of the pondweeds grow entirely submerged.

How are aquatic plants equipped for their watery lives?

Unlike algae, which are aquatics by nature, flowering plants are best suited for life on land, and species that thrive in the water have been modified over time. Their stems, for example, may have hollow, air-filled pockets, and they tend to be flexible and limber, yielding as the water moves.

Aquatic plants may also have air cells in their leaves and leafstalks, keeping them at the sunlit surface. Buoyant enough to support the weight of a frog, a water lily's round leaves float serenely at the surface. Push one down, and up it will pop. Water lilies have all their breathing pores located on the leaves' upper sides—a common adaptation in plants with floating leaves.

Floating leaves tend to be broad, making possible maximum exposure to the sun. In contrast, plants growing in fast water have slender threadlike or feathery leaves, offering minimum resistance to the current. Plants that grow totally submerged tend to have the same feathery type of foliage, and their leaves are often so soft that they collapse when the plant is removed from the water. Some plants have two very different sets of leaves—broad ones that float and feathery ones that stay submerged.

Why do water plants need roots?

Plants on land use roots mainly for absorbing water and nutrients and for anchoring themselves in place. By definition, free-floating plants have no anchors. One floating species, the water hyacinth, has thickly branching roots used for absorption; a few, such as the tiny duckweeds, have essentially dispensed with roots, absorbing water through their leaves.

Most water plants, however, have roots that hold them in place, keeping them in locations favorable to growth and preventing them from drifting elsewhere. Some, including the arrowhead and the water chestnut, have tuberous food-storing roots. Humans are fond of the succulent tubers, and waterfowl like them as well.

Which aquatic plant is the biggest?

Measuring some six feet across, the round, floating leaves of the Amazon water lily can easily support the weight of a child. The leaves have upturned edges, the saucerlike form seeming to help them ride over competing plants. A system of rigid, air-filled veins gives these huge leaves strength and buoyancy; special holes allow rainwater to drain away. Close-set spines on the undersides protect them against hungry herbivores.

When the blossoms of this giant open at sundown, they are pure white, and they give off a sweet pineapplelike odor that attracts beetle pollinators. About midnight the flowers begin to change to a deep purple-red hue and fold up, usually trapping eight or so beetles inside. When the sun sets again, the blossoms reopen, and the beetles emerge. They are well fed (the flowers produce a sweetish food), and they have a dusting of pollen to carry on to the next blossom.

What do the blossoms of aquatic plants look like?

Most aquatic flowering plants are pollinated by insects or wind, as are most of the species growing on land. Water milfoil is one of the many wind-pollinated species. Water lilies, pickerelweed, and many others attract beetles and flies to their showy blossoms. Water smartweed draws bees.

Plants that grow submerged have developed special methods to ensure pollination. *Vallisneria* (also known as ribbon grass, tapegrass, and water celery) sends its female flowers up to the surface on long stalks. There they

Charmed by the water lily's surface beauty, we seldom consider what lies below. Long stalks connect leaves and lilies to the anchoring roots.

float, buoyed by their long, water-repellent stigmas. The male flowers grow underwater, near the base of the plant. At maturity they break free and float to the surface, where they drift about until they contact female flowers. The familiar aquarium plant elodea, or waterweed, bears both male and female flowers at the surface. The male flowers pop open explosively, scattering pollen grains over the surface of the water.

Eelgrass, one of the few flowering plants in the ocean, is unusual in yet another way: its pollination takes place beneath the surface. The male flowers release cloudy masses of threadlike pollen grains, which drift across the eelgrass beds. When a pollen thread touches one of the long, forked stigmas of a female flower, it wraps itself around the stigma, and pollination takes place.

Do aquatic plants always reproduce with flowers?

A number of aquatic plants reproduce by budding off new plants as well as by flowering. Duckweed, in fact, seldom produces flowers, and the profusely flowering water hyacinth also reproduces mainly by budding. Some aquatic plants spread by means of portions that break off or are torn loose by storms or feeding animals. Water milfoil and others form special buds on their stems, which drop off at the end of the growing season and fall to the bottom. The following spring they sprout into new plants—a useful backup in case the previous year's seed production has failed.

What do aquatic plants do in winter?

In tropical climates aquatic plants have no winter worries, but those in harsher places must contend with surroundings that literally freeze. Pickerelweed and many other plants that bloom above the surface die back to the roots, sending up new stems and leaves in spring. Water lilies coil up their leafstalks and pull the leaves down below the reach of the ice; in spring the stalks uncoil, allowing the buoyant leaves to bounce back to the surface. In the case of water soldier, a floating plant native to northern Europe, the whole plant sinks to the bottom, and the leaves rot away.

Even in the Water, a Diversity of Form

Water crowfoot sometimes has two sets of leaves—feathery ones that are submerged and wider "floaters."

Buckbean lifts its leaves above the water. The plant is also called bogbean and water shamrock.

Water violet bears its feathery leaves —featherfoil is an alternative name— beneath the surface. This is the Eurasian species. The North American type has white blossoms.

The Ways of Vines

What special equipment do climbing vines possess?

Vines waste no energy in building a sturdy stem. Some succumb to gravity and merely creep along the ground. Others climb trees or trellises, flourishing only when they are securely attached and have grown high enough to be out of the shade.

How vines anchor themselves to a support differs according to species. Some, such as morning glories, pole beans, and kudzu, are twiners; that is, the entire stem winds about its support and spirals up toward the light. Others develop special attachment devices. Certain roses and other ramblers secure themselves with such sharp devices as prickles, hooks, and thorns. The root climbers (English ivy and poison ivy are examples) produce a profusion of often barbed or bristly side growths, which penetrate cracks and crevices and hold the vines in place. Often forming a tight latticework or net, these rootlets are most effective when clinging to a rough surface, but some can cling to surfaces as smooth as glass.

Tendrils, an extraordinary climbing mechanism, are used by plants as diverse as grapes, cucumbers, and peas. These slim, delicate outgrowths (sometimes from the leaves, sometimes from the stems) move back and forth as they elongate, their motion caused by unequal growth rates on the two sides. Once they make contact, they coil rapidly around the support. The tendrils of Virginia creeper and its close relative Boston (or Japanese) ivy have adhesive disks at their tips.

How do vines find something to climb?

Nature relies very much on chance, and not every vine seed happens to sprout where a supporting object is conveniently placed. If there are no tall plants, rocks, or other climbable objects nearby, young vines grow horizontally, sprawling over the ground as prostrate plants. If they get sufficient light, they may form an extensive carpet before their growing tips find something that they can attach to.

The tips of most vines are extremely active, "feeling around" constantly with a sort of rotary movement that makes certain no nearby opportunity goes unseized. In some species the tips wind around each other, becoming intertwined or braided in a tight ropelike structure that can lift itself much higher off the ground than can a single vine. Some vines, particularly those in the tropics, do not live long if they fail to find a support that can lead them to light.

What plant is known as the miracle vine?

Kudzu is an immigrant plant gone wild. Native to the Orient, this robust vine with bean-shaped leaves was planted in the southeastern United States for a variety of reasons—as an ornamental, as a fodder and hay crop, as a roadside erosion-stopper, and as a shade-producer. Kudzu grows with explosive vigor, and in certain circles it became known as the miracle vine.

But in some ways the miracle vine has become a nightmare, for throughout much of the region the vine has rampaged out of control. Trees as tall as a hundred feet have been smothered by this aggressive, high-climbing vine. Telephone and power poles have been pulled to the ground; whole buildings and large areas of woodland have been engulfed.

How are lianas different from other vines?

The ropelike vines used by the fictional Tarzan to swing from tree to tree are called lianas, a name referring not to any one species but to any woody-stemmed vine. Grapes and other woody vines of temperate climates are technically lianas, though the name most commonly refers to the enormous vines—some with stems as thick as a human body—that weave their way through tropical rain forests. In real life, monkeys and many other jungle creatures do indeed use these "bush ropes" as bridges and highways for traveling through the trees.

In many tropical areas every tree seems to carry at least one liana. Rooted in the soil, the vines climb the trunks of trees—some using hooks or adhesive disks, some simply by twining—and then spread in vigorous growth through the crowns, often a hundred feet or more above the forest

Clinging Vines and Climbing Lianas

1. Certain vines use tendrils to climb toward the sun. Highly sensitive to touch, these wiry structures seek support as they grow, then wrap themselves around the object and tighten their coils.

2. Clinging vines send out aerial roots from the sides of their stems. The roots grasp onto the tree trunk.

3. Hooks and thorns are another holding device.

4. These bush ropes, or lianas, twine their way up toward the sun.

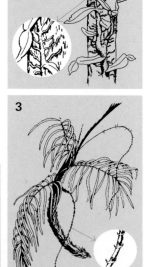

Three Different Ways of Climbing

Wiry tendrils, twining stems, and aerial rootlets help vines cling to their supports.

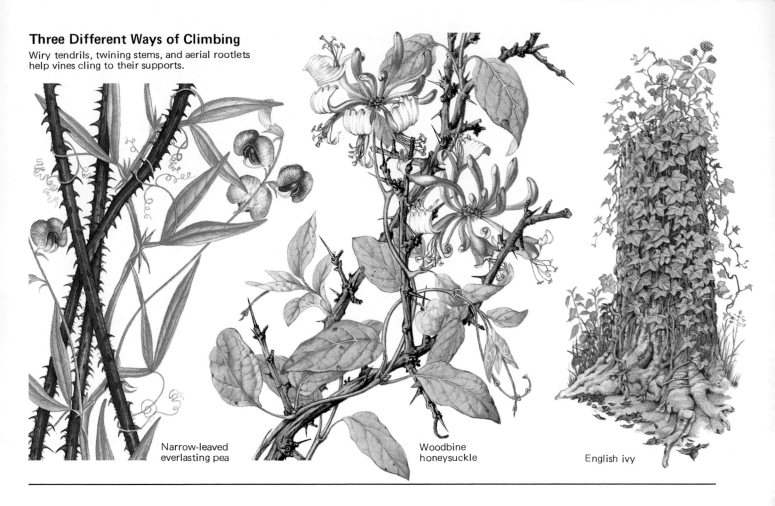

Narrow-leaved everlasting pea

Woodbine honeysuckle

English ivy

floor. They quickly fill in gaps where branches or entire trees have fallen.

Paradoxically, although these giants among vines depend on trees for support, lianas may themselves attain a total mass greater than their hosts. The weight sometimes causes huge branches to break, pulling much of the liana earthward as they go. Often these fallen vines grow in complex intertwining loops and tangles before they hoist themselves back into the forest's upper layers.

In what ways do people use vines?

Most vines grow in the tropics, and it is in the tropics that vines—their roots, fruits, leaves, and stems—have been put to the greatest use. Tough but flexible fibers from the palmlike leaves of the Panama-hat plant (or jipijapa)—a vine growing not in Panama but in the mountain forest of Peru and Ecuador—are used to make those popular lightweight straw hats. Vanilla comes from the fermented pods of the vanilla plant, a viny orchid native to Mexico

but now grown widely in warm climates around the world, particularly on Madagascar. The fish poison rotenone comes from Asian and South American vines.

Vines supply beverages too. Wines come from vines, of course (grape vines). Often considered a national drink of Brazil, guarana, concocted from the pulverized fruits of a shrubby vine, is a strong stimulant containing more caffeine than equivalent amounts of coffee or tea. Another drink is made from the sweet, juicy, aromatic passion fruit. Passionflowers are also appreciated for their flowers, whose structure reminded explorers of the Crucifixion of Christ.

What is rattan?

Most palms conform to the stereotype of straight-trunked trees with crowns of fronds, but a number of species are mavericks in this regard. Instead of developing their own trunks, they use the trunks and crowns of other trees to climb up to the sun.

Among these unpalmlike palms are the rattan palms, which grow on Pacific islands and in the tropics of Africa, Asia, and Australia. In most rattan palms, the woody, bamboolike, flexible stem (used for making baskets, furniture, and other items) is heavily spined beginning at a point about four feet above the ground. The spines help the palm cling to its support; barbed, whiplike tips on the fronds do the same.

Unlike most vines, rattans do not scramble to the tops of tall trees; they stay mainly at a medium height and then stretch from tree to tree. Of all the climbing plants, the rattans attain the greatest total length—some of them measuring more than 650 feet in length. Rattans have enormous quantities of water stored in their stems. A cut piece of rattan eight or nine feet long may yield several cups of pure, drinkable water. In a growing plant, water moves up the stem at a rate of five or six feet per minute, faster than in any other plant so far recorded.

127

Perching Plants

Why do plants grow on other plants?

Everywhere in warm climates trees are host to plants that grow attached to their trunks or sit on their limbs like birds on a roost. Among them are certain orchids, bromeliads, arums, cacti, ferns, mosses, liverworts, and algae—plants from unrelated groups that share the common feature of having no roots in the soil.

These are the epiphytes (*epiphyte* means "on a plant"), often dubbed air plants because they get their water mainly from the humid atmosphere. Epiphytes are not parasites. They manufacture their own food and do not harm their hosts except by their

An incredible variety of orchids blossom atop other plants. Some species develop a creeping form; others grow upright.

sheer weight on the branches (which sometimes break), or by usurping the air and space.

Epiphytes have adopted their high-living habit because it brings them into the sun. In the tropics perching plants are sometimes so abundant that it becomes difficult to distinguish a tree's real foliage.

How do plants manage to get up into the trees?

Epiphytes reproduce as other plants do—by seeds, spores, or other means, depending on the species. Though winds may blow seeds and spores to a lofty position, birds do much of the work for seed-bearing species. Using branches as perches, they eat the fleshy fruits, depositing the undigested seeds in a new location.

Which orchids live on trees?

Orchids growing in temperate climates, such as lady's slippers, tway-blades, and helleborines, are rooted in the soil. But in the tropics most of the thousands of orchid species are epiphytes, perching atop trees in order to ensure their place in the sun. Epiphytic orchids produce two types of roots. One kind anchors the plant to its host or support. The other protrudes from the plant, ending in a spongy, water-absorbing tip.

Orchids are not the only beautiful blossoms to grow perched atop other plants. Orchid cacti rival the true orchids—and in some cases surpass them—in the pleasure they give to the eye. Like most of the orchids, orchid cacti usually grow as epiphytes, anchored to the trunks and branches of trees at high elevations in tropical forests. Orchid cacti are among the species known as jungle cacti. Different in form from desert cacti, they lack the fearsome spines of their dry-country relatives (they have small bristles instead) and generally have long, trailing branches or flattened stems. The spectacularly blossomed houseplants known as Christmas cacti are jungle cacti, native to Brazil.

Which epiphytes are the most abundant?

Tropical orchids far outnumber any other epiphytes in terms of variety. But when abundance is measured, the bromeliads, found almost exclusively in the American tropics and subtropics, are unquestionably the winners. Bromeliads are mostly short-stemmed plants with stiff leaves rising in a rosette. Some produce plumed seeds easily transported by the wind; others have their seeds dispersed by fruit-eating birds. Bromeliads are popular as houseplants, many of them sporting handsome foliage as well as big, brightly colored blossoms. They are also popular in kitchens—not as living plants but as edibles. For the best-known bromeliad is the pineapple, which is a terrestrial species rather than an epiphyte; that is, it grows rooted in the ground.

The world's largest bromeliad grows high in the Andes mountains. Sometimes measuring more than 30 feet tall (that includes its flowering spike), it is not an epiphyte but a plant rooted in soil. Growing on it, however, is an epiphyte—the world's smallest bromeliad, a tiny 2-inch relative of Spanish moss.

How do epiphytes get the water they need?

By definition, epiphytes have no direct connection with the earth. A few species growing in the American tropics draw water in from streams (they send long aerial roots into the stream, then pipe the water back up as much as 60 feet), but epiphytes have no access to water in the ground. Like all other plants, however, they do need mois-

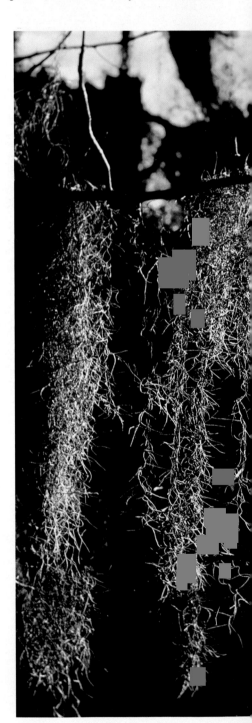

ture. How they obtain it depends on the type of plant.

Like desert plants, some epiphytes store water in thick leaves; many have waxy coatings on their leaves and stems, cutting down on water loss. Epiphytes can often absorb moisture directly from the atmosphere, using roots that protrude from the plant. (Other roots serve to anchor them to their perch.) Orchids put out finger-like aerial roots, tipped with "sponges" that collect water from the air. In the dry season they use their emergency supply—the water stored in swellings called pseudobulbs.

Ferns may catch and hold supplies of water in their cuplike bases. Bromeliads perched on tree limbs in the tropics are veritable cisterns: large ones hold several quarts of water in the cup formed by the overlapping leaves.

The thick roots of this strangler fig have braided themselves around another tree. Like other types of stranglers, strangler figs start out as perching plants.

Garlands of Spanish moss festoon trees in the southeastern United States. These perching plants have tiny green flowers, long stems, and no roots. If a stem breaks, both parts can grow into new plants.

How do strangler figs strangle their hosts?

Strangler figs, relatives of the edible fig, start out life as epiphytes, sprouting from seeds deposited by birds that have eaten the fruits. The germinating seed sends a small sprig of leaves upward, and threadlike aerial roots down toward the ground. Some roots wrap around the trunk; others drop straight down, spurring the growth of the entire plant when they burrow into the soil.

Soon the strangler develops a trunk of its own, part of it tightly wrapped around the host tree. Some of its broad crown may also be supported by the columnlike roots planted in the soil. Deprived of light by the strangler's dense canopy, constricted by its roots, and robbed of water and minerals, the host eventually falls victim to this vigorous killer. In time, only the hollow core in the center of the strangler remains as evidence of the extraordinary way this one-time epiphyte gained its independence.

Do epiphytes live only in jungles?

Although the struggle for a share of sunlight has drawn more kinds of plants into trees in the tropics than in cooler climates, the perching habit is not exclusive to plants in warm lands. In cool and temperate climates most epiphytes are such nonflowering plants as mosses, ferns, and algae. For many of them, not being rooted in the soil is nothing new; even down on the ground, they obtain moisture by other means than roots.

Nonflowering plants growing in the treetops may sometimes belong to the same species as those growing on the ground. It is not uncommon, for example, to see clumps of ferns at the base of a tree and a few adventuresome individuals of the same kind growing high on the trunk or perched out on a limb. Many mosses and liverworts cling to tree trunks, with only their need for moisture limiting how high they can grow. Algae form slippery coatings over the trunks and branches of trees. Such lichens as old-man's beard hang from the branches of trees in greenish-gray tufts, their appearance startlingly similar to that of Spanish moss, which—despite its name—is a flowering plant.

129

Wild, Wonderful Weeds

What are weeds?

Chrysanthemums and tomatoes are plants some people spend a great deal of time tending. But a tomato plant growing in a row of carrots or a chrysanthemum popping up among the petunias can, under the circumstances, be considered a weed. Weeds, in a general sense, are plants growing where they are not wanted.

Before they were "tamed," all of our cultivated crops and ornamental plants were in fact weeds. Interestingly, today many of them are incapable of making their way in the world on their own: the competition from the plants popularly known as weeds is just too great.

Weeds are typically tough, vigorous opportunists, generally capable of prolific growth under a variety of conditions. (Plants with specialized growth needs, such as rich, moist soil and an abundance of shade, rarely turn into weeds.) Often you see weeds in waste places—vacant lots, for example, or along the sides of roads.

Another general trait of weeds is their ability to produce an abundance of seeds and quickly colonize empty places. The seeds of some weeds have plumes with which they ride the wind (thistles and dandelions, for instance). Others carry such hitchhiking equipment as hooks (burdock), barbs (beggar's-ticks), and glue (peppergrass). Weeds also have an amazing ability to spread by means other than seeds. Year after year, perennial weeds sprout from their roots and underground stems, persisting even if their aboveground parts are cut off with a sickle or hoe.

Why do many of our weeds come from other places?

Like animals, plant populations commonly "explode" when moved to areas where they do not occur naturally and have no natural enemies to check their growth. Most such introductions come about accidentally, the seeds tucked into cargo or transported in some other way. But some plants are intentional transplants that turn into uncontrollable weeds when they escape into the wild.

Burdock, for example, was brought to North America by colonists who relished the roots as a vegetable. The plant's use as a food waned, but the burdocks have prospered as weeds, spreading from coast to coast. Similarly, the American prickly pear cactus was planted over large areas in Australia as a living fence. The aggressive cactus kept moving on its own, and within a short time became a prickly pest. Eventually, it was brought under control by introducing its natural insect foes from the United States.

Which plants are water weeds?

Algae are the first link in aquatic food chains. But algae "blooms" can sometimes exhaust the water's oxygen supply, leading to the death of animal life. Flowering plants can be equally troublesome, choking waterways and fouling fishing lines and lures. The water

Plantain

Great burdock

Dandelion

hyacinth, a South American species, got its start in the United States when a few "extras" were thrown from a rock-garden pool into a river in the South. The plant, attractive to some because of its spike of showy purple flowers, has since spread throughout much of the southeastern part of North America.

Are all weeds bad?
In a sense there is no such thing as a weed. One part of a dictionary's defi-nition of a weed is "a plant of no value"—but just about every plant has some redeeming feature. Thick growths of weeds prevent soil from eroding, and their tough, extensive root systems break up hard-packed soil. Plants with deep roots lift valua-ble minerals, including trace elements, to the surface, where they eventually become available to other plants.

Weeds are in some cases sources of medicines, dyes, and other useful products. Though we humans depend on weeds for food to a far lesser extent than do wild creatures, we eat such weeds as watercress, chicory, and dandelion greens. Weeds can be attractive too—their foliage delicate, their fruits fascinating, and their blossoms welcome bursts of color.

Chicory

Mullein

Motherwort

Grasses and Grains

How are grasses different from other plants?

Sedges and rushes are often confused with grasses, for all three usually have long thin stems and long, relatively narrow leaves with parallel veins. The stems furnish the best clue for distinguishing among the three groups. Grasses have round, hollow stems with solid joints called nodes. (A few exceptional species have stems that are completely solid.) In contrast, sedges usually have solid, three-sided stems with no joints. Rushes usually have wiry, round stems and bear their seeds in little pods.

Although the flowers of grasses are so small and inconspicuous that most people don't realize grasses have them, the flowers are indeed there, and botanists use them to differentiate among species. At the appropriate time of year, each grass plant bears numerous small flowers (the details can be seen with a hand lens), clustered in flower heads that are often branched and look somewhat like feathers. Some species have bristly flower heads; others are more like spikes. Grass flowers are pollinated not by insects but by the wind. Over time they have been stripped down to the bare essentials—reproductive parts shielded by tough, papery scales. In many grasses the flowers may pollinate themselves. Wheat is one of the plants in which self-pollination occurs.

Why do grasses cover so much land?

Grasses cover nearly one-third of the world's land area. They thrive atop mountains at the snow line and in depressions lying below sea level. They occur north of the Arctic Circle, at the equator, and south almost to the Antarctic ice cap. They grow on neatly tended lawns, in forest glades, and on such vast grasslands as prairies, savannas, pampas, steppes, and veldt.

Grasses do better than trees in so many places because they require so much less moisture. Most of a grass plant is underground, in the form of roots. In time of drought the grass becomes dormant, reviving when the rains return. It dies back to its root system in winter, then sends up new shoots in spring that will sow their own seeds. Some grasses are annual, living only one year and depending on seeds (rather than roots and seeds) for the next year's growth. Wheat, barley, rye, and wild rice are all annual grasses.

Grasses have another advantage over trees. Grass leaves grow continuously outward from their bases. If grazing animals nibble them down, the leaves keep growing out again. The same thing happens when man "grazes" his lawns with mowers. Grazed or mowed right down to the ground, grasses will come back again and again. Many species spread rapidly by sending out creeping stems beneath the ground or at the surface. These rhizomes and stolons, as they are called, send up new stems, so that a single grass plant may produce a large patch of vegetation. The dense sod that develops protects the soil very effectively against erosion.

Can grasses survive in water?

Although grasses are basically dry-land plants, over time some types have developed the ability to grow in water. One of these is rice, which is the chief food of more than half the human race. Rice is usually started in a special plot, then transplanted to a flooded

---

A Gallery of Grasses

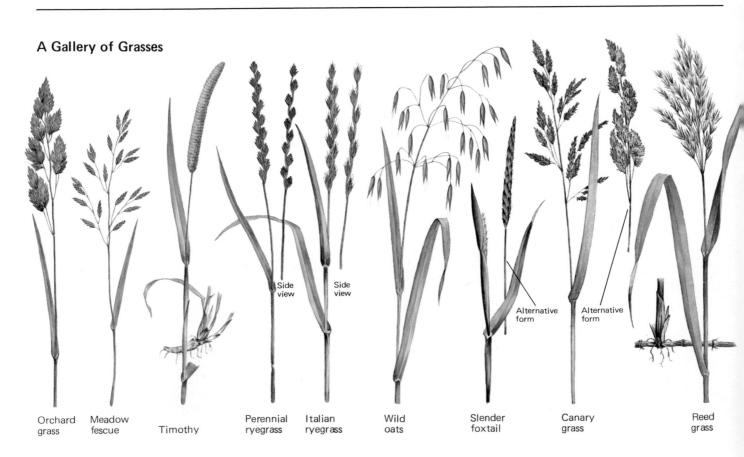

Orchard grass   Meadow fescue   Timothy   Perennial ryegrass   Italian ryegrass   Wild oats   Slender foxtail   Canary grass   Reed grass

field when the seedlings are four or five inches tall. Closely related to rice is wild rice, native to north-central North America. Indians traditionally harvested wild rice in canoes, bending the stems over the canoe and knocking the ripe grains into the bottom of the vessel. Much grain spilled into the lake, thereby assuring the reseeding of the crop.

Another aquatic grass is cordgrass, remarkable not just because it grows in water but because it can grow in salt water—specifically, saltwater marshes. Its root membranes screen out much of the salt from the water. Glands on its leaves excrete salt, and the salt that remains is concentrated in the cells of the grass plants in such a way that it does not interfere with their life processes. Interestingly, the places where cordgrass grows may not stay wet forever. Their underground connections bind the soil, and their waving leaves break the force of the sea. Eventually soil and sediments may build up, and the marsh will turn into dry land.

Which grass is the biggest?
Though reports tell of prairie grass that grew taller than a horse, and in Mexico a variety of corn grows 20 feet tall, the undisputed giant is bamboo. While we may think of bamboo as a tropical plant, some kinds grow high in the mountains of southwestern China, where winters are snowy and cold. In South America, bamboos grow up to the snow line of the Andes. There are native bamboos on every continent but Europe and Antarctica.

Bamboos blossom rarely. Twenty years may elapse between flowerings, and one Japanese species blossoms only once in 120 years. After flowering, a bamboo plant usually dies.

Bamboo shoots sprout from underground runners and are famous for their rapid rate of growth—sometimes as much as three feet in a single day. Gorillas, giant pandas, and humans enjoy eating the tender shoots. Once a bamboo stem is mature, it does not get thicker, but continues to grow only at the top. The tallest species, native to southern Asia, may reach 120 feet. Wherever they grow, bamboos form impenetrable thickets; the stems are so tough and so full of silica that they dull the sharpest cutting tool.

The Life-giving Grasses

Wheat, rice, corn, rye, oats, barley, millet, sorghum—the most important grasses of all are the cereal grains. The seeds of these grasses, especially the first three, are major items in the human diet. They are fed to livestock and poultry as well, and they supply products as diverse as starch, sugar, syrup, adhesives, and alcohol.

Each of these cereals is descended from a wild-growing grass whose seeds man collected and ate. Evidence suggests that wheat and barley may be the oldest cultivated grains, dating back at least to 5000 B.C. Corn may have been domesticated by 4000 B.C. Rice was being grown in China by 2400 B.C.

Over the centuries techniques have been developed for cultivating the grains, and the plants themselves have undergone enormous genetic change. In one monumental change, the grains have become dependent on man for survival. The seeds of wild grasses are loosely attached to the plant. In nature, this helps the grasses to spread their seeds; but in farming, it means that a great many seeds drop to the ground and are lost during harvest. Plant breeders have developed varieties of grain whose seeds are not easily dislodged. The most extreme example is corn, whose seeds are enclosed inside a tight husk.

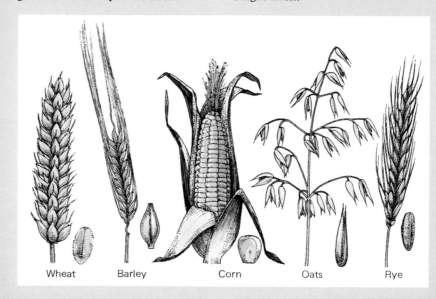

Wheat　Barley　Corn　Oats　Rye

Eating bamboo shoots is not the only way people use bamboo. The hollow stems can be cut into containers, for at each joint is a watertight partition. If holes are bored through the partitions, long stems can be turned into water pipes. Big stems are used for building houses and bridges; split and flattened, they make sturdy boards. Thin sections of split stems are woven into baskets and chair seats. Bamboo is also used to make paper pulp, as well as ropes, flutes, and hand tools of all descriptions.

Which grass is the sweetest?
About 300 B.C. a Greek scholar, Theophrastus, wrote about a "sweet salt"

that the people of India prepared from a reedlike plant. The sweet salt was sugar, and the reedlike plant he described was sugarcane. Sugarcane—there are many varieties—grows from 10 to 24 feet tall, with long, bladelike leaves. As the stalks mature, they turn a colorful mixture of deep red, purple, yellow, pink, and other rainbow tints. Most varieties produce a tassel of flowers at the top of the stem, but the seeds that develop from the pollinated flowers are rarely fertile. Commercial growers propagate sugarcane from sections of the stem. When buried, a section sends out roots and stems, and usually yields two or three harvests before replanting is required.

133

The Daisy Family

What's so interesting about a plain old daisy?

With its brightly colored center and fringe of petals at the rim, a daisy looks like just an ordinary flower. But things are not as simple as they seem. For in the central disk of the blossom are literally hundreds of individual tubular flowers, each capable of producing its own seed. Surrounding the disk are streamerlike rays. Popularly called petals, these flat straps are not petals at all but still more flowers. The ray flowers attract bees and other insect pollinators to the "business" part of the flower head—that is, to the disk flowers, where pollination occurs—and they serve as a convenient perching spot as well.

Do all composites have the same parts?

Daisies belong to one of the largest families of flowering plants, variously known as the daisy, the sunflower, and the aster family. With some 20,000 species, the group rivals the orchid family in diversity.

"Diversity" is in a sense a botanist's term, sometimes referring to differences between species that are not readily apparent to the untrained eye. In this family, however, there are some major subdivisions. Plants belonging to the family all produce composite blossoms—that is, ones composed of a number of individual flowers, typically arranged in tight flower heads. (Yet another alternative name for the family is the composite family.) The "standard" composite, such as a daisy or a sunflower, has disk flowers in the center and ray flowers at the edge. But there are many varia-

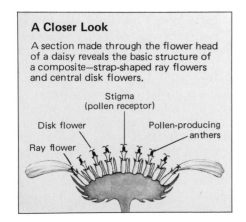

A Closer Look

A section made through the flower head of a daisy reveals the basic structure of a composite—strap-shaped ray flowers and central disk flowers.

Stigma (pollen receptor)

Disk flower

Pollen-producing anthers

Ray flower

A summertime field of daisies is impressive in its own right. But the effect is compounded when you realize that each blossom contains dozens of tiny flowers.

tions. Thistles and their cousins have no ray flowers—only disk flowers. And dandelions and chicory are among the composites that have only ray flowers—no disk flowers at all.

Does the daisy family contain any unique plants?

Though every species is by definition special, some are more unusual in appearance than others and more restricted in range. At one end of the scale for the daisy family is the common dandelion; at the other, the silversword. Silverswords grow high on the cinder-cone volcanoes in Hawaii, thriving in conditions hostile to other plants—extreme heat during the day, nocturnal cold spells, and practically no humidity or rain. Slim, pointed leaves form a big, spiked ball, blanketed by silvery hairs that reflect the intense sunlight and protect the plants' vital parts. The plant grows slowly for as long as 20 years. Then a leafless stem rises up from the center of the leaf ball. Along the sides of the stem a hundred or more small sunflowerlike blossoms appear, each with a yellow disk surrounded by purple rays. Its flowering completed, the plant dies and tumbles down the volcano, leaving behind the seeds of future generations.

Are sunflowers the largest of all flowers?

The giants among the wild sunflowers stand nearly 15 feet tall, and their huge flower heads may measure more than a foot across. Heads of some cultivated sunflowers reach twice that size. But even in these behemoths the individual flowers—brown in some, purplish in others—are small; literally hundreds are packed together to form the central disk. A sunflower blossom is not one large flower but a great cluster of tiny, densely packed flowers. So the sunflower in no way tops Indonesia's *Rafflesia*. In that extravagant species, just a single flower measures three feet across.

Which composites do we eat?

Without composites, salads would take on a very different appearance, and ingredients for them would be far more difficult to obtain. Lettuce, for example, belongs to the composite family (though few gardeners would be willing to have their lettuce "bolt" just to see its composite flowers). Endive is a leafy composite similar to lettuce; its leaves are bitter unless blanched as they grow. Chicory, still another leafy salad plant (it is marketed under the name Belgian endive), is more popular in its native Europe than in the United States, where it now grows as a weed.

Leaves are not the only parts of composites that we eat. The oyster plant, or salsify, has fleshy white roots with a flavor somewhat like oysters. Globe artichoke—the "ordinary" artichoke—is a coarse, thistlelike plant with big, round flower heads. Surrounding the clusters of small purplish flowers are the thick, overlapping, succulent scales so prized as items of food. The closely related cardoon is grown mainly for its celerylike stems, though its roots are sometimes eaten.

Which composites are valued for their beauty?

For its size, the daisy family contains surprisingly few species of economic importance, but the flowers it produces make an astounding contribution to the beauty of the earth. Whether you consider them weeds or wildflowers, the decorative value of such plants as chicory, hawkweeds, thistles, coneflowers, and goldenrods cannot be denied.

Some of the most popular cultivated flowers belong to the daisy family too, many of them so altered by selective breeding that they bear only the slightest resemblance to their wild ancestors. Once upon a time, zinnias were weedy Mexican plants with small, inconspicuous flowers. Dramatically transformed by horticulturalists over the years, zinnias now come in an incredible array of colors and forms. Literally thousands of varieties of dahlias have been developed—some coming into favor and then fading, others remaining popular year after year. Cosmos, asters, coreopsis, and chrysanthemums are other popular garden composites. Marigolds have a value beyond beauty. Their roots give off a chemical that kills pests, and the plants produce substances that actually burn up the tissues of insects trying to feed on their leaves.

The bachelor's button, or cornflower, is a composite with disk flowers only (no rays). The diagram at right shows the densely packed modified leaves (the involucre) that support a composite.

Disk flowers

Involucre (support)

Remarkable Roses

What do we mean by "a rose"?

Wild strawberries, mountain ash trees, raspberry bushes, hawthorns—the inclusion of many of the plants on these two pages may come as a surprise. For the subject under discussion is not only those beloved blossoms called true roses but also the other 3,000-plus species that belong to the same botanical family. Most are familiar plants, for perhaps the most remarkable aspect of roses is the extent to which they touch our lives.

How can you tell roses from other plants?

Next to their flowers, nothing about roses is more memorable than an encounter with their thorns. But though hawthorns, blackberries, and most cultivated roses are notorious for their prickly defense, many members of the rose family—among them, the fruit trees—are not so equipped.

The leaves of related plants often look quite unalike, and plants belonging to the rose family are no exception. Many, such as cultivated roses and mountain ash, have compound leaves (that is, each leaf consists of a number of leaflets); but such plants as apple

A single rose symbolizes beauty, caring, love. The astounding variety of cultivated roses that has been developed from wild species like this one bears witness to both the incredible diversity of nature and man's creative hand.

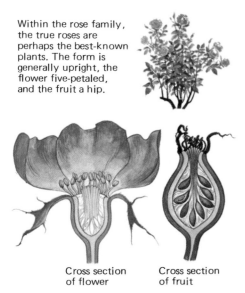

Within the rose family, the true roses are perhaps the best-known plants. The form is generally upright, the flower five-petaled, and the fruit a hip.

Cross section of flower   Cross section of fruit

and pear trees have simple leaves. To add to their diversity, the leaves of some species have smooth edges and others toothed. Nearly all species have a pair of leaflike appendages (called stipules) at the base of the leaf (where it joins the stem), but these are generally shed as the leaf develops.

In the rose family, and other plant families too, flowers are the most reliable means of identification. Excluding cultivated flowers, which almost by definition have been altered by man, flowers of species belonging to the rose family typically have five petals and five sepals (sepals are modified leaves, sometimes green and sometimes of other colors, that form a circle around the petals). Inside are numerous pollen-bearing stamens (the male parts) and the single central pistil (the female part).

Do all roses bear similar fruit?

One basic rule of botany is that fruits tell very little about relationships among plants. Not only do closely related species often have very different fruits; species that belong to vastly different groups may bear fruits that look pretty much the same.

Though blossoms of plants belonging to the rose family are structurally quite similar, once pollinated they develop in their own separate ways. Roses turn into rose hips, each hip a group of single-seeded fruits within a fleshy container. Peach, cherry, and plum fruits are all drupes, which contain a single seed at the center, a hard pit, and a juicy layer covering all.

Raspberry fruits are clusters of drupes. Still other members of the rose family, such as apples and pears, produce pomes—fruits with a fleshy layer and a central, usually five-seeded core.

How are almonds related to peaches?

The almond, one of the favorites of all nuts, comes from a peachlike fruit. With peaches we eat the fruits and throw away the seeds—and quite fortunately, too, for peach pits contain large amounts of highly toxic prussic acid. The seeds of apricots, cherries, and even apples also contain prussic acid, and so do bitter almonds. The ones we eat are sweet almonds.

In spring, almond trees, which grow to a height of about 30 feet and sometimes develop a delicate weeping form, bear showy pink flowers (the trees are sometimes grown simply for their ornamental value). After pollination these develop into fruits with an inedible flesh. As the fruits ripen, they shed their pits—that is, the almonds we eat, which have a high protein content (about 20 percent) and are also used as food flavoring and as a component of certain medicines. Oil from bitter almonds is processed too, but it is distilled to remove the toxic prussic acid.

What do true roses symbolize?

Before there were written records, people were admiring wild roses, and by the time scholars began to chronicle history, the rose was already an established companion of man. Luxury-minded Greeks reclined on beds of rose petals, and to this day "a bed of roses" is the epitome of ease.

The cultivation of roses—transforming the rather simple wildflower into more handsome forms—began in the Orient, under dynasties that predated the Greeks. The popularity of the rose spread throughout Europe, furthering the rose's role in symbolism, religion, and art. Throughout the ages, the rose—particularly the red rose—has been a symbol of caring and love. *Sub rosa,* said of something carried out in secrecy, is said to date from the Pope's placing of roses over confessionals. The rose is England's official flower, and in the United States the emblem of the District of Columbia and the states of New York, North Dakota, Iowa, and Georgia.

How have roses changed over time?

Wild roses may be white, pink, red, or yellow—but never blue; a blue rose, in fact, symbolizes the impossible. But rose breeders are moving toward this achievement, too, for in addition to every conceivable shade of the basic rose colors, they have added to their incredible array blossoms that are green, silvery, mauve, and violet.

Roses have been in cultivation for so many centuries that the precise wild ancestry of most varieties is no longer traceable. From several dozen species more than 5,000 varieties have been developed, ranging in size from dwarf plants no more than 6 inches tall to giant vines that can sprawl over 30 feet and to shrubs that may stand 10 feet tall. Their flowers are equally varied, ranging from miniatures less than an inch wide to mammoths some five inches across. Most have numerous petals—far more than the basic five.

What value do true roses have other than looks?

Those who have difficulty digesting or assimilating some kinds of vitamin C (ascorbic acid) rarely have problems when the source is the fruit of true roses, or rose hips. Oil obtained by distilling rose petals is the attar of roses used by the perfume industry—a costly product because about two tons of rose petals must be processed to get a pound of oil. Rose petals were long ago used in folk medicine, mainly as an astringent. Some say that rose petals were valued as food before beauty became their commanding attribute. Even today the petals are still a culinary item, added to salads primarily for brightness.

Two Representative Roses

Mountain avens is an alpine flower bearing big, beautiful blossoms and evergreen leaves.

Raspberries show several common rose-family traits—compound leaves, prickly stems, and leafy stipules where leafstalk meets stem.

Deadly, Delicious Nightshades

What are the nightshades?

The 2,000 species of plants belonging to the nightshade family range in size from small, delicate wildflowers to woody shrubs; a few even grow to the size of small trees. Some are extremely poisonous (the name is said to refer to the tranquilizing effect); some are valuable food plants. Diverse as these plants are, they all have five-petaled flowers shaped like wheels or funnels, with some additional technical characteristics that cause botanists to group them into the same family.

Why are the nightshades deadly?

Though not all plants belonging to the nightshade family are poisonous, the ones that are cause a variety of problems—severe digestive disturbances, hallucinations, interference with breathing and circulation, and sometimes even death. The causes are alkaloids the plants contain.

One of the most toxic nightshades is the jimsonweed; its name comes from that of Jamestown, Virginia, where a group of English soldiers were poisoned by eating it in 1676. The plant is tall and evil-smelling, with big, toothed leaves and spiny fruits. "Thorn apple" is another name. American Indians used its seeds in religious ceremonies for their narcotic effect. In more recent times, one of its poisonous alkaloids, scopolamine, has been used as a "truth serum."

A second killer is deadly nightshade, a native of Europe, also known as belladonna—Italian for "beautiful lady." (In the Middle Ages, women used drops from this plant to expand the pupils of their eyes, since large pupils were considered attractive.) Belladonna is the drug doctors use to dilate the pupils of their patients for eye examinations. Belladonna was used by practitioners of witchcraft to cause such hallucinations as a feeling of flying through the air.

Are potatoes deadly?

In the early 1700's the Swedish government was promoting a new crop, the potato. In the cool Swedish summer, the potato plants set fruit, and many peasants, thinking the berrylike fruits were meant to be eaten, did in fact eat them and became seriously ill. For all parts of the plant except the tubers—the part we eat—are poisonous. Even the green spots that develop on tubers are poisonous.

The potato originated in the bleak uplands of the Andes, in what is now Bolivia and Peru. No one knows how long ago man had begun to cultivate the wild potatoes that still grow there, but by the time of the Spanish conquest, in the 16th century, the Incas and their subjects were raising numerous varieties, with skins ranging in color from white and yellow to brown, pink, red, purple, and blue.

Although Sir Walter Raleigh and Sir Francis Drake have been credited with introducing the potato to Europe, it was probably the Spanish who did it first. Potatoes thrived in the relatively cool, moist European climate and in some places became more important than grain. Today potatoes not only are a major human food but are also processed for starch and alcohol.

Chinese lanterns bear fruits very different from those of other nightshades.

Bittersweet nightshade, a vine, produces berries that are poisonous but not fatal.

138

Peppers and Eggplants: Two Edible Fruits

Long before the coming of the Europeans to the New World, Indian civilizations from the Caribbean to the Andes were raising certain nightshade plants whose fruits tasted burning hot. The mouth-searing effect came from an irritating compound with a powerful action on such tender tissues as the lining of the mouth. Despite this, the Indians esteemed the fruits and used them liberally in their cooking. The Aztecs called the fruit *chilli*. We call them hot peppers. The flavoring paprika also comes from a member of the nightshade family, a sweet pepper. Both black and white pepper come from an Old World plant belonging to a completely different botanical family.

The eggplant is also the fruit of a nightshade—this one probably native to India (at least that is where it was first cultivated). During the thousands of years of cultivation, many varieties have been developed, including ones that differ drastically in color and size. A small-fruited white variety may have inspired the name "eggplant."

Eggplant

Pepper

Which of the nightshades was called the "love apple"?

When Spanish conquerors overran Mexico in the early 1500's, they found the Indians raising a small, soft-fleshed, sour fruit that looked a bit like an apple. The Indians called it *tomatl*, from which comes the modern name *tomato*. The Spaniards sent seeds back to Europe as a curiosity, but for years the tomato was considered poisonous. As often happened with exotic plants, the tomato acquired an undeserved reputation as an aphrodisiac and was dubbed "love apple."

The Italians were the first (in about 1550) to experiment with eating the supposedly dangerous and sexually arousing fruit. They found it quite safe, and since then tomatoes have been a mainstay of Italian cooking. Other countries were slower to take up the tomato, however. Thomas Jefferson grew tomatoes on his estate in Virginia in the 1780's and served them at his table. As late as 1900, however, many North Americans still believed that tomatoes were poisonous—although they did use the fruits as a base for catsup.

How are tomatoes related to potatoes?

Potatoes and tomatoes are both members of the nightshade family, and, curiously enough, there are some plants that yield both tomatoes and potatoes. This is not nature's way, of course, but a creation of man's: such plants are produced by grafting the stem of a tomato plant onto the roots of potatoes. Mail-order seed houses sometimes offer these plants as novelties. Though the crop you get is not particularly bountiful, the oddities are a sure-fire way of attracting attention.

Which plant produces paper lanterns?

The Chinese lantern—also called the Japanese lantern—isn't much to look at most of the year. Its leaves and flowers are inconspicuous, its form shapeless and undefined. But in autumn the plant comes into its own. As the fruits develop, the sepals (the parts cupping the flowers) become enlarged and bladderlike, enclosing the berry in a spectacular orange or blood-red "lantern" and transforming a rather ordinary-looking member of the nightshade family into one of the most extraordinary garden plants.

Where did petunias come from?

One of the mainstays of flower gardeners is the rugged, nearly foolproof petunia, one of the more vividly colored members of the nightshade family. Developed from wildflowers native to South America, petunias take their name from *petun,* a Brazilian Indian word for tobacco, which is a distant cousin. Several types of flowering tobacco, often called by the name nicotiana, are also popular garden ornamentals, prized for their graceful blossoms and for the delightful nighttime fragrance they emit to attract pollinating moths. Other nightshades raised to delight the eye include salpiglossis (also called painted tongue) and matrimony vine (a spiny shrub).

Which nightshade is grown for its leaves?

Shipmates of Columbus saw natives of the West Indies "drinking smoke" through a holder with forked ends that were inserted into the nostrils. The name for this holder was *tabaco* (some claim it was the name of a kind of cigar the Indians made), which the Spaniards took to be the name of the plant. A large-leaved, pink-flowered plant belonging to the nightshade family, tobacco is native to the New World. Although Indians from southern Canada to the Gulf Coast raised various types, experts believe that the chief cultivated species originated in South America, probably in Brazil.

Lilies of the Field

What defines a lily?

Whether or not the biblical "lilies of the field" (Matthew 6:28) were in fact true lilies is in dispute. For then, as now, "lily" was a name given not only to plants of the lily family (especially tiger lilies and close relatives) but also to a host of other plants with showy flowers. Some think the biblical text referred to the white Madonna lily, which belongs to the lily family; others, to anemones, attractive members of the buttercup family that were abundant on the Mount of Olives.

Typical members of the lily family grow from underground bulbs, which have a stem at their core and are surrounded by tightly packed food-storage leaves. The ordinary, above-ground leaves have parallel veins. The flowers, borne singly or in groups, are generally somewhat bell-shaped (lilies of the valley, for example) or triangular (trilliums), and they have six petallike parts. Extending from inside the flower are six prominent pollen-bearing stamens and, in the center, a large pistil with three compartments.

When a lily flower is pollinated, it develops into either a dry fruit or a multiple-seeded berry. Lily of the valley, asparagus, and several others in the family have the berry type of fruit. Most plants in the lily family are an-

Day lily

nual or perennial herbs—herbs, that is, according to the botanical definition, "plants that lack woody tissues." A surprisingly large number, including the 300 or so species of sharp-prickled greenbriers, are vines.

How tall do lilies grow?

When the word "lily" is mentioned, most people tend to think of attractive garden flowers rather than trees. But within the lily family are a number of tree-sized species, including about a dozen types of yuccas. Yuccas, most abundant in dry parts of Mexico and the southwestern United States, have clusters of stiff, pointed leaves (some go by the name of Spanish bayonet). The largest is the weird-looking Joshua tree, which bears bristling, brushlike clusters of leaves at the ends of its branches.

Even taller is the dragon tree, native to the Canary Islands but cultivated in warm climates throughout the world. Some individuals measure more than 50 feet tall. The dragon tree is a kind of dracaena, as are a number of house-plants valued for their clusters of palmlike, variegated leaves. (The word *dracaena* means "female dragon," for when dried the plant's juices are said to resemble dragon's blood.) Even the dragon tree can be grown indoors, though indoor specimens are unlikely to attain draconic size.

What do lilies smell like?

To many people the most aromatic parts of lilies are not the sweet-smelling blossoms but the pungent bulbs—specifically, the bulbs (but also the leaves) of onions, garlic, and their kin. These emit a highly volatile sulfur compound that mixes with eye secretions to form a mild sulfuric acid—and results in stinging, tearing eyes. Long used in folk remedies, these "stinking lilies" (all are members of the lily fam-

European smilax

Lily of
the valley

Fruit

Fruit

ily) are said to improve general circulation and blood pressure as well as helping some respiratory and digestive problems.

Though some bothersome weeds are wild species of onion (cows feeding on them produce onion-flavored milk), the common onion, cultivated at least since the days of the ancient Egyptians, no longer grows in the wild. Cousins that are cultivated include the shallot, with its clusters of small, mild-tasting bulbs used mainly for cooking. The slim leaves of chives, the gentlest of the common onion's relatives, flavor salads, cottage cheese, and various other dishes.

Which lilies are wildflowers?
Fortified by the copious supply of food stored in their bulbs, plants belonging to the lily family get off to a fast start in spring. Some, such as the woodland trilliums, add color to still-frosty landscapes. Among the most widespread are the mottled-leaved adder's-tongues (or dogtooth violets), Solomon's seals with their arching stems, the delicate star-of-Bethlehem, and day lilies, those orange-flowered natives of Europe that have spread throughout the world.

Which lilies are garden plants?
Lilies may be the oldest of all garden flowers, their popularity constant through the years. Many hybrids and varieties have been developed from the lilies that grow wild in the Northern Hemisphere. Among the favorites are the pure white Easter lilies, the red Japanese lilies, and the meadow lilies and others with yellow or orange flowers. Some, such as tiger lilies, are spotted. The striking blossoms of regal lilies, eight-foot-tall natives of China, are white on the inside, purplish on the outside, and yellow at the base.

Were there no lily family, springtime gardens would look quite different, for the family includes both the tulips and the hyacinths. Tulips are natives of the eastern Mediterranean (their name comes from the Persian for "turban"), though they have become so identified with the Netherlands that many people think of them as having originated in that low-lying land. Borne singly at the tips of stiff, straight stems and occurring in a phe-

This dazzling array says tulips, not lilies. But tulips do in fact belong to the lily family—a kinship revealed by details of the flower and the presence of bulbs.

nomenal rainbow of colors, tulips typically have the three sepals and three petals characteristic of the lily family. The hyacinth, also originally from the Mediterranean, bears clusters of bell-shaped flowers.

Why are certain lilies known as ferns?
No lily, of course, is truly a fern; for the most important consideration in determining botanical relationships is the method of reproduction. Ferns are spore producers; lilies reproduce by flowers and seeds. But because of their feathery, finely divided branchlets, certain plants of the lily family are popularly known as ferns. These are the asparagus ferns, cultivated as

houseplants because of their graceful appearance and trailing form.

Asparagus ferns will sometimes flower indoors, the structure of their inconspicuous blossoms confirming their relationship to other lilies. The young stems, or "spears," reveal another relationship—to the edible asparagus, which belongs to the same small group. Asparagus was valued as a medicinal herb before its culinary merits were fully appreciated. Native to the Mediterranean region, it now grows wild in temperate regions over much of the globe. The tender shoots are sometimes blanched as they grow but are much richer in vitamin A if allowed to remain green.

Clovers and Kin

How can you recognize clovers and their kin?

"Clovers and kin" refers to the botanical group variously known as the pea family, the bean family, or the legumes. The outstanding feature of this group is the fruit, a dry pod that typically splits along its sides when ripe. Inside lie the seeds, generally in a row along the underside. Some pods are smooth, others prickly or studded with warts. Some are constricted between seeds, so that the pod has the appearance of a string of beads. The plant known as the yard-long bean has pods measuring three feet long, as its name suggests; contrasting sharply are clover pods, of minuscule size.

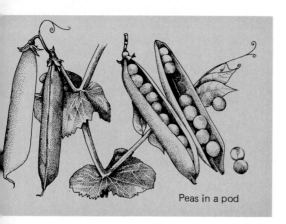
Peas in a pod

What does a clover blossom look like?

In the human world you can often figure out who is related to whom by the chin or the set of the eyes. Among plants, flowers are frequently the giveaway. In the plants belonging to the legume family, blossoms are often much like a sweet pea's—five-petaled and looking somewhat like a butterfly because of the two side "wings." Clovers have flowers that are pealike, albeit tiny and clustered together; so do lupine, Scotch broom, alfalfa, and vetch. Another group of legumes, including the acacias and mimosas, have round, fuzzy flower clusters—delightful "cushions" studded with yellow-tipped, pollen-producing stamens.

Intriguing in shape and often splendidly colored, the blossoms of clovers and kin are appreciated not just by humans but by insects too, which seek out the pollen and nectar that lie within. The flowers, however, are only part of the plants' allure to the animal world. Many creatures feast on the seed-containing pods; giraffes relish the acacia's leaves; and elephants strip off its leaves and bark, sometimes hungrily chewing up entire branches in the process.

Legumes have other traits in common. Usually the leaves are compound (composed of many leaflets) and are arranged in an alternate fashion (that is, not opposite one another on the stem). Fascinating to watch, the leaves of certain species are responsive to touch (the sensitive plant) or light (clover leaves fold up at night).

Can peas grow as tall as trees?

The ordinary garden pea cannot grow to the size of a tree—the plant lives only for a single growing season and will reach a maximum length of only six feet or so. But hundreds of the humble pea's relatives do grow to tree size, including the raspberry-jam tree of Australia (named for the scent of the freshly cut wood), the black locust, and the redbud, or Judas tree, whose purplish-red flowers are among the first to brighten the landscape in spring. Giants of the family include the Australian blackwood and silver wattle, which both top 90 feet; the North American honey locust, which occasionally reaches 140 feet; and *Albizia falcata* of Malaysia, which in 10 years shoots up to 100 feet. Its close relative, the silk tree, is a familiar backyard tree, popular for its fernlike foliage and its pink and white blooms.

Why are four-leaf clovers considered symbols of good luck?

To medieval Christians, the ordinary three-leaved clover was considered a charm against evil because its three leaves symbolized the Trinity. Four-leaf clovers became associated with good fortune because they are relatively rare. (It was once considered very *unlucky* to find and keep a five-leaved clover, but if you gave it away, it would bring good luck to giver and recipient alike.) The belief that four-leaf clovers bring good luck is only superstition, of course. But from another perspective clover and its relatives are indeed plants of good fortune. First and foremost, they add nitrogen to the soil, through the nitro-

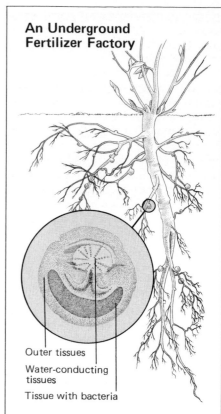

An Underground Fertilizer Factory

Outer tissues
Water-conducting tissues
Tissue with bacteria

If you pull up a clover or pea plant and look closely at its roots, you may spot little nodules. (The illustration above shows one such nodule.) These lumps are formed by bacteria on the roots that convert nitrogen from the air into a form stored in the soil—a service valuable to the world at large. Few plants other than legumes have nitrogen-fixing bacteria.

Clover not only improves the soil; it also supplies food for livestock and (as honey) for man.

Alfalfa, native to the Old World but now growing wild in North America, furnishes fodder.

gen-fixing bacteria that live on their roots. Then too, the family supplies one of the best pasture crops (alfalfa) for farm animals, and makes nutritious, protein-rich hay. Such legumes as soybeans and peanuts offer an abundance of protein in their fruits. And, as a fringe benefit, the clovers and kin yield a delicious honey.

Are any legumes bad to have around?
Agriculturally and nutritionally, we couldn't do without legumes. But this family of plants, like any other, has its black sheep—although "bad," of course, is a subjective word here, especially when one considers weeds. Some people deliberately plant clover to enrich their soil; others try their best to eradicate it, as a persistent weed. Though the legumes called tick trefoils blossom prettily in clearings, their virtues go unnoticed by people who meet up with their prickly seedpods, sometimes dubbed beggar's-ticks. The infamous kudzu is also a legume, imported to North America from the Orient. All too successful in its new home, it is overrunning buildings and forests in much of the Southeast. Paradoxically, though clover and alfalfa are important forage crops, a number of other legumes—the locoweeds and also the milk vetches—will poison and even kill grazing livestock.

Why don't all beans flower at the same time?
In the 1920's, scientists were puzzled by the behavior of some soybean plants. Although they had plenty of sunlight, water, and fertilizer, the plants stubbornly refused to flower until just before frost came and they were killed. By varying the factors involved, the researchers discovered that the beans would not flower in the long days of summer. They also found that there were other varieties of soybeans that would flower *only* when the days were long.

In the years that followed, it was learned that many kinds of plants will flower and fruit only when the day is of a particular length (that is, at a particular time of year), and that the triggering factor is the number of hours of darkness, not those of light. This responsiveness to light, known as photoperiodism, is not an arbitrary reaction, but one that enhances the plant's chances of survival and those of its seeds. Plants in different regions have developed their own photoperiods, keyed to completing the ripening of fruit before any killing frost; and growers can get plants to flower at the "wrong" time by adjusting the amount of light. Chrysanthemums, for example, are no longer just fall flowers; florists know enough about their response to light to get them to bloom the year round.

Nature's Candy Box

In ancient times the Greeks knew of a plant with pencil-thick roots that tasted sweet. *Glycyrrhiza* they called it—Greek for "sweet root." We call it licorice, chewing not on the roots but on a concentrated paste made from them. Licorice is not just a candy; it is used to flavor such diverse products as tobacco and cough drops, as an ingredient of shoe polish, and in fire extinguishers. About a dozen species grow wild in southern Europe, Asia, and the Americas. The pealike blooms can be blue, violet, yellow, or white.

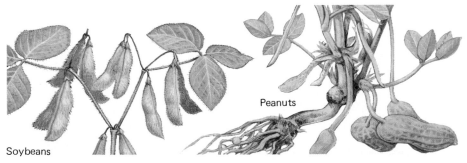

Soybeans

Peanuts

Which legumes do we eat?
Peas, beans, soybeans, peanuts, lentils—such protein-rich foods are staples in cupboards all over the world. In times gone by, peas were used, not as a green vegetable, but as a grain; left to dry on the vine, they were ground into flour and baked into bread. Sweet peas, popular for their sweet-scented blossoms, are not edible. Just the opposite, in fact: in large quantities, they are poisonous.

Peas originated in the Old World. Most of our beans, on the other hand, were developed by American Indians. Peanuts, whose pods grow underground, are native to Brazil. They emigrated to North America by a somewhat roundabout route, being shipped from South America to Portuguese colonies in Africa and then recrossing the Atlantic with the slave trade. Soybeans, in vogue today because they can be substituted for everything from meat and milk to rubber and soap (and, of course, are also an important livestock food), are native to the Orient.

The Cactus Family

Do all cacti live in deserts?
Cacti are all-American plants, generally thought to be native only to the New World. (Still controversial are the mistletoe cacti found in southern Africa, Madagascar, and Sri Lanka; though they have been growing there for centuries, their seeds may have been brought to the Old World by birds.) The hub of the 1,500 or so species is the desert and near-desert lands of Mexico and the southwestern United States. But cacti are not restricted to hot, dry places. They occur as far north as British Columbia and Nova Scotia, as far south as the tip of South America. Winter snow does not deter certain species; others thrive in the high humidity of the tropics.

Why does a cactus have spines?
Say "cactus" and most people think immediately of spines—an association manifested by such common names as pincushion, hedgehog, porcupine, eagle claw, and fishhook cacti. Although a few kinds of cactus are spineless, the stems of most are covered with a formidable array of sharp spines. The spines, of course, deter animals from making a meal of the fleshy stems—but that is not their only function. One effect of the many thousands of spines is to screen the sun's rays and help keep the plant cool. The spines trap an insulating layer of air close to the plant, and they reduce evaporation by breaking up drying winds and air currents. Spines also collect raindrops and dew, gently dropping the water beneath the plant, where it soaks into the soil and is eventually absorbed.

Botanically speaking, cactus spines are modified leaves growing from spots or bumps, called areoles, that occur in rows or spirals along the stem. Each areole is made up of two buds tightly pressed together. Cactus spines always occur in clusters (which differentiates cacti from similar-looking plants), and one spine is typically more prominent than the others. Spines come in an astounding variety of shapes. On some species they are short and stout; on others they are long and straight, like needles; still others bear curved, hooked, barbed, feathery, or hairlike spines.

Do any cacti have leaves?
A typical cactus manufactures food in the thin, green outer layer of its stem instead of in leaves. For in adapting to dry habitats, most species of cacti have modified their leaves into spines; too much water would otherwise be lost through the pores.

Not every species, however, has done away with typical leaves. The abundant prickly pears and chollas, collectively known as the opuntias, bear tiny awl-shaped leaves at the base of each cluster of spines. In this group, the leaves are shed as the spines develop. But in a few especially unusual species, such as the Barbados gooseberry (also called lemon vine), the leaves are retained throughout the life of the plant, masking its membership in the cactus family.

Which cactus looks the strangest?
The cactus family contains a number of bizarre-looking plants. Not only is the old-man cactus extraordinary in terms of size (one of the clan's Gargantuas, it grows to 40 feet); it also has a woolly mass of bristles, looking for all the world like long and unkempt gray hair. The old-woman cactus is similar but much more diminutive, rarely growing more than eight inches tall. Its soft, curly bristles have a silvery sheen. The spines of a tiny pincushion cactus are so finely divided that they look like down.

How long can a cactus go without water?
Desert cacti live where the rainfall is no more than 10 inches a year, most of it coming during a brief period in spring. In drought years, there may be no rain at all. To survive, a cactus must take full advantage of any rainfall, absorbing as much water as possible before it evaporates from the soil. Most species of cacti have sturdy taproots with sizable side roots that divide again and again to form a fine-meshed

Cacti Versus Succulents

Plants with thick, water-filled stems or leaves are known as succulents. Cacti are one type, recognizable because most kinds have clusters of spines and store water in their stems. Most other succulents, such as euphorbias, store water in their leaves, and their spines are not clustered.

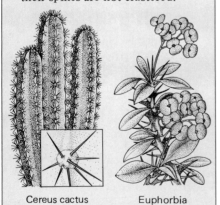

Cereus cactus   Euphorbia

Why a Saguaro Puts On Weight

In dry times the stem of the saguaro has deep, accordionlike pleats. But after a heavy rain the cactus takes up water and swells. The skin expands; the pleats almost disappear. Thanks to the stored water, and to the waxy, skin, a saguaro can survive several years of drought.

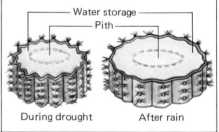

During drought   After rain

Blooming saguaro

Rains have come and gone in this Arizona desert, leaving a brilliant blessing of bloom. In drier times the saguaro is all that is there to capture the eye.

network. Every available drop of water is drawn into the plant and held in the fleshy stem.

A cactus may contain enough water to serve its needs for two years or longer. A plant filled with water is plump, but as the supply is used the cactus shrivels and wilts. Some may lose more water on the side facing the sun, causing the whole plant to lean. In certain places the barrel cacti typically bend toward the southwest, hence the name "compass cactus."

How big do cacti grow?
The stately saguaro is North America's tallest cactus, weighing 6 or 7 tons and growing as tall as 50 feet. Distinctive not just in size but also in shape, the typical saguaro has only a few branches, which rise from the central column a short distance above the ground. An inner skeleton of tough, woody ribs supports masses of pulpy, water-absorbent tissue; the heavy, waxy skin with its many spines keeps evaporation at an absolute minimum. The saguaro is scored with deep, accordionlike pleats that expand tremendously when the plant has absorbed its fill. Once full of water, it can survive several arid years, but growth occurs only after summer rains. In May and June, white blossoms appear, to be pollinated by the white-winged doves that often nest among the flowers. Saguaros are popular with other birds; woodpeckers and tiny owls occupy holes in the thick skin, and thrashers and wrens nest on the gently curving branches.

Are cacti of any use to man?
Until Europeans arrived in the New World, only the Indians knew about cacti. They cooked tender young pads and ate the fruit and seeds. Cactus spines served as needles; cactus fibers were woven into baskets and mats. The woody framework of tree cacti became furniture, poles, and fuel.

Brought to Europe as potential sources of medicines, cacti soon became appreciated for other qualities. Because of their intriguing forms, they are prized house and garden plants. As a bonus they offer spectacular blooms: some cacti only four or five inches tall have flowers measuring six inches across.

145

Ingenious Orchids

Do orchids always look like the showy corsage blossoms?

Orchid shapes in nature range from the relatively unremarkable to the extraordinary, including some fanciful blossoms that resemble insects, birds, and parts of the human body. Their colors range from corsage purple through the entire spectrum (even green) and also include white. Many orchids are strikingly decorated with dots, stripes, or patches of color—all patterns that guide insects with color vision to the precise portion of the flower where they can best accomplish their work of pollination.

Varied as they are, all orchids have the same basic flower form—three petallike sepals and three true petals, one of which is very different from the

Beauty and Function Allied

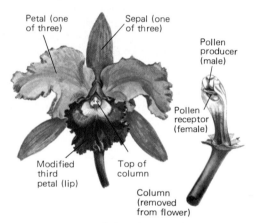

Petal (one of three)
Sepal (one of three)
Pollen producer (male)
Pollen receptor (female)
Modified third petal (lip)
Top of column
Column (removed from flower)

Ingeniously designed to expedite pollination, orchids have an elaborate petal that serves as an insect landing strip. The reproductive organs are fused into a long central column.

others. Generally a large, showy feature, this "maverick" petal often (as in the lady's slippers) takes the form of a deep pouch with an insect-attracting aroma. Another feature common to orchid flowers is a thick column, composed of fused male and female reproductive parts, which projects from the center of the blossom.

Thanks to the ingenuity of man (and also to orchids' propensity to hybridize), growers have been able to create thousands of new strains. The popular *Cattleya* corsage orchids are not the work of nature; they are among the hybrids of tropical American species specially bred to be spectacular and ornate.

How many different kinds of orchids are there?

If you look at various books about plants, you'll soon discover that few agree on the number of different kinds of orchids. Some say 10,000; others, 20,000 or 25,000; still others, as many as 35,000. The true figure will probably never be known, because it is always on the increase.

Orchids excite explorer and horticulturalist alike, and occasionally new species are discovered in far-off places. But such discoveries are in fact quite insignificant when compared with the other cause of the increase. With a talent possessed by few other plants, orchids hybridize freely in nature; that is, one species can—and often will—pollinate another, creating a new type of orchid. Hybrids that breed true may eventually become new species, and natural cross-pollination between a hybrid and the parent species creates a bewildering (and beautiful) array of forms.

Are all orchids jungle species?

The greatest variety of orchids grows in mist-drenched cloud forests high on the flanks of tropical mountains, where the temperature is cool and constant and the moisture supply relatively stable. But many tropical orchids grow in areas with dry seasons that are both long and hot. Some survive by absorbing the dew that condenses on them at night; others go dormant when conditions warrant, even shedding their leaves.

But orchids grow in unexpected places too. One species, dune helleborine, grows in sand dunes along the coasts of Great Britain and western Europe. Some grow atop rocks. And two Australian species spend their entire lives underground, never seeing the light of day and taking nourishment from decaying matter rather than making their own food.

Why do orchids smell so sweet?

Orchids are pollinated primarily by insects. Since insects have a far keener sense of smell than of sight, odors have, in the course of time, developed into an especially important way of bringing them in. In many cases, the larger blooms have only a faint odor, while the smaller ones smell the

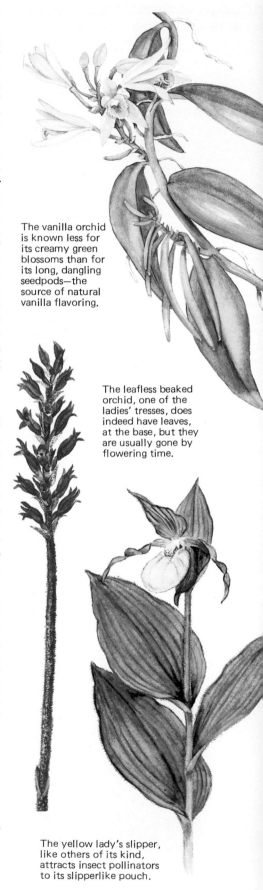

The vanilla orchid is known less for its creamy green blossoms than for its long, dangling seedpods—the source of natural vanilla flavoring.

The leafless beaked orchid, one of the ladies' tresses, does indeed have leaves, at the base, but they are usually gone by flowering time.

The yellow lady's slipper, like others of its kind, attracts insect pollinators to its slipperlike pouch.

strongest, as if to make up for the minuscule visual targets they offer.

Most orchids are pollinated by day-active insects, and so most species release their scent during the daytime. (There is nothing deliberate about this timed release; it is an adaptation that has developed over eons of time.) Others rely on night-flying moths and smell their sweetest at night. There are even orchids that attract both day and night insects and vary their fragrance to suit: one offers lily of the valley perfume by day and rose after dark. While most orchid scents are pleasing to humans, some definitely are not. Certain orchids smell like mothballs; others, pollinated by flies, smell like rotten meat.

Which orchids are the biggest?
In terms of sheer plant bulk, the largest orchid is *Grammatophyllum speciosum,* a native of Southeast Asia that has no common English name. This tree-dwelling giant (a great many orchids grow on tree limbs) has stems that measure an astounding 10 to 13 feet across. In length, however, it is surpassed by a vinelike climbing orchid from the same area, a species that grows to 130 feet. This orchid, which the local people call "bulb that makes us sick," is a saprophyte, a plant that takes its nourishment from decaying material rather than making it by the process of photosynthesis.

In terms of blossom size, however, these Asian orchids are not the biggest. The undisputed champion is the star of Madagascar, whose creamy-white blossoms measure eight inches across and have a nectar-bearing spur a foot or more in length. Charles Darwin studied this orchid in the 1850's and concluded that it could be pollinated only by a moth with a tongue as long as the spur. No such moth was known at the time, and other scientists scoffed. Forty years later the moth was found and Darwin was vindicated.

Why do orchids need other plants?
Orchids lack root hairs and are dependent on fungi living on their roots for absorbing moisture and minerals. The same fungi also play a vital role in an orchid's birth. Unlike the seeds of most other plants, the dust-sized orchid seeds contain no stored food sup-

This intricate bloom is one of the "toothy-tongued" orchids, named for the crests on the wide, scalloped lip. The flower takes two months to reach full glory.

ply that the seedlings can use. An orchid seed is doomed to die soon after sprouting unless it comes in contact with the right kind of root fungus to supply it with food. Over time, orchids have developed a kind of defense mechanism that protects them from an early demise: unless "turned on" by the fungus, they will not sprout in the wild.

For many years growers could not get orchid seeds to sprout. The only way they had of propagating these valuable plants was by dividing the roots. Then, through trial and error, they learned that sometimes the seeds would sprout in soil from the pot in which the mother plant grew. The reason was, of course, that this soil contained the appropriate fungus. Later, scientists discovered that the role of the fungus at this early stage is to break down complex substances into simple sugars needed by the embryo plant. Today orchid seeds are started

in sealed, germ-free flasks with a special nutrient solution. In the 1950's, a French scientist devised a way to clone orchids, using a few cells from the tip of a growing shoot. Now thousands of orchids are mass-produced by this method, which allows the perpetuation of prized hybrid blooms.

Which orchid is prized as a flavoring?
From a money-making point of view, the flowers themselves are the most important product of orchids. But long before orchids became popular as decorative objects, the Aztecs used the fragrant pods of the vanilla orchid to flavor their bitter beverage of cacao. Indians still gather the bean-shaped pods and cure them, using traditional fermentation techniques. Growing vanilla on various tropical islands is a laborious process too. Because the appropriate insects are not around to do the work, the pollination must be done by hand.

Danger: Poison

Which plant is the most dangerous?
Singling out the deadliest plant poison is impossible, since many, many factors influence how a poison affects its victim. Nor do poisons affect every species the same way or to the same degree. With respect to man, however, a few plants rank at the top. As such names as "death cup" and "destroying angel" suggest, amanita mushrooms are among the deadliest. Strychnine, found in a number of related tropical vines, shrubs, and trees, is notorious. The attractive red and black rosary pea, used for prayer beads, necklaces, and decorations, can kill. Oleander, an ornamental shrub, is so poisonous that people have died from using peeled oleander twigs for grilling meat.

How swiftly do poisons act?
While some poisonous plants produce symptoms almost immediately, others take longer to have their effect. Certain mushrooms, such as the jack-o'-lantern, cause instant vomiting; the acrid juice of buttercups works immediately too, causing a severe inflammation of the mouth and digestive tract. Water hemlock usually produces its initial symptoms of convulsions within half an hour of being eaten. On

Wild mushrooms can be deadly. Eat none unless an expert has said it is safe.

Panther amanita

Destroying angel

Death cup

the other hand, the effect of the deadly amanitas may not show up for 24 hours. Symptoms of eating *Cortinarius,* an orange-red mushroom, may not appear for as much as two weeks —and by then the victim may have forgotten what he ate, making treatment difficult or impossible.

What makes plants poisonous?
Dictionaries generally agree that a poison is a substance that chemically harms or kills an organism when the substance gets into its system or onto its skin. By this standard, experts believe that a relatively small percentage of the plants on our planet are poisonous, and the poisons produced by these plants vary in their virulence. Some are deadly; others merely make the victim temporarily sick.

Not all plant poisons act the same. Some affect the nervous system, causing weakness and paralysis; some interfere with the circulatory system and the heart; some disrupt the chemistry of the blood. Many irritate the skin and, if swallowed, affect the mouth, throat, and digestive tract. Certain plants cause the skin to become sensitive to sunlight, causing terrible burns; death may follow. And many plants affect humans by stimulating allergic reactions to their pollen or spores.

The poisons themselves are a bewildering array of glycosides, alkaloids, resins, and other complicated compounds, each of which affects victims in a different way. A poison that is deadly to one kind of animal may not be so to another. Fortunately, most poisonous plants must be eaten in rather large quantities to cause death.

Why are plants poisonous?
It is tempting to think that plants developed the ability to produce poisons as a defense against being eaten. To some extent, that may in fact be the case. Yet there is no plant that is not eaten by some kind of animal: even the death cup, *Amanita phalloides,* is eaten by snails with no apparent ill effect. Some animals actually incorporate the poison into their own bodies for self-defense. (One well-known example is the monarch butterfly, whose caterpillars feed on milkweed and are helped rather than harmed by the poisonous sap.) For this reason, many sci-

entists now tend to think that the poisons developed by accident and have persisted because they do not hinder the plants' survival.

Because they taste or smell unpleasant, many poisonous plants do escape being eaten by browsing or grazing animals. However, when food is scarce,

Poison hemlock has leaves like parsley and pretty white blooms. But its appearance belies its deadly nature: it was, in fact, the plant used to poison Socrates.

animals will feed on plants they would normally avoid. Domestic animals are particularly prone to eat poisonous plants. Sheep and cattle out on the range will eat such dangerous species as aconite (or monkshood), larkspur, and locoweed. Horses tied within reach of an oleander or a rhododendron bush will gladly snack on the poisonous leaves. Hungry cattle have often been poisoned by water hemlock and poison hemlock. Hogs devour poisonous roots. Even animals that are normally meat eaters may fall victim to plant poisons. For example, cats sometimes eat philodendron leaves and are poisoned thereby.

What causes milk sickness?

White snakeroot is said to cure snake-bite, but this carrotlike plant has other, more proven effects. During the pioneer days in North America, cattle often ate this thickly growing weed, and people who drank milk from the cattle were poisoned by it. Such milk sickness was a leading cause of death during the 19th century. Abraham Lincoln's mother is believed to have been one of the victims.

What is locoweed?

Early Spanish ranchers in the American Southwest noticed that their domestic animals acted peculiarly after eating certain wild plants. Horses behaved particularly strangely. They would stand around listlessly, seemingly unaware of everything that was going on, then become wildly excited, bucking and rearing uncontrollably. The Spanish thought the animals had gone crazy, and they named the disease *loco*—Spanish for "crazy." Plants that caused the loco sickness came to be known as locoweeds.

There are many species of locoweeds, all members of the clover family. Growing only where the soil contains selenium, they absorb that element and store it in their tissues. Animals that eat locoweeds accumulate selenium, which acts as a poison to their nervous systems. Locoweed is slow-acting, particularly in cattle and sheep. Before they are affected, these animals must eat several times their weight of locoweed over a period of six to eight weeks. Horses are more sensitive: they need to eat only about a third of their body weight to be affected.

Is there poison in your garden?

Imagine a typical garden in spring. Daffodils, snowdrops, and hyacinths blossom out; bleeding heart, lily of the valley, and mountain laurel follow. During the summer months delphinium and sweet pea brighten the garden. Perhaps some clipped yew bushes serve as a hedge.

It is a lovely garden, to be sure, but every plant growing in it has a dark, dangerous side. Nearly all parts of the yew are poisonous to man. The bulbs of daffodils, snowdrops, and hyacinths contain substances that can cause severe digestive distress, and so does bleeding heart. Lily of the valley contains glycosides that can stop the heart. Mountain laurel has poisonous leaves, as does rhododendron. (Honey made from rhododendron blossoms can be poisonous too.) Delphinium contains alkaloids that upset the intestinal tract and eventually paralyze the breathing muscles. Sweet pea can cause nitrate poisoning.

Even by going into the house you cannot escape. Dieffenbachia, or dumb cane, irritates the mouth, sometimes even making its victims temporarily mute. Poinsettia has an acrid juice that causes digestive problems. Amaryllis has a poison in its bulbs like that of daffodils. Even the berries of the holly and mistletoe we hang in our homes as Christmas decorations can, if ingested, do harm.

Beauty lies above and danger below. Admire the daffodil for its elegance, not its edibility; eating the bulbs is ill-advised.

Some Plants Are Even Poisonous to the Touch

Not all plants have to be eaten to do you harm. The three shown below are contact poisons: that is, toxic substances from them can penetrate the skin. Stinging nettles and at least one type of anemone (European windflower) also poison on contact.

Poison ivy, poison oak, and poison sumac are close kin, all belonging to a rather treacherous botanical group, the cashew family. Among the other toxic members are the lacquer tree, source of Japanese lacquer; and the ringhas, an Asian plant that yields an arrow poison. Even the hulls of the cashew nut are poisonous.

Poison ivy is one plant that shouldn't be touched—by humans, at least. Wild animals feed on the fruits.

Poison oak, like poison ivy, has three leaflets per leaf. Another shared feature is the white cluster of fruits.

Poison sumac is a swamp plant that grows as a tall shrub or small tree. It has white berries too.

Green Medicine

Can you tell what a plant will cure by the way it looks?

Lobed leaves for liver ailments, heart-shaped leaves for cardiac problems, nuts with brainlike convolutions for headaches—what a plant looked like was, in times gone by, a way of deciding which illnesses it could heal. According to this belief, called the Doctrine of Signatures, plants were put on this earth to help people, and their medicinal properties were suggested by their appearance, or "signature." The most potent signatures, indicating a cure-all, were human forms; of these, the most famous was that of the European mandrake, whose forked roots made it look somewhat like a man. Although at present mandrake is no longer in vogue, ginseng, which has similarly shaped roots, is still popular as a medicinal plant in various places.

The Doctrine of Signatures was abandoned long ago, but modern medicine nevertheless owes much to this old and unscientific belief. Its adherents made the first extensive catalogs and illustrations of plants, and these became the nucleus for the science of botany. Until recent times,

According to the ancient Doctrine of Signatures, a plant's curative powers are suggested by its appearance. Liverleaf, or hepatica, was said to cure liver disease.

botany and medicine were virtually one and the same.

Do any herbal remedies work?

From ancient times until rather recently, people healed themselves with plants. By far the majority of these remedies, even those given by the so-called "medicine men" and others supposedly privy to special knowledge, were useless—and, in fact, many were dangerous. But those potions that did work were turned to again and again, and the recipes for them passed on by word of mouth from generation to generation. Many of these remedies, both the good and the bad, were written down and published.

The very best of these old herbal remedies have, in fact, been incorporated in modern medicine. As an example, malaria has plagued people living or traveling in warm climates since ancient times. (It has probably killed more people than any other disease.) No cure was known until European explorers found the natives of South America treating themselves with a brew made from the bark of the cinchona tree. Early in the 1800's, the active ingredient—quinine—was isolated from the bark. By analyzing its structure, chemists created several synthetic drugs that work almost as well as natural quinine but do not have its undesirable side effects.

Similarly, Indian medicine men in North America commonly gave people whose joints were afflicted with arthritis a brew made of willow bark, a pain-relieving remedy also used by herbalists in Europe. An analysis of willow bark by scientists revealed a chemical they called salicin, and this became the base on which the most common pain-relieving drug in the world—aspirin—was synthesized.

Why don't all medicines come from plants?

In earlier times, doctors made medicines as well as prescribed them. They bought or collected herbs, mostly from local sources, and often also grew the most popular ones in their own home gardens. As medical science became more sophisticated, the job of making the medicines fell to the pharmacists. Even today the symbol representing pharmacists is a mortar and pestle, the equipment used for grinding and mixing medicinal herbs.

Though we no longer see druggists working with stems, leaves, flowers, and roots, nearly half of all our medicines still have direct plant origins. Many other medicines are synthetics that duplicate the plant products chemically. These can be made in the laboratory at a lower cost than it takes to obtain the natural ones from plants, and they allow purity, quality, and precise measures to be maintained.

Are there any plant remedies left to be discovered?

Probably less than 10 percent of the plants in the world have been tested to determine their possible usefulness as medicines. Most new discoveries are made by plant explorers, who find out which species are used by primitive peoples in remote areas (especially the tropics) to heal wounds, get rid of headaches, cure dysentery, or provide relief from other ailments. Their finds become grist for laboratory scientists, who determine whether the medicines do in fact have any real value.

Sometimes a laboratory discovery sets off a search. In 1949, for example, a doctor discovered a miracle medicine for arthritis sufferers—cortisone, which is a hormone secreted by the adrenal glands. But to get one gram of cortisone required processing thousands of cattle, and cortisone was prohibitively costly. Plant explorers began

Plants That Can Harm as Well as Heal

Medicinal plants are often a mixed blessing. Plant substances used in healing may act as stimulants or depressants to the circulatory or nervous system. One of the most potent of the plant medicinals, strychnine (derived from seeds of plants grown in the Philippines and the Orient), is a notorious stimulant. Curare, the deadly poison used by South American Indians to tip darts and arrows, is obtained from a closely related plant.

Digitalis, another strong stimulant, comes from the leaves of foxglove and has been used for centuries to treat people with weak hearts. In proper doses, castor oil (squeezed from the beans of a plant believed to be native to southern Africa) does no harm, but swallowing just two castor beans can kill. Opium, extracted from the seeds of a poppy and itself the source of morphine and codeine, and cocaine, produced from the dried leaves of the coca tree and once used as an anesthetic, are two examples of medicinal plant drugs that can be harmfully addictive as well as helpful.

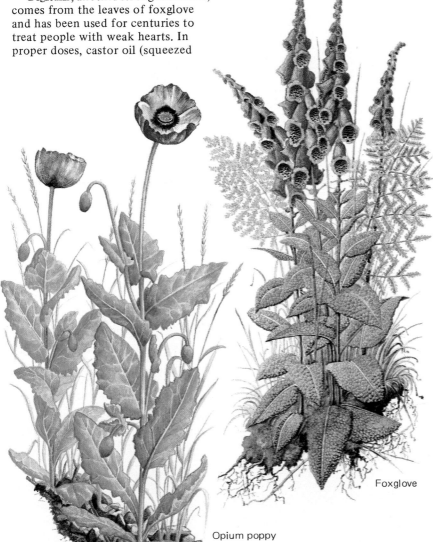

Foxglove

Opium poppy

searching for species containing chemicals that could be converted into cortisone. They focused first on an African plant that, many years earlier, the famous Dr. David Livingstone had said was a potentially powerful medicine. Though cortisone could indeed be made from the plant, the species was rare and could not be cultivated. Then a scientist developed a way of changing plant chemicals called steroids into cortisone. The richest source was a yam growing in the jungles of Mexico and Central America, and today many thousands of tons of these easily grown yams are processed every year to make cortisone at an affordable cost.

What kinds of medicines come from molds?

The most healing "new" medicines of this century are the antibiotics. The first was penicillin, its discovery credited to British scientist Alexander Fleming, in 1928. But even in much earlier times the Chinese were using molds to heal wounds, though the precise source of their healing power was then a mystery. Often people packed wounds with moldy bread; still others used warm mud. Nor was this hit-or-miss knowledge exclusive to the human species. When elephants cut their feet on rocks, they went instinctively to water holes and soaked their feet in the muddy shallows, actually healing their wounds with penicillin.

Aureomycin, streptomycin, and Terramycin are among the more than a dozen antibiotics now produced from molds. Some antibiotics are lethal only to particular types of microorganisms. But combined, they have become the most valuable of all the plant products that heal—if, of course, you consider molds plants. Lacking chlorophyll, they are fungi, and many scientists place them in a group separate from plants.

How do plants prevent illness?

Some illnesses—scurvy, rickets, beriberi—are the direct result of vitamin deficiencies. But in recent years it has been recognized that many other diseases can be attributed to poor nutrition. Preventing illnesses by maintaining healthy bodies has become the latest thing in medicine, and in this respect, plants are again major contributors. For in addition to supplying energy and body-building substances, plants are the primary sources of the vitamins and minerals essential to the proper functioning and well-being of our bodies. All of the plants we eat are in this sense green medicines, helping to eliminate the need for the plants that heal.

Aromatic Herbs

What sorts of plants are considered herbs?

Any nonwoody flowering plant, according to botanists, is an herb. That is a rather broad definition, one that includes almost everything except trees and shrubs. What most people have in mind when they think of an herb is a plant that—fresh or dried—is used as medicine or to flavor food. Over thousands of years, literally hundreds of plants have been experimented with for these purposes. Some of them probably poisoned their users, but others turned out to make ordinary or unpalatable foods tastier or to relieve common aches and pains.

Which parts of plants are the most aromatic?

In modern societies herbs are valued mainly for taste and scent, adding flavor and aroma to foods or, like lavender and lemon balm, perfuming the air. Most herbs concentrate their aromatic properties in their leaves. In the garden, constant clipping stimulates the plants to produce a succession of tender leaves, ready for immediate use or for drying or freezing. Basil, oregano, rosemary, and thyme are some of the popular leafy herbs.

Not all the herbs one buys in the market, however, are leaves. Caraway, anise, and coriander are appreciated for their piquant seeds, rich in essential oils; with dill, both seeds and leaves are used.

How do spices differ from herbs?

Unlike herbs, which generally are native to Mediterranean Europe, spices are usually products of the tropics—more particularly, of islands in the tropics. Cloves and nutmeg, for example, probably originated in the Moluccas, an exotic archipelago in the East Indies that was long known as the Spice Islands.

Herbs generally come from nonwoody plants, but most spices are harvested from trees. Cloves are the flower buds of a tree belonging to the eucalyptus family. Nutmeg is the kernel of a hard nut, and mace is its powdered outer covering. Cinnamon is the dried inner bark of the cinnamon tree. Ginger, however, is the somewhat biting flesh of a wildflower's underground stem.

What is a potpourri?

One of the pleasantest of summertime projects is the making of potpourri, a tradition in many places. Although recipes for potpourri (literally, "rotten pot") are almost infinitely varied, the basic ingredient is carefully dried rose petals; to these are added dried lemon balm, lemon verbena, or rose geranium and a sprinkling of ground cinnamon, allspice, or cloves. Sandalwood chips, patchouli (a musky Asian mint), and a few drops of distilled oil of roses or jasmine are exotic options. Fixatives to aid in retaining the fragrant or spicy odors are vetiver, the sweet-smelling root of a tropical grass, and powdered orris root. The mixture is allowed to ripen for a month or so, then stored in an apothecary jar and closely capped. When the lid is lifted, a heavenly aroma of flowers, herbs, and spices will pervade the room, a perpetual reminder of the bygone summer days.

Potpourris are not the only uses fragrant herbs may be put to. Fragrant sprays of fresh lavender, thyme, and mint were among the "strewing herbs" scattered on the rush-covered stone floors of medieval houses; trodden underfoot, they freshened the musty air. Sachets of dried lavender, thought to discourage moths and other insects, add refreshing fragrance to linen and clothes closets and bureau drawers. The nose of one family pet is titillated by the irresistible odor of dried catnip, a mint that has long since escaped from the herb gardens of Europe and North America.

Which herbs did witches use?

The cherished herbs of European gardens naturally figure in folklore and legend. Shakespeare's Ophelia was undoubtedly referring to popular lore when she called rosemary the herb of remembrance; the plant was thought to be beneficial in restoring a weakened memory. To the Greeks, rosemary was the symbol of the soul's immortality, while in medieval times it was a good-luck symbol and a protection against spells.

Anise seed was believed to avert the evil eye. Coriander and fennel, on the other hand, were used by witches in summoning demons. Dill, too, was an herb used in casting spells, although it also served as protection *against* a witch's spell.

By tradition, thyme was present in the straw of the manger at Bethlehem and so was included in Nativity crèches through the centuries. When knighthood was in flower, thyme was the symbol of courage; ladies embroidered sprigs of thyme on the scarves they gave to their knights. In a later age young girls made nosegays of thyme, with mint and lavender, hoping to attract a sweetheart.

Though the name "sage" may not be responsible for that plant's reputation as the herb of health and the aged, it is reputed to grow best for the wise. A physician's herbal from the 16th century called sage "of excellent use to help the memory, warming and quickening the senses." And a medieval proverb, credited to Saint Hildegarde, asks: "Why should a man die who has sage in his garden?"

Dill

Fragrant, tasty, and sometimes both, herbs such as these tantalize our senses and enrich our lives. Only occasionally is their appearance as striking as their other effects.

Thyme

Rosemary

Sage

Lavender

Plants in Our Lives

What good are plants?

First and foremost, we depend on plants to satisfy our hunger. But that is only part of the story. Even in these days of synthetic fabrics, our clothes and household belongings often contain natural fibers. Strong, pliable plant fibers are twisted into twine and rope. We look to our forests to supply lumber, plywood, and veneers, as well as wood pulp for paper.

Healthful low-fat oils are extracted from seeds; other plant oils are key ingredients in products ranging from soaps and cosmetics to varnishes and paints. Ethyl alcohol, the chief constituent of whiskey and the like, is fermented from molasses, potatoes, and grains. Plants can also be considered energy sources, and experiments with gopher weed, a plant common in the American Southwest, have raised hopes of a new commercially valuable one. The plant's milky sap contains hydrocarbons, just as crude oil does, and "gopheroil" can be refined in the same way to produce gasoline.

How do plants protect us from the elements?

In the tropics, where keeping warm is no problem, walls are often merely the closely set stems of plants—reeds, rattans, or palms. Air circulates freely through such walls, keeping interiors cool. Roofs are frequently thatched with palm leaves. The great chiefs' houses of New Guinea, for example, have sharply sloping roofs covered with palm fronds, impervious to even the severest tropical storm.

In England and Scotland, thatching with straw or reeds has been a traditional art—and a very impressive one, at that. Old-time thatchers pegged rows of bundles to the rafters, then added an outer row; a thatched roof may measure a foot thick.

Obviously, people sleeping blissfully in wooden houses or canvas tents owe their peace of mind to plants. Sometimes entire buildings consist of grasses or reeds. The Marsh Arabs of the lower Tigris and Euphrates valleys build elaborate houses of huge bundles of 20-foot reeds, the only material available for construction. Typical of some regions of Africa are circular grass huts; bamboos are important in the Orient.

What do plants have to do with civilization?

It's not too sweeping to say that the lives of human beings depend on plants. We breathe the oxygen that plants give off; we rely on plants and on plant-eating animals for our food. In fact, what we call civilization began some 10,000 years ago, when certain early peoples learned the art of exploiting food plants effectively. The place was Mesopotamia, in the area known as the Fertile Crescent. There nomadic hunters discovered that seed-bearing wild grasses—primitive forms of wheat and barley—could be sown and harvested, instead of being gathered at random. The oldest example of writing archaeologists have uncovered is a baked clay tablet from this area; on it, pictograms, or symbols, record sales and payments of taxes in grain.

Which leaves do we eat?

Through the ages human appetites have led to many experiments with eating leafy plants. Among those we eat raw or cooked are spinach, beet greens, Swiss chard, leeks, and kale. Edible stems of leafy plants include celery, fennel, rhubarb, and young shoots of asparagus and bamboo. Leafy salad makings are many and varied: head, bunching, and leaf lettuce; chicory, endive, and escarole; and—not to be overlooked—the spicy watercress leaves.

Leafy plants also supply us with stimulating beverages. Young leaves and buds of an Asian shrub related to the camellia are cured as black, green, and oolong teas. The dried leaves of a species of holly make the caffeine-containing South American drink called maté, or Paraguayan tea. Fresh or dried, leafy herbs are steeped in water to make refreshing teas.

A Plethora of Products From Palms and Pines

Date Palms

The long leaves of the date palm are a welcome gift from nature in North Africa and the Middle East. The intact fronds or fibers extracted from them appear in thatched roofs, baskets, ropes, mats, and even donkey saddles.
The fruit of the date palm is the date, a chewy substance eaten like candy or made into jam. Valuable because of their high content of protein, carbohydrates, vitamins, and minerals, dates are sometimes fermented to produce alcoholic beverages and vinegar. The ground-up seeds are used as livestock feed.
The trunk supplies timber for use in buildings, especially to make rafters, doorposts, and window frames. The sap can be drunk as is, or fermented and distilled.

Pines

The leaves of pines—that is, the needles—are distilled to yield pine-leaf oil, the refreshing fragrance used in soaps, perfumes, cosmetics, and other products. The needles themselves sometimes appear in sachets.
The fruit of a pine is the seed-containing cone, an item of far less nutritional value than a date palm's dates. The large seeds of pinyon pines are used as food.
The trunk is the most valuable part of a pine. One substance extracted from the bark is tannin, used by the leather industry. Of far more importance is the wood, an ingredient of everything from furniture to kitchen matches.
The gums and resins extracted from pines are the source of turpentine, the volatile substance used as a solvent and paint thinner. These products also appear in such diverse products as phonograph records, small parts for electrical and electronic devices, soap, ink, and even fireworks.

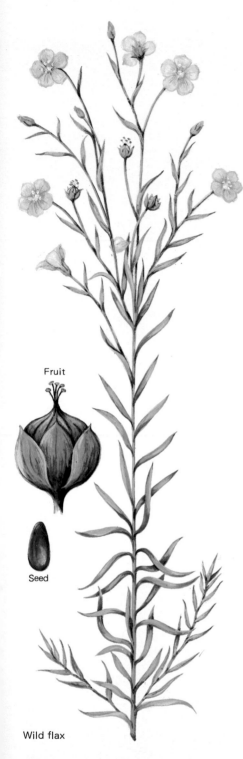

Fruit

Seed

Wild flax

What use do we make of plant stems?
Some 6,000 years ago Egyptians wrapped their dead in linen, a cloth made from the stems of flax. Still in demand for strong fabrics, such as carpets and fire hose, flax was formerly used for bed and table coverings, which are still, of course, called "linens" and stored in "linen closets." Jute, grown in India, is a stem fiber that is woven into a coarse fabric used for burlap sacks and as a backing for linoleum. Hemp, also a native of Asia, makes durable rope and cordage. Manila hemp, stronger than regular hemp, comes from the leafstalks of a plant related to the banana. Sisal, on the other hand, is a leaf fiber. It is harvested from a species of agave, native to Mexico and now grown in other dry tropical areas. Sisal is used mainly for cords and twine.

Where does paper come from?
The universal writing material without which our civilization would soon come to a halt gets its name from papyrus, a tall sedge that grows in the swamps of the Upper Nile. The ancient Egyptians split the long stems and extracted strips of pith. When two layers of pith, laid at right angles to each other, were beaten and pressed, the plant's adhesive juice held them together in parchmentlike sheets; the sheets were then pasted into rolls. One papyrus roll dates back to the First Dynasty (3100 B.C.).

The next major refinement in papermaking is credited to the Chinese. In A.D. 105 a government official discovered that the fibers of mulberry bark could be matted into a thin sheet. Later the Chinese made paper of cotton and linen rags. Papermaking spread along the caravan routes to North Africa, and the Moors carried paper to Spain. For centuries paper continued to be made by hand from rag pulp, just as the finest writing papers are at present. In 1840, however, a German discovered how to grind logs into wood pulp; a little later the process of treating the pulp with sulfuric acid to separate the fibers brought modern chemistry into the industry.

Where does cotton come from?
To the plants that produce them, the fine hairs within a boll or pod are a dispersal technique, a way of winging the seeds away from the parent and lessening competition between the two generations. To us, they constitute some of the most important plant products on earth.

Cotton comes from several annual plants that belong to the mallow family. Their leaves are large; their blossoms white, yellow, or purplish; and their fluff-filled pods an endless source of fascination to people seeing them for the first time. Cotton plants are native to subtropical America and Asia, and the Aztecs and Incas were among the ancient peoples who spun the short, strong fibers into thread.

The soft, glossy fibers called kapok are the product of trees—specifically, they come from the pod of a massive member of the silk-cotton family, called the ceiba tree. Kapok is nonabsorbent and a poor conductor of heat—an excellent (but somewhat outmoded) filler for life jackets, sleeping bags, and cold-weather clothing.

What is latex?
The hevea tree, Brazilian in origin but now cultivated mainly in the Far East, is the chief source of the latex from

Liquid oozing from this African tree will be turned into rubber. The tree secretes latex in response to injury.

which rubber is made. A milky substance that is about 30 percent rubber, latex is not a sap; it is, some scientists believe, a substance that protects the tree after an injury.

The chicle of chewing gum is also a latex from a tropical tree, the sapodilla of Central America. The first to enjoy chewing gum made from chicle were the Maya Indians of Mexico. Chicle is collected during the rainy season, boiled down, and molded into bricks; then it is ground, melted, flavored, and rolled into the familiar sticks or molded into pellets.

An ermine in white winter finery surveys its surroundings on a frosty November morning. In summer its coat is dark brown.

THE ANIMAL WORLD

Introducing the Animals

What is an animal?

The word *animal* comes from a Latin word meaning "breath" or "soul." We tend automatically to think it synonymous with "mammal." However, to scientists and many others, the animals include not only mammals but also birds, reptiles, fish, frogs, clams, lobsters, and insects—not to mention such humbler creatures as jellyfish and worms.

In the past, when the world seemed simpler, scientists classified all life into two kingdoms. Every living thing was either an animal or a plant. Today we know that life is far more complex, with a host of "lesser" species (such as myriad forms of bacteria) that fall into neither one kingdom nor the other.

How long do animals live?

Though the life span of an animal depends on a number of factors (among others, the availability of food and exposure to disease), each species also seems to have a built-in biological clock that controls its aging. Turtles and tortoises, with their slow metabolisms, are apparently the longest-lived creatures. The oldest authenticated tortoise was captured on the Seychelles Islands in 1766 and given as a mascot to the French garrison on the island of Mauritius. After falling from a gun emplacement 152 years later, it died. The age of the tortoise when captured is not known.

Among mammals, man, with his ability to control his environment and find cures for diseases, is the record setter. The great whales apparently have life spans approaching that of man; one fin whale, for example, is believed to have been an octogenarian. (The number of rings in a whale's waxy earplugs indicates its age.) Although in captivity elephants may live 60 or 70 years, their life spans are probably shorter in the wild. Among birds there are reliable records of parrots and swans more than 70 years old.

Which animal is the biggest?

Measured but never weighed, the champion is the gigantic blue whale, which has been known to exceed 90 feet. Whales can grow as large as they do because their weight is supported by water. A land animal equally large would be crushed by its own weight, unless it were built so massively that it could barely move. And getting enough food on land to fuel such an immense bulk would be virtually impossible.

The largest living land animal is the male African elephant, which can reach a height of 12 feet at the shoulder and weigh 8 tons. However, as millions of museum-goers know, the undisputed champions on land were the dinosaurs. Fossil remains prove that the well-known plant-eating *Brontosaurus* measured up to 70 feet from nose to tail. Scientists calculate that the animal when alive weighed some 30 tons. Even more massive was the gigantic *Brachiosaurus*, a browser that stood 40 feet tall and may have weighed as much as 80 tons. Others may have been larger still.

Which animal is the smartest?

Measuring the intelligence of animals is difficult at best. One problem is that most tests are based on things that we humans want the animals to do, such as sitting up on command or stepping on a treadle to get a reward of food. The animal's own needs and wishes are ignored.

Chimpanzees rank high, nearly everyone agrees. In the wild they use sticks as weapons and as tools to extract termites from their burrows. In captivity they learn tricks readily, and they can reason well enough to pile up boxes in order to reach a high object, or to fit together sticks for the same purpose. Experimenters have even taught chimpanzees to communicate with them in sign language.

Dolphins and killer whales have learned elaborate routines to entertain aquarium audiences. Thought by some to be even more intelligent than man (their brains are proportionately

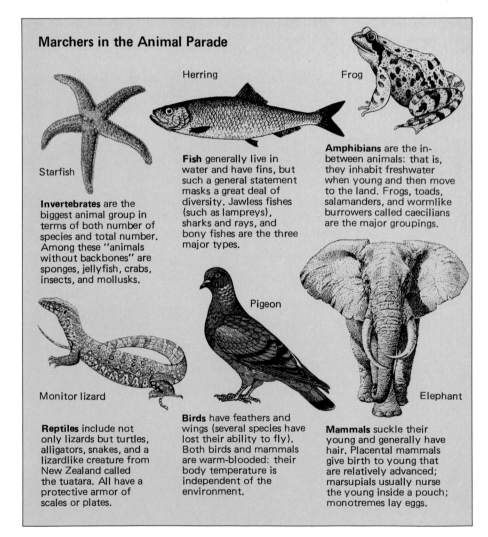

Marchers in the Animal Parade

Herring

Frog

Starfish

Invertebrates are the biggest animal group in terms of both number of species and total number. Among these "animals without backbones" are sponges, jellyfish, crabs, insects, and mollusks.

Fish generally live in water and have fins, but such a general statement masks a great deal of diversity. Jawless fishes (such as lampreys), sharks and rays, and bony fishes are the three major types.

Amphibians are the in-between animals: that is, they inhabit freshwater when young and then move to the land. Frogs, toads, salamanders, and wormlike burrowers called caecilians are the major groupings.

Pigeon

Monitor lizard

Elephant

Reptiles include not only lizards but turtles, alligators, snakes, and a lizardlike creature from New Zealand called the tuatara. All have a protective armor of scales or plates.

Birds have feathers and wings (several species have lost their ability to fly). Both birds and mammals are warm-blooded: their body temperature is independent of the environment.

Mammals suckle their young and generally have hair. Placental mammals give birth to young that are relatively advanced; marsupials usually nurse the young inside a pouch; monotremes lay eggs.

Kangaroos and Giraffes: Never the Twain Shall Meet

In no two locations on earth is the wildlife exactly the same; which species live in a particular place, and the proportions of each, are far too dependent on local conditions. But when wildlife is viewed from a global perspective, certain patterns become apparent—enough to enable scientists to divide the earth into six major "biogeographical" zones. Such divisions were first noticed for birds, but many other animals—plus some plants too—divide up rather neatly into the same categories.

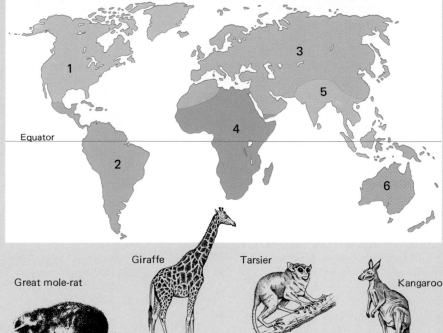

Equator

Pronghorn

Sloth

Great mole-rat

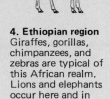
Giraffe

Tarsier

Kangaroo

1. Nearctic region
"Ne" refers to the New World, and the Nearctic is its more northerly part. Pronghorn antelope and giant sequoias are among the unique species.

2. Neotropical region
Associated with the southern part of the New World are such animals as toucans and sloths. Unlike those elsewhere, the monkeys here have grasping tails.

3. Palearctic region
This region includes northern Europe and Asia. It has much in common with the Nearctic, and it has fewer unique species than any other region.

4. Ethiopian region
Giraffes, gorillas, chimpanzees, and zebras are typical of this African realm. Lions and elephants occur here and in the Oriental region, to the east.

5. Oriental region
Not just the Orient but also India and various islands are included in this tropical region, which is bordered by the Himalayas in the north.

6. Australian region
Marsupials are the key animals here, with a far greater variety of these mammals than anywhere else. Eucalyptus trees grow in the wild.

larger), in scientific experiments they have shown great skill in telling the difference between objects of different sizes and shapes. Some observers claim that dolphins even can imitate human speech.

Other animals regarded as intelligent are elephants, horses, pigs, and domestic dogs and cats. Crows and pigeons have a limited ability to count. Parrots can imitate human speech, and mockingbirds have a vast repertory of the songs of other birds (they can mimic man-made sounds too)— but it is doubtful whether either talent helps the birds in the wild.

Who has the biggest appetite?
In proportion to its size, the hungriest animal is the shrew, which must eat several times its own weight every day because of its high metabolic rate. (A shrew's metabolism works so fast that its heartbeat sometimes goes as high

as 1,200 per minute.) A shrew is a creature, mouse-size or smaller, with a long pointed snout and a mouthful of sharp teeth. Active predators, shrews live mostly on insects and worms. Some have a poisonous bite.

In terms of total amount consumed, the great whales lead the list. A blue whale may devour up to eight tons a day of its preferred food—tiny, shrimp-like animals called krill. Yet even this titanic banquet amounts to only 4 percent of the whale's total weight—quite a difference from the proportion consumed by the voracious shrew.

Among land animals, the elephant is the biggest eater, munching from 300 to 500 pounds a day of leaves, bark, branches, grass, and other vegetable food. One reason for this high volume is that the elephant's food is low in nutritive value. In captivity, 100 to 150 pounds of hay, plus a few pailfuls of raw vegetables, is enough.

Who lives where?
From the tropics to the poles, there is almost no part of the earth where animals are absent. Even in bleak Antarctica, wingless flies and springtails live on or around the edges of meltwater pools; and the frigid seas surrounding the continent support an enormously rich pageant of life. In deserts where the ground literally becomes scorching hot, burrowing animals find cool shelter beneath the surface. Even the deep ocean floor, veiled in perpetual blackness and with a paucity of food, is home to a thinly scattered population of creatures adapted to pressures of several tons per square inch.

One phenomenon noted by scientists is that many different species occur in tropical areas, but in relatively small numbers for any one species. In colder regions, the number of species is relatively small and the number of individuals large.

The Need to Feed

Do animals have to eat every day?

Many an animal will gorge when food is abundant, then go for long periods without eating at all. Others fast—in a sense, a labor of love—for their offspring. The male gafftopsail catfish abstains from food for weeks at a time, holding in his mouth the eggs from the female until they hatch. For about two months a male emperor penguin incubates the single egg by holding it on his feet. The dutiful father-to-be loses a third or more of his weight; but when the egg hatches, he still manages to produce enough food from his crop to provide it with one or two days' worth of food.

Adult mayflies never eat. The mission of these ephemeral creatures is to mate and start a new generation, and the adults of many species live no longer than a day. For most animals, however, life consists largely of eating and avoiding being eaten.

How does diet change as an animal grows up?

With its hard beak, a tadpole scrapes algae from rocks and other submerged objects. But as the tadpole transforms into a frog, its mouth widens into a capacious insect-catcher. Its long, typically vegetarian digestive tract become proportionately shorter, a feature characteristic of a carnivore.

Other animals that undergo a drastic change in appearance and life-style change their diets too. Moth and butterfly caterpillars have strong jaws for eating plants; the winged adults suck up nectar through a slim proboscis. Mosquito larvae sieve microscopic plants and animals from the water. The adult females feed on blood; the males, on plant juices or not at all.

Among animals that care for their young, the parents may provide food very different from their own—as, in fact, human beings do. All mammals are suckled on milk at first, then change to their adult diets of plants, animals, or a combination of the two. The young of many birds are fed insects but shift to seeds as adults.

Which animals share?

Alone in an aquarium, a fish eats until satisfied, then quits. But if a second fish is added, the first fish begins gobbling food again. Competition makes both fish gluttonous—a fact generally true throughout the animal world, where the primary concern is individual survival.

But there are exceptions. When a kill is made, male lions typically eat first, then the females, and finally the cubs. If the number in the pride falls, cubs are given first choice. Wolves are noted sharers too, and will carry food long distances to females with pups.

Roosters practice "tidbitting" to help their hens find food. They pick up a choice morsel, then throw it to the ground and begin clucking excitedly to call the hens. Hens will do the same for their chicks. Sharing is also known among wild birds. Jackdaws have been seen loading their crops with food and then emptying out their bonanza some distance away so other jackdaws could eat too.

Who Eats Whom in the World of Nature

A domestic cat dining on canned tuna is the ultimate consumer in a long food chain. Most likely the tuna it is eating fed on cod or mackerel, which in turn consumed herring and other small fish. Herring eat tiny crustaceans, which sustain themselves on floating microscopic plants (called plant plankton). The plants are the producers, making food with the help of the sun.

At each step in a food chain, energy is lost. Biologists estimate, for example, that it takes as much as five tons of plankton to make just a single pound of tuna.

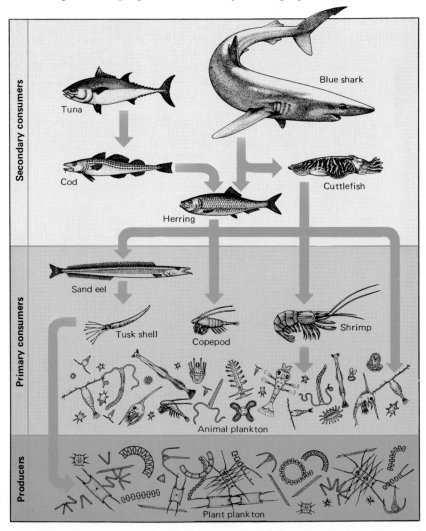

160

Lion and wildebeest, cheetah and gazelle, hunting dog and zebra—on the African savanna mighty hunters attack mighty prey. Smaller in size, but no less important, are such predators as meerkats, shrikes, and secretary birds.

Who saves food for another day?

A leopard kills an antelope, eats its fill, and drags the remains into the crotch of a tree, continuing to feast on the carcass for several days. Harvester ants put seeds in special granaries in their nests. If the seeds get damp, the ants bring them to the surface to dry. Sprouted ones are thrown away.

A host of rodents squirrel away food. Hamsters, pocket gophers, and chipmunks stuff their cheek pouches with food to tuck away in their dens. (Some foods are dried first.) Squirrels are famous for burying nuts, though

Shrikes sometimes impale and store prey on thorns or barbed wire.

sometimes these are rediscovered by other individuals than the ones that did the burying. Beavers cache their food underwater, where cuttings stay fresh when the pond ices over.

Pikas and some voles make "hay" by cutting grass and other green-stemmed plants, then curing them in the sun before they are stuffed into rocky niches. To keep these hoards from blowing away, the small mammals build a wall across the entrance with small rocks and pebbles. Shrews store snails and insects in their runways, and moles collect earthworms, biting off one end to immobilize them so they cannot escape. And familiar to everyone, of course, is the bone-burying habit of dogs.

Which animals are picky eaters?

Koalas are food specialists—"picky eaters," so to speak; these beloved marsupials eat only the leaves of eucalyptus trees. The caterpillars of many butterflies and moths subsist on diets of a few kinds (sometimes just one kind) of plants. Tapeworms, flukes, and many other parasites are equally demanding, some surviving only if they can find specific hosts.

Pandas eat bamboo shoots almost exclusively, occasionally supplementing this fibrous diet with grasses, flowers, and even small animals. Anteaters specialize in ants or termites. With their huge claws they rip apart nests, then pick up the insects with their sticky tongues—as much as two feet long in the giant anteater. Africa's egg-eating snakes eat only eggs.

Among birds, the Everglades kite of Florida and Central America feeds only on apple snails. As the name suggests, crossbills have strong tweezer-like bills, used to pluck seeds from deep in the scales of cones.

Such special diets as these supply the animals with all of their nutritional needs. But if the foods are somehow eliminated, by natural disasters or other causes, this unvarying focus on one or only a few kind of food can have a devastating effect.

Can any animals make their own food?

Bees, and also some wasps and ants, convert flower nectar into honey, storing it for later use. Some South American ants grow fungi in special gardens; like emigrants to a new land, the queens carry spores with them when starting new colonies. Giant clams host colonies of green algae in the soft, fleshy lining of their shells. By opening their shells and exposing the green cells to the sun, they put this food factory to work. The excess algae are absorbed as food.

None of these animals actually makes its own food from scratch. If the primitive "in-between" creatures with chlorophyll are excluded from the animal kingdom, then it is indeed true that no animals can independently produce food from raw materials.

How Animals Move

Can all animals move?

Such animals as sloths and snails are notoriously slow, but even such lethargic movements take them to safety, food, and others of their kind. Movement is characteristic of animal life. Even such animals as sponges, corals, barnacles, and oysters, all fixed in place as adults, have immature stages that can swim. Most also have moving parts as adults. For example, barnacles kick their "legs" to circulate water laden with food and oxygen through their bodies. Sponges do the same by lashing long whips on cells lining the body cavity.

How can animals walk upside down?

Performing a half-roll quicker than the eye can detect, a housefly lands upside down on the ceiling. As remarkable as the flip is the fact that the fly sticks there, and then nonchalantly walks about without falling off. The fly can defy gravity because of its feet. Between the two claws at the tip of each foot is a bladderlike structure covered with tiny hairs. Each hair secretes a glue that makes the "bladder" wet and sticky. In walking, the fly—which, like other insects, has six feet—picks up two legs on one side and one on the other, always leaving three legs firmly affixed.

In a rather awkward scramble, tree frogs can move about while upside down, using the suction pad at the end of each toe. But even more unusual are the little warm-climate lizards called geckos, which have tiny hooks on the bottom of their feet. These catch on the most minute irregularities in a surface—even on a seemingly smooth pane of glass.

How do legless animals move about?

An earthworm has two pairs of stiff bristles, or setae, sticking out from each of its many segments and anchoring the worm as it alternately stretches its body forward and then pulls up the rear. Each segment contains its own set of muscles that make it fatter and shorter.

A leech, closely related to an earthworm, has a sucker at each end of its body. With the rear sucker attached, the worm moves its body forward and attaches it at the front. When the rear sucker is released, the whole body is pulled forward, the middle temporarily forming a high loop. Inchworms, or measuring worms, are moth caterpillars that move in a similar fashion but use their front legs plus a set of false legs at the rear.

Starfish creep by suction too. Hundreds of little tube feet lining the groove in each arm work hydraulically, sticking to a surface when water is pumped out and then letting go as water fills them once again.

Locomotion in the Ocean—and Elsewhere

Bounding antelopes, jumping frogs, fluttering butterflies, prowling sharks—most animals, whether on land, in water, or in the air, move by contracting muscles. Often the muscles are attached to a rigid skeleton (a mammal's bones, for example, or a clam's shells). Such skeletonless creatures as jellyfish and squid use jet propulsion.

In Water

A paramecium uses hairlike cilia to swim. The cilia on the microscopic creature beat back and forth.

Jellyfish move by jet propulsion. When the animal contracts its bell, water is expelled, pushing the jellyfish the other way. When it raises the bell's sides, water rushes back in.

On Land

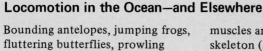

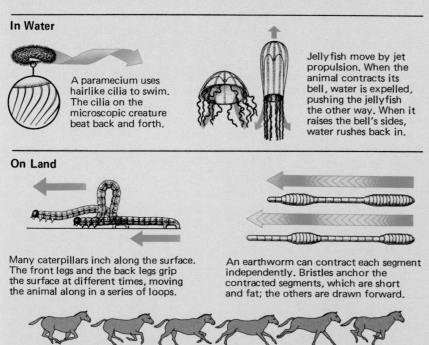

Many caterpillars inch along the surface. The front legs and the back legs grip the surface at different times, moving the animal along in a series of loops.

An earthworm can contract each segment independently. Bristles anchor the contracted segments, which are short and fat; the others are drawn forward.

Galloping horses take to the air: at one stage in a gallop all four feet are off the ground. As the drawings indicate, no two feet land or take off at exactly the same time.

In the Air

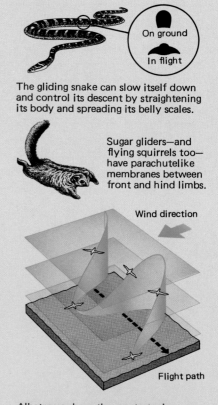

On ground / In flight

The gliding snake can slow itself down and control its descent by straightening its body and spreading its belly scales.

Sugar gliders—and flying squirrels too—have parachutelike membranes between front and hind limbs.

Wind direction

Flight path

Albatrosses have the greatest wingspan of any bird. Taking advantage of the variation in wind speed over the sea (it increases with height), an albatross glides down, then turns and is lifted up.

What makes fleas such good jumpers?

A common flea can make jumps spanning more than a foot—well over a hundred times its own body length. By comparison, a big kangaroo can leap only six times its body length—though such a leap may cover 40 feet.

The power for jumping, as well as for most other animal motions, comes from muscles. A muscle becomes shorter when it contracts and lengthens when it relaxes. One end of each muscle involved in motion is attached to a rigid portion of the animal's skeleton; the other, to such movable parts as legs and tails.

Kangaroos have an internal skeleton. In fleas, as in other insects, the skeleton is on the outside. The attachment of muscles to an external skeleton makes the most efficient kind of lever. As a result, a flea makes its spectacular jump without using any more energy than a kangaroo does in its proportionately shorter jump.

Which animals use jet propulsion?

In a pumping action, a jellyfish draws water into its bell and then contracts to force it out. The water is expelled in one direction, and the jellyfish moves in the other. But jet propulsion is not exclusive to jellyfish. Scallops clap their shells together to force out water, speeding away from the probing arm of a starfish or from another predator.

On the underside of a squid's body is a funnel-shaped tube through which a spurt of water can be released. By turning the nozzle forward, backward, or to either side, this torpedo-shaped mollusk can control its direction as it streaks through the water as fast as 20 miles an hour. Some squid build up their velocity and then explode from the surface, shooting up into the air.

What good are tails?

A typical fish can still swim without its tail—but not nearly as well. Side-to-side motions of both body and tail supply power for swimming, and the fish also steers with its tail. Crayfish move rapidly backward with a flip of the tail; a tadpole swims by wagging its tail. Tails are, in fact, the basic driving force for most aquatic animals.

Land animals use tails for grasping, supporting, signaling, and helping attract a mate. For terrestrial creatures

The fastest land animal is the cheetah, a sleek cat that reaches speeds of 70 miles an hour over short distances. Its runs are a series of leaps, with the momentum from one carrying through to the next. The claws act like spiked shoes.

tails are generally far less important in locomotion. A squirrel's bushy tail, however, becomes a stabilizer and rudder when it jumps; a bird's tail is a vital part of its flight mechanism; and such long-tailed runners as foxes use their tails as balancers.

Which animals are the fastest?

Because wild animals cannot be put on measured courses, judging their speeds accurately is difficult. Unintentional exaggerations are common. A slithering snake, for example, looks deceptively speedy, but few go faster than three or four miles an hour. Even the swift African black mamba does well to reach eight miles an hour.

Many sources call the spine-tailed swifts of Asia the fastest in the animal world: careful timing with a stopwatch indicates a flight speed of about 105 miles an hour. The plummeting dives of peregrine falcons have been clocked at 85 miles an hour—fast indeed, though their speed has sometimes been estimated at about double that rate.

The fastest runner is the long-legged cheetah, which can reach a speed of 70 miles an hour within a few seconds after starting. It can maintain this sprinting speed for only about 15 seconds, but that is generally long enough to catch such fleet-footed prey as antelopes. Antelopes are no slow-pokes themselves. They can accelerate quickly to 60 miles an hour and continue at that speed for several minutes, then run for half an hour or longer at nearly 40 miles an hour.

The fastest of fish are the marlins, swordfish, and sailfish, which often attain speeds of 45 to 50 miles an hour (possibly more in a spurting dash). Whales and porpoises can go only about half as fast—still speedy enough to pass most ships at sea.

Featherless Fliers

Which mammals take to the air?
The only animals that can truly fly are ones with wings, and the only mammals with wings are bats. All other "flying" mammals—colugos, certain possums, and flying squirrels—are really gliders. Incapable of sustained flight, they glide downward, their descent slowed by special membranes.

The greatest gliders of all are the colugos, also called cobegos and flying lemurs. The size of a domestic cat, the slender-bodied colugo of Southeast Asia (the other species lives in the Philippines) has a long neck and a doglike head. Stretched along each side from just behind its head to the tip of its long tail is its gliding membrane—a length of thin, leathery skin. Launching itself from high in a tree, a colugo can glide for several hundred yards. When it lands on a tree trunk, its mottled fur blends so well with the bark that the animal seems literally to disappear. A young colugo will cling to its mother as she glides.

Australia's gliding possums are the smallest gliding mammals; the most diminutive of these measure no more than six inches long—and half of the length is tail. These gliders are marsupials, carrying their young in a pouch.

Animals With Parachutes

All sorts of animals take to the air, but many are gliders, not true fliers. Such creatures as flying lizards have gliding membranes that slow their descent. This lizard has specially elongated ribs.

Another kind of lizard, the flying gecko, has skin flaps along its sides. When spread out, the flaps —and the webs on its feet—help it to glide from tree to tree.

Between the extremely long toes of some Asian tree frogs are enormous folds of skin. When the frogs jump from a high place and spread their toes, the webs become air-filled parachutes.

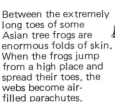

How far can flying squirrels fly?
Flying squirrels are wingless, but thin skin flaps stretching between the front and hind legs allow them to glide from tree to tree. In flight, the squirrel uses its tail like a rudder, to guide its direction; in landing, it lifts its tail and body at a steep angle so that it settles as softly as a falling autumn leaf. Most flights are relatively short, though some have been known to extend more than 150 feet.

Seeing a flying squirrel is for most people a rare event. Although some hollow trees may harbor several dozen of these creatures, they are nocturnal (all other squirrels are active during the day).

Grayish brown on the back and white on the belly, the flying squirrels of Europe and North America are as inconspicuous in looks as they are in life-style. But in Southeast Asia certain species are among the most colorful of all mammals—some even with patches of bright red. Giants in the clan measure nearly four feet long, including a bushy tail.

What are flying dragons?
In the jungles of Southeast Asia, an insect taking flight to escape a hungry lizard may find that the lizard is still in pursuit. Leaping from a branch, the kind of lizard popularly known as a flying dragon lifts the long ribs at the sides of its body and stretches loose folds of skin into "wings." The lizard's course is a downward slant, but sometimes it manages glides of 50 feet or more. By twisting its body, it can also steer itself to the left or right.

An unremarkable mottled gray or brown, flying dragons are not much to look at when resting camouflaged on the bark of a tree. When in flight, however, these lizards take on a different appearance. Their spread wings—sometimes displayed by the males during courtship—are bright yellow (or orange) striped with black.

Though in flight these lizards may look dragonlike to some, they are not at all draconian in size. Ten inches long, they are small indeed compared to some flying reptiles, or pterosaurs, of the past, whose wings spanned as much as 25 feet. Most of the thin, leathery skin forming a pterosaur's wing was stretched between the body

and an extraordinarily long little finger. Scientists believe the wings were excellent for gliding and soaring but lacked maneuverability.

Which insects fly the best?
Small though they are, insects—the only other true fliers besides birds and bats—are incredible aerialists: midges, for example, can vibrate their wings an astonishing 1,000 times per second. Dragonflies are the fastest insects and the ones with the greatest maneuvering skill. Though few insects fly for any distance at even 10 miles an

Like most insects, ladybird beetles have two pairs of wings as adults. Beetles use only the hind wings in flight; the others are protective.

hour, some dragonflies can cruise at 25 miles an hour and may in sudden bursts increase their speed to 35 or 40. They can also hover and make quick turns up, down, or to the side. No other insects match their agility.

Can spiders fly?
A great many small animals travel unintentionally on the wind. Even ones the size of frogs and fish may be sucked into the air by strong updrafts and then, miles away, showered back to earth. Such unwilling travelers have no control over the speed, direction, or duration of their flight.

Spiders are somewhat different. The young of certain species climb up plants (or onto rocks or other prominences) and begin paying out strands of silk that are lifted into the air by the slightest breeze. As one strand follows another, the pull eventually becomes strong enough to hoist the spider off its perch and into the air. Ballooning spiders have been found nearly three miles above the earth's surface and hundreds miles out at sea. Many spiders inhabiting oceanic islands could not have reached these remote areas except by ballooning.

How do flying fish take flight?

Travelers at sea are often delighted by the sight of schools of flying fish exploding from the surface in short, fin-rattling flights. Common in warm seas throughout the world, these bullet-shaped aerialists are bright blue above and silvery white below, a pattern typical of fish swimming in the open sea. Most are small, but some reach a length of a foot or more.

In flying fish, the extra-large lower lobe of the tail fin supplies power. As soon as the fish is airborne, it spreads its folded fins out stiffly at the sides. The paired front fins (called the pectorals) are broad and winglike in all species; but in some, the paired rear fins (the pelvics) are also enlarged—monoplane versus biplane types, so to speak.

Most flying fish skim the surface and remain airborne for only a few seconds. But if a fish is over a trough (or if it happens to be caught by a wind), its glide may be at a height of 10 feet or more. Sometimes when a fish drops low enough to get the long lobe of the tail fin back in the water again, it vibrates the fin vigorously and so builds up speed for staying aloft. There are reports of glides as long as a quarter of a mile. Why glide at all? Most likely the fish are trying to escape bigger ones—although one might prefer, of course, to think they are gliding for joy.

Why do animals fly?

Just as swimming moves creatures through water, so flying moves them through air. Flight takes animals to new sources of food. It allows escape from earthbound predators and makes possible long-distance migrations. It takes animals within range of prospective mates—and helps attract them as well. Who could fail to be impressed by the aerial acrobatics of the golden eagle, the long flight of the skylark, the hovering of the male hummingbird before his mate?

To escape a predator (or speed away from a passing ship), a flying fish takes to the air. Enlarged fins serve as wings. If the fish dips its tail in the water to get an extra boost, it may glide for hundreds of yards.

Mysteries of Migration

Which animals migrate?

Flocks of ducks and geese wing southward as autumn leaves fall, then return with the winds of spring. The seasonal flights of birds are familiar, conspicuous, predictable. But not all birds migrate—nor are birds the only animals that do. Caribou, wildebeests, elephants, and certain whales and bats are among the mammals making seasonal migrations.

Fish do it too. Trout, salmon, and shad travel up streams to spawn. Tunas, dolphins, jacks, and barracudas move southward to warmer waters in winter, then back north in spring; cod, mackerel, and pilchard are among the fish that leave cold coastal seas in winter and travel to warmer, deeper waters. Shrimp and squid make daily migrations from the depths toward the surface and back again. Giant sea turtles, some frogs and salamanders and a number of insects have migration patterns as regular as those of birds.

Where do fish go to spawn?

European and American eels spawn in the Atlantic Ocean, at the edge of the Sargasso Sea. After hatching, the young European eels steer toward Europe, 3,000 miles away and a three-year journey; the others head toward North America, a one-year trip of some 1,000 miles. Because their growth rates differ, the young of each population are about the same size when they reach the shores of their respective continents.

At this stage the eels look like miniature adults—that is, long, slender, greenish or brownish creatures with large mouths. Males remain near the mouths of rivers. Females swim far upstream, sometimes even slithering through wet grass to reach ponds or lakes. Several years pass before they mature and set out to complete their odyssey, returning to the Sargasso to spawn and die.

Salmon are reverse migrants, spawning in fresh water and maturing in the sea. Interestingly, migrating salmon can trace their way through a maze of tributaries to find exactly the stream from which, years earlier, they started their journey to the sea. Biologists have determined that each tributary has distinctive chemical properties with which the very young salmon are imprinted. In the sea, however, salmon use the sun as a compass.

Do animals always travel in groups?

Though animals moving in the same direction may appear to be traveling together, sometimes they are in fact making independent journeys. Hundreds of thousands of white storks, for example, cross the Strait of Gibraltar or move over the Bosporus in their seasonal journeys between Europe and Africa; but once past these funneling points, the flocks quickly spread as the birds go their own separate ways.

Traveling in groups permits young animals making the trip for the first

The migration of salmon is one of the wonders of nature—an amazing journey from spawning stream to sea and back again.

time to benefit from the experience of older individuals that have traveled the route many times before. During the day the migrants can see each other to keep together; birds migrating at night generally use call notes to keep in contact.

How do we know where migrants are going?

Much of what is known about the migration of birds and other animals has been learned by trapping them and attaching coded metal or plastic bands or tags. (A less frequently used procedure is to color-mark—that is, to dye—birds.) Mapping migration routes requires observations by many people from different locations—often over a number of years. Of the millions of animals banded and released, only a small percentage have been found again and the information sent, as requested, to a central agency where the records are kept. But this information has contributed greatly to our knowledge of where the animals travel and how long it takes them to get there.

Large flocks of birds migrating at night are tracked with radar. In some cases small radio transmitters can be fastened to individual animals, which are then released and followed. The beeping transmitters tell scientists exactly where the animals are. Called biotelemetry, this technique is most useful in tracking land animals over short distances, but it has also become a valuable tool for mapping the voyages of whales, sea turtles, and other marine creatures.

Do birds always follow the same routes?

Migrating birds kept in cages become restless as their usual time to migrate approaches; this happens even when they have been well fed and the temperature of their surroundings has been controlled. No one knows precisely what triggers the migration instinct (though day length is known to be important), but the internal clocks of some birds are so extraordinarily timed that in many cases they will depart on their journeys and arrive at their destinations on about the same date year after year.

Birds prepare for long trips by eat-

Champion Migrant

The Arctic tern is said to enjoy more hours of daylight in a year than any other creature on earth. This enviable situation is not without its drawbacks. To achieve its essentially endless day (which allows it to fish full time), it must journey twice a year from pole to pole—a round-trip flight of more than 20,000 miles.

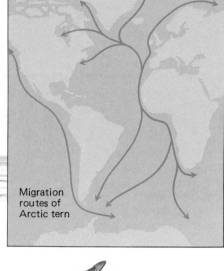

Migration routes of Arctic tern

These graceful birds, best identified in summer by their all-red bills, breed in Alaska, northern Canada, Greenland, the British Isles, and northern Eurasia. Surprisingly, banding experiments show that the birds nesting the farthest north are the ones that end up the farthest south. Some cross the Atlantic during migration.

ing large amounts of food and building up fat. Fat is their flight fuel, and some birds may increase their body weight by as much as 50 percent, particularly when their flights include long journeys over water. Many fly at night and spend most of the daylight hours feeding, replenishing exhausted energy reserves.

The traditional routes birds follow are called flyways. In North America there are four such corridors—one along each coast, one down the Mississippi Valley, and another extending in a north-south direction across the Great Plains. In the Old World, most birds flying from Europe to Africa and back again cross the Mediterranean at the narrow Strait of Gibraltar or the Bosporus, though a few kinds (mainly the smaller species) brave their way across the sea at its widest.

Do migrating birds ever get lost?

During the day, many birds orient themselves by the sun; at night, they may follow the stars. Some follow such prominent land features as river valleys, mountain ranges, and coasts. There is evidence, too, that certain species are "tuned in" to the earth's magnetic field, polarized light, infrared rays, or even slight changes in barometric pressure—extraordinary sensitivity that makes migration all the more miraculous to instrument-dependent man.

Migrating animals do make mistakes. Fog, rain, or a reversal in the prevailing winds can confuse animals temporarily, at least. Strong winds can also blow them off course. For most migrants, going off course is disastrous. Occasionally, however, new territories are colonized as a result.

Sounds and Signals

Which animals make faces?

With smiles, grimaces, frowns, and lifted eyebrows, we humans show our feelings and moods. Gorillas, chimpanzees, and other primates make similar facial displays. Dogs, wolves, and their kin convey anger by wrinkling the upper lip and baring their teeth; they show fear and submission by keeping their teeth hidden and laying their ears back. A few other kinds of mammals, especially those living in groups, also use facial expressions. But the faces of birds, reptiles, amphibians, fish, and invertebrates are relatively immobile, permitting little or no facial expression.

What body signals do animals use?

A dog wiggles its body and wags its tail as a way of showing pleasure. As an ultimate gesture, it may lie down and expose its belly—a sign among many mammals of submission to friend or foe. Ready to defend itself, a house cat stiffens its legs, arches its back, and lifts the hair on its back and tail. Fish sometimes show their moods by changing the position of their fins. Bird postures express fear or aggression, among other states. A graylag goose, for example, raises its head to threaten and lowers it in defense.

During courtship, males do most of the signaling—though often, of course, the female signals her assent. Male fiddler crabs wave an enlarged claw to attract a mate. Some kinds of spiders do elaborate dances in front of the female, identifying themselves thereby and preventing her from considering them prey; others strum her web before making their approach. Fish and salamanders may display spots of bright color, sometimes specially intensified for the breeding season. Certain lizards bob their bodies up and down; pheasants, peacocks, and other fine-feathered creatures display dazzlingly colored plumes.

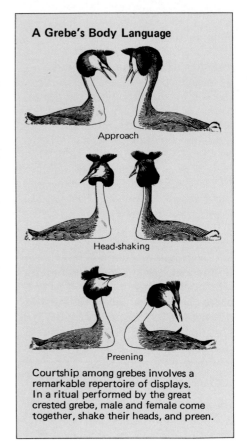

A Grebe's Body Language

Approach

Head-shaking

Preening

Courtship among grebes involves a remarkable repertoire of displays. In a ritual performed by the great crested grebe, male and female come together, shake their heads, and preen.

Why do birds sing?

Birds make sounds in their throats, much as we humans do. But their sound box, or syrinx, is at the bottom of the windpipe; our larynx is near the top. Such deep-voiced birds as whooping cranes and trumpeter swans have windpipes that measure an amazing three or four feet. A few species, such as the European white stork, are voiceless because they have no syrinx.

Most birds sing in the morning or evening and are quiet at midday. Whippoorwills sing in the twilight hours; mockingbirds and nightingales are nocturnal songsters. Although no two individuals sing exactly alike, to the trained human ear the song of each species is as distinct as its appearance—sometimes more so, in fact. Birdwatchers rely on sound to identify certain kinds of flycatchers, for example; they cannot tell the species apart by sight.

In nearly all bird species males are

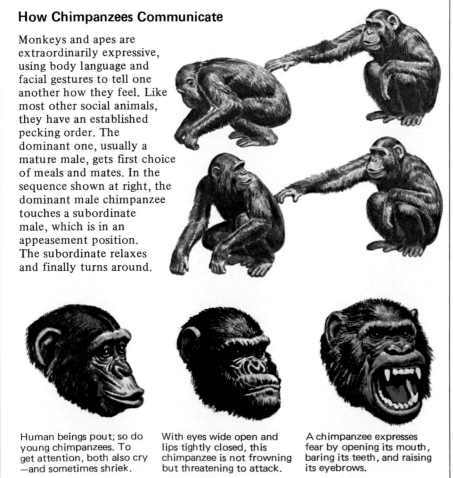

How Chimpanzees Communicate

Monkeys and apes are extraordinarily expressive, using body language and facial gestures to tell one another how they feel. Like most other social animals, they have an established pecking order. The dominant one, usually a mature male, gets first choice of meals and mates. In the sequence shown at right, the dominant male chimpanzee touches a subordinate male, which is in an appeasement position. The subordinate relaxes and finally turns around.

Human beings pout; so do young chimpanzees. To get attention, both also cry —and sometimes shriek.

With eyes wide open and lips tightly closed, this chimpanzee is not frowning but threatening to attack.

A chimpanzee expresses fear by opening its mouth, baring its teeth, and raising its eyebrows.

the more impressive songsters. They sing primarily to establish a claim to a territory, and some repeat their songs thousands of times a day, moving from perch to perch within their domain. Singing peaks just prior to breeding, and most species stop singing as the breeding season ends.

Song is not the everyday language of man (except in such artificial situations as musicals and operas)—nor is it that of birds. Birds communicate primarily with call notes, using them to scold, call young, beg for food, and help them stay together within a flock. Whether songs or call notes, their sounds are especially significant in forests, where often it is far easier to hear than to see.

How do insects make sounds?
Male mosquitoes intent on mating zero in on females by the distinctive whining whir of the females' wings. Crickets, grasshoppers, and katydids "sing" by stridulating—that is, rubbing one part of their body against another. (Only the males sing, and the songs of individual species are as different as those of birds.) Some grasshoppers have a row of slim pegs on the inside of each hind leg. To sing they lift their legs and draw the pegs across the stiff outer edge of the front wings. Crickets, katydids, and long-horned grasshoppers have a rough area, or file, near the rear of each front wing; the file is drawn over a thickened area

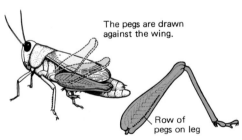

The pegs are drawn against the wing.

Row of pegs on leg

In making music, male grasshoppers use the leg as a bow and the wing as a violin.

Close-up of pegs in sockets

(the scraper) on the underside of the opposite front wing. Male cicadas make their shrill, monotonous calls by rapidly contracting and relaxing special muscles.

Mosquitoes perceive sound vibrations through their sensitive antennae. In short-horned grasshoppers, the "ears" are round membranes on the sides of the abdomen; in crickets and long-horned grasshoppers, on the front legs.

Who else communicates by sound?
As conspicuous as they are, the songs of birds and insects are by no means the only sounds in the animal world. Grasshopper mice put on near-operatic performances, standing on hind legs with head back and eyes half

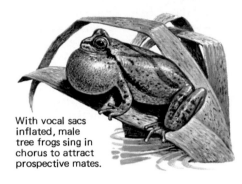

With vocal sacs inflated, male tree frogs sing in chorus to attract prospective mates.

closed as they utter high-pitched squeals. White whales, or belugas, have been dubbed sea canaries because of their melodious songs, and the hauntingly mournful dirges of humpbacked whales have become symbolic pleas for the preservation of their kind. Chirping and whistling beneath the surface, dolphins and porpoises are notable talkers. Such fish as drums and puffers also make underwater sounds.

Songs of frogs and toads range from birdlike chirps to rasps, croaks, grunts, and bleats. These amphibians sing by passing air over vocal cords; the sound then resonates in sacs puffed out from the throat. Choruses of males around lakes and ponds can be deafening—as is the roar of a far larger animal, the bull alligator, in spring.

What is a pheromone?
Recently scientists discovered that fire ants mark trails between food sources and their nests with an amazingly powerful chemical. Attractive only to other fire ants, this chemical is so potent that a trail a million miles long would take just a single teaspoonful.

Such social insects as ants secrete a number of pheromones; that is, chemical substances secreted by animals for signaling purposes. Some are alarm signals, which dissipate in less than a minute; those used to keep a group together last for a longer period of time. Pheromones are often sex attractants. Those released by female moths may be carried by the wind for a mile or more; males of a newt species create their own water currents, using their tails to send out pheromones.

Which animals have night lights?
Fireflies are soft-winged beetles with blinking taillights. Seen in the greatest numbers from midsummer until early fall, fireflies, or lightning bugs, usually start flashing at dusk and stop by midnight. Firefly flashes are sex signals. Lights from males are about twice as bright as those from females. Different species time their flashes differently, in many cases helping ensure that only members of the same species respond by flashing back.

In the American tropics certain kinds of click beetles glow at night.

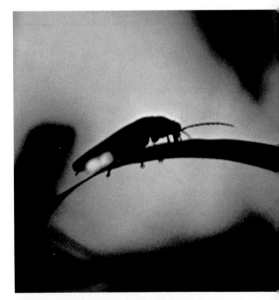

Flying lights on summer nights are fireflies, which use bioluminescence to attract potential mates. Hundreds of males flash in unison in the tropics.

One species has two green headlights, flashed when the beetle is at rest; when in flight, the beetle blinks a red abdominal light. With a glowing head and rows of lights along its sides, the larva of this beetle is called a railroad worm. Scientists believe such lights may be warning signals, helping keep predators at bay.

The Art of Camouflage

What good is camouflage?
In time of war, soldiers use camouflage to conceal themselves from the enemy. Animals use camouflage to hide from predators, prey, or both. In the case of humans, camouflage is an acquired trait; in wild animals it is a natural protective device, built into their bodies and behavior during millions of years.

Animals are often camouflaged by their colors, but shape and posture can also play a role. Camouflage typically enables an animal to blend in with its background, but this is not always the case: some species mimic others, and may be quite conspicuous as a result.

Why don't fawns look like does?
Newly hatched birds cannot fly; some newborn mammals cannot even stand up. Though very young animals often cannot flee from predators, in many species they are so well camouflaged that predators never see them at all. Plover chicks, for example, are sand-colored and speckled, matching the open beaches where they hatch. White spots dapple the brown bodies of fawns; young lions are spotted too.

Spots and streaks tend to blur and break up an animal's outline. But if the animal stands up or moves about, it casts a visible shadow. The shadow disappears when a plover chick or a fawn crouches down—evidence that camouflage can be a matter of behavior as well as appearance.

What is countershading?
Mackerel, striped bass, barracuda, salmon—a great many fish are dark on the back and light-colored on the belly. Seen from above by such fish eaters as ospreys and pelicans, the fish blends in with the water; seen from below, against the sunlit surface, the white belly seems to disappear. This color pattern is called countershading, and many birds have it too. One beautiful exception is the "upside-down" bobolink, which is completely black on its underside and has many white feathers on its back.

Why do tigers have stripes?
A tiger in a zoo is sure to catch your attention, but in a natural setting the big cat is far less visible. Tigers live for much of the year among tall, dry grasses and reeds. The tawny, dark-striped fur blends in with the vegetation, concealing the tiger from prey.

Bitterns, which are squat, brown, marsh-dwelling members of the heron family, also have stripes. At the first sign of danger a bittern freezes and makes itself as tall and narrow as it can, stretching out its body and pointing its bill toward the sky. If the wind is blowing, the bittern sways back and forth in rhythm with the reeds.

Zebras live in open country, where their stripes might seem to make them more conspicuous rather than less. Since this is unlikely to be true (it would hinder the zebras' survival), naturalists have looked for other interpretations. One possible explanation is that the stripes confuse lions and other predators by creating a disrupted image. Another is that at dawn and dusk, the times when the zebra's predators are most active, the black and white stripes blend together, producing a gray image that matches the dim light.

Why does the four-eyed butterfly fish have extra eyes?
In the Caribbean and other tropical waters, a number of species, including the four-eyed butterfly fish, bear a large, conspicuous spot on each side near the tail—a spot that, with its dark center surrounded by a light-colored ring, suggests an enormous eye. Scientists believe that such eyespots mislead predators, causing them to lunge for the tail instead of the head.

Insects have also developed such deceptive devices. Certain butterflies have not only prominent eyespots but also projections at the rear of each wing that resemble a head, antennae, and legs. Eyespots can sometimes function as threats: when menaced by a bird, a butterfly may suddenly open its wings, displaying a frightening "face" that startles the attacker. Certain caterpillars also use eyespots to scare off birds.

How do animals change color?
Ptarmigan change color every spring, molting the white winter feathers and growing a brown summer plumage. They molt again in fall. In contrast to such slow color changes, chameleons and a number of other animals are

How Animals Escape Being Noticed

Camouflaged by pattern, a bittern is even harder to see in reedy marshlands when it extends its neck, flattens its feathers, and points its bill toward the sky.

quick-change artists. Pigment cells in the skin are the agents of change.

By expanding and contracting its color cells, a flounder varies the amount of pigment that shows on its skin. It can imitate a light, sandy bottom; a dark, muddy bottom; or a mottled gravelly surface. In one experi-

In both looks and behavior, the Indian leaf bug is a startling imitation of a real leaf. It rocks back and forth, as if it were being blown by the wind.

Among the quick-change artists are flounder, bottom-dwelling fish with an incredible ability to match the color and pattern of their background. They prey on small animal life.

humidity. On occasion they also attempt to match their backgrounds.

Whether fish or frog, an animal taking on the color of its background is not making a conscious decision. The color change is a built-in, reflex action over which the animal has no voluntary control.

Is a dead leaf always what it seems?
A small fish approaches a dead leaf drifting down a South American forest stream. Suddenly the dead leaf lunges with open jaws, and the little fish disappears. The leaf was actually a leaffish, disguised by its leaf-shaped body, the short stemlike barbel on its lower jaw, and a tapering tail fin that mimics the tip of a leaf.

In tropical forests certain frogs and toads bear an incredible resemblance to fallen leaves. Their backs are pale and flattened, and flaps of skin protruding from the edge of the head and body give them a leaflike shape.

Insects, however, are the masters of the dead-leaf disguise. The wings of certain butterfly species not only look like leaves: they also have ragged edges and transparent spots that suggest the work of chewing insects. One grasshopper from Borneo has wings that, when folded, look like a dead, half-eaten leaf. The resemblance is not just in shape and color: the wings carry markings that look like leaf veins and spots of decay. Behavior is important too. When danger threatens, the grasshopper lies on its side, among genuine dead leaves.

Which animals use decoys?
A spider in Southeast Asia waits for prey at the hub of its big, circular web—a position in which it makes an easy target for spider-eating birds. The spider builds several false hubs on either side of the central hub and then weaves in remnants of its prey; the bodies serve as decoy spiders. Another species makes its decoys from pieces of lichen and bark.

Decoys deceive prey as well as predators. The alligator snapping turtle lies with its mouth open, wiggling its pink, wormlike tongue; when small fish are lured in, it snaps its jaws shut. Anglerfish have lures (sometimes even luminous ones) suspended over their mouths by a spine.

ment, scientists placed a flounder in a tank with a checkerboard bottom. Within a few hours, the fish had produced a recognizable imitation of the checkerboard pattern.

Certain other kinds of fish have similar color-bearing cells. So do octopuses and squid, as well as chameleons and certain other lizards. Some shrimps and crabs also have the ability to change color rapidly. Apparently, however, most of these animals change color when they experience such emotions as anger and fear. Frogs and toads change color not only with mood but with temperature and

171

Venomous Animals

Why are animals venomous?
Some animals run swiftly to catch prey or to escape predators; some take flight. Sharp claws or teeth help certain species to defend themselves and to capture food. Venoms are yet another weapon—a chemical one that can be used offensively (in subduing prey), defensively (as protection), or both. Birds are the only major animal group that apparently lacks venomous species; mammals include only a few (the platypus and certain shrews).

Venomous creatures are not necessarily aggressive ones. Those that protect themselves with venom are sometimes even brightly colored; their colors serve as a warning, and they use their venom only in self-defense.

How dangerous are bees?
In the natural world, of course, animals use venom against other wild animals. Although venoms do not necessarily harm human beings, what we in this human-centered world notice is their effect on man.

The stings of bees and wasps generally cause no more than localized swelling and a throbbing ache, both gone within several days at most. There are some people, however, who are highly sensitive to stings or have an unusual reaction to a particular insect's sting. In the United States insects are responsible for more deaths annually than are poisonous snakes.

Bees and wasps are not the only venomous insects. The fuzzy hairs or spines on some kinds of caterpillars, such as the larva of the io moth (one of the giant silkworm moths) and that of the puss moth, pack a stinging poison. With stilettolike piercing mouths, kissing bugs and their relatives wound the victim and then inject poison. The stings of some ants (fire ants, for example) are more dangerous and painful than bees'.

Bees, wasps, and ants are all closely related insects; and within this group of insects, only the females can sting. (The sting is a modified egg-laying tube.) Not all species have stings, but most of those that do can sting many times in succession. The honeybee, however, can do it only once. Its barbed sting, located at the rear of the body, lodges in its victim and is torn from the bee along with the venom sac. The sting cannot be withdrawn, and the honeybee dies.

Do black widow spiders really eat their mates?
To overcome the flies and other animals on which they feed, spiders wrap their victims in silk and inject a paralyzing or killing venom with their bite. Only a few spiders, however, are dangerous to man. Best known is the black widow. Though extremely painful, the bite of the female—recognizable because she has a red "hourglass" on the underside of her black abdomen—is rarely lethal. Males do not bite at all. Like the males of other spider species, male black widows die soon after mating. Some weakened individuals are captured and eaten by the female right after mating.

Why do scorpions sting?
A scorpion has a menacing weapon—a sharp, curved stinger at the tip of the long tail, which is held off to one side or arched over the back. Some of the nearly 700 species have only a mild venom; others (certain American and African ones) can be deadly to man. Scorpions can bite as well as sting. Found mainly in warm, dry regions, they are active at night, feeding on spiders (which are close relatives), insects, and other small animals. During

The scorpion uses the poisonous stinger at the tip of its tail to paralyze prey.

the day they hide in burrows, under stones and other objects, or indoors in such places as closets and shoes. They sting humans only in self-defense.

Compared with scorpions, which can grow to seven inches in length, pseudoscorpions are midgets; few measure more than a third of an inch. The poison in these creatures is in their pincers, not in their tails. Like scorpions, some pseudoscorpions live in houses, but these should not be considered pests: they feed on clothes-moth caterpillars and other destructive household insects.

Which is the most dangerous snake?
Rattlesnakes, adders, mambas, coral snakes, bushmasters, fer-de-lance, cottonmouths, copperheads, cobras—

Venom-Injecting Devices

Spider
Poison duct
Poison gland
Fang

Snake
Fang
Venom duct
Groove for venom
Opening where venom is forced out

Stingray
Spine
Teeth
Venom glands

Portuguese man-of-war
Uncoiled thread injects poison
Trigger (when touched, thread uncoils)
Barbs
Coiled thread
Poison sac

Honeybee
Venom sac
Valves control venom flow
Sting sheath
Bulb with venom
Sting
Barbs

all are venomous snakes and should be avoided, but they are not equally dangerous to man. Drop for drop, the most potent venom is believed to be that of the taipan, a large-fanged Australian snake. Australia is the only continent with more venomous than

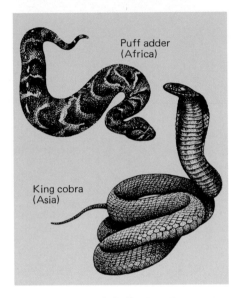

Puff adder (Africa)

King cobra (Asia)

nonvenomous species of snakes. The king cobra of Asia, which can reach a length of 18 feet, is the world's biggest venomous snake. Large individuals contain enough venom to kill 20 people or more. A snake's venom works primarily to immobilize and kill prey. The spitting cobra, however, uses its venom mainly in defense; it spits out the venom at an enemy's eyes.

Which poisonous animals live in the sea?
Scorpion fish, surgeonfish, stingrays, sea urchins, Portuguese men-of-war—more kinds of venomous animals are found in the sea than anywhere else. The stonefish, one of some 350-odd species of scorpion fish (all are armed with venomous spines), has an especially fearsome reputation. More people, however, are likely to come in contact with a stingray, which drives a sharp, barbed spine into the victim's skin when it lashes its tail.

Spines of some sea urchin species are hollow and venomous. Jellyfish, fire corals, and sea anemones can also sting. The Portuguese man-of-war, a tentacled creature with a purplish, sausage-shaped float, has as many as half a million stinging capsules, which

immobilize small animal prey and serve as an effective defense. All of the roughly 500 species of sea snakes are venomous—and the toxin of some is more potent than a cobra's. Cone shells, prized by collectors, can be deadly too. Unique among mollusks, the living snail shoots its hollow, harpoonlike tongue into the victim, then contracts a bulbous venom sac and pumps poison into the wound.

Although less notorious, a cabbage-sized jellyfish known as the sea wasp is ranked by some authorities as the most dangerous creature in the sea. Records kept for several decades at Brisbane, Australia, showed that sea wasps killed about five times as many people there as sharks did. These jellyfish, which drift into shallow areas and are difficult to spot, may have tentacles to 20 feet long, each containing hundreds of thousands of individually triggered stinging capsules. Death from the powerful venom may come within five minutes.

What is the difference between poisonous and venomous animals?
Venoms and poisons are both substances that can do harm. "Venom,"

however, is generally a more specific term, referring to substances produced by specialized tissues and introduced by means of a venom apparatus. A viper, for example, produces venom in glands in its head and injects the venom through its hollow fangs. Animals that are poisonous but not venomous can be harmful when ingested (the fish called puffers, for instance, are especially dangerous in this regard), touched (blister beetles), or both (certain frogs and toads).

Which animals are poisonous because of what they eat?
Many poisonous animals do not produce poisons themselves but accumulate them from their food. Green turtles living in Caribbean waters, where they feed almost exclusively on turtle grass, are not poisonous to man; but in the Indo-Pacific region, where they eat mainly jellyfish, they are. Hundreds of species of fish, especially in tropical seas, are poisonous because of what they eat. The poisons, believed to originate in marine plants, are ingested by plant-eating fish and then passed along to the plant eaters' predators, including man.

Bird eggs form part of the Gila monster's diet.

The desert "monster" is up to two feet long.

What is a Gila monster?
There are about 3,000 species of lizards in the world, and all of them can bite (most hold on with a viselike grip). Only two, however, are actually venomous: the Gila monster of the southwestern United States and adjacent areas in Mexico, and the closely related Mexican beaded lizard. Both are short-legged, thick-bodied reptiles

with fat tails; their scales do not overlap but fit together in rows like strings of beads. The poison glands are located in the lower jaw, and venom flows along grooved teeth into the bite wound. These sluggish lizards, which feed on bird eggs, nesting birds, and young mammals, do not attack human beings and will not bite them unless the "monsters" are molested.

Living Together

What enables deep-sea fish to glow in the dark?

Many fish inhabiting the deep sea carry their own lights. In a world where no sunlight penetrates, this luminescence is thought to serve such varied functions as attracting prey and enabling the fish to see nearby objects and recognize potential mates. In some species specialized cells belonging to the fish itself are the light producers. But more frequently it is bacteria living in the fish's tissues that do the work—and derive nourishment from their host in return. Some fish actually activate their bacterial "guests" by pumping oxygenated blood to them; others mask and un-mask the perpetually glowing bacteria by expanding or contracting cells in the skin.

How do anemone fish escape the anemone's sting?

Though they look very much like flowers, sea anemones are animals—predatory ones that capture small fish and other prey with tentacles that sting. But on tropical coral reefs brightly splotched fish known as anemone fish, or clown fish, actually shelter among the tentacles, protected from predators by the anemone's sting and from the sting by a mucous coating on their skin. The anemones benefit from the relationship, too: the little fish have

The Sting of Survival

How you perceive Portuguese men-of-war depends on your point of view. To some (humans included), their stinging tentacles are harmful or worse; but they offer safe harbor to the little man-of-war fish.

been observed nipping off diseased tentacles and cleaning debris from their hosts. Other fish have adopted the same survival technique; one species even spends its life among the deadly tentacles of the Portuguese man-of-war.

Which animals are "innkeepers"?

In mud flats along the California coast dwells a curious creature known as the innkeeper worm. The fat worm, which resembles a long pink sausage, lives in a U-shaped burrow—and so does some other animal life. Small fish called gobies take shelter in the mouth of the burrow (as many as two dozen have been found in a single burrow). Tiny crabs and two-inch scale worms take up residence in this convenient shelter. Even clams living outside the burrow stick their siphons into it, taking advantage of the current of water that passes through. The innkeeper worm apparently gains nothing from its "guests"—but they do not seem to harm it, either.

What do ants have to do with aphids?

Ants are fond of the sugary substances that aphids secrete as they feed on plants. Much as a human hand-milks a cow, the ants stroke the aphids' ab-

The gaudy little anemone fish has no special weapons of its own. It seeks shelter among the sea anemone's tentacles, remarkably immune to their poisonous sting.

domens to stimulate "honeydew" flow. Some species of ants build little enclosures of mud or chewed-up pulp around the aphids; when danger threatens, some carry off the valuable aphids in their jaws.

One North American species of ant keeps aphid eggs in its nest, tending them with as much care as its own eggs. In spring the aphid eggs hatch, and the ants put the baby aphids out to "pasture" on the roots of early weeds. Later, when farmers have planted their corn, the ants carry the aphids to the roots of corn plants. As the juice in one root becomes exhausted, the ants move the aphids to new roots.

Although the intensity of such a relationship may vary, the aphids involved in it benefit from the ants' attention. The ants, in return, get the sweet, nutritious honeydew. Ants and aphids—two very different sorts of insects—have an association that benefits both sides.

Do ant nests contain only ants?

More than 3,000 kinds of insects live in ants' nests—and more than a third of them are beetles. One kind of beetle secretes a substance favored by ants; using their front legs, the ants pick up the beetles and lick the tasty secretions. Often the beetles sit up and beg like dogs, waving their legs to attract attention. After letting an ant lick it, the beetle pushes its head out and opens its mouth. The ant responds by regurgitating a droplet of food.

The very existence of Europe's large blue butterfly is dependent on ants.

Large blue butterfly

Ants carry the caterpillar of this beautiful butterfly back to their nests. Though the caterpillar eats some of the ant larvae, its overall effect is more positive: it secretes a sugary syrup when the ants stroke it with their antennae and legs. Caterpillars of closely related species do this too, but they do not actually live in the nest.

Why do birds ride atop other animals?

In Africa a nature lover will often see birds riding on the backs of such large mammals as rhinoceros and buffalo. Some of these birds, such as the cattle egret, feed on insects stirred up by the plant-eating mammals; the tickbirds, also known as oxpeckers, patrol the hides of their hosts and eat ticks and other parasites they find on the skin. The winged passengers may be so bold that they even thrust their bills into the mammals' ears and nostrils to get at parasites—to the occasional annoyance of the host.

It is not only mammals that have birds on their backs. The big, ground-dwelling kori bustard—a distant relative of the cranes that may weigh as much as 30 pounds—often carries a smaller bird, called the carmine bee-eater. The exquisitely colored bee-eater eagerly snaps up insects flushed from the grass by the larger bird.

Is the honey guide really a guide?

Arctic foxes trail polar bears in order to scavenge on leavings of the larger animals' kills. For the same reason, pilotfish swim with sharks and other large fish. Jackals and hyenas often watch circling vultures, then follow them to carcasses to feed.

A great many creatures use other species in locating food. But there is one species that actually offers its services as a guide: an African bird known as the honey guide. As its name implies, the honey guide is fond of honey; it also eats adult bees, bee larvae, and beeswax.

Although the honey guide cannot raid a bee nest on its own, it has over time found a better way. When the honey guide discovers a nest of bees, it flies about the forest, uttering a special cry. The ratel (or honey badger), a mammal that shares with the honey guide a love for honey and bees, hears the bird and follows it to the nest. With powerful limbs and claws, it tears apart the nest and eats its fill; the honey guide feeds on what remains. Long ago, human beings learned to follow the honey guide—and the birds learned to rely on man as a partner in gathering food. Honey guides also have relationships with other birds: they lay their eggs in the nests of other species.

Riding atop a contented cow, the insect-eating cattle egret is alert to any little creatures the animal might disturb. Birds perched on other animals serve as sentries too.

Why do animals live together?

Among nature's most intriguing phenomena are the partnerships formed by different species. The name used for these relationships, *symbiosis,* comes from the Greek meaning "living together." Not all symbiotic relationships are the same. There are some, called commensal relationships, in which one partner gains a benefit while the other gains little or none but is not harmed. One example is the relationship between two types of fish—remoras and sharks. The remora, which is long and often striped, attaches itself to a shark (sometimes to another type of fish or a whale), using the sucker on its head. When the shark makes a kill, the hitchhiker briefly detaches itself to feed on the scraps. Another type of symbiotic relationship is parasitism, in which one partner benefits at the expense of others. Ticks and tapeworms are among the familiar parasites.

The third type of symbiotic relationship, called mutualism, is a true partnership in which both partners benefit. The relationship may be limited, as when zebras and wildebeest graze together on the vast African grasslands. Each species can survive on its own, but together their chances of detecting predators are improved because each contributes a specially keen sense. (Zebras have the better eyesight; wildebeest, hearing and sense of smell.) In a few cases the partners are so interdependent that one cannot survive without the other. Most mutualistic relationships probably lie somewhere in between.

Tool-Using Animals

How clever are chimpanzees?
Gorillas, baboons, orangutans, and other primates occasionally throw sticks or stones as weapons and use rocks to crack open nuts. Of all the apes, however, chimpanzees show the greatest versatility in the use of tools in the wild. With twigs stripped of their leaves, or with stiff grass stems, they probe into termite nests, then draw out the homemade "fishing rod" and lick off any insects. They also dip stems into bee nests for honey. With larger sticks they break open ant or termite nests; big sticks are also used as pries or digging sticks to get edible roots and tubers. Chewed-up leaves are poked into hollows in trees to sponge up water for drinking.

Which birds throw stones?
A tool has been defined as a means to an end, and for many animals that end is food. The Galápagos woodpecker finch holds a cactus spine or a slim, sharp twig in its bill, using it to probe under bark or into holes for grubs and other insects. When a prodded insect tries to make an escape, the finch shifts its tool to one of its feet, eats the morsel, and then puts the twig or spine back in its bill. The tool is then ready for reuse.

Like humans, some birds use stones as tools. For the European song thrush, a stone is an anvil for cracking open snail shells. Egyptian vultures pick up rocks with their bills and hurl them at ostrich eggs. If the shell does not break right away, they will repeat the pounding for half an hour or more. More common is the habit of throwing food against the rocks, rather than vice versa. The lammergeier, a large Old World vulture, has been known to drop bones from high in the air, shattering them on rocks so that it can get at the soft marrow. It is said to do this with turtles too. Gulls drop shellfish onto rocks to break them open.

Mongooses are weasellike mammals with similar habits. Some crack a bird's egg by holding it in their front paws and hurling it at a rock or tree trunk. Enterprising individuals may even throw the egg backward between their hind legs and kick it to give it an extra boost.

Which fish shoots water bullets?
For the six-inch archerfish, water has become a tool for getting food. The little fish, which lives in streams and swamps in Southeast Asia, cruises near the surface close to shore, looking for spiders, insects, or other small creatures on overhanging branches. When it sights a potential meal, it moves back and forth in the water, adjusting for distance and compensating in some unknown way for the bending of light rays by water. Then the archerfish spits "bullets" of water at the target, causing it to fall in the stream. Accurate to distances as great as four feet, it sometimes scores hits from even farther away.

What do elephants do when they itch?
An elephant with an itch in the middle of its back cannot scratch the itch with its feet; nor can the mammoth creature rub its back up and down a tree trunk as bears do. The elephant has been observed to pick up a stick with its highly mobile trunk and then use it as a scratcher. Mother elephants sometimes employ another tool, this one more of a weapon: an uprooted shrub or small tree may serve as a paddle for spanking misbehaving young.

Which insects work with tools?
Some wasps put pebbles to work. To prepare a nursery for the young, a female caterpillar-hunter wasp digs a tunnel in loose or gravelly soil. Then she puts back the loose material, carries away the big pieces, and plugs the opening with a carefully selected stone. Next she hunts for a caterpillar. After giving it a paralyzing sting, she carries it back to the nursery. She opens and cleans out the tunnel, then pushes the immobilized caterpillar inside and lays her eggs on it (the young wasps will eat it when they hatch). Finally she seals the opening with loose dirt and tamps it down with a small pebble held in her jaws.

How to Get Snails Out of Their Shells

Gourmets use special snail forks to extract the succulent morsel from its shell. Nature has other means. Holding on to a snail with one foot, the Everglades kite (an American bird of prey) pries out the food with its bill; the European song thrush (below and at right) actually breaks the shell, by banging it against a rock.

A song thrush often smashes snail shells against the same rock, popularly called its anvil rock.

As it balances a rock on its belly, a floating sea otter clutches a clam. The clam will be smashed against the rock.

What tools can be found in the ocean?
Even on land, where the two most frequently used tool materials—plants and stones—occur just about everywhere, tool-using animals are rare. In the sea, there are even fewer. The sea otter picks up a rock from the ocean bottom. Floating on its back, it puts the rock on its belly and then smashes its hard-shelled prey against the rock. Sea otters use another tool too—seaweed, which ties members of a family together, keeping them from drifting apart, or furnishes cover.

Certain hermit crabs pick up sea anemones and place them on their shells. For the crab, the stinging tentacles of the anemones serve as weapons and their bodies as camouflage gear. (The anemones get something out of it too—transportation.) The anemones are used as weapons, but can they be considered tools? Because the crab puts them in place, some biologists say yes; others find it difficult to consider any living object a tool.

Can you teach animals to use tools?
For animals, tool using may be largely instinctive—an inborn compulsion that gives them a seeming wisdom without need for thought. But they can learn such habits too. For circuses and other types of shows, numerous kinds of animals—from fleas to chickens, parrots, dolphins, and even the big cats—have been trained to perform a variety of acts involving tools. Most are deceptive: though the animals appear to possess skills or reasoning powers, their actions are in fact conditioned responses. They are performing for particular rewards—usually food.

In Africa baboons have been trained to use simple tools to dig vegetables or pick fruit. Though not always willing or dependable, these ground-dwelling monkeys will indeed work for their keep. Many primate species have been tested in laboratories to determine their tool-using ability. When they are shown how an object can be used to help them attain a goal, most are quick to imitate. They can master only simple one-step tasks, however. Even the quick-witted chimpanzee is stumped when one tool must be used to make another. Its skill is limited to attaining immediate and direct goals.

Animals Without Backbones

What sorts of creatures don't have backbones?

Lobsters and ladybugs, sponges and spiders, mosquitoes and mussels, corals and clams—about 95 percent of all living animal species are creatures without backbones, called invertebrates. Since the group includes huge numbers of animals with nothing in common except their lack of a backbone, their differences are far more remarkable than their similarities. Some are carnivores, some herbivores, some parasitic on other forms of life. Speedy runners contrast with marine drifters and those that never move at all. Sizes range from microscopic to more than 50 feet.

How can an animal survive without a backbone?

Most animals have skeletons that support—and sometimes protect—their tissues, and the bony internal skeleton of mice and men is but one of several variations on a theme. Some invertebrates have internal skeletons too, albeit made of different materials. Sponges, for example, have an intricate framework of silica or other substances to stiffen their flaccid bodies. Since a sponge does not move about or change its shape, it does not need more of a skeleton.

Two major groups of invertebrates are noted for their *external* skeletons—that is, skeletons that enclose the body rather than stiffening it on the inside. Clams, snails, and most other mollusks have shells made of calcium carbonate, the same substance that makes up limestone. Arthropods, the group that includes insects, spiders, and crabs (as well as many others), have external skeletons of chitin, which is chemically similar to plant cellulose. Here too, the formula is varied. Most insects have thin, flexible skeletons, while lobsters and crabs have harder ones.

What prevents a jellyfish from collapsing?

Though flabby in appearance, a jellyfish is actually firm to the touch. Even though it has no internal skeleton or external shell, the creature is able to maintain its shape. This is due partly to the fact that the animal's gelatinous mass is interlaced with tough fibers of connective tissue. In addition, jellyfish are kept rigid because they pump themselves up with water, rather like a rubber raft that becomes rigid when filled with air. Sea anemones and worms have a similar type of support, called a hydrostatic skeleton.

Why are most invertebrates small?

Although a few invertebrates grow quite large (the biggest is the giant squid), most are small compared to man and the majority of other vertebrates. One reason is that most lack internal skeletons. As an animal grows, it becomes increasingly difficult for an external skeleton (such as a crab's) to accommodate the creature inside. If the skeleton becomes strong enough to withstand the pull of the animal's muscles, it becomes too heavy to allow the animal much mobility. Squid can grow to giant size partly because, unlike most other mollusks, they have no external shells.

The weight limitation is much less in water than on land, and the world's biggest invertebrates live in the sea. The sedentary giant clam of South Pacific coral reefs grows to more than four feet wide and weighs up to a quarter of a ton. Giant squid can reach a length of 55 feet (including tentacles) and weigh well over a ton. In

---

The Amazing Diversity of Invertebrates

As the nine groups represented here make clear, the word "invertebrate" says nothing about an animal's looks. Life-style is as varied as appearance. Sponges remain fixed in place; blue crabs are good swimmers; and jellyfish are among those that float in the sea. Millipedes crawl on their "thousands" of legs. Tarantulas are nighttime hunters, and butterflies sip flower nectar during the day. Moon snails drill holes in clamshells to get out the meat; starfish pry them apart. The most ubiquitous scavengers are the earthworms, which feed on dead material in the soil.

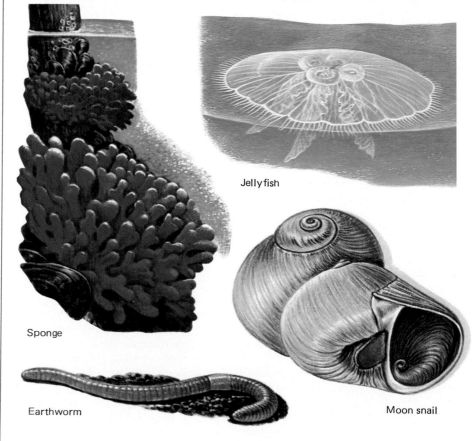

Jellyfish

Sponge

Earthworm

Moon snail

contrast, the largest free-living land invertebrate is an Australian earthworm measuring "only" 10 feet long.

How do invertebrates reproduce?

Animals without backbones form a very diverse group, and their modes of reproduction are equally varied. Among the simpler creatures, such as sponges and corals, the same individual may reproduce both sexually (by releasing fertilized eggs) and asexually (by dividing in two). Jellyfish have a more complicated life cycle. The free-floating, bell-shaped form, called a medusa, produces eggs that hatch into tiny larvae. These sink to the seafloor, where they grow into sedentary individuals that produce row upon row of buds. When the buds break off, a new generation of free-floating jellyfish takes shape. Among some invertebrates, such as butterflies and crabs, male and female come together to mate. But sea urchins and many other aquatic creatures shed eggs and sperm simultaneously in the water and leave fertilization to chance.

Do animals without backbones care for their young?

The female octopus guards her eggs, cleans them, and oxygenates them with gentle jets of water. Some female spiders carry their eggs and newly hatched young on their abdomens; some starfish carry their young on their backs, between their spines. The social insects—bees, wasps, ants, and termites—carefully rear their young to adulthood. Female scorpions and certain starfish are among the invertebrates that carry their eggs inside their bodies until they hatch; in some species the eggs are actually nourished similarly to the way a mammalian embryo is. For most kinds of invertebrates, however, there is no parental care.

How intelligent are invertebrates?

In proportion to its size, the octopus has the largest brain of any invertebrate. Most invertebrates need little of what we call intelligence to get through their daily routines (instinctive responses are enough to ensure survival); many, including sponges and starfish, do very well with no brain. Yet invertebrates sometimes appear to have the ability to learn. Such humble creatures as flatworms (planarians) can be trained to run simple mazes. Spiders learn to weave better webs by trial and error, and domesticated honeybees have learned to recognize the color of their painted hive.

How do starfish open clams?

Gripping a clam with its dozens of sucker-tipped tube feet, a starfish exerts a steady pull with its arms until the beleaguered mollusk weakens. The clamshells open, and the starfish turns its stomach inside out, forcing it into the gap between the shells and digesting its victim alive. That, at least, was the theory until quite recently. But scientists who watched starfish feeding learned that in many cases the clam's shells left a small gap even when tightly closed. This gap is big enough for the starfish to insert its stomach, and widen the gap as the victim's muscles are digested.

Not all starfish feed in this manner. Species with short, stubby arms swallow their prey whole, spitting out the shell afterward. Some species feed not on clams and other bivalves but on hermit crabs, sea urchins, or even other starfish. The big crown of thorns starfish feeds on live coral animals, causing widespread destruction of reefs in the process.

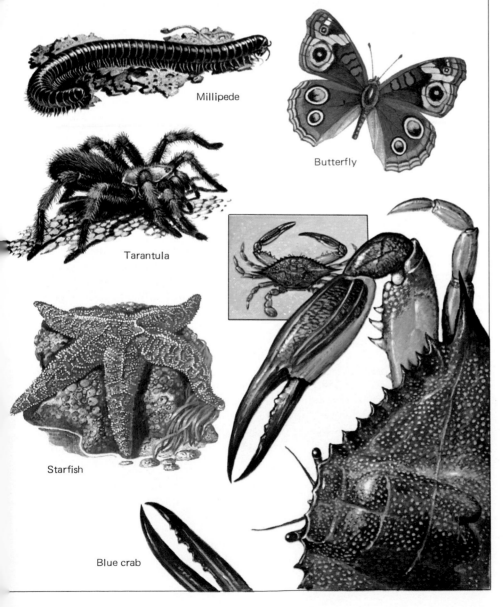

Millipede

Butterfly

Tarantula

Starfish

Blue crab

Many Kinds of Mollusks

Which animals are mollusks?

Snails and mussels represent the two most familiar groups of mollusks, the single-shelled animals (univalves) and those with pairs (bivalves). The eight-plated chitons, tentacled tusk shells, and squid and octopuses are also mollusks. Though most mollusks have shells and a well-defined foot, a more general feature is the fleshy mantle that encloses the animal's body. Many mollusks also have a radula—a hard, tooth-bearing "tongue" that scrapes away plant tissues or tears up animal flesh.

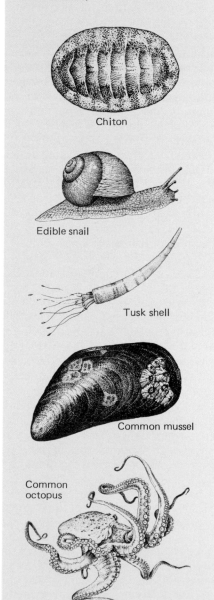

Chiton

Edible snail

Tusk shell

Common mussel

Common octopus

Do all mollusks have shells?

It is for their shells that mollusks are most appreciated (their edibility is a prized feature too). Beachcombers delight in the exquisite colors and patterns, especially those of tropical shells; such "decorations" as spines and knobs enhance the appeal. Fascinating too is the very diversity. Tusk shells, turret shells, glass snails, slipper shells, bubble shells, razor clams, turban shells, keyhole limpets—names like these only hint at the shells' different forms.

Not every animal with a shell is a mollusk, of course (turtles have them too); nor is every mollusk shelled. Those of squid and cuttlefish lie inside the body, greatly reduced in size (the squid's shell is the "pen" and the cuttlefish's the cuttlebone); octopuses, sea slugs, and most land slugs have none at all. Shell-less mollusks have developed other sorts of protection. For example, sea slugs defend themselves with "borrowed" stings—cells recycled from such prey animals as sea anemones and jellyfish. Sea slugs, also known as nudibranchs, are far more beautiful than their name implies. Their stunning coloration is, in fact, associated with their sting: like a skunk's conspicuous pattern, a sea slug's vivid color often warns other animals to stay away.

Which mollusks are dangerous to man?

Considering the large number of mollusks (more than 40,000 species) worldwide, few indeed are directly dangerous to man; and most of those are confined to tropical seas. Especially venomous is Australia's blue-ringed octopus, which inflicts a paralyzing dose of neurotoxin in its painful bite. Certain cone shells can deliver a deadly sting with the barbed tip of their radula (tongue). Though cone shells may sting a collector in self-defense, they normally use poison to kill prey—mainly other mollusks.

Why do clams have siphons?

Clams need a current of water in order to breathe, and also to bring them particles of food (the clam filters these out in its gills). Water enters a clam through one siphon, and exits through another. Thanks to these tubular

structures, the creature can stay buried in the muddy or sandy bottom, with only its siphons extending up into the water.

Different species of clams have siphons of different lengths. Such deep-digging burrowers as razor clams have very long siphons; species that burrow only a short distance beneath the surface have far shorter ones. The arrangement of siphons also varies. Some clams have two completely separate siphons (sometimes of different lengths); in other species, the two are joined together at the base or fused throughout their length. Siphons can be retracted into the shell, but those of gaper clams are so large that they cannot be withdrawn completely; and so the shell gapes open.

Why do oysters make pearls?

Unlike edible oysters, which live in muddy temperate waters, pearl oysters prefer the clean sandy bottoms of tropical seas. There they form pearls in response to irritation—as a defense against the invasion of their body by a grain of sand (or sometimes a parasite). Secreting nacre, or mother-of-pearl, around the foreign object in thin, regular layers, the oyster takes several years to build up a smooth, lustrous pearl. Early in this century the Japanese discovered that pearls could be deliberately cultured by inserting a piece of shell into the oyster—a process known as seeding.

Oysters are not the only mollusks that form pearls. Freshwater mussels produce red or pinkish pearls, which were formerly in great demand for jewelry. The iridescent inner shell of both abalones and freshwater mussels is used as a source of mother-of-pearl for buttons. A large button industry grew up along the banks of the Mississippi (where mussels are plentiful), but dwindled after cheaper, mass-produced plastic buttons replaced the genuine article.

How strong is a limpet's grip?

Pounded by the waves, mollusks on exposed rocky shores live a precarious life. Such snails as topshells and periwinkles are easily dislodged and rolled about by the tides; but a limpet can withstand the strongest breakers by using its foot as a suction pad. Pull-

Can mollusks see their surroundings?

Throughout the animal world the ability to see is coordinated with style of life. Mammals that burrow may have poor eyesight or none at all (the eyes of certain moles are covered with skin); certain burrowing snails are sightless too (their chemical and tactile senses are well developed). In contrast, land snails use their eyes, which lie at the tips of long tentacles on the head, to explore terrain.

Unlike snails, clams and other bivalve mollusks have no well-defined head, and their eyes—as well as the other sense organs—often lie at the edge of the fleshy mantle, which overhangs the body and is attached to the shell. Unusual bivalves because they can swim, scallops have several extraordinary rows of eyes visible between their shells. The octopus has large, lidded eyes.

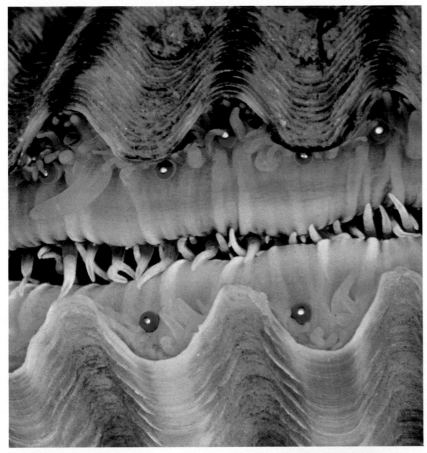

Beautiful blue eyes look out from a scallop's fleshy mantle; tentacles sensitive to chemicals and touch also respond to the outside world. Although scallops detect motion and shadow, they do not perceive form.

Scallops swim jerkily by jet propulsion, shooting out water when they shut their shells. The muscle used to close the shells is what we eat.

ing a limpet away from a rock requires a force of more than 60 pounds.

Many people who have seen limpets attached to a rock do not even realize that the drab-colored bumps they are looking at are animals; the bumps do not move and are hard to the touch. But limpets do not always remain fixed in place. This mollusk comes to life after dark, roaming over the rocks on its fleshy foot and feeding on algal growths. After feeding it always returns to the same depression, then maneuvers about until the fit is precise. Abrasion from the shell and acid secretions from its foot continue to hollow out the depression.

How fast is a "snail's pace"?

Although shells offer protection, they also hamper mobility. The round-mouthed snail of Europe creeps along at a speed of an inch a minute; other kinds move only slightly faster. Progression is slow, but—as in the fable of the tortoise and the hare—the creature gets where it is going.

A snail crawling up the glass of a fish tank reveals a great deal about snail locomotion. A series of muscular waves passes up the sole of the foot, showing up as dark bands; as many as ten bands may be present at any one time. To smooth their path, snails—and slugs too—secrete mucus, forming a track of lubricating slime that allows them to traverse rough patches of soil and helps them retrace their steps.

Why do snails and slugs come out at night?

During the day snails and slugs often cluster together in such damp places as underneath stones and rotten logs. Because their soft bodies are susceptible to drying out (this is especially true of slugs without shells), they emerge only when conditions are suitable—after a rain or at night, when the air is cooler and much more humid at ground level.

Water loss is a special problem during certain seasons. Before winter sets in, a snail secretes a double layer of mucus over the opening to its shell; the mucus hardens and reduces water loss. Many types of snails hibernate in this state. Conversely, in hot, dry places snails may not come out of their shells during summer.

The Octopus and the Squid

How many arms does an octopus have?

Though octopuses and squid are mollusks, on them the fleshy foot typical of such mollusks as snails and clams has developed into grasping arms that grow out from the head. For this reason, octopuses, squid, and their relatives are called cephalopods (Greek for "head-foot").

Different groups of cephalopods have different numbers of arms, or tentacles. Octopuses, as their name suggests, have 8 and squid 10. On squid two arms are much longer than the others; normally kept retracted, these are shot out to capture prey or in defense. Cuttlefish, which look like flattened squid (one common species is elaborately striped), are 10-armed too. Arms on all three are laden with suckers. Those of an octopus are plain and fleshy; cuttlefish and squid have suckers rimmed with teeth.

Why do squid squirt ink?

When attacked, a squid ejects a dark, thick cloud of ink, which does not spread in the water but forms a blob of roughly the same size and general shape as the animal's body. At the same time the animal becomes pale. An assailant tends to attack the dark ink cloud (which is much more visible than the animal itself), and the squid jets off to safety. Sometimes a squid ejects a more fluid ink, which spreads rapidly through the water and forms a "smoke screen" through which nothing can be seen. It may also temporarily numb a predator's sense of smell.

Squid usually produce a blue-black ink; octopuses and cuttlefish eject black and sepia-brown inks respectively. The word *sepia*, in fact, comes from the Greek for "cuttlefish," and cuttlefish ink was for centuries used as a writing fluid.

Do giant squid really exist?

The smallest adult squid grows to a mere $\frac{3}{4}$ inch in length; the largest ever measured, an individual stranded in 1888 on a New Zealand beach, was 57 feet long (about 90 percent of that was arms). Giant squid are relatively unknown creatures (they spend most of their time in deep water), and there is some evidence that they grow much larger. Sperm whales that fed on giant squid may bear sucker scars from the

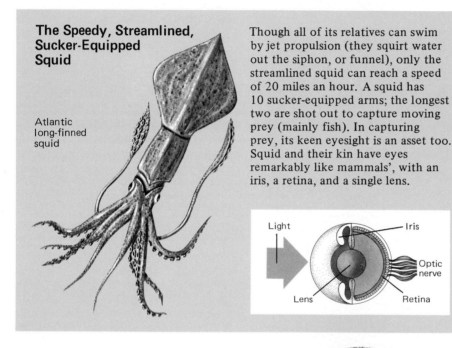

The Speedy, Streamlined, Sucker-Equipped Squid

Atlantic long-finned squid

Though all of its relatives can swim by jet propulsion (they squirt water out the siphon, or funnel), only the streamlined squid can reach a speed of 20 miles an hour. A squid has 10 sucker-equipped arms; the longest two are shot out to capture moving prey (mainly fish). In capturing prey, its keen eyesight is an asset too. Squid and their kin have eyes remarkably like mammals', with an iris, a retina, and a single lens.

Light
Iris
Optic nerve
Lens
Retina

Octopuses have eight suckered arms, joined together at their bases by a web. Protruding from the head are the eyes; on the underside is the parrotlike beak. The baggy body contains the internal organs.

squid on their bodies. A battle with a 50-foot squid leaves scars 4 inches across, and whalers have found scars measuring 18 inches across—suggesting squid far larger in size.

Like squid, octopuses range in size from midgets to giants. One Pacific octopus caught in a fishing net off Alaska had an arm span of 32 feet (its body, however, was less than 18 inches long). The common octopus, found in warm waters worldwide, occasionally reaches an arm span of 10 feet, with a body 9 inches in diameter. An octopus of this size weighs 40 to 50 pounds.

What do squid and octopuses eat?

Although all cephalopods have a hard, strong beak (a big squid can bite through heavy steel wire), their diets are not all the same. An octopus, which lives on rocky bottoms, preys principally on lobsters and crabs. Lurking in a rocky crevice and matching its color to its background, the octopus seizes a crab in its sucker-studded tentacles and dispatches it with a bite of its powerful beak, aided by poison from its salivary glands. The poison is apparently absorbed by the crab's gills, not injected by any fangs on the octopus.

A squid generally preys on schools of fish, though large squid often follow schools of smaller squid and feed on them too. Squid kill by taking a bite out of the back of a fish and severing the spinal cord. Sometimes they sweep through a school of panic-stricken fish, taking only one bite from each victim and leaving the rest.

How do octopuses move about?

Living on the seafloor, an octopus generally crawls on its tentacles. Remarkably, octopuses have been seen crawling out of the water to capture crabs on land; but they cannot survive long out of their element unless kept cool and moist. If necessary, the animal can swim. By flapping the webs between its tentacles, it propels itself slowly through the water; if threatened, it can make a rapid escape by jetting water from its siphon.

How smart is an octopus?

A cold, diabolical intelligence is a quality that writers commonly attribute to the octopus and its tentacled kin. Octopuses, squid, and cuttlefish do indeed have large brains (they are the only mollusks that do), but their intelligence appears to be limited.

Of these big-brained animals, the octopus has been the most intensively studied. Octopuses have learned to negotiate mazes and to respond to such cues as colored lights and objects of different size and shape. On the other hand, they cannot figure out how to extract a crab—their favorite food—from an open-topped glass jar. Octopuses are highly curious, a trait that is usually linked to intelligence. In nature they sometimes build shelters out of loose rocks, which also implies a certain degree of intelligence. Though captured octopuses have an uncanny ability to escape from their containers, this is due not to reasoning but to their ability to make tentacles and body extraordinarily flat (almost as thin as a sheet of paper) and then ooze out through cracks.

Does any octopus have a shell?

The unlikely hero of an 1857 poem by the famed American Oliver Wendell Holmes is a small cephalopod with a face full of tentacles—about 60 in males and up to 94 in females—and a typical mollusk shell. The chambered nautilus (*nautilus* means "sailor") is the only living cephalopod with a complete external shell, since octopuses and their kin generally have only remnants of shells, or none at all.

The nautilus shell is an engineering marvel, divided internally into a series of compartments that the animal builds as it grows. As the nautilus outgrows its quarters, it adds more shell to form a new, larger compartment at the open end. (Using the gas in the compartments, the nautilus can regulate its buoyancy and float or sink to the bottom, where it hunts for crabs and other prey.) The lustrous, pearly shell, striped a rich red-brown, is coiled like an old-fashioned cornucopia.

Ancient Greek and Roman seamen sometimes caught sight of what appeared to be a tiny boat sailing over the surface, trailing long arms. The paper nautilus, or argonaut (named after the legendary sailors that sought the Golden Fleece), is an eight-armed mollusk. Two arms on the female have tips that broaden out and look like miniature sails, and glands on each of these arms secrete half of a papery shell. When the shells are brought together, forming a "boat," they become a brood chamber for the eggs. The shell also serves as shelter for the female; the male, which is much smaller, sometimes lives there too.

The chambered nautilus has far more tentacles than octopuses and squid, and its tentacles have no suckers. Its most unusual feature, however, is its shell. Exquisitely patterned on the outside, the shell is divided into internal chambers.

Armored Crustaceans

What sort of armor does a crustacean have?

As the land teems with insects, so does the water with crustaceans, especially coastal waters and the surface layer of the open ocean. Shrimp, lobsters, and crabs—all delicious items of food—are part of the marine crustacean world. Freshwater lakes and rivers are well supplied with crustaceans, including lobsterlike crayfish, delicate fairy shrimp, water fleas (sometimes used to feed aquarium fish), and cyclops, named after the one-eyed giants of Greek mythology.

Like insects, crustaceans are arthropods—animals with jointed legs and a skeleton on the outside of the body. The crustacean skeleton contains four layers; one is pigmented and all but the innermost are hardened by calcium salts. At some stage of their lives most kinds of crustaceans have segmented bodies (you have to turn a crab over to see its segments) and one pair of limbs on each segment; a crab has 19 segments (though some are fused) and 19 pairs of limbs. The limbs should more properly be called appendages, for not all look like ordinary arms or legs: some are modified as jaws, antennae (crustaceans generally have two pairs), reproductive structures, or other specialized parts.

What is a soft-shelled crab?

The only way an armored crustacean can grow is to burst out of its skin—that is, to molt. Before a crab or other crustacean molts, it absorbs much of the calcium from its shell. The calcium will be used to stiffen the soft, wrinkled new shell lying underneath. Blood flows back into the body from the pincers; this causes them to shrink and enables the crustacean to pull them out of the shell. The animal backs out of its skeleton through a slit across its back. Crabs, shrimp, and lobsters shed their skins in a single piece—a remarkable feat, considering the irregular nature of the crustacean body. The molt is so complete that even the stomach lining is shed.

A soft-shelled crab is a crab that has just shed its skeleton; the new one has not yet formed. No one particular species of crab is called the soft-shelled crab, though in North America the term often refers to the blue crab, an attractive edible creature found along the east coast. Female blue crabs, lobsters, and certain other species mate in the soft-shelled stage.

Fishermen seeking soft-shelled crabs look for hard-shelled ones showing certain telltale signs. Crabs about to molt, called peelers, are kept in floats until a few hours after they have molted and are then sold as the delicacies known as soft-shelled crabs.

How do barnacles catch their food?

Crustaceans are generallly aquatic creatures, and most of them can crawl or swim. Barnacles, however, spend their adult lives firmly fixed in place; only the larvae from which they develop move about. In fact, it was not until larval barnacles were discovered that scientists identified barnacles as crustaceans rather than mollusks, which they outwardly resemble because of the shell.

A barnacle's armor is its shell, made up of individual limy plates that vary in number according to species. When covered by water, a barnacle opens its plates, unrolls and thrusts out its bris-

Acorn Barnacles: An Inside Look

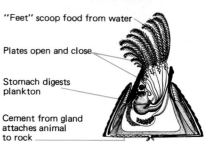

"Feet" scoop food from water

Plates open and close

Stomach digests plankton

Cement from gland attaches animal to rock

tly limbs, and scoops up food particles suspended in the water. People enthralled by rocky coasts sometimes assert that there is no sound more evocative of their beloved shores than the "whispering" of barnacles—the faint clicking sound made as, one by one, they shut their shells with the ebbing of the tide.

Though most people associate barnacles with rocks, the six-plated rock dwellers called acorn barnacles are not the only types (long-stalked goose barnacles are also common)—nor are

---

Midgets and Giants of the Crustacean Clan

The world's biggest crustacean is a crab—specifically, the Japanese spider crab, which can measure 18 inches across its body and an incredible 12 feet from the tip of one leg to another. Lobsters, more commonly measured by weight (some weigh more than 40 pounds), are far larger than most other crustaceans. The others shown here, which usually measure only a fraction of an inch, are too small to be well-known.

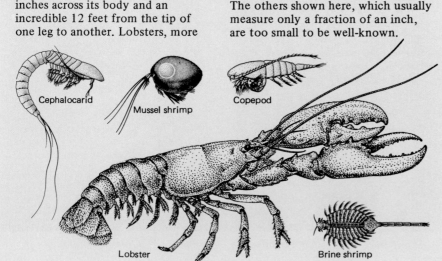

Cephalocarid

Mussel shrimp

Copepod

Lobster

Brine shrimp

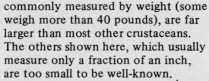

A male fiddler crab waves its enormous claw, warning off rivals and attracting mates. Like certain other crustaceans (most notably shrimp), fiddler crabs can change color, becoming paler or darker in rhythm with the tides.

rocks the only objects to which they cling. Barnacles attached to driftwood may be swept to shore. Some foul ships. And nearly any marine creature, be it whale, jellyfish, sea turtle, shark, crab, or even sea snake, may carry its share.

How fast can crabs move?
Though certain crabs are powerful swimmers (the rearmost legs of the blue crab and its relatives function as paddles), others are champions on land. Pale-colored ghost crabs, which live in burrows above the high-tide line, can run more than five feet a second. The motion is sideways but sometimes circular as well; the crab may turn as it runs, allowing muscles on each side to perform equal work.

Why do lobsters turn red when boiled?
Blending in with the ocean bottom, living lobsters are usually a mottled green and black. When placed in hot water, however, these big-clawed crustaceans turn a brilliant red. Pigments in the lobster undergo a chemical change in the presence of heat, forming a compound that colors the animal red. But unlike color changes in living animals, the chemical reaction that occurs when you boil a lobster cannot be reversed; the lobster stays red.

Which crustaceans live on land?
Temperatures on land are far less constant than in the sea, and terrestrial animals are faced with the danger of drying out. Few crustaceans have adapted to life on land. Those that have are generally active after dark. Pill bugs, for example, feed at night on decaying vegetation and take shelter under bark, in damp leaf litter, and in rotting logs. The name comes from their habit of rolling up into tiny balls, which protects them from enemies as well as conserves moisture.

The most famous land crab is the South Pacific robber (or coconut) crab, a type of hermit crab that takes its name from its habit of walking off with such human possessions as cooking utensils and shoes. Adults weigh up to six pounds, have well-developed pincers and sharp-pointed legs, and are best known for their ability to climb trees. Tree climbing helps them escape predators—and also the heat—and once up in a tree, they find new items of food (mainly soft fruits). Even these crabs, however, have a connection with the sea: females return there to deposit their eggs.

Are horseshoe crabs as dangerous as they seem?
With horseshoe-shaped shield and long, spikelike tail, horseshoe crabs may look rather frightening to beachcombers who come across molted skeletons or spot live individuals mating in shallow water or laying their eggs. The brown creatures can grow to more than 20 inches long, and on the underside are five pairs of vicious-looking pincer-tipped legs. Despite their appearance, horseshoe crabs are not harmful to man (they scavenge for food along the ocean bottom)—nor are they really crabs at all. They are more akin to spiders and scorpions than to their fellow residents of the sea.

Incredible Insects

Which insects eat the strangest foods?
Tobacco merchants are sometimes plagued by small beetles that feed on stored tobacco of all kinds but show a preference for cigars and cigarettes. The bread beetle has equally exotic tastes. Its grubs, which in the past infested the hardtack biscuits of seamen, eat dry wood, hot peppers, and even dried ginger. The same grubs are among the most destructive of bookworms, devouring bindings, paper, and paste. In one case, a single grub gnawed its way straight through 27 volumes on a shelf.

The wine-cork moth lays its eggs on the corks of wine bottles—and when the eggs hatch, the caterpillars eat their way into the corks. One beetle that normally eats wood has formed the habit of gnawing holes in the lead sheathing of telephone cables. Water vapor gets into the holes, condenses, and shorts the wire out—all of which has earned the insect the name short-circuit beetle. Certain beetles have been put to work for science. Muse-

ums use scavenger beetles to clean the last shreds of flesh and sinew from the bones of specimens. The beetles do a far better job than humans could, and they do it without getting paid.

Which insect is the biggest?
Some 300 million years ago, prehistoric dragonflies with a wingspan of 30 inches flitted through forests. Today, the greatest wingspan belongs to the Atlas moth, a "mere" 10 inches across. The longest are tropical stick insects, which grow to 13 inches. The majority of insects, however, are small—less than a quarter inch in length. Possibly the smallest are the fairy flies (actually miniature wasps), which are only a hundredth of an inch long and could pass through the eye of the smallest sewing needle.

How long do insects live?
Most insects live for only a single year or less. An Oriental cockroach has a life expectancy of about 40 days; the common housefly from 19 to 30 days.

Mosquitoes live from 10 days to 2 months. Among insects, industry brings no reward of a secure old age; although a worker ant may live as long as 6 years, it is believed that few live for more than 1.

The adult life of some insects is extremely short. Adult mayflies live less than a day. As the name suggests, a 17-year cicada lives 17 years, but it spends most of that time as a larva underground, sucking juice from tree roots. The adult cicada lives only a few weeks. The longest-lived insect known to science is the queen termite, which may live for decades. One queen ant cared for by a scientist reached the 15-year mark; a queen honeybee may live 8 years.

Are insects the same as bugs?
To scientists a bug is a member of a particular group of insects, called the Hemiptera. This word is Greek for "half-wings," and refers to the appearance of a bug's front wings, which are thick and leathery at the base and thin and transparent at the tip. More to the point for man, bugs have sharp beaks that pierce plants (or sometimes animals) and suck out juices.

Most bugs are land dwellers, but a number, including backswimmers, water striders, and giant water bugs, make their home in the water. In the United States giant water bugs often reach two inches or more in length, and one extra large species in South America measures more than four inches long.

How good is an insect's eyesight?
An insect sees the world very differently from a human, for its eye is built on a different plan. Whether housefly, hornet, butterfly, or beetle, all insects have compound eyes, made up of separate units. (Some species also have simple eyes.) Certain moths and dragonflies have as many as 30,000 units in each eye; ants may have as few as 6. Each unit has its own lens, or facet, so that the insect sees a mosaic image, something like the dots of a greatly magnified newspaper photograph. Because the facets of an insect's eye have a fixed focus and cannot be adjusted for distance, insects see shapes poorly. On the other hand, compound eyes are excellent for detecting motion

Two Different Patterns of Growth

In the animal world, the difference between young and old is often not just a matter of size. Most insects change dramatically with age. A beetle egg hatches into a larva, which molts several times and develops into a pupa. The adult body forms during the pupal stage. When metamorphosis is finished, the adult emerges. The larvae of dragonflies and some other insects do not pass through a pupal stage.

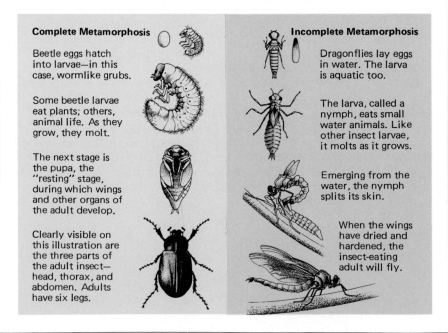

Complete Metamorphosis

Beetle eggs hatch into larvae—in this case, wormlike grubs.

Some beetle larvae eat plants; others, animal life. As they grow, they molt.

The next stage is the pupa, the "resting" stage, during which wings and other organs of the adult develop.

Clearly visible on this illustration are the three parts of the adult insect—head, thorax, and abdomen. Adults have six legs.

Incomplete Metamorphosis

Dragonflies lay eggs in water. The larva is aquatic too.

The larva, called a nymph, eats small water animals. Like other insect larvae, it molts as it grows.

Emerging from the water, the nymph splits its skin.

When the wings have dried and hardened, the insect-eating adult will fly.

The glimmering surface of an insect's eye looks like a mosaic—and that is indeed what it is. An insect's compound eye has as many as 30,000 units, each with light-sensitive cells and a lens.

and thus avoiding predators or tracking down prey.

With eyes that cover most of their heads, flies and dragonflies have almost 360° vision; they can detect predators coming at them from behind, above, and below. Ants, which spend most of their time underground, get along with rudimentary eyes, and some species are blind.

Why do mosquitoes suck blood?

Mosquitoes' reputation for peskiness is only half deserved, for only the females of the blood-sucking species suck blood. The males live on plant juices and nectar. A mosquito does not have biting jaws. Instead, its mouthparts are modified for piercing and sucking. As the mosquito penetrates the victim's skin with its needlelike proboscis, it injects saliva laden with a substance that keeps blood from clotting. It is a reaction to this substance that causes the subsequent itching and swelling of a mosquito bite.

Mosquitoes belong to the fly clan, and numerous other species—including blackflies, horseflies, deerflies, and greenhead flies—share the bloodsucking propensity. In these insects, too, only the adult females suck blood; males live on nectar and pollen. Both male and female African tsetse flies, carriers of deadly sleeping sickness, feed on blood.

Why are there so many insects?

We live in an insects' world. There are more species of insects than of any other animal, and insects outnumber any other group in a count of heads. Insects live from the tropics to the polar regions, in rain forests, deserts, and man-made structures; some even live in salt lakes and petroleum seeps.

A combination of factors accounts for the insects' phenomenal success. Their small size helps them hide from enemies and enables each individual to live on a minimum of food. The short life cycle of most insects, which causes a quick turnover of generations, allows them to respond quickly to changes in the environment—a new insecticide, for example. Perhaps most important is the incredible rate of reproduction. It has been calculated that a single pair of houseflies could produce 191 quintillion (191 followed by 18 zeros) descendants in four months if all survived and reproduced.

What would the world be like without insects?

If man could instantly eliminate all insects, the world would be a vastly different place. In some ways it would be much pleasanter, for there would be no biting flies or mosquitoes. Without the crop-destroying and disease-transmitting insect pests, it would be a healthier place, too.

Without insects as pollinators, however, many plants, including important food and forage crops, could not reproduce. Lacking ants to aerate the soil, land in many parts of the world would become poorer. Without bees, we would have no honey or beeswax; fireflies would no longer brighten summer nights. Many insect-eating songbirds would vanish, as would many reptiles and amphibians. Even such game fish as trout, which at certain times depend heavily on insects, would have a harder time surviving.

Representatives of a Remarkable World

Incredible indeed is the number of insect species: 800,000 and still counting. Here are but a few of the different types.

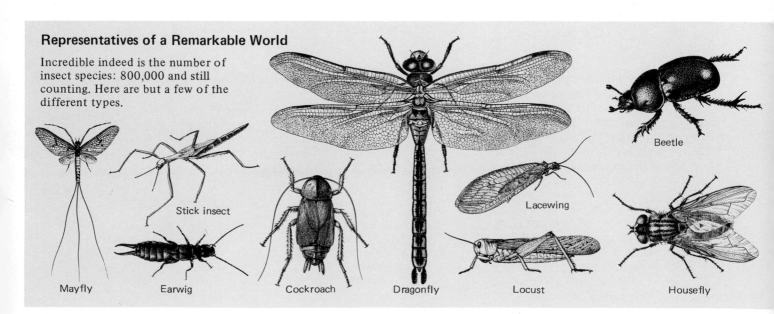

Mayfly · Stick insect · Earwig · Cockroach · Dragonfly · Lacewing · Locust · Beetle · Housefly

Butterflies and Moths

What is the difference between butterflies and moths?

If you pick up a butterfly or a moth by its wings, your fingers may become covered with a fine dust, made of tiny overlapping scales. Butterflies and moths belong to the group of insects called Lepidoptera; the name means "scaly wing," and it is the scales that give them their color and pattern. Where the scales are lacking, the wings are transparent.

Though many people distinguish between butterflies and moths by

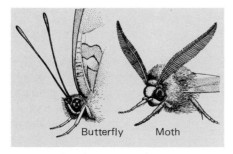

Butterfly   Moth

color (butterflies are often the more brightly colored), other features are better for telling them apart. Butterflies have slim bodies and moths stout ones. Even more significant, though less conspicuous, are the antennae: the antennae on a butterfly are long, slender, and tipped with knobs, while those of moths are hairlike or feathery. Most moths fly at night; butterflies are active during the day.

Not all species follow these "rules." Skippers, for example, are active during the day and have antennae more like butterflies' than like moths', but they have fat bodies and are often somberly colored.

Are butterflies as fragile as they look?

With their eye-catching colors and fragile wings, butterflies may look like easy prey—but they are not as defenseless as they seem. Certain species are unpalatable (the monarch, for example). Butterflies with false head markings (eyespots on their wings, and tails that resemble antennae) encourage predators to bite on portions where the bite will not be lethal. A butterfly can survive a torn wing. Species that show vivid colors in flight may be superbly camouflaged when they alight. The butterflies known as dead-leaf mimics are masters of de-

ception. At rest they display their brownish underwings, whose shapes and patterns look extraordinarily like dead leaves.

Adult butterflies and moths can fly from predators, but caterpillars do not have the option of speeding away. The caterpillars of certain species have bad odors or tastes; the hairs of furry individuals may sting or produce a rash on human skin. Some caterpillars drop from their perches on silken threads when disturbed, then climb back when the danger has passed. Camouflage is important to survival. Many match the leaf or stem color of the plants on which they feed. Bagworms, which are the caterpillars of certain types of moths, travel about in silken cases plastered with pine needles, twigs, or other plant debris.

How do silkworms make silk?

A great many caterpillars are silk producers; they use the threads as ropes on which they can crawl and swing, or make cocoons of them. The most prolific are silkworms (the caterpillars of Asian silkworm moths), whose silk glands may form more than a quarter of their weight. The silk glands open into a spinneret on the caterpillar's lip. When secretions passing through the spinneret come in contact with the air, they harden, forming a two-part

thread with a core and a sheath. Caterpillars feeding on different foods may spin silk of different colors.

Which butterfly is the biggest?

To visitors from temperate lands, butterflies in the tropics may seem incredibly large. The wings of Queen Alexandra's birdwing, a spectacular butterfly from New Guinea, span nearly a foot. Certain moths—Hercules moths of Australia and New Guinea, Atlas moths of Southeast Asia, and Brazilian owlet moths—grow even larger. At the opposite extreme is a British moth with a wingspan of less than a tenth of an inch. Some 20,000 species of moths have wingspans measuring half an inch or less. The smallest of the butterflies are the blues, of temperate lands.

Which places have the most butterflies?

Butterflies and moths occur on every continent except Antarctica. Some species live north of the Arctic Circle; some range up mountains to the snow line (as high as 20,000 feet in the Himalayas). But in number of both species and individuals, butterflies and moths are by far most abundant in the tropics, where food is available the entire year. In tropical South America, for example, there are about 6,000

Monarch butterfly

Caterpillar

Chrysalis

Life's Dramatic Changes

In the insect equivalent of an ugly duckling's turning into a swan, butterflies and moths change dramatically during their lives. The eggs hatch into caterpillars, which eat, grow, and molt several times. The caterpillar, or larva, changes into a pupa, which in moths is covered by a cocoon.
The butterfly pupa is called a chrysalis. From the pupa emerges the winged adult.

In the monarch butterfly the extraordinary transformation from egg to adult may take as little as two weeks. After several molts the striped larva pupates, forming a colorful, dangling, hard-shelled chrysalis.

What do butterflies do in winter?

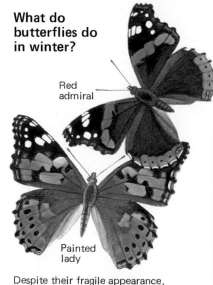

Red admiral

Painted lady

Despite their fragile appearance, butterflies have amazing endurance. Painted ladies that develop in North Africa fly to Europe in spring.

Most butterflies and moths living in temperate regions spend the winter as eggs or pupae. A few species, such as the red admiral, winter as adults, hibernating in tree hollows, rocky crevices, or debris. Most remarkable of all are the ones that migrate. In North America hundreds of millions of monarchs fly southward in late summer; painted ladies undertake seasonal flights in both the Old World and the New. Some moths migrate too, but because they are nocturnal, less is known about them.

named species of butterflies. By comparison, North America has about 700 species, and Europe only 400.

What do butterflies eat?

Adult butterflies and moths sip fluids—mainly flower nectar but also tree sap, juices from overripe fruit, and other liquids. When not in use, the tubular proboscis through which they suck fluids is coiled under the head.

Caterpillars have quite different food requirements from the adults. Newly hatched caterpillars do not have to search for their meals, for their food is near where they hatch; females tend to lay their eggs on food the caterpillars can eat. Though the caterpillars of certain species are scavengers (clothes moth caterpillars, for exam- ple, eat wool, fur, and feathers), and a few prey on other insects, most feed on plants; they may eat stems, leaves, flowers, fruits, or seeds. Many species specialize in certain kinds of plants (monarchs eat mainly milkweeds, and red admirals nettles). Ravenous, round-the-clock feeders, caterpillars are often damaging pests in fields and forests. They do form food for wildlife, however—and when they grow up they are both beautiful and beneficial, especially as pollinators, in the natural world.

How can a moth find its way in the dark?

Butterflies are inactive at night, rest- ing mostly alone but sometimes in groups occupying special "roosts." Most moths, on the other hand, take flight as daylight fades. They rely mainly on odors and sounds, rather than eyesight, to find their way. Their sense of smell, located largely in the antennae, is amazingly acute, and they are able to detect sounds far be- yond the range humans can hear. A moth, using the "ears" located in membranes on its body (butterflies have no comparable hearing organs), can pick up the high-frequency pulses used by insect-hunting bats. If a bat is homing in, a moth will quickly drop to the ground to escape being caught.

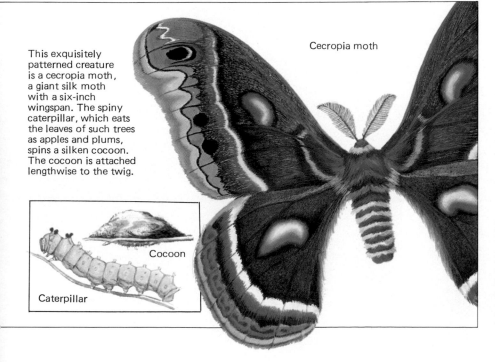

This exquisitely patterned creature is a cecropia moth, a giant silk moth with a six-inch wingspan. The spiny caterpillar, which eats the leaves of such trees as apples and plums, spins a silken cocoon. The cocoon is attached lengthwise to the twig.

Cecropia moth

Cocoon

Caterpillar

Termite Societies

What is a white ant?

If you dig into a rotting log, you may see numerous whitish, soft-bodied insects creeping along channels in the damp wood. Although superficially they look like ants (and are often called white ants), they are termites.

Both termites and ants are social insects, living in colonies whose members are organized into castes. Biologically, however, they are very different insects and—if examined closely—even look somewhat different. A termite's antennae are straight; an ant's are bent. On ants, but not on termites, the two main parts of the body (the thorax and abdomen) are separated by a thin "waist."

Are termites really blind?

A termite colony may contain more than a million insects, and some 95 percent of these belong to the worker caste. Grublike and blind, the wingless workers use the senses of smell, taste, and touch to explore their world. The workers, though seemingly handicapped, are responsible for constructing and maintaining some of the biggest, most elaborate animal homes on earth. They also collect food for themselves and the other castes.

In most species the soldier caste is blind and wingless too. Generally big-headed and with powerful jaws, the soldiers defend the colony against ants and other invaders. Certain species rely on chemical defense: through a projecting snout, the soldiers eject a sticky substance, entangling and killing any intruders. Sometimes the soldiers use their broad, flat heads as plugs, inserting them into holes in the nest and keeping them there until repairs can be made.

Reproductives make up the third caste. Termite colonies usually have a royal couple, a king and a queen. Kings and queens that came from another colony have large eyes, although the eyes are of little use once the nest has been constructed (thereafter, the royal couple never goes outside). Kings and queens that are replacements for the founding couple have smaller eyes.

A Termite Mound Is an Air-conditioned Home

Though the very size of a termite mound may be impressive, the interior is amazing, too. Passages in the walls supply air conditioning: warm air rises, gives off heat, and flows back down.

Compared with the workers, a queen termite is immense.

The termite queen, which occupies a royal chamber deep inside the mound, is the colony's biggest member by far: the king that mates with her, the workers that feed her, and the soldiers that defend her are all much smaller. A record setter among insects, the queen may live for decades.

How are colonies formed?

A swarm of bees has a single queen and numerous workers. In contrast, all the termites in a swarm are capable of reproduction; there are no workers.

After the short swarming flight, a female termite sheds her wings, performs a courtship dance, and produces a chemical that attracts a mate. The two then seek a nest site, the male walking directly behind the female with his antennae in constant touch. When they find a suitable nest site, they mate.

Eggs laid by the female, or queen, hatch into miniature adults, called nymphs. The first nymphs to hatch are fed predigested food by the king and queen. Thereafter all of the royal couple's needs are attended to by the nymphs and the workers that develop from some of them. (The others become soldiers.) The king and queen live in a special chamber near the center of the nest. His only duty is to mate from time to time; hers is to lay eggs (she may lay more than 30,000 in a day). In one African species the queen grows to 2,000 times the size of the workers thronging at her side.

How do termites manage to digest wood?

Though termites feed on wood, many if not all species cannot digest the wood by themselves. Cellulose-digesting protozoans in their digestive systems usually do the work. Without these protozoans, a termite would die.

Termites are not born with these welcome guests. Young ones get them from the predigested food provided by other members of the society. Each time a termite molts, it loses the protozoans. As it shares food with other termites, it is infected anew.

In the tropics many species lack these cellulose-digesting protozoans. Some grow fungi in their nests, eating both the decayed substances produced by the fungi and the fungi themselves. Others feed on grass that is carried into the nest and cured; still others eat decaying matter in the soil.

Despite the wood-eating propensity of certain species, termites are not all bad. In a natural setting they hasten the recycling of wood into compounds useful to other forms of life. In the tropics termites perform the same function as earthworms do in more temperate lands: they churn organic matter into the soil, aerate it, and supply channels through which mineral-laden water can move.

Which termites don't live in wood?

Termites that eat wood do not necessarily stay where they eat. Dry-wood species, which form small colonies (often of only several hundred individuals each), do actually nest in wood, but the damaging pests of temperate climates live mainly in the soil. Workers belonging to these subterranean species travel through tunnels from the soil to sources of food. If their wood supply does not touch the soil directly (a wooden house built atop a foundation, for example), they construct enclosed runways or even free-standing tubes.

Termites in dry savannas build impressive aboveground nests—some dome-shaped, some pyramidal, some with pinnacles or chimneys rising 30 feet above the ground. Most structures are double-walled. The outer wall, as hard as concrete, consists of bits of soil cemented together. The inner wall and channels are lined with carton—a softer compound of chewed-up plant material mixed with saliva and other substances.

In the humid tropics termites build nests in trees. The nests, made of carton, may have shingled outsides, which help them shed rain. Covered runways connect nests to the ground.

The magnetic, or compass, termites of northern Australia construct wedge-shaped nests. The broad, flat sides always face east and west and the thin ends north and south—an orientation believed to help control the temperature inside the nest.

Which animals eat termites?

In the tropics, where termites are commonest, such mammals as anteaters, pangolins, and aardvarks have made termite-eating their specialty. Using the powerful claws on their front feet, these animals tear nests apart and then pick up the crawling insects, dozens at a time, with their sticky tongues. Termites are especially vulnerable when they swarm and leave the nest. Then birds, ants, and other insect eaters move in rapidly to feed on the slow-moving creatures.

Though it looks as if it were made of ashes, this termite mound has been constructed of ash-colored soil.

In tropical rain forests some termite nests are covered with "shingles," which help prevent water from soaking in.

Made of red clay particles cemented together with saliva, termite mounds dot the African savanna. Some "chimneys" reach heights of 30 feet.

Makers of Honey

Does the queen bee rule the hive?

Though the queen is the most important single individual in honeybee society, she in no way rules the hive. She does produce hormones that control various aspects of bee behavior. (Picked up by the workers as they groom her body, these hormones circulate rapidly throughout the hive as the workers exchange food mouth to mouth.) The queen's chief function, however, is to produce eggs.

The queen is the only sexually developed female in the hive (the workers are undeveloped females), but she is little more than an egg-laying machine. She cannot take care of her own young, and she is totally dependent on the workers for food and care. As a crowning indignity, her brain is smaller than those of the workers—the true rulers of the hive. It is they who "decide" when and where to gather nectar, when a queen should be replaced, and when a swarm should set out to found a new colony. By building honeycomb cells of different sizes, they even determine whether the eggs the queen lays will develop into males or females.

How busy are bees?

In spite of their reputation, bees are not all diligent workers. A scientist once kept tabs on a colony in a glass-sided hive. One worker bee, identifiable by the tiny dots of paint with which it was marked, did absolutely nothing for 68 hours and 53 minutes. Most bees, however, are driven by instinct to work at various tasks.

All worker bees are female, and the jobs they do are governed by age. Like butterflies and moths, bees develop from egg to larva to pupa to adult. After a worker emerges from the pupa, it cleans out brood cells and makes them ready for the next batch of eggs. When food-secreting glands develop in its head, the worker starts feeding the colony's young larval bees. When the wax-producing glands in the worker's abdomen mature, it switches to building comb and concentrating nectar into honey. During the third week of adult life, it begins to take short orientation flights, learning the location of the hive in preparation for its work outdoors—the gathering of nectar and pollen.

Without pollinating bees, the flowering world would not be nearly so rich.

In the hive, bees are rather disorganized workers. If one bee adds a bit of wax to a comb, another may bite it off and take it somewhere else. However, the essential tasks eventually get done. When nectar is plentiful, bees work around the clock in the hive. Field bees operate during daylight hours.

How do bees make honey?

The process of honey making begins when a worker bee visits a flower and sips nectar. The bee stores the nectar in a special sac and flies back to the hive. There it regurgitates the nectar and passes the thin, runny fluid to a house bee, which mixes it with glandular secretions in its mouth and evaporates some of the water.

The bee then deposits the nectar in an open cell in the comb. Other house bees fan the open cells continuously with their wings, evaporating water and completing the transformation of the nectar into honey. The process takes about three days. Cells filled

Dances With Deeper Meaning

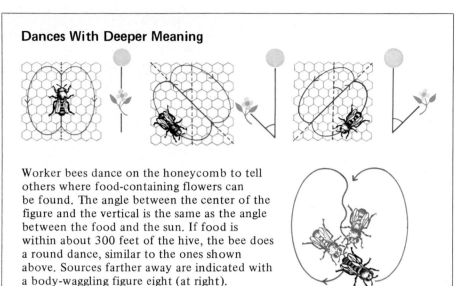

Worker bees dance on the honeycomb to tell others where food-containing flowers can be found. The angle between the center of the figure and the vertical is the same as the angle between the food and the sun. If food is within about 300 feet of the hive, the bee does a round dance, similar to the ones shown above. Sources farther away are indicated with a body-waggling figure eight (at right).

with finished honey are sealed with an airtight cap of wax until the bees need the food. The colony's survival in winter depends on an ample supply of this vital food.

Are drones really lazy?

For untold generations, humans have looked on the drone—the male honeybee—as the embodiment of laziness. A drone's purpose in life is to mate with a queen. Its legs lack baskets for gathering pollen, and its tongue is too short to sip nectar. Indeed, it cannot even feed itself, but must beg food from the worker bees.

Necessary as they are, drones are a drain on the hive's resources. Only a few drones of the hundreds that develop in a thriving colony each year fulfill their reproductive mission. Immediately after doing this, they die.

What do bees eat?

Bees are not predators; only the females can sting, and they sting only in self-defense, not to capture prey. Adult bees feed on nectar, which supplies energy, and on pollen, which is rich in proteins and vitamins. Most young larvae are fed a white jelly produced by the worker bees; after several days, they are switched to a mixture of pollen, nectar, and jelly. Queen larvae, however, are fed a special jelly, called royal jelly, which is richer in vitamins but contains less protein than ordinary larval food.

Where does beeswax come from?

A honeybee produces wax on the underside of its abdomen. The bee scrapes off the wax with its legs, then chews it up to make it soft and easy to mold into the six-sided cells of the comb. The shape of the cells is the most efficient in terms of space. Wax combs contain both cells for storing honey and others where eggs are laid and the larvae develop into adults. Though beekeepers use various methods to keep honey and brood combs separate, in nature the same comb serves both purposes.

Wild honeybees build combs in rock crevices and hollow trees, or in such remote parts of buildings as the space between the walls. In the tropics they may simply hang their combs from the branches of trees and shrubs.

Why do bees swarm?

Buzzing loudly, a great, dark mass of bees, seeming to seethe as the bees crawl over one another, clings to a branch or the side of a building. Although the swarm looks menacing, the dense formation is part of a natural process by which a bee population grows and extends its territory.

Bees may swarm for several reasons, including a shortage of food or an overzealous owner who keeps opening the hive. But often they swarm when the hive is overcrowded and food is plentiful. The workers prepare for swarming by building large numbers of brood cells. As the time for swarming approaches, many of the workers stop going out to the field to forage and instead remain inside the hive, gorging themselves on honey. Then the current queen and about half the workers depart from the hive. They settle temporarily on a convenient branch, with the queen in the middle of the mass of workers. Scout bees go out to search for a suitable home, and a new colony is founded. Workers rear a replacement queen in the old hive.

Bees That Aren't Honeybees

Honeybees live together in enormous numbers (a hive may contain 80,000 bees), and members of a colony are divided into several castes. Each caste has a different function. Bumblebee society is similar, but colonies are much smaller. Less familiar are the solitary species— among them the carpenter bees, leaf-cutting bees, and mining bees. In these species each female makes her own nest and supplies it with food. Cuckoo bees lay eggs in other bees' nests, much as certain cuckoos parasitize the nests of other birds.

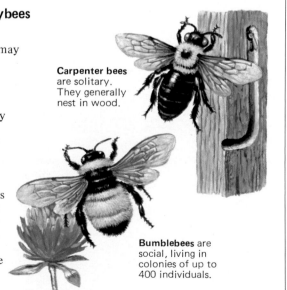

Carpenter bees are solitary. They generally nest in wood.

Bumblebees are social, living in colonies of up to 400 individuals.

Trappers and Hunters

The Web of Death

Not all spiders spin silken webs; nor are spiders the only creatures that manufacture silk. Their web-spinning habit is, however, their most intriguing feature—and one that should be extolled rather than decried. The most elaborate webs, those of the orb weavers, are made in a mere 60 minutes.

The web of a garden spider or other orb weaver traps prey in the sticky spiral at its center; other strands are spun of a drier silk. When an insect flies into the web, the threads vibrate or become taut, telling the spider that a victim is at hand. Some spiders wait at the center of the web; others hide nearby, relying on a special thread to signal when something is in its web.

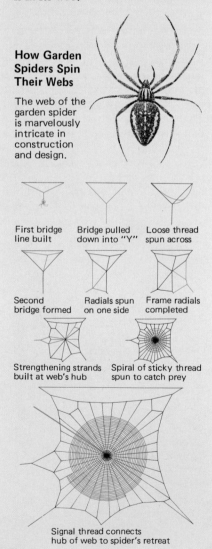

How Garden Spiders Spin Their Webs

The web of the garden spider is marvelously intricate in construction and design.

First bridge line built

Bridge pulled down into "Y"

Loose thread spun across

Second bridge formed

Radials spun on one side

Frame radials completed

Strengthening strands built at web's hub

Spiral of sticky thread spun to catch prey

Signal thread connects hub of web to spider's retreat

How strong is spider silk?

Spider silk is the strongest natural fiber known, and even steel drawn out to the same diameter is not as strong. The giant webs of a South Pacific spider are strong enough to be used as fishing nets. Closely related spiders in the American tropics produce equally sturdy silk—and in unbelievable amounts. A scientist once stripped 6 feet of silk a minute from one of these spiders and stopped after some 450 feet had been extracted. The spider was capable of producing still more.

What are cobwebs?

When people think of spiderwebs, an image of the spirals spun by orb weaver spiders often comes to mind. But these are not the only spider-built snares. Cobwebs, for example, are sheets of silk made of many hundreds of tiny threads strung between heavier guy lines. The spider hides at the edge of the web (or beneath it) and rushes out to grab entangled prey.

Other spiders spin different types of traps. The funnel weavers make irregular webs that narrow at one end and usually pass under a rock or into debris; there the spider waits for a vibration in the silk, which signals a catch. A purseweb spider builds a silken tube that extends from an underground burrow up the trunk of a tree. It camouflages the tube with debris. If an insect lands on the tube, the spider bites through the silk and makes its kill. The prey is pulled through the silk and consumed, the remains are pushed out, and the tube is patched.

The bolas used by human hunters is a cord with heavy balls attached to its ends. Bolas spiders have a comparable weapon: a thread of silk tipped with glue and held in the claws. When a moth or other insect inspects the dangling lure, the spider whirls the weapon. The thread wraps around the victim, which is then hauled in.

Do all spiders spin webs?

All spiders catch living animals, but not all spiders build webs or other types of snares. Spitting spiders, for instance, squirt a sticky secretion onto prey, moving in rapidly to inflict a lethal bite. Other spiders are simply agile hunters. The jumping spiders, which—in contrast to most web-spinning spiders—have excellent vision, may jump several times their own length to make a catch.

Crab spiders are camouflaged hunters that can vary their color according to background. They perch on flowers or leaves with legs spread apart—ready to grasp insects that come close—and inject a potent venom with their bite.

How big an animal will spiders eat?

In the 1700's scientists scoffed when a naturalist painted a picture of a giant tarantula crouched over a dead hummingbird in the tropics. A hundred years passed before another naturalist confirmed that such spiders, which measure as much as 10 inches across the legs, do indeed stalk and kill birds. Their prey includes lizards, small rodents, and other sizable animals.

Like spiders, certain insects have surprisingly large prey. Giant water bugs, which grow to $4\frac{1}{2}$ inches long, eat tadpoles and fish. Swift, bold robber flies are active hunters that kill bumblebees. Praying mantises hunt rather passively, the front of their body erect and their strong front legs folded. They lunge forward to grab grasshoppers, frogs, lizards, and even other mantises.

What is the difference between insects and spiders?

Though frequently grouped together, and in fact closely related, insects and spiders are not the same. Spiders have eight legs and insects six. Insects generally have two pairs of wings and spiders none. Insects have three body segments; on spiders, the head and the thorax—the middle section—are combined. The traits that separate adult insects from spiders are not necessarily found in the young. Larval insects, for example, are wingless and in some species have no legs.

Which insects hunt spiders?

Predator-prey relationships are not always as simple as they seem. Spiders generally prey on insects, but there are some insects that hunt insect-eating spiders. Best known is the tarantula hawk, a gunmetal-blue wasp with long, spiny legs. Only an inch long or less, the tarantula hawk fearlessly attacks spiders twice its own size, battling them for an hour or more. Rarely does the spider emerge victorious; the wasp typically delivers one or more paralyzing stings.

Like most other spider-hunting wasps, the tarantula hawk drags the victim to a burrow and stuffs it inside. It lays an egg on the immobilized spider, seals the opening to the burrow, and sets out in search of another spider. The wasp larva that hatches from the egg has a handy (and still-living) supply of food.

What is a mosquito hawk?

Flying back and forth over lawns and other open areas on summer evenings, rattling their wings as they swoop and turn, are animals called mosquito hawks. They are insects—more precisely, dragonflies—that feed on mosquitoes and similar prey.

A dragonfly holds its legs together in flight, forming a traplike basket in which it makes its catch. The prey, passed immediately to the mouth, is generally eaten while the dragonfly is airborne. Young dragonflies, called nymphs, are predatory too. A nymph, which lives in water and cannot fly, has a long, hinged lower lip. The lip can be thrust out with great speed, and has clawed lobes at the tip, which catch aquatic insects and small fish.

A Tiny Lion in Its Lair

If an ant walks into a funnel-shaped pit in sand or in loose, dry soil, the bottom may erupt as a creature hiding underneath flips its head and showers the sides with sand. The ant slides to the bottom, prevented by the barrage from climbing out of the pit. Waiting at the bottom is a powerfully jawed ant lion, the larva of an insect that in its adult form looks much like a damselfly. Not all species of ant lions build pit traps; some merely rush out from under such hiding places as rocks.

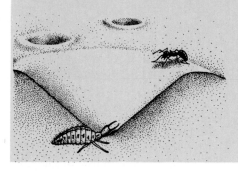
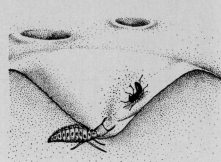

What is a masked bedbug-hunter?

The masked bedbug-hunter, a member of the assassin bug family, does indeed have a penchant for bedbugs, but this creature will eat other insects if bedbugs are in short supply. If you pick up a masked bedbug-hunter, it will inflict a piercing, stinging bite. The larva is covered with a sticky secretion to which dust, lint, and other debris cling, concealing it like a mask.

The tiger beetle larva is another deceptive hunter. It digs burrows in sandy soil and then spends most of its time at the top. The flat head, which lies at a right angle to the body, fits like a lid over the opening; hooks on a humped area on the back anchor it in place. If an ant or other insect crawls near, the larva flips out of its burrow, stretching its body but still holding with its hooks. It grabs its victim with its jaws, then withdraws into the burrow and feeds.

Mighty Hunters Despite Their Size

Although insects and their kin are generally small, this does not mean that their hunting techniques are any less impressive than large animals'.

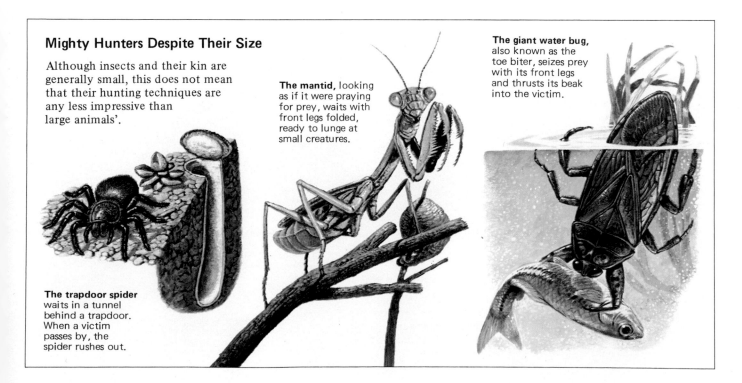

The trapdoor spider waits in a tunnel behind a trapdoor. When a victim passes by, the spider rushes out.

The mantid, looking as if it were praying for prey, waits with front legs folded, ready to lunge at small creatures.

The giant water bug, also known as the toe biter, seizes prey with its front legs and thrusts its beak into the victim.

How Fish Survive

What do fish eat?
Herring strain tiny living creatures from the water that passes over their gills. Suckers draw in bottom ooze with their protruding snouts and sift out organic matter. Paddlefish use the paddlelike snout to detect swarms of the microscopic life on which they feed. Minnows and other fish that include plants in their diets grind up food with special teeth.

Most fish eat other animals, swallowing their food whole or in big chunks. They use their teeth not for chewing but for grabbing, holding, or tearing. Sharks and barracudas in the sea and pikes in lakes and streams are among the creatures whose sharp teeth help them capture prey. The teeth of a parrot fish are fused into a powerful beak, allowing it to crunch hunks of coral to extract the soft coral animals from the limestone skeleton.

Are piranhas really man-eaters?
To people who attribute human qualities to wildlife, these 12-inch South American fish appear vicious and bloodthirsty. Any blood or commotion in the water attracts piranhas in large numbers, sending them into a feeding frenzy. Using their razor-sharp teeth, piranhas can, within minutes, chop up and consume animals the size of pigs. Ordinarily they make their meals of smaller prey. Piranhas might best be regarded not as vicious creatures but as skilled hunters. There are no authenticated records of human deaths caused by these predatory fish.

Why don't fish drown?
When you watch a goldfish gulping water, rhythmically opening and closing its mouth, you are seeing it breathe. Fish take oxygen from water rather than air. Instead of drowning in water, they require it for life.

From the mouth, water passes over the fish's gills, which are fleshy filaments with blood vessels lying close to the surface. In the gills carbon dioxide, which has been carried away from body cells by the blood, is exchanged for oxygen dissolved in the water. Gills function so efficiently that they can take up about 75 percent of the available oxygen.

How much oxygen is in the water influences which fish live there. Because trout need large amounts of oxygen, they inhabit cold water, which holds more oxygen than warm water does. In contrast, carp and catfish thrive where the oxygen content is low—in sluggish streams, for example.

What is roe?
Unusual among fish are species that give birth to live young, including guppies, swordtails, and many sharks and rays. Although some rockfish off the California coast produce as many as 30,000 young at a time, the usual number of live young produced by any species is far less.

In contrast, such egg-laying fish as mackerel, cod, sturgeon, flounder, and carp may lay several million eggs at one time. At spawning time the eggs —often referred to as roe, especially when wrapped in the ovarian membrane as in the living fish—may account for a quarter of the female's total weight. Although most fish provide no parental care, some, such as sea horses and sticklebacks, build nests or guard the young. This is typically the responsibility of the male.

Do fish ever sleep?
Fish have no eyelids and cannot shut their eyes. But they do rest or sleep regularly. Yellow perch and mullet, for example, travel in schools during

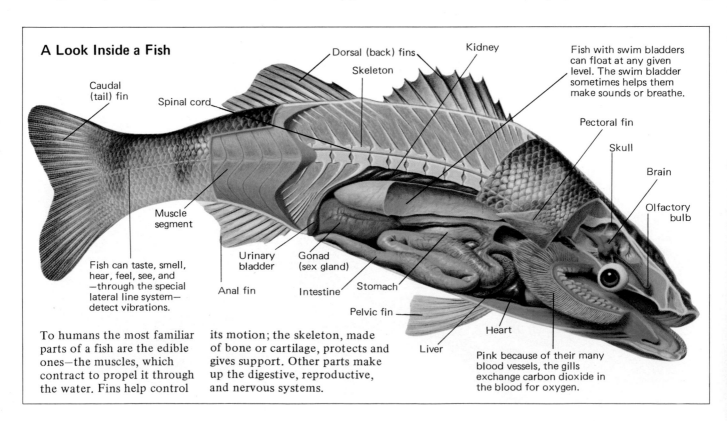

A Look Inside a Fish

Caudal (tail) fin

Spinal cord

Dorsal (back) fins

Skeleton

Kidney

Fish with swim bladders can float at any given level. The swim bladder sometimes helps them make sounds or breathe.

Pectoral fin

Skull

Brain

Olfactory bulb

Muscle segment

Fish can taste, smell, hear, feel, see, and —through the special lateral line system— detect vibrations.

Urinary bladder

Gonad (sex gland)

Anal fin

Intestine

Stomach

Pelvic fin

Heart

Liver

Pink because of their many blood vessels, the gills exchange carbon dioxide in the blood for oxygen.

To humans the most familiar parts of a fish are the edible ones—the muscles, which contract to propel it through the water. Fins help control its motion; the skeleton, made of bone or cartilage, protects and gives support. Other parts make up the digestive, reproductive, and nervous systems.

Different Shapes, Different Styles

When people hear the word *fish*, they tend to think of creatures shaped like the surgeonfish shown at right. But fish vary in shape according to life-style and habitat. Eels and other speedy bottom dwellers have slim, snakelike bodies; pike are among the arrow-shaped fish that wait for prey and then rapidly attack.

Surgeonfish

Eel

Pike

the day; at night the schools break up, and the fish rest individually on the bottom. Some wrasses take naps by diving headfirst into the soft bottom and wriggling out of sight. Other fish lie on their sides, lean against rocks, or crawl into crevices. Parrot fish secrete mucous "blankets" around themselves, spending an hour or more every evening "getting ready for bed."

How do fish swim?

Completely encased in a shell-like covering, a trunkfish swims awkwardly by moving its fins. The graceful rays flap their side fins like wings. Eels wriggle their bodies in flowing S shapes, like snakes. Such typical fish as bass and groupers swim by wagging the body from side to side.

When a fish swims, the driving force comes from the strong W-shaped muscles along each side of the body, which account for as much as three-quarters of the animal's weight. (These muscles are the part of the fish we commonly eat—that is, the flakes or chunks that separate easily from each other when the fish is cooked.) Fish generally use their fins for steering, braking, or holding their position.

How can you tell a fish's age?

In most species of fish, the scales develop within a few weeks after hatching and eventually cover the body in overlapping rows. Atop the scales is a thin, transparent membrane secreting a mucus ("slime") that seals in body fluids and helps protect the fish against disease.

Instead of overlapping like shingles on a roof, the very hard scales of gars —cigar-shaped fishes from North and Central America—fit against one another like bricks in a wall. Sturgeon have similar scales, which form an armor on certain parts of the body.

The scales of sharks and rays are toothlike, with a hard outer coating of enamel over a core of dentine and pulp. Still others—certain catfish, for example—have no scales at all.

The total number of scales on most fish remains the same throughout their life. Scales, however, increase in size as a fish grows, and their growth lines, like rings in the trunk of a tree, tell the history of the fish. From a single scale a scientist can tell how old the fish is, how old it was when it first spawned, when it grew the fastest, and how many times it has migrated.

Which are the biggest and smallest fish?

To fishermen, the biggest fish are always the ones that got away. But the giant among fish would show no interest at all in baits or lures: whale sharks, which may reach lengths of 40 feet and weigh more than 20 tons, feed on plankton, the tiny plants and animals forming the great pastures of the sea. At the opposite extreme are gobies living in lakes in the Philippines. These diminutive creatures are harvested commercially and cooked into fish cakes, though it takes many thousands of them to weigh a pound. Measuring less than half an inch long as adults, they are not only the world's smallest fish but the smallest animals with backbones.

Wagging Its Way Through Water

When a fish swims, waves of muscle contractions pass down the side to the tail. The numbers at right show the sequence of tail movements. When muscles on the left side contract, the tail swings to the left.

Sharks and Rays

Is the great white shark the largest shark?

Although the great white shark has the most fearsome reputation (as the world's biggest flesh-eating fish), it is not the world's biggest shark. The whale shark grows to 40 feet long or more and can weigh 25 tons, and is not only the largest of sharks but the largest of all fish. Like the great whales, whale sharks feed on the smallest marine organisms, straining them from the water flowing over the gills. Basking sharks, with similar habits, are the second largest species.

Which sharks are dangerous?

Some 25 of the 250 species of sharks are classified as dangerous to man. In terms of size, strength, and aggressiveness, the worst is the great white; the largest individual ever caught measured more than 30 feet. Many of the requiem sharks are also dangerous to man. Of these, the tiger shark, known to feed on such diverse items as seabirds and saltwater crocodiles, has the worst reputation for attacking human swimmers.

What happens when a shark loses a tooth?

The most famous feature of sharks is their teeth—specifically, the sharp, cutting teeth of such active hunters as the great white, blue, and mako. Sharks have more than one set of teeth (some have as many as five). As the teeth are worn down, they fall out and are replaced by new ones growing behind. Keeping up with the shark's growth, the new teeth are slightly larger than the ones they replace.

To humans, who have only two sets during a lifetime (the milk teeth and the adult), the rate at which sharks wear out and replace teeth is astounding. In a single decade, a tiger shark can shed as many as 20,000 teeth.

How did devilfish get their name?

Among the features distinguishing sharks from the closely related rays are the rays' enlarged pectoral fins, which look like part of the body and are commonly called wings. Manta rays tend to be big fish. The giant manta has a wingspan of more than 20 feet and a recorded weight of some 3,500 pounds.

What makes sharks different from other fish?

Most of the fish shown at right are easy to recognize as sharks: they have sickle-shaped tails, prominent dorsal fins, pointed snouts, and underslung jaws. Not all sharks have these traits in common, however, and other features are more universally shared. Sharks and their relatives, the skates and the rays, have skeletons of cartilage rather than bone. They have multiple gill slits and many teeth.

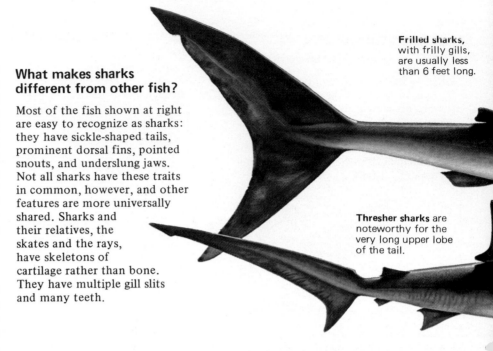

Frilled sharks, with frilly gills, are usually less than 6 feet long.

Thresher sharks are noteworthy for the very long upper lobe of the tail.

The Shark's Kin

Though closely related to sharks, rays are quite different in shape: they have flattened bodies and enlarged side fins (the "wings"). Biggest of the group are the mantas, with wingspans greater than 20 feet. Mantas have special head fins, used to funnel food into the mouth.

Pacific manta

Mantas are famous for making spectacular leaps, followed by resounding cracks as their massive bodies reenter the water. They do not feed on prey as large as their size might seem to warrant; instead, they use a special pair of head fins to sweep small animals into the mouth.

Often looking rather sinister, mantas were believed by seamen to portend doom. "Devil rays," some call them; another name is devilfish. Octopuses, which are not fish but mollusks, are called devilfish too.

What is a mermaid's purse?

Even when it comes to breeding, sharks make good use of their teeth. A male horned shark lashes out at the female with a set of specially developed teeth; male rays give mates prenuptial "love bites." Unlike most other kinds of fish, sharks and rays actually mate.

What happens next depends on the kind of shark. Whale sharks and dogfish are among the sharks that lay eggs. In skates, which are a type of ray, the eggs develop inside a leathery

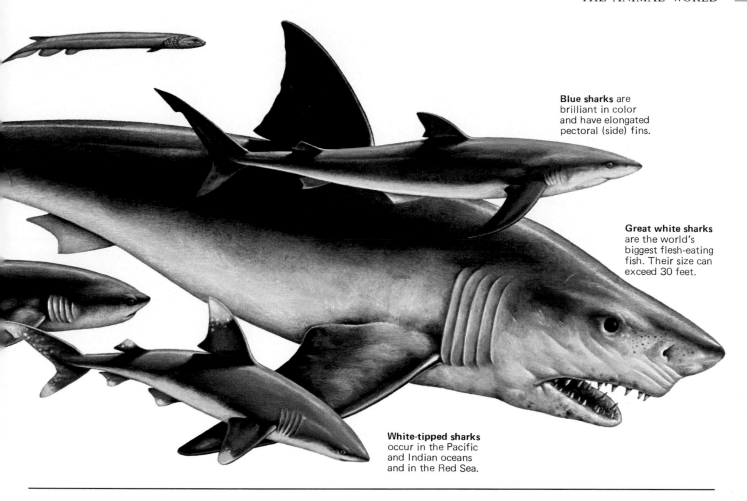

Blue sharks are brilliant in color and have elongated pectoral (side) fins.

Great white sharks are the world's biggest flesh-eating fish. Their size can exceed 30 feet.

White-tipped sharks occur in the Pacific and Indian oceans and in the Red Sea.

"mermaid's purse." Mermaid's purses have anchoring tendrils in the corners, but they often wash ashore—much to the fascination of beachcombers, who may not know precisely what they are.

In contrast to dogfish and skates, most other sharks do not lay the eggs; instead, the female retains them in her body until they hatch. Some sharks give birth directly to live young.

Why does sharkskin feel so rough?
Sharks feel rough to the touch. Unlike trout and other bony fish, which generally have flat, interlocking scales, sharks and the closely related rays have a thick hide studded with small, toothed scales. Each scale does in fact resemble a tooth, with a hard layer of enamel-coated dentine and a central pulp cavity well-supplied with blood vessels and nerves. Like hairs on a dog or cat, the scales point backwards; if you stroke the skin forward from the tail, you feel the full effect of the many pointed teeth. The skin of certain sharks was once sold as sandpaper.

Sharks do not glisten like other fish, and the fabric called sharkskin tends to have a dull finish.

Shark scales do not increase in size through the animal's life, as do the scales of a bony fish. Instead, new scales develop between existing ones to cover the growing shark.

Why do sharks have slits in their sides?
A fish breathes by moving water through its body. Water enters the mouth, passes over the gills, and exits through openings near the head. As water passes over the gills, oxygen is exchanged for carbon dioxide.

In a trout or other bony fish, "used" water exits through a single opening, covered by a bony flap, on each side. A shark has five to seven openings (gill slits), each covered by a flexible skin flap, on each side.

Do sharks ever stop swimming?
Underwater films of sharks show them as restless creatures, moving in and

out of the camera field with a ceaseless glide. Unlike most other fish, sharks do not have a gas-filled swim bladder, which helps control buoyancy. Their lift comes from their side fins and their large, oil-filled liver. If a shark were to stop swimming, it would sink.

Some species do rest on the ocean bottom. Carpet sharks have been observed lying down with tails curled like sleeping cats. Bull and lemon sharks enter underwater caves and rest on ledges or wedged in between overhangs and the sandy floor.

Do all sharks live in the sea?
Sharks tend to be associated with the ocean, especially the warmer seas. Though some species, such as the frilled shark, live in deep water, most occur in shallower areas. Occasionally sharks are sighted far upstream in major rivers. The bull, river, and sharp-nosed sharks are among the species known to penetrate fresh water; the bull shark has been found as far up the Mississippi as Illinois.

199

Strange Fish

Why do sea horses have such strange-looking snouts?

A sea horse neither looks nor acts like a typical fish. Protruding from its head is a tubelike snout, useful for probing into crevices and sucking up food; its body is scaleless and encased in bony rings. A sea horse spends much of its time upright in the water, its horselike head held at right angles to its body, and its slim, finless tail wrapped around a seaweed for support. It stays in a vertical position when it swims. The odd little fish moves through the water with surprising speed and grace, fanning its winglike dorsal fin so rapidly that the fin turns into a blur.

A sea horse's breeding habits are unusual too. The female passes her eggs to the male, who incubates them in his brood pouch until they hatch. When he flexes his body, the young are expelled into the sea.

Which fish breathe air?

Almost by definition, a fish takes in oxygen from the water, using its gills. But from time to time gars, bowfins, and other residents of slow-moving waters gulp air at the surface. Even more remarkable is the lungfish, which has a swim bladder, richly supplied with blood vessels and connected to the mouth, that functions like a lung. Far better adapted for using oxygen in the air than oxygen dissolved in water, lungfish cannot survive if they do not take in oxygen regularly at the surface.

Lungfish live in stagnant pools in

Lungfish possess a swim bladder that functions like a lung. They take in air at the surface, using air instead of water as a source of vital oxygen.

Africa, Australia, and South America. If its pool dries up, a lungfish may burrow into the mud and secrete a protective coating of slime around its body. It breathes through a small air hole. When rains come and the pool fills, the fish wriggles out of its "cocoon."

Are eels fish or snakes?

Though long, slim, and snakelike, eels are indeed fish—but not your usual fish. Their fins, compared with those of most other fish, are different in structure (they have no spines) and number (in most species the dorsal, tail, and anal fins are joined into one long, continuous fin). Many species lack paired side fins. Few have scales.

Morays, which live in crevices or holes in coral and other rocks, are perhaps the most notorious eels: they have numerous sharp teeth and a reputation for being venomous (which is now believed to be undeserved). With a third or more of its body extending out from its shelter, a moray grabs at whatever swims close.

Can fish walk as well as swim?

The paired fins on the sides of a fish are the counterpart of a land animal's limbs, and in some cases they are strong and stubby enough to allow the fish to walk. Frogfish, goosefish, and a number of other bottom dwellers walk underwater on short, stout fins. Mudskippers that live along mangrove shores in the Indian and Pacific oceans stay on shore when the tide goes out. Using their front fins as legs, these bulbous-eyed fish either walk or hop about on the mud like frogs. In the same regions are found climbing perch, or walking fish, which hoist themselves onto mangrove roots. Occasionally they stroll on land.

When food is scarce (or under certain other conditions), the walking catfish stands up on its stubby, leglike fins and walks on land, searching for a more suitable home. Since escaping from aquariums in Florida in 1968, these thick-skinned creatures, which are native to Asia, have prowled their way over most of the southern half of the state.

Which fish swim on their sides?

Ocean sunfish, or molas, are poor swimmers, and these giants (some

weigh more than 600 pounds) are often sighted floating on their sides. But the flatfishes—such bottom dwellers as flounder, halibut, sole, and plaice—have no options in orientation: their body plan is adapted to a sideways life.

A flounder or other flatfish starts life looking like most other fish but soon

A Shifting Eye

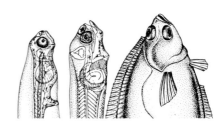

Early in life a flatfish turns to one side, and the surface becoming the underside loses its pigment. One eye migrates, so that both eyes are on top; the mouth may turn upward too.

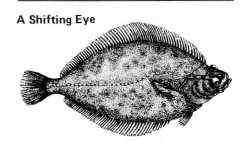

Very young flatfish looks like a normal fish.

On ½-inch larva, eye begins to migrate.

Older fish has both eyes on same side.

begins to lean to one side. Slowly one eye migrates, traveling almost completely across the head so that both eyes are on the same side. The lower, or "blind," side of the fish becomes pale or white. In many species the mouth twists upward too.

How do electric fish generate electricity?

Although human beings have used electricity for only about a century, fish have been using it for millions of years to protect themselves, stun their prey, and find their way through turbid water. They are the only animals, in fact, that can generate and discharge electricity in significant amounts—an ability sure to amaze visitors to aquariums with "performing" electric fish.

Fish generate electricity in modified muscle tissue and are immune to their own shocks, presumably because of the insulating layers of fat. A big electric eel—a South American freshwater fish more closely related to minnows than to true eels—can give off more than 600 volts. Some electric eels are 8 feet long and weigh 100 pounds, and their electric organs account for half their weight. Large torpedo rays (these marine creatures are also known as numbfish) can produce 200 volts; electric catfish (from tropical Africa), 50. Most other electric fish produce far weaker shocks.

Do any fish "go fishing"?

Goosefish in cool Atlantic waters are big creatures (they measure as much as 4 feet long and weigh more than 50 pounds) with mouths so cavernous that they can swallow fish nearly as large as themselves. Their sharp teeth curve backward, like snakes', making

escape impossible once a victim is inside the trap.

A goosefish fishes for its meals, using a fleshy-tipped filament—a rod and a lure—developed from the first dorsal (back) fin. The lure hangs directly in front of the fish's mouth and is waved about. When prey is lured in, the goosefish opens its mouth, letting the sudden rush of water carry the meal inside. More than 200 other marine species fish for their meals. Anglers that live in the dark ocean depths have luminous lures, and also stomachs that can stretch to several times normal size.

Why do puffers blow up like balloons?

Puffers, which live in warm seas throughout the world, are not fast swimmers. When a puffer senses danger, it quickly inflates its body—some species by gulping in air, others by taking in water, still others by doing both. (Once inflated, it may turn

belly-up and float to the surface.) Most would-be attackers are so startled by this sudden and dramatic change in the puffer's size that they

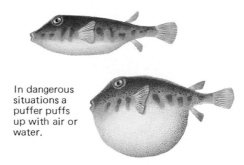

In dangerous situations a puffer puffs up with air or water.

hurry away. As soon as the danger is past, the puffer deflates.

The porcupine fish, a relative of the puffers, can also inflate its body, but it does not float to the surface. When it swells up, the spines on its scales stand out stiffly—and the porcupine fish becomes as unapproachable as the mammal for which it is named.

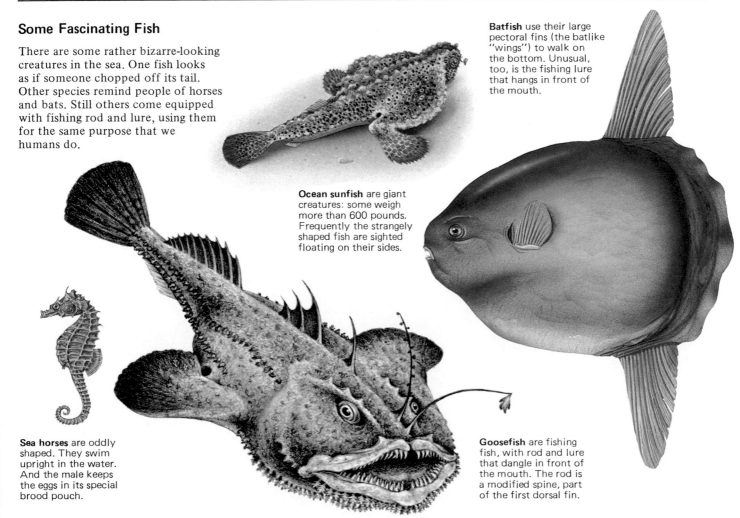

Some Fascinating Fish

There are some rather bizarre-looking creatures in the sea. One fish looks as if someone chopped off its tail. Other species remind people of horses and bats. Still others come equipped with fishing rod and lure, using them for the same purpose that we humans do.

Batfish use their large pectoral fins (the batlike "wings") to walk on the bottom. Unusual, too, is the fishing lure that hangs in front of the mouth.

Ocean sunfish are giant creatures: some weigh more than 600 pounds. Frequently the strangely shaped fish are sighted floating on their sides.

Sea horses are oddly shaped. They swim upright in the water. And the male keeps the eggs in its special brood pouch.

Goosefish are fishing fish, with rod and lure that dangle in front of the mouth. The rod is a modified spine, part of the first dorsal fin.

201

Amphibians

What is an amphibian?
Amphibians are animals that lead a double life. Their name comes from the Greek *amphi,* meaning "both," and *bios,* "life," since most amphibians are at home in two worlds—on land and in water. They typically begin life as aquatic larvae or tadpoles that breathe through gills; they then undergo a remarkable transformation to land-dwelling adults.

Frogs and toads make up the largest, most familiar group of amphibians. Found almost worldwide, they thrive in habitats that range from steaming tropical rain forests to cold northern bogs. A few species even tolerate semidesert conditions.

The second group of amphibians includes the long-tailed, lizardlike salamanders and newts. Native mostly to cooler regions of the Northern Hemisphere, they skulk beneath rocks and rotting logs to keep their thin skin from drying out.

The final group, the tropical caecilians, hardly fit the amphibian mold at all. They are mysterious wormlike creatures, most of which spend their entire life burrowing underground.

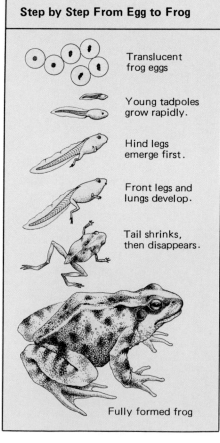

Adult bullfrog

Tadpoles

How does a tadpole become a frog?
A tadpole begins life as a tiny, tailed, fishlike creature. Breathing with gills and rasping on plants with a beaklike mouth, it eventually transforms into an adult by a process known as metamorphosis. The first sign of change is the pair of legs that develops at the rear of the tadpole's plump body. Forelegs soon emerge, and the tadpole becomes more and more froglike in appearance. Lungs eventually take the place of gills, the tail disappears, and the tadpole becomes a miniature copy of the adult.

All these changes take time, the amount depending on species, water temperature, and other factors. Some types of frogs and toads metamorphose within a matter of days or weeks; others take several months. The tadpole of the North American bullfrog, by contrast, may not develop fully until it is more than a year old.

Step by Step From Egg to Frog

Translucent frog eggs

Young tadpoles grow rapidly.

Hind legs emerge first.

Front legs and lungs develop.

Tail shrinks, then disappears.

Fully formed frog

How do frogs and toads find mates?
Every year, when conditions are right, many kinds of frogs and toads leave dry land and head for traditional mating pools. In temperate climates most migrate in spring, at the end of a dormant period. In the tropics the breeding urge is triggered by the onset of the rainy season.

Frogs and toads seem to be guided to mating areas by sight and smell, but they are also attracted by the croaking calls of others of their kind. They produce the calls by vibrating their vocal cords; inflatable air sacs at their throat serve to amplify the sound. The results can be deafening. A chorus of tiny spring peepers, all singing in unison, can fill the night with song.

The call of each species is as individual as bird songs; experienced listeners can identify many frogs and toads by voice alone. The North American carpenter frog, for example, sounds like a carpenter hammering nails, and a bullfrog's *h-h-rrumph* is unmistakable. But whatever their song, all the performers in the springtime choruses have similar aims. The bellowing bullfrogs, piping tree frogs, and trilling toads are all announcing that they are males of a certain species and are ready to mate.

Can salamanders sing?
The voiceless newts and salamanders are essentially silent. But whether they migrate to spawning pools or mate on dry land, they are able to recognize others of their own species just as surely as frogs and toads can. Sight, touch, and smell take the place of voice, and many engage in elaborate courtship displays. Twisting, nuzzling, and tail waving all play a part in the complex "dances" that lead to successful mating.

Where do amphibians lay their eggs?
Most amphibians lay eggs—sometimes by the hundreds—in ponds and slow-moving streams, where water keeps the shell-less eggs from drying out. Some species attach their eggs individually to the leaves of underwater plants. Others lay eggs in long, mucus-covered strands that resemble strings of beads, and still others lay them in large clumps.

But not all amphibians return to

water to spawn. Many salamanders build nests among damp vegetation, beneath rocks, or in crevices in rotting logs. Some tropical tree frogs go a step further, building bubble nests among branches and leaves that overhang water. The female produces a fluid that she beats to a froth with her hind legs, and deposits her eggs in the mass of foam. When the larvae hatch, they fall from the foam nest and land in the water below.

A few other frogs and toads bury their eggs underground. And a very few do not lay eggs at all. They give birth to fully developed young.

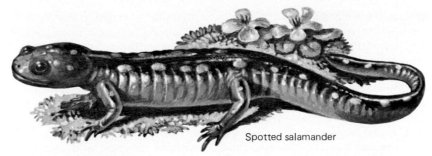
Spotted salamander

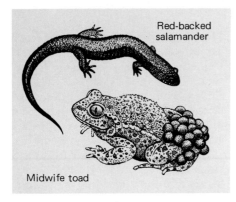
Red-backed salamander

Midwife toad

Do amphibians ever tend their eggs?
Most amphibians simply lay eggs and abandon them to their fate, but some are diligent parents. The females of many salamanders guard their eggs and sometimes the young as well. The North American red-backed salamander will even guard eggs that another female lays in her nest.

Some of the frogs and toads are even more unusual. The European midwife toad gets its name from the habits of the male. After mating, he winds the strands of eggs around his hind legs and carries them there until they are ready to hatch. At just the right moment he returns to water, where the tadpoles emerge and swim away. South America's Surinam toad is even more unusual. In a rolling water ballet, the male maneuvers newly laid eggs onto the female's back. Her skin immediately swells and encases each egg in a protective pocket where the young develop without going through a true tadpole stage. After two months or so, the miniature toadlets begin to emerge, fully formed and able to fend for themselves.

Are all salamanders alike?
Although many salamanders are drab and inconspicuous, others—like the American spotted salamander—are mottled and streaked with patches of brilliant color. Among the showiest of all are some of the European newts; the males, adorned with a crest along the back, resemble little multicolored dragons.

Salamanders also vary greatly in their habits. Most live on land as adults, hiding by day in damp, dark places and coming out at night to feed.

How do amphibians breathe?
Tadpoles breathe with gills, which some aquatic salamanders retain even as adults. But while mature frogs and toads have lungs, they get most of the air they need through their moist skin. Oxygen passes easily through the porous membranes to the blood-filled capillaries beneath. So effective is this method of breathing, in fact, that the adults of more than half the salamander species have no lungs at all.

What do amphibians eat?
The tadpoles of frogs and toads are vegetarians, though larval salamanders feed on tiny aquatic animals. But as adults all amphibians are meat eaters. Most species have long, extensible tongues that dart out with lightning speed to snap up any small creatures moving nearby. Larger prey is grasped with the forelegs. Insects are the mainstay in the diet of most amphibians, but various species prey on everything from earthworms and spiders to fish and crustaceans. American bullfrogs have even been known to dine on small mice.

Can frogs climb trees?
Most frogs live on land and in water, but the widespread tree frogs spend

Others spend their entire life in water, retaining feathery external gills even as adults. And a few blind, colorless species live in the perpetual darkness of caves.

The size range of these elusive amphibians is tremendous. The smallest are pygmies less than two inches long. The largest American species is the aquatic hellbender, which can grow to three feet in length. But the goliath of them all is the rare Japanese giant salamander, a stream dweller that may reach 5 feet and weigh 50 pounds.

most of their time high in the treetops. Sucking disks on the tips of their toes enable them to climb vertical tree trunks, clamber about in the foliage, hang from the undersides of leaves, and perform other acrobatic stunts. Some tropical species do not even leave the trees to breed. They lay their eggs in bubble nests or deposit them in pockets on the female's back. Others, such as the North American spring peepers, throng to ponds and marshes, where they are well known for their amazing choruses; during the mating season, one frog begins to chirp and, within moments, is joined by all the other peepers in the area.

Do toads cause warts?
Despite their own warty appearance, toads do not cause warts. But many amphibians do secrete poisons that are mildly irritating to human skin. Toads often have prominent poison glands behind their eyes, and some salamanders have them on their tail to ward off predators. Most notable are South America's brilliantly colored arrow-poison frogs. For countless generations, local Indians have extracted the frogs' poison. Just a dab of it on an arrowhead is enough to instantly paralyze small birds and monkeys.

Reptiles

Are snakes really slimy?

Despite the common belief that reptiles are slimy, snakes and other reptiles are covered with scales and dry to the touch. Scales are outgrowths of the skin that often cover the animal's entire body. Although in some species they are nearly invisible, in most they form a conspicuous, tilelike coat. Turtles have hardened scales fused into a rigid shell; crocodiles have a more flexible suit of armor.

Scales protect a reptile against predators and help conserve body moisture, but these are not their only functions. Certain lizards have scaly ruffs, crests, or fans that can be raised to scare a foe or court a mate. Geckos can hang from a ceiling, thanks to specialized scales on their feet. Fringed footscales on desert lizards act like snowshoes, allowing the reptiles to run atop loose, shifting sand.

Which reptile is the biggest?

The largest land animals ever known, the dinosaurs, were reptiles, but living species do not even remotely approach these champions in size. Today's record setters are such crocodilians as the Madagascar crocodile and the long-snouted Indian gavial, which can reach an awesome 30 feet in length; though less bulky, such snakes as pythons and anacondas reach comparable lengths. The longest venomous snake, the king cobra of tropical Asia, can reach 17 feet—and has a bad disposition to match. The biggest lizard, capable of overpowering pigs and other large prey, is Indonesia's 12-foot Komodo dragon. The leatherback turtle, which glides through the sea at speeds of nearly 20 miles an hour, can weigh almost a ton.

What does "cold-blooded" mean?

Unlike birds and mammals, reptiles are cold-blooded. A reptile lacks internal mechanisms for controlling its body temperature, which changes along with the temperature of its surroundings. When the air temperature drops to below about 65°F, most reptiles become sluggish and inactive; at 125°F, they die from overheating.

By behaving in certain ways, reptiles can to some extent regulate their body temperature. In the morning they often soak up the sun's energy on a rock. During the heat of the day they may lift themselves high on their legs, allowing the air to cool their bodies. Some seek shelter at this time; others cool themselves by panting.

Being cold-blooded saves energy for the animal concerned. A two-pound rabbit, which uses 80 percent of the energy from its food just to maintain its body temperature, must eat more than an iguana (a type of lizard) weighing 10 times as much.

How do snakes manage without legs?

To anyone watching a snake, it is immediately obvious that the snake's lack of legs allows it to accomplish things it might otherwise not be able to. Snakes can easily slip into holes and cracks, move over rough terrain, and squeeze through heavy brush.

To move fast, snakes writhe in S-shaped curves, but they can also glide forward in a straight line by hitching the scales on the underside up and forward, one section at a time. Many species can climb trees by hooking the scales onto the bark. Once into the branches, the snake can span large gaps, using its body as a bridge.

Representative Reptiles

Although some people equate reptiles and snakes (the word *reptile*, in fact, comes from the Latin for "creep"), snakes are not the only members of the group. Turtles are encased in a bony shell. Lizards include chameleons, horned "toads," and Gila monsters. Crocodiles represent the fourth major type.

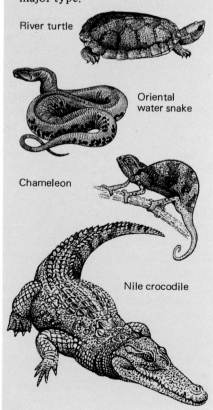

River turtle

Oriental water snake

Chameleon

Nile crocodile

How do snakes shed their skin?

A snake molts periodically, leaving behind a tissuelike impression of its body, scales and all. (A lizard molts too, but its skin tears off in pieces.) Before it molts, the snake's eyes cloud over, and the reptile goes into hiding until they clear. When the snake emerges, it brushes against rough surfaces, causing the old skin to be pulled away.

A rattlesnake adds a new rattle to its tail every time it molts.

Scare tactics used by the Australian bearded lizard include an open mouth and distended throat. This threat posture calls attention to the spiny "beard," which is made up of modified scales. The lizards feed on insects.

Why does a lizard sometimes lose its tail?

For most lizards the tail is a rudder, helping the animal rapidly change direction. Lizards that run on their hind legs use the tail as a counterweight. Chameleons can grasp branches in monkey fashion with their tails. Some desert lizards have tails armored with spikes, used as clubs to ward off predators; others, such as the Gila monster, store fat in the tail.

It is sometimes to a lizard's advantage to lose its tail. When a hawk or other predator grabs the tail (which may be brightly colored or waved about), the tail breaks off, and the lizard scampers to safety. The severed tail continues to wiggle, further diverting attention away from its owner, which grows a replacement within a month or two.

Do snakes lay eggs?

An egg is a package well designed for the early stages of life. On a reptile egg the tough shell protects the embryo from drying out while at the same time allowing oxygen to enter. A thin membrane, richly laced with tiny blood vessels, lines the interior of the shell, acting as a lung and keeping the liquid portion from leaking out. The egg white serves as a shock absorber, as insulation against rapid temperature change, and as a depository for waste products from the embryo. The yellow, or yolk, is the developing reptile's food supply.

Despite all the advantages of the reptilian egg, a number of species bear live young. Sea turtles and many other aquatic reptiles do leave the sea and lay eggs on land; but their eggs and young (and sometimes the adults too)

are vulnerable to land predators. Sea snakes, in contrast, give birth in the ocean, avoiding the hazardous journey onto land. The most northerly lizards and snakes also bear live young.

Which reptiles make the best mothers?

Most reptiles provide little or no parental care beyond laying the eggs in places favorable to the development of the young. The crocodilians—true crocodiles, alligators, caimans, and gavials—are unusual. The female lays her eggs in a hole she has dug or in a mound made of soil and decaying leaves. Instead of walking away after depositing her eggs, she guards them throughout their incubation, turning them periodically to maintain an even temperature and level of moisture. When the young hatch, the mother hears them peeping, helps them dig their way out, and in some species carries them down to the water. Certain species establish nursery areas in the swamps, guarding the young there for several months. Sometimes the males assist in caring for the young.

How can you tell alligators from crocodiles?

Armor-plated and closely related, alligators and crocodiles look and behave very much alike. True crocodiles live in tropical regions around the world. Of the approximately 10 species, most have pointed snouts. Alligators occur only in the southeastern United States and China, and their snouts are

Siamese crocodile

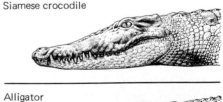

Alligator

broader and rounder. Crocodiles look more ferocious than alligators because their teeth are generally larger and a greater number protrude when the mouth is closed.

Turtles and Tortoises

What's the difference between turtles and tortoises?

Turtles, tortoises, terrapins—reptiles with shells go by a variety of names. Those who distinguish between the three terms generally consider a tortoise any land turtle with elephantlike legs. *Terrapin* is reserved for several freshwater species valued commercially for their edible flesh. *Turtle* refers to the others, and often to the group as a whole.

How do turtles survive without water?

In reality as well as in the human mind, turtles tend to be associated with water. Most species live in fresh water or alternate between fresh water and land; sea turtles leave their warm oceans only to lay eggs on land. A number of turtle species, however, seldom—or never—set foot in water, and several have adapted to desert life. Most desert tortoises stay in the shade (if there is any) during the hottest part of the day or burrow into the sand. Using their beaklike jaws, they can chomp through tough vegetation. Although they will gulp great quantities of water when it is available, they can survive on liquids from cacti and other water-storing plants.

Which turtles don't have shells?

The typical turtle shell is made of bony plates fused to the underlying bones, leaving only the limbs, neck, and tail free. (The single exception is the leatherback, an enormous sea turtle whose shell, made up of small bony plates embedded in the skin, is not fused to the bones.) The shell is covered by a layer of hard scales.

Generally a turtle retracts into the shell by crooking its neck into a vertical curve. Certain tropical freshwater species, called side-necked turtles, withdraw by folding the neck sideways. Some species, such as North America's box turtles, have a hinged lower shell, allowing them to enclose themselves completely in the "box."

Terrestrial turtles have the thickest shells. Over time many aquatic species have reduced their shells and therefore their total body weight. Leatherbacks are a prime example. Snapping turtles have very small lower shells, or plastrons (the upper part is called the carapace). Soft-shelled turtles—freshwater creatures known as flapjack turtles because of their flat, circular shells—lack the hard covering usually found on the shell. A leathery skin covers it instead.

What is tortoiseshell?

Gleaming when polished and with a striking pattern, tortoiseshell has in the past come mainly from the hawksbill turtle, a species native to warm seas in both the Old World and the New. Tortoiseshell is made from the hard scales covering the bony shell. Fortunately for the hawksbill, genuine tortoiseshell has largely been replaced by plastics for hair ornaments and other decorative products.

Which turtle has a built-in lure?

Earthworms, jellyfish, cacti, clams—turtle food varies according to species and also according to habitat. The green turtle, a marine species, feeds mainly on seaweed. Land turtles, such as box turtles and desert tortoises, are primarily vegetarians, but they feed

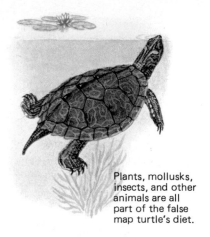

Plants, mollusks, insects, and other animals are all part of the false map turtle's diet.

on earthworms and grubs too. Many freshwater species eat mostly animal life. In the Amazon region the matamata hides in muddy water, wiggling fleshy fringes on its jaws to lure fish within reach. Like most other turtles, the matamata has powerful, sharp-edged jaws. Matamatas and other species have no teeth.

Who eats turtles?

Whether aquatic or not, all turtles lay their eggs on land, generally burying them or covering them with leaves.

Turtle Types

The 200-plus species of turtles differ in size as well as form. The largest is the leatherback, whose shell is nearly seven feet long; the Australian snake-necked turtle is among those only a foot long or less.

Leatherback

Australian snake-necked turtle

Snapping turtle

Green turtle

Leopard tortoise

Spiny soft-shell

South American river turtle

Such animals as raccoons, snakes, foxes, and large birds eat eggs and hatchlings. And despite their shells, adults are not always immune. Some hawks will carry a tortoise high into the air, dropping it onto rocks to smash the shell. Hyenas and alligators can crush a turtle's shell in their powerful jaws. Certain fish eat small aquatic turtles—and so do some larger turtles. Sharks prey on adult turtles in the sea. All species, of course, are vulnerable to man.

Are turtles really slowpokes?

The typical turtle moving about on land does nothing to dispel the notion that turtles plod through life. But not all turtles are slowpokes. Sea turtles have flipperlike legs, which propel them through the water at speeds of nearly 20 miles an hour; as anyone bitten by a snapping turtle has surely discovered, many freshwater turtles can strike with lightning speed at prey or in self-defense. A turtle's generally slow-paced life is a help as well as a hindrance, enabling the armored reptile to sustain itself with a minimal expenditure of energy.

Can turtles hear?

For a long time turtles were believed to be deaf, even though they were known to have ears and to make booming and groaning sounds occasionally. Only recently has it been recognized that these sounds are organized into regular patterns and that turtles are capable of perceiving a wide range of water- and airborne sounds. Most species see well too (even when submerged) and have excellent color vision. Smell is also important in their lives.

Where do turtles go in winter?

Turtles, like other reptiles, are not active in the cold. With the coming of cool weather, land species in temperate regions bury themselves under leaves or in the soil; aquatic ones, in the mud of lakes and ponds. Dormant turtles stop breathing through their lungs. Because their life processes slow down so much, the small amount of oxygen that is absorbed through the skin is sufficient to keep them alive. In tropical areas some turtles become inactive in hot, dry periods.

On the Galápagos Islands both tortoises and cacti reach giant size. The lumbering tortoises may weigh more than 500 pounds; cacti grow to 15 feet.

How big do turtles get?

Although most turtles weigh a few pounds or so, different kinds vary greatly in size, as might be expected in animals that occur in a wide range of habitats. Some of the mud turtles weigh only a few ounces. The largest freshwater species, North America's alligator snapping turtle, can exceed 200 pounds. The largest land turtles, which sometimes weigh more than 500 pounds, are tortoises from Aldabra Island in the Indian Ocean and the Galápagos in the eastern Pacific. Remarkable for more than size alone, giant tortoises have been known to live for more than a century. In size, however, they are surpassed by sea turtles; the leatherback can reach a whopping 1,500 pounds.

Birds: Built for Flight

In what ways are birds built for flight?
The demands of flight have molded nearly every part of a bird. The entire bird has become streamlined for flight. To maximize power and minimize weight, muscles and bones have been modified. To meet high energy requirements, birds have developed extremely efficient lungs and circulatory systems. Diets are high in energy-rich foods; digestive systems are geared to rapid processing. Unique to birds, feathers are important for flight and supply the bird with insulation.

How are the wings constructed?
Birds literally fly with their arms. On the wing are sections corresponding to our own upper and lower arm, wrist, and hand. Unlike the human arm, however, a wing rotates freely only at the shoulder joint.

The muscles of the wing itself are involved mostly in folding the wing or in controlling the movements of individual feathers. They are small, so the bulk to be moved through the air is low. Power for flight comes from huge muscles attached to the breastbone and connected to sinewy tendons that attach to the wing bones. As the breast muscles contract, they pull the tendons, which in turn move the wings in a rope-and-pulley action. One set of breast muscles powers the downstroke; a smaller set, the upstroke.

Skin and feathers cover the wing. Small feathers called coverts streamline the bird and serve as protection, while very large ones, the flight feathers, make up the sail area needed to stay aloft.

What is special about bird bones?
To fly, birds need to be strong yet lightweight. Many species have hollow bones braced and reinforced by tiny cross ribs. Air spaces in the bones link up with the lungs through a network of air sacs—a feature furnishing a reserve air supply as well as a ventilation system for the muscles.

Bird bones are strengthened by being fused. The fusion is especially evident in the spinal column and the rib cage, which tend to be more rigid than in other animals and thus supply solid anchorage for moving the wings and legs. As compensation for this rigidity, birds have extremely flexible necks.

Massive Muscles, Hollow Bones

For flight any animal must be strong yet lightweight. Many bird bones are hollow and reinforced internally with struts. Massive breast muscles power the downward motion of the wing; smaller ones move it up. Feathers, too, are built for flight. At the wings' outer edges are the primaries, which supply propulsion and control. Others furnish lift.

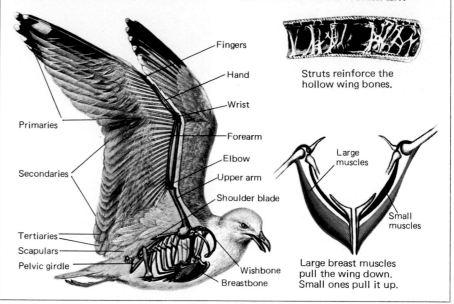

Struts reinforce the hollow wing bones.

Large breast muscles pull the wing down. Small ones pull it up.

How do birds manage without hands?
Since birds use their front limbs as wings, tasks that in many animals are performed by the front limbs must be accomplished by other means. Birds use their hind limbs for walking, running, and jumping. Climbing and swimming also get help from the hind limbs, but these activities may involve other structures too. In South American rain forests, a young hoatzin climbs with special claws on its wings; parrots use their bills. Some water birds use half-open wings as paddles, while land birds that have fallen into water may row to safety with their wings. Birds pick up objects with their bills. Some, such as parrots, hawks, and crows, can also manipulate objects with their feet.

Why do turkeys have light and dark meat?
The meat of poultry is muscle tissue, made up of two different types of fibers. Capable of rapid contraction, white muscle fibers, fueled by the sugar glycogen, are involved in quick movements. Their blood supply is limited, however, and they are relatively inefficient in refueling and removing waste products. Birds with mainly white muscle on the breast are incapable of sustained flight.

In contrast with white fibers, red fibers are narrow, well supplied with blood vessels, and somewhat slower to contract. Chickens and other ground birds that use their legs almost continuously have a preponderance of red fibers in their leg muscles, which appear darker than those of the breast. Such birds as swallows, which use the wings constantly and spend relatively little time on foot, have dark breast muscles and pale thigh muscles. Burning fat instead of glycogen, red fibers power sustained flight.

Which senses are needed for flight?
Birds use their eyes constantly, spotting obstacles with them, locating food, judging distances, and navigating by the stars. Their vision is among the best in the animal kingdom. Another sense important in flight is that of balance and position. A large part of a bird's balance is accomplished anatomically: the weight and location of each body structure are optimum for efficient flight. The fluid-filled inner ear acts as a balancing organ,

Epitomizing the miracle of flight are gulls aloft, which flap their wings more slowly than birds with smaller wings.

working like a gyroscope to judge deviations from the horizontal and to help birds maintain level flight.

Neither as obvious nor as well understood is the constant use of touch in flight. Air currents, always changing in direction and force, move across the plumage. In the skin at the base of each feather are nerve endings sensitive to feather movements caused by air currents. A bird can move each feather independently by contracting muscles near the base. Thus the sense of touch helps birds adjust feather position, allowing them to exploit air currents in the best possible way.

Why don't birds get tired?

Beating its wings several times a second, a tiny warbler may fly nonstop for 10 hours or more. Birds can cover tremendous distances before showing signs of fatigue—a stamina due largely to the remarkable synchronization of all the body systems. The muscles that power the wings also contract and expand the rib cage, filling and emptying the lungs. As a result, the breathing rate keeps pace with the beating of the wings.

In structure and function bird lungs are unique. When a bird breathes, some air passes from the bronchial tubes directly into the lung and on through subdividing passages and the minute tubules where oxygen reaches the blood. Much more of the air intake bypasses the lungs and goes into a series of air sacs, which branch to many areas of the body. This air retains its oxygen, and when the bird exhales it passes back through the breathing tubules of the lungs, allowing the bird to obtain oxygen on both inhalation and exhalation.

Wings Make the Difference

Though all wings are basically the same, a bird's life-style is tied in with its wings. Such ground birds as pheasants and quail have short, rounded wings, which allow nearly vertical takeoffs and quick escapes. Swallows, swifts, and other open-country speedsters dart on narrow swept-back wings. Such large, soaring land birds as condors and eagles have long, broad wings.

Swifts are the most aerial of birds. Their legendary swiftness comes partially from the long, pointed wings.

Short, rounded wings are the rule among pheasants, which fly almost straight up when trying to escape.

Condors are soaring birds. Long, broad, and slotted, their wings allow tight control in turbulent air.

The Importance of Feathers

Why do birds have feathers?
Although feathers make birds beautiful to both humans and prospective mates, their primary "purpose" has nothing to do with attractiveness. Feathers insulate a bird and help it to fly. Insulation is the more important function; a number of birds, such as ostriches and penguins, get along very well without the ability to fly. Strong and lightweight, feathers trap a body-warmed layer of air close to the skin and form such efficient insulation that birds can survive bitter cold if they have enough food.

The Phenomenal Feather

Thanks to their intricate design, ruffled feathers can be almost magically restored. Extending from the central rachis are barbs made of hundreds of barbules, which hook onto the adjacent ones.

— Barb

— Rachis

— Barbule

— Shaft

What is down?
A wing feather is a marvel of construction. From the stiff yet flexible central shaft spring fine filaments called barbs. Each barb has a central shaft fringed by smaller ribs called barbules. The barbules are equipped with tiny hooks that mesh with neighboring barbules and hold the feather together in a flat, smooth web. If the feather becomes disarranged, the bird needs only to draw it through its beak to zip everything back into shape.

The feathers on the wing and tail are called flight feathers. Body, or contour, feathers are much like flight feathers except that often only the barbules near the tip have hooks for interlocking; the others are loose and fluffy. A third type of feather, the filoplume, has a thin, naked shaft with a few scraggly barbs at the tip. Feathers of the fourth type, down, have a short shaft with a tuft of many barbs sprouting from the tip. The barbs are fluffy because they do not interlock. Down acts as extra insulation. Bird nestlings are covered with down feathers, and the adults of many species have a warm undercoat of down.

How do birds keep clean?
When used in reference to humans, the word "preening" is virtually a synonym for vanity. For birds, however, preening is required to keep feathers in good condition. A bird begins this conditioning operation by rubbing its beak over an oil gland at the base of its tail. Using its beak as an applicator, the bird spreads the oil over a patch of feathers, then runs them through its

Preening is vital to the life of this godwit—and to all other birds.

beak, nibbling as it goes. This process straightens rumpled barbs and zips their hooklets back into place besides removing dirt. Doing one area at a time, a bird preens its entire body, paying particular attention to the flight feathers. Pigeons and herons are among the birds lacking oil glands. Instead of using oil, they preen with the fine powder produced by specialized powder-down feathers.

How many feathers do birds have?
Only a relatively few birds have had their feathers actually counted. Not surprisingly, the smaller the bird, the fewer it is likely to have. The diminutive ruby-throated hummingbird was found to have 940 feathers. The number for most songbirds runs between 1,100 and 4,600 feathers. A plucked Plymouth Rock hen yielded 8,325; though much larger, a bald eagle had only 7,180. Water birds, which require good insulation, are the most densely feathered of all: a mallard duck has about 12,000 feathers, and a patient researcher counted more than 25,000 on a swan.

Birds tend to have fewer feathers in summer than in winter, when they need extra insulation against the cold. In one study, white-throated sparrows taken in February averaged more than 2,600 feathers per bird; in October, slightly more than 1,500.

Although the lightness of feathers is proverbial, they make up a surprisingly large proportion of most birds' weight. A 9-pound bald eagle was found to have more than 1¼ pounds of feathers, which together weighed more than twice as much as its bones.

What makes a flamingo pink?
Zoos and aviaries once had a problem with flamingos: although the birds appeared healthy, they were not pink but an unattractive white. The problem was in their diet, and feeding shrimp to the caged birds restored their brilliant color. For the red pigment of flamingo feathers, like the yellow on a canary and almost all the other reds, yellows, and oranges in birds, comes from natural pigments called carotenoids, which are incorporated into a feather as it grows. Blacks and browns come from the pigment melanin, also found in human hair

and skin. The lovely blues, however, are produced not by pigments but by the scattering of light. Green results from a layer of yellow pigment overlying the blue-producing portion.

Which birds have unusual feathers?
In a sense, all bird feathers are unusual, for you can often identify a bird by only a single feather. But some species have strikingly specialized plum-

A Show of Pride

Peacock plumage is among nature's most ornate. This species displays both its wings and its train.

Lyrebird males have extra tail feathers and extraordinary plumes. The outer pair on this species measures nearly two feet long.

age. Feathers involved in display, such as the resplendent plumes of a peacock's train or a lyrebird's tail, are among the most extraordinary. Certain insect eaters have bare bristles around their mouths. Herons are among the birds with patches of special powder-down feathers, which they use in preening.

Is a bald eagle really bald?
Penguins have feathers more or less evenly distributed over their bodies. But although most other species appear to have feathers growing all over,

this is not the case. Feathers tend to grow in patches, called tracts, separated by bare skin. On a plucked chicken, feather tracts can easily be seen: areas that were feathered are covered by small protuberances (the feather follicles), while the featherless areas are smooth.

Even though birds may have featherless areas, the bare skin there is usually protected by feathers growing nearby. Many vultures, however, have naked heads and sometimes naked necks—a trait believed to be connected with the carrion eater's habit of plunging its head inside a carcass as it feeds. America's magnificent bald eagle is also a scavenger, but its head is not really bald: like hairs on a human patriarch, the feathers on the adult's head are a glistening white.

Why do birds molt?
Tough and resilient as they are, feathers fray and wear out with use. Periodically they must be shed, or molted, and replaced by new ones. In most species only a few feathers are shed at any one time, so that the bird always has enough to cover its body and to fly. Notable exceptions are ducks and other waterfowl, which are so heavy-bodied that they would have trouble flying without all their wing feathers. They shed and replace their flight feathers all at once, undergoing the summer molt in a protected place.

Growing new feathers takes energy, and molting must be synchronized with periods when the birds are not involved in such strenuous tasks as breeding or migrating. Usually there is a single annual molt. Birds that migrate long distances molt twice a year, and so do those living in thorny scrub or other habitats that cause extra wear and tear to the feathers.

Do birds look different after they molt?
A herring gull hatches from the egg with a camouflaging coat of gray down spotted with black. As it acquires its flight feathers, it becomes dark brown. In successive molts the gull lightens in color until it assumes the crisp, pale gray and white "uniform" of the breeding adult.

In many species young birds look different from adults. Adults, how-

ever, do not always look the same. Ptarmigan are white in winter to match their snow-covered habitats; by summer they have molted to a mottled brown that blends in with the rocks or vegetation. Males that sport bright-colored breeding plumage shed the

Mandarin duck

Male

Female

Whiskered, crested, and with "sail" feathers along the back, the male mandarin duck looks quite striking at breeding time. In other seasons its plumage is more like the female's.

attention-getting feathers as the mating season draws to a close. The male scarlet tanager, for example, changes his springtime red for a dull green.

Feather color can change without a molt. Sunlight may cause colors to fade; so can the wearing away of the tips. Many a pelican's white neck feathers turn yellow from the preen oil they absorb. For the same reason, gull feathers may turn pink.

Masters of the Air

Can all birds fly?

Not all birds are masters of the air, for over time some have lost the ability to fly. Though no kind of penguin can fly, many other flightless birds belong to groups—the cormorants and the parrots, for example—with species that can. These flightless birds are usually found on islands that at one time had no predators; today, however, dogs, mongooses, and other introduced predators complicate their lives. Such very large birds as ostriches and emus are flightless too. Although they cannot escape by flying away, they run fast and defend themselves with powerful limbs.

How does a hummingbird suspend itself in midair?

Only a few birds, such as kingfishers and sunbirds, can hover in midair, and none has skills to match those of the hummingbirds, which can hover, fly backward, and fly upside down. Since the hummingbird's wing is used for long periods without rest and moves faster than other birds', the breast muscles are huge in proportion to the bird's size. The hand portion of the wing is the longest part, while the arm is quite short. The fusion of the wrist and the elbow joints welds the wing into a strong frame.

A hummingbird beats its wings in a figure eight—that is, down and forward, then up and back. In forward flight, propulsion is generated on the downstroke only; but both the downstroke and the upstroke supply lift. In other birds only the downstroke does this. In hovering, the hummingbird tilts its body and wings toward the vertical, a position in which the wings supply lift but not propulsion.

Why do eagles soar?

Nearly all types of birds will glide occasionally, for short periods at least. Even hummingbirds may interrupt their humming flight to sail from flower to flower on motionless wings. Birds save energy by gliding instead of flapping all the time.

Such heavy birds as swans and bustards glide only when landing, and in general small birds cannot glide effectively for extended periods of time. For some other species, however, gliding is not just an alternative means of flight. Certain hawks, as well as eagles, pelicans, and storks, fly mainly by soaring—that is, gliding upward. Longwinged in proportion to body size, these birds use rising air currents to power their flight. This type of gliding cannot occur when the air is still.

Air rises as local currents along cliffs and mountains and as more widespread movements created by the heating of the air. Known as thermals, heat-caused currents develop when the sun's reflected heat warms air near the ground, making it lighter and

A Pair Share in Midair

Birds of prey are superb fliers. Among the aerial acrobats in the group is the marsh hawk, or hen harrier, which passes food to its mate in flight. Male and female differ in color, but both have white rumps.

The male drops prey to his mate, which rolls over to make the catch.

Female in flight

causing it to rise. Air in a thermal moves upward in a great spiral, the entire air mass forming a large dome. Thermals tend to be absent over large bodies of water and at night. With few exceptions soaring birds avoid sea crossings; nor do they fly after dark.

Birds in a thermal rise in large circles to great heights, progress forward by gliding downward, reach the next thermal, and then rise in circles once again. In this way large distances can be covered in a single day, and over time, migrants can soar across thousands of miles.

Why are seabirds such good fliers?

The rising air currents that power the soaring flight of birds over land are absent over the sea. So although such seabirds as albatrosses, shearwaters, and boobies fly mostly by gliding, they use a technique radically different from gliders on land.

In a technique known as power gliding, seabirds take advantage of winds blowing horizontally across the ocean.

How a Hummingbird Hovers

Though birds generally use their wings to propel themselves forward, a few, such as ospreys and kingfishers, can hover in the air. The most impressive are the small, glittering hummingbirds of the Americas, which pause in front of blossoms to draw in nectar. When a hummingbird hovers, the bird slants its body upward, causing the main flight feathers to beat horizontally. As the sequence above illustrates, the wings move in a figure-eight pattern.

The air currents close to the water surface are slower than the winds higher up. Seabirds typically glide downward until they just skim the surface. They use the momentum from the glide to climb, and then turn abruptly into the wind. The wind supplies lift, causing the birds to rise into increasingly faster winds. Eventually they turn and glide downward once again.

How do birds take off?

For most birds landings and takeoffs are the most difficult part of flying. In takeoff, achieving enough momentum to become airborne is the major problem. Hummingbirds vibrate their wings even faster than usual, then release their grip on the perch. Such songbirds as robins and sparrows launch themselves by jumping into the air and rapidly beating their wings. To build up speed, cranes and other heavy land birds run into the wind with wings outstretched. Loons, which have their legs positioned so far to the rear that they are unable to take off from land, are among the water birds that run over the surface to take off. Some ducks take flight by jumping vertically into the air.

Though they seem true masters of the air, frigate birds and swifts generally cannot become airborne from the ground. They take off only from an elevated perch, by falling and then spreading their wings. Their feet are useless for walking.

How do birds land?

A bird getting ready to land glides on motionless wings, then tilts its body upward while dropping and fanning its tail. To help with braking, the legs come downward and forward; many web-footed birds spread their feet. Additional control is supplied by the alula, a tuft of feathers on the thumb.

Beauty on the Wing

Flying gracefully and continuously, swallows catch insects on the wing and swoop down over the water to take a drink. The species shown here is the barn swallow. Among the most cosmopolitan of birds, barn swallows breed in Europe, North America, Asia, and Africa. They rarely land except to gather mud for the nest. Male barn swallows, which have longer tail streamers than the females (the left-hand bird in the pair is a female), usually carry the mud; the females build the nest. Swallows make some very long migrations: barn swallows fly from Norway to South Africa—7,000 miles.

In pursuit of flying insects, swallows change direction almost constantly.

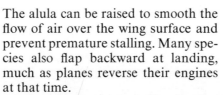

Swallows not only feed in flight: they also drink while on the wing. The mouth opens amazingly wide.

The alula can be raised to smooth the flow of air over the wing surface and prevent premature stalling. Many species also flap backward at landing, much as planes reverse their engines at that time.

When landing, a bird turns its forward motion into a controlled stall to cushion the impact; if the bird does not slow down enough or a gust of wind causes overshooting, injury may result. Birds trying to touch down on an elevated perch aim for a point slightly below the target, then glide upward at the last moment, using gravity to slow their flight.

Touchdown and Takeoff

When landing, a duck flies low over the water and splashes down, braking with its webbed feet and using its wings to "backpedal" and reduce speed. When taking off from water or land, a bird must get air moving over its wings, which is how it achieves lift. Such ducks as pochards patter over the surface, flapping their wings until they gain enough momentum for takeoff.

Finding a Mate

How do birds tell males from females?
In his bright red plumage a male cardinal is easy to tell from the brownish-yellow female. The male mallard has a glossy green head, but the female, like so many other female ducks, is more plainly marked. Orioles, woodpeckers, hummingbirds, buntings, pheasants—in color and pattern, the males of a great many species look quite different from the females to both birds and humans. Birds can be duped if the special markings are changed. For example, the males of certain woodpecker species sport a mustache. If a mustache is painted on the female, her mate will attack her as he would a genuine male.

Where the sexes look alike, behavior may differentiate male from female. A male penguin puts a pebble at the feet of a prospective mate. If he has chanced on an uninterested female, the offering is ignored. A male given the pebble may attack. An interested female, however, will acknowledge the gift by a receptive bow, and the courtship gets underway.

Why does a blue-footed booby have blue feet?
Male birds do most of the courting, drawing the attention of females with songs and displays. The "selling" techniques of each species are unique, for courtship activities serve not only to attract a partner but to prevent birds of different species from mating with one another. Generally only the appropriate species responds.

In courtship birds may display such special features as crests and wattles. A puffin shows off its gaudy bill, ringed with bright red, yellow, and blue. The eye-catching feet of the blue-footed booby are lifted into the air, as if to make certain they are seen. A male European redstart advertises by perching in front of a prospective mate. With head low and neck outstretched, he hisses and displays the yellow interior of his mouth, fanning his red tail feathers at the same time.

Some South American hummingbirds do dramatic aerial dances. Sandhill cranes may leap an amazing 15 feet into the air. Skylarks spiral upward nearly out of sight, then hover, turn, and descend—singing impressively all the while.

Do birds mate for life?
At least 90 percent of all birds remain faithful to their mates at least until the young are reared. If the same pair mate again the following season, their

Many Ways to Woo a Mate

Ruffed grouse attract females with sound—drumming sounds made by birds standing on logs and beating their wings. When a female approaches, the male displays by strutting about and elevating his tail.

Ruffs are shorebirds that use ornate feathers to advantage. The males gather together on dancing grounds (usually open hillsides) and perform in front of rival males, fluffing out their ruffs. Winter males look plain.

Cranes love to dance—by themselves, with their mates, and in groups. They leap from the ground, circle one another with quick steps, stretch, bow, and throw sticks into the air.

courtship is brief, and they nest and start a family more quickly than firsttime mates. Geese, swans, albatrosses, and probably some eagles and owls are among the few birds believed to mate for as long as both partners survive. In contrast, certain species of grouse and other chickenlike birds take several mates during a season.

Are birds affectionate?

Fragile in the beginning, the bond between a mated pair is strengthened by continued courting. In certain birds, the bond eventually becomes very strong. If the mate of a goose is shot, for example, the surviving bird may show an obvious reluctance to leave.

Males of some species bring food to their mates. The male belted kingfisher provides a fish, turning it around so the female can swallow it headfirst. Male hawks sometimes pass food to their mates in midair. Pigeons and doves "bill and coo" (the male inserts his bill into the female's and regurgitates partially digested food). Often the female bends low and begs for food, acting much like a fledgling bird. Females of certain species may have as much as 50 percent of their food delivered to them—gifts all the more valuable because breeding females burn up so much energy in building nests and producing the eggs.

Other gifts are more symbolic. A female waxwing may accept a berry from her mate and then almost immediately pass it back. Male roseate spoonbills bring sticks, while other species present pebbles or grass. Jackdaws, gannets, and cormorants are among the birds that preen their mates. This serves not only to clean feathers that are otherwise hard to reach but also to strengthen the bond between mates—the true interpretation of such "affectionate" acts.

When do migrating birds pair off?

Like other birds, most species that migrate mate in the general area where they nest. But ducks and other birds that nest in the Far North, where the nesting season is brief, may court and even mate long before they reach their nesting grounds. Getting the preliminaries out of the way early gives them more time to rear their young. White-rumped sandpipers winter in

Argentina, 7,000 miles from where they nest. After months of feeding and resting, they molt into breeding plumage and begin breeding activities. By the time many of these shorebirds arrive in the Far North, they are paired off and ready to nest.

What is a territory?

Male birds often stake out territories, which they defend against intruders. In most species the male first establishes a territory and then courts a mate, but some select a territory only after they have paired off. In ducks and other birds that have already mated by the time they reach the breeding area, the female typically chooses the territory. The male defends the territory but leaves after the eggs are laid.

Robins and robin-sized songbirds usually command territories of about an acre, but they require less space in areas where food is especially abundant. Territories of birds nesting in dense colonies may be no larger than the reach of their bills. At the opposite extreme are the eagles that defend territories of 50 square miles or more.

Lacking true territories, male prairie chickens and grouse gather at communal arenas, called leks, where each male performs in a small court. The males, which often use these same "booming grounds" for many years, patter about, strut, bow, and make booming noises by drawing in air to expand their air sacs and then letting it out. The hens walk among the performers and choose mates (often several each), then go off alone to nest and rear their young.

Do birds ever fight for mates?

Actual physical battles are rare in nature. Male birds, for example, often defend breeding territories more by warning than by actually fighting. Threat behavior is an important part of bird life, and aggressive males do not restrict their pugnacity to birds of the same species. Mockingbirds, robins, blue jays, and many others will chase any invader, be it a squirrel, a dog or cat, or a human intruder.

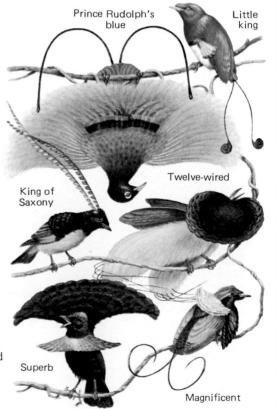

Birds of Paradise Put On a Spectacular Show

Australia and New Guinea have some 40-odd species of birds of paradise, each with more richly decorated males than the other. For instance, the male magnificent bird of paradise (lower right) sports a metallic-green bib, a golden cape, and bare, curling quills. Gripping a sapling in his display court, where he performs in front of the females, he points his bill toward the sky, spreads his cape, and fluffs out his glossy green plumes, all the while frantically dancing up and down the sapling. Some species hang upside down. As the males shown at right dramatically illustrate, fluffy plumes, extravagantly long pennants, crests, capes, and bibs abound among these ornate birds. Many take their names from 19th-century royalty.

Prince Rudolph's blue

Little king

King of Saxony

Twelve-wired

Superb

Magnificent

Building a Nest

What good is a nest?

Birds whose young are well developed when they hatch often do not construct nests. Sandpipers and plovers lay eggs in shallow depressions or scrapes; ostriches, in deeper pits. A fairy tern glues its eggs to a branch. An emperor penguin holds its egg on its feet, enveloped by a fold of skin.

For the species that do build nests, the nests protect eggs and young from excessive heat and cold, and help contain the warmth from the parent during incubation. Sometimes fiercely defended by the adults, nests permit young birds to develop in relative comfort and safety during their period of total dependence.

Who does the building?

Males of many species select a nest site within their territories, but the females usually help in the actual building. In some species, such as robins and red-winged blackbirds, the females both choose the site and build the nest. Cooperative nest building occurs among many birds. Male pigeons and doves collect nesting materials, which the females then arrange. With ravens, both partners gather material, but only the females work on the nest. Among woodpeckers and kingfishers, mates dig out the holes together. Swans and birds of prey also cooperate on their nests.

Which birds can sew?

For nesting materials most birds depend on plants. Wooded areas furnish the widest variety, ranging from hefty sticks to fine twigs, rootlets, and strips of bark. Hummingbirds use lichens. The tailorbird, an Asiatic warbler, selects large leaves still on the branch, stitches the edges together, and nests inside. Such meadow nesters as song sparrows and bobolinks use grasses and weeds. Not surprisingly, aquatic species—most diving ducks, coots, and grebes—collect water plants.

Birds make ingenious use of many other materials, some natural and others man-made. Wool, feathers, and spiderweb are in common use. Mud forms the nest of swallows and flamingos. Chimney swifts cement their nests in place with saliva. Rags, paper, and plastics end up in many a nest.

Who lives in apartment houses?

For centuries birds have used nesting sites provided by man. In Europe storks have traditionally nested on chimney tops; swifts prefer chimneys to natural crevices. Pigeons long ago deserted cliffs for the ledges of buildings. Owls nest in barns and belfries; swallows and phoebes, under bridges and on interior beams. House sparrows, of course, take their name from where they nest.

Birdhouses provide accommodations for such hole nesters as bluebirds, nuthatches, and even certain ducks (the wood duck often uses man-made boxes). House wrens, which will nest in any hollow object—a rusty tin can, an unused flowerpot, an old shoe hanging in a shed—obviously appreciate human donations. In Indian villages of the past, purple martins nested in hollow gourds hung on saplings. Today martins, among the most effective of insect eaters, are cherished inhabitants of localities across North America, living in special bird-sized apartment houses set on tall poles.

Nests of Sticks, Nests of Stones

Great blue herons construct stick nests in trees. Dozens of birds, including other kinds of herons, may use the same tree. Nests are often lined with grass or moss.

Goldcrests, a type of kinglet, suspend their finely woven nests from a branch.

Baya weavers build flask-shaped nests entered through a woven tunnel.

Ringed plovers use a scrape on the ground, lined with shells or stones.

Tailorbirds stitch leaves together, making a container to hold the nest.

Emperor penguins make no nests. The male holds the one egg on his feet.

Do all birds incubate their eggs?

In Australia and on nearby islands, pheasantlike birds called megapodes (the name means "large-footed") bury their eggs in a mound. When the chicks hatch, they dig their way out and then fend for themselves—the only birds in the world to have no contact with their parents.

Megapode mounds, which are piles of earth and leaves, can be enormous. One built by scrub fowl—scrub fowl, mallee fowl, and brush turkeys are the three types of megapodes—was 15 feet wide, 10 feet high, and 60 feet long. Heat produced by the combination of sun and fermenting vegetation spurs the development of the eggs. During the long incubation period (up to eight months), the parents monitor temperatures in the mound by digging down to the eggs and probing with their bills. The male mallee fowl has the most difficult monitoring job. By constantly scraping sand away to allow the eggs to cool or piling it back to raise the temperature, he keeps the eggs at just about 92°F.

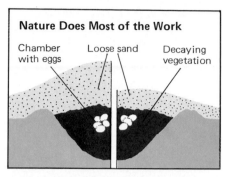

Nature Does Most of the Work

Chamber with eggs — Loose sand — Decaying vegetation

Decaying vegetation as well as the sun warm the mallee fowl's eggs. The male adds or removes the insulating sand as needed.

A huge mound of sand and vegetation, the mallee fowl's nest is built by the male (right). The female is about to lay an egg.

How does a robin build its nest?

Of all the varied forms of nests, the commonest is probably the cup, favored by robins, finches, and most other small land birds. Cup nests are constructed by compacting the materials, not by weaving them together.

A female robin does the building herself, though the male helps out by bringing her materials. She begins by crouching and spinning around on a suitable site—a horizontal limb, the fork of a tree, or a convenient ledge. Sometimes she tries out a number of spots. Using both her beak and her feet, she makes a framework of sizable twigs and weed stalks. Standing in the middle, she draws finer materials around her to form the sides. Then, pressing with breast and wings as she turns around in place, she molds the mass into a compact cup. Next she makes a lining of mud and grass, shapes it into a cup, and finally adds a soft, dry inner lining. Building the nest takes from 6 to 20 days.

Why do birds live in colonies?

More than 95 percent of all seabirds—from penguins to petrels, gannets to guillemots—and almost 15 percent of other species are colonial nesters. Colonies bring potential mates in contact with one another. Stimulated by the calls and actions of their neighbors, birds form pairs, mate, and nest within a few days of one another—which means that all the chicks hatch within the same period and so predators, who cannot eat *all* of them, take a smaller toll. A colony also furnishes quick replacements for lost mates and information about available food. Colonial nesting allows for cooperative defense: to rout an intruder, enormous numbers of birds in a tern or gull colony will rise up from the ground.

How do birds hide their nests?

Keeping the young safe from predators, be they other birds, snakes, or mammals, is vital to any species. Among birds, the choice of a nest site is all-important. Many depend on concealment—camouflaging the nest with leaves, for example, or building it inside a burrow. Inaccessibility is an advantage, too. The top of a tall tree, a seaside cliff, and a small, isolated island may offer safety from ground-dwelling predators. Tropical orioles called oropendolas suspend elongated, baglike nests from the tips of slender branches, foiling snakes and other tree-climbing predators.

Raising the Young

How many eggs are laid at a time?

Domestic hens, bred for productivity and fed a special diet, have been known to lay more than 350 eggs a year. In nature, no bird approaches this record. Clutch size ranges from a single egg, as in the albatross, to the 20 eggs of the Old World partridge. In general, small birds lay larger clutches than large birds, but this is far from universally true. The tiny hummingbird, for example, lays only 2 eggs, while the huge ostrich produces 10 to 12.

Most birds, even those with large clutches, lay only one egg every 24 hours and do not start to incubate until the clutch is complete. This ensures that all the eggs will hatch at the same time. Among birds where both parents share the task of incubation, however, egg warming begins as soon as the first one is laid, and the young hatch out at intervals.

Where does the shell come from?

The shell is the finishing touch on an egg, which begins as a ripe yolk moving out of a female's ovary into her oviduct, where fertilization occurs. A short distance down the oviduct, special glands secrete a thick coating of albumen, or egg white, around the yolk. The albumen, which is 90 percent water, supplies water to the growing embryo and for the first few days cushions it against shock. Further cushioning is supplied by two twisted cords called chalazae, which connect the yolk to both ends of the egg.

When the albumen-coated egg is about halfway down the oviduct, other glands secrete a thin, semiporous membrane—the skin that sticks to a hard-boiled egg when you try to peel it. Near the end of its journey, the egg acquires its shell, composed of calcium carbonate crystals. For most birds, producing an egg takes about 24 hours, and forming the shell takes from 18 to 21 hours of that time. Because the shell's crystals support each other like stones in an arch, the completed egg can stand a great deal of steady pressure—yet at hatching time it gives way relatively easily to the probing of the chick.

Why do birds have to sit on their eggs?

Left to itself, a bird egg would not hatch, for the embryo cannot develop when its temperature is less than about 80°F. Parent birds usually keep the eggs warm with their body heat. For this purpose the insulation afforded by feathers is a hindrance (they block the transfer of body heat), and most species molt some belly feathers at incubation time. Generally only the females develop a bare brood patch. A dense network of blood vessels brings additional heat to the skin.

During incubation, birds turn the eggs several times a day, either with their bills or by the squirming of their bodies as they settle into position. This turning keeps the eggs evenly heated and, more important, prevents the embryo from sinking to one side. After the eggs hatch, parents continue to brood until the chicks can maintain a steady body temperature—an ability that may take days or weeks, depending on the species.

How does a baby bird get out of the egg?

At hatching time a bird fills the eggshell almost completely. In its rapid growth it has used up all the egg white and nearly all the yolk. The chick must break out of the egg or perish.

In preparation for hatching, the chick has been active for several days, rocking and rolling about inside the shell. A day or two before hatching, the chick thrusts its beak into the air space at the wide end of its egg and begins to take slow breaths. It also

A Labor of Love

Plovers perform a famous distraction display. When danger threatens, the parent pretends to be injured (often by feigning a broken wing) and diverts attention from the eggs or chicks.

Grebes carry their chicks on their backs, and sometimes even dive with the chicks on board. Young grebes are fed by their parents until they can fly. In certain species this may take several months.

Phalaropes are not like other birds. The females are the more brightly colored individuals (the bird shown standing is a female), and it is they who court their mates. Males incubate the eggs and feed the young.

begins to cheep. In such birds as quail and pheasant, which have large clutches, this cheeping synchronizes hatching: all the eggs hatch within a few hours of each other.

Regardless of species, the chick has a protuberance called an egg tooth on the end of its bill and a powerful "hatching muscle" on the back of its neck. Using these, it pecks a hole in the end of the egg and breathes the outside air. After resting, the chick slowly revolves in the shell, chipping a circular groove all the way around. This may take from a few hours (in grebes) to several days (curlews). After a long rest, the chick gives a powerful heave with its neck, the end of the shell falls off, and the bedraggled bird emerges.

Are all birds born with feathers?
A newly hatched duckling, a ball of yellow fluff, is born with its eyes open and is able to feed itself and run about within a few hours. In contrast, a baby robin is born naked, blind, and totally unable to fend for itself. All it can do is beg. Until it has developed feathers and muscles, it is totally dependent on its parents for food.

Such birds as ducks, whose young are born nearly self-sufficient, are called precocial, from the Latin for "early ripening." Those like the robin are termed altricial, from the Latin for "one who nourishes." Between the two extremes are many birds born with varying degrees of self-sufficiency or helplessness. Gulls, for example, have a warm coat of down when they hatch but depend on their parents for protection and food.

What is the cuckoo's secret of success?
The European cuckoo is notorious for the habit of depositing its eggs in the nests of other birds, leaving the involuntary hosts with the work of incubating the eggs and feeding the young. The cuckoo parasitizes some 300 species. Remarkably, it even lays eggs that resemble those of its host—the better to make sure its eggs are treated like those of the foster parent.

Not all cuckoos are parasites: more than half the species (including those in North America) raise their own young. Nor is the parasitic habit limited to certain cuckoos. Nearly 80 others, including some ducks, cowbirds, and honey guides, lay eggs in nests of other species. Newly hatched honey guides, which occur in Asia and Africa, are born with sharp hooks on their bills, used to nip the host's young to death. Some of the cuckoos eliminate competition by removing the host bird's eggs and young from the nest. The young of many parasitic species, however, are raised peaceably with their foster siblings.

A huge young cuckoo begs for food.

Newly hatched, a cuckoo ejects its host's eggs.

European cuckoos lay eggs in other birds' nests. They may remove the eggs of their hosts.

What keeps parent birds on the job?
A pair of barn swallows was once clocked feeding insects to its young at the phenomenal rate of once a minute. Although a few birds, such as albatrosses, bring food only once every few days, many others do it several times a day or more. In both incubation and feeding the young, it is instinct that drives the hardworking parents—instinct so powerful that a mated pair sometimes compete for the privilege of incubating, actually pushing each other off the nest.

In contrast with the urge to incubate, which is triggered by the presence of egglike objects in the nest, the feeding instinct is stimulated partly by the cries of the young and partly by the brightly colored insides of their open mouths. Occasionally the instinct is so strong that birds will feed the young of other species. A naturalist once observed a pair of flycatchers that lost their nest in a storm. The next day they were force-feeding young blackbirds in a nearby nest and actually driving the natural parents away. The record for feeding strange babies, however, must surely belong to the bird—a cardinal—that was seen feeding goldfish in a garden pool.

How Birds Find Food

What does "eat like a bird" really mean?
A bird is literally hot-blooded, with a body temperature of from 105° to 111°F. Maintaining this high temperature requires constant stoking with fuel. Small and medium-sized birds expose a greater surface area in proportion to their size than large birds, and so they lose body heat more rapidly. During their waking hours, many small birds eat almost all the time.

Before long migration flights, birds eat huge quantities of food. Some increase their body weight by 50 percent or more, storing their fuel as fat. Females also eat a great deal before laying eggs. Many birds start the day with a big meal and then eat heavily again in the evening to keep themselves supplied with energy throughout the night. A bird's body temperature may drop at night, indicating a slowed metabolic rate. The temperature of some Andean hummingbirds falls more than 40 degrees; only the decreased burning of fuel allows these diminutive creatures to survive the hours when they cannot feed. In winter the temperature of the poorwill—a relative of the whippoorwill that lives in the western United States—drops to below 40°F. The birds become dormant, or hibernate, more because of lack of food than because of the cold.

How do birds manage without teeth?
Because birds are toothless, they cannot chew their food. Instead, they swallow food whole or use sharp-edged bills to tear it or cut it into pieces. Food passes through the mouth into the throat and then the stomach. The first part of the stomach has digestive glands. In the gizzard, which is the second part, the food, already somewhat softened by digestive juices, is ground or mashed by the powerful muscular action of the hard, ridged walls. Many seed eaters regularly swallow grit and small stones, which make the gizzard an even better grinding machine. Birds digest food more quickly and more thoroughly than most other types of animals.

What is the crop?
Midway in the throat of many birds is a pouch—called a crop, or craw—where quickly swallowed food is temporarily stored. Thanks to the crop, a bird can eat much more than its stomach will hold. Though food held in the crop may be softened by saliva, the crop has no digestive glands, and food is not digested there. Many birds, in fact, carry food long distances in their crops and then regurgitate it to feed their young. When food is bountiful, some fill their crops so full they cannot fly. Others stuff first the crop and then the full length of the throat. The excess—a fish tail, for example—hangs out the mouth.

When do storks eat mice?
Though in the tropics birds may eat the same kinds of food year round, diets in temperate regions commonly change with the seasons. Blackbirds mainly eat seeds most of the year, but in midsummer they take advantage of the abundance of insects and may eat nothing else. White storks, which ordi-

Marsh hawks hunt birds and other small animals.

Frigate birds steal other birds' catches.

Gannets dive from great heights.

Spotted sandpiper

Masked booby

Lesser black-backed gull

Osprey

Eurasian spoonbill

Royal terns

Whooper swans

Sanderlings

American avocets

Oystercatcher

Northern phalarope

Mallard

Skimmers skim the surface for food.

Shags dive for fish, as do other cormorants.

Black guillemot

Birds of Sea and Shore
Though all the birds in this assemblage would never occur together in one place, a great variety of birds can coexist at the sea or shore. Each has a different niche: that is, different species feed on different food and in different locations. For example, the ternlike skimmers take small fish and other creatures from near the surface, while loons, which have heavy bones, dive deep.

Loons are deep divers.

What Bills Tell You About the Birds

Nightjars, related to whippoorwills, gulp nocturnal insects on the wing.

Godwits pick up small aquatic prey with the long, up-curved bill.

Whimbrels are shorebirds with down-curving bills.

Crossbills use their bills to pry open cones.

Orioles snatch caterpillars and other insects in trees.

Grosbeaks are stout-billed seed eaters.

Woodpeckers have straight bills and long tongues. This species, the green, eats mainly ants.

narily eat frogs and fish, may shift to mice during drought.

In experiments, young birds given a particular food and then offered a variety showed a preference for what had been offered first. This suggests that parent birds, which bring food to their young, have a strong influence on the offspring's diet. What birds eat often changes as they mature. Young birds that eat only worms, insects, fish, or other small animals may be strictly vegetarian as adults.

Why aren't all bills the same?

Bills like the robin's are quite versatile, helping the animal do everything from pulling worms out of the ground to pecking fruit and plucking insects from leaves. In contrast, birds with less varied diets have bills shaped to help

procure their specific food. A finch's wedge-shaped bill, for example, is designed to crack seeds. Using its tongue, the bird fits the seed into a groove in the upper part of the bill and then presses the sharp-edged lower part against it. The seed may be moved several times to cut through the husk in different places. Eventually the soft kernel inside is released.

With its stout, powerful bill, a parrot can crack nuts and—using the sharp, down-curved tip—deftly pick out the meaty center. Parrots hold food in their feet. A toucan uses its big, seemingly unwieldy bill to snip off fruit and then slice it into bite-sized chunks. (Brightly colored, the bill is also said to intimidate predators.) Nighthawks, swifts, and other species that catch insects in flight have short

bills and wide mouths, which become gaping traps. Nuthatches have slim, tweezerlike bills that probe into crevices and under bark. Woodpeckers in search of wood-boring insect larvae chisel with stout bills.

An oystercatcher's blunt bill pries open mollusk shells. A woodcock's long one is hinged at the tip, enabling the bird to grab a worm while its bill is deep in mud. Male and female huias, New Zealand birds that are now extinct, had differently shaped bills. The male's, used for digging into wood, was straight and stout; the female's, a slim, down-curved probe.

Which birds steal their food?

All birds compete to get their fair share, but some have made thievery a way of life. Seabirds called skuas—or jaegers, which means "hunters" in German—pirate most of their food. When a tern or gannet is sighted carrying a fish, one or more skuas give chase until it relinquishes its catch. Sometimes the victim will even regurgitate food stuffed in its crop. In tropical seas frigate birds steal from such fish eaters as pelicans and cormorants. Bald eagles regularly swoop onto fish-carrying ospreys to force them to drop their load. Although pilfering is less common among land birds, European blackbirds may relieve thrushes of as much as a tenth of their earthworm catch.

Which birds help one another?

Most birds are fiercely independent and have no concern for others except their mates and young. Among the few that cooperate in getting food, white pelicans form a crescent-shaped line on a lake. Each bird flails the water with its wings as the line moves toward the shore. Fish driven ahead of the birds become a milling mass as the line tightens and the water becomes shallower. The pelicans then sweep their pouched bills back and forth through the water, making their catch. Cormorants also fish together at times.

Many land birds feed in flocks, some of which are made up of several species. But there is no real cooperation within a flock. Birds at the rear fly over the group to reach a forward position, where they have first choice of the available food.

The Biggest Birds

Which are the world's biggest birds?
Weight is a hindrance to flight, and so the largest birds are flightless. The champions are the African ostrich, the South American rhea, the Australian emu, and the cassowary of Australia and New Guinea. Except for the cassowaries, which are jungle dwellers, all live in grasslands or semideserts.

Ostriches are the record setters. With a height of up to 8 feet and a weight of as much as 300 pounds, the male ostrich—females are smaller—is taller than a human and outweighs most of us. Ostriches are also the fastest runners among birds; over short distances, they have been clocked at 40 miles an hour.

Why do cassowaries have helmets?
Cassowaries are notably short-legged and stout-bodied. Their coarse wing feathers—which look more like hair than normal feathers—hang down the sides. The face is vividly colored, and two of the three species have dangling red neck wattles.

But it is the bony casque, or helmet, that most significantly sets cassowaries apart from other large flightless birds. Flattened like a blade and perched on the forehead, the helmet is believed to protect the head of the cassowary as the bird makes its way through thorny undergrowth. Also of advantage in such tangled vegetation is the coarse, drooping plumage: far less delicate than those of other birds, the cassowary's feathers are less likely to get damaged as it moves along.

How can you tell the big birds apart?
To many people ostriches, emus, and rheas all look pretty much the same. The main differences among the three involve proportion and size. Ostriches and rheas have longer necks and legs than emus. Rheas are smaller and more slender than ostriches; emus are heavy, bulky birds. Plumage varies too. Only the emu is thickly feathered throughout (except for two areas of bare skin below the face). Ostrich wings and tails have long, curly plumes. The body of a rhea is covered with soft, loose feathers; an emu's, with hairy, coarse, drooping plumage. Only in a zoo, however, or between the covers of a book would you see all three together. In nature they live oceans apart.

Why do birds that are flightless still have wings?
Useless for flying, the weak wings of an ostrich nevertheless help the bird survive. When running at high speed, ostriches—and rheas too—balance themselves with their wings, particularly when making the quick turns and changes of direction by which they evade pursuit. In the hot, dry Australian bush, emus cool themselves by holding out their wings.

Wings play a role in courtship too. Rheas display by fluttering their small, normally inconspicuous wings. Male ostriches use theirs in a stately ballet, alternately flapping the plumed wings and bowing to the right and left, then throwing themselves down and stirring up the sand with their wings, as if hollowing out a nest.

Though the biggest birds are flightless, they are by no means helpless. They need not depend on wings to lift them out of danger, for these birds are protected by their very size and also by their strong legs and muscular thighs. Both ostriches and cassowaries can deliver lethal kicks. Ostriches have two stubby toes on each foot (they are the only birds with just two toes)—a trait that increases strength and thrust. Cassowaries have three long ones, with nails as sharp as razors. Emus and rheas have three too.

How big is an ostrich egg?
As befits the world's largest bird, ostriches lay the world's biggest eggs—up to $3\frac{1}{2}$ pounds. Male ostriches incubate at night; the drabber, less conspicuous females take over during the day. Among rheas, cassowaries, and emus, all the work of incubation is done by the male, which often sits tight for up to 40 days, scarcely leaving to eat. Once the eggs hatch, the male oversees the care of the chicks.

Despite similarities in their looks, the big flightless birds have different family lives. Two of them, emus and cassowaries, form pairs. Male ostriches and rheas, in contrast, maintain harems of up to half a dozen females each.

Emus and cassowaries make flat nests of grasses and leaves. Ostrich and rhea nests are mere scrapes in the ground, often too small to accommo-

Who's Who Among the Biggest Birds

Ostriches are the champions, growing to 8 feet tall and 300 pounds in weight.

Rheas are the South American counterpart of Africa's ostriches.

Cassowaries live in Australia and New Guinea. Note the bony helmet.

Emus of Australia have plumage that droops like the cassowary's.

eggs are occasionally discovered in the streambeds and swamps of Madagascar. Weighing some 20 pounds, the largest ones measure 3 feet around, big enough to contain about 8 quarts of fluid. Analysis of the eggshells shows that some elephant birds were alive less than a thousand years ago.

Other examples of flightless giants were the moas of New Zealand, roughly contemporary with the elephant birds. Some were more than 10 feet tall and weighed 500 pounds. Hunted for food and other purposes, moas were extinct or nearly so—sources differ—when Captain Cook arrived in New Zealand in 1769. In Australia an aboriginal tribe handed down legends of a giant bird and made rock carvings of the creature's huge tracks. The legends may have had some basis in fact: bones and eggs substantially larger than those of present-day emus have been found.

Appearing ever so proud because of its elongated neck, the ostrich can easily spot grassland predators. Its unusually long eyelashes give it a distinctive look.

date all the eggs laid by the various females. Harem-forming males have been known to retrieve eggs laid outside the nest and roll the eggs into place with their bills.

How did the elephant bird get its name?

An Arabian legend tells of a gigantic flying bird, the roc, that could carry off an elephant to feed its young. In truth, however, flightless birds hold the record for size in the past as well as the

present. For there were once birds—flightless ones—even larger than the modern ostrich, and these may have been the inspiration for the legend.

Island conditions—lack of predators, little competition for food—seem to have produced some exceptionally large forms. On the island of Madagascar lived the extinct giants called elephant birds, the largest of which was an ostrichlike species more than 10 feet tall and weighing about half a ton. Well-preserved elephant bird

Dwarfing the Maori chief at the right, the New Zealand moa, now extinct, towered some 10 feet above the ground. Elephant birds of Madagascar, also now extinct, were equally tall.

Ducks, Geese, and Swans

What do waterfowl have in common?
Ducks, geese, and swans usually feed in and nest near water; many even mate while they are afloat. Certain traits fit them for aquatic life. Plumage is thick and waterproof, for example. Webs between the birds' toes improve their ability to swim.

The differences among waterfowl, especially in size and color, are often more evident than the traits they share. Of the three groups, the largest in size are the graceful, long-necked swans; the trumpeter swan, in fact, is considered the heaviest of all flying birds. Geese are smaller and less aquatic in habits than swans.

Short-legged and short-necked, ducks are the smallest waterfowl. In breeding season, the plumage of many males is brightly colored and sometimes splendidly iridescent (the mallard's brilliant head is an example); after breeding they molt into plumage that resembles the females'. In contrast, geese and swans look essentially the same the year round, and there is little difference between the sexes.

Why do geese fly in formation?
Although a few species, such as the Hawaiian goose (or nene), do not fly long distances, most waterfowl are strong fliers, and long migrations are typical of many ducks and geese. The record holder within the group is the blue-winged teal, which breeds on the North American prairie and flies as far south as Argentina—a journey of more than 6,000 miles.

Canada geese flying in characteristic V-formation are a familiar sight. The lead goose does most of the hard work of overcoming air resistance, and geese toward the rear, spread out to the right and left, take advantage of currents stirred up by the birds flying ahead. By some sort of mutual arrangement, other geese relieve the lead bird from time to time.

Do geese keep their mates for life?
Mated pairs of geese and swans develop a special relationship, called a pair bond, that is constantly maintained. Sometimes living for many years, the birds form long-lasting—often lifelong—unions. Partners acknowledge each other by sessions of mutual preening and by rituals in

Small, Medium, and Large

Largest among waterfowl are the swans, long-necked and usually white as adults. Ducks are the smallest; geese lie in between. The most colorful waterfowl are the male ducks, like the mallard shown here.

Whooper swan
(adult and immature)

Mallard
(male)

Canada
goose

which they dip the head and bill. In the mutual greeting ceremony of swans, heads literally turn; in the triumph ceremony, which occurs after the male has driven off an intruder, the pair celebrate by waving their heads in unison and calling excitedly.

Pair bonds scarcely exist among ducks. As soon as incubation begins, the drakes desert their mates and go off to join their fellows in bachelor colonies. Ruddy ducks, a North American species, are unusual in that the male helps care for the young.

How do ducks talk to one another?
Except for the aloof and stately swans, waterfowl are gregarious by nature. They usually feed and migrate in flocks, and communication between individuals in the group is essential. A flock of ducks about to take flight indicates its intention by visual signals—shaking heads or lifting chins. Threatening birds (most notably swans) lift their wings and ruffle their feathers in an attempt to look more dangerous.

Courtship displays are also a type of communcation. Waterfowl experts recognize two kinds—social display, aimed at attracting as many potential mates as possible, and directed display, aimed at facilitating mating with a particular female. A female mallard uses a social display when she dashes among a group of males, nodding her head and holding her body flat in the mating position. In a spectacular directed display, the male ruddy duck cocks his stiff tail over his back, inflates his neck, and beats his breast with his bright blue bill.

Auditory signals, or calls, are important too. Grunts, hoots, honks, and hisses keep a flock in contact, warn off intruders, or attract mates. Males generally make most of the noise.

Where does eiderdown come from?
To be near their food supply, most ducks, geese, and swans choose nest sites adjacent to water. Swans and geese pick slight elevations, preferably on small islands; ducks, thick vegeta-

tion at or near the water's edge. Certain birds use loftier sites. Tree-nesting species include the wood duck, which prefers a hole high over water; the bufflehead, so small it can squeeze into a woodpecker hole; and the goldeneyes, diving ducks that require larger cavities.

Neither tree nor ground nesters carry building materials to the site. Females of ground-nesting species collect stems and leaves lying within reach as they sit on the site. As the nest progresses, they pluck special downy feathers from their breasts to make a soft, warm lining. (Eiders are famous for the quantity and superlative quality of their down.) When the female leaves her eggs, she covers them with down.

Why do ducks waddle?
When swimming, ducks and other waterfowl advance the foot with toes closed and the web on the foot folded. Then the foot is dropped backward and the toes unfolded, which pushes the bird forward. Though waterfowl propel themselves with alternate strokes of the feet, they can change direction the way rowers do, by stroking more often on one side.

Where the legs are on a duck varies according to species. Such divers and underwater swimmers as the mergansers have their legs placed well to the rear, which impedes their walking on land. The ruddy duck, a small diving bird, is so handicapped in walking that it rarely leaves the water on foot. Geese, swans, and surface-feeding ducks, whose legs are centered under the body, are better equipped for moving on land.

Why do ducks tip upside down?
One way to sort out the waterfowl is by feeding habits: some dabble, some dive, and some graze. Dabblers take their food, mostly pondweeds, from the surface or from the bottom in shallow water by "upending"—that is, immersing head and neck while the rest of the body projects above the water. Such ducks as mallards, wigeons, and pintails are upenders.

Dabbling ducks have flattened bills edged with plates called lamellae, which strain out edible matter as water is squeezed through. Waterfowl

diving for animal life have different bills. Mergansers have long, narrow bills equipped with toothed plates adapted for grasping slippery fish. Eiders and scoters have hard, sharp bills used like pickaxes to dislodge mussels and other food.

Swans and geese are grazers. A swan submerges its long neck and plucks water plants. Geese feed on land, grazing on tender grass or succulent sprouts of grain. Tougher vegetation can be sheared off with the sharp bill.

Ducks Differ in Looks and Lives

Ruddy ducks belong to a group of divers known as stifftails. They often swim with their short, spiky tails held erect.

Pintails are dabbling ducks, tipping up their bodies as they search for aquatic food. Remarkably graceful whether in water or in the air, these rather shy birds are among the fastest-flying ducks.

Wood ducks nest in tree holes and man-made nest boxes. They feed on the seeds and leaves of aquatic plants.

Common eiders, famous for the down they use to line their nests, dive for mussels and other marine animals. Like many other male ducks, eider drakes molt into eclipse plumage after the breeding season.

225

Great Birds of Prey

What makes birds of prey such good hunters?

Hawks and their relatives vary enormously in size. The smallest are tiny 2-ounce falconets of the Asian forests; the largest, South America's impressive harpy eagle, which can weigh more than 15 pounds. In most species the females are larger than the males.

With such wide variation in size, it is not surprising that different species hunt in different ways and for different foods. Hawks that feed on ground-dwelling prey usually hunt from an elevated perch—a fence post, a utility wire, the exposed limb of a tree. Scanning the ground intently until they see movement, such birds drop down onto their prey. Kestrels and most other grassland hunters hover in the air as they hunt. An eagle locates most of its prey while soaring, though the golden eagle often hunts on foot or waits motionless until a gopher or prairie dog pops up from its burrow. From atop a perch the honey buzzard watches wasps returning to their underground nest, then digs up the nest and gulps down the grubs.

All birds of prey, including owls as well as hawks and their kin, have excellent eyesight. On their feet are sharp talons for grasping and holding; hooked beaks with a sharp cutting edge help tear flesh. A falcon breaks the necks of birds and small rodents with the toothed edge of its bill. Snail-eating kites have slender hooked beaks with which they extract the snail "meat" from the shell. Osprey feet have roughened soles, an aid in holding slippery fish.

How do ospreys catch fish?

An osprey hunts by soaring above a body of water, sometimes hovering as it fans its wings. When it spots a fish swimming at or just below the surface, the osprey, also known as the fish hawk, dives with wings held high and feet thrown well forward. When necessary, it plunges in, making a tremendous splash. Once the fish is caught in its talons, the bird rises, shakes its wet feathers, and flies off to a customary perch, carrying the fish headfirst in its talons. Ospreys are often robbed by winged pirates—bald eagles in North America, fish eagles in Asia and Africa.

Where do you find the most birds of prey?

Two contrasting environments vie in popularity among day-active birds of prey. Of the 289 species of hawks, eagles, and falcons, 112 are most commonly found on grassy savannas with scattered trees, a habitat that covers large areas of East Africa and of South America too. Savanna species range from the secretary bird, a curious-

Seen from a distance, a bird of prey in flight can be recognized by type, though usually not by specific species. The six types shown here differ noticeably in size and in the shape of the wings and tail. Below are examples of all but the harrier.

looking creature with long legs and a black-tipped crest, to the African chanting goshawks, which in the breeding season chant melodiously from the tops of trees. A close second in number of species is the tropical forest, home to such birds as bat falcons and monkey-eating eagles. Though some forest species may soar above the canopy or hunt along the edges, most never leave the shelter of the deep forest.

Not all birds of prey are associated with wild places. Many thrive around farms, doing the farmer a good turn by feeding on pests. Falcons commonly hunt for small prey in towns and cities in Europe, Africa, and Asia; in North America, one celebrated peregrine nested for 12 years on a Montreal insurance building. The birds of prey that do best in cities are those that scavenge for food. (Despite their non-predatory habits, such species are classified as birds of prey because of their close similarities to the predatory species.) Indian cities, for example, swarm with vultures and other scavenging birds called kites. New Delhi has been credited with the highest

Peregrine falcons nest on cliffs and ledges, sometimes on city buildings.

Honey buzzards, like other buteos, have broad wings and short tails. They feed on insects and honey.

known concentration of any breeding bird of prey—more than 2,400 pairs of black kites, the species believed to be the most abundant bird of prey.

Why do hawks turn cartwheels?

Among the hawks, eagles, and falcons, courtship displays vary from soaring and calling—by the male or by both sexes—to highly elaborate sequences of climbs and dives. In one undulating display, the male dips in flight with wings partly closed, then regains his original height by shooting upward, vigorously flapping his wings. Sometimes male and female dip and rise together in this frequently repeated maneuver.

In the most spectacular display—cartwheeling, or spinning—the male dives on the female from a height, forcing her to roll over and present her claws; the pair then lock talons and whirl down through the air, tumbling over and over each other as they descend. Anyone fortunate enough to witness this whirling display will always remember the thrill.

What sorts of nests do birds of prey build?

Falcons make do with a bare ledge on a cliff, but other birds of prey construct some type of nest. When trees are available, nests are built in them; otherwise, some species will use the ground. Nests vary from fragile platforms of twigs and leaves, occupied for a single season by such relatively small kinds as the sharp-shinned hawk, to huge piles of sticks collected over the years by eagles and ospreys.

Both male and female usually take part in nest building. Established nests may be used by a succession of pairs, or a new nest may be built on top of the old. (Golden eagles in Scotland are reported to have occupied one such series of nests for more than 75 years.) The finishing touch on the nest, be it old or new, is a lining of fresh green leaves, which the female presses into shape with her breast.

Why is the firstborn better off?

As a rule, birds of prey lay no more than four eggs, and often they lay only one or two. Eggs in the larger clutches are laid at intervals of two to four days. The female starts to incubate

with the first—and there is thus considerable variation in the size of the nestlings. The first one to hatch has a great advantage over its fellows. The parents feed the larger, more alertly begging chicks first and may neglect the others entirely, leaving the weaker young to die from starvation.

The chief cause of death, however, is sibling aggression. In this fratricidal strife, the older offspring savagely attack the younger, often driving them from the nest. The parents do not interfere. In the case of such endangered species as the European white-tailed or the Spanish imperial eagle, concerned conservationists often remove the second nestling and place it in the nest of a chickless foster parent. After the young eaglet has grown its feathers, it is returned to its own parents. If all goes well, the number of young eagles fledged is doubled—a great help to the survival of the larger species, which do not breed every year.

Ospreys hover over water, plunge onto a fish, and carry it headfirst in their talons to a perch.

Goshawks, with their short wings and long tails, are classified as accipiters.

Golden eagles are among the biggest birds of prey. Note the mighty talons.

All About Owls

Why are owls so steeped in legend?

Though seldom seen, owls figure importantly in the art and folklore of nearly every culture. Many people have believed that owls are wise and are capable of predicting births, deaths, and other significant events. Some consider them portents of doom: an owl perching on or near a house, they feel, is bad luck.

Experts have suggested that people's fascination with owls stems in part from the birds' human appearance—more specifically, from such childlike traits as a large head, chubby body, and big, round eyes. The association between owls and misfortune stems perhaps from the fact that these silent hunters are nocturnal. The night, of course, is often equated with evil.

Are owls as wise as they seem?

If wisdom is being silent and assuming a solemn expression, then owls are surely wise. If wisdom is—as some define it—the ability to predict the probable outcome of events, then owls compare unfavorably with apes, elephants, porpoises, parrots, and perhaps even octopuses. Most of an owl's behavior is instinctive, though the bird has the capacity to remember and the ability to learn new habits for a limited number of novel situations. Owls kept as pets—not a recommended practice—seem able to recognize their owners, friends, and other household pets. Owls remember the localities where they were successful in finding prey, but they will often return to those places for some time after the prey supply has been exhausted.

How can owls hunt at night?

Like many other nocturnal animals, owls have big eyes. Located at the front of the head rather than at the sides, they allow for three-dimensional vision, which is vital in judging the distance and size of a moving target. Unlike human eyes, those of owls are immovably fixed in their sockets. This does not mean that the bird cannot see to the side: in following the movement of an object, it can turn its head upside down and nearly all the way around. This extraordinary ability has given rise to the myth that an owl will turn its head far enough to

wring its own neck if a person walks in circles around it. Actually, upon reaching the limit of its neck's flexibility, the owl merely whirls its head rapidly in the other direction.

Adapted for night vision, the sensory portion of the owl's eye—the retina—is densely packed with light re-

Although they have a narrow field of vision, owls can turn their heads upside down.

ceptors exceptionally sensitive to low levels of illumination. The pupil of the eye can open wide, admitting a maximum amount of light.

Owls are superb at detecting prey—and they are also superb at approaching without being detected. Their flight is silent. Flight feathers on the wings are fringed, which muffles the noise of air passing through.

What is an owl pellet?

Owls are animal eaters, hunting such creatures as rodents and other small mammals (the commonest prey), birds, snakes, lizards, frogs, and even insects and fish. Larger species tend to take larger prey: the eagle owl of Europe and the great horned owl of the Americas, each more than two feet tall, are capable of seizing and killing skunks and cats.

Owls have developed the same weapons—hooked beaks, stout legs, and long talons—as eagles and hawks. Owls capture prey with their feet and then drive claws into the victim; sometimes the capture is followed by a lethal bite with the beak. Claws and beaks are in proportion to prey size. The great gray owl of the Far North feeds mostly on such small rodents as mice and voles. Although it is as big as the great horned owl, its claws and beak are much smaller and weaker.

Whenever possible, prey is swallowed whole—skin, feathers, bones, and all. Indigestible matter, compressed into oval pellets, is regurgitated the next day. Such pellets often accumulate beneath roosting perches and furnish an accurate record of the bird's diet.

Night and Day in an Owl's Life

Most owls are nighttime hunters, capturing such small animals as mice and voles with powerful, sharp-taloned feet. The birds roost during the daytime, often in tree holes or out on a limb. Shown here is a tawny owl, an Old World bird of the woodlands that is closely related to North America's barred and spotted owls.

Short-eared owls are among the species that hunt during the day. These open-country birds, which nest on the ground, are good mousers.

Long-eared owls do have ears, but—like other owls'—theirs are hidden at the sides of the head. What you see are tufts of feathers.

Barn owls nest in barns and other buildings. Well-liked because of their soulful faces, these rodent killers should be admired for that role too.

What do owls do when it's too dark to see?

On the darkest nights many species rely on hearing rather than sight. Extremely sensitive, the ears—not to be confused with the tufts on such species as the long-eared and the great horned owl—are hidden among feathers behind the eyes. In some owls the ear openings are asymmetrical, allowing the bird to determine the direction of a sound because the two ears receive it at slightly different times.

Do all owls hoot?

To owls vocal signals are far more important than visual ones. The birds have a large vocabulary of sounds, including hoots, whistles, shrieks, screams, chatters, laughs, and growls. They also produce sounds by clicking the beak or by clapping the wings.

Different species of owls have widely different calls. The boreal owl has a rapid series of whistles, the flammulated owl emits a single deep hoot, and the barn owl makes all sorts of strange-sounding noises. Since larger owls often prey on the smaller ones, the calls of smaller species have a ventriloquial quality, hiding the source from both other owls and man.

What do owls do in the daytime?

As the sun rises, most owls go to sleep, resting in deep shade on large tree branches, often near the trunk. Others hide in holes in trees or in the ground. Inconspicuous because of their mottled gray or brown plumage, many assume postures that make them look like tree stubs or large pieces of bark.

Not all owls are night owls. Many hunt during daylight if food is scarce or if they have a large brood, and a few, including the short-eared owl, are primarily daytime hunters.

Which birds fly about at night?

Best known of the nocturnal birds besides owls are the nightjars, long-winged birds that are more often heard than seen. The whippoorwill is one example. Songbirds generally migrate at night, and many ducks and geese continue their foraging in the dark. On moonlit nights the handsome black skimmer, an American relative of the terns, pursues fish by flying low over the water with its lower jaw cutting the surface like a knife. The aptly named night herons may be feeding nearby.

Sensational Songbirds

Can all songbirds sing?
Perhaps the most interesting fact about songbirds is that there are so many different kinds. Almost half of the world's birds, about 4,000 species, are classified as songbirds because of their specialized sound-producing structures. Not every species sings well—or even at all. The best efforts of a raven, for example, produce only a deep, hoarse croak.

For all the songbirds' diversity—they range from 24-inch ravens to 3-inch flower peckers, from inconspicuous wrens to gaudy tanagers and iridescent sunbirds—they share certain traits. Only the dippers have adapted to water; all the rest are land birds. Except for such hole nesters as nuthatches, most build cup- or basket-shaped nests, usually in trees or bushes but sometimes—like the nest of the ovenbird—concealed on the ground. As parents, songbirds are exemplary, tirelessly popping morsels of food into the gaping mouths of helpless young and continuing to feed them until the offspring are well on the way to independence.

Where songbirds live depends on what they eat. The majority are insect eaters, like warblers, or fruit eaters, like orioles. Where these foods are lacking, songbirds are scarce. Mountaintops are sparsely populated. Deserts have relatively few songbirds; icy Antarctica has none.

Why don't birds fall off a branch when they sleep?
Songbirds are classified as perching birds because of the way their feet grasp a branch. A percher's secret lies in the position of its toes. Robins and other songbirds have four toes, three pointing forward and one, stronger than the others, pointing to the rear. As the bird alights, its hind toe closes

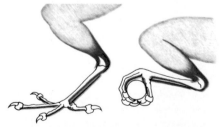

A songbird's foot has four toes, which are clearly visible as the bird walks on the ground. When the bird alights on a branch and bends its legs, the toes afford a tight grip.

Not All Songbirds Are Sensational Songsters

Songbirds are generally small, but not all of them are diminutive creatures. Nor does every species make beautiful sounds. What all the 4,000-odd species—nearly half the world's birds—have in common is something far less obvious: their ability to perch. Adapted to cling to branches and reeds (and telephone wires too), the feet of a songbird automatically tighten when the creature alights.

Nightingales look rather ordinary but sing extraordinary songs. These Old World birds are in the thrush family.

Yellowthroats, the males masked like bandits, sing out *witchery, witchery.* They range over most of North America.

House sparrows are more chirpers than singers. Both the black-throated male and the female make unmusical sounds.

around the branch from below while tendons automatically pull all the toes tight. This action prevents the bird from tumbling off its perch.

Songbirds have adapted to perching elsewhere than on trees. Swallows, which have small, weak feet, favor utility wires; meadowlarks sing from fence posts; marsh wrens balance on waving reeds. In ground-walking birds like pipits and horned larks, the perching foot has been slightly adapted: toes are longer and claws straighter than the typical bird's. Bark-clingers like nuthatches and brown creepers have strong, curved claws. The dipper's grasping feet enable it to walk underwater on slippery rocks.

Which are the finest songsters?
By tradition, the bird with the most beautiful song is the nightingale, a brown and white European representative of the thrush family, all of whose members are notable songsters. Singing by day as well as after dark, nightingales pour out a rapid succession of rich, liquid phrases, interspersed with harsher notes. If the nightingale has a rival on the other side of the Atlantic, it is the hermit thrush, whose flutelike

Black-billed magpies are noisy chatterers. Like their relatives the crows, they are exceptional songbirds because of their size.

Winter wrens sing cheerily in both the Old World and the New. All other wrens occur only in the Americas.

Bohemian waxwings, elegant birds with feathery crests, have weak voices. A flock can be heard to twitter in flight.

tounding. Some species, like the zebra finch, are somber in their dress. Firetails, twinspots, and waxbills are touched with brilliant red, and the Gouldian finch is a medley of primary colors. These birds never become very tame, and their chirpy, buzzy songs are almost inaudible, but their lively dispositions make up for these deficiencies. Sociable birds, they do not thrive when caged alone, but in company they breed readily.

What does a mockingbird mock?

A bird that takes its name from its ability to mimic, as does the mockingbird, is surely a champion of the art. Ornithologists have recorded mockingbird imitations of at least 30 species of birds as well as of other animals and the sounds of machines. The mocker has a bubbling song of its own too. Like the nightingale, it sings by night as well as by day. Typically, a mockingbird repeats each phrase three or four times before passing on to the next. In Australia, the spotted bowerbird is an accomplished mimic, with an equally diversified repertoire.

What good are songbirds?

To most people the melodious music, beautiful plumage, and intriguing habits of the cherished songbirds are benefits enough, but there are other, more tangible ones. Nectar-eating honeycreepers of tropical America, Australian honey eaters, and African sunbirds pollinate the flowers they visit. Such species as waxwings help plants reproduce by eating their berries and spreading their seeds. By burying acorns, blue jays plant oaks.

On balance, songbirds repay occasional raids on fruit and other crops by their services in holding back the population of insect pests. Barn swallows and martins consume huge quantities of mosquitoes and flies. Meadowlarks and bobolinks feast on grasshoppers. Warblers search foliage for leaf-destroying insects; chickadees seek insect eggs in bark. Caterpillars are the preferred food of titmice; orioles eat even the gypsy moth's hairy caterpillars. Starlings, condemned by almost everyone for their untidy roosts, can often be seen probing a lawn for the grubs of Japanese beetles and other destructive species.

song echoes through northern forests.

Nightingales and skylarks are dear to poets. Shelley called the skylark "blithe spirit," and Wordsworth, "ethereal ministrel." Showering the earth with melody, the skylark sings unceasingly in its vertical ascent, sings as it hovers on beating wings, and sings as it descends. In England the skies over moors and downs are sometimes full of skylarks, all making music at the same time. In North America the meadowlarks, more closely related to blackbirds than to skylarks, are cherished for their clear, plaintive songs.

Where did canaries come from?

In the 16th century, the ancestors of tame canaries were brought to Europe from the Canary Islands. The wild birds, greenish with darker streaks above and yellowish green below, did not look much like the family pets of today. Through selective breeding, many color phases—including the familiar bright yellow plumage—and various elaborately crested and collared forms have been developed.

As cage birds, canaries are rivaled by a variety of small finches from Africa, Asia, and Australia. The diversity of plumage color and pattern is as-

Unusual Birds

What makes a bird unusual?

For one reason or another, some of the almost 9,000 known species of birds bid for special attention. One compelling reason is rarity. The species in question may have never been widespread; perhaps, like the kagu of New Caledonia, it has always lived in only one remote spot. In many cases the bird's habitat has been destroyed, as has happened with the forests along rivers in the southern United States, where the ivory-billed woodpecker may or may not still exist.

Sheer beauty is another reason some birds are memorable. South America's appropriately named resplendent quetzal, with its long green tail, is a vivid example. Other birds—spoonbills and puffins, for instance—are noteworthy for some unusual structure, such as an oddly shaped or oversized beak. Still others, such as the bower-building bowerbirds, stand out for their behavior. Hornbills qualify on two counts—the peculiar bill and their fascinating way of protecting mother and young. By anyone's standards, they are truly unusual birds.

Why do bowerbirds build bowers?

Male bowerbirds of New Guinea and Australia, close relatives of the birds of paradise, build elaborate display arenas. Using small sticks and twigs, they erect domes, maypoles, or pyramids. They clear the space around the bowers, removing leaves and debris, and decorate the area with fresh flowers, fruits, moss, mushrooms, pebbles, or shells. Each species has its own preference in decorations.

The male satin bowerbird of eastern Australia erects an avenue—that is, a long strip marked off by two walls of fine twigs, built about a foot apart. Painting with a wad of bark (an unusual instance of tool-using by a bird), he coats the inner surfaces with a paste of charcoal dust or other pigment, mashed berries, and saliva. The area is decorated with feathers and assorted objects, often man-made and mostly blue, a color harmonizing with the male's glossy blue-black plumage. When a female enters, he puts on a display. The two may then mate.

What do hornbills do with their bills?

A large, curved bill, which in some species is surmounted by a helmet, is the hornbill's most outstanding feature. Usually hollow or honeycombed inside, the helmet is lighter than it looks. The bird uses its bill like an arm in adroitly plucking fruits, even small berries, from a branch. Hornbills live in forests in Asia and Africa. In tropi-

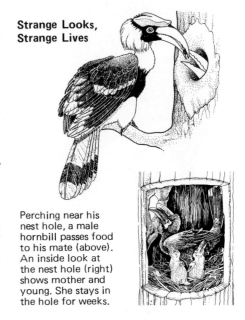

Strange Looks, Strange Lives

Perching near his nest hole, a male hornbill passes food to his mate (above). An inside look at the nest hole (right) shows mother and young. She stays in the hole for weeks.

cal America toucans have similar—though helmetless—bills.

Hornbills nest in holes, but they are by no means typical hole-nesting birds. Instead of flying in and out of the hole, the female seals herself in, using a mixture of mud, droppings, and saliva applied with quick, nibbling motions of her bill. The male helps from the outside. While the female incubates, the male feeds her through the narrow opening that remains. When she finally breaks out of the protective chamber, possibly several months later, the young replaster the slit from the inside, walling themselves in until they are fledged.

How does a flamingo feed?

A flamingo's beak, with its sharp bend in the middle, may look peculiar, but it is in fact a very efficient filter. When the long-necked, long-legged bird—some kinds are pink and others mainly white (the food they eat also affects color)—holds its beak in the usual position, the large, trough-shaped lower part is underneath the smaller upper mandible, which fits it like a lid. The flamingo turns its beak upside down when feeding. Inside the structure, the bird's thick, fleshy tongue acts like a suction pump. When the tongue is retracted and the beak slightly opened, food-rich water enters. With the beak closed and the tongue pushed forward, water is forced out through slits. Food particles are retained.

How to Impress a Female

To attract mates, male bowerbirds turn into architects. The type of bower they build varies according to species. (There are some 18 species, all in Australia or New Guinea.) Made of sticks, the bowers are often decorated with small objects. The male displays there, and then mates. Nests are built elsewhere.

Decorated with assorted objects, the satin bowerbird's bower is an avenue lined with twigs. Here, the male is displaying with a flower in his bill.

The golden bowerbird piles up twigs around a tree (left). The gardener bowerbird uses a walled garden with a roofed hut for display (right).

A cleared "court" decorated with bits of vegetation, shells, and even beetle wings is used by the male Archbold's bowerbird when he performs.

232

What is a kiwi?

The kiwi of New Zealand is a small flightless bird the size of a chicken (the name is also used for a type of fruit). Kiwis, named for their call, are strictly nocturnal. Though these birds are the national emblem, few New Zealanders—indeed, few people—have ever seen them in the wild. The elusive creatures hide in burrows by day and feed at night by probing for worms and insects. They have long, pliable beaks with nostrils at the tips, and are among the few birds using the sense of smell to locate food. Coarse, shaggy plumage is another unusual feature.

Why does a puffin's beak look so strange?

Solemn-looking and comical at the same time, the puffin inevitably suggests a clown. Both sexes sport the strikingly patterned beak, which plays a part in courtship. After the breeding season the colorful outer plates are shed, and the birds are left with smaller, duller bills.

A puffin's bill is more than an orna-

Puffins are irresistible even without a dangling load of fish. The colorful bill is the bird's most unusual feature.

ment. When the bird returns to its burrow from a trip to sea, its beak is crammed with neat rows of sand eels or other small fish. How a puffin manages to retain the first fish while opening its beak to capture the others is somewhat of a puzzle. One suggestion is that the tongue may be used to clamp each succeeding fish against the roof of the mouth.

Which are the rarest birds?

Today there are at least 100 bird species with fewer than 2,000 living individuals. Island creatures are especially threatened (Hawaii has some 15 endangered birds, including its unique honeycreepers), but which is the rarest cannot really be determined. Not only would the answer change over time; there are also several borderline species—the ivory-billed woodpecker, for one—that may no longer exist.

The partial recovery of the whooping crane and the trumpeter swan in North America has demonstrated that, given careful monitoring and conservation measures, limited success in rescuing endangered species is possible. For some species wildlife experts consider captive breeding programs the ultimate solution.

In a life-giving kiss a flamingo uses its oddly shaped bill to pass food to its chick. The chicks, whose bills are less curved, are fed special secretions.

233

The Ways of Mammals

Nineteen "Typical" Mammals

There is no such thing as a typical mammal. Sizes range from that of the mighty whale to the minuscule shrew; their homes, from the air (bats) to the sea (whales and walruses). Anteaters specialize in eating ants, while the walrus takes mussels and crabs, and certain rodents consider everything food. Kangaroos hop, manatees swim, monkeys climb, and colugos glide from tree to tree. Magnificent antlers, an enormous snout, an armor of scales—mammals are, in sum, splendidly diverse.

Spiny anteaters and the duck-billed platypus are the world's only mammals that lay eggs.

Kangaroos protect their young in pouches. Like other marsupials', their newborn are very undeveloped.

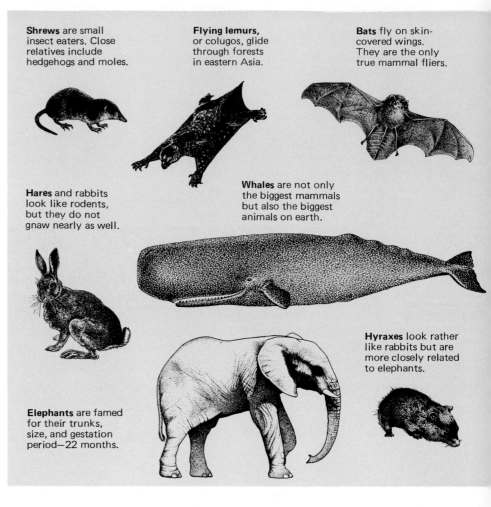

Shrews are small insect eaters. Close relatives include hedgehogs and moles.

Flying lemurs, or colugos, glide through forests in eastern Asia.

Bats fly on skin-covered wings. They are the only true mammal fliers.

Hares and rabbits look like rodents, but they do not gnaw nearly as well.

Whales are not only the biggest mammals but also the biggest animals on earth.

Elephants are famed for their trunks, size, and gestation period—22 months.

Hyraxes look rather like rabbits but are more closely related to elephants.

What is a mammal?

Adaptability is surely the hallmark of the mammals, a group so successful that its members range from pole to pole and can be found in the air and in water as well as on land and in the trees. Mammals range in size from the 100-foot blue whale, the largest animal ever to grace the earth, to the pygmy shrew, which measures less than 4 inches long. All mammals are warm-blooded, breathe air, and have hair and a backbone, and their females produce milk. Their brains are bigger and more complex than any other animal's.

Do all mammals reproduce in the same way?

Of the 4,000-odd species of mammals the most numerous are the placentals, which have a structure—the placenta—that connects the developing embryo with the mother. Lions, elephants, mice, horses, and hippos, among others, are all placental mammals. The second group, the marsupials, give birth to young that are at a very early stage of development; to continue growing, they generally must crawl into their mother's pouch. Kangaroos and opossums are marsupials.

Spiny anteaters, or echidnas, and the duck-billed platypus are the only egg-laying mammals, technically known as monotremes. The least common of the mammals, monotremes live in Australia and New Guinea. They hatch from eggs warmed outside the mother's body. Like all other mammals, they require mother's milk, but how they get it is more haphazard. The platypus, for example, licks milk droplets off hairs attached to pores on its mother's belly.

How does mother's milk vary from species to species?

While milk is the food of all young mammals, its composition is not al- ways the same. The fat, protein, sugar, and water content of milk varies according to species, the environment, and the infant's age.

Just after giving birth, a seal produces milk that is about 53 percent fat. From this, the richest milk produced by any mammal, the pup develops an insulating layer of blubber, for soon it must relinquish its birthplace on land for the frigid sea. The Atlantic gray seal gains about 4 pounds every day, approaching a weight of 100 pounds when it is weaned a mere two weeks after birth.

Whales and other mammals that never leave the water also produce rich milk. Whale calves add nearly 200 pounds daily; baby blue whales double their birth weight in just 7 days. It takes a domestic cow 47 days—and a horse, 60—to perform the same feat.

Both Bactrian camels and kangaroo rats live in dry places, but the camel's milk is 87 percent water and the rat's

234

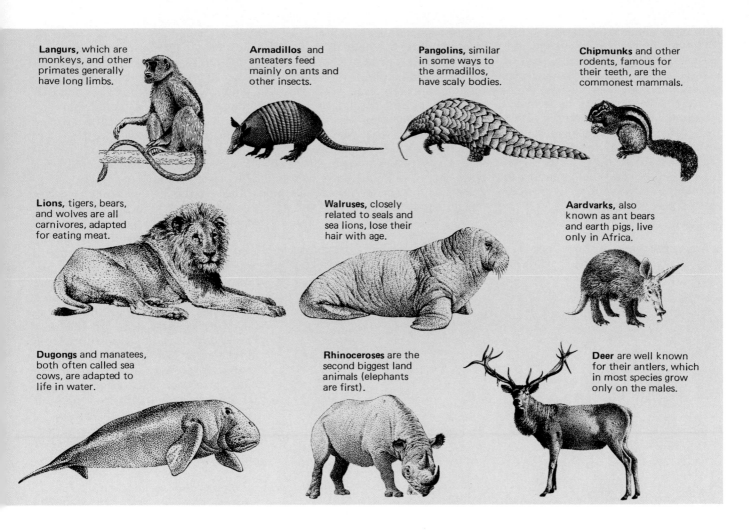

Langurs, which are monkeys, and other primates generally have long limbs.

Armadillos and anteaters feed mainly on ants and other insects.

Pangolins, similar in some ways to the armadillos, have scaly bodies.

Chipmunks and other rodents, famous for their teeth, are the commonest mammals.

Lions, tigers, bears, and wolves are all carnivores, adapted for eating meat.

Walruses, closely related to seals and sea lions, lose their hair with age.

Aardvarks, also known as ant bears and earth pigs, live only in Africa.

Dugongs and manatees, both often called sea cows, are adapted to life in water.

Rhinoceroses are the second biggest land animals (elephants are first).

Deer are well known for their antlers, which in most species grow only on the males.

only 50. The contrast may be due to a difference in daily rhythm. The kangaroo rat confines its activity to the nighttime, but the camel is active during the daylight, and so must provide more moisture for its young.

How do mammals talk with one another?

Although some scientists consider speech a distinctively human trait, others believe that the complex songs of certain whales and the vocal signals of porpoises are languages too. Researchers teaching sign language to great apes argue for an even less human-oriented definition of language—one that appreciates the mind of the animal attempting communication as well as the message.

In any case, to transfer information it is not necessary to have a spoken language. Mammals communicate by sounds, touch, visual clues, and odor. A prairie dog barking, a calf nudging

its mother's udder, a timber wolf with its tail raised, a dik-dik antelope brushing its scent glands against the grass—all are sending signals to others of their kind, signals as clear as those of humans saying, respectively, "Look out!," "I'm hungry," "*I'm* in charge," and "This place is mine."

Why do animals have hair?

Hair, made of a sulfur-based protein called keratin, is a mammal's insulation, retaining internally produced heat. (Birds accomplish the same thing with feathers.) But hair has taken on other roles as well. It can serve as feelers, as do the whiskers of a cat. Even whales, which lose most of their hair before they are born, generally have sensitive bristles on their heads. The spines on porcupines and echidnas are examples of hair stiffened and transformed into defensive weaponry. Claws, nails, and hooves essentially are modified hair. Hair also serves to

camouflage, as on spotted fawns, or to warn, as on striped skunks. By flattening out the hairs covering its tail, a flying squirrel gets some help in controlling the direction of its glide.

Which animals work as teams?

As might be expected, teamwork is most likely among mammals living in groups—among them wolves, hyenas, wild dogs, baboons, prairie dogs, and chimpanzees. When threatened by a wolf pack, musk oxen form a defensive circle, with horns pointed outward and cows and calves protected in the center. Not only do lionesses hunt for the rest of the pride, frequently aiding each other in the stalk and kill; they share too in caring for the cubs. Porpoises cooperate in hunting; and when a member of their group is injured they support it on the surface so it can breathe. On occasion they have extended such assistance across species lines, to humans in trouble in the sea.

235

Family Affairs

How big are animal families?

An animal family may be as small as a mother dolphin and her single calf or as large as that of an old matriarch elephant, which includes her daughters and their offspring. The basic mammal family is mother and young, and that is true even among such harem-forming animals as the fur seals. A male fur seal jealously guards his females, but he pays no attention to their pups and cannot really be considered part of the family.

Which mammals mate for life?

In most species of mammals, male and female come together only to mate. Among those that form longer-lasting relationships are wolves, gibbons, beavers, and chinchillas, all of which stay paired for many seasons. The red fox falls in between. About midwinter the male seeks a mate. Inseparable for the next seven to eight weeks, the two mate, hunt, and prepare a den together. As the time of birth nears, the female retires to the den and will not allow the male to enter. He continues, however, to leave prey at the entrance and joins the family several weeks after the cubs are born. When the youngsters are old enough to fend for themselves, the fox family splits up. The male does not necessarily take the same mate the following year.

Where do animals hide their young?

Elephants, rhinos, moose, and many other mammals—typically, species that are usually moving about—raise their young out in the open. The majority, however, provide their young with some sort of shelter. Such mammals as squirrels and raccoons make cozy nests of leaves or use plant-lined hollows in trees. Many, including marmots and voles, rear their young in burrows. Bear dens are generally holes dug into a slope; polar bears dig in the snow. African warthogs are burrowers; so are hyenas, which may move into an abandoned warthog burrow. Carnivores may find it convenient to take over burrows of their prey or other animals, enlarging them if necessary for their own use. Wolves sometimes use old fox dens.

Which newborns can fend for themselves?

A young wildebeest in Africa is born with its eyes open and with a well-developed coat of hair. Within a few minutes it can stand; within a day it can run well enough to keep up with the herd. A hunting dog, from the same part of Africa, has its eyes closed at birth. Bears are born in an even less developed state, not only blind but naked and often weighing less than a pound.

In general, plant-eating mammals are more fully developed at birth than predators. One of the main survival traits of such creatures as deer and wildebeest is the ability to hide or run from danger—and the sooner they can do it, the better. A young carnivore, in contrast, has much to learn about hunting, and develops its skills during a long period of time.

Who uses baby-sitters?

Baby-sitting is not a human invention. When a pack of hunting dogs goes out in search of prey, the younger pups are left behind at the den, guarded by sev-

Nuzzled by its mother, a fawn nurses every four hours. Fawns are weaned four months after birth but may stay with the mother for up to two years.

eral females. Wolves often leave their cubs under the watchful eye of an "aunt." Lions do something similar, though the guardian is perhaps not so much an official baby-sitter as a lazy female who hopes to get her food the easy way—not by hunting but by sharing what the other adults bring back. Regardless of her motives, the cubs do get protection as a result.

Though an elephant herd moves as a unit, and so has no need of baby-sitters, adults and adolescents will take care of a calf that is not their own, comforting it and picking it up when it stumbles. Sometimes a nursing elephant will even suckle another mother's calf.

What do parents teach their young?

Though fawns, baby rabbits, and other young plant-eating mammals usually have little to learn beyond how to conceal themselves and escape, such skills do not always come naturally. When danger threatens, a doe may nudge her fawn into a concealing thicket; from repeated experience, the youngster learns where it can hide. Animals learn the signals their species uses to communicate by observing how parents and other adults react. By imitating the parent, they also learn what kind of food to eat.

Young carnivores must learn much more demanding skills—how to stalk, ambush, and kill. Scientists believe that much of the play these animals

Several months old, a young baboon still rides on its mother's back. Primates take a long time to grow up.

engage in is actually training for adulthood. Mostly, however, the lessons occur when the youngsters accompany their parents and imitate them. Young mink and raccoons, for example, watch their mothers turn

Though this elephant calf is cooling off very close to its mother, chances are that the rest of the family—its grandmother, aunts, and cousins—are nearby.

over stones in a streambed to look for crayfish. Young lions and wolves go with their elders on hunts.

In some species the parent takes a more active role in training. A house cat will bring an injured mouse home as practice for her kittens. The mother cheetah cripples and retrieves a young gazelle. Though cruel by human standards, these activities are necessary for survival, for only through practice does a young predator learn how to kill.

What role do fathers play?

In nature the father's role is often limited to mating, but in many species the male does contribute to the care of the females and young. Among zebras and their relatives in the horse family, the stallion acts as a sentinel and defends his harem and their offspring against attack. Male lions defend the territory of their pride, driving off competing predators. Male wolves are excellent parents even by human

standards, not only defending their families but bringing meat for the cubs and the nursing mother.

How do families break up?

As a young mammal develops, it becomes less and less dependent on its mother. It explores its environment, plays with its siblings or other youngsters, and begins to nibble solid food. Eventually, the mother uses bites, kicks, butts, or cuffs—the behavior varies according to species—to discourage her offspring from nursing.

Young males, often driven from the group as they reach adolescence, may form bachelor herds until they can win acceptance into another group. In a herd of guanacos, South American relatives of the llama, the ruling adult male drives off both sexes when they are a year old. Among solitary animals, the family unit may simply split up when the young can fend for themselves, as among foxes; or the mother may drive them away, as does a bear.

Amazing Marsupials

How did marsupials get their name?
When the explorer Vicente Pinzón brought an opossum from the New World to the Spanish court about A.D. 1500, he persuaded the king and queen to feel inside the animal's pouch. This was Europe's first official experience with the mammals called marsupials, as scholars have termed the animals with a "little bag" (technically known as a marsupium) on the underside. Marsupials are born at a very early stage of development, and the pouch is used to carry them about.

Not all female marsupials, however, have true pouches. Marsupials with enclosed pouches include koalas, kangaroos, and the larger species of American opossums. The Australian mulgara, a kind of marsupial mouse, has only folds of skin to shelter its young. The Latin American rat opossums and the ant-eating Australian numbat are among those with no pouches at all. In such species only the mother's fur protects the newborn; unweaned but bigger offspring are carried on the mother's back.

Marsupials are by no means equally distributed throughout the world. The members of the approximately 250 species, ranging in size from so-called marsupial mice less than five inches long to seven-foot kangaroos, live in Australia and neighboring areas and in North and South America. The Australian area has the greatest number and diversity, including the koalas and kangaroos.

How small are marsupials when they are born?
When young marsupials leave the womb, they are amazingly small. The marsupial mouse is as tiny as a grain of rice; the koala, as big as a bumblebee. The internal organs of most newborn marsupials are incomplete, and their hind legs are only nubs. But these diminutive creatures can smell and, using their front legs, climb. Their survival depends on the strength of their grasp, for they must pull themselves unaided through as much as eight inches of tangled hair into the mother's pouch—the life-giving nursery where they get their milk. Once the newborn has its mouth around the nipple, it becomes firmly attached.

How far can a kangaroo hop?
As might be expected of a group with so many species, marsupials do not move in any one particular way. Most have larger and stronger hind legs than forelegs. The climbing and burrowing ones, however, have a more even balance between front and back. Koalas and opossums are adept climbers whose padded paws, sharp claws, and flexible feet permit secure movements on trees. This is true of the gliders too, animals that somewhat resemble squirrels and can swoop from tree to tree by using skin flaps on their sides like a parachute.

Wombats and marsupial moles are burrowers equipped with powerful, spadelike claws on their front feet. The mole excavates with its claws and fills in with its hind legs, sometimes traveling short distances on the surface; the stocky, badger-sized wombat digs tunnels up to 100 feet long.

Kangaroos, of course, are quite different. They hop on their hind legs, using the tail for balance when speeding along and as an extra limb when moving on all fours. In open places the big kangaroos can travel 40 miles an hour for short distances, bounding 25 feet or more at full stretch.

Do possums really play dead?
When threatened, the Virginia opossum—the only marsupial native to North America—hisses at first and discharges a bad-smelling liquid. But if these devices fail to drive off the aggressor, the opossum lapses into a comatose state. With tongue hanging out, it lies still. Its limbs are stiff and without apparent sensation; its breathing and heartbeat become so slow as to be imperceptible. Even under ordinary circumstances opossums and other marsupials have a slower metabolism than other mammals, and their body temperature is lower and their heartbeat slower than those of other mammals of comparable size.

Are koalas really bears?
The early European colonists in Australia named local forms of wildlife after the European animals they most resembled. The marsupial mouse, the native cat, the Tasmanian wolf—all are marsupials that look and behave somewhat like the unrelated animals for which they are named. Sometimes even scholars were confused. Koalas, for example, were given a scientific name meaning "pouched bear." Although these charming little creatures may look like teddy bears, their way of life is more like that of leaf-eating monkeys in the forest.

Marsupials in Australia, like other mammals elsewhere, play various roles. Kangaroos and wallabies are the large grazers; wombats and marsupial moles, the burrowers; Tasmanian devils and the almost extinct wolves, the carnivores. The most numerous are the insect eaters—among them the numbat, woolly cuscus, and striped possum.

Long Day's Journey

Marsupials are different from other mammals because their embryos spend so little time inside the mother's body. Though tiny and immature, the newborn is able to climb up to the mother's pouch, following a track in the fur. There it clamps on to a teat and begins to nurse. The first time a red kangaroo leaves the pouch is six months after birth.

Slightly more than a month after its conception, the newborn kangaroo leaves its mother's reproductive tract.

The baby climbs some six inches up to the pouch—an enormous journey for an animal less than an inch long.

Inside the pouch, the young kangaroo, known as a joey, suckles at a teat. It is weaned after about seven months.

Red kangaroos are the dominant wild grazers on Australian grasslands. Bigger than the females, the males can weigh more than 200 pounds. They fight each other using their arms.

Tasmanian wolves, largest of carnivorous marsupials, may or may not be extinct. They rely—or relied —not on speed but on endurance for running down prey, including kangaroos.

Marsupial mice are not plant eaters (as are most true mice elsewhere), feeding instead on insects and other small animals. The flattened head is said to help the mouse probe among crevices.

Tiger cats are tree climbers with long bodies, short legs, and feet that grip bark. They occur on the ground too. Mainly nocturnal, they eat small animals and eggs.

Numbats eat mainly ants and termites, ripping open termite mounds with strong claws on their front feet and thrusting the long snout and sticky tongue into crevices.

Marsupial moles, like similar creatures elsewhere, rarely appear above the surface. Using their nails, they dig for worms and insects. They sense prey by touch, not sight.

Bats: Mammals That Fly

What kind of animal is a bat?

People probably have more wrong ideas about bats than about any other animals. These creatures of the night are thought of as weird birds or flying mice and as portents of doom or—contrariwise—symbols of good luck.

Bats are mammals, albeit extraordinary ones. The only true fliers among mammals (flying squirrels glide rather than fly), they range in size from the so-called flying foxes, with five-foot wingspans, to the Philippine bamboo bat, whose wings span a mere six inches and which weighs only

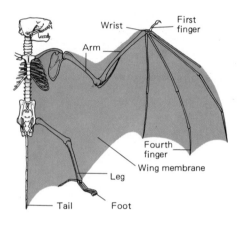

The most extraordinary feature of a bat's skeleton is the amazingly long fingers. Note the wing membrane, a double fold of skin supported by bones.

a twentieth of an ounce. Bats abound in the tropics. Fewer than 40 species live in North America, while about 100 have been counted in West Africa alone. With some 850 species, bats are more varied than any other mammal group save the rodents. About one out of every four or five species of mammals is a bat.

How do bats fly?

A bat's wing and life-style are closely related. A free-tailed bat—so named because its tail projects beyond the flight membranes—has long, narrow wings, well suited for long-distance travel. The insect-eating Indiana bat has short, wide wings permitting quick turns. Nectar-feeding species, which hover over flowers, have wings that arch upward in the middle.

Many bats cannot get enough lift from their wings to raise themselves into the air. Free-tailed bats, which hang on the ceilings of caves to rest,

must drop about six feet before becoming airborne. Vampires leap into the air before spreading their wings.

Where do bats spend the winter?

In temperate regions insect-eating bats, like insect-eating birds, have trouble finding food in winter. Some make long-distance migrations. Free-tailed bats that summer in the United States may travel a thousand miles to winter haunts in Mexico. Others fly up to several hundred miles between central and northern Europe. A bat that was banded in the Soviet Union was recovered in Bulgaria, more than 700 miles away.

Indiana bats are among those that spend the winter hibernating in caves. Not just any cave will do: bats require places where temperatures remain low—but above freezing—and relatively constant. Their body temperature drops during hibernation, and the metabolism slows down, which means the animal requires less food (it lives

off body fat). Certain species also lower their body temperature when they roost during the day.

Which bats eat bananas?

In at least one way bats are friends of man: most kinds catch insects on the wing and at times consume enormous numbers of pests. Not all bats, however, are insect eaters. Bananas and other fruits form the diet of flying foxes in Asia and Australia. Others—the long-tongued bats of tropical America, for instance—consume flower nectar and pollen, pollinating the plants in the process. The tongue of such species is not only long but also hairy; this allows the animal to probe into flowers and pull out food.

Fishermen bats are among the most extraordinary types, gaffing fish with elongated claws as they sweep low over the water. Mice, frogs, bird nestlings, and even other bats are hunted by the Indian false vampire, a seemingly fastidious creature with the habit

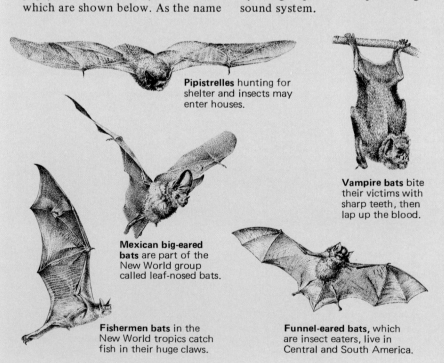

Beyond the Vampire, Variety

There are two very different sorts of bats—fruit bats, one of which is the flying fox shown on the facing page, and all the others, some of which are shown below. As the name implies, fruit bats eat fruit, finding their food by smell and sight. Most other bats zero in on flying insects by using a special echo-producing sound system.

Pipistrelles hunting for shelter and insects may enter houses.

Vampire bats bite their victims with sharp teeth, then lap up the blood.

Mexican big-eared bats are part of the New World group called leaf-nosed bats.

Fishermen bats in the New World tropics catch fish in their huge claws.

Funnel-eared bats, which are insect eaters, live in Central and South America.

Issued at a rate of up to 200 a second, high-pitched sounds—most are beyond the range of human hearing—stream from the bat's head. Those that strike flying insects, fruit, or other targets bounce back to the bat, whose brain analyzes the echoes and determines what and where the object is. Echolocation works in a flash. A bat can find an insect, chase it, and eat it in half a second.

What do bats do during the day?

Nearly all bats roost during the day in dark, quiet places. Caves are favored by many; attics, hollow walls, and the proverbial belfries are popular sites. The tent-making bat bites partly through the ribs of palm fronds, making them droop to form a weatherproof shelter. Tiny bamboo bats enter bamboo stems through cracks, then roost inside the hollow portions. More than a dozen of these bats may roost together, anchoring themselves with foot pads that act like suction cups against the smooth walls.

In Asia and Africa, gaudy, orange-red creatures known as painted bats roost in clumps of dead leaves, bird nests, and hollow tree trunks. Tomb bats, as the ominous-sounding name implies, like to roost in old ruins and tombs. Huge numbers of flying foxes—up to 100,000—form community roosts in trees. Bats tend to be gregarious, and cave dwellers perhaps most of all: a free-tailed bat colony in the southwestern United States may number up to 60 million individuals.

Do bats make good mothers?

Bats are born blind and furless. A very young bat, which has strong hind legs but not much in the way of wings, spends much of the time clinging to its mother's underside. Certain species carry their young when they go out to feed; others may leave infants in a communal roost. Usually the mother can identify her own baby when she returns to the roost. Especially when bats live in huge colonies, however, a nursing mother may feed the first infant she encounters upon her arrival home. Like other mammals, bat mothers nurse their youngsters on milk. Small species are weaned several weeks after birth; larger ones take as long as five months.

Its fur tells you this bat is a mammal—and a beautiful one indeed. This individual belongs to a group known as flying foxes, which feed on bananas and other fruit.

of plucking birds and skinning mice before eating them.

In contrast with false vampires, true vampire bats eat blood, although not in the way many people think. Small animals with bodies no longer than a human hand, vampires, which live in warm parts of the Americas, alight too gently to awaken the sleeping victim—a cow perhaps, a bird, or even a human. Using teeth as sharp as razors, they scoop out tiny pieces of skin, just deep enough to draw blood. While an anticoagulant in the bat's saliva keeps the blood from clotting, its tongue inverts, creating a trough through which the blood flows into its mouth. The vampire does not really suck blood but laps it up with dazzling speed. A single vampire may drink up to three gallons a year.

How do bats find their way at night?

Like many other nocturnal animals, the bats called flying foxes have well-developed eyes. Most other species, however, use sound rather than sight to navigate at night. A sonar system called echolocation enables them to avoid obstacles and locate food.

Life-and-Death Echoes

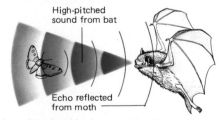

High-pitched sound from bat

Echo reflected from moth

Sounds emitted by insect-eating bats bounce off objects they hit. A bat can tell from the echo where and what the object is. Insects may be snapped up in half a second.

Remarkable Rodents

Why are there so many rodents?

Remarkably, rodents account for about half the known species of mammals, and as individuals they may well outnumber all the other mammals put together. One reason for their abundance is the phenomenal reproductive rate of the smaller species: a house mouse may begin breeding five weeks after birth and have more than 50 young a year. Rodents have a great talent for adapting to diverse conditions, too. Squirrels wax fat begging food in parks. House mice and rats turn man's habits of cultivating crops and storing food to their advantage; muskrats and nutrias thrive in irrigation ditches and artificial lakes.

Do mice really eat cheese?

Though rodents are basically plant eaters, certain ones search out different foods. In addition to fruits and greens, the agoutis of South America eat shellfish. Muskrats occasionally take fish, crayfish, and freshwater mussels. The Australian water rat is almost entirely carnivorous, preying on snails, fish, shellfish, frogs, and even waterfowl.

Mice will indeed eat cheese, and also bacon, peanut butter, bread crusts, and a wide range of other foods we humans should prefer keeping for ourselves. In a natural setting mouse food includes seeds, buds, shoots, fruits, nuts, and insects—for most species, at least. The grasshopper mouse of western North America hunts scorpions and even other rodents, killing them with a bite on the neck.

Why are mice so small?

In times past, certain rodents grew very large. An extinct beaver from North America was the size of a small black bear, and South America boasted a rodent that, to judge from its bones, was as big as a wild boar and had a head the size of a bull's. The largest of all living rodents is the capybara of South America, which may tip the scales at more than 100 pounds and measures 4 feet from its horselike muzzle to the base of its inconspicuous tail. Beavers may reach a body length of more than 3 feet and weigh almost 75 pounds. Porcupines and muskrats are somewhat smaller.

Mice and most other modern rodents, however, are small. Thanks to their diminutive size, each individual needs little food and can survive times

The world's largest rodent is South America's capybara, or water pig, which measures four feet long. It inhabits lowlands and has webbed feet.

of scarcity, when larger animals might starve. A small animal, though attractive to predators, can hide just about anywhere. Large animals mature late and bear relatively few young; small ones mature early and during their brief lives have many young.

What is a trade rat?

The globular nest of the pack rat, built of sticks, grass, bones, and anything else around, is decorated with a variety of bright, shiny objects—pebbles, bits of colored glass, coins, watches, eyeglasses, even false teeth. When pilfering such treasures under cover of darkness, pack rats often leave other objects, as if in exchange. Early settlers, who believed the rat was actually making a trade, called it the trade rat. Modern scientists are convinced that pack rats are neither turning in one object for another nor trying to conceal thefts by substituting different items for the stolen ones. Instead, the rat is simply picking up an object and dropping another because it cannot carry both.

Do rodent teeth ever stop growing?

Prominent chisellike incisors that grow throughout the animals' life are the rodents' outstanding feature. The very name *rodent*, in fact, means "one who gnaws." Rodents gnaw for two reasons—to eat, of course, and also to keep their front teeth from be-

Just About Anywhere Can Be Home

In terms of sheer numbers rodents are surely the most successful of all mammals. Sometimes helped by man, these toothy creatures have spread over the globe, from the Arctic to the tropics, from desert to rain forest, from mountain to lowland. Rodents live underground, at the surface, in trees, in water—and in buildings too.

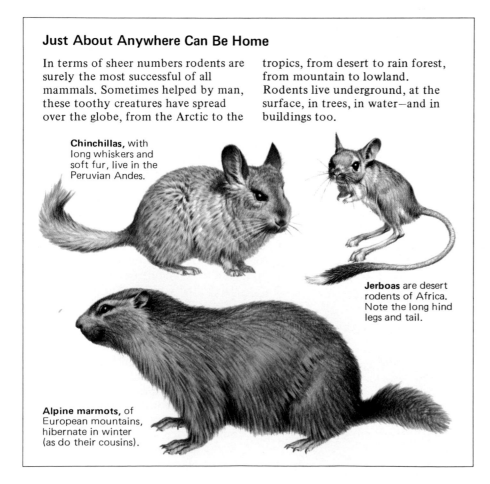

Chinchillas, with long whiskers and soft fur, live in the Peruvian Andes.

Jerboas are desert rodents of Africa. Note the long hind legs and tail.

Alpine marmots, of European mountains, hibernate in winter (as do their cousins).

coming overgrown. If a rodent fails to keep its incisors worn down, the teeth may eventually grow through the animal's throat or skull.

Rodent teeth are astonishingly durable. Mice and rats can gnaw through lead cable sheathing and concrete, and a porcupine is reported to have eaten its way through a glass bottle, perhaps because the bottle had traces of salt, from a human hand.

Not all animals with chisellike incisors are rodents. Once classified with mice and rats, rabbits and hares have been split off from their cousins be-

cause of differences in blood chemistry and the arrangement of their teeth. Many mouselike animals, such as shrews and moles, are not rodents either. Their mouths are filled with needlelike teeth, and they are entirely carnivorous. Rodents for the most part subsist on plants.

How smart are rodents?
European hamsters, which have formidable appetites, stock their burrows with as much as a bushel of potatoes and grain per hamster. The golden hamster—the familiar pet—does like-

wise when living in the wild. Beavers supply their lodges with lengths of saplings and branches, feeding in winter on the succulent bark. Chipmunks, squirrels, and pocket gophers store food in their dens or cache it outside.

Although by storing food for the winter animals seem to display foresight, scientists believe such activities are guided by instinct, not intelligence. But when it comes to solving problems, rodents do show some aptitude for learning. Squirrels not only learn how to beg for food but display an infuriating ability to circumvent devices put up to protect bird feeders from their raids. The most intelligent rodents are apparently the rats. In laboratories they have solved complex problems when motivated by rewards of food, and they appear to have a good deal of ingenuity. In one case, experimenters left large dog biscuits within reach of the rat cages. The rats grasped the bulky treats with their agile forepaws, tilted them on edge so that they would pass between the wires, and pulled them in—a neat example of an animal's ability to perceive spatial relations.

Which rodents bark and which ones whistle?
Squirrels chatter in high-pitched voices. Mice squeak. Porcupines growl—when confronting an enemy, that is; at other times they grunt, a fact that may account for their name, a variation of the Old French for "prickly pig." The capybaras of South America grunt like pigs too and show their contentment with low, clicking sounds. The gopherlike tuco-tuco, another South American creature, calls its name as it tunnels.

Other rodents communicate with different calls. Prairie dogs sound the alarm with sharp barks; the hoary marmot of the northern Rockies has a whistlelike call that carries as far as a mile. A number of rodents show anger by noisily grinding their teeth; the skunk-sized maned rat of East Africa will do so if merely looked at. The grasshopper mouse of western North America sometimes stands on its hind legs and howls like a miniature wolf. The cane rat of West Africa calls out incessantly—a metallic *boing*—as it makes nocturnal forays for food.

With bristling whiskers and prominent ears, the perky deer mouse looks ever so alert. This elfin creature, also called the white-footed mouse, eats fruit.

The Cat Clan

What sort of creature is a cat?
To the ordinary person, the word "cat" may conjure up images of soft fur and a gentle purr. The scientist more likely thinks of teeth. Cats have fewer teeth—no more than 30—than other carnivores. When hunting, they use their large canine teeth to seize and hold victims. Scissorlike premolars shear off chunks of flesh and bone. The cat's abrasive tongue rasps meat from bones. Acute hearing, large eyes, long whiskers, and retractable claws—they can be pulled in when running—are other feline traits.

There are 30-odd species in the cat clan, whose members range in size from 800-pound tigers to Asia's 3-pound rusty-spotted cat. Certain European and African wildcats are the species believed to be the closest relatives of our household friends.

How do cats hunt their prey?
Though one species, the Asian flat-headed cat, relies heavily on fruit, felines are predominantly meat eaters. Most often they hunt at night or in the early morning, making their kills from concealed locations. Such large cats as lions, tigers, jaguars, and leopards stalk the prey first, moving their supple bodies as close as they can without being detected. A sudden rush or leap brings down the victim, which is killed with a bite to the back of the head or throttled with a hold on the throat. The cheetah is the only cat that chases down its quarry, though—like most other cats—it lacks endurance and will give up a chase if the prey eludes it long enough.

Of all the big cats, only the lion hunts in groups. While one lioness circles to one side of a herd of zebra or other prey, several others distract the targets by advancing in the open from another angle. When the ambush is ready, a charge from the advancing lions moves the herd toward the waiting claws of the other. Lions often steal kills from other animals, especially hyenas and cheetahs. Except for the cheetah, all big cats scavenge as well as hunt.

What makes a man-eater?
The lion, tiger, jaguar, and leopard all have reputations as man-eaters. In most cases studied, the cat turned to killing people for one of three reasons. Some individuals were old or injured and unable to catch their usual prey. Occasionally they developed the man-eating habit because food was scarce, or they learned the habit from their mothers. Whatever the reasons, man is not a cat's natural prey.

Are lions the only cats that roar?
Some scientists separate cats into those that roar and those that do not. Only the big cats have an elastic ligament connecting the voice box to the skull. Lacking this, the small cats and the cheetah cannot roar.

Instead of roaring, the cougar, which is considered a small cat even

Like domestic cats, lions lick their fur. One lion often grooms another, cleaning parts they cannot reach themselves and also helping reinforce social ties.

Shown here in Florida, where it has nearly disappeared, the mountain lion ranges from Canada to southern South America. It is known by many names: cougar, catamount, panther, painter, puma.

though it may weigh more than 200 pounds, gives birdlike calls. Researchers doubt that it screams, as has sometimes been asserted. The cougar, also called mountain lion, panther, and puma, makes rumbling purrs indicating pleasure. Small cats purr while inhaling or exhaling; big cats purr only when exhaling.

Cheetahs make birdlike sounds too, including a "stutter call" that resembles the cooing of pigeons. The sounds are related to courtship, mating, and—with different inflections—communicating with the young. Myth has it that tigers imitate the call of their deer prey. In reality, the *pok* sound of tigers, similar to that made by certain deer, announces their presence at a kill before another animal intrudes.

Why do cats' eyes shine?
Research on domestic cats, which is believed to be valid for wild ones too, indicates that the feline eye is six times more sensitive to the blue end of the light spectrum than ours, and that it adjusts faster to darkness than does the human eye. Behind the cat's retina (the sensory membrane lining the eye) is a layer of highly reflective cells, which collects light from dim sources. It is this layer, called the tapetum, that makes cats' eyes glow when light shines on them.

The pupil of a cat's eye, through which light enters, is a compromise between the requirements of night vision and those of daylight. Generally, the big cats have round pupils and the small ones slit, or spindle-shaped, pupils (like those of domestic cats). A slit pupil can be wider when opened and narrower when closed.

Do black panthers really exist?
Cats are camouflaged creatures. The tiger's stripes work well in India's long grasses, while spots and rosettes on cheetahs, leopards, and jaguars imitate the play of light and shadow in a forest or on a plain. Occasionally, genetic mutation causes color and pattern to vary. Black panthers, once considered a separate species, are now thought to be melanistic leopards—ones with excess black pigment in the fur. In the right light the spot pattern, which is black against black rather than black on yellow, shows up. Black panthers are fairly common in India but rare in Africa. Cougars and jaguars sometimes have black fur too.

How well can cats climb trees?
Most small cats are excellent climbers. Asia's clouded leopard hunts in the treetops and runs headfirst down trunks. Equally acrobatic is the Latin American margay, which descends headfirst in a spiraling motion or leaps to the forest floor. Both species can

hang from limbs by the claws, using only one foot.

Big cats get up into the trees too. Using its strong, sharp claws, the African lion sometimes reaches a height of 20 feet above the ground. Forest-dwelling tigers have been reported nearly as high. None of the other large cats, however, approaches the leopard in climbing strength and agility. One 130-pound individual dragged a 200-pound young giraffe up a tree for safekeeping, feeding on its private cache for several days.

Which cats can swim?
Scientists believe that drinking water may not be as important to cats as to many other mammals, and some experts think that fresh meat contains enough fluid to slake a predator's thirst. Certain species do use water as a source of food. The jaguar and the jaguarundi, both New World species, hunt along riverbanks. Jaguars eat turtles and will sometimes take on an eight-foot alligator, breaking its neck and ripping open its hide.

Cats can usually swim if they have to, but their abilities and apparent interest in doing so vary. Lions dislike getting wet. Tigers, on the other hand, readily swim in pursuit of prey. They also jump into water to play or, on a hot day, soak for hours immersed up to their necks.

Wolves and Wild Dogs

Where do wild dogs live?

Except on Antarctica and many oceanic islands, wild dogs of one sort or another roam over most of the world's land areas. Even Australia, where marsupials abound, has the dingo. Scientists believe dingoes are descended from half-wild dogs that escaped from the camps of primitive people thousands of years ago and that have fended for themselves ever since. Australia also has red foxes, introduced from Europe.

Red foxes, in fact, are the most widespread of all wild dogs. Various species range through much of the Americas, Eurasia, and parts of Africa. Wolves, though less numerous, are also found over an immense area—across northern North America and Eurasia, with scattered populations as far south as Italy and Spain.

Wild canines tolerate a wide range of living conditions. The Arctic fox roves across tundra and ice packs in the Far North, while the small-eared dog prowls the humid jungles of Amazonia. Other species thrive in forests, deserts, grasslands, and on high, dry mountain slopes.

How big are wild dogs?

Wolves are the largest of the wild canines. A prime male can weigh in at 120 pounds or more, although the majority average 100 pounds or less. Most wild dogs are much smaller. Fifty pounds is big for a coyote; 15, for a red fox. Smallest of all is the fennec, a delicate little fox of the Sahara and Arabian deserts. It weighs only about three pounds.

Just as they differ in size, so the wild dogs are quite varied in appearance. Some, such as the African hunting dog and the maned wolf of South America, are lean and long-legged; others, like the raccoon dog of Eurasia and the South American bush dog, have chunky bodies and stubby legs. The snow-white Arctic fox and the bat-eared fox of Africa look much like other foxes. But the Arctic fox has tiny ears, the bat-eared fox enormous ones.

How do wild dogs hunt?

Wolves, red dogs (or dholes), and African hunting dogs are social creatures that live and hunt in packs. By joining forces to pursue and catch their prey, wolves, for example, can overtake and

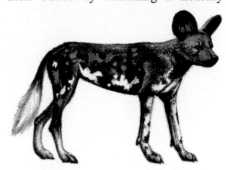

Hunting in packs, African wild dogs prey on antelopes and other animals.

kill animals as large as moose. However, recent studies have shown that members of a wolf pack show a keen perception of the vulnerability of their prospective victims. They do not risk their bones by attacking a healthy adult moose. The majority of all prey taken are old animals handicapped by physical ailments or other conditions, and those less than a year old.

Other dogs live alone or in small family groups. Coyotes may pair up for years or live a solitary life. But even lone coyotes team up in killing prey that is too large or fast for one alone to overcome.

Why do wolves howl?

Lone wolves howl to keep in touch with other members of the pack, but sometimes the entire pack gathers together and howls as though singing in chorus. Scientists are not sure of the reasons for these noisy get-togethers; it is believed they may serve to strengthen social ties among members of the pack. Many other sounds communicate information in the highly organized wolf pack, which is headed by a dominant male and female. A growl by the dominant male keeps his subordinates in tow. Brisk barks warn of danger. And a nursing female "speaks" to her pups in soothing whimpers.

Body language is also important. Pack members greet the dominant male with a nuzzling, nipping ceremony. He in turn may assert his dominance with a gentle but unmistakable nip on the neck of a pack member. Tail, ear, and head movements are among the many other signals used by members of the pack.

A dominant male announces his authority with a mock bite on the neck of a subordinate wolf, which assumes a submissive stance.

Group howling sessions by wolves seem to be happy occasions, accompanied by much milling about and tail wagging.

The kit fox of western North America is typical of the dogs that live and hunt alone. Prowling by night, it listens and sniffs for traces of mice and other small animals. When it detects a victim, the fox usually catches it with a sudden pounce, before the prey animal realizes what is happening.

Do all dogs eat meat?

Just as many pet dogs enjoy vegetables and other table scraps, most of their wild relatives dine on varied fare. A few, including the African hunting dog, the red dog (dhole), and the gray wolf, feed almost entirely on meat—although in a pinch even these may take vegetable matter. Coyotes vary their diet with berries and other fruits. The maned wolf is even more versatile; sugarcane, nuts, and fruit form an important part of its diet.

The red fox is another opportunist. Mice and other small rodents are the mainstay of its diet, but it also eats beetles, crickets, and grasshoppers, as well as fruits and other plant materials. The Arctic fox dines on fish and sometimes even seaweed. But the crab-eating fox of South America, despite its name, does not specialize in crabs; it eats a variety of small animals and—when it can find them—enjoys turtle eggs as well.

In typical canine fashion, a red fox pauses on its rounds to scratch an itch.

Why do dogs bury bones?

Domestic dogs retain many of the habits of their wild ancestors. One is the tendency to bury bones, a holdover from the instinctive urge of many species to store food. A red fox with more food than it can eat will dig a hole and bury the surplus for later use. The Arctic fox, which has to cope with worse winters than any other dog, frequently caches food during the summer months, then retrieves its hoard when the hard times of winter hit. Oddest of all is the pampas fox of South America. It piles up all sorts of inedibles, from twigs to bits of cloth, and stores them away like a pack rat, a strange habit that no one has been able to explain.

Can dogs climb trees?

Unlike cats, most dogs have claws that are rather blunt, more suited for running than for holding prey or climbing trees. But there are exceptions. The corsac fox of Asia is an agile climber. So is the American gray fox, which has claws that are sharper and more hooked than those of other dogs. The gray fox often climbs trees to scan the countryside, eat fruit, or escape enemies. Sometimes it even dens among the branches.

If it finds a tilted trunk or a sloping branch that leads aloft, the gray fox simply runs up from ground level. But it also climbs nearly vertical trees by clinging to the trunk with its forepaws and shoving with its hind feet. Once in the treetops, the fox easily leaps from limb to limb. To get back down to earth, it scrambles headfirst.

Are foxes really smart?

The red fox has long been a symbol of cleverness and cunning, and in fact often acts in ways that seem extremely crafty. Trappers seeking red foxes must sterilize their equipment to rid it of human odors, or the foxes will not come near. The foxes also manage to dig up hidden traps and set them off without being caught. When hunted by hounds, they often double back on their own tracks or run along fences or fallen logs to throw the dogs off their scent. Red foxes also manage to fare quite well in heavily populated areas, including big cities. They have even been known to use a pedestrian underpass rather than cross a highway.

On the other hand, red foxes can be extremely reckless. They often come running in response to an imitation of their bark, regardless of danger. They readily return to areas where they have been heavily hunted in the past and frequently pass up safe hiding places while being pursued. So whether or not the red fox is especially intelligent is an open question. But certainly its feats have enriched our folklore and literature.

Of Seals and Sea Lions

How are seals different from sea lions?

Few mammals are so adapted to aquatic life as the seals. Seals, sea lions, and walruses, together known as the pinnipeds ("fin-footed"), have webbed flippers instead of paws or feet. Their bodies are streamlined and covered with short, dense fur. Valves keep water out of their ears and nostrils when they dive.

True seals, the group that includes the harbor, leopard, and elephant seals, are the most aquatic. On land their hind flippers are useless, and so

Sea lions and fur seals have ear flaps and can turn their hind limbs forward.

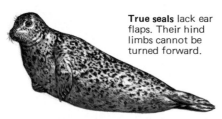

True seals lack ear flaps. Their hind limbs cannot be turned forward.

the animals wriggle or clumsily hump along. Sea lions, fur seals, and walruses can turn the hind flippers under the body, using them as legs for moving on land. Another difference becomes visible when you observe the animals at close range (say, in an aquarium). Sea lions and fur seals have small ear flaps. True seals, along with the walruses, have none at all.

Do all seals live in the sea?

More than a thousand miles from the nearest ocean, large numbers of seals spend their entire lives in Siberia's mile-deep Lake Baikal. The Caspian seal lives in the brackish waters of the Caspian Sea, and a few harbor seals inhabit Canadian lakes. All other seals are marine. Of them, only the Mediterranean and Hawaiian monk seals live in warm seas. The one species that lives near the equator, the Galápagos fur seal, thrives there because of the cold Humboldt Current.

Where can you find a million seals in one place?

Seals gather on the shore to breed, sometimes in enormous numbers. On the Pribilof Islands off Alaska, the summer seal population may reach a million. Male fur seals arrive at the Pribilofs in May, and the most vigorous ones—usually those about 10 years old—immediately claim portions of the beach. Old, battle-scarred bulls and those still too young to win in the breeding competition form isolated bachelor groups. From time to time a young bull tries to take over a territory. The fights are savage, but rarely is a combatant killed. The loser merely returns to, or becomes part of, the bachelor group.

In late June or early July the females, or cows, arrive and are herded into harems. Though a bull may command a harem of 50 or more, he must be on guard constantly to prevent other beachmasters from stealing his cows. Protecting harems from rivals is so time-consuming that bulls subsist on stored fat rather than taking time to catch and eat fish and squid.

Pregnant from the previous season's mating, each cow gives birth to a single pup within a week of her arrival. The pups grow rapidly on their mothers' rich milk and can swim within three weeks. By October, the seals go back to the sea.

How deep can seals dive?

Most seals can stay underwater for 15 or 20 minutes before surfacing for air, and during that time they can dive several hundred feet. California sea lions have been trained to retrieve objects from depths greater than 500 feet, but the champion diver is the Weddell seal of the Antarctic. Weddell seals have remained underwater for nearly an hour, and pressure gauges attached to them have recorded dives exceeding 1,800 feet.

Being mammals, seals need air; they cannot take in oxygen from the water. Seal blood has about five times as much oxygen-carrying hemoglobin as human blood; that means the ani-

Elephants of the Sea

Largest of all the seals, the huge elephant seal may reach a length of 20 feet, measure nearly 15 feet around its middle, and weigh as much as 3½ tons. Its name comes not only from its size but also from the male's elephantlike trunk. Though normally the snout hangs limply over the mouth, at mating time the male inflates it with air, lifting it straight up or curving it down into the mouth, where it amplifies his roars.

Despite their size, elephant seals are graceful swimmers and can dive to depths of more than 200 feet. One species breeds in the Pacific, mainly off California and Mexico; the other, in subantarctic waters.

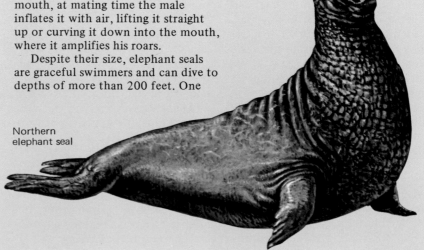

Northern elephant seal

mals take a large amount of oxygen with them when they dive. During dives, the heart rate slows to 15 beats a minute or fewer, significantly lowering the amount of oxygen the seal requires. The body temperature also drops. Strange as it may seem, a seal expels most of the air in its lungs before it dives. This is believed to prevent it from getting the bends.

How do seals stay alive under the ice?
When ice begins to cover the polar seas, seals chew holes big enough to allow them to poke their snouts—and hence their nostrils—into the air. As the ice thickens, the seal continues chewing to keep the breathing hole open. Each seal may have a dozen or more air holes, which it sometimes shares with others. Seals also breathe through natural cracks in the ice and take advantage of air pockets where the ice has buckled up.

Still somewhat of a mystery is how seals locate their air holes when coming up from a dive. Since they have no trouble finding breathing holes in the dark, it is believed that the animals use echolocation—sound signals similar to those of dolphins and bats. During the daytime they may perceive the holes as slightly lighter areas in the ice.

Do crab-eating seals really eat crabs?
All seals eat animals rather than plants. Although most make their meals of fish, squid, or octopuses, some—the crab-eating seal of the Antarctic, for one—rely on other sorts of food. Despite its name, this seal does not eat crabs. Instead, it subsists largely on krill, the shrimplike creatures that abound in cold polar seas.

Who eats seals?
Few predators are big enough to tackle seals, but large sharks and killer whales do regularly feast on them, particularly the vulnerable young. Leopard seals are notorious killers of other kinds of seals (they also eat penguins and fish); polar bears eat seals too. In rare instances seal pups on the ice have become victims of foxes, wolves, and bald eagles. But the seals' greatest enemy over the years has been humans, who have hunted them for their fur, oil, and meat.

A walrus's tusks—marvelously modified teeth that grow to more than two feet long—are weapons, dredges, and ice picks. One tusk on this walrus broke while in use.

Why does a walrus have tusks?
Just as the land has its tuskers, the elephants, so does the sea. A big bull walrus of the Far North may weigh as much as 3,000 pounds, and its tusks may measure more than 2 feet long and 10 inches around at the base. The female, weighing about half as much, has proportionately smaller tusks. Those of the young barely project beyond the lips.

Walrus tusks are elongated teeth—specifically, the upper canines. (Elephant tusks are modified incisors rather than canines.) At one time it was believed that a walrus used its tusks to dredge or rake the bottom for clams and other shellfish. Though this is now questioned, the impressive teeth are known to serve as ice axes when the animal hauls itself out of the water and also as chisels to open air holes in the ice. Tusks become formidable—and sometimes lethal—weapons in repelling polar bear attacks.

Hooves, Horns, and Antlers

What's the difference between horns and antlers?

From Africa's vast herds of antelope to the moose of northern forests, animals with prominent headgear are common throughout the world. Deer, moose, caribou, and elk all have antlers—solid, bony structures that usually develop branches and tines. Antlers are not permanent. They fall off after the mating season and grow back within several months.

Antelope, buffalo, sheep, cattle, and goats bear horns rather than antlers. A horn is made up of a bony core covered by hard tissue more like that of fingernails than bone. Growing throughout an animal's life, horns can be an awesome sight. Gazelle horns stretch for nearly three feet; a water buffalo's, for more than six. Bighorns in the Rockies have massive, curving spirals. Nyalas and greater kudus, two African antelopes, carry magnificent twisted horns. Of all the horned creatures, only North America's pronghorn sheds its headgear annually—and only the outer sheath, at that. The bony core is permanent.

American elk, like European red deer, have antlers with many points.

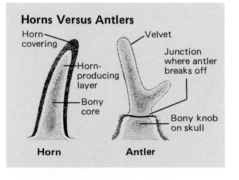

Horns Versus Antlers

Horn covering
Horn-producing layer
Bony core

Horn

Velvet
Junction where antler breaks off
Bony knob on skull

Antler

Bison, or buffalo, are massive animals with horns and a woolly "cape."

What good are antlers?

To the human eye, horns and antlers look like an excellent defense against predators. But though some creatures—musk oxen, mountain goats, and occasionally deer—do use their headgear to fight off foes, protection is not the primary purpose. Instead, animals use horns and antlers against their own kind, threatening, ramming, and pushing them—even fencing with them—to resolve questions of territory, strength, and sexual dominance.

During the breeding season male bison lock horns, keeping their heads together while pushing one another around. Dall sheep literally bash their heads together, then pause to compare horns; only rams bearing horns of equal size will compete intensely. Red deer and others may lock antlers so tightly that they cannot disengage—a test of strength ending in starvation for both.

Horns and antlers are convenient for other purposes, including scratching one's back and digging up food. Scientists have also suggested that the growing horns serve to cool an animal, allowing heat from their blood vessels to escape to the outside.

When don't deer have antlers?

Deer shed their antlers after the mating season—in the Northern Hemisphere, in early winter. A layer of specialized skin, called velvet, nourishes the growth of antlers and guides the formation and branching of tines. In the velvet is an intricate network of nerve fibers, which makes the tissue highly sensitive and is thought to keep the animal from treating its developing antlers too roughly. Antlers grow extraordinarily fast beneath the velvet—in elk and caribou, an estimated inch every two days. Nerve growth must keep pace, and nerve fibers in these animals' antlers are believed by some scientists to grow faster than those in any other mammal.

Not all deer develop antlers. In most species—the white-tailed and the red deer, for instance—only the males carry the headgear, using it to fight against rivals. In musk deer, however, neither the male nor the female has antlers. Serving somewhat the same function as antlers are three-inch-long tusks on the males.

Of what medicinal value are horns and antlers?

For centuries antlers have been gathered in Asia and sold to herbalists, who extract substances from the velvet by drying, grinding, and bleaching. The antlers' reputation for curative powers may indeed be deserved: in them scientists have found a number of hormones thought to help heal wounds and alleviate some symptoms of old age. Rhinoceros horns, made of filaments more typical of hooves than horns, are widely believed to have other powers, as aphrodisiacs. There is no medical evidence to support this myth, which has resulted in the near-extinction of rhinos in Asia. Demand for deer antlers has also pressed certain species.

What keeps fawns safe from attack?

No young animal is entirely safe, but each species has developed ways of improving the odds. Of critical importance to a baby that stays put is camouflage—the spotted coat of the fawn, for instance. In addition, among hoofed animals the mother licks her baby dry from head to toe, which removes most of the baby's scent. Predators often sense the presence of prey by smell rather than sight.

How big is a moose?

Moose, known in Europe as elk, are the world's largest deer. (The pudu of South America is the smallest.) Their antlers may spread across six feet; standing six feet at the shoulders, an adult may weigh as much as 1,500 pounds. Moose do not reach such a hefty size by eating meat. Like all hoofed animals, they are plant eaters, browsing on leaves and twigs and wading into lakes and rivers in search of water plants. The moose snips off vegetation with its tongue and uses its heavy lips to manipulate food.

How fast is the pronghorn?

Pronghorns are designed for running. Their lungs and windpipe are large; their hooves are twice as big as a deer's and the heart twice the size of that of a domestic sheep of comparable weight. Just how fast pronghorns can run is subject to debate. Some sources report top speeds of 40, 50, or even 60 miles an hour in short bursts, with a sustained pace of about 30 miles an hour. With the possible exception of a racehorse, the pronghorn is North America's fastest mammal. Among its relatives only India's blackbuck, which is said to have outrun cheetahs on occasion, challenges its swiftness.

For pronghorns, blackbucks, and other hoofed animals, running when threatened is a basic rule of survival. When faced with a lion or other carnivore, even the powerfully built Cape buffalo, which can weigh several thousand pounds, prefers to flee. The ability to run is, in many species, present virtually from birth. A baby wilde-

Pronghorns lose the forked outer covering of their horns at the end of the breeding season every year. The bony core remains.

beest, or gnu, can stand up within 10 to 20 minutes, and a little pronghorn can outrun a human adult a mere hour after birth. Adapted for running, the foot of such an animal is a characteristic cloven hoof. Angled so the creature runs on tiptoes, the hoof allows greater speed, traction, and maneuverability.

How do deer talk with one another?

Deer can be noisy animals at times. In the breeding season sika deer in Asia whistle; red deer and elk proclaim their presence by bugling—a combination of roars, whistles, and grunts that can be heard for several miles.

Not all mating signals of hoofed animals are spoken ones. The male musk ox announces the onset of mating by emitting a musky scent from facial glands. When the breeding season begins, the prominent nose of the male saiga antelope, a curious-looking creature that lives near the Russian-Chinese border, swells like a balloon.

Alarm too is often communicated by means other than sound. When a white-tailed deer is startled, the tail snaps up like a flag. Pronghorns use both visual and chemical alarm signals. Long white hairs on the rump spread out into an oval "flash patch" that fellow pronghorns can observe from miles away. Those receiving the signal immediately pass along the alarm. To alert animals not in the line of sight, the pronghorn releases a strong scent—one that even we humans, with our rather weak olfactory sense, can smell a hundred yards away.

Moose are the world's largest deer, and antlers on the males are of a size to match. Some measure more than six feet across.

Mammal Oddities

What has a tail like a beaver and a bill like a duck?

When European scientists first saw specimens of the Australian platypus in 1797, they were convinced that the skins were a craftily contrived hoax. For the two-foot-long platypus is indeed an improbable creature. Covered with dense fur as soft as a mole's, it has a ducklike snout, webbed feet, a beaverlike tail, and, in the male, venomous spurs on the hind legs. Most astonishing, this strange little mammal hatches from an egg.

At dawn and at dusk, the platypus emerges from its streamside burrow to feed. Using its tail as a rudder, it swims close to the stream bottom and probes with its soft, sensitive bill for crayfish, worms, and other creatures hidden in the mud.

Once a year the female lays one or two eggs and then incubates them in a grass-lined nest in her burrow. Although she lacks teats, the young are able to feed by lapping up milk that oozes from her mammary glands onto the hair on her belly. The world's only other egg-laying mammals are echidnas, or spiny anteaters, found in Australia and a few nearby islands.

How slow is a sloth?

Several species of sloths inhabit the tropical forests of Central and South America. They spend most of their lives high in the treetops, hanging upside down from branches. Long, curved claws hooked over the limbs keep these animals from falling as they munch on leaves, fruits, and twigs. Sloths move along the branches at a snail's pace, averaging only about 6 feet per minute. Even when they are in a hurry, they can manage only about 12 feet per minute. Sloths are slower still on the rare occasions when they descend to earth. After crawling backwards down their tree trunks, they can scarcely drag themselves across the ground as they seek another tree to climb.

What are sea cows?

Except for whales, sea cows are the only mammals that spend their entire lives in water. Two types of these big, gentle, slow-moving plant eaters—manatees and dugongs—live in warm, shallow seas, estuaries, and rivers.

A three-toed sloth climbs laboriously up a tree. Long hooklike claws afford a firm grip when it assumes its usual posture—hanging upside down from a branch.

Manatees are found on both sides of the Atlantic. Dugongs dwell mainly on the fringes of the Indian Ocean and the nearby South Pacific.

Both types, up to 10 feet or so in length and weighing several hundred pounds, have torpedo-shaped bodies with big rounded heads and small piglike eyes. Their forelimbs have been modified into flippers and their broad flattened tails serve as rudders.

Despite their homeliness, sea cows are also called sirens, for they are believed to have inspired the mermaid myth.

How do anteaters catch ants?

Of the three kinds of anteaters that inhabit the New World tropics, the most impressive is the giant anteater. It is some six feet long and adorned with a spectacular plumelike tail. Like its smaller kin, it uses its powerful claws to rip open ant and termite nests. It then pokes its slender snout into the opening and laps up the little insects with a long wormlike tongue that is coated with sticky saliva. It consumes as many as 30,000 termites and ants in a single day.

In Africa the unrelated aardvark leads a similar life. (Its name is Afrikaans for "earth pig.") Looking like an animal made from spare parts, the aardvark has a piglike snout, donkey-

The giant anteater has a tongue nearly two feet long.

like ears, a stout body, and a thick tail like a kangaroo's. It too tears apart termite nests, then picks up the insects with its long thin tongue.

Why do hippos yawn?

The name hippopotamus means "river horse," and these amphibious giants of tropical Africa do indeed spend much of their time in the water of rivers, lakes, and ponds. They emerge at night to graze on grasses and other land plants, but pass most of the daylight hours floating in the water with only their ears and the top of the head visible. Their frequent yawns bare their big teeth and are threat gestures rather than signs of boredom.

Hippos can swim surprisingly well considering their short legs and bulky bodies. (Males may weigh as much as four tons.) The great beasts, in fact, are agile swimmers from the moment of birth; young hippos are born underwater and swim even before they walk.

How long are porcupine quills?

The common North American porcupine wears an arsenal of some 30,000 needle-sharp quills on its back and tail. Varying from one to as much as five inches in length, they usually make any intrusion on the porky's

privacy a painful experience. Only the weasellike fisher and a few other predators have learned that the porcupine is highly vulnerable if it can be flipped on its back to expose its soft, spineless belly.

Contrary to folklore, the porcupine cannot shoot its quills. But it can and does lash its tail and so drive them deeply into the snout of an attacker. The quills are tipped with backward-pointing barbs. Not only are they difficult to remove; if left alone they actually work their way deeper into the flesh.

Other porcupines have quills of varying lengths. Most impressive are those of the Old World crested porcupine. It bristles with a formidable array of miniature harpoons, each one up to 18 inches long.

Which mammals wear suits of armor?

Among the strangest-looking of all mammals are the ant- and termite-eating pangolins of Africa and Asia. Long-nosed, long-tailed, and slender, they are covered with hard, loosely overlapping scales and look vaguely like oversized animated pinecones. A pangolin foils would-be predators by curling up into a tight scaly ball, with head and soft underside tucked safely inside.

But the best known of the armored mammals are the insect-eating armadillos of the Americas. The smallest ones, the fairy armadillos, or pichicia-

The nine-banded armadillo ranges from Argentina to the southern United States.

gos, are only about 6 inches long; the largest, the giant armadillo of Brazil, is 4 feet long and weighs more than 100 pounds.

The armadillo's armor consists of bony plates, usually arranged in neat rows over most of the head and body. When danger threatens, most species first try to hide, often by burrowing quickly into the ground. But in an emergency, many resort to the same

Tiny Tarsiers Are Champion Jumpers

Tarsiers are primitive primates that inhabit the jungles of the Philippines and nearby islands. The largest are only about 6 inches long with 10-inch tails. Active by night, tarsiers sleep during the day, clinging to upright branches. They are agile jumpers in their nocturnal pursuit of insects, leaping as much as six feet from tree to tree and managing to cling even to vertical tree trunks. On the ground they hop like frogs and sometimes cover five feet in a single jump.

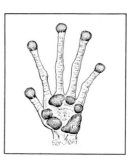

Adhesive disks on their toes help tarsiers cling to all sorts of surfaces.

tactic as pangolins: they roll themselves up into a ball, completely protected by their hard outer shell.

Are pandas as playful as they seem?

Pai-hsiung, the Chinese name for the giant panda, means "white bear." And these strikingly patterned black and white creatures, up to 5 feet long and weighing as much as 300 pounds, are indeed bearlike in build and shuffling gait. (Some scientists have said that they are members of the bear family; others, that they are more closely related to raccoons.) Because of their lovable looks, pandas are popular zoo animals, and their undeniably playful antics add to their appeal.

Unknown by Westerners until 1869, the pandas now live only in a very limited region in China. There they lead solitary lives, except when they meet to breed, and spend much of their time munching on bamboo shoots. Because of their rarity in the wild, these comical creatures enjoy full government protection in China.

Invaluable Animals

Where did pet dogs come from?
Though the origins of the partnership between man and dog are lost in prehistory, archaeological finds in Siberia suggest it is more than 10,000 years old—the oldest long-term relationship between animals and man. The main ancestor of the domestic dog is believed to have been the wolf. A now-extinct species of wild dog from Russia may also have contributed to the bloodlines of man's best friend.

Scientists believe that the dog-man relationship began in various ways. Wolves almost certainly scavenged around campsites; people may even have tossed them scraps and bones. Humans certainly kept orphaned and abandoned cubs as pets. During centuries of association with man, the wild animals gradually developed into dogs. In time, man learned how to breed them purposefully, selecting stock for particular qualities. The oldest known breed, developed before 3000 B.C. in the Middle East, is the saluki, a hunting dog similar to the greyhound.

Why do sheep have such curly wool?
Wild sheep have straight hair and only a scant undercoat of wool—a far cry from the farm animals' fleece. Curly

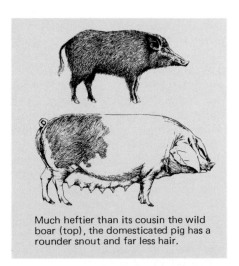

Much heftier than its cousin the wild boar (top), the domesticated pig has a rounder snout and far less hair.

wool probably appeared as a chance mutation several thousand years ago and was then selectively bred into sheep by man. Another change is that, over the centuries, domestic sheep have stopped shedding their wool in spring, as their ancestors did. Man now takes care of its removal.

Dogs and pigs have shorter faces than their wild relatives. Domestic pigs are roly-poly; wild ones are tough and lean. Dogs come in a whole range of hues, with only a few breeds retaining the gray-brown coloration of their wolf ancestors. Most other domesticated animals have experienced similar changes over time.

Is taming an animal the same as domesticating it?
A performing dolphin, a circus lion, and a pet raccoon are all more or less tame, but none is domesticated. A fully domesticated animal is one that lives with man, is protected and in most cases fed by him, and breeds in captivity, usually under man's control. Its movements are controlled: for example, sheep are driven from pasture to pasture by shepherds instead of being left to wander on their own.

There are exceptions, of course. The domesticated elephants of Asia are not bred in captivity; rather, they are captured in the wild and then trained. Many house cats roam freely and breed indiscriminately. At the other extreme is the mink, raised in confinement for generations but in no way tame.

Can domesticated animals do without us?
Science fiction scenarios contemplating the destruction of mankind sometimes involve ferocious packs of domestic animals gone wild. In fact, however, the chance that a domesticated species could survive without our help is by no means good. Dogs, for example, might make it, with the exception of such specialized breeds as toy poodles, dachshunds, and great Danes. The breeds that survived would be those most like the "natural dog" or its wild wolf ancestor—the German shepherd, for instance.

In the western United States, mustang horses and wild burros, descendants of animals imported by Spanish colonizers, have thrived so well that, with their predators eliminated, they have become a nuisance—a fate all too common for imported species. The famed Texas longhorn, descended from stray Spanish cattle, proliferated in the Texas scrublands and became the original basis of the ranching in-

dustry in the West. Like the more specialized dogs, however, such breeds as Percheron horses and Jersey cows would soon disappear without attention from human caretakers.

Why don't people keep koalas as pets?
Chickens and pigs for food, sheep for food and clothing, horses for transportation and sport, dogs for sport, companionship, and guard duty—domesticated animals perform a variety of services for their human keepers. Many different creatures have been tamed, but only a relative handful, including cattle, goats, chickens, and ducks, are raised globally. Donkeys, camels, water buffaloes, elephants, and llamas are of regional importance.

At various times people have tried to keep such unlikely creatures as antelope, moose, foxes, and hyenas, but

Exotic Beasts of Burden

For centuries elephants have pulled plows, hauled timber, carried people and goods, and performed in circuses.

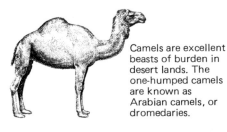

Camels are excellent beasts of burden in desert lands. The one-humped camels are known as Arabian camels, or dromedaries.

they proved to be not entirely satisfactory as associates. To be a successful candidate an animal must be tractable enough for man to manage; it must be able to tolerate people; and, generally, it must be able to reproduce in captivity. Domesticated animals have to be reasonably easy and inexpensive to feed and care for. And, of course, there must be a demand for the creature or its products.

The American bison, or buffalo, is too aggressive and powerful to be raised in large numbers for meat and leather. Zebras, trained to pull carriages, failed because they were too intractable for general use. The cuddly koala would surely be a popular pet,

Evidence that animals have been domesticated for thousands of years, the wall of an Egyptian tomb shows cattle being milked.

but it can live only on a special—and expensive—eucalyptus-leaf diet.

What are some exotic uses of animals?

The ancient Egyptians attempted to domesticate many animals, including cats, baboons, and gazelles, but undoubtedly their most bizarre enterprise involved raising hyenas for meat. A famous tomb painting from about 2500 B.C. shows a pair of hyenas being held down on their backs while slaves force food down their throats to fatten them up. The ancient Egyptians would also drive herds of pigs across fields at planting time. Rooting in the soil with their snouts, the pigs turned over the soil as efficiently as the crude plows and digging sticks of the time. The pigs also manured the soil as they plodded along, and their hoofprints made holes the right depth for planting grain.

Among the other animals put to esoteric uses are the geese brought into cotton and strawberry fields to eat up unwanted plants. For centuries cormorants, long-necked birds related to the pelican, have been used in the Orient to catch fish. In medieval England, pigs were trained for the hunt (commoners were forbidden to keep hunting dogs). In France today pigs are used to locate truffles, the prized fungi that grow entirely underground.

They Serve Us Well

Cows, horses, sheep, pigs, goats—many hoofed animals have been domesticated. Cattle are usually bred for milk or meat. Horses have been bred for various purposes too. There are now more than 200 kinds.

Guernsey cow   Shetland pony   Clydesdale horse

Wildlife in Danger

How many kinds of animals are extinct?

In some ways, extinction is part of the natural scheme of things, for species have been vanishing virtually since life began. While it is impossible to know exactly how many kinds of animals have disappeared, scientists estimate that they amount to perhaps 90 percent of all the species that have ever lived.

At certain times in the earth's history, moreover, the rate of extinction has accelerated. The pace quickened some 65 million years ago, when the dinosaurs all disappeared. And the

Mighty dinosaurs once ruled the earth. But all died out from natural causes some 65 million years ago.

Tyrannosaurus

rate has jumped again in modern times. Since 1600, more than 200 species of mammals and birds have died out, along with countless other creatures, large and small.

A major problem today is that humans are able to change the natural environment so rapidly that many kinds of animals are unable to adapt to the altered living conditions. If we could control these forces of change, perhaps they would pose less of a threat to wildlife.

Does hunting endanger wildlife?

In the past, unregulated killing of wildlife for various purposes did indeed contribute to the extinction of species. The great auk, a flightless seabird of the North Atlantic, was killed so relentlessly for food and fish bait that by 1844 it had vanished from the earth. Slaughter for hides and meat played a major role in the extinction of

the quagga, a South African zebra, and in the last century the North American bison was nearly exterminated for similar reasons. Killing for commercial and subsistence purposes continues to threaten various cats, whales, sea turtles, and certain other types of wildlife.

Such slaughter is no longer considered hunting. Today hunting in many countries is a legally controlled activity in which the taking of meat and fur are secondary values. Hunting is restricted to certain species, and the animals are harvested under regulations designed to limit the annual kill to a number that will be replaced in the following breeding season.

What is the worst threat to wildlife?

Late in the 19th century, on an island off New Zealand, the lighthouse keeper's cat killed a dozen or so small birds within just a few weeks. Too late, they were identified as a species of wren unique to the island. The cat had killed them all.

Domestic Animals Can Spell Danger for Wildlife

Man's animals, roving free, pose a threat to native wildlife in many parts of the world. By competing for food and living space, sheep, goats, cattle, pigs, and other domestic livestock can gradually crowd wild species out of existence.

Overgrazing, especially by goats, can even transform once-productive pastures into wastelands. The wild animals shown at the right are among the many kinds that are threatened by domestic livestock on the loose.

"As dead as the dodo" is no mere figure of speech. The last of the big birds were killed about 1680.

Seldom, however, does a species vanish from a single cause. Dodoes—flightless birds the size of turkeys—once thrived on the Indian Ocean island of Mauritius. Many were killed for meat, but the big, ground-nesting birds suffered even more from rats and pigs that ate their eggs. Even if they had not been hunted, wolves and tigers would have declined in numbers because so many humans have moved

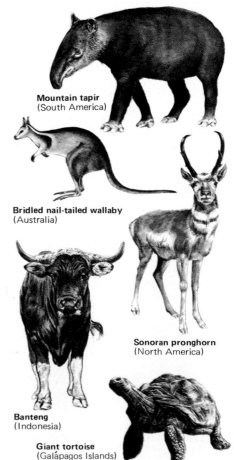

Mountain tapir
(South America)

Bridled nail-tailed wallaby
(Australia)

Sonoran pronghorn
(North America)

Banteng
(Indonesia)

Giant tortoise
(Galápagos Islands)

into their domains and destroyed the wilderness these big predators need.

Destruction of habitat is, in fact, the greatest threat of all to the world's wildlife. Overgrazing by livestock, pollution of air and water, the felling of forests and construction of towns and factories—these are the kinds of things that most effectively squeeze wild animals out of existence.

Which species is in the most trouble?

There are many ways to judge the degree to which a species is imperiled. The most obvious is by numbers. The echo parakeet of the Indian Ocean island of Mauritius probably numbers only about half a dozen birds—mainly as a result of habitat destruction. The Javan rhinoceros, another critically endangered species, has dwindled to only a few dozen individuals, harassed by poaching and the elimination of the deep forests it inhabits.

Extinction, however, is not just a numbers game. The Tokyo bitterling, a small minnow, still numbers at least a thousand, yet it is very much in danger. Urban sprawl and pollution threaten to destroy the few tiny streams in the Tokyo area that are the only home of the species.

What is being done to save wildlife?

International agreements play an important role in protecting endangered wildlife. Scores of countries have agreed to prohibit trade in the hides of threatened species such as the cheetah and the snow leopard, or in live animals such as the rare imperial parrot from the Caribbean island of Dominica. Another international agreement attempts to control the hunting of whales.

Private organizations such as the World Wildlife Fund and the International Union for the Conservation of Nature and Natural Resources also are working to protect wildlife. Their activities range from establishing parks and reservations to breeding wild animals in captivity. Educating the public is all-important.

Private conservation groups, for example, helped the Peruvian government establish a reserve in the Andes for the vicuña. This little relative of the llama had been almost exterminated for the sake of its fine wool.

Three Threatened Birds on the Rebound

A helping hand from humans has brought many a threatened species back from the verge of extinction. The nene, a native Hawaiian goose, was once hunted almost out of existence; breeding the survivors in captivity produced enough offspring to replenish the wild population. North America's wild turkey suffered from overhunting and habitat destruction; capturing and transplanting the remaining birds have restored the turkey to most of its former range. Pesticides were the brown pelican's problem. DDT in its diet so weakened its eggshells that the birds were unable to reproduce. When DDT was banned, the birds began to breed successfully again.

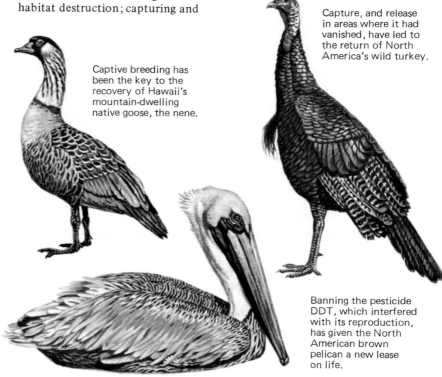

Captive breeding has been the key to the recovery of Hawaii's mountain-dwelling native goose, the nene.

Capture, and release in areas where it had vanished, have led to the return of North America's wild turkey.

Banning the pesticide DDT, which interfered with its reproduction, has given the North American brown pelican a new lease on life.

With protection from poachers and maintenance of their habitat, the animals gradually increased in numbers and some have been captured and transplanted to other parts of the country. In time there may be enough vicuñas for some to be safely harvested for their pelts, and the wool sold for the benefit of the local people.

Standing stiffly on a mound, a male vicuña proclaims ownership of his territory.

How can individuals help?

People can help protect wildlife in simple, direct ways. They can maintain a bird feeding station, confine the family dog at night so that it cannot harass deer and other wild animals, or put a bell on the cat to warn the birds it stalks. They can also act in indirect ways—by refusing to buy products made from rare animals, by becoming aware of events that affect wildlife in their own communities and around the world, and by prodding lawmakers to pass sound conservation legislation. And they can join forces with thousands of other citizens in supporting organizations that are devoted to the preservation of nature and of all the wild creatures with whom we share our planet.

Flamingoes, scarlet ibises, egrets, and other long-legged waders share the bounty of food in a Venezuelan lagoon.

MANY WORLDS OF LIFE

Desert Animals

Are deserts really deserted?

By definition, a desert is an area able to support relatively little life, and it is indeed true that parts of some deserts are barren wastelands. Most deserts, however, play host to a surprising variety of both plants and animals.

During the heat of midday, a visitor may see nothing more than a few birds and perhaps occasional lizards or insects. But as the air begins to cool toward evening, the desert comes to life. Jerboas, foxes, snakes, ground squirrels, and a host of other creatures emerge from hiding and begin to feed. Bats and owls wing through the night sky seeking prey. Another burst of activity comes at daybreak. Then, as the sun begins to rise in the sky, the lull descends once again over the seemingly deserted desert.

What do desert animals eat?

Predators—lizards, snakes, jackals, foxes, hawks, and the like—are fairly common in deserts. But as in every habitat, the most abundant creatures are the plant eaters.

Hordes of insects feast on the desert plants, especially after rains, when dormant vegetation comes back to life. Antelopes, camels, and other grazers munch on the tough stems and leaves of shrubby plants and the juicy stems of succulents. Some rodents gnaw on fleshy bulbs and tubers, but the majority feed almost exclusively on the plentiful seeds scattered over the desert floor.

Gerbils, jerboas, and some kangaroo rats store food when it is available, then live on these caches in times of scarcity. Gila monsters and fat-tailed geckos also prepare for hard times; they gorge when food is plentiful and store the excess as fat in their tails.

Where do the animals find water?

Desert water holes are busy places. Birds and some of the larger mammals visit them regularly to drink. But many other desert dwellers are able to survive far from any water source.

For a few, the moisture of morning dew is sufficient to fill their needs. Predators receive much of the liquid they require from the body fluids of their prey. Succulent plants are an adequate source for many of the herbivores. Oryxes, gazelles, and some of the other grazers can survive indefinitely on the meager amount of water in the plants they eat.

Among the desert's most remarkably adapted animals are jerboas and kangaroo rats, two types of rodents that need not drink any water at all. They manage to get by on the small amounts that are released as a by-product of digestion.

Why are so many desert creatures pale?

A large number of desert-dwelling birds, mammals, reptiles, and other animals are noticeably lighter in color than members of the same species or closely related ones living in other regions. The pale tones are part of a desert animal's cooling system, for light colors reflect the sun's hot rays and dark colors absorb them. Light colors also serve as camouflage, making the animals more difficult to see against the pale, dry desert floor.

A few animals, especially among the lizards, have such finely attuned

How do desert lizards cope with high temperatures?

Lizards, like other reptiles, are cold-blooded: their body temperature varies with that of their surroundings. But by changes in behavior, many species maintain a fairly constant temperature throughout the day. Typically, they bask in the sun during early morning hours, and so warm themselves. In midmorning they hunt for prey. If it becomes too hot, they may raise tail and body off the ground to keep cool. At midday the lizards retreat to the shade of their burrows or into sheltered rock crevices, then become active once more in midafternoon. Late in the day, they bask again, absorbing the heat of the fading sun before retiring to their burrows for the chilly desert night.

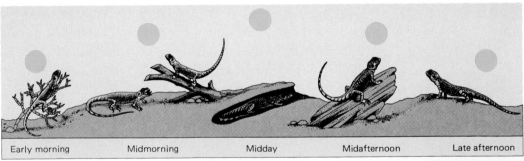

Early morning　　　Midmorning　　　Midday　　　Midafternoon　　　Late afternoon

As soon as they emerge from their burrows in the morning, most lizards bask in the sun to warm up before setting out on their daily rounds. When the sun is high in the sky at midday, they hide in their burrows, then reemerge to bask again late in the day as temperatures fall.

To every rule there are exceptions: North America's desert iguana is one of the species that prefer high temperatures and are most active toward midday.

In the Arizona desert, a Gila woodpecker perches at its nest hole in a saguaro, while an elf owl peers from an abandoned woodpecker hole. Drinking at the water hole are diminutive Gambel's quail. The distant saguaro holds the nest of a Harris's hawk.

temperature-control systems that they actually change color as the day progresses. They are dark in the morning, gradually turn pale by midday when the sun is blazing, and then darken again in the evening.

What kinds of birds live in deserts?

Insect eaters are the commonest kinds of desert birds, followed by seed and fruit eaters. Least numerous are hawks and other birds of prey. Most desert birds have no special adaptations to desert life and must remain within flight range of a water source. Some, such as owls and nightjars, are nocturnal, but most are active in early morning and evening; during the heat of midday they rest wherever they can find shade.

The reproductive cycles of many desert birds are linked to the arrival of rains, when food becomes most plentiful. In the driest years they may produce fewer young or fail to breed at all. Like the birds themselves, their eggs need some protection from the intense midday sun. Most birds nest in the shade of dense vegetation, in tree cavities, or in crannies among the rocks. Of the ground-nesting species, only the ostrich produces eggs large enough to withstand more than brief exposure to direct sunlight.

Why do desert foxes have big ears?

The smallest of all foxes, the fennecs of the Sahara, are only about 18 inches long, with 12-inch tails. But their pointed ears are almost 4 inches high—nearly a fourth of their body length. The little kit foxes of the American Southwest also have disproportionately large ears. With these sensitive detectors, the night-hunting predators can pick up the slightest sounds made by insects, rodents, or other potential prey stirring in the darkness.

The big ears of jackrabbits, which share the desert with kit foxes, are protective devices, warning them of approaching predators. But in these and other animals, oversized ears serve yet another purpose. Well supplied with blood vessels, they are heat radiators that help keep the animals cool.

Why do camels have humps?

Tales of camels plodding through the desert for days with little food and no water are no exaggeration, for these creatures are remarkably well adapted to desert life. Contrary to the common belief, however, a camel does not store water in its stomach or its hump.

Unlike most other mammals, a camel does not have a layer of fat under its skin. Instead, the fat is accumulated in the hump. When food and water are scarce, the camel utilizes this reserve for energy and as a water source. When the fat breaks down, hydrogen is released and combines with oxygen to form water. The animal also uses water from other body tissues in a similar way.

A camel can go for several days without drinking. As its tissues dehydrate, the creature can lose as much as 25 percent of its weight without suffering. But when it does find water, a thirsty camel may drink up to 30 gallons in 15 minutes. The water passes rapidly into its body tissues and soon revives the "wilted" beast.

Some Desert Look-alikes With Similar Life-styles

In the desert, as elsewhere, similar living conditions often result in similar adaptations of unrelated creatures. Thus, kangaroo rats of North American deserts and African jerboas not only look alike; they lead similar lives. Among the other animals with counterparts in distant deserts are kit foxes and fennecs, American jackrabbits and Old World desert hares, and certain snakes.

Kangaroo rat (North America)   **Jerboa** (Africa)

Large hind legs and a hopping gait enable these little desert rodents to make quick escapes from predators.

Kit fox (North America)   **Fennec** (Africa)

Oversized ears help these nocturnal desert foxes detect prey in the dark. They also serve to radiate excess heat.

Sidewinder (North America)   **Horned viper** (Africa, Asia)

Nearly identical in appearance, both of these desert snakes skim across loose sand with similar twisting motions.

How Desert Plants Survive

Why do deserts suddenly burst into bloom?

A square foot of desert soil commonly contains many thousands of seeds, produced by plants that grow with astonishing speed after seasonal rains. A few are so fast that they sprout, flower, and bear seeds in less than two weeks, quickly transforming a barren landscape into spectacular gardens filled with fragrance and color.

Seeds generally do not germinate when first touched by moisture: most need to be thoroughly soaked. An inhibitory chemical in seeds of certain species must be washed away before germination can occur—effectively delaying the appearance of seedlings until the soil is damp enough for their growth. In deserts most seeds sprout during the second, not the first, rains to follow their formation. Some stay in the soil for a number of years, waiting until conditions are just right.

What is a living stone?

Many animals escape the hot desert sun by burrowing into the soil. Surprisingly, a group of plants native to southwestern Africa are essentially burrowers too. Some living stones, as these plants are called, grow in sand with only their "windows"—portions of the leaves where light can enter—exposed at the surface. Others look so much like the pebbles and small rocks strewn over the desert that they are impossible to find until they flower. Then the tips of the leaves separate, allowing the remarkably large bloom to emerge.

Surviving where the average annual rainfall may be less than half an inch, many living stones receive most of their water from fog that drifts in from the sea. Living where they do, they need to reduce moisture loss. The "burrowing" habit lessens their exposure to the sun.

Do deserts have trees?

Typical broad-leaved trees—say, a maple growing out in the open—do not do well in deserts, for their spreading crowns let too much water escape from the leaves. Among the trees most characteristic of arid lands are the many kinds of acacias. Most have umbrella-shaped crowns, but when the amount of water available becomes insufficient for their needs, their leaves fold and droop, then fall. New leaves appear after the rains.

Many tree-sized plants growing in deserts look rather bizarre. The baobabs of Africa have enormously swollen trunks of spongy wood. The thick, water-storing trunk of Baja California's boojum tree has a scattering of slim, thorny branches that bear leaves only when water is plentiful. The ocotillo, a shrub belonging to the same family as the boojum tree, is a clump of stiff, leafless woody stems much of the year, but blazes with scarlet flowers when the rains come. Joshua trees in the southwestern United States and kokerbooms of southwestern Africa (also known as quiver trees because of the quivers made from the fibrous core) are other desert trees.

Why don't plants wilt in the desert sun?

Lacking the luxury of an unlimited supply of water, plants that grow in deserts conserve what water they get. In certain species a waxy coat on the leaves or stems helps reduce water loss. Others have dense mats of sil-

Even without their feathery blooms, living stones from southern Africa would be extraordinary plants.

Deserts are not necessarily deserted. At the base of these mountains in California, winter rains have stimulated a lush display of bloom.

very "hairs" that reflect the rays of the sun. As water becomes scarce, some plants shed their leaves. In many, the tiny openings (stomata) through which gases are exchanged are in deep pits—an arrangement that keeps loss of water by evaporation to a minimum.

Do century plants really bloom every hundred years?

For 10, 20, even 50 years—but never as long as a hundred—the century plant is merely a ground-hugging cluster of leaves. "Merely" is perhaps an inappropriate word for this kind of agave, native to deserts in Mexico and the American Southwest: its leaves may measure 10 feet long, and they come armed with sharp teeth.

A mature century plant is not just a cluster of leaves. Shooting up 20 feet or more from the leafy rosette is a stalk with yellow blossoms. Once the flowers are pollinated, fruits form, drop to the ground, and give rise to new century plants. The parent plant dies after its single season of bloom.

Do cacti make good houseplants?

Desert plants are popular as houseplants because they are not very demanding, and also because in many cases they look rather odd. The peanut cactus, the fishhook cactus, the old-man cactus—these are not your typical leafy green plants.

In addition to various kinds of cacti, desert plants grown indoors include the crown of thorns and other euphorbias, jade plants and other crassulas, sedums, aloes, and living stones. All store water in fleshy leaves or stems.

Even these tough desert dwellers are not indestructible. They do best when their natural habitat is duplicated as closely as possible, which generally means a high temperature and a great deal of light. Although water in excess of what they normally get in nature will not kill them, the soil must be porous, so that water will drain off. Water needs are greatest when the plants are growing rapidly—something that can easily be detected by an observant eye. For species native to the Northern Hemisphere, spring is the typical growing period, followed by a resting period when they should be watered only every few weeks.

Prairies and Pampas

What is the difference between prairies and pampas?

A sea of grass billowing in the wind, an open vista unbroken by trees, extending for miles, bounded by the circle of the horizon and the sky—this description fits both the prairie and the pampa. The difference is in the name. By tradition, *prairie* is the term used for the grasslands that cover much of the western United States and Canada, while *pampa* refers to the grasslands of Argentina. *Prairie* is an old French word for "meadow"; *pampa*, the Spanish version of an Indian word meaning "plain."

These are not the only local names for grasslands. Near the northern rim of South America, the mighty Orinoco River flows through vast grasslands called *llanos*—Spanish for "flats." In southern Africa there is the veldt, whose name is Dutch for "field." The largest uninterrupted grassland in the world, known by its Russian name, the steppe stretches from central Europe far east into Siberia.

Why do sea gulls live so far from the sea?

In Salt Lake City, Utah, stands a statue of a gull, honoring the birds that devoured a plague of insects and saved the corps of Mormon pioneers. Then, as now, the gulls nested on islands in Great Salt Lake. The lake is far too salty for fish; the gulls eat grasshoppers and other insects in nearby grasslands.

Though the heart of a dry grassland may seem a surprising place to find birds associated with water, ducks and geese are no strangers to the moister, cooler grasslands. For although prairies, steppes, and pampas are relatively dry, they are far from waterless. Rivers rising in mountains or in rainy uplands cut through the grasslands. Water is stored in depressions, either natural or man-made. Melting snow at the end of winter or downpours during the rainy season soak the soil and create temporary streams and shallow ponds.

Grasslands are home to hundreds of species of birds, large and small. As might be expected in treeless areas, many make their nests on the ground. Most eagles are tree nesters, but Siberia has a ground-nesting species; in

Streams wind through North America's tallgrass prairie (above), where "tall" means plants growing up to 12 feet high. Trees may occur in moist places. The Argentine pampa (right), covering nearly 300,000 square miles, is an enormous grassland. Its soil was washed down over the centuries from the Andes.

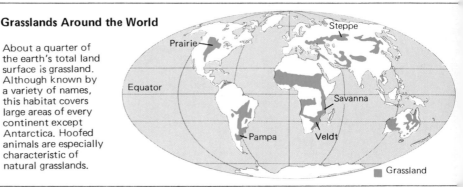

Grasslands Around the World

About a quarter of the earth's total land surface is grassland. Although known by a variety of names, this habitat covers large areas of every continent except Antarctica. Hoofed animals are especially characteristic of natural grasslands.

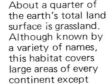

North America tiny owls nest in burrows. Also living in grasslands are the world's most massive birds—the ostrich of Africa, the ostrichlike rhea of South America, and the emu of Australia. All are too heavy to fly. Certain other species, like the big kori bustard of Africa, approach the weight limit for flight and prefer to run rather than fly.

What creates a grassland?

A broad belt of coniferous forest extends clear across northern Siberia. South of the dark green forest stretches the tawny, treeless steppe. Why do these neighboring regions have such a very different plant life?

Actually, several factors determine whether a given area will be covered with trees or grass. Rainfall is perhaps the most basic. Trees need more moisture than grasses; where average rainfall over the years is less than the critical minimum, trees do not survive, and grass covers the land. Even though the total amount of rain is enough to support trees, they may not thrive where there is a long dry season. This is the case on the llanos of Colombia and Venezuela. In other cases, the grassland may be studded with widely spaced scrubby trees and bushes, giving it the appearance of a park. Most of the great grasslands of Africa are of this type, known as savanna.

garoos, live in herds. Certain major predators, including lions and African hunting dogs, also live in groups.

Another common adaptation to grassland life is the burrowing habit. Prairie dogs in North America, vizcachas in South America, susliks in Asia—all are rodents that burrow beneath the grass. Their tunneling turns over the soil on a grand scale, helping to increase fertility.

Staying Out of Sight

Animals on a grassland, especially small ones, need some place to hide. South America's vizcachas take refuge in tunnels (a network of tunnels is called a vizcachera). The guinea pig, also of South America, lives at the surface and hides among tufts of grass.

Plains vizcacha

Pampas guinea pig

Wind is another factor in creating and maintaining grassland. Where winds are strong and steady, they may steal more water from a tree's leaves than the plant can replace through its roots. Grasses, with their relatively small leaf area, do not suffer this fatal dehydration. In the dry season, fires driven by the wind sweep across vast expanses of grassland. Whether caused by lightning or set by man, the fiercely burning fires devastate trees. Grasses, however, soon sprout again from undamaged roots.

As on the original prairies of North America, the grass itself may form a dense, continuous mat of sod in which tree seedlings cannot gain a foothold. Hoofed animals and other grazers and browsers may destroy young trees and bushes, creating grasslands. So does man, by clearing vast areas in the quest for timber and pastureland.

How did buffalo help extend the prairie?

Before the Europeans came, large areas of the United States east of the Mississippi River were covered with grass—yet the climate and soil conditions favored forests. Many scientists believe that, in addition to the effects of periodic fires, the great herds of bison, or buffalo, helped to create these eastern prairies by trampling and feeding—activities that destroyed young forest growth. In time, the old trees died, and there were none to replace them. The grasses, unlike the trees, grew back after being grazed and took over.

Scientists have seen how even today elephants are contributing to the spread of grassland in Africa. Elephants eat tree leaves and twigs, among other things, and often they destroy the trees on which they feed. An entirely different type of vegetation takes over when the trees are gone.

What special traits do grassland mammals share?

By definition, a grassland is an open environment. It has little in the way of hiding places and few obstacles that would interfere with the running of a herd. Animals living in grasslands, especially the hoofed mammals—bison, wild horses, and the like—tend to be wary and fast. For safety, many plant eaters, such as Australia's kan-

Are grasslands crawling with insects?

Though in many cases it is mammals and birds that capture our attention, insects are by far the most numerous grassland animals. They include beetles, aphids, flies, bees, wasps, butterflies, and especially crickets and grasshoppers, which may well outnumber all the rest. When grasslands are brought under cultivation, some insects become highly destructive agricultural pests. In nature, however, they supply food for birds, reptiles, and small rodents (and also pollinate many crops). These in turn are eaten by larger creatures. Generally the insects are kept in balance with their environment by the insect eaters, but in certain years they increase to plague proportions. The dreaded locust swarms (actually, grasshopper swarms) of the Middle East and Africa are perhaps the most notorious.

Those Sociable Prairie Dogs

Just how sociable are prairie dogs?

As prairie dogs go about their business of eating and of maintaining their burrows, the colony in which they live has a certain resemblance to a human town. A dog town, however, is not a true community but an aggregation of smaller units.

A prairie dog coterie is an extended family, usually consisting of an adult male, several females, and their young. Each female has her own burrow. Every member of the coterie knows every other member, and they literally keep in touch by frequently grooming each other and kissing—touching noses or teeth. Sometimes a pair will sit together, the arm of one over the shoulder of the other.

Typically occupying a little over half an acre of ground, a coterie is defended against all other prairie dogs. Individuals belonging to different coteries are chased away. Two or more adjacent coteries make up a ward, which is usually separated from other wards by such natural barriers as hills or streambeds. Two or more wards make up a town. In the past, prairie dog towns grew and coalesced until they reached immense size. One famous example in Texas was estimated at the turn of the century to cover an area 100 by 240 miles and to contain perhaps 400 million animals.

How do prairie dogs talk with one another?

Early explorers named these delightful creatures "prairie dogs" because of their sharp, high-pitched yap; they are really rodents, not dogs. When other prairie dogs hear the barking alarm call, they go on alert. A special call that warns of a hawk or an eagle sends them scurrying into their burrows. Another call doubles as a territorial warning and an all-clear signal when danger has passed. When giving it, the prairie dog flings its body into an upright position; young ones often fall over backward before they have mastered the maneuver. There are other calls too, including defense barks, snarls, chuckles, screams of fear, and tooth-chattering.

What do prairie dogs use as lookout posts?

Marking the main entrance to the burrow—for emergencies, most have more than one entrance—is a mound of dirt excavated from the tunnel. Black-tailed prairie dogs build a high, conical mound and tamp the dirt firmly, using their noses as rams. Other species make loose dirt piles. Often the exit has a low mound around it too.

The mound, or mounds, serve to keep rain from flooding the burrows and are also used as lookout posts for spotting eagles, coyotes, and other enemies. Prairie dogs keep the grass around their burrows nibbled short, and carefully cut down tall weeds. Often the area around the mound is completely bare, increasing their field of vision.

How deep do the burrows go?

Though no two are exactly alike, a typical prairie dog burrow plunges steeply into the earth for 4 to 10 feet, then rises slowly to within a few feet of

Above Ground and Below: Two Different Lives

Prairie dogs live their lives both at the surface and underground. Daylight hours, in which such activities as feeding, defense, communication, and play occur, are spent outside the burrow. Dug as deep as 10 feet, prairie dog burrows supply shelter, though some predators will enter them too.

Eating prickly pear

Recognition embrace

Family members at play

Alert posture while eating

Sentries

Greeting kiss

Nest chamber

Toilet chamber

the surface. Below the main entrance is a ledge that serves as a listening post. Prairie dogs going up and down the tunnel can also use this as a passing place.

Usually the main tunnel has side branches that open into rooms— grass-lined nesting chambers, toilet chambers, and tunnels for refuge in case of flooding. There may be a special nursing chamber for a mother and young infants. Whatever its design, the burrow is always changing as its residents dig new chambers and seal off the old.

Do prairie dogs eat owls or vice versa?

Beetles, spiders (including the poisonous black widow), toads, salamanders, ground squirrels, cottontails, mice, bull snakes, box turtles—wild creatures of all types live or take refuge in prairie dog burrows. Folklore has it that the rodents share their homes amicably with rattlesnakes and burrowing owls. In actuality, these animals do use the burrows, but the prairie dogs abandon their homes soon after the unwelcome guests take over. When owls first move in, a round of predation takes place. The owls are believed to eat young prairie dogs; the rodents, in turn, eat the birds' eggs and chicks. (Not strictly vegetarians, prairie dogs also eat grasshoppers and other insects.)

One kind of predator, the weasellike black-footed ferret, not only feeds almost exclusively on prairie dogs but depends on their burrows for dens. The ferret now stands on the brink of extinction because man has drastically reduced the prairie dog population.

Are prairie dogs found only on prairies?

The prairie dog's realm stretches from southern Saskatchewan through the United States and into northern Mexico. On the east, it reaches into Kansas and Nebraska; on the west, Utah and Arizona. While the most numerous and most social species lives on the plains, others inhabit high plateaus, mountain meadows, and near-deserts. The plains- and desert-dwelling species have black-tipped tails; the others, white-tipped ones.

What is a suslik?

Though the prairie dog is unique to North America, grasslands elsewhere have rodents living similar lives. The 15-pound plains vizcacha of Argentina, which resembles a huge guinea pig, digs extensive underground mazes and piles up such hard objects as stones and bones at the entrance to its burrow. From central Europe to southern Siberia is suslik territory. The suslik, more carnivorous than the prairie dog, is a ground squirrel that feeds on small birds, mice, and insects as well as on plants. The steppe lemming, another colonial animal, shares the same general area. The South African ground squirrel is amazingly like the prairie dog in its habits of visiting fellow squirrels and basking in the sun.

Living in colonies has many advantages, chief among them an efficient warning system and the availability of mates. In southern Africa not only ground squirrels but also certain carnivores, the meerkats, live in colonies. These odd-looking creatures live in bands of up to 50 animals, sleeping in interconnecting burrows. By day the band wander in search of insects, spiders, and other small prey. Meerkats are fond of sunning themselves at their burrow openings, and they often prop themselves up on their tails, sitting in an upright position like inquisitive prairie dogs.

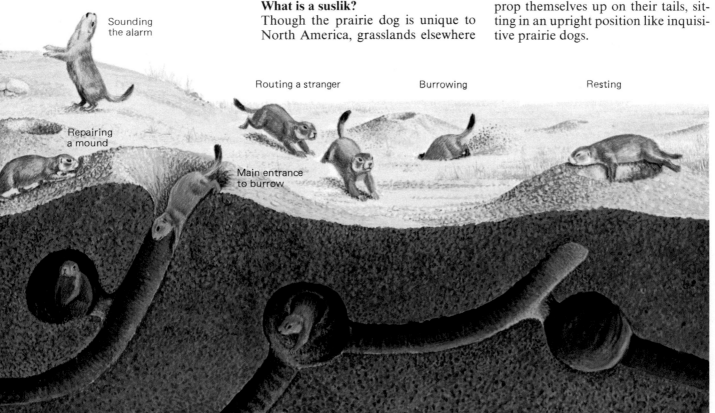

Sounding the alarm

Repairing a mound

Routing a stranger

Burrowing

Resting

Main entrance to burrow

The African Plains

Why do zebras live in herds?
Zebras migrate in large herds, which are usually loose gatherings of zebra families mixed with wildebeest. Being together gives safety: the more eyes, the better the chance of spotting trouble. The herd also offers possibilities for escape. A pursued animal can run into the herd and vanish, its individuality lost in the throng. Hiding is difficult on Africa's open plains, and fleetness saves lives.

A mixed herd—that is, one composed of different species—offers a variety of vantage points. For example, when ostriches mix with wildebeest and zebras, the ostrich's keen eye gives a periscopic view that augments the others' sense of smell. Giraffes, by virtue of their height, are even better equipped to sight stalking predators.

What are klipspringers and dik-diks?
Africa has more than 70 different kinds of antelope, and klipspringers and dik-diks are among the tiniest. Measuring about 20 inches tall at the shoulder, the klipspringer prefers rocky places and often stands perched on the tips of its diminutive hooves.

Dik-diks are 14 inches tall at most. As they flee through tall grass, leaping several times their height to see what lies ahead, they look, some say, like bouncing balls.

Most African antelopes prefer dry, open areas, where they often form enormous herds. Waterbucks and duikers (whose name means "diver," from the habit of diving into thick cover when disturbed) are among those living in marshes and forests.

Why do elephants roll about in the mud?
For much of the year, water in the African grasslands is scarce. In sand-choked riverbeds, elephants scoop out pits with their feet. When the pits fill with water, the elephants drink; when they leave, the "cistern" is available for use by rhinos, birds, and other wildlife. To cool off, elephants take showers—sprinkling themselves with water from the trunk—and roll about in the mud. This packs the mud down and produces huge, firm-bottomed pans. Rainwater collecting there may last well into the dry season—another bonus for animal life.

Most other animals, of course, cannot dig wells. Enhancing their water supply, gerenuks and oryxes, two kinds of antelopes, feed at night, when foliage has the greatest water content and dew may add moisture to each bite. Black rhinoceroses chew succulent leaves and stems for moisture, then spit out the indigestible fibers. The rabbitlike hyrax gets almost all of the water it needs from plants, and from the by-products of food assimilation. It seldom drinks.

How do elephants affect the land?
Standing 10 feet tall at the shoulder and weighing 6 tons, an adult bull elephant requires a quarter ton of grass, leaves, and fruit a day. To meet their needs the animals uproot trees, bulldoze branches, and pull out tussocks of grass. Such breaking and "mowing," combined with trampling, lets light into tangles of tall grass, promoting the growth of other kinds of vegetation. Ordinarily elephants travel slowly over extensive areas, and so lessen their effect in any one place. Nowadays, however, herds are largely restricted to parks and reserves, and where numbers swell excessively, damage ensues.

How big are the African herds?
Five million square miles of Africa—nearly half the continent—is carpeted with grass. In times past, great herds of grazing animals spread on every side as far as the eye could see. At present, the largest herds are limited to national parks, such as Tanzania's Serengeti and Kenya's Tsavo. Serengeti contains herds with as many as 50,000 gnu, or wildebeest (*wildebeest* is an Afrikaans word for "wild ox," though the animal is really an antelope). Mixing with the wildebeest on migration are a million Thomson's gazelles and 200,000 zebras.

Though by definition grazers depend on grass, not all species are competing for the same food. Zebras, for example, eat tall grasses down to a certain height; wildebeest graze plants clipped by zebras and also the fresh growth that follows rain. Shown here are not only grazers but also such browsers as elephants and giraffes. Which part of the savanna each lives in depends on the food and water needs of the individual species.

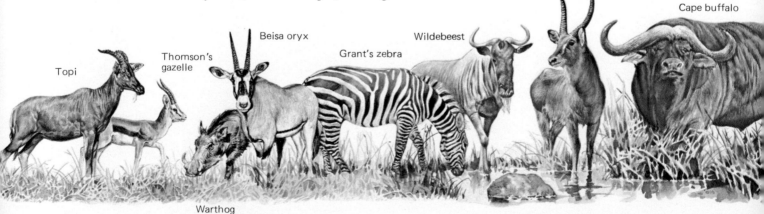

Topi
Thomson's gazelle
Beisa oryx
Grant's zebra
Wildebeest
Waterbuck
Cape buffalo
Warthog
Dry Grassland
Moist Grassland

Why do trees have haystacks?

Haystacks on trees on the African plains are the work of weaverbirds, sparrowlike creatures that in the breeding season are often splendidly plumaged in yellow or red. Weavers build hanging nests at the tips of tree limbs or tall grass stems. Though most species use such flexible plant materials as grass, a few prefer coarse twigs.

Weaverbirds are the most numerous birds on the African savanna. The nests built by different pairs are often so close together that they seem like chambers within a communal whole rather than separate structures. A single colony may include more than a thousand nests, and as successive generations add to the structure, the haystack effect intensifies.

Who is the elephant's closest living relative?

Next to elephants, rhinoceroses are the world's largest land animals. The white rhino, an endangered species of the African plains, weighs up to four tons; the black rhino, which favors thorn scrub, weighs about a ton and a half. Other rhinos live in India and other parts of Asia.

The African Savanna's Most Abundant Birds

Among the most impressive of nature's architects are the weaverbirds, which live not only on the African plains but elsewhere in Africa and in Asia. Using its beak and feet, the bird builds a grass ring around a support (left). A nest chamber is built outward (center) and a roof added (right). An entrance hole is left on the underside.

Though it is easy to see similarities between rhinos and elephants (size, leathery skin, and the like), the two are in fact *not* closely related. The closest kin of the elephant is actually the hyrax, an animal of rabbit size. Hyraxes have small ears, short legs, and virtually no tails. They live in trees or in rocky places in various parts of Africa and feed on leaves and fruit.

What good are long trunks and necks?

An elephant's trunk helps it drink, make noise ("trumpet"), and smell. By showering water and dust, it respectively keeps the animal cool and wards off insects. The female uses it to steer infants and chastise young. Most important, the trunk is used for picking up food. This unique structure can handle objects as big as a tree and as small as a seedpod—or a peanut.

By contrast, the tallest land animal, the giraffe, has a long neck, which allows it to browse on vegetation some 15 feet above the ground. (The leaves of acacia trees are its main food.) The animal's massive 25-pound heart can pump blood against gravity up to the head. Conversely, when the giraffe browses on low foliage or drinks, special valves in the blood vessels close, preventing a dangerous rush of blood to the head.

In different parts of the African savanna, soil and water conditions vary, and hence the plant and animal life. There are four major zones, each with characteristic mammalian species.

Giraffe

East African eland

Gerenuk

Black rhino

African elephant

Bushbuck

Dik-dik

Dry Thorn Scrub

Greater kudu

Blue duiker

Riverine Forest

Predators on the Plains

Why are lions such successful hunters?

Unlike wolves, lions do not run in packs. Nor are they solitary, as are leopards and cheetahs. The lion's family unit, or pride, typically revolves around an adult male, who often lives with one or two subordinate males and several related females and young. Adult males are the ones with impressive manes.

Three or four members of a pride often hunt together—a procedure unusual among cats, which rarely cooperate in a hunt or in other endeavors. A solitary hunter, such as the cheetah, must kill daily to feed its young and has to leave them alone while it hunts. Lions working together can take more, and larger, prey—animals as big as a three-quarter-ton buffalo, a hippopotamus, or a young elephant separated from its parents. Each adult lion needs 12 to 15 pounds of meat a day on the average, though the pattern is to gorge, then fast. If the hunt is unsuccessful, lions can rob other animals of food. At the ap-proach of these great cats, hyenas or leopards feeding on a kill draw back; vultures flutter aside. Within the pride, lions will share a kill and take turns guarding the food while one after another leaves to drink.

How do crocodiles attack?

The best known of the approaches that lead predator to prey is active patrol, a method commonly used by lions and other big cats. Crocodiles, however, lie in wait. Though on land they can barely move, they are agile in the water and lie there with only eyes and nostrils above the surface. When an antelope starts to drink, the crocodile clamps onto its muzzle and knocks it off balance with a swish of the tail. The victim is pulled underwater, then dragged ashore.

Why do animals head toward a fire rather than running away?

To jackals and hyenas, vultures spiraling through the air indicate the location of a carcass and the promise of a meal. They are not the only animals responsive to signs of food as well as to the food itself. Smoke from a grass fire, for example, attracts certain predators. Because flames send insects, lizards, and rodents fleeing, birds fly in to feast. Bee eaters and rollers, both members of the crow family (rollers are named for their habit of somersaulting in flight), perch on tree limbs, then swoop in as insects leap just beyond the flames. Such birds of prey as grasshopper buzzards and kites dive into smoke clouds and seize large insects. Once the blackened ground has cooled, marabou storks snap up lizards, rodents, and other fire victims.

Rain clouds are another sign read by predators. Termites swarm in response to rain, and insect-eating falcons fly in to feed on such swarms. Frogs and toads emerge in the rain to feed on insects—but may vanish instead into a bird's gullet.

How did the secretary bird get its name?

Three feet tall and standing erect, the secretary bird is crowned with feathers that look like old-fashioned quill pens thrust behind its ears, and is dressed in a businesslike blackish gray and white; hence its name. This bird of prey stalks the ground for snakes, insects, and mice. Although it is startling in appearance, its habits are by no means unique: many other winged creatures are predators on the African plains. Patrolling for similar prey are ground hornbills, turkey-sized birds that call with deep notes and flock together by the score. The martial eagle is big enough to kill impala calves. Bateleur eagles soar above the grasslands, surveying 200 square miles a day for carrion and prey. Snake eagles specialize in snakes and lizards, although they also take frogs, rodents, and birds. Fish eagles swoop down to catch fish and sometimes waterbirds. Pel's owls live by fishing too.

How do animals avoid being eaten?

The ground-dwelling baboons seek safety in groups, traveling in bands of 100 to 200 animals. The fierce males can ward off such small enemies as wild dogs; elaborate warning systems protect against larger predators. Baboons vary their alarm calls according to the degree of danger. Cheetahs are

The African plains feature big predators and also big prey. Here, chasing a gazelle through the grass, is a cheetah, the fastest-running wild animal on earth.

Unique to Africa's open country is the secretary bird. Though it can fly, this bird of prey is mainly a ground dweller. It hunts for rodents and other small animals.

Are all meat eaters killers?

In packs of up to 30, hyenas scavenge kills of such predators as lions, cheetahs, and hunting dogs. Recently, field researchers have seen them making their own kills. Hyenas are alert animals with sharp senses of sight, smell, and sound. Jaws are strong enough to crush bones; teeth are adapted for tearing meat. As opportunity presents itself, these maligned creatures hunt for prey or scavenge.

Many other flesh eaters are opportunists. As a whole, members of the dog family are less particular than cats and likelier to feed on carrion. Africa has two dogs, the wild (or hunting) dogs and the jackals. Wild dogs hunt in packs of up to 60 individuals, killing animals as big as a wildebeest and challenging even the lion. More often,

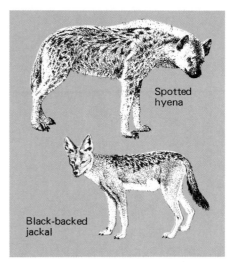

Spotted hyena

Black-backed jackal

however, they will settle for rodents or the kill of a leopard or cheetah. The jackals, in contrast, roam singly, in pairs, or in family groups. Although they hunt such grazers as Thomson's gazelles, they also scavenge. For flesh eating does not depend on hunting alone: there is cleanup too.

Are predators cruel?

Lions dashing after antelope and fish eagles swooping down for fish do so for the same reason that flamingos strain out small organisms from the water and beetles chew into leaves: each has over time developed certain ways of obtaining food. The roles of predator and prey are neither good nor evil, neither kindly nor cruel. It is their, and nature's, way.

regarded as a minor threat. Leopards often kill front-line defenders. Lions cause total panic, sending baboons screaming toward the trees.

Such hoofed animals as antelopes and zebras feed close to baboons and flee when the alarm is sounded. The baboons, in turn, profit from these creatures' ability to smell. If an antelope or zebra breaks into a run, the baboons leap to the alert.

The alarm calls of a baboon troop

are only one of the many defenses animals have against predators—defenses so effective that how predators ever succeed is as basic a question as how prey animals avoid being eaten. In fact, it is a rule of nature that hunters miss their prey as often as they catch it—and even more often in many cases, especially among birds that specialize in taking other birds on the wing. Merlins, a kind of falcon, fail 95 percent of the time.

The Many Faces of Forests

What is a forest?

Dictionaries define a forest as a large area densely covered with trees. But to naturalists a forest is far more than trees alone. It is an intricately interwoven community of living things, animals as well as plants, that range in size from microorganisms to great oaks and mighty sequoias.

In this forest community, each member plays a role in the continuing cycle of life, death, and rebirth. Some insects pollinate the trees, while others destroy them by eating leaves and wood. Squirrels devour tons of nuts, but bury others that survive to become mature trees. Some fungi infect living trees and kill them; others play a major role in breaking down dead plant and animal material and so releasing their locked-up nutrients to nurture new generations of living things. Deer, bears, birds, beetles, butterflies, and a host of other wild creatures all make the forest their home and contribute to its web of life.

How many kinds of forests are there?

The vast coniferous forests of Siberia; the maples in New England forests, ablaze with autumn color; a European beech wood, suffused with sunlight filtering through the leaves—all these are among the many faces of forests. So too are the rain forests of Amazonia, the thorny acacia forests that cover parts of Africa, the majestic eucalypts of Australia, and the redwood groves on the California coast.

The map at the right shows the broad zones of different types of forest that cover much of the earth's land area. Each type differs from the others. And each type includes many variations on the same theme. The trees of the tropical rain forests of South America, for example, are different from those found in Africa. But the forests in both places resemble each other in many ways, for they result from similar conditions.

Why do forests differ from place to place?

Conifers dominate the broad belt of forest that spans northern Eurasia and North America. Farther south, deciduous forests covered most of the eastern United States when the first European colonists arrived. Climate is one key to the puzzle of why such forests differ, for trees are adapted to different climatic conditions. Conifers flourish in high latitudes because they can withstand wind and cold better than broad-leaved trees can. But if conditions are more favorable for broad-leaved trees, they tend to crowd out the conifers.

Climate also varies with elevation. For each increase of 1,000 feet above sea level, the average temperature drops about 3.5 Fahrenheit degrees. In the Himalayas, lush tropical rain forest in the southern foothills gives way at higher elevations to broadleaf trees such as oaks and magnolias. These in turn are replaced by conifers on higher, colder slopes.

Soil is another factor. Conifers can survive on poorer land than broadleaf trees; thus pines dominate the zone of poor, sandy soil in the southeastern United States. Isolation, too, can play a role. Long separated from any other landmass, Australia has forests dominated by members of a single family of trees, the eucalypts.

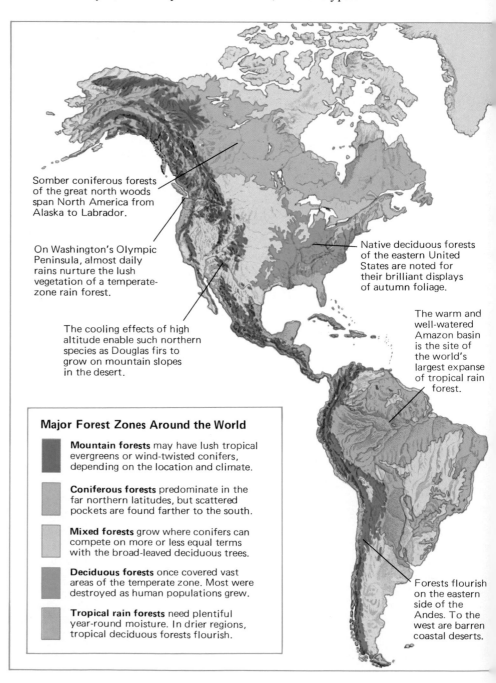

Somber coniferous forests of the great north woods span North America from Alaska to Labrador.

On Washington's Olympic Peninsula, almost daily rains nurture the lush vegetation of a temperate-zone rain forest.

The cooling effects of high altitude enable such northern species as Douglas firs to grow on mountain slopes in the desert.

Native deciduous forests of the eastern United States are noted for their brilliant displays of autumn foliage.

The warm and well-watered Amazon basin is the site of the world's largest expanse of tropical rain forest.

Forests flourish on the eastern side of the Andes. To the west are barren coastal deserts.

Major Forest Zones Around the World

Mountain forests may have lush tropical evergreens or wind-twisted conifers, depending on the location and climate.

Coniferous forests predominate in the far northern latitudes, but scattered pockets are found farther to the south.

Mixed forests grow where conifers can compete on more or less equal terms with the broad-leaved deciduous trees.

Deciduous forests once covered vast areas of the temperate zone. Most were destroyed as human populations grew.

Tropical rain forests need plentiful year-round moisture. In drier regions, tropical deciduous forests flourish.

Do forests ever change?

If living conditions are right, any bit of bare land eventually reverts to mature forest as the result of a long series of changes. First weeds and shrubs move in, only to be replaced in time by a young forest of hardy, sun-loving "pioneer" trees. Eventually other types of trees, shade-tolerant ones, sprout in the undergrowth and finally crowd out the pioneer species.

This final stage, called the climax forest, theoretically could remain unchanged for centuries. As individual trees died, they would be replaced by others of the same species. But in fact even climax forests are not immutable. They can be destroyed by diseases, plagues, or disasters such as forest fires. When this happens, the succession begins anew; eventually the climax forest again covers the land.

Are there forests without trees?

It is hard to imagine a forest without trees, but in fact some so-called forests contain no true trees. High in the rugged mountains of southwestern China grow dense forests of bamboo, actually oversized members of the grass family. Here live such rarities as the giant panda and the snow leopard.

In parts of the Himalayas there are forests of tree-sized rhododendrons. Elsewhere these plants grow as shrubs; here they sometimes reach heights of 80 feet and turn entire mountain slopes red when they bloom. Tree ferns are another kind of plant that is not really a tree. But in some places they grow in pure stands, forming lovely, sun-spangled groves.

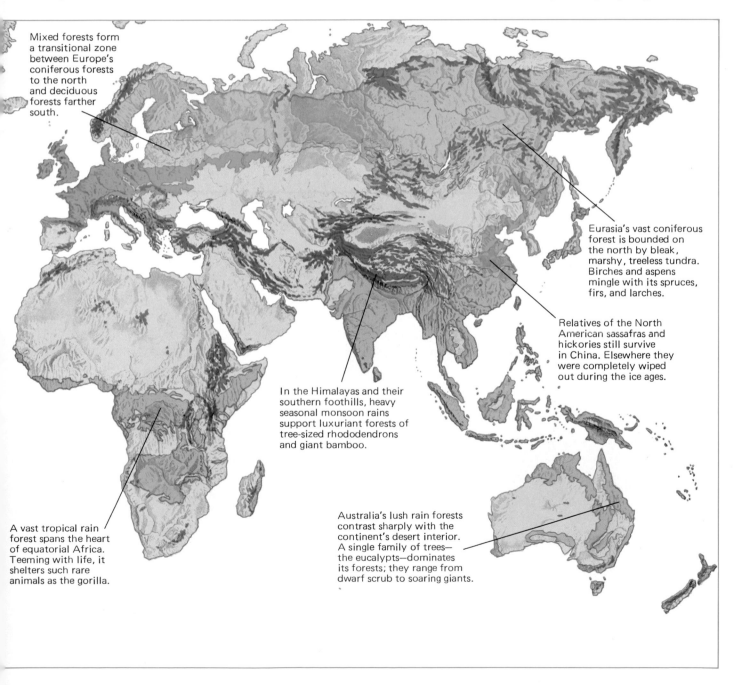

Mixed forests form a transitional zone between Europe's coniferous forests to the north and deciduous forests farther south.

Eurasia's vast coniferous forest is bounded on the north by bleak, marshy, treeless tundra. Birches and aspens mingle with its spruces, firs, and larches.

Relatives of the North American sassafras and hickories still survive in China. Elsewhere they were completely wiped out during the ice ages.

In the Himalayas and their southern foothills, heavy seasonal monsoon rains support luxuriant forests of tree-sized rhododendrons and giant bamboo.

A vast tropical rain forest spans the heart of equatorial Africa. Teeming with life, it shelters such rare animals as the gorilla.

Australia's lush rain forests contrast sharply with the continent's desert interior. A single family of trees—the eucalypts—dominates its forests; they range from dwarf scrub to soaring giants.

The Great North Woods

Where is the great north woods?

Just south of the Arctic tundra, a broad belt of forest circles the Northern Hemisphere. This great north woods, also known by its Russian name, taiga, is the largest forest in the world. Whether in Eurasia or in North America, it looks much the same everywhere, for nearly all the trees are spruces, firs, and other conifers. To the south, the taiga gives way to mixed forests, or, in drier regions, to grasslands and deserts.

Living conditions are harsh in the north woods. During the long winter, temperatures far below 0° F are commonplace, and much of the subsoil remains permanently frozen. Precipitation amounts to only about 20 inches a year, but evaporation is so slow that the surface is sodden all summer long. Decay takes place slowly; beneath the dense stands of trees, a cushion of fallen needles cov-

ers the poor, acid, waterlogged soil. Despite such adversity, the northern conifers manage to thrive where few other trees can survive.

Why are there so many lakes and ponds?

During the ice ages, great continental ice sheets covered much of these far northern lands. Spreading slowly southward, they gouged out countless basins and dropped debris that formed natural dams. Lakes and ponds now occupy these depressions, which are linked by networks of streams and slow-moving rivers.

The streams and standing waters add a welcome note of variety to the great north woods. Along their borders grow thickets of hardy alders, birches, willows, and other broad-leaved shrubs, along with various herbs. Such plants are the major source of food for beaver, moose, and

many other herbivores. Here too live such creatures as mink and otter, along with loons and other waterbirds that wing their way north each spring to nest and rear their young in this watery wilderness.

Are pine needles palatable?

The needles of most conifers are tough, coated with a waxy cuticle, and filled with resin—all of which makes them unpalatable to the majority of animals. However, various kinds are important to deer, and many mammals large and small munch on young needles and buds from time to time. Among birds, only the blue grouse in North America and the Eurasian capercaillie rely on a diet of needles and buds, especially in winter. So do a few insects. Sawfly larvae and spruce budworms can denude entire forests when they appear in great numbers.

The abundant crops of conifer seeds are a much more significant food source. Crossbills, nutcrackers, jays, grosbeaks, and other birds feast on them, as do moles and chipmunks and other rodents. Among the champion seed eaters are red squirrels. With their chisellike teeth, the squirrels cut off each cone scale, then shuck out the small seed at its base. By the time a red squirrel finishes a meal, the ground beneath the tree where it is feeding may be littered with the remains of dozens of cones.

Are insects just a summertime food?

During the short summers in the north woods, hordes of flies and mosquitoes hum through the forest, and legions of caterpillars feed on the buds and shoots. Warblers and flycatchers are among the many kinds of insect-eating birds that fly in from the south to feast on this bonanza. They remain to nest and rear their young while food is plentiful and then, as autumn approaches, return to the south.

Even in winter some of the year-round residents continue to feed on a diet of insects. With their sharp, powerful bills, woodpeckers chisel deep into wood to get at larvae resting in their burrows. Other birds such as chickadees and nuthatches probe for insect eggs, pupae, and dormant adults that are hidden under bark or tucked into crevices.

Two Birds of the Northern Coniferous Forest

Capercaillies, widespread Eurasian grouse that are nearly the size of turkeys, are among the year-round residents of coniferous forests. Although they dine on fruits and berries in summer, the mainstay of their winter diet is the needles and buds of conifers. In spring, the males fan their tails and perform an elaborate courtship display.

Capercaillie

Red crossbill

Crossbills, found in far northern woodlands around the world, specialize in a diet of conifer seeds. The crossed tips of their bills are used as forceps, and enable the birds to probe between overlapping cone scales and extract the seeds that are tucked in at their bases. In years when few cones are produced in the north, large flocks of the sparrow-sized birds often roam far south of their usual range.

In a forest in Finland, snow signals the onset of winter, the season of hardship for creatures of the great north woods.

How do mammals survive the winter?
Although most birds of the north woods head south in autumn, the mammals remain year round. Some are as active in winter as in summer. Voles and lemmings, for example, keep warm by remaining in tunnels beneath the snow, where they continue to feed on lichens, seeds, and tender roots. Moose plod through the snow, browsing on twigs of fir, willow, birch, and aspen. Snowshoe hares are versatile feeders, taking even the pungent spruce. Porcupines gnaw on bark and twigs. And the predators—wolves, foxes, lynxes, martens, and the like—are always on the prowl.

A few mammals prepare for winter and its food shortages. Beavers build up larders of cut branches that remain fresh and supple in the storage piles under the ice. Squirrels and chipmunks put away hoards of seeds to tide them over the cold months.

Woodchucks and ground squirrels are among those that avoid the rigors of winter by going into hibernation and living off stored fat. Black bears, on the other hand, simply go into a deep sleep. They may rouse from time to time and even wander about to find a new resting place before settling in for another siege of cold.

How do lynxes hunt?
Though rare in northern Europe, lynxes are still quite numerous in the North American taiga. The stub-tailed cats sometimes kill prey as large as deer. But their main food is hares.

Usually they stalk their quarry until close enough to pounce and kill. Or they may crouch in the snow, waiting for an unwary hare to venture close enough to be taken.

The fortunes of the two animals are closely linked. In some areas snowshoe hares have a strikingly regular population cycle. From a low of only a few individuals to a square mile, the number of hares gradually increases about every 10 years to a peak of several thousand. Then, for reasons not fully understood, the population plummets. Lynx populations follow the same pattern, gradually increasing as their chief prey becomes more abundant and then dropping to a low about a year after the dramatic decline in the number of hares.

Temperate Woodlands

What kinds of trees grow in temperate forests?

Broad-leaved deciduous trees—oaks, beeches, maples, and the like—are the dominant species in most temperate woodlands. They thrive where summers are long, winters are not too severe, and adequate precipitation is spread fairly evenly through the year.

The most extensive temperate deciduous woodlands are found in the Northern Hemisphere. Such forests once covered most of eastern North America. A broad belt of similar forests stretched across much of Europe, and others flourished in eastern Asia. In most places the original forests were long ago cut down for lumber and fuel, and the woodlands were converted into farms and cities. Except for a few virgin stands of deciduous trees, the remaining temperate woodlands are at least second growth.

Are there any conifers?

Toward the northern fringes of the temperate woodlands, more and more cold-tolerant conifers begin to mingle with the deciduous trees. Mixed forests, in fact, form a broad transitional

A morning mist diffuses the light filtering through the treetops in a New England woodland dominated by deciduous trees.

zone between temperate woodlands and northern coniferous forests in many parts of the world.

But even farther to the south, there are extensive "islands" of conifers on the cool upper slopes of mountains. Rising high above the surrounding deciduous woodlands, the Alps, the Pyrenees, and the highest peaks of the southern Appalachians are capped with cold-tolerant conifers. At lower elevations, pockets of hemlocks and other conifers often grow on north-facing slopes of valleys and ravines.

How do these forests change with the seasons?

While northern coniferous forests remain green and somber throughout the year, temperate woodlands undergo dramatic changes. The first great transformation comes in early spring, when sunlight floods the forest floor. Boosted by food reserves stored in roots and bulbs, masses of wildflowers burst into bloom, set fruit, and in many cases die back even before the trees are fully leafed out.

In summer the leafy canopy lets only a dappling of sunlight reach the ground. Relatively few herbs and shrubs prosper in this dim light. The main activity takes place overhead, where tree leaves are manufacturing food for growth. Insects feed on the fresh green leaves, and birds feast on the abundant insects.

Autumn supplies a bounty of acorns, beechnuts, and other mature fruits that nourish a host of woodland creatures, from squirrels to wild turkeys. But the shorter days and cooler nights usher in the next big change. Leaves no longer produce chlorophyll and their summer green fades, revealing hidden pigments in yellows, reds, and other hues. In places like New England, the woodlands are ablaze with color; elsewhere the show is more subdued. Finally the leaves are shed, winter—the season of rest—arrives, and through the cold months the trees stand bare-limbed and dormant until warm weather returns.

What happens to the fallen leaves?

The temperate woodland floor is a kind of giant, self-sustaining compost heap, where nutrients are continually recycled. Every autumn, uncountable

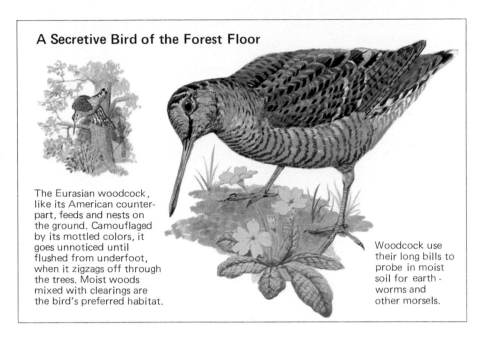

A Secretive Bird of the Forest Floor

The Eurasian woodcock, like its American counterpart, feeds and nests on the ground. Camouflaged by its mottled colors, it goes unnoticed until flushed from underfoot, when it zigzags off through the trees. Moist woods mixed with clearings are the bird's preferred habitat.

Woodcock use their long bills to probe in moist soil for earthworms and other morsels.

millions of leaves flutter to the ground. But the unending rain of organic debris also includes such things as broken branches, bud scales, insect droppings, and even entire trees.

Worms burrow through the fallen debris, feeding on it and helping to break it down. So do insects and other small animals. But the main decomposers are fungi and bacteria. Throughout the warm months they attack the accumulated litter, releasing essential nutrients as they convert the debris into a thick, rich layer of humus. And every spring this fertile soil promotes new growth that, at season's end, will contribute still more organic material to be recycled on the forest floor.

How do woodlands change from top to bottom?

In most mature woodlands, as in other forests, the vegetation grows in distinct layers. The tops of the tallest trees form the canopy, the leafy crown. Below this is the understory of shorter, shade-tolerant trees. Lower still is the shrub layer. The herb layer, closest to the ground, is made up of ferns and other low-growing plants.

This layering of the vegetation promotes diversity among the forest's animal life. Some creatures, such as squirrels, are opportunists that regularly commute between the canopy and the forest floor. Others tend to

stick to the levels that best fulfill their living requirements. Hawks and owls, for example, nest in the canopy, where their eggs and young are well concealed from other predators. Woodcock, in contrast, spend most of their time on the ground; there they nest and probe in the soil for earthworms, their favorite food.

Has cutting the forests harmed wildlife?

Human tampering with deciduous woodlands has exterminated some wild creatures and greatly reduced the numbers of others. The European bison, once widespread, now survives only in a few forests in Poland and the Soviet Union. In North America the ivory-billed woodpecker is extinct or nearly so, the victim of the destruction of the mature bottomland woodlands it needs for nesting and feeding.

But others have benefited from the cutting of forests and the creation of clearings. In North America, for example, there are many times more white-tailed deer today than there were when the Europeans first discovered the continent. The clearing of the forests and the subsequent regrowth of many of them resulted in a patchwork of open fields, brushy areas, and dense woodlands. The fields and brushy areas supply more than ample food for the deer; the nearby forests, places of refuge.

Tropical Rain Forests

How much rain does it take to make a rain forest?

The climate of a tropical rain forest is not one that changes with the seasons: it is, in fact, the most uniform climate on earth. Rain falls regularly (sometimes almost daily), totaling a minimum of 80 inches—and often exceeding 150 inches—a year. Rain forests are warm as well as wet, although not fiercely hot. The temperature usually stays about 80° F.

Just how large is the largest rain forest?

Girdling the land areas of the globe in the region of the equator are vast areas of tropical rain forest. West and central Africa have some, primarily in the drainage basin of the Congo River; so do parts of Asia, Australia, Central America, and especially South America. No other rain forest can compare in size with that of the Amazon, which covers an astonishing 2 million square miles—a third of the South American continent.

There and elsewhere, however, the rain forests are rapidly being cut and bulldozed to supply lumber and to free the land for other uses. Once the trees are gone, the land loses much of its animal life and its meager fertility. Effects are felt far beyond the area: birds breeding in temperate lands far to the north, for example, may live in the forest for most of the year.

How rich is life in a rain forest?

Tropical rain forests have greater diversity of trees and other plants than any other habitat. In a temperate woodland the variety of trees is small—often about a dozen species. In contrast, some 150 types of woody plants may be found on just two or three acres of northern Australian rain forest; some rain forests of Southeast Asia support more than 200 kinds of trees. Wildlife is similarly diverse. Exploring a single river in the Amazon basin, researchers counted almost 500 species of birds.

Plant or animal, rain forest life is so varied it often seems more abundant than it really is. For although a great many species occur there, the total population of any one species is usually small. A particular type of rain forest tree, for instance, may occur only once every several acres—in striking contrast to an oak or beech forest, dominated by the tree for which it is named.

Where do lemurs live?

Wild lemurs live in only one area of the world—on Madagascar and nearby islands. These woolly primates, which feed on insects and plants, are mainly forest dwellers. Species known as gentle lemurs live in bamboo thickets; ring-tailed lemurs (the ones usually seen in zoos), in drier, rockier places. With the exception of the indri, which is tailless, all have long, bushy tails.

Which resident is the biggest?

In the rain forest treetops large size can be a hindrance, and such arboreal creatures as squirrels and sloths are small to medium in size. Although by no means as common as in open country, some larger creatures do occur in

From the Treetops to the Forest Floor

The dense foliage in a tropical rain forest prevents nearly all the sunlight from reaching the ground, making living conditions very different in the treetops and on the forest floor. As a result, wildlife occurs in layers rather than as a random mix. The animals shown here are from South America, but those living in other rain forests display similar preferences for a particular layer.

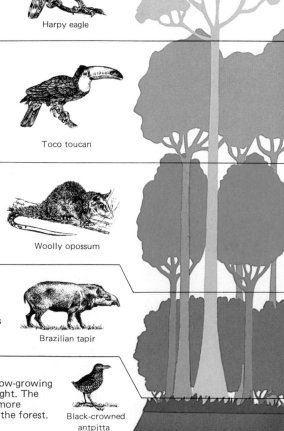

The emergent layer—the "attic"—is formed of the isolated tops of the tallest trees, which rise as much as 300 feet above the forest floor. This is the domain of the great birds of prey, which use the treetops as perches for sighting quarry.

Harpy eagle

The canopy, generally 150 to 250 feet above the surface, is the rain forest's "ceiling." Composed of the crowns of closely spaced trees, this sunny layer offers the most food and shelter and contains the most animal life.

Toco toucan

The understory is the layer directly beneath the canopy. Living space there is supplied by the long, narrow crowns of the shorter trees and by the trunks of the canopy trees.

Woolly opossum

The shrub layer is not a dense one; plants in it are widely scattered. From this layer such large ground-dwelling mammals as tapirs take their food.

Brazilian tapir

The ground layer, made up of low-growing plants, receives practically no light. The temperature and humidity are more constant than anywhere else in the forest.

Black-crowned antpitta

A perpetual mist softens this scene in a Costa Rican cloud forest and nurtures the growth of swordlike perching plants.

rain forests, both in the trees and on the ground. Tapirs, stocky relatives of the rhinoceros, live in South America and Asia, foraging in wetlands and sometimes on sugar plantations. Leopards occur in the Old World; jaguars, in the New. Above all, there are the elephants; for though elephants in Africa prefer the savanna, Asian elephants—smaller but still impressive—seek out the forest.

What are kinkajous?
Many a mammal of the Amazon rain forest is a climber, using its tail as a fifth limb for swinging through the trees. Spider and howler monkeys do this; so does the kinkajou, a yellowish, three-foot-long relative of the raccoon. Kinkajous, like raccoons, are primarily nocturnal. Sometimes called honey bears, these creatures use the long, slender tongue to feed on honey, insects, and fruit.

What is a cloud forest?
Blanketed by fog and colder than a tropical rain forest, cloud forests clothe mountain heights in several parts of the world—most notably in Central and South America. Thanks to the airborne moisture, perching plants, or epiphytes, thrive without roots or soil; the forest there nurtures a thousand kinds of orchids alone. Prevailing winds in this region blow from the east, dropping their moisture as they rise over the mountains. Some leeward slopes of the Andes, which may experience rain only once or twice in a human lifetime, are covered not by cloud forest but by desert.

In East Africa cloud forests are dominated by 60-foot tree heaths, cousins of plants growing no more than knee-high on Alaskan muskeg and Scottish moors. Heath thickets mix with giant lobelias and groundsels, members of the daisy family that send up 30-foot stalks. Downslope, tall bamboos dominate; upslope are lichens and moss, then perpetual snow and ice.

Are rain forests the same as jungles?
Even though tropical rain forests are often called jungles, the two are not the same. A jungle is a tangle of vegetation in which vines, branches, and brush intertwine in a mass that is nearly impenetrable at ground level. In contrast, rain forests are covered by a green canopy, made up of the crowns of trees, that filters out all but about 1 percent of the sunlight. Because so little sun passes through, plant growth beneath the canopy is relatively open—a far cry from the impenetrable jungle. About the only places in a rain forest that qualify as jungle are those where the big trees have been cleared or along riverbanks and other natural openings.

Jungle Monkeys

What makes primates such good climbers?

Most primates—primates are the mammal group that includes monkeys and apes—are designed for climbing. On nearly all species the arms are longer than the legs. For a maximum grip on branches and other rounded surfaces, limbs have separate digits (that is, fingers and toes). Apes and Old World monkeys have a grip-facilitating thumb, powerful hind limbs, and large feet for leaping and balance. On some New World monkeys a prehensile tail—one equipped for grasping—functions as a fifth limb.

To travel from tree to tree, primates need not descend. The gibbon's long arms, which hinder movement on the ground, end in hooklike hands that allow the acrobatic ape to swing through the trees with maximum speed. An orangutan moves its heavy body from tree to tree by bending the tops until the next perch is within reach of its powerful arms. Its feet clutch objects so well that they serve almost as another set of hands.

How fierce are gorillas?

Many animals have stereotypes based on appearance, but few have suffered as much in this regard as gorillas. Long-term field studies of the fast-disappearing mountain species show them to be not fierce beasts but gentle vegetarians; they spend most of their day playing, resting, and foraging.

Gorilla

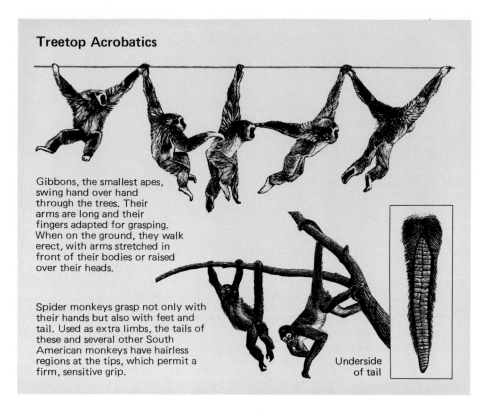

Treetop Acrobatics

Gibbons, the smallest apes, swing hand over hand through the trees. Their arms are long and their fingers adapted for grasping. When on the ground, they walk erect, with arms stretched in front of their bodies or raised over their heads.

Spider monkeys grasp not only with their hands but also with feet and tail. Used as extra limbs, the tails of these and several other South American monkeys have hairless regions at the tips, which permit a firm, sensitive grip.

Underside of tail

A large ape with impressive canine teeth and a loud threat display, the male gorilla is more bluff than bite. When agitated he beats his chest, gives a series of calls, places plant materials in his mouth, tears up vegetation, stands erect, and crashes through the underbrush in a charge that almost always stops short of the target. Such behavior usually drives away unwelcome visitors, be they gorillas, other large animals, or man.

Which ones eat meat?

Though most monkeys and apes feed mainly on nuts, fruits, and other plant materials, many also eat insects, eggs, and small lizards. The African chimpanzee is believed to make frequent use of meat, taking baby antelope, bushpigs, and red colobus monkeys. Cooperative hunting by male chimpanzees in Tanzania's Gombe National Park results in an annual kill of 60 to 70 animals.

Why do primates pick at one another's fur?

Certain primates spend hours each day removing flakes of skin, insects, and other debris from one another's coats. This behavior, called grooming, is more for social than hygienic purposes. Among such animals as chimpanzees and baboons, which frequently associate in large groups, grooming helps reinforce friendly relations, and it is often used to placate dominant or aggressive individuals. Female gorillas, for instance, spend far more time grooming the dominant male than one another.

How do monkeys and apes learn?

In primate society the basic unit—educational and otherwise—is mother and young. Mothers supply their young with food, warmth, security, and, at least initially, transportation. Very early they learn to respond to their mother's gestures and calls.

Though born with a strong grip, young monkeys must learn how to climb. Watched over by their mothers, they start on low branches and work their way up. Some adult monkeys taste foods to show their weaned offspring which ones are suitable and which are not. Monkeys are weaned at a younger age than apes and so have a shorter time to learn. A spider monkey, for example, is weaned at six months; orangutans take three or four years and chimpanzees five or six.

What are monkey tails like?

One major difference between monkeys and apes—gibbons, orangutans, gorillas, and chimpanzees—have no tails. On a monkey, tail length is usually correlated with body length, but some large species, including mandrills and Japanese macaques, have only stumps.

Tails can serve as balancing poles, flying equipment, or extra hands, depending on the monkeys to which they are attached. Old World monkeys, such as langurs, mangabeys, and patas monkeys, use their hair-covered tails as rudders or air brakes when the animals leap from tree to tree, or as props to support them on the ground. New World monkeys, such as howlers, spiders, and woollies, have tails with sensitive hairless ridges on the inside tip. The spider's tail is so deft it can pick up a peanut—yet is strong enough to support the monkey's full weight.

Who climbs trees?

Like other residents of a tropical forest, different kinds of primates live at different heights. Leaf-eating monkeys cluster at the top of the forest canopy; monkeys with more varied diets—macaques and capuchins, for example—range from mid-tree height down to the forest floor.

Weight plays an obvious role in determining who climbs trees. In the treetops the small red colobus monkey munches on flowers and leaves; more than a hundred feet below, an adult male gorilla may browse on the ground. Female gorillas, which are smaller, and young climb trees to feed, play, and rest. The ground, of course, offers less protection. Sleeping there is unusual among apes—some big gorillas do it—and unknown among wild monkeys, even those that spend most of the day on the forest floor.

Relatives Keep Their Distance

Among the most beautiful monkeys are the 20 or so species of guenons, which come in a number of colors and often have such special markings as a spot on the nose. Guenons live in African forests, where different species occupy different levels. Dianas, for example, prefer the treetops; the red-tailed spends the day on the forest floor.

1. Diana monkey
2. Spot-nosed monkey
3. DeBrazza's monkey
4. Mona monkey
5. Mustached monkey
6. Talapoin monkey
7. Red-tailed monkey

Mountain Wildlife

How are mountains like layer cakes?
Any mountain, whether it rises from the green valleys of Europe, like the Matterhorn, or from the dry highlands of Africa, like Kilimanjaro, resembles a gigantic layer cake. Each layer constitutes what biologists call a life zone, with its characteristic plants. (Animals tend to arrange themselves in similar fashion, although they often move about from zone to zone.) Which species live in a given zone depends on soil, prevailing winds, rainfall, and especially temperature. For each 1,000-foot rise in elevation, the temperature falls by several degrees—on the average, that is. Temperatures drop less rapidly in the tropics.

On mountain ranges of different continents, the zones of life show striking parallels. In parts of Europe and North America, for example, the lowest zone is a mixed forest of broadleaved trees and conifers, which often adjoins mountain meadows and park-

The European chamois, cautious on narrow ledges, can leap a 20-foot-wide chasm with confidence.

lands. This is the winter range of such hoofed animals as deer and elk, which move to the evergreen forests of higher elevations in summer. Smaller animals of the forested levels include rabbits, hares, squirrels, and porcupines—food for foxes, coyotes, bobcats, and members of the weasel family. Above the timberline, mountains feature such surefooted hoofed creatures as Rocky Mountain goats and bighorn sheep, European ibex (a wild goat), and chamois (related to American mountain goats.) Furry marmots enliven the rocky slopes.

Which trees grow where?
In temperate regions the lowest windward slopes usually get plenty of precipitation. There the forest consists of moisture-loving species—such broadleaved trees as maples, beeches, elms, and oaks, and some hemlocks and other conifers. In the higher, cooler coniferous zone various spruces, firs, and pines grow straight and tall; Engelmann spruce, noble fir, ponderosa pine, and mountain pine are among the species associated with mountains. As elevation increases, trees become smaller until near the timberline only stunted conifers and willows hold on to life. This is the habitat of the oldest living things on earth—the gnarled, twisted bristlecone pines of the American West. Some specimens are close to 5,000 years old.

In the tropics dense rain forest occupies the lowest zone. In the New World dozens of species of tall, massive trees with buttressed trunks crowd together in a small space. Where fog blankets an area, rain forest is transformed into cloud forest. Twisted, widely branching trees are draped with such perching plants as orchids and moss. At high elevations in Borneo and New Guinea, northern pines and magnolias mingle with such southern conifers as podocarps. Australian mountain forests are mainly eucalyptus. Everywhere, tree ferns and clumps of bamboo contribute to the lush tropical look.

A trio of Rocky Mountain goats play follow-the-leader on a precipitous cliff in Canada's Jasper National Park.

Why don't mountain goats fall?

Life among the crags and chasms of the high peaks depends on agility, a head for heights, and the ability to leap without fear. Ensuring a firm, nonslip grip on unstable rocks, the mountain goat's spreading, cloven hooves have two tough, pliant pads with soft centers that act like suction cups. Though wild goats can climb almost vertically up the face of a cliff, these surefooted creatures sometimes do fall—victims of rockslides and avalanches, a significant cause of death. A golden eagle may dive on a newborn kid, slamming into it at 80 miles an hour and knocking it off a ledge. But even the rare grizzly that invades high meadows avoids the male goat's sharp horns and aggressive defense, and predators are generally not a problem for adults.

The chamois, cousin of the Rocky Mountain goat, leaps over rocks and chasms in the Alps and other European mountains. Higher on the slopes is the ibex, with long, back-sweeping horns. Other hoofed mountain dwellers include the shaggy Himalayan tahr, closely related to ibexes, and such wild sheep as Europe's mouflon and North America's bighorn.

What sort of bird is a condor?

Mountains furnish refuge, roosts, and breeding territories for some of the world's most impressive birds. The Andean condor—one of the largest of all flying species, with its incredible 10-foot-wide wings—breeds on inaccessible ledges from Venezuela to Tierra del Fuego. Condors are vultures. Carrion eaters like other vultures, Andean condors often visit the coast, where they feed on dead fish.

Only slightly smaller than the South American bird, the California condor is restricted to a reserve in the coastal mountains of that state. A low reproductive rate (a single egg is laid every other year), illegal killing, and loss of habitat have brought the species close to the point of no return.

Clinging to existence in high, remote areas of Europe, Asia, and Africa is the lammergeier. The name means "lamb vulture." Unusual in appearance (it has a bearded head), the lammergeier has an intriguing feeding habit as well. The bird has often been observed carrying a bone in its feet, like an osprey with a fish. Having split the bone by dropping it from a height, the vulture descends to feast on the marrow.

Vultures are, of course, not the only mountain bird. The mighty golden eagle, a spectacular flier, is found in temperate areas throughout the Northern Hemisphere. Rosy finches and white-tailed ptarmigan in North America, hill star hummingbirds in South America, snow finches and wall creepers in Eurasia, malachite sunbirds in Africa—these are among the smaller feathered forms.

Are mountains devoid of life in winter?

Active throughout the year, such hunters as the rare, beautiful snow leopard of the Himalayas move to lower slopes in winter. So do the wapiti, or American elk, and many other large creatures. But migrating to warmer lowland areas is not always the answer. Such rodents as voles take advantage of heavy snows by digging tunnels. The temperature there is sometimes 70 degrees warmer than the outside air, and they can feed all

In winter furry little pikas, close cousins of rabbits, feed on plants that they dried and stored during the summer.

winter on roots and other vegetation. Hares spend the winter actively hopping about, feeding on bark and twigs and seeking shelter beneath snow-weighted branches of spruce or fir.

Where hot springs exist, animals are quick to take advantage of the benefits supplied. Bison in North America's Yellowstone National Park, mountain sheep on Asia's Kamchatka Peninsula, and snow monkeys (macaques) in Japan head for hot springs and the surrounding heated ground. There they feed on green plants all winter and enjoy the sauna-style living.

Life Above the Timberline

Where is the timberline?

Trees, like other green plants, are sugar factories. Because a certain level of warmth is necessary for them to operate efficiently, temperature determines how high on a mountain trees occur. Summer is what counts, not winter; when trees are already dormant, increased cold matters little.

The critical point is a July average of 50° F. Trees cannot grow where summers are cooler, whether that happens high on a mountain or toward the poles. Such a limit is called the timberline, or tree line, and precisely where it occurs depends on local climate. In the Alps it is at about 5,500 feet; in the Himalayas, at about 15,000 feet. Toward the poles the timberline lies much lower than it does closer to the equator.

How difficult is life at the top?

Above the timberline the temperature at the ground surface may be more than 100° F at noon and fall to below freezing at night—a fluctuation challenging indeed to plant life, which also faces an abbreviated growing season at high elevations. Supplying a head start for the next generation, one species of grass has seeds that germinate while still on the parent plant.

For insects, high mountains do not make hospitable homes. Because of the scarce food supply and the cold, grasshoppers and others develop at a slowed pace. Wind can be either a help or a hindrance. To avoid it, butterflies skim low to the ground, and many mountain insects have no wings. Among the delightful exceptions are the Apollo butterflies. With wings proportionately larger than those of other butterflies, they sail on the wind rather than lying low. Their dark color helps them stay warm and active.

Air at high elevations is thin, with little oxygen. To enhance its oxygen-carrying capacity, the blood of llamas, Andean relatives of the camel, has an extraordinarily high red cell count. Where llamas live, air pressure and oxygen are so low that ignited matches will not continue to burn.

Why are some plants hairy?

Fine hairs coat the stems, leaves, and sepals of many alpine flowers, trapping heat—as does the fur of a mammal—and raising the plants' temperature higher than the air's. The hairs of snow-growing willows are actually two-toned—translucent at the top, which allows sunlight to penetrate, and dark at the base, to absorb radiant heat. On some alpine plants matted hairs deflect wind and prevent excessive drying, which is often a problem on mountains. In contrast, plants living in the Himalayas are subject to monsoon rains and get too much water. Their hairs help them to shed the rain.

Edelweiss—"noble white"—is perhaps the most celebrated of alpine flowers. Sometimes called flannel flower, this yellow-blossomed member of the daisy family has white, woolly leaves that spread out into a star. Its home is the mountains of Europe (specifically, the Alps, the Pyrenees, and the Apennines), where it grows to elevations of about 10,000 feet.

How high on a mountain will you find bird life?

Close relatives of crows known as choughs breed at 16,000 feet in the

---

High Life and Low: The Patterns Are the Same

High on a mountain such as this one in Europe, food resources are scant and animals not particularly abundant. But from a general perspective life above the timberline is not dramatically different from life elsewhere. Many species found here also occur in other places; rock ptarmigan, for example, live on the northern tundra too. Species more or less restricted to mountains, such as the mountain ringlet and the alpine chough, have close relatives at lower elevations. Nor are life-styles above the timberline unique. Hares nibble on plants; weasels hunt hares.

Mountain ringlets, like most other satyr butterflies, have eyespots.

Alpine gentians set seed every year— an unusual habit for a mountain plant.

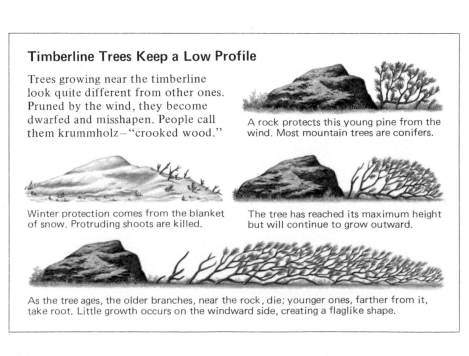

Timberline Trees Keep a Low Profile

Trees growing near the timberline look quite different from other ones. Pruned by the wind, they become dwarfed and misshapen. People call them krummholz—"crooked wood."

A rock protects this young pine from the wind. Most mountain trees are conifers.

Winter protection comes from the blanket of snow. Protruding shoots are killed.

The tree has reached its maximum height but will continue to grow outward.

As the tree ages, the older branches, near the rock, die; younger ones, farther from it, take root. Little growth occurs on the windward side, creating a flaglike shape.

Himalayas and have been recorded at more than 26,000 feet. In the Andes, condors range above 20,000 feet; eagles, vultures, and other soaring birds frequent the 13,000-foot level on the Ethiopian plateau. For birds to manage at such high elevations requires a high degree of adaptation since their huge energy output demands large amounts of oxygen.

Why do pikas make hay while the sun shines?
Guinea pig–sized relatives of rabbits, pikas live in the mountains of western North America. In summer pikas harvest the tender growth of heather and other plants, carrying bundles crosswise in their jaws and placing them on sun-heated rocks to dry. Although the haystacks are usually small, they may hold a bushel of material, the product of several days' work. In winter, when pikas stay active beneath the snow and in rock crevices, the sun-cured hay means food. Such a supply must meet the animal's needs for six to eight months—needs that are greater than in other seasons because so much body heat is lost to the air.

Alpine choughs, a type of crow, live on Everest and other Himalayan peaks as well as in the Alps.

Purple saxifrage sends its roots into rock crevices. The name comes from the Latin for "breaking rocks."

Three-leaved rushes may look like grass, but they are really more closely related to lilies.

Rock ptarmigan, members of the grouse family, have a rapid wingbeat.

Crane flies look like mosquitoes but do not bite. Their long legs are easily broken.

Mountain hares are also called blue and northern hares. Larger than rabbits, hares have long hind legs and ears.

Forget-me-nots on mountain slopes tend to be smaller than lowland species.

Ermine, known also as stoats and short-tailed weasels, are active hunters.

Sheep's fescue, a grass good as pasture for sheep, grows in dense tufts.

285

The Arctic Tundra

Why doesn't the tundra have trees?

In the Far North willows are about the only trees—*if* you call them trees. They stand mere inches high, the growth rings in the woody tissue so close-set it requires a microscope to count them. Narrow rings, of course, indicate slow growth. Trees grow tall only by manufacturing large amounts of food, and apparently cells cannot do this fast enough in the cold. Trees do not occur where July temperatures average below 50° F.

The Arctic tundra, known by a Lapp word for this kind of land, blankets 5 million square miles—one tenth of the earth's land surface north of the tree line. (Since the comparable latitudes in the Southern Hemisphere are covered with water, there is no such thing as "Antarctic tundra.") Plant growth here is limited not only by cold but also by wind, drought, and the long winter darkness. A permanently frozen layer of soil, called permafrost, stops roots from pushing deep; even if a plant's growing tips could endure the harsh conditions, it could not form a root system capable of supporting much in the way of height. Soil is poor and constantly churned by alternate freezing and thawing. Furthermore, the soil lies insecurely over the permafrost. Whole slopes creep and slide, and only masses of shallow roots let plants ride along.

What is the difference between reindeer and caribou?

In looks and behavior, reindeer and caribou are very much alike. All that separates these two hoofed mammals is their range—wild reindeer live in Eurasia and caribou in North America—and the fact that reindeer, but not caribou, have been domesticated. They are generally considered members of the same species.

In only two places in the world, East Africa and the Far North, can you see wildlife clear to the horizon. The vast African herds comprise several species; the northern ones, only the caribou. "Only" is perhaps an inappropriate word: a caribou herd may include tens of thousands or more.

Migrating caribou calve on the tundra and winter in sparse forests to the south. (Other individuals stay in the forest all year.) Although these animals can smell food plants—they specialize in reindeer moss, a type of lichen—under fluffy snow, they cannot paw down to it once the snow has compacted. It is snow, not cold, that prompts migration.

How do polar bears hunt seals?

Polar bears drift hundreds of miles from land, riding ice floes. Though they swim well, paddling with their great paws, they hunt not only from the water but also from the ice. The preferred prey is seals, which gnaw breathing holes in the ice. Such holes

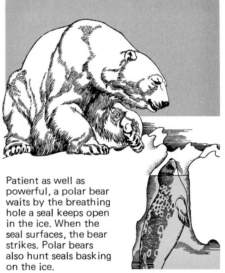

Patient as well as powerful, a polar bear waits by the breathing hole a seal keeps open in the ice. When the seal surfaces, the bear strikes. Polar bears also hunt seals basking on the ice.

are clues to the victim's whereabouts, and if they become snowed over, bears find them by smell. Scooping out the holes so they can reach in freely, the bears lightly backfill so that nothing looks disturbed. Then they wait. It may be a long vigil, for a seal uses more than one hole. When a seal finally surfaces, the bear uses claws and teeth to draw the prey onto the ice. The polar bears feast on the blubber and internal organs; ravens and Arctic foxes claim the leftovers.

Polar bears are mammals of the land as well as the sea. The huge creatures, which measure 10 feet long and weigh half a ton, can lope along at 25 miles an hour. When on land, especially in autumn, they are plant eaters rather than hunters.

Caribou: Nomads of the North

Old World reindeer and New World caribou are thought to belong to the same species.

The only species of deer in which both sexes have antlers, caribou have another unique feature: they are the only deer to associate in such enormous herds. Tens of thousands or more migrate together across the tundra. The land endures such an onslaught only because they snatch a mouthful and then move on; they do not deplete the lichens on which they largely feed. Also, their hooves splay out, preventing the soil from turning into a quagmire. Helping them tread on snow and ice, the feet of caribou and polar bears are broader than those of their kin to the south. The ptarmigan's feathered toes, which its grouse relatives do not have, serve as snowshoes and insulation.

Some Animals Have Snowshoes

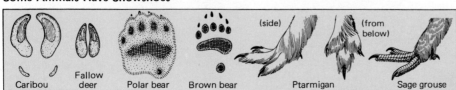

Caribou | Fallow deer | Polar bear | Brown bear | (side) Ptarmigan (from below) | Sage grouse

A Summer Visitor and a Stay-at-home

With the return of the sun above the tundra horizon, literally millions of birds flock to this northern nursery to nest. Insects, seeds, and berries are plentiful, and unbroken daylight permits nonstop feeding. Shorebirds and waterfowl are the most numerous summer visitors; ptarmigan and snowy owls may stay around all year.

A hillock is used as a roosting and nesting site.

The snowy owl's flight is silent.

Loons fly with rapid wing-beats, keeping the head lower than the body.

Arctic loons, known as black-throated divers in Britain, nest beside tundra lakes and winter on coasts to the south.

Snowy owls are hardy tundra birds that hunt lemmings, hares, and ptarmigan. If the food supply fails, they fly south.

How does wildlife cope with winter?

As winter approaches, ptarmigan molt from brown to white, the new plumage camouflaging these chickenlike birds in the snow. Feathery tufts grow on their feet, enlarging the foot on the downstroke and serving as built-in snowshoes. At night or on cold days, ptarmigan dive into the snow or dig down through it. They feed on willow buds as they go.

Arctic foxes and certain weasels and hares also turn white in winter, making them less conspicuous as predators (the fox and weasel) or as prey (the hare). A rare color phase of the Arctic fox is pale blue in winter.

Arctic foxes, like ptarmigan, have snowshoes, but theirs are made of fur rather than feathers. They increase the effective size of the foot and thus help support body weight in snow besides keeping warmth in. Fur is a powerful defense against the cold. Long hairs shielding a thick, felted, almost airtight fleece keep a musk-ox warm in winter. Musk-oxen are, in fact, the only land mammals that can simply wait out a northern storm. Other crea-tures use trees or snow as cover, but musk-ox bands, typically numbering 20 to 30 animals, do nothing more than bunch around their young for optimum warmth and face into the wind. When necessary they can endure a blizzard for days, standing the whole time and living off fat from around-the-clock summer feeding. Grasses and dwarf shrubs are their favorite foods.

Who preys on whom?

In northern lands the wolf reigns as predator king. Such large mammals as caribou and moose offer it the best return for energy spent, but such smaller creatures as lemmings, voles, hares, or nestling birds will do. Wolves can also scent seal pups on land and capture seals basking on the ice.

The Arctic fox, which weighs only about a tenth what the wolf does, prefers lemmings. If need be, it feeds on birds, eggs, berries, and whatever can be scavenged; in winter it follows polar bears and wolves, filching from their kills. Arctic foxes locate voles—small rodents—under snow by listen-ing for faint scratchings and squeals, then leap into the air and land stiff-legged to break the crust of snow. With nose and forepaws held together, the hunters are ready to dig and bite.

Are wolverines related to wolves?

Thirty-pound wolverines lumber through northern parts of North America and Eurasia (many other Arctic animals occur in both the Old World and the New). Despite the name, they are related not to wolves but to weasels. Wolverine fur is generally thicker than wolf fur and has more oil.

Wolverines hunt aggressively both from trees and from the ground. While patrolling for food, they may travel nonstop as much as six or seven miles. Diet embraces just about anything with fur or feathers. The animal's scientific name—*Gulo gulo*—translates as "glutton," and Siberian trappers reported finding a wolverine cache with some 20 fox carcasses and 100 ptarmigan. Wolverines also eat carrion, which they locate by watching for converging ravens and gulls.

The Bountiful Ocean

What lives in the ocean?
The ocean teems with all sorts of life: great schools of fish, whales and dolphins, giant squid, wandering sea turtles, seals, and hosts of other creatures. But the most abundant form of life is plankton, the uncountable hordes of tiny drifters that swim only feebly or float passively with the currents in the surface layers of the sea.

Plankton includes both plants and animals, most of them microscopic in size. A sampling taken with a fine-meshed net would yield multitudes of diatoms and other one-celled algae along with many kinds of very small animals. There would also be large numbers of slightly bigger animals that feed on the plants, on the smaller animals, and on each other. Among the many other creatures of the plankton are miniature shrimplike animals called copepods, most of them smaller than grains of rice; the eggs and larvae of such creatures as fish and squid, whose adult forms can swim; and predatory arrowworms, transparent little animals that are all but invisible save for the tiny dots of their eyes.

Is plankton important?
Just as animal life on land depends ultimately on plants, all other life in the sea (except for the larger seaweeds) is nourished by planktonic plants. Though microscopic in size, these superabundant algae form the basis of ocean food chains.

Copepods, for example, feed mainly on diatoms and other one-celled algae. They are eaten in turn by herrings, anchovies, and other small fish that are the food of larger fish, squid, and other predators. At the top of the food chain are the biggest carnivores, such as killer whales, sharks, and giant tunas, on which few or no other animals prey. Thus, however indirectly, even they rely finally on the energy produced by the microscopic planktonic plants.

Does plankton stay put near the ocean surface?
During World War II seamen on board U.S. naval vessels were mystified when their sonar indicated dangerous shoals where their maps showed deep water. Stranger still, other ships passing over the same areas found no sign of shallows.

Oceanographers, called in to solve the mystery, discovered what they called the "deep scattering layer," or DSL, which seemed to be causing the false sonar readings. It moved close to the surface at night and descended to deeper water during the day.

Researchers eventually learned that the DSL is actually composed of planktonic animals and the larger creatures that prey on them. At sunset the animals of the DSL begin their nightly journey to the surface to feed on planktonic plants; by day they return to depths of 2,000 feet or more. Sonar beams, reflected off their bodies, give the misleading reading of shallow water.

Where is ocean life most plentiful?
The algae on which all other ocean life depends thrive best in coastal seas. There the water is richest in dissolved mineral nutrients, the natural fertilizers that support vigorous plant growth. Many of the minerals are washed down to the sea by rivers flowing off the land. Another means of transport is vertical currents, called upwellings, that carry minerals from ocean depths to the surface.

Along the west coast of South America, for example, such upwellings support one of the richest fisheries in the world. Millions of tons of plankton-eating anchovies are netted there each year, along with tuna and other fish that feed on the anchovies. Enormous colonies of seabirds also thrive on the teeming throngs of fish. Thick deposits of their droppings, called guano, which have accumulated on islands and cliff tops, are harvested for fertilizer.

Every few years shifting currents cause the upwelling to slow down or temporarily stop, and so demonstrate

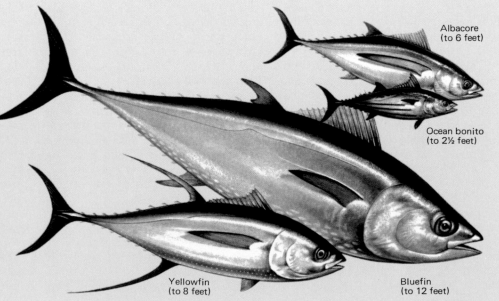

The Tunas: Tireless Rovers of the Open Sea

Among the top predators in oceanic food chains, the tunas are fast-swimming and far-ranging. Knifing through the water at top speed, they snap up herring, mackerel, flying fish, squid, and other prey. Large schools travel through tropical and temperate seas around the world, where they are avidly pursued by commercial and sport fishermen. Many are notable for their long-distance travels; giant bluefins regularly cross the entire Pacific Ocean between the coasts of California and Japan.

Albacore
(to 6 feet)

Ocean bonito
(to 2½ feet)

Yellowfin
(to 8 feet)

Bluefin
(to 12 feet)

its importance. The once bountiful harvest from the sea dwindles to a trickle until conditions return to normal and nutrients once again begin to nourish life near the surface.

Do any big animals eat plankton?

The majority of plankton eaters are relatively small, but some surprisingly large creatures also depend on a diet of plankton. Crab-eating seals of Antarctic waters, despite their name, feed mainly on krill, small shrimplike crustaceans. They gulp mouthfuls of water, then force it out through tiny openings between their teeth, trapping the krill inside.

The huge basking shark, which reaches lengths of 30 feet or more, and the even larger whale shark also are peaceful plankton eaters. They strain it from the water with a sievelike system of projections on their gills. But the largest of the plankton eaters are the baleen, or whalebone, whales. Fringes of baleen plates hanging from the roofs of their mouths act as strainers that filter out krill and other small creatures. Blue whales, the largest animals that have ever lived on earth, are one of the species that feed on this tiny floating food of the sea.

Which fish swim the fastest?

Fish speeds are notoriously difficult to calculate, and many conflicting claims have been made as to which are the speediest. Some say that sailfish and swordfish are the champions, reaching speeds of 50 miles or more an hour. Other top contenders are some of the streamlined tunas, which can easily slice through the water at more than 40 miles an hour. As might be expected, all the fastest fish are large predators, specialized for the chase. Usually, however, fish conserve their energy by cruising along at moderate rates, and resort to their top speeds only when pursuing or being pursued.

Why are albatrosses special?

In past centuries, sailors sometimes blamed albatrosses for causing dangerous winds and storms. In fact, the great seabirds appeared at such times because, without a strong wind to ride, they are almost helpless; their long narrow wings are designed for gliding, not flapping flight.

Shearwaters are birds of the open sea. They skim just above the waves, dipping down now and then to nab small fish and other morsels.

Storm petrels flit and hover above the waves, sometimes pattering their feet on the surface as they search for food.

Shearwaters and Storm Petrels Shun Land Except to Nest

Among the small seafaring relatives of albatrosses are the gull-like shearwaters and the smaller, wide-ranging storm petrels. Completely adapted to life at sea, the birds return to the land only to breed on remote islands or isolated mainland cliffs. Most species approach their nesting colonies only under the cover of darkness, and many breed in shallow underground tunnels. Both parents care for the single chick, which is ready to take up a life of its own at sea when it is about two months old.

Unequaled in their ability to ride on the wind, albatrosses are perhaps the most truly marine of all birds. Most seabirds stick to coastal waters and return to land at night to rest. Albatrosses, in contrast, travel over the open sea for months at a time, covering thousands of miles. The big birds, in fact, spend most of their lives at sea, coming to land only to breed. They can drink saltwater without harm.

Albatrosses are found in both the Northern and the Southern Hemisphere but are most common south of the equator. One native of the southern oceans, the wandering albatross, is the largest member of its family. Its 11-foot wingspan exceeds that of all other birds, including even the Andean condor. Smaller, similarly adapted relatives of the albatrosses include fulmars and shearwaters.

The Ways of Whales

What sort of creature is a whale?
Though over the centuries people have confused whales with fish, by 350 B.C. at least one individual, Aristotle, knew that the two were very different. In his writings he noted that since whales had blowholes instead of gills, they must possess lungs, making them mammals instead of fish.

Some species dive several thousand feet deep to feed and can stay underwater for more than an hour. All must, however, surface for air. Before drawing in a fresh supply, they force warm, moist breath out of the blowhole, forming the spout, which at a distance is often far more visible than the whale itself. For not only do whales tend to be camouflaged by color; when they breathe, often only their blowholes and surrounding areas are brought above the surface. The rest remains hidden.

Shaped for life in the sea, whales do not look like typical mammals. They have flippers instead of forelegs. Hind legs remain as mere vestiges inside the body. Hair lingers as bristles rather than heat-retaining fur; insulation is supplied by blubber.

Are all whales the same?
Blue, white, gray, humpbacked, bottle-nosed—as the names suggest, color and form vary from species to species. Size is even more diverse: the 80-plus species range in size from the renowned big blue, which has exceeded 100 feet, to several warm-water species smaller than human beings.

Scientists divide whales into two major groups: the toothed and the baleen whales. Among the larger kinds, only the sperm whale has teeth. The others—the blue and the humpbacked, for example—have a curtain of plates made of baleen, a fibrous material much like a fingernail. Baleen functions as a strainer, separating small bits of food from the water.

How big is the biggest whale?
For sheer bulk, whales easily outstrip all other animals of any place and any time. Mature blue whale females, larger than the males, average 85 to 95 feet long. Total body weight approaches 100 tons, with oil-rich blubber accounting for nearly a third of that. The heart alone weighs half a ton. Yesterday's dinosaurs seem puny by comparison; today's elephants and rhinos, almost runts.

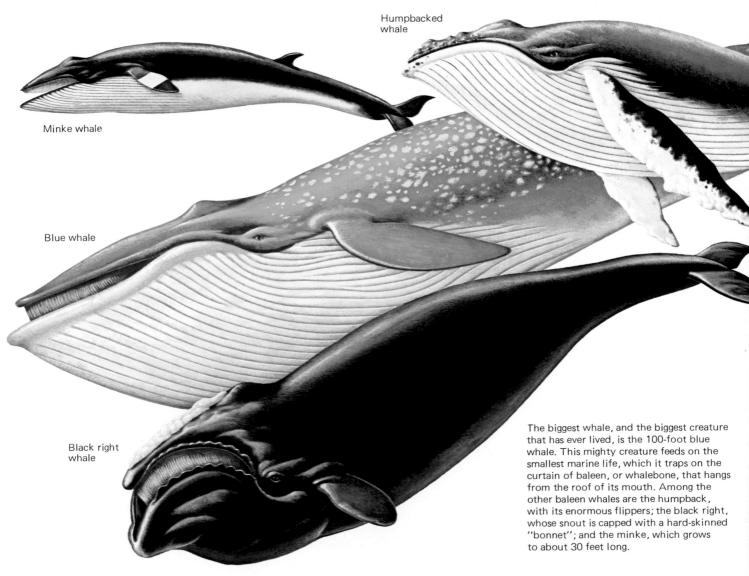

Humpbacked whale

Minke whale

Blue whale

Black right whale

The biggest whale, and the biggest creature that has ever lived, is the 100-foot blue whale. This mighty creature feeds on the smallest marine life, which it traps on the curtain of baleen, or whalebone, that hangs from the roof of its mouth. Among the other baleen whales are the humpback, with its enormous flippers; the black right, whose snout is capped with a hard-skinned "bonnet"; and the minke, which grows to about 30 feet long.

Common dolphin

Sperm whale

Narwhal

Bottle-nosed whale

Toothed whales range in size from the sperm whale, which can measure more than 60 feet, to dolphins and porpoises less than 10 feet long. Instead of teeth, narwhals of the Far North have tusks. Killer whales eat everything from other whales to fish and shellfish. Pilot, sperm, and bottle-nosed whales specialize in squid and the related cuttlefish and octopuses.

Killer whale

Pilot whale

Only the oceans—more precisely, only the cold oceans—can support animals of such enormous size. Vast supplies of the small plants and animals known as plankton (Greek for "drifting") in the Arctic and Antarctic are food for the largest whales. In just one day a single whale can strain out a ton of food—mostly inch-long planktonic relatives of shrimp, called krill.

How do whales talk with one another?
Southern finbacks do not follow regular migration routes, yet these baleen whales congregate each summer in places where food is abundant. Somehow they must communicate to one another precisely where plankton "pastures" are the richest; some sort of contact must knit widely scattered individuals into a herd.

In the chill darkness of the ocean, neither eyes nor noses can gather much information. Hearing seems to fill the gap. Although a whale has no vocal cords, air forced past valves and

flaps that are associated with the blowhole produces a range of clicks, moans, whistles, and even songs. Communication is not the only function of sound. "Reading" the sound waves rebounding from objects, toothed whales navigate and find food, much as bats do when echolocating in flight.

What do killer whales kill?
Killer whales, or orcas, grow to only about 30 feet long, but they will fearlessly attack bigger whales, ripping out tongues and biting flippers and flanks. More often the prey is smaller—fish, squid, seals, dolphins, and porpoises. In swimming, the killer whale's high back fin and its flippers act as stabilizers; large tail flukes help the spindle-shaped creature speed through the water. Killer whales are the fastest of all whales.

In captivity, killer whales sometimes display a trait their name does not even remotely imply: devotion.

Netted individuals may be followed by free whales, who press close to the net and communicate through the mesh. There is the story, too, of a male killer whale, newly placed in an aquarium and long without food, who finally took a fish from the trainer. Instead of eating it all himself, he took it to another newcomer—a female whale—and shared it with her.

Do whales always stay in one place?
The great whales make the longest migrations known among mammals. From the Pacific coast of Mexico, where they give birth in winter, gray whales swim 6,000 miles to the icy Arctic, where they feed unceasingly on the abundant life. Humpbacks also feast in the north, then migrate for the winter to Hawaii or Mexico, or to Bermuda and the Caribbean islands. In the Southern Hemisphere, baleen whales follow comparable migration patterns, leaving polar feeding sites for warmer calving grounds as winter approaches. The survival of the young—and therefore of the species—may require warm water, for the newborn have little blubber.

The Depths of the Sea

What's it like beneath the sea?
The ocean depths are a strange environment. Even in the clearest water, no light is visible to the human eye at more than about 650 feet below the surface. The heat of the sun's rays is absorbed by the upper layers, and temperatures hover near freezing. The water pressure is tremendous. Increasing 15 pounds per square inch with every 33 feet of depth, it amounts to almost 5,000 pounds per square inch at 10,000 feet.

Although animals are less numerous than in the upper layers of the sea, many creatures manage to survive in this frigid, never-changing environment. A few are blind, but most can see in light so dim it is imperceptible by humans. Many also produce their own light in specialized cells scattered over their bodies. Water pressure is not a problem either. The outward pressure of fluids in the animals' body tissues equalizes the pressure of the water weighing down on them.

Where does food come from?
Food is scarce in the depths of the sea. No plants can survive in this sunless world. Instead the basis of most food chains is the constant rain of plant and animal materials that falls slowly from the surface layers. Scavengers feed on these bits and pieces, and predators eat the scavengers and each other. Food is also imported by "commuters"—fish and other creatures that make nightly journeys to the surface to feed. When they return to the depths by day, they may become food for the predators there.

Are there monsters in the deep?
Survival is a particularly harsh struggle in the ocean depths, for food is scarce and hard to find in the dark. Fish must be able to seize and hold prey, even when it is bigger than they are. Adapted to a life of hunting, many of the fish do indeed look monstrous. They have large, glaring eyes and huge, gaping mouths edged with teeth as sharp as daggers. All that mitigates this frightful appearance is that most are only a few inches long.

Among the "monsters" are such species as dragonfish and viperfish, armed with long, curved teeth. Another, the gulper, has enormous jaws

and an expandable stomach; a six-inch specimen once was found to have swallowed a fish nine inches long. Anglers dangle luminescent lures in front of their sharp-toothed jaws, thus enticing prey within easy striking distance. Not all dwellers in the deep are bizarre, however. Many of the sea urchins, sea anemones, and others look much like their relatives that live in shallower water.

How do deep-sea animals produce light?
A surprising number of the creatures of the deep, from fish to squids and shrimp, are equipped with their own tiny built-in flashlights. The arrange-

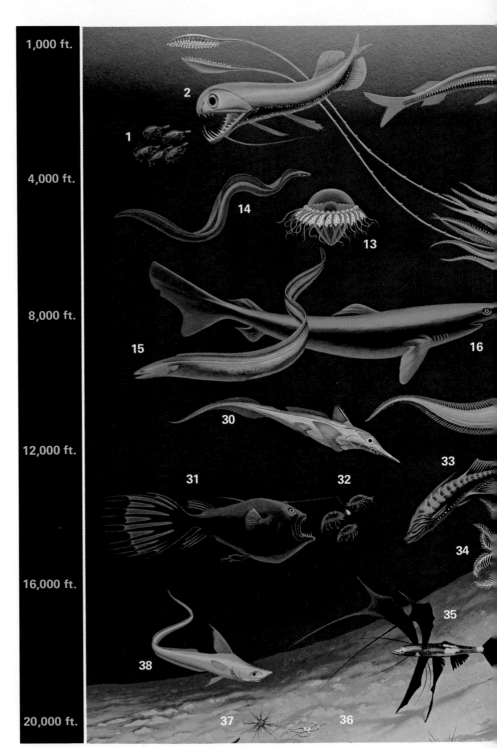

1,000 ft.

4,000 ft.

8,000 ft.

12,000 ft.

16,000 ft.

20,000 ft.

ment of these light organs varies from species to species. On some creatures the lights are dotted here and there; on others, they are arranged in long rows or patterns. There may be lights around the eyes, on trailing tentacles, on tails, or even on the roof of the mouth. Generally the lights can be turned on and off at will.

In some cases the lights are produced by colonies of luminescent bacteria that live in the animal's light organs. Other creatures are equipped with special light-producing cells.

This ability to produce living light serves its owners in many ways. It enables animals to recognize others of their own kind, and find mates or stick together in schools in the inky darkness. It helps them find prey animals or, in the case of anglerfish, attract them with lumininous lures. It can even be used in self-defense. When attacked, certain deep-sea squids send out a cloud of luminous ink that confuses pursuers and enables the squids to escape under the "cover" of light.

Secretive Citizens of the Hidden World of the Deep

Despite eternal darkness and a scarcity of food, the depths of the sea are host to a surprising array of animals. Permanently anchored to the ocean floor are such creatures as sea anemones, sponges, sea lilies (long-stalked relatives of starfish), and sea pens (feathery cousins of corals). Brittle stars, sea cucumbers, sea urchins, and many others travel on and under the bottom mud. And swimming in the inky waters above are such strange creatures as luminescent little hatchetfish, some with bodies as thin as wafers, and gulpers, practically all head and gaping jaws.

1. Shrimp	18. Anglerfish
2. Dragonfish	19. Sea spider
3. Viperfish	20. Sea anemones
4. Spirula	21. Blind lobster
5. Halibut	22. Sea cucumber
6. Hatchetfish	23. Sea urchin
7. Sea pens	24. Octopus
8. Tulip sponges	25. Gulper
9. Barrel sponges	26. Amphipods
10. Greenland shark	27. Brittle star
11. Euphausiid shrimp	28. Blind lobster
12. Deep-sea squid	29. Brotulid fish
13. Jellyfish	30. Chimaera
14. Conger eel	31. Anglerfish
15. Deep-sea eel	32. Amphipods
16. Portuguese shark	33. Bristle mouth
17. Lantern fish	34. Sea lilies
	35. Tripod fish
	36. Brittle star
	37. Sea urchin
	38. Rattail

Sea Islands

How do islands form?
The islands of the world fall into two basic categories. Some, like Great Britain and Japan, are continental islands. They are fragments that have been separated from a continental mainland by such long-term events as changing sea levels and movements of the earth's crust.

Oceanic islands, in contrast, rise directly from the ocean floor. Most, such as Iceland and Tahiti, are the result of volcanic activity. Living organisms can also play a role. Coral forms the rim of many volcanic islands, and it sometimes grows on shoals to form islands such as the Bahamas. Mangroves are another island builder; in shallow seas their stilted roots can trap enough debris to form new islands.

How does life get to islands?
Birds and bats can simply fly to newly formed islands. Among the other airborne colonists are windblown seeds, spores, spiders, and insects. Some arrive as hitchhikers on birds. Mud on the feet and feathers of birds on one island near Java yielded 21 kinds of seeds. Snails and insect eggs also have been found in such mud.

Other colonists arrive by sea. Some seeds can survive long journeys in salt water. Plants occasionally come as rafts of vegetation that was torn from mainland shores, then swept along by currents. Stowaways arrive on the rafts, including insects, lizards, and other animals. The famous tortoises of the Galápagos Islands probably drifted there from South America aboard such rafts.

What usually arrives first?
Newborn volcanic islands are devoid of life or even soil. Seabirds and seals can use them for breeding or resting since these animals get their food from the sea. But other animals must await the arrival of plants. The pioneers usually include mosses, ferns, and other plants that reproduce by spores. Minute and incredibly numerous, spores can travel far and wide on the wind.

Some seeds also travel well, especially those adapted for riding the wind or clinging to birds. Seeds of a dandelion relative, for instance, are known to have been dispersed by wind from Australia to New Zealand, more than 1,000 miles away, and then on to some of the islands of Polynesia.

Waterborne seeds generally are less successful; only those of seaside species are likely to reach suitable habitats. Among the successful island castaways are coconuts, mangroves, and morning glory vines; all are common on many tropical coasts.

Do all the immigrants survive?
The majority of plants and animals that land on oceanic islands soon die, for they can prosper only if they come ashore at a place where their basic living requirements will be met. The windblown seed of an upland grass is doomed if it settles on a tidal mud flat. Pond weeds must find their way to ponds; plants of the forest floor need a leafy canopy overhead.

Animal immigrants must find suitable food sources. On islands already populated, newcomers rarely compete successfully with established species that need the same food. An insect-eating lizard, on the other hand, would not compete with resident lizards that relied on plants and so would have a better chance.

Animals are faced with another obstacle. A lizard or dragonfly can leave descendants only if it arrives with others of its own kind or finds a potential mate already living on the island. The exception, of course, would be a female bearing fertilized eggs.

What is special about island life?
Over time, island life becomes so distinctive that it seems odd in comparison with life elsewhere. In adapting to their new environments, many plants and animals, in fact, develop into completely new species, unique to particular islands.

Flightlessness, for example, is common among island birds. The Galápagos cormorant and New Zealand's kiwi are among the many that have lost the ability to fly, possibly because, in the absence of predators, there was no need to make quick escapes. Many island insects, from grasshoppers to

The Varied Descendants of a Common Ancestor

The vanga shrikes, a family of about 12 species unique to Madagascar, are strikingly varied in appearance and especially in bill shapes. All are thought to be descended from a single ancestral type. Over time, differences developed in their bills and feeding habits, enabling them to coexist without competing. The helmet bird can manage prey as large as lizards, the blue vanga is an insect eater, and the sicklebill probes in crevices for its prey. Finches in the Galápagos and Hawaiian honeycreepers are other examples of descendants of an island colonist that have diversified and become adapted to exploiting various foods.

Blue vanga

Sicklebill

Helmet bird

The Komodo dragon, up to 12 feet in length, is the world's largest lizard. It lives on a few small Indonesian islands.

butterflies, also have small, useless wings or no wings at all.

Giantism is another tendency. Some of the now extinct elephant birds of Madagascar and moas of New Zealand stood more than 10 feet tall. Still surviving in the Galápagos and on certain islands in the Indian Ocean are giant tortoises, which can weigh several hundred pounds each. Plants, too, from sunflower relatives to cacti, may grow to tree size.

Islands can also be arks, preserving the descendants of creatures that have vanished elsewhere. Lemurs, primitive relatives of apes and monkeys, once were widespread in many parts of the world. Such primates now survive only on Madagascar. Tenrecs, another specialty of Madagascar, are found nowhere else. Some of these strange little mammals resemble hedgehogs; others, mice, moles, and other creatures.

How do newcomers affect islands?

Limited in size and surrounded by water, islands offer no escape for land-bound species faced with competition from animals introduced by humans. The results have been disastrous. Even centuries ago, stowaway rats became established on islands with no native mammals. To control rats, in more recent times the mongoose was introduced into Hawaii and islands in the Caribbean. Instead it exterminated native ground-nesting birds. Long ago, European seafarers released goats on islands to provide ready meat supplies. The goats devoured everything in sight, transforming brushlands into wastelands and wiping out wildlife dependent on native plants.

Plants can cause problems too. On the Hawaiian island of Kauai, blackberries have escaped from cultivation and turned upland forests into formidable tangles. Unable to withstand these weedy aggressors, the native plants may well be on their way to extinction. The best hope for island life is that any future introductions will be made with extreme caution, and that some islands will be preserved as sanctuaries for their unique cargoes of indigenous species.

Some Staple Foods of South Sea Islanders

Traveling from island to island, the ancient peoples of the South Pacific brought with them a wide variety of cultivated plants, including taro (its edible tubers are the main ingredient of Hawaii's famous poi), sweet potatoes, coconut palms, and breadfruit trees. All of them are still grown on islands in warm regions around the world.

Taro   Sweet potato   Coconut   Breadfruit

Coral Reefs and Atolls

How do coral animals get together to form a reef?

Surprising to many people is the fact that coral comes from living things, and that those living things are animals. But coral animals do not actually get together to form a reef. When corals reproduce, free-swimming larvae hatch from fertilized eggs. Eventually they settle on a suitable surface, secrete their limestone cups, and then produce replicas, called buds, that remain attached. As the corals continue to bud, a colony forms. In this way a single animal no larger than a fingernail can generate a reef.

Reefs grow upward as generations of corals produce limestone, die, and become, literally, the base for a new generation. Over the ages, they can grow to enormous size. Australia's Great Barrier Reef—the largest structure on earth created by a living thing—is nearly 1,300 miles long and covers some 80,000 square miles.

Where do reefs develop?

Coral reefs, built a fraction of an inch at a time by multitudes of tiny animals, lie within a belt around the mid-section of the globe. In the Western Hemisphere the belt extends from northern Florida to southern Brazil; in the Eastern Hemisphere, it includes Madagascar, the northeastern coast of Australia, and various islands of the Indian Ocean and the South Pacific.

Within this belt, not all locations are suitable for reef growth. Coral animals flourish only in relatively shallow seas that are warmer than 70° F, free of sediment, and exposed to direct sunlight. Where wave action is strong, coral colonies grow in flat or rounded masses; in sheltered waters the slender or branching forms include sea whips, sea fans, and staghorn coral. Breaking the power of the waves, full of intriguing crevices and crannies, a coral reef is a home—and restaurant too—for myriads of fascinating forms of life.

Are all reefs the same?

Reefs vary enormously in structure and complexity. The simplest type is the fringing reef, which grows close to shore and extends out like a submerged platform. Fringing reefs are the ones most accessible to human visitors; some can be reached without a boat. Barrier reefs also follow the coastline, but are separated from it by wide expanses of water. The finest, most extensive example is the Great Barrier Reef off northeastern Australia.

A roughly circular ring of reefs surrounding a lagoon is an atoll, a low-lying island common in the Indian Ocean and the South Pacific. Scientists believe that an atoll begins to form when reefs envelop the base of a volcanic island. Eventually the volcano sinks, leaving a central lagoon and an encircling ring—the tropical island of dreams and legends.

Which animals don't live in reefs?

For diversity of animal inhabitants, in both color and shape, few habitats can compete with a tropical reef. Except for mammals and insects, almost every major group of animals is represented. Clawless spiny lobsters and timid octopuses find openings in the coral rock. Tube worms spread flowerlike crowns of tentacles from the leathery stalks of their bodies. Sea urchins with long, needle-sharp spines and snails with brilliantly patterned shells creep

The Living Coral Animal

Mention coral, and most people think of a piece of white, stony substance, often intricately sculptured. But the word "coral" also applies to the tiny animals that create such treasures of the sea. Kin to the jellyfish, a living coral animal, or polyp, is shaped like an open-mouthed sac and fringed with

The large polyp is a star coral, a stony reef-building species. The smaller ones are solitary corals and may be stony or soft.

over the reef. Sponges of many colors encrust the coral or grow in branching or rounded masses. Giant clams in Indo-Pacific reefs have yard-wide fluted shells. Sea turtles laze at the surface above the reef or rest on the coral. Poisonous sea snakes abound in reefs throughout tropical seas.

Fish come in a wide variety of sizes, with habits to match—from huge solitary sharks on the prowl to dense schools of tiny damselfish. Big fish called groupers make friends with divers; snakelike moray eels capable of inflicting severe bites lurk in holes; strong-toothed parrot fish crunch up the reef. Though many species are as striking to the eye as circus performers, the dots on a coral cod or the stripes on an angelfish are not attention-getting devices: they help break up the fish's outline, making it almost invisible against the multihued coral.

Defensive tricks protect less conspicuous creatures. When a spiny puffer is threatened, it blows itself up like a ball. The triggerfish uses its dorsal fin to wedge itself so tightly into a crevice that it can hardly be dislodged.

How an Atoll Is Formed

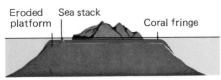

When a volcano erupts from the seabed, it may grow above the surface and form an island. Steeply sloping sides are scored by gullies and bathed in vapor.

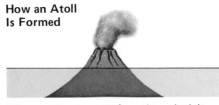

The volcano is now extinct. The sea has eroded the cliffs, leaving a platform with an offshore "stack." Coral fringes the island. Onshore, rocks crumble into sand.

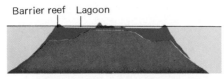

The island sinks. Only the tip of the volcano is now visible, surrounded by a lagoon and guarded by a barrier reef. Eventually the reef alone will remain as an atoll.

stinging tentacles. Polyps of most species live inside protective limestone cups. A coral animal feeds by sweeping the water with its tentacles and stunning microscopic prey. When not feeding, or when disturbed, it withdraws into the cup. Living corals are often gorgeously colored. Coral rock is mostly white, but prized red and black varieties are sometimes found.

Structure of a Polyp

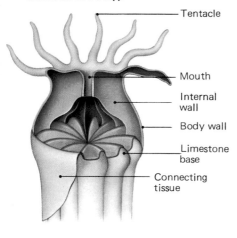

- Tentacle
- Mouth
- Internal wall
- Body wall
- Limestone base
- Connecting tissue

Stonefish, which look like chunks of coral encrusted with bits of debris, can kill waders who step on their venomous spines.

Why do fish congregate in certain places?

When divers first began to explore coral reefs, they were surprised to find crowds of fish in some locations. Closer observation revealed that the fish were waiting to be cleaned. Certain small fish, mostly members of the wrasse family, feed on parasites and the diseased or dead tissue of larger fish. Such cleaners take up stations at various spots on the reef, and the larger fish visit them there. The relationship benefits both parties. Cleaning fish are assured of a regular food supply; client fish stay in good health.

Certain shrimp are also cleaners. One species seems to cater particularly to the predatory moray eel, waving its long, brightly marked antennae to attract the eel's attention and then climbing aboard to do its work. Only seldom does an eel make a mistake and eat the cleaner.

A school of fairy bass busily feeding among colonies of living coral brightens the precipitous face of a Red Sea reef, off the tip of the Sinai Peninsula.

Life on Sandy Shores

Where are all the animals?

To the casual visitor, a sandy shore may seem empty of animals—with the obvious exceptions of bathers, shell collectors, surf fishermen, and raucous gulls. Yet this appearance is deceptive: beneath the surface the sand is literally crawling with life.

Hundred of holes visible at low tide, V-shaped or ribbonlike trails, even moving hills of sand—all are signs of unseen animals. Small holes signal the burrows of ghost shrimp or mole crabs; larger ones are made by clams. Pencil-thin protruding tubes mark the burrows of plumed worms. Conical mounds of black mud roof the homes of lugworms, popular with fishermen as bait. Heart urchins, flattened relatives of the long-spined, deepwater sea urchins, make V-shaped trails. Ribbonlike trails may lead to a sand dollar or a burrowing starfish. A moving hill of sand reveals the presence of a predatory moon snail.

Animal life seeks protection against enemies as well as the elements. Sand supplies cover; so do dunes behind the beach, with their beach grasses and other plants. Dunes are home to such small creatures as spiders, digger wasps, and grasshoppers. Rabbits and mice leave tracks in the sand. Snowy owls may roost among the dunes in winter; terns and gulls nest there.

Who lives above the high-water mark?

The typical sandy shore has four zones—the dunes on the landward side, then the upper beach, the tidal zone, and the inshore area. Generally the last of these, which is always submerged, is the most hospitable to life, and the upper beach the least.

At the boundary between the upper beach and the tidal zone, ebbing waters deposit their relics—seaweed, barnacle-encrusted driftwood, black egg cases from skates (fish related to sharks), strings of papery egg capsules from the snails called whelks. Scavenging gulls, clouds of buzzing flies, and hordes of beach hoppers, or sand fleas, feed on what the sea has delivered. Above the high-water mark food—and therefore life—are scarcer. The summer sun beats down with blazing force, drying the surface and heating it to a temperature that burns bare feet. Just a few inches below, however, the sand is cool and moist. Many animals escape the extremes of heat and dryness by burrowing. Microscopic creatures—one-celled protozoans, roundworms, and very small crustaceans—spend their lives in the thin film of seawater filling the spaces between grains of sand.

Ghost crabs are among the few larger—but by no means conspicuous—forms of life. Pale, sand-colored creatures, they make themselves invisible by crouching down and "freezing." Much of the time they stay in deep burrows, and it takes a careful eye to detect their tentative motions. Several times a day a ghost crab may scuttle sideways over the sand down to the water's edge to moisten its gills. The animals feed mostly at night.

What is a sand dollar?

Most shells found by beachcombers were once part of a clam, snail, or other mollusk. Flat ones with a pattern of holes resembling a five-petaled flower are, however, from a different

animal—the sand dollar, a type of sea urchin. Sand dollars live around the globe in northern seas, on sand flats and in deeper water.

Like other sea urchins, a sand dollar is covered with spines—in this case, a velvety coat of short, purplish spikes. The mouth, on the underside, is equipped with chewing jaws. Tube feet, arranged in the shape of a flower, protrude through holes in the shell, which is known as the test. They are used in breathing, feeding, and moving about; a sand dollar travels with a wavelike motion of its feet and spines.

What happens when the tide comes in?
Animals in the tidal zone, alternately washed and exposed by the sea, are most active when water covers their homes. Ghost shrimp leave their burrows to forage. Generally buried in deep sand, vast numbers of mole crabs—inch-long, egg-shaped crustaceans—spread their feathery antennae to strain food from the water. Parchment worms busily circulate water and sand through U-shaped tubes. Extending their tubelike siphons, razor and soft-shelled clams suck in vast quantities of water.

When the food-laden waters recede, most burrowers shut down operations. Clams retract their siphons; filter-feeding worms lie quiescent. Only a few predators, such as moon snails and whelks—these prey mainly on buried clams—continue the business of feeding.

Where do sea turtles lay their eggs?
Sea turtles spend most of their lives in the water, feeding mainly on submerged grasses (the green turtle) or small marine animals (the leatherback, the largest turtle). When it is time for breeding, the females haul themselves onto widely separated beaches in warm areas around the world. Using their front flippers to fling out great quantities of sand, they scoop deep holes well above the tide line. The hole is widened by movements of the female's body and deepened by her back flippers.

Each clutch may contain more than a hundred eggs, deposited one by one, seemingly with great effort. The female weeps copiously during the process. Liquid "tears," actually the animal's way of getting rid of excess salt, also keep the eyes free of sand. When all the eggs have been deposited, the turtle fills in the hole with movements of the tail and back flippers, carefully smoothing over the site. Heat from the sun-warmed sand incubates the eggs.

Horseshoe crabs, not true crabs but related to the spiders, also deposit their eggs on beaches. In late spring, multitudes of these armored, long-tailed creatures crawl out onto the Atlantic shores of North America. The females, larger than the males, scoop out shallow pits in the sand and deposit several thousand eggs. Clinging to the females, the males fertilize the eggs, which soon become covered with sand by lapping waves. Two weeks later, they hatch. High tides carry the baby horseshoe crabs out to sea.

Are sea cucumbers animals or plants?
Sea cucumbers have elongated bodies, shaped like cucumbers, and they tend to stay in one place. These are, however, the only ways in which they resemble plants. They are animals related to starfish. Like the starfish, some species use tube feet to move about; others burrow through the sand. In places where the animals are large (they can grow to more than three feet long) and numerous, they are sometimes eaten by man. *Trepang,* a Malay word, and *bêche-de-mer,* French for "sea grub," are names by which they are known.

A Sampling of Life at the Shore

1. Beach hoppers, or sand fleas, are kin to crabs.
2. A ghost crab burrows on the upper beach.
3. Parchment worms use "paddles" to move water through their burrows.
4. Small coquina clams dig in below the surface.
5. A mole crab puts its antennae into water to filter out food.
6. A trumpet worm builds a tapered tube of sand.
7. Sanderlings seek food from incoming waves.
8. The moon snail, which has an enormous foot, preys on clams.
9. Quahogs are clams that have thick, hard shells.
10. The channeled whelk cracks a victim's shell with its own.
11. Lady crabs look fierce because of the pincers.
12. Sea cucumbers are cousins of starfish.
13. Flounders have both eyes on the top.
14. Sand dollars often lie half-buried in the sand.

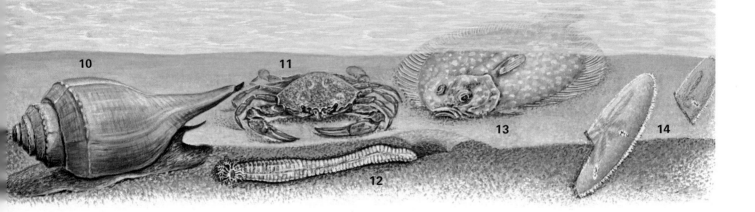

Rockbound Seacoasts

Who lives where on rocky coasts?

At low tide, broad horizontal bands of color are generally visible on rocky shores. Each band represents a different community of living things that vary in their ability to withstand exposure to the air. Lichens live in the uppermost zone, which is moistened only by the splashing of the waves; near the high-water mark, there is usually a stripe of blue-green algae. Among the few animals in this most exposed zone are land insects and air-breathing varieties of the little snails known as periwinkles.

Below this is the intertidal zone, alternately exposed to the air and covered by the sea. The most characteristic animals here are acorn barnacles, which encrust the rocks with a band of white shells. The commonest plants are branching, ribbonlike rockweeds.

Life is most abundant in the bottom zone, where the rocks are exposed only by the lowest tides. Jungles of kelp and other algae supply shelter for starfish, sea urchins, crabs, and a wealth of other animals. Beyond this is the realm of fish and the creatures of the open sea.

How can life survive in the surf?

Waves crashing endlessly against rocky shores pose a special challenge to all the creatures that live there. The two most common secrets of survival are to hide from the surf or to hang on for dear life. Many animals find refuge under rocks or in crevices. Some sea urchins use their spines to brace themselves in rock cavities. And rock clams and certain worms actually bore holes into soft rock.

But the most numerous survivors in the surf are the clingers. Seaweeds are permanently anchored to the rocks by rootlike holdfasts. Barnacles fasten themselves to the rocks with an amazingly strong gluelike secretion, mussels with a system of minute guy ropes. Sea squirts, sponges, and sea anemones are among the many others that are permanently attached. Limpets, snails, and other mollusks, in turn, cling to the rocks with muscular feet that act like suction cups.

Can mussels move about?

Mussels live from the middle to the lowest level on rocky shores, often attached to the rocks in enormous clusters. Each one fastens itself in place by means of numerous tough threads formed by the secretions of a gland on its fleshy foot. The secretions harden on contact with the water into slim fibers called byssal threads. The many threads form a remarkably strong attachment to the rock.

Mussels wedged tightly together in beds are unable to change position and so remain permanently attached to the same spot. A single mussel, however, by stretching its foot for leverage, can exert enough force to break the threads, then move to a new position and reattach itself.

What happens when the tide is out?
Most fish and other mobile animals simply move offshore at low tide, though some find temporary refuge in tide pools. Other animals withstand brief exposure to the air by hiding in damp crevices, where they are protected from direct sunlight. Many keep themselves moist by sheltering in the sodden tangles of seaweed.

Permanently attached animals such as mussels and barnacles can't go into hiding. Instead, they seal their shells tight at low tide, trapping a bit of the sea inside to keep themselves moist. Limpets resort to a similar tactic. At high tide these mollusks are up and about, scraping algae from the rocks with their filelike tongues. At low tide each one returns to its home base, a shallow depression it has etched into the rock. There it clings tightly with its muscular foot, awaiting the wash of the next incoming tide.

Are tide pools hazardous habitats?
When the tide ebbs, pools of water are left behind in low places in the rocks. Large, deep pools usually present few problems for their inhabitants. But only the hardiest creatures can survive in pools that are shallow or flooded only by the highest tides.

On a summer day, such pools can become as warm as bathwater, and in winter, freezing cold. Evaporation can make the water intolerably briny, or a sudden downpour can freshen it too much for creatures of the sea. Or oxygen may be so depleted that the animals suffocate.

Even so, a surprising variety of plants and animals manage to cope with the changing conditions in tide pools. From algae and sea anemones to starfish and sponges, they make exploration of these miniature oceans a never-ending delight.

Can starfish swim?
Starfish, of course, are not fish at all. They are echinoderms, members of a group of animals that also includes sea urchins and sand dollars. Instead of swimming, starfish creep about on hundreds of rubbery tube feet, each tipped with a suction cup and projecting from grooves on the underside of the arms. The tube feet are also used for clinging to rocks and, in some species, prying open clamshells.

The common starfish has 5 arms, but some species have as many as 40. If one of the arms should happen to break off, not only does the starfish survive, it soon grows a new arm in place of the lost one. Even more remarkable, if enough of the central body remains attached to the broken-off arm, the fragment eventually grows into a complete new starfish.

Zones of Life on a Rocky Shore

Plants and animals on rocky coasts live in fairly well defined zones; which zone depends on their ability to survive exposure to the air. Little besides lichens and blue-green algae lives on the highest rocks, moistened only by splashing water. Life is more plentiful in the intertidal zone, which is alternately covered and exposed by the tides. The lowest zone, bared only by extreme low tides, supports a lush growth of seaweeds inhabited by hosts of fish and other marine animals.

1. Lichens	12. Brittle star
2. Blue-green algae	13. Jonah crab
3. Rough periwinkles	14. Kelp
4. Acorn barnacles	15. Northern starfish
5. Limpet	16. Redbeard sponge
6. Blue mussels	17. Lumpfish
7. Dog whelk	18. Sea cucumber
8. Rockweed	19. Sea squirts
9. Smooth periwinkle	20. Bread crumb sponge
10. Sea urchin	21. Blackfish
11. Irish moss	22. Blood star
	23. Sea anemone

Seaside Birds

Why are seagulls white?

Very few gulls have pure white plumage. Many show gray on the back or black on the wings, and several species—among them the lava gull, from the Galápagos, and Heermann's gull, from western North America—are dark all over. Most adult gulls, however, appear white at a distance. Although in certain cases the white serves as camouflage (for the ivory gull of the Far North, for example), sometimes it may do just the opposite, making the bird more conspicuous rather than less. Because of their white feathers, birds feeding at sea are visible at some distance; other gulls can fly in to the same spot and benefit from the food. The whiteness of gannets and certain other seabirds may function in a similar way.

How does an oystercatcher open oysters?

Long, stout, and flattened at the sides like a chisel, an oystercatcher's beak is an efficient tool for opening two-shelled mollusks—not only oysters but also mussels and clams. Barnacles and limpets are pried off rocks. The sturdy beak makes mincemeat of such softer items as sea urchins and crabs; in Britain, the birds often feed inland, dining on insects and worms.

An oystercatcher intent on catching oysters must wait until the tide recedes and the beds are exposed. Oysters feeding in shallow water open their shells. The bird inserts its beak between the shells and, using it like a lever, cuts the muscle uniting the two halves. It then withdraws the succulent meat.

Oystercatchers are not the only shorebirds with intriguing ways of obtaining food. In the Antarctic, sheathbills steal eggs and chicks from penguin colonies. Elsewhere, turnstones turn over stones in search of small forms of animal life.

How did the skimmer get its name?

Old-timers called the skimmer the scissorbill or cutwater. Flying just above the water and using its unique beak like a scoop, the skimmer quite literally skims its food from the surface. No other bird uses its beak in precisely the same way, for no other bird has precisely the same kind of beak.

Shorebirds and Seabirds

Most seaside birds belong to one of two groups. Shorebirds, such as sanderlings, typically feed at the water's edge. The species classified as seabirds, including gannets, come ashore only to nest.

Roseate terns, with their long tail streamers, are among the most graceful of birds. Terns and their close relatives, the gulls, are considered shorebirds.

Sanderlings snatch food from the water's edge. Like many other shorebirds, they develop brighter colors for the breeding season. The bird shown here is in winter plumage.

Dunlin flying in huge flocks along the shore at high tide look, as the illustration above suggests, like clouds of smoke. In winter and on migration these tundra-nesting shorebirds frequent coastal areas, especially mud flats. Dunlin chicks lack the black belly of the adult.

The skimmer's lower jaw, or mandible, is much longer than the upper, which fits neatly inside it when the beak is closed. The flexible, sensitive lower mandible, held at an angle, knifes through the water; when it strikes a small fish or crustacean, the upper one snaps shut.

When feeding, skimmers are noisy birds, uttering short, yelping barks. Active at dawn and dusk, they fish mainly at night, when their aquatic prey rises to the surface. By day, they rest in sociable groups on sandy beaches. Close relatives of terns, skim-mers nest mainly on offshore islands. The various species are most abundant in tropical Asia and Africa.

Why do cormorants sit with outstretched wings?

Long-necked, long-billed fish eaters related to pelicans, cormorants are excellent swimmers and divers, but their feathers, lacking in oil, become waterlogged. To dry out, they sit with spread wings on such perches as rocks, buoys, and piers. Of the 30-odd kinds of cormorants, some occur only along coasts, others near fresh water, and

Fulmars look much like gulls, but tube-like nostrils reveal their kinship with the albatrosses. These seabirds nest on precipitous cliffs in the North.

Gannets can often be seen from shore plunge-diving into the sea with angled wings. These fish eaters, like many other seabirds, are white overall. Gannets and their close relatives, the boobies, have large webbed feet and feather-less patches of skin on the face. They can seal their nostrils when they dive.

ward to make its catch. After swallowing the fish underwater, the gannet surfaces and takes flight.

Why do seabirds use the same cliffs year after year?

Uncountable millions of seabirds, such as gannets and fulmars, gather each year to nest and rear young on rocky coastal cliffs. Near these giant assemblages the sound is deafening—a cacophony of screams, cries, squawks, and the constant whistling whir of wings. For centuries seabirds intent on nesting have returned to such famed spots as Bonaventure Island off the east coast of Canada, Noss in the Shetland Islands, Skomer off the coast of Wales, and St. Kilda off western Scotland. Birds nesting for the first time, sometimes after spending several years at sea, are homing in to the place where their lives began. Older individuals are returning to a location where nesting sites and food were available in previous years.

How do birds arrange themselves on a cliff?

A dozen or more species may nest on a coastal cliff, each at a preferred height above the sea—a natural division that has developed over time to keep competition for nesting space at a minimum. Gannets typically use sites at the very edge. Narrow ledges are packed with kittiwakes, razorbills, fulmars, and murres. Gulls and petrels nest at the top of the cliff; cormorants and black guillemots, at the base.

As in so many other habitats, wildlife arranges itself into zones—and as elsewhere, the arrangements are not hard and fast. If a gannet cannot find a suitable spot at the top of a cliff, it will take a broad, flat ledge lower down. If every ledge is occupied, kittiwakes will move to the top.

Most territorial disputes occur between members of the same species, who seek out the same sort of site. Though nests appear to be scattered haphazardly, their spacing conforms to a rigid pattern when conditions permit: from the center of one nest to that of another is a distance of at least 2½ feet. As the number of birds at a site grows, the colony typically expands in area rather than by crowding the nests more closely together.

still others near both. One species, the Galápagos cormorant, is flightless.

Why do gannets waddle when they walk?

Gannets, occasionally called sea geese, are somewhat similar to true geese in size and shape. Like geese, these seabirds have short legs located far to the rear of the heavy, streamlined body. Thanks to the position of the legs, and to its huge, webbed feet, a gannet can swim fast and dive nearly a hundred feet deep. But those same big feet and short, rearward-placed legs

are an encumbrance to the birds on land: gannets sway back and forth in a wobbly walk.

Gannets in flight are very different. With long wings spanning as much as six feet, they fly rapidly and gracefully. When a school of fish is sighted, the bird plummets into the sea, sometimes from as high as a hundred feet above the surface. Usually gannets travel in flocks, and so when one bird dives, its companions quickly follow suit. The dive typically takes the bird deeper in the water than the fish are swimming, and it swiftly planes up-

Coastal Wetlands

What sorts of places are coastal wetlands?

Sandy shores and rocky coastlines form clear-cut boundaries between land and sea. In sheltered shallows the transition is often more gradual. In the tropics and subtropics, for example, muddy seacoasts and estuaries are commonly fringed with dense thickets of mangrove swamps. Sediments trapped among the tangled roots of the trees slowly extend the shoreline outward into the sea.

In temperate regions, coastlines protected from the surf are frequently edged by extensive saltwater marshes. These are dominated by vast tracts of salt-tolerant grasses, along with other plants that can survive periodic flooding by the sea. The marshes sometimes include large areas of open water and are typically crisscrossed by meandering channels where seawater streams in and out with the ebb and flow of the tide.

Other coastal wetlands are found at the mouths of some of the world's great rivers, where fresh water mingles with the sea. The Mississippi delta is North America's most notable example. Major wetlands in Europe include Las Marismas, the marshlands at the outlet of the Guadalquivir in Spain, and the Camargue, a watery wilderness on the Rhone delta in France. In Asia, enormous mangrove swamps fringe both the Ganges and the Mekong deltas.

How do crabs hide from the tide?

At low tide, the mud flats of salt marshes and mangrove swamps come alive with crabs of many kinds. The little crustaceans scuttle about in search of food left by the receding water. Certain kinds scrape off some of the green algae covering the mud; others eat bits and pieces of plants and other organic debris. Most conspicuous are the fiddler crabs; each male is adorned with one exceptionally large, usually brightly colored claw that is used to attract mates and threaten rivals.

When the water begins to return with the rising tide, the swarms of crabs quickly disappear. They retreat into burrows in the mud where they are protected from the wash of waves and currents that might carry them out to sea. Even when feeding at low tide, the crabs often duck into their burrows to escape herons, raccoons, and other predators that come to feast on the mud flats. People walking nearby elicit the same response.

Do mammals like marshes?

Muskrats are perhaps the best-known mammals that live in salt marshes. (They are also found in freshwater wetlands.) Other residents and visitors include various water-loving mice, rats, and shrews, along with larger creatures such as mink and raccoons.

In some areas, animals not normally associated with water have found sanctuary in the wilderness of coastal wetlands. In Europe, for example, red deer and wild boar have turned to wetlands such as Las Marismas for refuge from civilization, and wolves prowl the swamps and marshlands of the Danube delta.

Mangrove swamps also have their contingents of mammals. Several kinds of monkeys, for instance, are very much at home among the tangled mangroves of Southeast Asia. One, the long-tailed macaque, or crab-eating monkey, forages on mud flats for its favorite food. Another, the proboscis monkey, named for the males' bulbous snouts, lives only in the mangrove swamps of Borneo, where it feasts peacefully on mangrove leaves.

Where do muskrats live?

Water-loving muskrats occur across most of North America and are also found in Europe, where these rodents were introduced accidentally. Individuals living along rivers dig burrows in the banks, but in marshes, where muskrats are most at home, they build dome-shaped lodges out in shallow water. These haystacklike heaps of cattails, reeds, and other vegetation are several feet high and project above the surface. Underwater entrances lead to a snug, dry chamber above water level, where the animals rest and raise their young. Walls a foot or more thick protect the muskrats from the weather and from predators of the

Muskrat

outside world. Inside the nest, the muskrats keep cool in summer and warm in winter.

Much like the legendary gingerbread house, the domed lodges also furnish emergency rations. In winter when weather is severe and food outside is scarce, the resourceful muskrats can simply munch on the vegetation that makes up the walls of their lodges.

In North American salt marshes, diamondback terrapins venture out on the mud at low tide to hunt for fiddler crabs and other prey. Ribbed mussels are embedded in the mud nearby.

Birds of American salt marshes include large numbers of red-winged blackbirds and secretive clapper rails that slip quietly through thickets of cordgrass. The two domes in the open water are muskrat lodges.

Are birds abundant?

Coastal wetlands around the world abound with birds of many sorts. Secretive rails and bitterns slip through the grasses of salt marshes. When the tide is out, sandpipers and other shorebirds probe in the mud flats for prey. Herons and egrets wade in the shallows, while gulls, terns, and ospreys patrol the air overhead. Songbirds are abundant, and open areas of water often attract immense flocks of ducks and geese. Salt marshes, in fact, are some of the most important wildlife refuges, especially as stopping places for migrants and wintering grounds for concentrations of water birds.

Like marshes, mangrove swamps are havens for large numbers of birds. In addition to plentiful food, they afford secure, elevated nesting sites. The mangroves that fringe the Florida Everglades, for instance, are famous for their great nesting colonies of herons, egrets, ibises, pelicans, roseate spoonbills, and other birds.

What good are wetlands?

Many people view coastal wetlands as wastelands that should be drained and filled to provide space for housing developments, marinas, industrial sites, and similar uses. Fortunately, many others now understand the real worth of wetlands and are working to assure their preservation.

Coastal swamps and marshlands serve as storm buffers, protecting mainlands from the full fury of storm-driven seas. They are havens for a wealth of wildlife. But their greatest value is as one of the most productive habitats on earth.

Acre for acre, a field planted with sugarcane is the only land that produces a greater volume of plant material per year than a coastal salt marsh. Not only does this huge volume of vegetation nurture the teeming life of the marsh itself; its decay releases nutrients that enrich nearby coastal seas. Plankton proliferates and so does all the marine life that depends on it, including many species of incalculable commercial worth. The wetlands are irreplaceable in another way as well. They are essential as nurseries for the young of many of these same marine creatures, from shrimp to snapper and mighty tarpon.

Some Salt Marsh Plants

Sea lavender, which thrives in salty soil, supplies splashes of color in many seaside salt marshes.

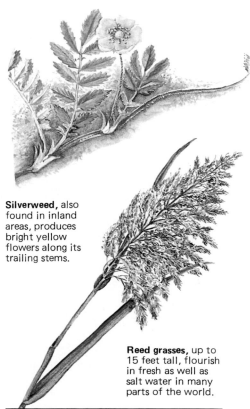

Silverweed, also found in inland areas, produces bright yellow flowers along its trailing stems.

Reed grasses, up to 15 feet tall, flourish in fresh as well as salt water in many parts of the world.

Life in Running Water

Which is the biggest river fish?

Though the oceans are home to the world's largest fish—the giants are whale sharks and basking sharks—some rivers support fish of enormous size. The champions are the primitive, armored sturgeons; the beluga, the species breeding in the Volga River (like many other sturgeon, belugas move between fresh water and salt water), reportedly reaches weights of more than a ton. The wels, a Eurasian catfish, can top 600 pounds; a giant Nile perch, 300. In the shallow backwaters of the Amazon, air-breathing fish called arapaimas reach lengths of 16 feet and weigh some 400 pounds. Arapaimas acquire oxygen by using simple lungs rather than gills.

Where do kingfishers fish?

The fish-eating kinds of kingfishers hover above water or hunt from a perch, plunging down to seize their prey with their long, narrow, sharp-pointed bills. North America's belted kingfisher, which takes lizards and other land animals in addition to fish, hunts in lakes, streams, and coastal areas; its nests are dug in stream banks and cliffs. The European kingfisher, a petite bird, lives along slow rivers and streams and also near ponds. The Amazon kingfisher fishes along jungle streams. Australia's little kingfisher, only 4½ inches long including the bill, finds its prey in mangrove swamps as well as other aquatic places.

Not all kingfishers fish. The forest kingfishers, with broader, flatter bills than the fish-eating species, specialize in insects (Africa's gray-headed kingfisher does this), reptiles (Australia's kookaburra), and even earthworms (New Guinea's shoe-billed kingfisher, whose extraordinary bill does indeed look somewhat like a shoe).

How are rivers like highways?

Any aquatic creature that spends one part of its life in brooks or streams and the other in the ocean must use a river as a highway. Most salmon breed in headwater streams far inland and require rushing water to spawn. The young swim downstream, then mature in the sea. When the fish enter a river once again, they hurl themselves upstream, tearing their fins and battering their bodies during this return journey. Salmon generally do not feed

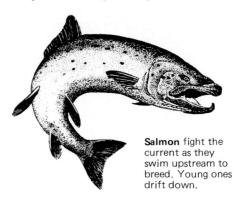

Salmon fight the current as they swim upstream to breed. Young ones drift down.

during this part of their lives, and most survive only long enough to spawn.

Rivers bear a constant traffic of migrants besides supporting their own communities. Among the many other animals that travel the rivers are the freshwater eels, whose migration pattern is the opposite of the salmon's—that is, they breed in the ocean and mature in fresh water. Certain crabs migrate a hundred miles upstream to grow and spawn each year.

Where do mink live?

Excellent swimmers, mink are among the relatively few mammals associated with flowing water; both the North American species (the one usually raised on fur farms) and the Eurasian species favor forested rivers and streams. These long, slim members of the weasel family hunt such animals as fish, rodents, and frogs; ducks and poultry are also taken. Close relatives of mink, otters of many kinds also occur in rivers around the world. The giant among them, a South American species, is more than six feet long.

Which insects spend their youth in swift streams?

One important feature of insects is that their lives undergo dramatic change. Immature forms often look very different from adults, and habitat may change too. The caterpillarlike caddisfly larvae, for example, live in streams and other wet places; woods and fields are among the homes of the mothlike adults.

The caddisfly spends more time as a

Fast Streams Mean Fewer Birds

Although the birds found near flowing water are many and varied, few species are associated with fast-flowing streams; the water there offers little in the way of food. Among the exceptions are torrent ducks. Living near streams in the Andes, these birds, with their long tails and elongated bodies, are superb swimmers. Their homes afford no room for takeoffs and landings: they leave the water by jumping onto rocks and dive to get back in. Torrent ducks search under rocks for stonefly larvae, and are also believed to take mollusks and fish.

Mountain streams in the Andes are also home to a species of dipper; other kinds live in Eurasia and North America. These short-tailed, wrenlike birds walk underwater or swim by using their wings. With their thin bills, they probe the bottom for insect food.

Dippers walk underwater in search of small prey. This is the European species.

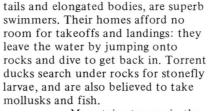

larva than as an adult—nearly a year, as opposed to a month. Though they often go unnoticed, caddisfly larvae are, to those in the know, a most exceptional form of life: they build themselves portable homes, which serve as housing and later as the structures in which they pupate (comparable to a moth's cocoon). The cases of certain species, built of bits of wood or bark, have a few slender twigs that act as rudders to keep them pointed upstream. Others are made of pebbles, with a pair of stones on each side for ballast. Caddisfly constructions occasionally furnish food rather than shelter. Some species make fishing nets of strong silk woven into measured rectangles and stretched out between submerged rocks. When particles of food lodge in the mesh, the larva pulls them into its case. Torn nets are speedily replaced.

Blackflies are among the many insects whose larvae—in this case, dark little sticklike forms attached by suckers to underwater rocks—live in brooks. If the larva is dislodged and whirled downstream, it slowly travels back to its site of attachment by reeling in a silken lifeline. Feathery appendages on the head filter food from the current. The adult females, notorious for their small, potent bites, feed on blood.

Battling the Current

Swift currents may fling animals against rocks or sweep them to places where living conditions are not as suitable. Suction cups help certain insects fight the current; others are protected by their flattened shapes.

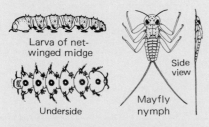

Larva of net-winged midge

Underside

Side view

Mayfly nymph

Suction cups on the underside of net-winged midge larvae help them hold on to rocks.

The flat body of a mayfly nymph reduces the likelihood of its being swept away.

Mountain streams open up the forest, offering vistas as well as contrast. Animals find such places inhospitable, but they are by no means devoid of life.

The Pond World

Where is all the life in a pond?
The surface of a pond is an elastic plain, home to specialized forms of life. Such large-leaved plants as water lilies make use of surface tension to support their foliage (air cells in the leaves also keep them buoyant), as do the world's smallest flowering plants, the duckweeds. Water striders and whirligig beetles, with water-repellent bodies and feet, skim across the surface, food for fishing spiders buoyed by water-repellent hairs. On the underside of the surface film, aquatic snails crawl slowly along. Plants constitute a miniature world of their own, inhabited by insect larvae, planarians, hydras, and more.

Water shaded by the broad leaves offers a cool, quiet habitat for certain fish. But most pond creatures are invisible to the naked eye—the single-celled protozoans, for instance, and the curious rotifers, whose heads are tipped with a "wheel" of rapidly beating hairs. At the bottom of the pond spraddle-legged dragonfly nymphs stalk their prey; snails and crayfish—crayfish resemble miniature lobsters—scavenge for food. Insect larvae and burrowing worms constantly churn the mud, enhancing its fertility.

How do beavers affect other wildlife?
No other wild creature has as extensive an impact on the land and its life as the beaver. Large dams built by these impressive rodents can flood hundreds of acres and create extensive wetlands. Trees and other plants are flooded and die; the homes of mice, shrews, and many other animals are destroyed. But nature soon adjusts. Fish may prosper in beaver ponds,

some swimming upstream to spawn. Waterfowl, herons, kingfishers, and other aquatic birds come to feed or nest. Moose and deer wade in the shallows and browse along the shore.

Who breathes through snorkels?
Some aquatic animals—among them, fish, tadpoles, and young salamanders—have gills, which take in oxygen from the water. Hibernating turtles, which lie immobile at the bottom of a pond, also absorb oxygen from the water. Many other aquatic species, however, are dependent on oxygen in the air. Freshwater beetles carry an air supply beneath their wing covers. When it is frightened or pursuing prey, a fishing spider dives beneath the surface, taking with it air trapped among its hairs. Such creatures as mosquito larvae and water scorpions breathe through tubes protruding above the surface—natural snorkels, so to speak.

How do insects hunt underwater?
Young dragonflies, called nymphs, bear little resemblance to the dazzling creatures often seen winging their way over ponds. For one, the nymphs are wingless and aquatic; they swim rather than fly, using a sort of jet propulsion. Whereas the adult catches insect prey in flight, trapping victims in the basketlike arrangement of its legs, the nymph has an actual weapon—a hinged lower lip. When the nymph spots potential prey (usually another insect, but sometimes a tadpole or small fish), the lower lip unfolds, shooting outward. Hooks at the tip fasten on the prey, inject a tissue-dissolving enzyme, and retract,

Water birds need not swim to move about.

pulling the morsel against the nymph's chewing jaws.

Other small aquatic hunters include the grublike larvae of the phantom midge (the adults resemble mosquitoes), which scoop up crustaceans with their huge hinged beaks. Glassy and transparent, the larva is almost completely invisible except for silvery horseshoe-shaped tubes at the ends. These tubes function as buoyancy reg-

Built by the Busy Beaver

One of the most impressive animal architects, the North American beaver builds dams and lodges of branches, sticks, and mud. The dam creates a pond in which lodges can be built. The lodge, which measures six or more feet across and extends several feet above the water, is home to the beaver family. (Instead of lodges, Eurasian beavers generally use riverside burrows.) Branches anchored in the bottom mud nearby are used for winter food.

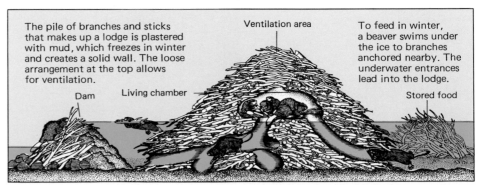

The pile of branches and sticks that makes up a lodge is plastered with mud, which freezes in winter and creates a solid wall. The loose arrangement at the top allows for ventilation.

Ventilation area

To feed in winter, a beaver swims under the ice to branches anchored nearby. The underwater entrances lead into the lodge.

Dam   Living chamber   Stored food

The beavers' dam, lodge, and pile of stored food are shown here in a cutaway view.

In a Kenyan lake, this little crake—like its relatives the coots and gallinules—can step from one lily pad to the next.

ulators: at night, when they are inflated, the larva rises to the surface and hunts for prey.

Elongated, sticklike bugs known as water scorpions crawl about on aquatic plants. Although these creatures bite when handled, their hunting technique involves legs rather than jaws. When an insect or small fish approaches, the water scorpion quickly clamps its long, scythelike legs together, and the victim is trapped.

How does a backswimmer swim?
Aquatic insects are a varied group, not only in appearance but in how they swim. Whirligig beetles spin about in circles; water striders seem to skate. Backswimmers and water boatmen, two kinds of beetles, row with long, hair-fringed legs. At the surface, the backswimmer swims upside down.

One of the strangest swimming aids is a chemical produced by certain land beetles when they fall into a pond. The chemical destroys the water's surface tension at one end of the insect; at the

Whirligig beetle   Water strider

other, the remaining surface tension pushes against the beetle, causing it to shoot across the pond.

What is special about water fleas?
Tiny, transparent relatives of lobsters and crabs, water fleas progress through the water with flealike jerks. They are far more interesting than the name implies. For instance, they do not need males to reproduce. Eggs develop into females without fertilization, and only under certain unfavorable conditions, such as a scarcity of food, do some develop into males.

Remarkable too is this little creature's blood. When the oxygen content of the surrounding water is low, the blood becomes bright red, rich in

oxygen-carrying hemoglobin; when the water is well aerated, the blood gradually turns pale. Water fleas are also responsive to temperature changes. In summer they tend to develop long spines, which increase their surface area and help them stay afloat. In winter their round, compact bodies are buoyed up by the colder, denser water.

Do leeches really suck blood?
Though some species are scavengers, many leeches—worms generally associated with ponds and other bodies of water—feed on the blood of such vertebrates as turtles and fish. A blood-sucking species, such as the European medicinal leech (used in the past to heal bruises and treat certain diseases), clamps onto the victim with the hind sucker and wounds and feeds with the smaller, toothed one in the front. A chemical produced by the salivary glands prevents the blood from clotting. Because a leech's digestive tract has blood-storing pouches, a single meal can last for several months.

Swamps and Marshlands

What sort of place is a wetland?
The rather general definition of a wetland—a combination of shallow water and soggy soil—masks the great variety that exists within this common habitat. In many parts of the world wooded swamps and reed- or cattail-filled marshes extend over vast tracts of low-lying land. In Africa, for example, the enormous areas watered by the White Nile are papyrus-choked marshes called the Sudd. The lower reaches of the Amazon, in contrast, are heavily forested swamps, or *igapos;* some are flooded annually and others permanently wet. In North America the Okefenokee—the name means "shaking water"—is a mix of baldcypress swamps, prairielike marshes, and quaking bogs.

Surprisingly, the waters in most large marshes and swamps are slowly on the move. In Africa shallow sheets

Cattails: More Than Just Fluff

Spreading rapidly, the stout, creeping roots of cattails help stabilize marsh soils. The dense, leafy growth shelters nesting birds and other animals; the velvety flowering spikes ripen into cottony fluff and seed-filled nutlets.

of water from the Okovanggo River turn the surrounding region into a gigantic, sloshy marsh. In the Florida Everglades, water flows almost unseen through the saw grass prairie. Such slow, persistent currents prevent stagnation. Tannin, which is leached from the roots of such trees as cedars and colors swamp water brown, helps keep it sweet and fresh.

What happens when wetlands dry up?
Wetlands contain shallow water, and sometimes none at all. Those that are bone-dry at certain times of year present special problems for wildlife. One solution is a life cycle that calls for breeding and laying eggs in the wet season, as the amphibious frogs, toads, and salamanders do; by the time the water around them dries up, they have become air-breathing adults. Many insects, including dragonflies, damselflies, and mayflies, also take advantage of seasonal rains.

A second solution is estivation, the hot-weather equivalent of hibernation. In African marshes and elsewhere, tortoises, frogs, lungfish, and catfish burrow into the mud before it dries up and cakes, and remain there until released by the wet-season rains. American alligators spend the dry part of the year in water-filled pits. Excavated by the powerful reptile's tail and snout, the pits, known as 'gator holes, are a great boon to other wildlife. Snakes gather around them; otters and raccoons, herons and wood storks, feed on fish trapped by slowly evaporating water. Thanks to the alligators, all such creatures have a better chance of surviving.

What is a wiggler?
All of the some 2,500 species of mosquitoes lay their eggs in water. There the larvae, or "wigglers," feed and grow, then change into active pupae, or "tumblers," before transforming into winged adults. Some go through their entire life cycle in only a week; others may require several months.

Mosquitoes breed prolifically in the standing water of marshes and swamps. The larvae and pupae are excellent foods for fish and other aquatic creatures, and the adults supply meals for fellow insects—dragonflies and damselflies, for example—

and insect-eating birds. Sometimes, however, the mosquitoes become so abundant that they descend on potential victims in buzzing black clouds. Only animals that can submerge or that have good protection—tough hides, impenetrable shells, thick plumage, or heavy fur—can endure the onslaughts of these pervasive, persistent blood drinkers.

Surprisingly, some wetlands are almost without mosquitoes. In certain coastal areas, the rafts of eggs and the developing larvae and pupae may be carried out of the wetlands and into brackish or salt water before they can mature. In other swamps and marshes, the water is too acid for young mosquitoes to survive.

Which birds can walk on water?
One expects birds to wade or swim, but a number of species have another

Tall, feathery papyrus, a tropical sedge, borders the waters of a Ugandan swamp. Where the soil offers support, date palms take root.

On flaring bases slender baldcypresses, also known as swamp or pond cypresses, rise in a North Carolina swamp. This American tree is a close relative of the dawn redwood, first found in China in 1941.

way of moving through water: they walk on top. One such bird is the coot, a dark gray, ducklike denizen of wetlands across Eurasia and North America. A coot has outsized feet with flaplike lobes along the toes. To rise from the water, it beats its wings and feet vigorously—to build up speed—and then scurries over the surface, making spray fly.

Often called "lily trotters," jacanas—slim-necked waders of tropical and subtropical marshes—can walk over a carpet of floating plants without ever sinking in. Like coots, they have exceptionally long toes and toenails, which help them spread their weight and keep their balance.

Which big animals live in marshes and swamps?
The majority of wetland wildlife—insects and amphibians, for instance

—are on the small side, but larger animals are not lacking. As in other habitats, some of these, like the alligator, python, and jaguar, are predators. Beavers, muskrats, tapirs, and coypus, also called nutrias, are among the plant-eating species.

In many cases wetland animals have special traits that make them better adapted to a semiaquatic life. The Asiatic water buffalo, for example, has hooves that spread widely under its weight. Supported by such footgear, the hefty animal can wade through chest-high mud without becoming mired—a valuable asset for the creature in the wild and one prized by humans, who use the buffaloes as draft animals in rice-growing regions. The sitatunga, an antelope living in the papyrus marshes of the Sudan, is among the other species with broadly splayed hooves.

Why don't swamp trees topple?
Soggy soil offers little support for trees. Species that grow in swamps—the presence of trees separates swamplands from marshes—have developed various adaptations to keep from falling over. One is a trunk with a swollen base, which enables such trees as the baldcypress to sit as solidly as tenpins, even though they grow in deep water. On mangroves and baldcypresses woody "knees" protruding above the water are not supporting structures but breathing devices that supply the underwater roots with oxygen.

Another anchoring device is the buttress, a flangelike growth from the base of many tropical swamp species. The screw pine, or pandanus, of Asia and Pacific islands rises high above the ground on stilt roots. Stiltlike prop roots support mangroves in brackish coastal swamps throughout the world.

Life Underfoot

What kinds of animals live underground?

Birds, bees, badgers, earthworms, turtles, toads—a host of creatures of all kinds have learned to exploit the hidden habitat beneath the soil. Some, such as moles, spend virtually their entire lives in the perpetual darkness of this underground world. Others use burrows only as temporary refuges for themselves or their young. Mining bees and hunter wasps, for instance, lay their eggs in burrows that they have provisioned with food for their developing larvae, but do not use the burrows themselves.

To varying degrees these are conspicuous creatures. But the most numerous inhabitants of the soil are the teeming throngs of living things too small to be seen without magnification. A single cupful of soil can contain many millions of protozoans, minute spiderlike mites, and tiny nematodes, or roundworms. Creeping and crawling between individual grains of soil, they spend their time feeding on decaying plants and animals, on each other, and on the roots of living plants.

How do burrowers dig?

Stout forelimbs armed with powerful claws are the hallmarks of such champion burrowers as moles and badgers. Such other mammals as gophers and chipmunks are not so conspicuously equipped for digging, yet all are accomplished burrowers. Some dig with their forelimbs and kick the dirt out

---

A Bee's Underground Nursery

Mining bees dig deep, branching tunnels to raise their young. Each branch ends in a cell that the female provisions with a ball of pollen and nectar. She lays an egg on the pollen ball, which the larva eats after hatching. It pupates in the brood cell, and eventually surfaces as an adult insect. Some of these tireless miners are solitary; other species live in large colonies.

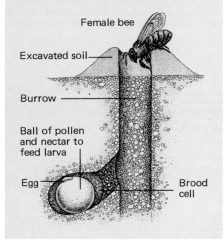

Female bee

Excavated soil

Burrow

Ball of pollen and nectar to feed larva

Egg

Brood cell

---

with their hind feet. Others carry it to the surface cradled between their front legs and their bodies.

Insects show a similar range of adaptations. Some of the burrowing bees and ants laboriously haul dirt and pebbles to the surface. Hunter wasps kick it out of the way. Mole crickets, like the mammals for which they are

---

named, have greatly enlarged forelegs especially designed for digging. Like most other kinds of burrowers, some drop their diggings in piles around the entrance, and some scatter the debris, obscuring the opening.

Is flooding a problem?

Too much water is a constant hazard for underground animals. Saturated soil, for example, brings earthworms to the surface where they wait helplessly for the water to recede. Flooding occasionally evicts larger animals from their burrows as well. As a precaution, woodchucks and others frequently do their digging on slopes; slanting the tunnels upward from the entrance provides further protection from flooded living quarters. Plains-dwelling prairie dogs, on the other hand, heap mounds of dirt around the entrances to their burrows. These damlike barriers not only keep water out of the underground chambers. They are fine places for basking in the sun and serve as lookout posts for surveying the surrounding countryside.

Are burrowers safe from predators?

From the smallest to the largest, every creature living in the soil is a potential meal for someone else. Those that venture above ground must constantly be on the alert for predators. But even in their burrows they are not entirely safe. Ground beetles, centipedes, and other hunters are always on the prowl for small prey. Snakes, weasels, and other creatures also slip into burrows to catch their inhabitants.

Safety is probably one reason why many burrowers equip their homes not only with a main entrance but also with a couple of additional entries. They can duck into these plunge holes to elude outside attackers or use them as escape hatches if the marauder is already inside. Wood rats in North American deserts sometimes barricade the entrances with piles of cactus spines—a deterrent to at least some predators. And aardvarks sometimes "shut the door" behind them by plugging up their tunnels, perhaps to keep out unwanted intruders.

Can birds live in burrows?

Just as nests in tree cavities afford a measure of protection from preda-

---

How do moles get about underground?

Although they are found across much of North America and Eurasia, moles are seldom seen, for they spend most of their lives underground. As they tunnel in search of earthworms, insect grubs, and similar prey, moles "swim" through the soil by pushing the dirt aside with their powerfully clawed, paddlelike front feet. Their sensitive snouts and keen sense of smell apparently are very helpful for navigating in the underground darkness. The ability to detect vibrations in the soil is useful

Mole

for locating prey and escaping from enemies. Moles' eyes, in contrast, are not very effective. Tiny and in some species covered by skin, they probably serve only to distinguish darkness from light.

An Abundance of Burrowers Large and Small Find Refuge in the Hidden World of the Soil

Kingfishers like this European species dig nest tunnels in steep banks, usually near the streams and lakes where they fish. The eggs are laid on bare ground in a chamber at the end of the tunnel.

Earthworms of more than 2,000 species are found throughout much of the world. They play an invaluable role in enriching soil and improving its texture.

Spadefoot toads seem to melt out of sight as they dig backwards into sand and loose soil. They emerge at night to feed on insects and other small prey.

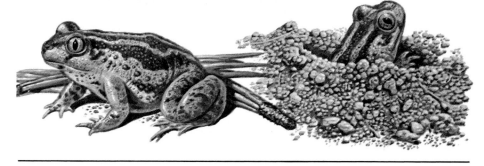

can, in fact, become a crowded dormitory. Gopher tortoises of the American Southwest dig burrows up to 40 feet long. Frogs, toads, snakes, burrowing owls, insects, and a variety of other creatures soon move in to share the accommodations supplied by the tortoises.

The tuatara, a primitive lizardlike reptile that lives on islands off New Zealand, is another tolerant landlord. Although tuataras are predators, they pay no attention when petrels move into their burrows to nest and raise their young. Sometimes they even turn the tables and move into burrows already occupied by petrels.

How do earthworms help the soil?
Like most other burrowing animals, earthworms act as living plows. Charles Darwin, the first scientist to focus attention on their importance as soil-builders, calculated that on an acre of good soil, worms can bring as much as 18 tons of subsoil to the surface each year. They do this by literally eating their way through the earth, digesting its content of dead leaves and other organic material, and eliminating the rest on the surface as coiled nutrient-rich castings. Their constant mixing and loosening of the upper layers of the soil also permits air to penetrate and water to percolate through, thus improving it as a living place for plants.

Can burrows be used more than once?
The gregarious European badgers live in family groups that occupy the same burrows for generations, as do North American gophers and some other rodents. Many of these perennially used burrows become complex networks of tunnels containing a variety of chambers for special uses such as resting, raising the young, sanitation, and food storage. Prairie dogs are renowned for their intricate burrows.

Even burrows that are only used for a season or two, then abandoned, are frequently reused. Animals such as foxes and skunks commonly live in underground dens for at least part of the year. Although they can dig for themselves, they will also take over old burrows of woodchucks and simply remodel them to suit their own needs. Fox dens are recycled too, by wolves.

tors, so burrows serve as secure nesting sites for a surprising assortment of birds. Many kinds of seabirds, from storm petrels to puffins, literally go underground during the breeding season. The Eurasian shelduck regularly nests in abandoned rabbit burrows among coastal dunes, and the North American burrowing owl takes over prairie dog dens. Kingfishers, showy motmots of the New World tropics, and Old World crab plovers are among the other burrowing birds. But perhaps the most widespread species is the little bank swallow, which ranges all across North America and Eurasia. Taking advantage of manmade excavations as well as natural embankments, the birds nest in large

colonies. Sandbanks are often pockmarked with entrances to the nesting tunnels of dozens of pairs.

Do burrowers ever share their homes?
Both ants and termites play host to a variety of interloping insects. Most are petty thieves that steal food from their hosts, but some are stealthy predators that dine on eggs, larvae, or even adult ants and termites. A few pay for their keep with services. One kind of cockroach that lives with fungus ants in the American tropics earns its welcome by licking the soldier ants and keeping them clean.

Large burrows also attract uninvited guests. A hospitable host's home

City Wildlife

Does city wildlife include anything besides pigeons?

Pigeons are among the most numerous urban animals, but they are by no means all there is. Other winged residents include certain kinds of gulls, crows, vultures, and storks. Hedgehogs abound near European population centers; foxes and martens (a type of weasel) have been sighted in or near New York and Copenhagen respectively. The coyote's howl is familiar to Los Angeles hillside residents, the jackal's call to people in some African and Asian cities.

By definition a city is a large concentration of humans living on land that is for the most part no longer in a natural state. Whether a plant or animal survives in a given city depends on the habits, hardiness, and adaptability of the species, and the kind of habitat on the city's outskirts. In some cases the presence of a particular plant or animal reflects the tolerance people have—or do not have—for the species. City dwellers in Western countries often welcome squirrels; sharing urban space with animals is routine in Hindu and Buddhist cultures.

How do plants move into cities?

A city's plant life is a mixture of native and imported species. Paris, London, Tokyo, and Delhi all have wild patches of "North American" goldenrod; some have the South American shaggy soldier. In Buenos Aires the European garden chrysanthemum grows wild; in San Francisco, the European wallflower. A study in the Polish city of Poznan revealed that more than half the 550 plant species counted were exotics, mostly from western Asia and southeastern Europe. A few were native to the Americas, and one to Africa.

Such imported species are often the progeny of plants that were cultivated in gardens and then "escaped" with the help of the wind. Plants also travel when their undigested seeds pass through birds and other animals, and certain species begin their wild existence as discarded fruits and vegetables. Once they get started, plants often spread rapidly in unoccupied places. Fifteen years after bombing laid waste a 100-acre area in London, 342 species were growing on ground where fewer than a hundred had been previously found.

Plants take over vacant lots and colonize gravelly railroad beds. They sprout along roadsides and around reservoirs, on embankments, under hedges, in lawns and parks, and even in sidewalk cracks. Sunny openings are preferred by ragweed, various mustards, asters, and goldenrod. Ivy tends toward the shade of bushes, fences, and walls. In warm, damp climates ferns grow out of standing walls, drawing nutrients from bricks, mortar, and the organic debris trapped in between.

So long as their needs for water, sunlight, and nutrients are satisfied, wild plants—certain ones, at least—will thrive in cities. Such species as horse chestnuts and ginkgoes do well despite the presence of pollutants and other growth-limiting factors.

Where can you find animals in a city?

Given adequate food and cover, indoors or out, wildlife can occur just about anywhere. Swifts and martins build nests inside buildings or under eaves; pigeons roost along a ledge. Monkeys and bats occupy Asian temples. City parks—especially large, open parks like the big ones in New York, San Francisco, Munich, London, Amsterdam, and Delhi—are home to diverse animal life.

Manicured cemeteries afford sanctuary for birds. A long-eared owl moved into Moscow University's botanical gardens to feed on sparrows. Opossums sheltered in a hedge near the headquarters of the Los Angeles police department. Peregrine falcons have been introduced to various North American cities, making their homes on skyscrapers there.

Birdwatchers who explore garbage dumps near cities find much to hold their attention, but other sorts of animals live there too. The Canadian town of Churchill has shared its dump with polar bears. In Africa, scavengers may include hyenas, jackals, and an occasional warthog, as well as vultures and marabou storks.

What do zoos do for wildlife?

Zoos are, of course, a guaranteed place to see animals in the city. Few creatures there can be considered

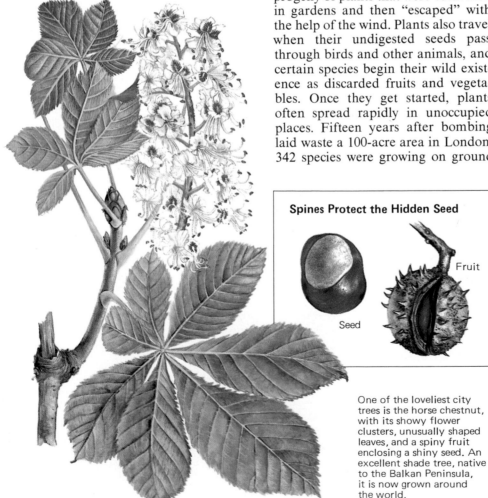

Spines Protect the Hidden Seed

Seed

Fruit

One of the loveliest city trees is the horse chestnut, with its showy flower clusters, unusually shaped leaves, and a spiny fruit enclosing a shiny seed. An excellent shade tree, native to the Balkan Peninsula, it is now grown around the world.

Wings Over the City

Pigeons cannot be ignored. They coo, they court, they conduct their lives as if their sole purpose were to remind us that cities are not ours alone. Starlings too insist on being noticed, but such high-density species are not the only birds. Gulls, crows, nighthawks, falcons, swifts —anyone alert to nature's sights and sounds can spot quite an array.

Viewed with objectivity, the starling is a gorgeous bird.

Whether it be Venice (right), Vienna, or Valparaíso, nearly every city in the world has pigeons galore.

wildlife—probably only the free-living hangers-on, such as squirrels and birds, which inhabit the surrounding parkland and scavenge for food. But zoos do far more for wildlife than provide sanctuary for animals. Major ones have research operations concerned with the conservation and perpetuation of species in the wild, and all perform an immeasurable role in educating the public about wildlife.

Have pigeons always lived in cities?

Wild pigeons are not city dwellers. As their alternative name rock dove suggests, these blue-gray birds prefer to nest and roost on rocks in such natural settings as cliffs and gorges. Thousands of years ago, some of these birds in Eurasia were domesticated, first for

their meat and then for their message-carrying services. (Pigeons are fast, with flight speeds measured at more than 80 miles an hour, and they have a remarkable ability to find their way home, even over hundreds of miles.) Pigeons living in towns and cities are the half-wild descendants of those domesticated birds, their lives made easier and their numbers enhanced by human handouts.

Is the presence of wildlife in the city good or bad?

Caterpillars chomping away at a carefully nurtured garden, squirrels gnawing through telephone cables, termites undermining a home—wildlife around people can be a nuisance or worse. Certain diseases have been

linked to bird droppings, and rabies can be transmitted by such creatures as foxes, skunks, and bats. But the infinitely varied music of songbirds, the delicate flutter of butterflies, the soft furriness of a scampering squirrel—all these elicit a different response. The presence of animals and greenery in the city offers beauty, serenity, and a sense of oneness with nature.

Homes built for people shelter wildlife too. The house mouse is among the uninvited guests.

Life Everywhere

Can animals live inside leaves?

Green growing leaves are an important food source for all sorts of animals, from cattle to caterpillars. While most do their munching from the outside, a few are small enough to burrow inside the leaves themselves. If you've ever seen a living leaf marred by a zigzag whitish line, you've seen the work of one of these tiny tunnelers. The culprits are leaf miners, the larvae of certain kinds of moths and flies that eat the inner tissues of leaves while leaving the upper and lower epidermis intact. Typically, their winding tunnels start out narrow and become ever wider, marking the growth of the insect larvae as they eat their way through the leaves.

What are oak apples?

Globular swellings, sometimes as big as table tennis balls, often form on the leaves and twigs of oaks. Called oak apples, they are a type of plant gall. The larva of a gall wasp lives inside each "apple" and feeds on the swollen plant tissue. Other kinds of plant galls, each with its own characteristic form, are caused by various flies, midges, aphids, and other insects, as well as by mites, bacteria, fungi, and other organisms. In most cases, the abnormal plant growth is thought to result from substances secreted by the parasite. Sometimes the parasite's mere physical presence interferes with normal plant growth. Whatever their causes, the galls usually supply safe haven and a ready source of food for the creatures that live hidden inside.

Is Antarctica devoid of life?

Except for the penguins that come ashore by the millions to nest, and a few other kinds of birds, life on the frozen continent is sparse indeed. Yet it does exist. Here and there, slow-growing mosses, lichens, and algae have gained a foothold on bare ground, where they absorb heat from the rocks on sunny summer days. A specialized type of lichen has also been found growing just under the surface of porous sandstones. (The fungal filaments penetrate minute pore spaces in the rocks.) The scanty land vegetation offers food and shelter to a few hardy animals such as tiny insects and mites, including a type of wingless fly that is only about one-fifth of an inch long.

There is also some aquatic life. Dense shore-to-shore mats of algae have been discovered growing in the frigid water at the bottom of deep lakes that are permanently covered with thick layers of ice. Animal life in temporary ponds formed by melting snow includes microscopic rotifers, water bears, and other kinds of invertebrates. Amazingly adapted to the Antarctic cold, these tiny creatures can remain frozen in their ponds for years at a time yet, when thawed out, become as lively as ever.

Are there tadpoles in treetops?

In tropical rain forests, water collects in the cuplike leaf bases of bromeliads, epiphytic plants of the pineapple family that grow high on the branches of forest giants. Investigators have found that these miniature ponds serve as homes for an amazing variety of life. Insect larvae, midget crustaceans, aquatic worms, and even the tadpoles of certain types of tree frogs are among the many creatures that live in these tiny ponds perched high in the treetops.

A Bromeliad Brimming With Life

Flatworm
Harvestman
Mosquito larvae
Tree frog
Crab

A cross section of a bromeliad shows pools of water between its leathery, overlapping leaves. These ponds perched high in the treetops supply homes for a variety of creatures both large and small.

Tree cavities can also collect rainwater and turn into pools that teem with life, especially crustaceans and various insect larvae. Among the most common in both temperate and tropical regions are the larvae of mosquitoes. These abundant pests are likely to lay their eggs in any body of standing water they encounter.

Can animals live in caves?

A number of creatures such as bats, bears, and certain birds take advantage of the shelter afforded by caves. While these must emerge regularly to forage for food, there are certain other animals that spend their entire lives in caves. Various kinds of fish, salamanders, insects, and crayfish are among the creatures that have become adapted to life in total darkness.

Eyes are useless in this lightless environment, and many of the permanent cave dwellers are blind. They find their way around by touch, smell, or echolocation. Some can locate prey in water by sensing the vibrations caused by even the slightest movement. Since pigments are also useless, cave creatures tend to be colorless or even transparent.

No plants can grow in the dark interiors of caves. As a result, full-time residents must rely on food imported from the outside world—plant and animal remains that are washed in by

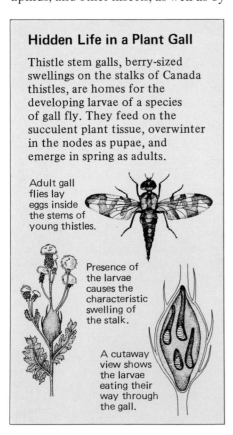

Hidden Life in a Plant Gall

Thistle stem galls, berry-sized swellings on the stalks of Canada thistles, are homes for the developing larvae of a species of gall fly. They feed on the succulent plant tissue, overwinter in the nodes as pupae, and emerge in spring as adults.

Adult gall flies lay eggs inside the stems of young thistles.

Presence of the larvae causes the characteristic swelling of the stalk.

A cutaway view shows the larvae eating their way through the gall.

storms, the bodies of animals that crawled in and died, and the droppings of birds and bats. Scavengers feed on this organic debris; predators in turn track down the scavengers in the strange, silent world of caves.

Do frogs live in deserts?

If the water is not too salty, permanent pools and springs in deserts, like ponds everywhere, frequently have their own complements of fish, aquatic insects, and other water animals. Even the temporary pools caused by infrequent downpours can harbor life.

In the arid Australian outback, for example, the appearance of temporary ponds stimulates amphibians known as water-holding frogs to mate and lay eggs. The fast-growing tadpoles mature into adult frogs in as little as two weeks. Then, as the ponds begin to shrink, the frogs store water inside their bodies. After becoming round and bloated, they burrow deep into the mud beneath the disappearing ponds, coat themselves with mucus, and await the return of rain to reproduce once more.

Tiny tadpole shrimp of the American Southwest survive in a somewhat similar way. Their eggs, lying dormant in the soil, hatch as soon as a temporary pool forms. Within a matter of weeks, the little crustaceans mature and produce a new generation of eggs. The adults die when the ponds dry up. But the eggs can endure many years of drought before hatching when it rains once again.

Where can you look for life?

From the depths of the ocean to the tops of the mountains, nearly every nook and cranny of the surface of the earth is exploited by some form of life. Even a single blackberry bush in a British hedgerow, like the one shown below, welcomes a constant parade of residents and visitors, from birds and butterflies to tiny leaf-mining insects. For the careful observer of the natural world, the drama of life on earth is constantly taking place all about us—if only we open our eyes to see.

Ripe fruits furnish a feast for many. Butterflies suck the juice from mushy berries; flesh flies and wasps pierce the skin to get at the juicy pulp; birds eat the berries whole.

Comma butterfly

Red admiral

Transparent tracery on the reddened leaf marks the trail of a leaf-mining insect larva; it ate its way between the leaf's upper and lower epidermis.

Banded snail

Flesh fly

Stinkbug sucks sap.

Blackbird wipes seeds from bill after eating fruit.

Wasp

Crane fly trapped in spider's web

ILLUSTRATION CREDITS

Some of the artwork in this book has previously appeared in other Reader's Digest publications. The sources of such illustrations are identified by the following initials:

ADAC   *Der Grosse ADAC—Führer Durch Wald, Feld und Flur*
AF   *Animal Families*
AFTR   *America From the Road*
AIA   *Animals in Action*
AOC   *Atlas of Canada*
BBB   *Book of British Birds*
BBC   *Book of the British Countryside*
BTB   *Back to Basics*
DATG   *Drive America: Traveler's Guide*

FWA   *Fascinating World of Animals*
IGG   *Illustrated Guide to Gardening*
JON   *Joy of Nature*
LMK   *Library of Modern Knowledge*
LOE   *Life on Earth: A Natural History*
LWA   *The Living World of Animals*
NAW   *North American Wildlife*
NLL-B   *Nature Lover's Library: Field Guide to the Birds of Britain*
NLL-F   *Nature Lover's Library: Field Guide to the Wild Flowers of Britain*
NLL-T   *Nature Lover's Library: Field Guide to the Trees and Shrubs of Britain*
NWW   *Natural Wonders of the World*

OAWN   *Our Amazing World of Nature*
OC   *Outdoors Canada*
OMW   *Our Magnificent Wildlife*
SA   *Southern Africa: Land of Beauty and Splendour*
SNE   *Splendeurs Naturelles de l'Europe*
SNI   *Splendore della Natura in Italia*
SOS   *Secrets of the Seas*
SVPM   *Secrets et Vertus des Plantes Médicinales*
SWA   *Scenic Wonders of America*
SWC   *Scenic Wonders of Canada*
TAWN   *The Amazing World of Nature*
TUS   *These United States*
WAU   *Marvels and Mysteries of the World Around Us*

1 Edward S. Barnard. 2-3 M. P. Kahl. 4 SVPM. 6 *left* NASA; *right* Frans Lanting. 7 *left* Steven Fuller; *right* David O. Johnson. 8-9 NASA. 10 LMK. 11 *top* AOC (George Buctel); *bottom* OC (George Buctel). 12 *upper left* (diagram) LMK; *top right* (8 photos) Lick Observatory Photographs; *bottom* JON. 13 *upper left* LMK; *bottom right* Helmut K. Wimmer. 14-15 *top* Bob Clemenz Photography. 15 *bottom* FWA. 16 George Buctel (after LMK). 17 *top* Richard W. Brown; *lower left* National Oceanic & Atmospheric Administration. 18 OC (George Buctel). 19 WAU. 20-21 *top* Harry Engels. 21 *bottom right* JON. 22 Helmut K. Wimmer. 23 Leo Ainsworth, courtesy of the National Severe Storms Laboratory, NOAA. 24 Richard Edes Harrison © *Smithsonian* magazine. 25 *upper right* NWW; *bottom* Richard Edes Harrison © *Smithsonian* magazine. 26 & 27 Lee Boltin. 28 *left* BBC; *upper right* Runk-Schoenberger/Grant Heilman Photography, specimen from North Museum, Franklin & Marshall College; *lower right* Lee Boltin. 30 Photographic Library of Australia. 31 *left* David Muench Photography, Inc.; *right* NWW. 32 Ward W. Wells. 33 *left* WAU; *right* NWW. 34 TUS. 35 *top* Alfredo MacKenney; *bottom* JON. 36 SNI (Luciano Corbella). 37 Galen A. Rowell. 38 WAU. 39 *top* JON; *bottom* Barry C. Bishop. 40 *left* JON. 40-41 SNE. 42 *bottom* SWA. 42-43 *top* Hans Schönwetter. 44 JON. 45 Aerophoto Eelde. 46 *left* FWA; *right* JON. 47 *left* Kingsley C. Fairbridge; *right* FWA. 48-49 H. C. Berann, under the supervision of Prof. Bruce Heezen (Lamont Geological Observatory) and Marie Tharpe (U.S. Oceanographic Office)/© Verlag Das Beste GmbH, Stuttgart. 50 *center* SNI (Luciano Corbella). 50-51 *top* Paisajes Españoles. 51 *right* Art Clifton/Camera Hawaii. 52 Paul Hague. 53 *top* Janet Tenenzaph; *bottom* SWC (George Buctel). 54 *top* George Buctel (after LMK); *bottom* Janet Tenenzaph (after LMK). 55 *left* Peter G. Sanchez; *right* LMK. 56 NWW. 57 David Muench Photography, Inc. 58-59 *top* Loren McIntyre. 59 *bottom* SWC (George Buctel). 60 *left* Janet Tenenzaph. 60-61 *bottom* Matti A. Pitkänen. 61 *top right* SWA. 62 WAU. 63 *top* Janet Tenenzaph; *bottom* Les Line. 64 Janet Tenenzaph. 65 *left* SWA; *right* Jeremy Schmidt. 66-67 SNE. 67 *bottom* Janet Tenenzaph. 68 SWC (George Buctel). 69 *top* © Pierre A. Pittet, Geneva; *lower* JON. 70-71 *bottom* George Holton/Photo Researchers. 71 *top* JON. 72-73 Frans Lanting. 74 *left* D. P. Wilson/Eric & David Hosking. 74-75 David Muench Photography, Inc. 75 *center* Satour; *right* Josef Muench. 76 Janet Tenenzaph (after LMK). 77 SVPM. 78 *center* BBC; *bottom* NAW. 79 *top* NAW; *top right* Chrile/Mauritius; *bottom* NAW. 80 *left* LMK; *right* Gilbert Nielsen. 81 NAW. 82 *upper* BBC; *bottom* JON. 83 Larry West. 84 *top* Heather Angel; *lower*

SVPM. 85 *left* Detail from painting by Alex Ebel from *Childcraft—The How and Why Library* © 1982 World Book, Inc.; *right* SVPM. 86, 87, & 88 SVPM. 89 *left* JON; *bottom* LMK; *right* NLL-T. 90 *left* SVPM; *top* JON; *bottom* AFTR. 91 *upper left* SVPM; *lower left* NAW; *upper & lower right* DATG. 92 *upper left* NAW; *bottom left* SVPM; *right* NLL-F. 93 *top left* NLL-F; *inset* SVPM; *bottom* SVPM. 94 *left* LMK; *right* John Dawson from *Biology Today*. Copyright © 1972 by Communications Research Machines, Inc., a Division of Random House, Inc., by permission of the publisher. 95 Constance P. Warner. 96 *bottom left* JON; *bottom right* LMK; *upper right* IGG. 97 *left* Morris Karol; *right* SVPM. 98 *left* LMK; *center* SOS; *right* LMK. 99 *left* JON; *top* LMK; *bottom* SOS. 100 *upper left* JON; *bottom* SVPM; *right* NAW. 101 *left* NAW; *right* JON. 102 *left* Stuart Umin; *right* SWA. 103 BBC. 104 JON. 105 *top* SVPM; *bottom* SWC (Anker Odum). 106 JON. 107 *left* LMK; *right* NLL-T. 108 Roland C. Clement. 109 *top center* Edward F. Anderson; *right* Photographic Library of Australia; *bottom* NLL-T. 110 JON. 111 BBC. 112 *top* Gilbert Nielsen; *bottom* LMK. 113 SVPM. 114 *left* Thase Daniel. 114-115 SVPM. 116 SVPM. 117 *top* William H. Harlow; *bottom* NAW. 118 SVPM. 119 *left* SVPM; *right* Heather Angel. 120 *left* OMW. 120-121 David Muench Photography, Inc. 122 *top* Durward L. Allen; *lower* JON. 123 *top* NAW; *right* SVPM. 124 *left* Gilbert Nielsen; *right* NLL-F. 125 NLL-F. 126 *bottom left* SVPM; *remainder* Reprinted from *Tropical Queensland* by Stanley and Kay Breeden by permission of Collins Publishers. 127 NLL-F. 128 *top* JON. 128-129 Ken Lewis/Earth Scenes. 129 *center* R. E. Hutchins. 130-131 SVPM. 132 & 133 BBC. 134 *left* NAW; *right* Gilbert Nielsen. 135 SVPM. 136 *left* JON; *top* Gilbert Nielsen. 137 & 138 SVPM. 139 IGG. 140 *top* NAW; *bottom left & right* SVPM. 141 Gottlieb Hampfler. 142 *left* IGG; *top right* LMK; *bottom right* NAW. 143 *left* JON; *right* SVPM. 144 *left* IGG; *right* SWA. 145 David Muench Photography, Inc. 146 *left* JON; *right* NAW. 147 James H. Carmichael, Jr. 148 NAW. 149 *bottom left* JON; *right* SVPM. 150 SVPM. 151 NLL-F. 152-153 SVPM. 154 LMK. 155 *left* SVPM; *right* Firestone Tire & Rubber Co. 156-157 Steven Fuller. 158 FWA. 159 *map* LMK; *No. 2 & No. 3* FWA; *remainder* LMK. 160 LMK. 161 *top* Roger McKay; *lower left* NAW. 162 LMK. 163 Shep Abbott. 164 *left* FWA; *right* BBC. 165 Patrick G. Bryan; *inset* FWA. 166 Glenn Gallison/National Park Service. 167 *map* SOS; *center* NLL-B. 168 *lower left* OMW; *upper right* BBC. 169 *left* BBC; *center* NAW; *right* Kathy & Alan Linn. 170 K. H. Himmer. 171 *top* N. Smythe; *lower* Douglas Faulkner/Sally Faulkner Collection. 172 LMK. 173 *left* FWA; *right* NAW. 174 *bot-*

tom Graham Pizzey; *top* SOS. **175** *left* BBC; *right* NAW. **176** NLL-B; *inset* BBC. **177** Jeff Foott. **178-179** NAW. **180** FWA. **181** *upper* William H. Amos; *bottom* JON. **182** *upper left* NAW; *inset* LMK; *bottom* SOS. **183** Douglas Faulkner/Sally Faulkner Collection. **184** *bottom left* FWA; *upper right* NAW; *lower right* LMK. **185** E. S. Ross. **186** LMK. **187** *top* N. Smythe; *bottom* FWA. **188** *left* BBC. **188-189** *bottom* NAW. **189** *top left* NAW; *top right* JON. **190-191** AF. **192** © Robert P. Carr. **193** *top* FWA; *bottom* NAW. **194** *spider* FWA; *webs* LMK. **195** *top* FWA; *bottom* NAW. **196** SOS. **197** *top* NAW; *bottom* AIA. **198** *lower* NAW. **198-199** SOS. **200** *left* SOS; *upper right* FWA; *lower right* BBC. **201** NAW. **202** *left* NAW; *bottom* LMK. **203** *left* FWA; *top* NAW. **204** *left* FWA; *right* NAW. **205** *top* M. K. Morcombe; *right* LMK. **206** *upper right* NAW; *bottom* FWA. **207** David Cavagnaro. **208** AIA. **209** *top* Gilbert Nielsen; *bottom* AIA. **210** *left* BBB; *right* NLL-B. **211** *left* FWA; *right* NLL-B. **212** *lower left* AIA; *upper right* NLL-B. **213** *top* NLL-B; *bottom* BBC. **214** *upper left* NAW; *bottom left* NLL-B; *right* NAW. **215** LOE. **216** *herons* Guy Coheleach; *goldcrest* BBC; *remainder* LMK. **217** *top* Janet Tenenzaph; *center* David G. Corke. **218** NLL-B. **219** *left* BBC; *right* NLL-B. **220** AIA. **221** *top & right* NLL-B; *inset* JON. **222** FWA. **223** *left* © Leonard Lee Rue III; *right* SOS. **224 & 225** NLL-B. **226** *center* NAW. **226-227** NLL-B. **228** *upper* OC; *bottom* NLL-B. **229** NLL-B. **230** *bottom* Janet Tenenzaph. **230-231** *yellowthroat and magpie* NAW; *remainder* NLL-B. **232** *lower left* LMK; *upper right* LMK & FWA. **233** *bottom* M. P. Kahl; *right* NLL-B. **234 & 235** FWA. **236** William J. Weber. **237** *left* OMW; *top* Stanley Breeden. **238** LMK. **239** SOS. **240** *left* BBC; *bottom* FWA. **241** *top* Graham Pizzey; *bottom* BBC. **242** *bottom* JON; *upper right* FWA. **243** © 1981 Paul E. Meyers. **244** Thase Daniel. **245** Charles Fracé. **246** *upper right* SOS; *bottom* SWC (Anker Odum). **247** © Leonard Lee Rue III. **248** AFTR. **249** *top* © Leonard Lee Rue III; *bottom* FWA. **250** AFTR; *inset* FWA. **251** AFTR. **252** N. Smythe. **253** *upper left* SOS; *center* AFTR; *upper right* FWA. **254** FWA. **255** *top* The Metropolitan Museum of Art, Rogers Fund, 1948; *bottom* DATG. **256** *left* JON; *top right* SOS; *bottom right* OMW. **257** *upper* AFTR; *bottom* LWA. **258-259** David O. Johnson. **260** *upper* LMK; *bottom* NAW. **261** *top* JON; *bottom* FWA. **262** *left* E. R. Degginger. **262-263** David Muench Photography, Inc. **264** *top* Lynn M. Stone/Bruce Coleman Inc.; *lower* OMW. **265** *left* Francisco Erize/Bruce Coleman Inc.; *right* FWA. **266-267** OC (Anker Odum). **268-269** OMW. **269** *top* FWA. **270** Guy Coheleach. **271** *left* Thase Daniel; *right* FWA. **272-273** JON. **274** NLL-B. **275** Matti A. Pitkänen. **276** Richard W. Brown. **277** NLL-B. **278** JON. **279** Thomas P. Blagden, Jr. **280** *bottom* OMW; *upper right* FWA. **281** AF. **282** *left* JON. **282-283** Jeff Foott. **283** *right* JON. **284** *left* JON. **284-285** ADAC. **286** *caribou* NAW; *remainder* FWA. **287** NLL-B. **288** SOS. **289** NLL-B. **290-291** SOS. **292-293** SOS. **294.** SOS. **295** *top* James A. Kern; *bottom* SOS. **296** *left* FWA; *right* Keith Gillett. **297** *left* FWA; *right* Carl Roessler/Animals Animals. **298-299** SOS. **300-301** SOS. **302-303** NLL-B. **304** *bottom* JON; *right* NAW. **305** *left* JON; *right* NAW. **306** *bottom* NLL-B; *upper right* FWA. **307** *left* From *The Ecology of Running Water* by H. B. N. Hynes, published by the Liverpool University Press; *right* Richard W. Brown. **308** *bottom* FWA. **308-309** *top* Thase Daniel. **309** NAW. **310** *left* NAW; *right* E. S. Ross. **311** David Muench Photography, Inc. **312** *upper* BBC; *lower* SOS. **313** *upper* NLL-B; *middle* JON; *lower* NAW. **314** SVPM. **315** *upper left* NLL-B; *upper right* Richard L. Scheffel; *lower right* NAW. **316** *left* BBC; *right* JON. **317** BBC. **319** SVPM. **320** NAW. **321-336** *zebra* JON; *remainder* FWA.

Efforts have been made to contact the holder of the copyright for each picture. In several cases these sources have been untraceable, which we sincerely regret.

INDEX

Aardvark

B

Bee

Bulbs, 101, 111, **111**
Bullfrogs, **202**
Bumblebees, 193, **193**
Burdocks, **130**
Burrows and burrowing, 312–313, **312–313**
 flooding and, 312
 grasslands and, 265
 mutualism and, 313
 of prairie dogs, 266–267, **266–267**
Bushbucks, **269**
Bustards, kori, 175, 264
Buteos, **226**
Butterflies, **179,** 188–189, **188, 189,** 284, **317**
 large blue, **175**
 moths vs., 188, **188**
Butterworts, 116, **116**
Buzzards, honey, **226**
Byssal threads, 300–301

Camel

Cacti, **100,** 128, 144–145, **144, 145,** 263
 leaf modifications of, 144
 other succulents vs., **144**
 water absorption and storage in, 144–145, **144**
Caddisflies, 306–307
Caecilians, 202
Calcium, 184
Caldera, 36, **36,** 60
Calyx, 92
Cambium layer, 106, **106**
Cambrian period, 29
Camels, 234–235, 261
Camouflage, 170–171, **170, 171,** 251, 296
 dead-leaf disguise in, 171, **171**
 decoys in, 171
 eyespots as, 170
 pigment cells in, 170–171
Canada geese, 224, **224**
Canaries, 231
Canary grasses, **132**
Canyons, 56–57, **56, 57**
 erosion in formation of, 56, **56**
 submarine, 48
Cape buffalo, **268**
Capercailles, 274, **274**
Capybaras, 242, **242,** 243

Carbon dioxide, 14
 fish and, 196, 199
 photosynthesis and, 104–105
Carboniferous period, 29
Caribou, 286, **286**
Carnivorous mammals, 236, 237. *See also*
 Predators; Scavengers.
Carnivorous plants, 116–117, **116, 117**
Carotenoids, 210
Carpenter bees, **193**
Casques, 222, **222**
Cassiopeia, 12, **12**
Cassiterite, 27
Cassowaries, 222, **222**
Caterpillars, **162,** 188–189, **188, 189**
Catkins, 93, **93,** 94, 103
Cats, 244–245, **244, 245**
 calls of, 244–245
 climbing ability of, 245
 eyes of, 245
 hunting tactics of, 244, 270, **270**
 man-eating, 244
 teeth of, 244
 water and, 245
Cattails, 310, **310**
Cattle egrets, **175**
Caves, 66–67, **66–67**
 formation of, 30, 66
 life in, 316–317
 size of, 67
 surface signs of, 67
Cave systems, 66–67, **66**
Cecropia moths, **189**
Cell structure, 74
Cellulose, 74
 digestion of, by protozoans, 191
Cenozoic era, 29
Century plants, 263
Cephalopods, 182–183, **182, 183**
 feeding habits of, 183
 ink in defense of, 182
 intelligence of, 183
 locomotion of, 182, 183
Cereal grains, 133
Chalk, 28, 52
Chambered nautiluses, 183, **183**
Chameleons, **204**
Chamois, 282, **282**
Charge, electrical, 20
Chatoyancy, 27
Cheetahs, **163,** 244–245, 270–271, **270**
Chemical weathering, 30
Chernozem, **44**
Chestnuts, horse, **103,** 314, **314**
Chicle, 155
Chicory, **131**
Chimpanzees, 158, 168, **168,** 176, 177, 280
Chinchillas, **242**

Chinese (Japanese) lanterns, **138,** 139
Chinook, 15
Chipmunks, **235**
Chitin, 178
Chitons, 180, **180**
Chlorophyll, 74, 102, **102,** 104–105
 algae and, 76
 luminous mosses and, 82
Chloroplasts, 104
Choughs, 284–285, **285**
Chromium, 27
Chrysalis, 188, **188**
Chrysoberyl, 27
Cinnabar, 27
Cirques, 42
Cirrocumulus clouds, **19**
Cirrostratus clouds, 19, **19**
Cirrus clouds, 19, **19**
Cities, 314–315, **315**
 animals in, 315, **315**
 pests in, 315, **315**
 plants in, 314, **314**
Clams, 180, 298–299, **299,** 300
 siphons of, 180, 299
Clay, 45
Climate, 18, 44, 272, 278
 in Arctic and Antarctic, 70
Climax community, 122–123
 forest, 273
Cloning, 101, 147
Cloud forests, 279, **279,** 282
Clouds, 14–23
 hail formation and, 17
 types of, 19, **19**
Clovers, **92,** 142–143, **142**
Club mosses, 84–85, **84**
 reproduction of, 84
 spread of, 84, **84**
 true mosses vs., 84
Coastal seas, 288–289
Coastal wetlands, 304–305, **304**
 birds in, **304,** 305
 conservation of, 305
 mammals in, 304, **304**
 vegetation in, 305, **305**
Cobras, 173, **173,** 204
Cobwebs, 194
Cockroaches, **187**
Coco-de-mer, 98, **98**
Coconuts, **295**
Cocoons, 188, 189, **189**
Cods, **160**
Cold-blooded animals, 204
Cols, 42
Colugos (flying lemurs), 164, 234, **234**
Columbia Plateau, 36
Comets, 10, 13, **13**
 orbits of, 13
Comma butterflies, **317**

Deer

Giraffe

Hare

Ibis

compound eyes of, 186–187, **187**
feeding habits of, 186
flying, 164, **164**
grasslands and, 265
growth patterns of, 186, **186**
high altitudes and, 284, **284–285**
longevity of, 186
predatory, 194–195, **195**
reproduction rate of, 187
singing of, 169, **169**
sizes of, 186
social, 190–193, **190, 192–193**
spiders vs., 194
stinging, 172
tool-using, 176
types of, **187**
See also specific insects.
Invertebrates, **158,** 178–195
intelligence of, 179
parental care among, 179
reproduction of, 179
sizes of, 178–179
skeletons of, 178
See also specific invertebrates.
Irish moss, **77**
Iron, 27
Islands, 294–295
continental, 294
giantism and, 223
oceanic, 294–295
volcanic, 25, 37, 48, 294, 296
Ivy, English, **127**

Jellyfish

Jacanas (lily trotters), 311
Jackals, 271, **271**
Jack pines, 123, **123**
Jaguars, 244–245, 279
Japanese (Chinese) lanterns, **138,** 139
Jellyfish, **162,** 173, **173,** 178–179, **178, 293**
venomous, 173, **173**
Jerboas, **242,** 260–261, **261**
Jimsonweeds (thorn apples), 138
Joshua trees, 109, 140, 262
Jumping spiders, 194
Jungle cacti, 128
Jupiter, 10, **10**
Jurassic period, 29
Juvenile hormones, 115

Kangaroo

Kames, **42,** 43
Kanchenjunga, **39**
Kangaroo rats, 234–235, 260, **261**
Kangaroos, **159,** 234, **234,** 238, **238, 239**
Katydids, 169
Kelps, 76, **77,** 300, **301**
Keratin, 235
Kettle lakes, **42,** 43, 60
Kilimanjaro, Mount, 18, 34, 38
Killer whales (orcas), 291, **291**
King cobras, **173,** 204
Kingfishers, 306, **313**
Kinkajous (honey bears), 279
Kites, 226–227
Everglades, 161, **176**
Kit foxes, 247, 261, **261**
Kiwis, 232, 294
Klipspringers, 268
Koalas, 238
Kokerbooms (quiver trees), 262
Komodo dragons, 204, **295**
Kori bustards, 175, 264
Krakatoa, 34–35, 123
Krill, 249, 289, 291
Krummholz, 284, **284**
Kudus, **269**
Kudzu, 126, 143

Lion

La Brea tar pits, 29
Lacewings, **187**
Ladder lichen, 81, **81**
Ladybird beetles, **164**
Lady crabs, **299**
Lady's slippers, yellow, **146**
Lakes, 60–61, **60, 61**
crater, 36, **36,** 60, **60**
life cycle of, 122
sizes of, 61
Lamellae, 225
Lammergeiers, 176, 283
Landslides, 30, 31
Langurs, **234**
Lapilli, 34

Latex, 155, **155**
Latitude, 18
Lava, 28, 34, 36, 37
Lava tubes, 37
Lavender, **153**
Lead, 27
Leaf bugs, Indian, **171**
Leatherback turtles, 204, 206, **206**
Leaves, 104–105, **104, 105**
color change in, 102, **102,** 277
decay of, 277
insects burrowing in, 316
shedding of, 102–103
simple vs. compound, 105, **105**
Leeches, 162, 309
Legumes, 96, **96,** 142–143, **142, 143**
edible, 143, **143**
photoperiodism of, 143
pods of, 142, **142**
Leks, 215
Lemurs, 278, 295
Leonid meteor shower, 13
Leopards, 244–245, 257, 279, 283
Leopard tortoises, **206**
Lepidoptera, 188–189, **188, 189**
metamorphosis of, 188, **188, 189**
seasonal behavior of, 189, **189**
sizes of, 188
Levees, **54,** 55
Lianas, 126–127, **126**
Lichens, 74, 80–81, **80, 81**
compound nature of, 80, **80**
longevity of, 81
reproduction of, 80
rock-dissolving acids in, 44
seashores and, 300, **301**
types of, 81
uses of, 81
Licorice, **143**
Life zones, 282, 298–301
Light, 11, 14–15
colors and, 14–15
photoperiodism and, 143
photosynthesis and, 104
plant movements and, 112–113, **112, 113**
speed of, 11, 20
vision of deep-sea fish and, 292
Lightning, 20–21, **20**
Light-producing organisms, 169, **169,** 292–293, **293**
Light-years, 11
Lily family, 101, **101,** 140–141, **140, 141**
edible members of, 140–141
flower structure of, 140
Lily trotters (jacanas), 311
Limestone, 26
Limpets, 180–181, 300–301, **301**

Lions, **161,** 235, **235,** 237, 244–245, **244,** 270

Liverworts, 75, 82

Living stones, 262, **262**

Lizards, 204–205, **204, 205,** 260–261, **260**
   flying, 164, **164**
   regeneration in, 205

Llamas, 284

Llanos. *See* Grasslands.

Loam, 45

Lobsters, 184–185, **184, 293**

Locoweed, 149

Locust, black, **88, 103**

Locusts, **187**

Long-eared owls, **229**

Loons, **220, 287**

Lords-and-ladies, **93**

Luminous mosses, 82

Lumpfish, **301**

Lungfish, 200, **200**

Lung lichens, 81, **81**

Lynxes, 275

Lyrebirds, **211**

Monkey

Maars, 36, 60

Macaques, 281
   Japanese (snow monkeys), 281, 283
   long-tailed (crab-eating monkeys), 304

Madagascar, wildlife of, 295
   elephant birds, 223
   lemurs, 278
   traveler's-trees, 108

Maelstroms, 47

Magma, 34
   dome mountains and, 38
   igneous rocks and, 26
   thermal areas and, 64–65, **65**
   volcanic landforms and, 34, 36–37, **36, 37**

Magpies, black-billed, **231**

Malachite, **26,** 27

Mallards, **220, 224**

Mallee fowl, 217, **217**

Mammals, 158, 234–253, **234–253**
   adaptations to winter of, 275, 287
   baby-sitting among, 236–237
   burrowing, 312
   communication among, 168, 235
   cooperation of, 235
   definition of, 234

development at birth of, 236
   family life among, 236–237, **236, 237**
   flying, 164
   reproduction, types of, among, 234
   See also specific mammals.

Manatees, 235, 252

Mandarin duck, **211**

Mandrakes, European, 150

Mangroves, 63, 99, **99,** 294, 311

Mangrove swamps, 63, 304–305, 311

Man-of-war, Portuguese, 172–173, **172,** 174, **174**

Man-of-war fish, 174, **174**

Manta rays, 198, **198**

Mantid, **195**

Marble, 27

Marmots, alpine, **242**

Mars, 10, **10**

Marshes, 62–63, 304–305, **304,** 310–311
   swamps vs., 62

Marsh hawks (hen harriers), **212, 220**

Marsupial mice, **239**

Marsupial moles, 238, **239**

Marsupials, 234, **234,** 238–239, **238, 239**
   nursing of, 238, **238**
   pouches of, 238

Masked bedbug-hunters, 195

Matamatas, 206

Mauna Kea, 34, 38

Mayflies, **187**

Medusa, 179

Meerkats, 267

Megapodes, 217, **217**

Melanin, 210–211

Mercury (metal), 27

Mercury (planet), 10, **10,** 12

Meristematic tissue, 100–101

Mermaid's purses, 198–199

Mesopotamia, 154

Mesosphere, 14

Mesozoic era, 29

Mesquites, **120**

Metals, 27

Metamorphic rocks, 26, 39

Metamorphosis (of insects), 186, **186,** 188, **188,** 192

Meteorites, 13

Meteoroids, 10

Meteorology, 19

Meteors, 13

Meteor showers, 13

Mexican big-eared bats, **240**

Mexican jumping beans, 113

Mica, 26

Mice, **239,** 242–243, **243**

Mid-Atlantic Ridge, **24,** 49

Midges, phantom, 308–309

Midwife toads, 202, **203**

Migration, 166–167, **166, 167**
   of bats, 240
   of butterflies, **189**
   errors in, 167
   individual vs. group, 166–167
   preparation for, 167
   reverse, 166
   timing of, 167

Mildew, 78

Milk, 234–235

Milk sickness, 149

Milky Way, 10–11

Millipedes, **179**

Minerals, 26–27, **26–27,** 44
   identification of, 26

Mining bees, 312, **312**

Mink, 306

Minke whales, **290**

Miocene epoch, 29

Mistletoe, 118–119, **118**

Mistral, 15

Mites, 312

Mixed forests, 272, **272–273,** 276–277

Mixed herds, 268, **268–269**

Moas, 223, **223,** 295

Mockingbirds, 231

Molds, 78–79, **79**

Mole crabs, 299, **299**

Mole-rats, great, **159**

Moles, 238, **239,** 312, **312**

Mollusks, 180–183, **180, 181, 182, 183,** 298
   bivalve vs. univalve, 180, **180**
   eyes of, 181, **181**
   feet of, 180–181
   mantle of, 180, 181
   radula of, 180
   venomous, 173, 180

Monarch butterflies, **188**

Mongooses, 176, 295

Monkey puzzle trees, 109, **109**

Monkeys, **235,** 280–281, **280, 281,** 304
   apes vs., 281
   prehensile tails of, 280–281, **280**

Monocots, 98, **98**
   dicots vs., 98, **98**

Monotremes, 234

Monsoons, 21, **21**

Moon, 12
   distance from earth, 12
   phases of, 12, **12**
   size of, 12
   tides and, 46, **46**

Moons, 10

Moon snails, **178,** 298, **299**

Moose, 251, **251,** 275

Moraines, 40, **40–41,** 42–43, 60

Moray eels, 200, 296, 297

Morels, **78**

Rhinoceros

Snail

Salt lakes, 61, 68
Salt marshes, 62, 304–305, **304**
  birds in, **304,** 305
  conservation of, 305
  mammals in, 304, **304**
  vegetation in, 305, **305**
Samaras, 96
San Andreas Fault, 33
Sand, 45, 50–51, **51,** 298–299
Sand dollars, 298–299, **299,** 301
Sand dunes, 30, 50–51, **51,** 69, **69,** 123,
  298
  life on, 123, 298
  types and formation of, 69, **69**
Sanderlings, **220, 299**
Sand fleas (beach hoppers), 298–299, **299**
Sandpipers, spotted, **220**
Sandstone, 27
San Francisco earthquake (1906), 33
Saponins, 115
Sapphires, 27
Saprophytes, 147
Sapwood, 106, **106**
Sargasso Sea, 46, 166
Satellites, natural, 10, 12
Saturn, 10, **10, 13**
Sausage trees, 109
Savannas, 264, **264**
  elephants and, 268
  herds on, 268, **268–269**
  predators on, 270–271, **270, 271**
  water scarcity in, 268
Saxifrage, purple, **285**
Scallops, 181, **181**
Scavengers, 271, 292, 315, 317
Scissorbills (cutwaters, skimmers), **220,**
  302
Scorpions, 172, **172**
Scouring rushes, 85
Screw pines (pandanuses), 311
Sea anemones, 174, **174,** 177, 292, **293**
Seabirds, 212–213, 302–303, **302–303**
  nesting of, 303
Sea caves, 53
Seacoasts, rocky, 30, 52–53, **52, 53**
  life on, 300–301, **301**
  zones of, 300–301, **301**
Seacoasts, sandy, 30, 50–51, **50**
  life on, 298–299, **299**
  zones of, 298–299
Sea cows, **235,** 252
Sea cucumbers, **293,** 299, **299, 301**
Sea geese (gannets), 303, **303**
Seagulls, **209,** 302–303
Sea horses, 200, **201**
Sea lavender, **305**
Sea lettuce, 76, **76**
Sea lions, 248, **248**

Seals, 234, 236, 248–249, **248**
  crab-eating, 249, 289
  diving ability of, 248–249
  predators of, 249, 286, **286**
  sea lions vs., 248, **248**
  social behavior of, 248
Seamounts, 49
Sea otters, 177, **177**
Seas, coastal, 288–289
Seashores. *See* Seacoasts, rocky;
  Seacoasts, sandy.
Sea slugs (nudibranchs), 180
Seasons, 11, **11,** 21, 102–103
Sea squirts, **301**
Sea stacks, 53, **53,** 296
Sea turtles, 206–207, **206,** 299
Sea urchins, 292, **293,** 298, 300–301, **301**
Seaweeds, 76–77, **77,** 300, **301**
Secretary birds, 270, **271**
Sedimentary rocks, 26, 28, 36
Seed leaves (cotyledons), 98–99, **99**
Seeds, 88–89, 92, 94, 96–99, **98,**
  99, 100, 101, 294
  desert plants and, 262
  fruit and, 96–97
  sizes of, 98
  spores vs., 88
  spreading of, 98, **98**
  sprouting of, 99, **99**
  uses of, 99
  vegetative reproduction vs., 100–101
Seismographs, 33
Sepals, 92, **92,** 96
Sequoias, **75,** 90–91, **90**
Setae, 162
Shags, **220**
Shale, 26
Sharks, **160,** 198–199, **198–199,** 289, **293**
  gills of, **198,** 199
  mating activities of, 198
  migration of, 199
  skin of, 199
  swim bladder absent in, 199
  teeth of, 198
  viviparous, 199
Shearwaters, 289, **289**
Sheathbills, 302
Sheep's fescues, **285**
Shield volcanoes, 34, **34**
Ship Rock Peak, 36–37
Shooting stars, 10, 13
Shoreline vegetation, 122
Short-eared owls, **229**
Shrews, 159, 234, **234**
Shrikes, **161**
Shrimp, **160,** 184, **293,** 298–299
  tadpole, 317
Sidewinders, **261**
Siliques, 96, **96**

Silkworms, 188
Sills, 37
Silt, 45
Silurian period, 29
Silverswords, 135
Silverweeds, **305**
Sirius, 12
Siroccos, 15
Skates, 198–199, 298
Skeletons, 163, 178
Skimmers (cutwaters, scissorbills), **220,**
  302
Skuas, 221
Skylarks, 214, 231
Slate, 26
Sleet, 17
Slime molds, 79
Sloths, **159,** 252, **252**
Smilax, European, **140**
Snails, **178,** 180–181, **180,** 298–299, **299**
Snake-necked turtles, Australian, **206**
Snakes, 172–173, **172, 173,** 204–205, **204**
  locomotion of, 204
  molting of, 204, **204**
  venomous, 172–173, **172, 173**
Snapping turtles, **206**
Snow, 16–18, 20, 40, **275**
Snowflakes, 17, **17**
Snow leopards, 257, 283
Snowshoe hares, 275
Snowstorms, 21
Snowy owls, 287, **287**
Social insects, 190–193, **190, 192–193**
Soft-shelled turtles, **206**
Soil, 30, 44–45, **44, 45,** 272, 286
  organic material in, 44, 45
  types of, 44, **44**
Soil creep, 31
Solar eclipses, 12, **13**
Solar energy, 11, 15, 104
Solar system, 10, **10**
  location in Milky Way, 11
Solifluction, **71,** 286
Solstice, summer, 11
Solstice, winter, 11
Songbirds, 230–231, **230–231,** 305
  perching of, 230, **230**
  pest control and, 231
  songs of, 230–231
Sori, 86
Sorrels, wood, **113**
Sound, speed of, 20
Soybeans, **143**
Spadefoot toads, **313**
Spadixes, 92, **93**
Spanish moss, 83, 129, **129**
Sparrows, house, **230**
Spathes, 92, **93**
Specific gravity (of minerals), 26

Turtle

Tortoises, 206–207, **206, 207, 256,** 295
    dry land species of, 206
    turtles vs., 206
Toucans, **278**
Tracts (of feathers), 211
Trade rats (pack rats), 242
Trade winds, 14, **15**
Transpiration, 107, **107**
Trapdoor spiders, **195**
Traveler's-trees, 108
Tree ferns, 87, 273
Tree frogs, **164, 169,** 203
Tree heaths, 279
Tree line (timberline), 284, 286
Trees, 89–90, **89, 90,** 93, **93,** 108–109,
    109, 262
    age and growth of, 90, 106–107, **106,**
        107
    blossoming, 93, **93**
    broad-leaved, 102–105, **102, 103, 104,**
        105, 276–277, **276**
    competition of, 120–121, **120**
    coniferous, 88–91, **88, 90, 91,** 123,
        123, 274, 282
    deciduous, 102–103, **102, 103**
    forests of, 272–279, **272–273, 275,**
        276, 278, 279
    healing of, 106, **107**
    man and, 154–155, **154, 155**
    mountains and, 282, 284, **284**
    rings of, 107, **107**
    roots of, 110–111, **110**
    succession of, 122–123, **122**
    swamp, 311, **311**
    transport of water in, 106–107, **107**
    See also specific trees.
Triassic period, 29
Triggerfish, 296
Trilobites, **28**
Tropical rain forests, 272, **272–273,**
    278–279, **278**
    diversity of life in, 278
    jungles vs., 279
    soil in, 45
    transition of, to cloud forests,
        282
Troposphere, 14
Truffles, 79
Trumpet worms, **299**
Tsunamis (tidal waves), 33, **33**
Tubers, 101, **101,** 111, **111**
Tulips, 141, **141**
Tuna, **160,** 288–289, **288**
Tundra, 71, **71, 273,** 274, 286–287
Turbidity currents, 48
Turkeys, wild, **257**
Turnstones, 302
Turquoise, **27**

Turtles, 204, **204,** 206–207, **206, 304**
    dormancy of, 207
    locomotion of, 207
    predators of, 206–207
    shell construction of, 206
    sizes of, 207, **207**
    tortoises vs., 206
    types of, 206, **206**
Tusk shells, **160,** 180, **180**
Twigs, age of, 107
Twiners (vines), 126
Twisters (tornadoes), 23, **23**
Typhoons, 22

Vulture

Ultraviolet radiation, 14
Umbra, 12, **13**
Underground stems (rhizomes), 100–101,
    100, 111, **111,** 132
Undertow, 51
Upwellings, 288
Uranus, 10, **10**

Valley (Alpine) glaciers, 40–42, **41,** 60
Valleys, canyons vs., 56
Vampire bats, **240,** 241
Vanga shrikes, 294, **294**
Vanilla orchids, **146,** 147
Vegetative reproduction, 100–101, **100,**
    101
Veins (of plants), 105, **105**
Venice, **315**
Venomous animals, 172–173, **172, 173**
    aquatic, 173, 180
    poisonous animals vs., 173
Venus, 10, **10**
Venus's-flytraps, 117, **117**
Vesuvius, Mount, 34
Vicuñas, 257, **257**
Vines, 126–127, **126, 127**
Viperfish, 292, **293**
Vipers, horned, **261**
Viviparity (in animals), 196, 199
Viviparity (in plants), 99, **99**
Vizcachas, **265,** 267
Volcanic ash, 34–35
Volcanic dikes, 37, **37**
Volcanic islands, 25, 37, 48, 294, 296
Volcanic necks, 36

Volcanoes, 25, 34–38, **34, 35, 36**
    atolls and 296, **296**
    formation of, 34
    sea salt formation and, 46
    types of eruptions of, 34
Vulcanian eruptions (volcanic), 34
Vultures, 176, 211, 283

Whale

Wadis, 21
Waialeale, Mount, 18
Walking catfish, 200
Wallabies, **256**
Walruses, 234, **235,** 248–249, **249**
    tusks of, 249, **249**
Wapiti (American elk), **250,** 283
Warm-blooded animals, 204
Warthogs, **268**
Wasps, 176, 312, **312,** 316
Water, 14, 16–17, 18
    cave formation and, 66
    erosion and, 30–31
    fish and, 196
    as habitat for plants, 124
    in photosynthesis, 104–105
    in soil, 45
    surface vs. groundwater, 64
    transport in trees of, 106–107, **107**
    underground, 64–65, **64, 65**
    world's supply of, 16
Waterbucks, **268**
Water buffalo, 311
Water bugs, giant, 186, 194, **195**
Water crowfoot, **125**
Water cycle, 16–17, 46
Waterfalls, 58–59, **59**
    discharge of water from, 58
    heights of, 58
Water fleas, 309
Waterfowl, 224–225, **224, 225,** 305
    communication among, 224
    feeding habits of, 225
    locomotion of, 225
    migrations of, 224
    pair bonding of, 224
Water-holding frogs, 317
Water lilies, 124–125, **124,** 308, **308–309**
Water scorpions, 309
Water shamrocks (bogbeans, buckbeans),
    125
Water snakes, oriental, **204**

Zebra

Page numbers in **bold** type refer to illustrations.

Reader's Digest Fund for the Blind is publisher of
the Large-Type Edition of *Reader's Digest.* For
subscription information about this magazine,
please contact Reader's Digest Fund for the
Blind, Inc., Dept. 250, Pleasantville, N.Y. 10570.